MOBILIZING THE MASSES

ODORIC Y. K. WOU

Mobilizing the Masses

Building Revolution in Henan

STANFORD UNIVERSITY PRESS
STANFORD, CALIFORNIA
1994

Stanford University Press
Stanford, California

Printed in the United States of America

CIP data appear at the end of the book

Published with the assistance of
China Publication Subventions

Stanford University Press publications are
distributed exclusively by Stanford
University Press within the United States,
Canada, and Mexico; they are distributed
exclusively by Cambridge University Press
throughout the rest of the world.

In Memory of My Sister,
Henrietta Man-chu Ng

Acknowledgments

This study is drawn mostly on the research currently being done by the Chinese scholars in various research establishments in Henan, in particular those in the Henan Party Archives, in the Henan Local Gazetteer Bureau, and in the Henan Academy of Social Sciences. Without their meticulous research and scholarly assistance, this study would have been very different. Particularly helpful to me were Hu Siyong, Wang Tianjiang, Wang Quanying, Zhang Ying, Pang Shouxin, and Feng Wengang of the Henan Academy of Social Sciences, Li Guoqiang, formerly of the Henan Local Gazetteer Bureau, and Le Baoshan, formerly of the Henan Academy of Social Sciences and presently of the Guangzhou Academy of Social Sciences. To them I wish to express my sincere appreciation.

I also acknowledge with thanks the help of Yu Yanguang of Jinan University, Chen Zhoutang of South China Normal University, Lu Yao and Ge Maochun of Shandong University, Wei Jiting of Hunan Normal University, Huang Yan of the Guangdong Academy of Social Sciences, and Yang Shenzhi of the Hunan Academy of Social Sciences. I would like to thank the following institutions for letting me use their libraries: the Henan Academy of Social Sciences, the Hunan Academy of Social Sciences, Shandong University, South China Normal University, Hunan Normal University, Princeton University, Columbia University, and the University of Hong Kong. I especially want to thank Nelson Chou for his assistance in making some research materials readily available to me.

The study has greatly benefited from the comments and critical reading of the manuscript or some chapters by Joseph Esherick, C. Martin Wilbur, Charles Tilly, Lyman P. Van Slyke, Susan Naquin, Stephen C. Averill, Linda Bell, Judith Miller, J. Kenneth Olenik, Thomas Curran, and Ka-che Yip. My gratitude goes to James Harrison, who suggested that I focus my work on the masses. I am indebted to Ira Cohen for pointing out to me the significance of peasant routine and routinization. The idea of working on the social movement in Henan originated at the "Workshop on Rebellion and Revolution in North China" at Harvard University in 1979. Chapters of this study were subsequently presented as research papers at the Modern China Seminar, Columbia University, conferences of the Mid-Atlantic Region of the Association for Asian Studies, meetings of the Historical Society for the Twentieth Century in North America, and the annual conference of the American Historical Association. To those participants who commented on my papers, I am thankful.

I thank Li Yu-ning and M. E. Sharpe for permission to reproduce in modified form my article "The Chinese Communist Party and Labor Movement: The May 30th Movement in Henan" (*Chinese Studies in History*, Fall 1989: 70–104) as Chapter 1 of this book.

The research and publication of this book were made possible by the generous financial support of the research council of Rutgers University, which financed my trips to China, and by a grant from China Publication Subventions. The book has greatly benefited from the editorial advice of Peter Golden, Roger Whitney, Jan Johnson, and Muriel Bell. Their efforts have made it more readable. I owe much obligation to my wife Kan for her support and encouragement at various stages of the book's progress.

I alone am responsible for the interpretation of events presented here, and for any defects.

O.Y.K.W.

Contents

Maps

Tables

MOBILIZING THE MASSES

Introduction

Revolution is a familiar political phenomenon in the twentieth century. The study of revolutions has always been a field of intense interest for historians, political scientists, sociologists, and anthropologists, and scholarly works have analyzed all types of revolutions. Some deal with revolution within a single nation, while others investigate and compare revolutionary processes in several nations.[1] For a long time the "Great Revolutions" in Russia and France have been a favorite subject of academic inquiry,[2] and lately the study of revolutionary processes in developing nations has become popular as well.[3]

Scholars engage in academic exchanges on the causes of revolution, the revolutionary process, and the political, social, and economic factors that contribute to the success or failure of revolutions. Revolution theorists write about issues such as social setting, organizational forms, leadership, strategies and tactics, ecological factors, revolutionary locations, participants and responses, motivations, and the impact of market forces on the revolutionary process. Their treatments of proletarian and peasant-based revolutions are diverse; there is no lack of analytical frameworks for the study of revolutions. Paradigms that immediately come to mind are the aggregate-psychological approach, the resource mobilization perspective, moral economy, social exchange theory, and the social structural approach.[4]

Scholars studying the Chinese revolution energetically ask fundamental questions: What type of revolution was the Chinese revolution? Was it a nationalistic or a social revolution? Which factor ultimately contributed more to the Communist triumph, organizational weapons or social reforms? What motivated Chinese peasants to participate? Peasant-based revolutions invariably involve two different but intricately interrelated processes, a political and a social process. In order to succeed in a revolution, rebels have to seize state power. As social revolutionaries aiming to change the countryside, they must redefine social relations and transform rural sociopolitical structure.

In studying such major changes as peasant-based revolution, it is imperative that investigators use the tools of political analysis to carefully examine the power interplay at regional, national, and international levels, as well as to look into such social factors as land tenure arrangements, rural social relationships, and community cohesion in villages. An examination of elite power politics is as critical as an investigation of peasant revolutionary potential and rural involvement. Overemphasizing elite power politics often results in overlooking the dynamics of the masses. Overstressing mass politics can lead investigators to lose sight of the basic political processes at work. Students of peasant-based revolution must somehow achieve a critical balance between those two analytical approaches.

Power Politics

Those who take the view that revolution is a form of political action invariably focus on political factors like the interplay of power, organizational forms, and historical conjunctures. Charles Tilly is the principal proponent of such a political approach.[5] His resource mobilization perspective is based on the theory of elites, which depicts society as characterized by a disparity of power. It looks at social movements as political processes aimed at establishing control over resources. Social movements are collective phenomena. Their outcomes involve power transfers. A revolutionary situation is characterized by multiple sovereignty, with contenders exerting claims on the governing polity. The key to the emergence of a social movement is a significant and rapid growth in resources. Resource mobilization theorists believe that group interests, movement organizations, repressive state power, relationships with the authorities, political opportunities, and cost and rewards are crucial analytical factors in the understanding of social movement activities. The theory also concentrates on external groups, on persons and institutions outside of the collectivity. Such a perspective places heavy emphasis on the mobilization process and on the deliberate actions taken by revolutionaries to aggregate resources, to organize, and to seek power.[6]

There was a tendency for early studies of the Chinese revolution to concentrate on its political aspects. Some view the Communist movement as the expression of self-serving conspiracies by the Chinese Communist Party. Others stress the movement's "organizational weapons." The latter view is partly attributable to those who want to divert attention from the interpretation, expounded in the Communist literature, of the Chinese revolution as essentially a social revolutionary movement aimed at alleviating the suffering of an impoverished peasantry. But the political interpretation is mostly ascribable to a common perception that Communist revolutionary success was purely a function of the party's political and military leverage. After all, the Chinese Communist Party and its Red Army played a crucial role in leading the peasant masses to a revolutionary triumph. If one perceives social revolution as "guided political action," then one tends to underscore the organizational and military factors.[7]

Recent scholarship on the Chinese Communist revolution also pays increasing attention to the political dimensions of the revolution. Adopting an analytical approach similar to Charles Tilly's resource mobilization, recent scholarship views the Chinese revolution as a political phenomenon characterized by organized activity. The movement's effectiveness, popular mass support, and Communist revolutionary strategies vary according to the strength of the state, the elite power, shifting military situations, forms of community institutions, the growth of party and military organizations, the availability of political opportunities and political choices, "countervailing factors," such as the strength of the state and rural elites, and the intervention of international events.[8] Particular stress is placed on organization as the crucial factor in Communist success.[9]

While stressing the political process, there is a tendency for scholars to highlight historical conjuncture and the international situation prevailing at the time of the revolution. International warfare has been singled out as a catalyst, and foreign incursion looked upon as a dynamic activating force that rallied peasants to the Communist cause. The Japanese invasion, some argue, dramatically changed the power balance in China and thus drastically altered the course of the revolution.[10] During the 1930s, the Communist movement was nearly crushed by repressive Guomindang forces, but international war suddenly reversed the Communists' fortune.

The resistance war against Japan provided the Chinese Communists with new political opportunities for a revolutionary resurgence. Intervention of international forces compelled the Nationalist government to cede strategic ground and to arrive at a tactical compromise with the Chinese Communists in a united front against the foreign invaders. Chalmers Johnson goes even further, insisting that conditions of war and Japanese terrorism had produced so much rural dislocation, political anarchy, and bitter hatred against the foreign invaders that the peasants were completely transformed in the process into nationalistic masses. In wartime, peasants were not only susceptible to Communist political appeals, but "the pre-political peasantry," Johnson contends, "was introduced to the concept and goals of the Chinese national community."[11]

Using power politics to analyze revolutions certainly enables us to find out how revolutionaries achieve power. Resource mobilization is a very effective tool for such political analysis. But there is often a tendency for resource mobilization theorists to place too much emphasis on social organizations, power, and coercion in the creation, containment, and repression of revolutionary movements. Consequently, they undervalue the role of socioeconomic forces in shaping the revolution.[12] They fail to pay much attention to individual participation in the movement, and occasionally overlook the role of movement ideology. By focusing strongly on the political sphere and on power, resource mobilization theory overestimates elite involvement. By accentuating external forces, it undervalues the potential of indigenous forces and the "political capabilities of the movement's mass base," and fails to recognize that indigenous social networks can be sources of insurgent leadership and antecedents of later revolutionary organizations.[13]

Social Revolution

Revolution theorists who perceive peasant-based revolutions as a social process or a social revolution often concern themselves with a different set of issues. Their primary objective is to seek an understanding of the revolutionary potential of the peasantry. The basic question they ask is, How do we explain the mass base of a peasant revolution? As Theda Skocpol puts it, "What makes peasants revolutionary?" "What kinds of social structure and historical situations produce peasant revolutions and which ones inhibit them?"[14] Their analyses focus on identifying the motivation behind peasant participation and the organizational forms that facilitate revolution.

What motivates people to revolt? Classical theorists frequently use an aggregate-psychological perspective to explain the outbreak of revolution. Violent political action is normally caused by discontent and by a society undergoing a process of breakdown.[15] The breakdown is often induced by a depressed economy, internal civil strife, a crushing defeat in war, or the highly disruptive and polarizing effects of commercialization. Human aggressive behavior, that which we find in a revolution, for example, is a direct response to frustration. According to Ted Gurr, the likelihood and intensity of civil violence are determined by the severity of relative deprivation.[16] Even if the economy is not undergoing a downturn, as in the case of the French economy during the French Revolution, frustration, James Davis explains, can engender an intolerable gap between expectation and gratification that propels aggrieved people to resort to violent action to correct that discrepancy. Hence, relative deprivation frequently provides the necessary motivation for aggrieved individuals to join a revolution.[17]

The debate over the viability of using the relative deprivation theory or rural immiserization as an explanatory variable for peasant revolutionary involvement is very much alive in the China field because of the Communist use of class conflict theory in explaining revolutions. Chinese Communist scholars have amassed a sizable amount of socioeconomic data to show that peasant revolts are an expression of rural hardship and tension. They argue that peasant involvement in the Communist movement was a result of revolutionary programs aimed at alleviating the economic suffering of impoverished rural peasants. Material interests are viewed as the primary motivating force for peasant revolutionary participation. Using the class conflict framework, Robert Marks maintains that the principal issues in the study of the rural revolution in Haifeng in 1911 are control of land, surplus extraction and exploitation, class relations, the intrusion of the capitalist market, and class consciousness.[18]

Some scholars find the theory of immiserization of the Chinese peasantry and the economic determinants of the Communist-peasant alliance unconvincing. Chalmers Johnson, for instance, admits that rural misery might have been an inducement for traditional peasant rebelliousness, but insists that it fails to explain adequately the wartime peasant-CCP alliance. He cites the Communist prewar failure in using radical class warfare and property redistribution to win mass support. Moreover, the moderate land policy the Communists promulgated in wartime did not radically alter the pattern of land ownership, a change that would have served as an economic appeal to landless and land-hungry peasants. Instead, the mild Communist policy of rent reduction and debt resolution was designed to foster class cohesion for national defense. Johnson concludes, "In retrospect, the Communist Party was successful only when it ceased acting solely for the sake of the peasantry and began acting on the side of the peasantry instead."[19]

Others admit that rural misery is a crucial variable but find it to be merely a partial explanation for peasant involvement in the revolution. Tetsuya Kataoka refuses to accept the powder keg explanation of social revolution and contends that chronic rural poverty alone rarely explodes into revolution. According to him, rural distress "was indeed a factor in the Communist revolution," but only a "passive" factor.[20]

Mark Selden, in his studies of the Communist revolution in the Shaanxi area, also views agrarian revolution as the key to peasant support, but he too is convinced that rural misery alone cannot explain the rise of peasant movements. "If peasant discontent provides the major impetus to revolution," he notes, "discontent alone cannot define the revolutionary situation. The transformation of discontent into revolution faced the intense opposition of the warlord and landlord masters of Shensi and all China."[21] There is a general consensus among China scholars that economic motives are necessary but clearly not sufficient in explaining revolutions.

Those using theories of relative deprivation and class conflict to interpret revolutionary movements often face two problems. First, it is not easy to demonstrate that aggrieved individuals are capable of perceiving deprivation collectively, as a group or a class. Second, even if they are capable of this perception, it is difficult to show that the aggrieved can then transform deprivation into a popular motivating force that disposes them to engage in collective action to correct the situation. The leap from perception to collective action is complex and difficult to prove. Frustrated individuals may or may not be easily disposed toward aggressive behavior. Surprisingly, people do have a high degree of toleration for frustration. Moreover, there are alternative responses to aggressive behavior, for instance, self-blame, blame of other people, resignation, and withdrawal. The association between psychological tension and social action is often very weak, but intervention from external allies, such as the Communist Party, can alter the situation. Intense politicization and mobilization can bring peasants to an awareness of their class interests and channel their energies toward collective action.

Recent theoretical debate over the motivation behind peasant involvement in revolution has turned to the issue of whether peasants, in joining a revolution, are motivated primarily by moral values or by a desire for material gains. Moral economists perceive peasant revolution as the violent result of a breach of the agrarian moral contract. According to James Scott, principal advocate of the moral economy theory, peasants normally live at an economic level close to the margin of subsistence. Their actions are therefore governed not by profit maximization but by risk aversion and subsistence security. In peasant communities, there is a subsistence ethic based on a right to subsistence and the principle of reciprocity. Elites are compelled by this subsistence ethic to take into account the needs of the poor. When the elites violate this shared moral standard, they trigger violent peasant protests. The violation is especially acute in times of subsistence crisis, when peasants are thrown below the level of subsistence. When this happens, all forms of protest, including revolution, are justified and sanctioned. Moral economists hold that peasants are moral communitarians and that there is a normative basis for peasant action. Peasant revolution is therefore viewed as the product of a breach in the communal moral code and as a consequence of peasant moral outrage.[22]

Social exchange theorists, however, refuse to accept the assumption that peasants, in their participation in a revolution, are motivated by communal interests and shared moral values. Samuel Popkin contends that peasant decision making is essentially rational. In deciding to join a revolution, peasants hope to maximize their personal and family, rather than communal, welfare. They seldom act as a group fighting for common interests. Free-rider problems and mutual mistrust splinter peasant communities and undermine their solidarity.[23] In explaining peasant behavior, social exchange theorists argue that economic incentives, trade-offs, material rewards, and sanctions are crucial factors that induce peasants to join a revolution. Revolutionaries and the peasantry engage in social exchange, trading material benefits for political support.[24]

China scholars participating in the moral economy debate raise the following questions: What kind of political action did the peasants take in the Chinese revolution? How dynamic a role should we assign them? Was the Chinese revolution a movement from the bottom up, or from the top down? If we view peasants as traditionally active in folk politics and subsistence crisis revolts, and if peasant-based revolution is an expression of anger resulting from a violation of their moral ethic, then the Chinese revolution can be perceived as a kind of autonomous political action of the peasantry. Peasant communities can be seen as possessing a certain degree of innate dynamism that, in times of subsistence crisis, can propel the peasantry into violent revolutionary action. But if peasants are essentially passive followers and have to be provoked into political action by outside forces, then the Chinese revolution should be looked at as a kind of guided political action.

Ralph Thaxton, a hard-line moral economist, assigns the Chinese peasantry a much more dynamic role in the revolution. He views the Chinese revolution as essentially a folk revolution. Rejecting the idea of the Chinese peasantry as merely "passive rural people" who are a "receptacle of outside influence," Thaxton assigns a high degree of innate political energy to these rural cultivators. According to Thaxton, peasant revolutionary initiative is embedded in folk culture. Peasant counterculture and survival strategies can "define their own passage to power" and shape the course of political struggle. He goes to the extreme of asserting that the revolution is guided by "instructions from the village world." To a moral economist like Thaxton, the CCP was able to gain legitimacy in the rural world only by "dancing to the demanding tunes of a decentralized peasant movement, not by orchestrating its own centrist plan for power."[25]

Steven Levine, on the other hand, rejects outright the image of a self-generated revolutionary movement in the countryside. In his study of the Communist revolution in Manchuria, Levine fails to find a revolutionary impulse among the peasantry. He instead places heavy emphasis on the political aspects of the revolution, for instance the role of the Chinese Communist Party and its organizational strength. He does not think that the CCP was simply riding to victory on the crest of rural insurrection. To Levine, the Chinese peasants were basically a passive group of cultivators. In their quest for power, the Chinese Communists deliberately and persistently provoked these rural cultivators into excessive violence. Communist revolutionary success depended on military strength and effective political organizations. The Communists, Levine notes, "did not simply lead the rural revolution to victory, the Communists *created* [emphasis mine] the revolution."[26]

Subscribing to the social exchange theory, Levine explains that the Communist ability to mobilize the peasants was based essentially on an exchange of material benefits for political support. Thaxton has argued that, at the incipient stage of the revolution, the Communists were operating in a bankrupt peasant economy. They did not possess enough resources to dispense any to the peasants in exchange for support.[27] But Levine maintains that the Communists came to Manchuria with an established organizational structure. New recruits were motivated by Communist success on the battlefield, which gave them a sense of security. The growing Communist military superiority convinced them that the revolution offered an opportunity for status advancement. The villagers, as rational decision makers, carefully weighed the costs and benefits of their choice, but they were aware that failure to join the revolution might entail popular sanction.[28] Levine demonstrates that the Communist movement and social exchange in Manchuria benefited tremendously from the Communists' success at organization and power building in North China.[29] This leaves Thaxton's question unanswered, however: Without resources to dispense, how did the Communists initially carry out a meaningful social exchange with the North China peasants?

Finding out what motivates peasants to participate in revolution is only one of the problems we face in understanding peasant-based revolutions. Another is understanding how peasants achieve the organizational capability required for a large-scale revolutionary movement.

Traditional peasant rebellions are mostly spontaneous amorphous political actions. Peasant movements are usually inhibited by diverse peasant interests, family-based cultivation that involves little or no cooperative effort, a tradition of non-violence, parochialism, and closed village society. But peasant-based revolution is a large-scale collective action involving a large number of peasants. Such an agrarian movement requires a certain degree of coordination, as well as effective leadership and organizational forms.

Social structuralists have a particular interest in peasants' organized capacity for collective action. Many believe that such an organized capacity can either come from existing peasant organizations or be created by outside organizers. Theda Skocpol points out that "peasant organized capacity is explained by structural and situational conditions that affect: (1) the degrees and kinds of solidarity of peasant communities; (2) the degrees of peasant autonomy from direct day-to-day supervision and control by landlords and their agents; and (3) the relaxation of state coercive sanctions against peasant revolts."[30] Peasant insurrectionary capacity is therefore directly related to community solidarity and peasant autonomy. Certain social structure and institutional forms possess an insurrectionary potential that can facilitate peasant revolutionary movements. Others do not. In order to identify peasants' insurrectionary potential, Skocpol and Eric Wolf urge students of revolutions to pay more attention to social structural factors such as institutional forms, socioeconomic relations between upper and lower classes, and community arrangements in agrarian societies.[31]

Social structuralists are also concerned with the question of what types of peasants are most prone to revolution. If social revolution is an agrarian conflict between classes, certain forms of class relations produce higher rural tension and therefore are more conducive to revolution. Which types of rural social arrangements generate intense tension and thus are more likely to produce agrarian insurrections? Arthur Stinchcombe argues that family-sized tenancy, in which landlords and tenants share the proceeds, is more likely to produce class tension and encourage agricultural tenants to support a revolution.[32] Jeffrey Paige believes that sharecropping arrangements and migratory labor, which give the peasant solidarity and a willingness to take risk, are more conducive to revolution.[33] Some structuralists, however, maintain that peasant insurrectionary capacities are highly dependent on the peasants' autonomy, that is, whether the cultivators are outside the landlords' direct control and therefore possess the ability to challenge the landed upper classes. Wolf insists that poor peasants are too dependent on landlords and hence lack the "tactical leverage" to resist the rural elite. Middle peasants, on the other hand, command an independent economic base and tactical political resources and are more likely to be revolutionary.[34]

This debate also brings up a related issue: the locus of revolutionary activities. Is it possible to locate centers of revolutionary strength? Should one look for revolution in locations with high rates of tenancy or in sites where smallholders predominate? Roy Hofheinz, in his study of revolutionary movements in Guangdong and Hunan, cautions against using a single social index such as land tenancy to measure peasants' revolutionary potential. He notes that "there appears to be a negative relationship between areas of unequal land distribution and areas where the Communist movement blossomed."[35] Hence, should we look for revolutionary activities in certain tactically advantageous terrains, for example in inaccessible mountain redoubts and bandit lair areas? After all, many Communist bases were located in weakly controlled border areas where rebels could easily escape state repression by taking refuge in another province. Do revolutions occur in what Wolf calls the "marginal geographical areas" where peasant insurgents have a tactical advantage? After identifying the locus of revolutionary activities, do we find a geographical continuity in peasant revolution? Are revolutionary centers often in a state of flux and do they continue to shift over time? Is there an "ecological determinant" to revolution?[36]

Further, do we find revolutionary movements in locales where the impact of capitalist forces is strong and where society is undergoing radical structural changes? Do we find revolution occurring, for example, in commercial zones? Western capitalism is often perceived as a highly disruptive force that frequently changes the social fabric of the countryside. Penetration by market forces often causes major rural economic dislocation. Capitalist forces often change rural land tenure, open previously inaccessible villages to the global market, alter social relationships, and undermine state and traditional rural authorities. Commercialization changes crop patterns, improves the transport system, and eventually broadens peasants' outlook. Capitalist expansion also creates a power crisis, which often leads to the reshaping of class alliances. A society penetrated by capitalist forces is therefore more vulnerable to major revolutionary changes. Is there a correlation between revolution and modernization? Does European capitalism promote peasant revolution?

The Study of the Revolution in Henan

These academic exchanges have brought up varying and conflicting issues and theories to be tested and resolved. This study of the Chinese revolution in Henan builds on these scholarly exchanges and attempts to test these theories. However, it is my conviction that when studying such a complex movement as a peasant-based revolution, one should definitely move away from a monocausal explanation. No single overarching theory can adequately explain a multifaceted revolutionary peasant movement, and the investigator is well advised to take an interlocking multiple-factor approach instead. In his study of Chinese peasants, Daniel Little notes that a plurality of theoretical analyses is neither inconsistent nor conceptually indecisive. "The investigator must recognize that the phenomena are complex, embodying a variety of social processes; a plurality of theories may well be needed to identify the causal properties of these processes."[37]

Crucial factors such as peasant values, political processes, social structure, and institutional forms all come together and interact in a revolution. It is the interplay of these factors that one should look for in a revolutionary movement. Therefore, the aim of this study is to look for the kinds of social structure and historical situations that produce revolution. It identifies the motives of peasant participants and searches for the organizational forms that facilitate or impede the movement. It examines the social and ecological conditions under which a revolutionary movement occurs.

This study seeks to understand the Chinese revolution as a dual process of power politics and social revolution. In the revolution, Communist contenders built up both political and military power in order to topple the ruling state. At the same time, they actualized a social revolution. As Yung-fa Chen has shown in his work on the Chinese revolution in central China, the key to understanding the revolution is to find out what actually happened.[38] In order to see the revolutionary process at work, one has to focus on how the Communists actually mobilized the masses. What factors facilitated and what factors inhibited mobilization? Only by examining the dynamics of mass mobilization can one analyze the ever-shifting Communist revolutionary strategies and tactics at work. This study focuses on the interaction among the Communist revolutionaries, the rural elites, and the peasant masses, and delves into the conflicts between revolutionary goals and peasant parochial interests.

The Chinese revolution unfolded within a cycle of disintegration and reintegration. China in the twentieth century experienced internal turmoil, external invasion, and sociopolitical breakdown. The Chinese nation was then reintegrated and rebuilt by the Communist revolutionaries. It is therefore important to identify the forces emanating from the domestic power crisis and the international military intervention that shaped the course of the revolution.

The revolution was a protracted movement that spanned 25 years.

Within that extended process were revolutionary continuities as well as changes. The Chinese Communists acquired their revolutionary experience incrementally. Certain revolutionary strategies succeeded while others failed and eventually were abandoned. In the process, many strategies were modified. It is fascinating to see how the Communists incessantly adapted and adjusted their strategies throughout the revolution.

The Japanese invasion of China was a cataclysmic event that radically changed the course of the revolution. After the outbreak of the Sino-Japanese War, the revolution entered a new and more dynamic phase. It is my contention, however, that the prewar Communist experience—its recruitment methods and revolutionary tactics, for instance—forms an integral part of the total Communist revolutionary legacy. The prewar and wartime revolutionary experiences should be viewed as interrelated parts of the same process. Separating the two periods serves only to truncate the revolution. Hence this study traces the Chinese revolution from the early mass movement of May 30, 1925, to its successful conclusion in 1949. Over this quarter of a century one can see the gradual maturation of the revolution.

Any study of the Chinese revolution has to look at urban-rural linkage. The revolution was a circular movement that shifted from the cities to the countryside and then back to the cities. It started as a proletarian revolution in urban centers but was soon forced out of the cities by the Guomindang. The revolutionaries then learned to operate in a rural environment and began entrenching themselves in the countryside. By that process the revolution was radically transformed into a peasant-based revolution. However, revolutionary activities were still conducted, although clandestinely, in urban centers, which were repeatedly tapped for revolutionary leaders. The ultimate goal, as Mao put it, was "to encircle the cities from the countryside."[39] A study of a peasant revolution has to take into account its urban connections. It is important to trace the full urban-rural-urban revolutionary trajectory. How did the urban-rural linkage work in the Chinese revolution? Is there a "geographical continuity of peasant revolution"?[40] What is the underlying logic for the shift in revolutionary location?

Studies of peasant-based revolutions tend to place too much emphasis on the role of the peasantry. Eric Wolf calls his work *Peasant Wars of the Twentieth Century*.[41] James Scott also stresses the revolutionary potential of the peasantry. Most studies of the Chinese revolution suffer from an intense focus on either the Chinese Communist Party or the peasant masses, to the exclusion of the rural elite. When elites are brought into the picture it is often the urban elite or the student intellectuals who formed the bulk of the Communist cadres. The rural elite are invariably considered feudal remnants, the logical targets in a revolutionary class struggle.[42] Yet a peasant-based revolution cannot succeed until the power of the predominant rural elite is substantially undermined.

Both Barrington Moore and Theda Skocpol call attention to the gentry's tenacious hold on power in Chinese society. A successful peasant-based revolution entails a fundamental alteration of social relationships and a transformation of the political structure at the grass-roots level. Unless one can illustrate the process by which rural elite power is eroded, one will find it difficult to explain how the peasantry comes to power. This study focuses on the erosion of the power of the rural elite as a key factor in understanding peasant revolutions. What was the nature of gentry power in the Chinese countryside? What social and political forces facilitated the breakdown of that power? How did revolutionaries, rural elites, and peasants interact in a revolutionary situation? All these questions are central to inquiry into a peasant-based revolution.

In analyzing a revolution, one needs to look at both its temporal and spatial dimensions. Whether there is an ecological determinant to revolution is still debatable. There is no doubt that Communists operated in different environments, each with its particular set of problems and obstacles. Revolutionaries are required to formulate and adapt their strategies in accordance with the social structure and parochial interests of each locality. Different areas experience varying degrees of political breakdown and therefore generate different problems requiring different solutions. Operating conditions sometimes define the revolutionary process in a particular locality. James Polachek demonstrates in his study of the Jiangxi Soviet that the Communists had to employ different strategies to tackle different problems in the highland and lowland communities.[43] This study analyzes the diverse mobilization tactics the Communists used to promote the revolution in differing ecological environments, for instance in the highland and lowland communities on the Henan-Hubei border, the floodplain of eastern Henan, the lakeside communities in northeastern Anhui, and the Taihang mountain region in northern Henan. By comparing different ecological areas it is possible to analyze the intricate interplay of ecology, social structure, parochial interests, and Communist mobilization.

This study does not deal with high-level power conflicts within the Chinese Communist Party. It is not my intention to belittle those conflicts and decisions; earlier studies of the Chinese revolution have adequately addressed these issues, and it is more fruitful for me to focus on the implementation of policies at the local level. This study will show that the success of certain policies varies from place to place, depending on the social environment and particular needs of that locality. The study is region-specific, concentrating on the province of Henan. By focusing on one region, an investigator can carefully examine the revolutionary process and policy implementation.

Communist revolutionaries always operated under local conditions, were involved in certain local power politics, and addressed certain needs of the local peasantry. It is imperative to pay particular attention to localities, if possible at the county, the subcounty, and even the village level. Mass politics are invariably related to community issues and community politics. Unless one can closely examine mobilization at the grass-roots level, one is not very likely to find out what makes the peasant revolutionary. The study of peasant-based revolutions also requires tracing how revolutionaries penetrate settled peasant communities. How do revolutionaries develop local roots in the countryside? How do they overcome the problem of suspicion of outsiders that sociologists often encounter in their rural studies? How do they create power out of nothing at the start-up stage of the revolution? This study takes an empirical approach. Whenever possible I use concrete cases, those at the county and subcounty levels, to illustrate the revolutionary process.

I have chosen Henan for testing the theories about revolution and its processes for the following reasons: the marked ecological diversity of the different socioeconomic zones in the province enables us to chart the revolutionary processes in distinct ecological environments; the chronic warfare in Henan that spanned the warlord period and the Sino-Japanese War (even during the Nanjing period, the province was far from unified and the GMD never really established a firm rule here) lets us take a close look at the processes of war and revolution; and the economic poverty and constant flooding problems in this area allow us to analyze the relationship between economic impoverishment and peasant revolutionary potential.

Henan is located in the central-eastern part of China, around the middle and lower course of the Yellow River. The province shares a border with Shandong and Anhui in the east, Hebei and Shanxi in the north, Hubei in the south, and Shaanxi in the west. A comparatively poor area, Henan nevertheless produces a number of agricultural products, including wheat, rice, sorghum, corn, cotton, beans, and sesame. On the whole, the province can be divided into two major agricultural zones: the wheat/sorghum-growing area in the north, and the rice paddies in the south.

The introduction of railroads in Henan in the late Qing and early Republican period dramatically changed the province's socioeconomic structure (see Map 1). Certain areas rose to economic power and prosperity while others retrogressed. Agricultural products, formerly carried by inland waterways, were gradually shifted to transport by rail. Consequently parts of Henan, particularly areas formerly dependent on water transport, steadily declined. On the other hand, new centers of trade sprang up like a string of beads along the Beijing-Hankou and Longhai lines. In a previous study, I traced the transformation of three ecological zones—the underdeveloped west, the low-lying degenerating zone in the east, and the developed zone along the railroads and in the northern part of the province—with the introduction of railway transport into the province.[44]

Henan is a land of marked diversity. The western and southern sections form the poverty-stricken backyard of the province. The area is essentially a mountainous region. A series of ranges, the Taihang, the Funiu, the Tongbai, and the Dabie, divide that part of the province. In the late Qing and Republican periods, much of the production of this underdeveloped corridor was consumed locally, with little left for marketing. There was a conspicuous absence of commercial activities in the region, and many of the county towns looked deserted or were nothing more than shanty towns. Western Henan had traditionally been the lair of such famous bandits as Wang Tianzong, Bai Lang, and Lao Yangren, whose gangs roamed Henan and neighboring provinces. Within this area there developed a unique bandit tradition known as the *lulin*, or the "green forest" tradition. The uninterrupted social conflicts caused by banditry led travelers to designate the province "bandit-ridden Henan."

Eastern Henan is a low-lying area that forms a segment of the North China Plain. Watered by the Huai River in the east and the Wei River in the north, this eastern flatland is agriculturally rich but has always been flood-prone. The Yellow River is best known as "China's sorrow." The Huai, too, silted most of the time, often overflows its banks, causing misery for local residents. Many of the rivers fell into disuse with the building of the new rail networks. Continuous silting and long-term neglect created chronic flooding problems for the entire region. The introduction of the railway system also brought about a degeneration of the urban centers in the area. Formerly bustling salt- and grain-marketing centers along the Wei, such as Huaxian county seat and Daokouzhen, fell into decay. The port of Zhuxianzhen on the Huai lost most of its waterborne traffic to the railway and also declined and became a depressed town.

In contrast to the underdeveloped and degenerating areas, the

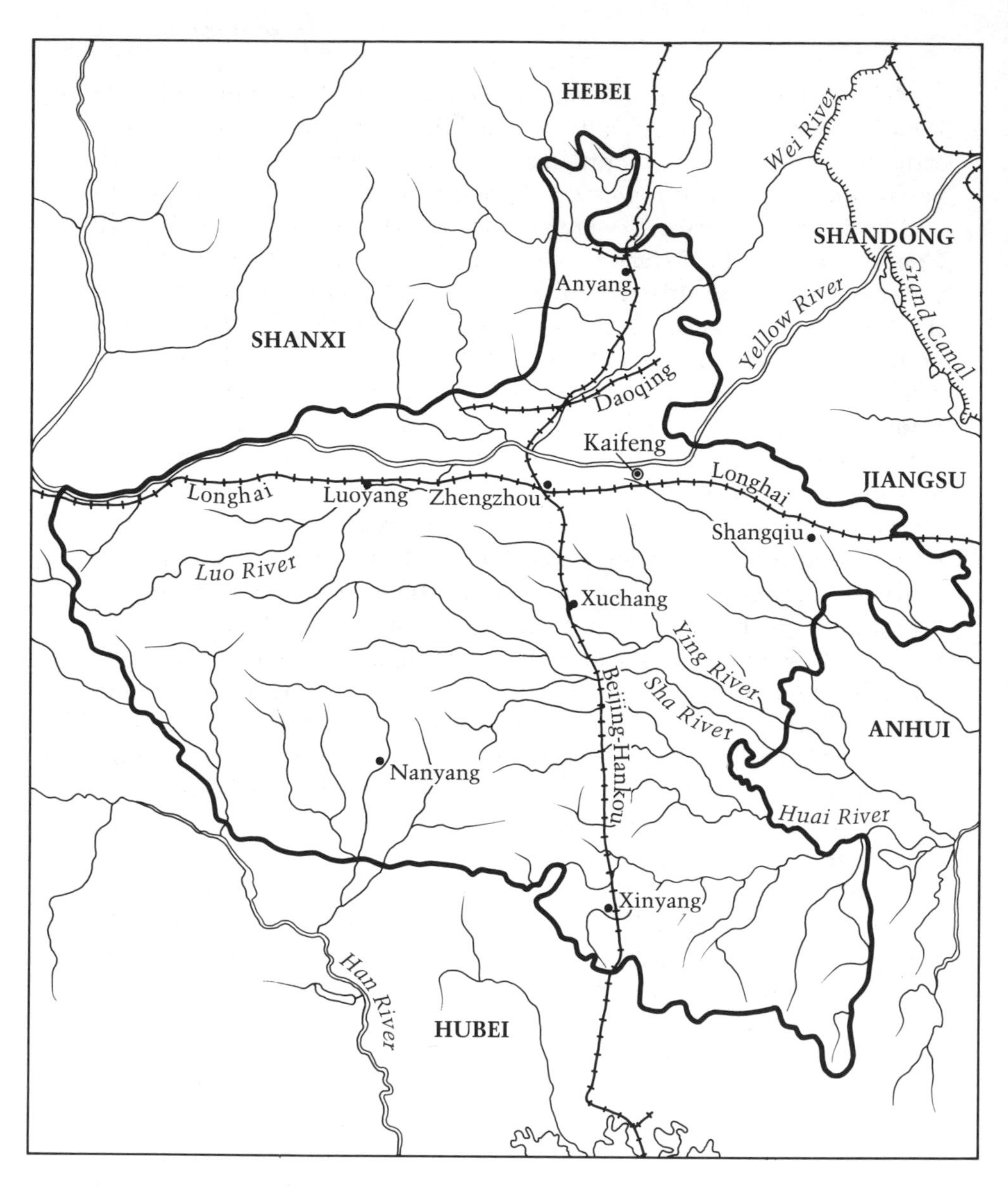

Map 1. Henan rail transport and drainage systems.

T-shaped developed zone running along the Beijing-Hankou and Longhai railroads, as well as the northern part of the province, sprang to life with the coming of the rail system. Cash crops were introduced to Henan by the railways. Long-staple American cotton, for instance, came to such cities and railway towns as Anyang, Minxian, and Lingbao. Peanuts were grown along the eastern stretch of the Longhai line around the provincial capital of Kaifeng. Tobacco, introduced by the British-American Tobacco Company, covered roughly 20–40 percent of the cultivated acreage and became a highly profitable cash crop for farmers around the rail town of Xuchang. Counties on both sides of the Daoqing railway in northern Henan were brought to life by the coal-mining industry. At the foot of the Taihang Mountains stand the Jiaozuo mines owned by Peking Syndicate Collieries and Zhongyuan Mining, the two most productive mining operations in the province. The concentration of commercial activity and light industry in this area, such as cotton spinning in Anyang and flour milling in Xinxiang, made the northern region the most developed zone in the province.

Because of its centrality within China, Henan has traditionally been known as Zhongzhou (the central prefecture) or Zhongyuan (the central plain). Its central location historically made Henan a strategic military area known as *bingjia bizheng zhi di* (a place always contested by all military strategists). In military terms, the province has been regarded as the bridge between northern and central China. Invading troops from the north found this province to be the gateway to central China. The fact that the Beijing-Hankou and Longhai railroads crisscrossed Henan and met at Zhengzhou gave the province added strategic importance. Modern warfare is always conducted along lines of transportation. Military strategists often call Henan "a hub linking all other parts of the nation" (*sitong bada*), or "a perfect battlefield but a difficult place to defend" (*ke zhan er bu ke shou*). Henan has historically been the site of famous battles, and in modern times the province was the battlefield for the Northern Expedition, the so-called Zhongyuan Campaign between Chiang Kaishek and Feng Yuxiang, as well as battles in the Sino-Japanese War. Such an ecologically varied and strategic area is ideal for the analysis of the process of a peasant-based revolution.

The amount of rich information pouring out of the People's Republic lately makes it impossible to discuss Communist activities in the whole province. There were six Communist border bases in Henan in the Sino-Japanese War period, and an exhaustive study of Communist activities in all six bases would take several monographs. Therefore I have to be highly selective, and this work focuses on the eastern part of Henan, in particular the Huaibei region. Except for the chapter on the Taihang Mountains, which is included for comparative purposes, the study deals with the following border bases: the Yu-E (Henan-Hubei), the Eyuwan (Hubei-Henan-Anhui), the Yuwansu (Henan-Anhui-Jiangsu) and the Sui-Qi-Tai (Suixian, Qixian, and Taikang counties in eastern Henan). The Yuxi (West Henan) base is conspicuously absent from this book, not because the base is insignificant but because materials on West Henan were unavailable while the study was being completed.

On the other hand, many of these Communist bases bordered on two or three provinces and it is impossible to study Communist activities in these areas without touching on the neighboring provinces. The study of early land reform in the Eyuwan area takes us into Hubei province. The study of Communist activities in the Yuwansu base area takes us to the Hongze lakeside in the northeastern part of Anhui province. All these adjacent territories formed integral parts of the border regions linking them with Henan.

A few words should be said about the meaning of the term "masses" as used in this study. The term does not mean simply the proletariat and the peasantry. According to Deng Zihui, the political commissar of the New Fourth Army, the term "masses" means "the masses of the people" (*renmin tazhong*). As defined by Mao Zedong at the Seventh People's Congress, it has a rather broad meaning that includes urban workers, peasants and all other "laboring people" (*laodong renmin*) such as the urban poor, independent laborers, free professionals, handicraftsmen, and intellectuals. It also includes the "free bourgeoisie" (*ziyou zichan jieji*), the "enlightened gentry" (*kaiming shishen*), ethnic minorities, overseas Chinese, and all "patriotic elements."

Among these broad masses of people, the Chinese Communists clearly distinguish the core and the peripheral groups. The core group, or the "main body" (*zhuti*), encompasses workers, peasants, and all "laboring people." These formed the party's "principal forces" (*jiben liliang*) and the "basic masses" (*jiben qunzhong*).[45] On the other hand, cadres were told not to ignore the elite, a strategy that grew out of the sheer necessity of the time. The Communists, operating in a non-confrontational atmosphere under United Front tactics and New Democracy in wartime, had broadened their coalition targets to include even landlords and merchants. Thus cadres were instructed to make friends and work with the "enlightened gentry" and the "free bourgeoisie," even though they were told to be aware of the "conservative and vacillating" attitudes of landlords and merchants. At some point in the course of the revolution, Deng Zihui said, the party would have to part company with these "unreliable classes."[46] In mobilizing the masses, the Communists were instructed to make a clear distinction between these two groups. The definition was kept deliberately vague so as to retain flexibility in their coalition strategy.[47] This study examines not only the Communist mobilization of the "basic masses" but also that of the peripheral elements, the merchants and landed gentry.

This study is based mostly on party archival and local historical materials gathered during recent research trips to Henan.[48] Valuable new party materials have been pouring out of China since the mid-1980s as the Communist Party compiles its own history. Veteran revolutionaries, most of them octogenarians now, were instructed by the party to put down their revolutionary experience in writing before it is lost. Lately, multivolume sets of revolutionary reminiscences and party archival materials have been published for the benefit of domestic party historians.

There is also a nationwide movement underway to compile county gazetteers. County gazetteer bureaus are being set up all over China for the special purpose of gathering the necessary materials. For years, county historians have been collecting material not only on the political, social, and economic conditions of their localities, but also on Communist revolutionaries and revolutionary events that occurred in their particular counties. Multivolume biographies on county revolutionaries are now available. Particularly useful for this study were party work reports, *caijing* or reports on the finances and economy of the border bases, prefectural party archival materials (for example, those of Xinyang, Anyang, and Shangqiu), and materials published by the county gazetteer bureaus. Many of these are *neibu* (for restricted internal use only). Without this information it would be impossible to examine the Chinese revolution in depth and detail. All these intense research activities in the People's Republic have given us a more complex picture of the revolutionary process, and at the same time have simplified the historian's task of writing on the revolutionary history of a specific region.

EARLY MOBILIZATION

CHAPTER I

Mobilizing the Proletarians: The May 30th Movement

To the early Chinese revolutionaries, a Communist revolution meant a proletarian revolution, not a peasant revolution. According to Lenin, the process of revolution in a feudal or semifeudal nation like China had to go through two distinct stages. The first was a national-democratic revolution. At that stage, the principal conflict was between semifeudal China and the imperialist powers. The proletariat, vanguards of the revolution, were told to put aside their differences with the national bourgeoisie for the moment and to cooperate with them in order to drive out the imperialists. Only after the national-democratic revolution had been accomplished should the revolution then move to the second and higher stage, that of a socialist revolution. Although Lenin regarded the agrarian problem as a central problem of the revolution and thought the proletariat and peasants should forge an alliance against capital, he assumed that in the first anti-imperialist stage the peasantry would not be the central class of the revolution but a subordinate ally of the urban social classes.[1]

During the national-democratic stage, the locus of revolutionary activity was invariably in the urban centers. Revolutionaries were instructed to infiltrate urban industrial establishments, to exploit socioeconomic grievances in order to arouse the workers, and to lead them in antiforeign movements. At this stage CCP leaders such as Chen Duxiu were much more interested in a proletarian than a peasant revolution. This study, therefore, begins with the May 30th Movement of 1925. The May 30th was the urban proletarian movement that provided the Communists the opportunity to mass-mobilize the Chinese people. Party membership showed phenomenal growth, and the movement propelled the Communists to power.

In studies of the Chinese revolution there is often a tendency for scholars, particularly Communist scholars, to give undue weight to socioeconomic factors. This is inevitable. Materials on social injustice and economic hardship are readily available because research establishments in the People's Republic churn them out day after day. Although no student of history would deny that a good knowledge of the socioeconomic conditions of oppressed classes is absolutely essential to understanding the reasons behind social conflicts, an overemphasis on societal breakdown frequently obscures the actual cause of a movement and sometimes skews the entire picture. Socioeconomic factors may tell us something about group or class interests, but they might not explain the timing of an outbreak or the success or failure of a movement. As Charles Tilly and other social historians have repeatedly argued, it takes more than frustration and aggression to bring people together in collective violence. Collective action requires leadership, organization, mobilization, and integration, that is, a body of people to orchestrate the activity. It also requires "the opportunity to act together" and to seize collective control over resources needed for action. A repressive or a tolerant government can greatly alter the cost and chance of success of a collective action.[2] This chapter examines the socioeconomic, political, and organizational factors in the May 30th Movement and discusses their impact on strike activity. It shows that in the May 30th period, a political factor—party politics—played as important a role as socioeconomic conditions in shaping the labor movement in Henan.

Socioeconomic Factors: Matters in Dispute

A study of any discontent connected with the work place is always crucial in an analysis of strike activity, even though one might not wish to emphasize economic factors as the sole determinant of a labor movement. Industrial issues such as low wages, long hours, harsh treatment of workers, and union recognition have always been fundamental matters of disagreement between workers and management. China is no exception. In Henan in the 1920s, the industries involved in the May 30th labor disputes consisted of the railways, textiles, and mining, mostly congregated in the northern part of the province. The railway industry was unionized in 1922, when the Communists took advantage of Wu Peifu's "protection of labor" policy to set up a number of "recreation clubs" along major rail lines. But the union movement was crushed by Wu in the February 7, 1923, labor incident in which the Party attempted to set up a general union by combining the workers' clubs of all sixteen stations.[3] It was not until late 1924, with the collapse of Wu's rule in the province, that the Communist Party began to revitalize some of these local unions and the union movement spread to other industries.

Each industry, however, had its own individual conditions of employment and thus its own set of problems. The railways, composed mainly of the Beijing-Hankou, Longhai, and Daoqing lines, had a longer history than the other industries. Most of these lines were constructed and, in some cases, still owned by foreign powers; the engineers and top managers were foreigners—French and Belgians. Conflicts between Chinese foremen and the foreign managers were frequent.[4] Railwaymen were divided by function into the train crew, track workers, and railway workshop employees, but the basic difference was between the skilled and the unskilled, clearly reflected in the two-tiered structure of their wages. Skilled railwaymen, or the "elite" workers (*guizu xing de gongren*), as they were known, were the engineers, coal burners, and workshop employees. The base pay of the engineers (*kai che*) was C$30 a month, and they worked a ten-hour shift.[5] With on-the-road expenses and overtime, they sometimes received C$100 a month. The incomes of the coal burners (*shao huo*), who also received on-the-road expenses and overtime, and the workshop mechanics, were high. A bureau head could get as much as C$600 a month.[6]

The lower tier, the unskilled laborers, were the helpers (*bang gong*), both on the train and in the workshop, the train-washers (*ca che*), the track workers (*xiu lu gongren*), the handymen (*xiao gong*), the station workers (*zhang fu*), and the coal transporters (*tai mei*). These were mostly middle-aged men; many were seasonal workers drifting between cities and the nearby countryside. Some were apprentices. Not only were their wages low, (monthly pay for track workers was between C$7.50 and C$12.00, and for others as low as 24 cents a day), part of it was deducted by the foremen. Some workers were known to have to forfeit as much as three months' pay as commission to foremen or overseers. On top of that, payment was always in arrears. Most worked a ten- or twelve-hour day; the coal transporters had a seventeen-hour day.[7] On average, they worked 292 days a year.

Aside from the pay issue, there were other grievances. Train workers were always subjected to the violent behavior of the militarists. Engineers had little job security and coal burners were frequently replaced by favorites of ministry or bureau officials. If they made the slightest mistake, they would be suspended or removed from their jobs. They did not complain about working overtime or at night, but thought that they were entitled to double pay. For unskilled workers, the promotion process was slow: it took two or three years for a train washer to become a helper, another one to three years to become a coal burner, and an additional five to ten years to go from a third-class engineer to first-class engineer. It seems that relations between workers and foremen were close. Workers must have accepted wage deduction by the foremen, though they complained about other deductions.

In the railway industry, the two fundamental issues were wage increases and union recognition, which the union incessantly demanded. The railwaymen also wanted the union to handle all disciplinary actions, hiring, and firing. The union was fighting for better employment conditions and benefits: half a day's rest for the washers after cleaning the engine; twenty days of paid holiday a year; free travel for themselves, members of their families, and union members; accident compensation and paid sick leave; pensions; and even such minor things as free work clothing for all outdoor workers.[8]

Textile workers were mostly unskilled and poorly paid. Workers were paid either by the piece, for example by bale or cartload of yarns produced, or by the hour or month. The average monthly wage was C$4.80, much lower than that of the railwaymen. Most of the workers earned less than 30 cents a day. Working hours were long, normally twelve to fourteen hours daily. In Yufeng Cotton Mill in Zhengzhou, two-thirds of the workers, including child laborers, worked a twelve-hour day. The work force in the textile industry consisted mainly of seasonal workers, with a large group of female and child laborers (in Yufeng Cotton Mill, female and child labor accounted for about a third of the work force). This was simply because spinning and weaving had traditionally been the woman's job at home, and much of the work required little or no skill and could be done by a child. Female and child workers were usually paid a third or half of the regular wage. Most of the piece-rate and hourly-rate workers received their pay in copper cash; workers often mentioned receiving a daily wage of 100–200 cash or a monthly wage of less than six strings of cash. Wages in the textile industry in North China were much lower than in the south. A skilled northern worker received only 280 cash a day, while those in the south earned 509 cash. As usual, part of their wage was automatically deducted by the foremen. It was also customary for laborers to give foremen and overseers "gifts."[9]

Since the textile industry had a sizable number of female and child workers, in addition to the usual pay raise the unions demanded three eight-hour shifts for child laborers and paid maternity leave for female workers. They hoped to shorten the working hours of male laborers to ten hours a day. Other issues reflected in their demands included paid sick leave, two holidays a month, wage payment in silver dollars instead of copper cash, an hour of lunchtime and the right for family members to bring lunch to the mill between eleven and noon, improved lighting in the workplace, schools for workers, three month's extra pay plus travel expenses for ex-provincial workers fired from their jobs, and such routine issues as union recognition, accident compensation, and union authority in hiring and firing.[10]

The coal mining industry faced a different set of problems. The industry had two mining sites in Henan, Jiaozuo and Liuhegou (near Anyang). In Jiaozuo, there were three types of mines: those of the Peking Syndicate Collieries, a British-owned establishment dating back to the end of the Qing dynasty; those belonging to the Zhongyuan Mining Company, an enterprise owned by Chinese merchants; and a whole array of native mines known as small pits (*xiao yao*), all of them either unmechanized or semimechanized and using old-fashioned production methods (*tu fa*). The Peking Syndicate Collieries was a huge foreign establishment with a work force of 10,000 (6,000 in the summer) and an annual production of 560,000 tons. Zhongyuan Mining was of a similar size, with an estimated 11,200 workers and annual production of 830,000 tons.[11]

Before 1927 all coal mines used the contract labor system for recruitment, with foremen as recruiting agents. It was an oppressive system; not only did miners have to give the recruiting agent a fee of C$10 (equivalent to a month's pay) and part of their wages, but they were usually required to give the foremen "gifts" and stay in the living quarters and gamble in the gambling houses run by these foremen. The foremen treated the laborers harshly, scolding and beating them and frequently cheating them by manipulating the currency exchange rate. Nevertheless, contract labor remained an established recruitment practice until the Communists fought for its abolition. The workers maintained some kind of amiable relations with the foremen in spite of this oppression, probably because they were highly dependent on them for their jobs. The workers' targets of hostility were not the foremen but the overseers and bosses.

Labor in the coal industry was differentiated into contract or "external" labor (*wai gong*) and hired or "internal" labor (*li gong*). Hired labor consisted mostly of skilled workers such as mechanics, electricians, and administrators. Of the 6,000 workers in the Zhongyuan Mines in 1934, only 800 (13 percent) were hired labor. Wages for the hired laborers ranged from C$6 to C$55 a month, with half of them receiving roughly between C$6 and C$9.[12] Contract laborers were those performing manual labor, such as digging, transporting, screening, sacking, and piling up coal. The majority were natives of neighboring counties. Half were young adults (ages fourteen to eighteen) or children, with child laborers receiving half the adult wage. Unlike the hired laborers, who received monthly pay, contract labor was paid daily. There were three classes of contract labor: first class (*ta gong*), second class (*er gong*), and unskilled (*xiao gong*), with pay scales ranging from 13 cents to 16 cents a day.[13] Some unskilled laborers worked under an apprentice system. There was also a marked distinction in the living conditions of contract and hired laborers. The living quarters for hired labor were more comfortable, while contract labor lived in overcrowded housing. Those who brought their families with them usually lived in the coal pit.

The quarryman's life was one of extreme hardship. The men entered the pit early in the morning and did not emerge till dusk. After coming out of the pit they took a bath, went to the food store to have a meal, and then headed for the gambling house. If they lost money in the game, they would go right back to the pit to work a night shift.[14] Most of them worked an eight-hour day but some worked longer, and there was no extra pay for overtime. Except for the Zhongyuan mines, which gave workers two holidays a year—Labor Day and National Day—there were no holidays for miners. Accidents in the pit were frequent. There was no insurance nor much accident compensation for the disabled or for the families of workers who were killed on the job (normally a C$100 lump sum for the family of the deceased). Once a mine collapsed and killed ten miners, and instead of paying the families of the deceased accident compensation, management told the remaining workers that what had happened was ill fate, and persuaded them to give up a day's pay to set up a Daoist temple for their own protection.[15]

There were some fringe benefits for the miners. In the Zhongyuan mines, for example, the company built ten primary schools and a playground for the miners' children. Water and coal were always free. Some form of rudimentary medical care for the wounded was available. A company store sold daily necessities at a reduced price.[16]

Working conditions in the native-owned mines (*tu yao*) were deplorable. The number of workers in these mines was no fewer than in the mechanized mines (*da jing*, or large pits). Some native-owned mines had already been taken over by large companies such as the Peking Syndicate Collieries. In 1922, the Peking Syndicate took over 98 mines by force and "purchased" 38 others from native owners. Kou Yingjie, the local warlord, supported the British appeal to close down these mines, but in early 1930, 41 native mines remained in operation in the vicinity of the Peking Syndicate Collieries. Groups of miners were normally contracted for by the big mining companies or by indigenous merchants under the contract mining system (*bao cai*) to extract coal jointly from a number of mines.[17]

Daily wages for workers in the native-owned mines were high, 50 cents a day. But the miners worked long hours, at least a straight 24-hour shift, frequently continuously for two or three days. A fixed quota was set for them, for instance 200 baskets of coal, and they were not allowed to leave the pit until the quota was fulfilled. In the morning a foreman led a couple of pit workers down the mine, each bringing with him a basket, a few steamed buns, and his tools—a pick, a shovel, and an oil lamp. At the end of the pit they had to crawl. Ventilation was so bad that the lamp went out and they worked in suffocating darkness. The miners were all bare to the waist; children were completely naked. The coal dug up by the adult miners was hauled by children to the opening, transferred to a sack, and reeled up either by manpower or by a machine. Then it was moved to open ground, where the coal screeners separated it by size. Baskets of screened coal were carried to another area to be stored. Much of this work was done by minors. Of the 4,700 workers in the Zhongyuan native mines, 40 percent were young adults and 10 percent children.[18]

In general, the trade union movement in Henan was still in its infant stage. Although a number of small railroad unions were set up as early as 1922 after an understanding was reached between Li Dazhao and Wu Peifu, who then drew up a policy for the "protection of labor," the union movement was quickly aborted by the February Seventh Strike of 1923, when the Zhili warlord used his troops to crack down on Beijing-Hankou strikers. Afterward, a very feeble underground labor movement barely survived in a few railway centers (Xinyang, Daoqing, and Anyang), as well as in the Yufeng Textile Factory in Zhengzhou. It was not until after the collapse of Wu's power in the Second Zhili-Fengtian War, and under the more cordial political atmosphere of Guominjun rule (which will be dealt with later), that trade unions began to resurface in the province.[19] But in the beginning, trade unions remained a rather feeble force. In industries where bargaining did not exist and unions were not legal institutions, union recognition was a major issue in disputes. Unionists fought for their existence as well as for a voice in shop floor issues such as discipline, suspension, and discharge of workers. In the railway, textile, and mining industries in Henan, workers scratched out a bare existence. Wages and work conditions always formed the predominant issues in the strikes, followed by other terms of employment: worker's compensation, paid holidays, double pay for overtime on holidays and Sundays, schooling for workers' children, and better housing for families. Resolution of these issues often transformed strikes into intense urban warfare. Although wages and work conditions were much worse in the native enterprises than in foreign-owned establishments, in a period of antiforeignism firms such as the

British Peking Syndicate Collieries were always singled out by radicals as targets of hostility. The labor movement in Henan therefore must be looked at as an integral part of a broader, nationwide antiforeign movement sparked by the May 30th Shanghai Incident.

Political Factors: The Opportunity to Act Together

Discontent motivates workers to act together in strikes, but the success of their collective action depends on the strength or weakness of the government's repressive mechanisms. There is a range of actions the government can take against labor organizers, such as forbidding assemblies, infiltrating unions with spies and informers, outlawing or arresting activists, cracking down on dissident organizations, or simply exerting military force. A government can collaborate with foreign authorities to repress labor agitations directed against foreign-owned industries. On the other hand, government patronage and tolerance can facilitate a labor movement and cut the cost of collective action, giving the contenders an opportunity to build and expand their organization. A government favorably disposed toward workers can accord the movement protection.[20] It was under government patronage that the labor movement in Henan began to grow and spread during the May 30th period.

Opportunity arrived with the collapse of Wu Peifu's rule in the area at the end of the Second Zhili-Fengtian War. By the end of 1924, the political environment in China had changed dramatically. The southern government under Sun Yatsen had emerged as the center of national revolution and the major vehicle of Chinese nationalism. Rebuffed by the West and frustrated by his inability to obtain loans from western powers, Sun had turned to the Russians for aid. In January 1923, he signed a joint declaration with the Soviet representative Adolf Joffe, who promised Sun Russian support of Chinese national reunification. Under the Sun-Joffe agreement, Chinese Communist members were allowed to join the Guomindang as individuals. The understanding initiated a period of CCP-GMD cooperation under the so-called First United Front. To help Sun reinvigorate the Guomindang, Mikhail Borodin was sent by Soviet ambassador Leo Karakhan to act as adviser to the Nationalist leader. After arriving in Guangzhou in October 1923, Borodin began reorganizing the Guomindang and building an army under the complete control of the Nationalist Party.

The Second Zhili-Fengtian War also radically altered the power structure in North China. The war ended with Feng Yuxiang turning against his superior Wu Peifu and winning a civil war against the Zhili clique. The power of the Zhili military faction under Cao Kun and Wu Peifu came to an abrupt end. Feng was in control of Beijing; the Guominjun, under the leadership of Feng, Hu Jingyi, and Sun Yue, became the dominant force in North China. In the aftermath of the war, Duan Qirui, the provisional chief executive, and Feng Yuxiang cabled Sun, inviting the Nationalist leader to come north to work with them to reunify the nation. In November 1924, Sun declared that he would go to Beijing "to plan China's unification and reconstruction."[21] It was against the backdrop of a rapidly changing and cordial political atmosphere that the Russians began to enlist the support of Feng Yuxiang in their opposition to Manchurian warlord Zhang Zuolin. Subsequent rivalry between Feng Yuxiang and Zhang Zuolin gave the Soviet Union the opportunity to exploit the situation in its bid for power in China. Searching for a military force willing to oppose the increasing power of the Japan-dominated Zhang, the Russians found their target in the Guominjun, whose generals were also looking for support in their climb to power.

Through an introduction from Xu Qian, a member of the Central Executive Committee of the GMD, and Li Dazhao, the head of the CCP Northern Bureau, Feng met with Soviet ambassador Karakhan on October 27, 1924. Feng and the ambassador reached an agreement under which Feng and Hu Jingyi, the commander of the Second Guominjun, each sent 25 high-ranking army officers to the Soviet Union for military training. In early 1925, at the suggestion of the GMD and Li Dazhao, the Russians decided to give substantial support to Feng to "set up a revolutionary movement modelled on Guangzhou." A resolution was later passed by the Soviet government to send Feng military advisers and to assist him in arming the Guominjun.[22]

It was under the umbrella of Russian-CCP-GMD-Guominjun cooperation that Hu Jingyi and his Second Guominjun became targets of Russian influence. A Guomindang member, Hu was sympathetic to Sun Yatsen's revolutionary cause. While stationed in Beijing and Tianjin, he was approached by the Chinese Communists and the Russians. Through Kan Xingfu, a Beijing University professor, Hu was contacted by Li Dazhao, who had recently returned from the Soviet Union.[23] A preliminary understanding between Hu and the Russians was reached in the Soviet embassy in Beijing in December 1924.[24] The Russians agreed to supply Hu with arms in return for a free hand for the Chinese Communists to conduct their activity in North China. With Guominjun support, Li rehabilitated the Beijing-Hankou Railway General Union and freed labor activists who had been imprisoned by Wu Peifu after the failure of the 1923 Beijing-Hankou labor strike. In mid-

December, Hu, accompanied by Communists Liu Tianzhang (a military commander) and Qu Wu (a Beijing University student), went to Henan to take up the post of military governor of the province.[25]

Details of the understanding were not worked out until the Guominjun had set up its headquarters in Kaifeng. At the end of December, through his Communist intermediary, Hu extended an invitation to Ambassador Karakhan and Li Dazhao to come to Kaifeng for a discussion.[26] Karakhan accepted the invitation and came to Kaifeng, but the actual negotiations were conducted by Li Dazhao. The Guominjun commander requested that the Russians give him military support and advisers, assist him in reorganizing his army, and help him set up a Whampao-type military academy. Hu also used Henan's strategic location to plead for a large share of Soviet arms for the Guominjun. In return, he promised to let Li Dazhao send him "a group of young Communists to assist him in his administration." He would also allow the Chinese Communists a free hand in promoting labor and peasant movements in his province.[27] Karakhan agreed to these terms. The accord was probably finalized in Beijing on January 29, 1925, between Hu's delegates and A. L. Guecker, the Soviet military attache.[28]

In the meantime, Li arranged with Hu to appoint A. I. Klimove, an old party leader from the Maritime Territory and Siberia, as his adviser. Soviet specialists left for Zhengzhou in February.[29] Communist activists joined Hu's administration at the same time:[30] Yang Xiaochu, a Beijing University student, served as Hu's assistant in the stamp duty office, and Hou Youke was assigned by Hu to be in charge of provincial tax reform. A number of Communist leaders, including Wang Ruofei, the head of the Henan-Shaanxi Regional Committee, Xiao Chunu, publisher of *Henan Critics*, Li Quishi, a student activist, and Zhang Kundi, a labor leader active in the Beijing-Hankou union since 1922, were ordered to Henan by Li Dazhao.[31] As Hu had fulfilled his side of the bargain, the Russians proceeded to work out a plan for military cooperation with him. On March 12, 1925, Hu's commanders and the Soviet advisers held a conference at which they discussed such questions as the building of armored trains and improvement of the local Guominjun arsenal. The group of Soviet specialists was about to leave for Kaifeng when they received news of the sudden death of Hu and immediately changed their destination to Kalgan, the site of Feng's headquarters.[32]

Hu's successor Yue Weijun was a very different man.[33] Unlike Hu, Yue had little interest in the revolutionary cause of the south. His primary goal was to consolidate his power base in Henan as rapidly as possible. Yue also maintained close ties with Wu Peifu, his former superior. At the end of May, having arrived in Zhengzhou and taken up his post as head of the Henan-Shaanxi Regional Committee, Wang Ruofei found that Yue was very suspicious of the Communists and that he often kept his distance from the Guomindang. Wang immediately reported the changes to Li Dazhao. Upon receiving the report, Li instructed Wang to devote his attention to seizing power at the local level. Wang was ordered to focus on building a model battalion and on winning the support of "the young military and progressive intellectuals" in the area.[34] Wang in turn directed the Communist cadres to concentrate on building up political power in the counties.[35] For the time being, while he was seeking Russian support and expecting a shipment of arms from the Soviet Union, Yue played the role of obedient follower of the revolution. He adopted a tolerant attitude toward the Communists in the area and was very cooperative during the May 30th Movement, directing his generals to support the antiforeign effort.

The Guominjun was a complex military force. Many of its members were from Shaanxi and had been followers of Hu Jingyi, but some were traditional Henan soldiers. Others were former subordinates of Wu Peifu and Liu Zhenhua, the two warlords of the Zhili clique. Those who came from Shaanxi were originally part of the National Pacification Army under the leadership of Yu Youren, a veteran Guomindang member, and some of the commanders were pro-Guomindang and sympathetic toward the revolution. The Guomindang set up special headquarters within the Second Guominjun, and both the Chinese Communists and the GMD were allowed to propagate freely in areas under the jurisdiction of these pro-Guomindang generals. Commander Deng Baosan, for instance, was himself a revolutionary who issued messages calling upon the masses to fight for their freedom.[36] Thus the Communists and the Guomindang had some influence over the Guominjun leaders.

A study of the behavior of the Guominjun commanders in the May 30th Movement is essential to our understanding of the labor movement. Most significant was the attitude of Yue Weijun, who not only personally participated in the movement but also made contributions to the strike fund to support the workers in Shanghai and headed the fund-raising committee of the Society for the Support of the Shanghai Incident. On Yue's order, many Guominjun officers took part in mass meetings; some even became oratorical agitators. He Sui, commissioner of aviation for the Third Guominjun, sent two airplanes to help the propagandists drop leaflets in the Zhengzhou-Luoyang area. Student and worker protests would never have attained such a magnitude if Yue, his officers, and the county mayors had not lent their support. Even when Duan Qirui's Beijing government, under pressure from the foreign community, ordered Yue to restrain the students and the strikers, the

Guominjun commander refused to budge. When the British brought direct pressure on Yue to cancel the boycott against British goods, Yue contended that because the treaty had explicitly forbidden foreigners from directly doing business in the interior, and since foreign trade in the interior was conducted through Chinese middlemen, the British had no right to interfere and claim reparations for goods destroyed in the boycott.[37]

Another militarist who gave the movement strong support was Fan Zhongxiu. Fan was a former subordinate of Wu Peifu who defected to the South in 1923. In the following year, Fan and his troops were reorganized by Sun Yatsen into the Henan Army for National Reconstruction. At the end of the Second Zhili-Fengtian War, Feng Yuxiang openly invited Sun to come north "to discuss national affairs with him." It was under this collaboration between Sun Yatsen and the Guominjun that Hu Jingyi allowed Fan's army to station itself in Henan. Sympathetic toward the southern revolutionary cause, Fan was an ardent supporter of the May 30th Movement. He donated C$50,000 to the strikers in Shanghai and directed all the military instructors in his training regiment to contribute seven copper cash a day to the cause. In Linying, where his troops were stationed, he set up the Military Academy in Support of the Shanghai Incident to politicize his officers. In addition to basic military science, they were taught modern Chinese history and Sun's Three Principles of the People.[38] During the miners' strike in Jiaozuo, Fan openly supported the strikers and even suggested that Chinese banks and merchant associations in Henan issue "patriotic bonds" to raise money to build indigenous factories to absorb the striking workers.[39]

It was in this favorable political environment that the Henan General Union was founded. The labor movement received recognition from the government and support from the militarists from the outset. Feng Yuxiang sent his representative to the union's founding ceremony to give the workers a talk on Leninism and Sun Yatsen's Three Principles. Zheng Xiang, another Guominjun commander present at the ceremony, gave a speech telling the workers that they and the Guominjun were working for the same cause—the revolution—and therefore should assist each other.[40] The reason the Guominjun officers were so supportive of the labor movement in Henan was obvious: they were seeking Soviet military support. The Russians and the Communists had great influence over the troops. Soviet advisers, often accompanied by Chinese Communist interpreters, served in the Guominjun units.[41] Many of the instructors in the Guominjun training regiment came from the Whampao Military Academy and had been sent by the

South under Guomindang-Guominjun cooperation.[42] Some Guominjun officers, such as Fan Zhongxiu, were true followers of the revolution; others just tagged along because it was Guominjun policy.

Such military support gave labor leaders a chance to take to the streets and agitate in the workplace. But ultimate success depended on the amount of resources, particularly financial, these leaders could amass to sustain the strike. Adequate strike funds were needed to enable laborers to hold out as long as they wanted. The nationwide movement to raise funds to support the strikers in Shanghai after the May 30th Incident gave Henan leaders the opportunity to obtain funds for local use. A fund-raising committee was set up on June 19, 1925, that brought together all the power holders in the province: Yue Weijun (chairman), the garrison commander, the secretary of the provincial administration, the head of the Henan Department of Industry, the *daotai* of Kaifeng, the head of the board of education, and leaders of other public organizations such as the merchant association, the provincial assembly, and Zhongzhou University.

The goal was to raise C$100,000. The students had already collected C$10,000 and were to raise another C$10,000 (C$6,000 from the schools and C$4,000 from the teachers). Contributions were to be automatically deducted from teachers' salaries. Each county school was required to raise C$40. The rest was allocated in the following way: C$40,000 from businesses, C$20,000 from the military, and C$20,000 from politicians. Native banks and merchant associations would advance C$30,000 to be sent to Shanghai immediately.[43] Most of the donations, in fact, came from business circles. Huaxin Textile Mills donated C$1,000. Others donated under coercion, in particular those with foreign connections. Zhao Zhongtao, the manager of the British-American Tobacco Company, and his staff were paraded through the streets and released only after agreeing to pay a fine of C$5,000.[44] In other cities, students seized cigarettes from retailers and forced merchants to pay a fine.[45] Indigenous merchants actively supported the movement because they stood to gain the most from it. Boycotts of foreign goods had practically destroyed the market for foreign merchandise. The Nanyang Brothers Tobacco Company realized a C$40,000–C$50,000 increase in cigarette sales during the movement.[46] Sales of other indigenous commodities, such as fabric, soap, and towels, brought in extra profit. When threatened by student radicals, most stores switched their goods to native commodities.

It would be difficult to say what percentage of the funds raised were actually forwarded to Shanghai and how much was retained to support local strikes, but a contemporary news report on the conflict between

Zhang Bochen (the head of the merchant association and chair of the executive committee of the Society for the Support of the Shanghai Incident) and Li Zhenying (the society's deputy and secretary of the Beijing-Hankou Railway General Union) sheds some light on the matter. According to the report, a total of C$10,000 was raised, but Li only forwarded C$2,000 to Shanghai, leaving C$8,000 unaccounted for.[47] Since Li, a Communist, was the main organizer of the strike, it seems likely that much of the money donated was channeled into the local labor movement.

Organizational Factors: Party, Unions, and Leadership

Given Henan's geographical isolation and low degree of industrialism, the only way for strike actions to be effective was to build sufficient collective support and an efficient labor organization to coordinate activities. A rudimentary form of labor organization did exist in Henan in late 1922 and early 1923. In the fall of 1922, the Labor Secretariat of the CCP had successfully transformed the Laojun Societies (a worker organization with a strong Daoist influence) on the Longhai line into the Longhai General Union. Similar efforts were made to build workers' recreation clubs along the Beijing-Hankou line. Simultaneously, a Communist by the name of Li Zilong had used his social ties to Ren Youmi, a former secretary to Feng Yuxiang and then the mayor of Kaifeng, to secure a position as director of education. He then used his influence to organize 3,000 students into a "Youth Improvement Recreation Club." In early 1923, the Labor Secretariat took the initiative in attempting to integrate the workers' clubs from sixteen stations into a Beijing-Hankou Railway General Union. The attempt was crushed by Wu Peifu, then military commissioner. The labor movement in Henan was nipped in the bud. Labor leaders were either apprehended or went underground.[48] For the next year or so, the party concentrated its effort on infiltrating local high schools. A branch of the Socialist Youth League was set up in the First Normal School in Kaifeng in February 1923, and "Henan Socialist Study Association" was formed in neighboring Qixian in August 1924.

When the understanding between the Chinese Communists and the Guominjun was reached, all the labor leaders arrested in the February 1923 strike were released. The Labor Secretariat seized this favorable political opportunity to send a group of Communist activists to rehabilitate the labor unions on the Beijing-Hankou, Longhai, and Daoqing lines. On February 7, 1925, in commemoration of the labor incident of 1923, a Second National Congress of Railwaymen was held in

Zhengzhou. It was attended by 45 delegates from the three lines and by unionists from as far away as Hamburg, Moscow, and Singapore. The Second National Congress not only revitalized but also legitimized the labor movement in Henan. Between February and May 1925, nine railway unions with a total membership of more than 4,200 were rehabilitated.[49] The offices of the Beijing-Hankou Railway General Union and the All-China Railwaymen's General Union were turned into operational centers for the Communists. From their bases along the railways the Communists fanned out to neighboring areas to set up trade unions in coal mines (Jiaozuo, Liuhegou, and Xin'an), textile mills (Yufeng, Anyang, and Xinxiang), the Kaifeng arsenal, an egg factory, and a government mint.[50]

From February to May 1925, the party rapidly rebuilt its organizations in Henan. Party organizations and Communist Youth Leagues were set up in the major railroad centers of Kaifeng, Zhengzhou, and Xinyang. In March 1925, a CYL headquarters was formed in Kaifeng which became the center for directing student movement in Henan. Outside labor activists, working through the students, began to infiltrate schools, mines, and railroads in the province. The rehabilitated party itself consisted of a three-level hierarchical structure in the province, the locality, and the plant. The chain of command started at Li Dazhao's North China Regional Committee in Beijing, which oversaw all operational activities in North China, including those in Henan. Kaifeng, the provincial capital of Henan, was the center for directing all provincial activities. A Henan Labor Union was set up there in September 1925, following a wave of labor strikes, but the capital was overshadowed by the railway center of Zhengzhou.[51] Because the revitalization of the labor movement had begun with the rebuilding of the railway unions, all party activities were directed from Zhengzhou. Aside from the usual local Communist Party and the Youth League, all major organizations such as the Guomindang headquarters, the Beijing-Hankou Railway General Union, and the All-China Railwaymen's General Union were located there. Even when the party later decided to form a regional organization (the Yu-Shan quwei, or Regional Committee of Henan and Shaanxi), it chose Zhengzhou as the site of the regional headquarters.[52]

Provincial-level leaders consisted mainly of ex-provincials.[53] When the opportunity arose for the Communists to rebuild the party structure in Henan, Li Dazhao ordered a group of activists from Beijing, Shanghai, and Hankou to Zhengzhou. All party secretaries held dual membership in the Communist Party and the Guomindang.[54] Most of the leaders were May Fourth intellectuals and veterans of the labor movement.[55] Labor leaders like Li Zhenying, Zhang Kundi, and Liu Wensong had been active on the Beijing-Hankou line back in the days of the first strike wave in 1923; they were all reassigned to the same line after rehabilitation.[56] Others were labor activists from other provinces. Wang Hebo, for instance, had been a labor organizer on the Jinpu line as early as 1916 and was elected an alternate member of the CCP Executive Committee before receiving his assignment as head of the All-China Railwaymen's General Union.[57] The party at that time regarded Henan as one of its central operational centers, second only to Guangdong and Shanghai. The party's special relations with the Guominjun, and the centrality of Zhengzhou, where two major rail lines (the Beijing-Hankou and the Longhai) crossed, gave the province added significance. The number of high-level leaders injected into the province by Party Central suggests its importance as an operational base.

Henan was sectored into various zones, all centered at major railway towns and each under the direction of a local leader: Anyang (Yang Jieren), Xinyang (Liu Shaoyou), Luoyang (Ma Liangchen), and Jiaozuo (She Liya). Of these zones, Anyang (or Zhangde, as it was called then), located at the heart of the relatively industrial north, was the most important. Since the Communists were devoting most of their attention to urban insurrections at the time, the north, which embraced most of the provincial mining, railway, and textile industries, became their main area of operation. At the local level, leadership was held by natives. The head of the Anyang operation, Yang Jieren, was a native of Qinyang in southern Henan. Yang had been a work-study student in France for two years before returning to China in 1923. In December 1924, he headed the Anyang operation and was in charge of the rail section between Xingtai (Shunde) in Hebei and Xinxiang in Henan.[58] Thus he had authority over an operational zone consisting of Xingtai, Xinxiang, Weihui, Liuhegou, Jiaozuo, and Anyang counties, roughly the area north of the Yellow River.

The Communists operated in three areas: the railway, the schools, and the mines. It was at the railroad, given its importance and the long history of Communist activity in the industry, that the Communists set up their base of operations. They formed three party cells among the railwaymen: a ten-person cell (the largest) among the maintenance crew; a cell among train workers; and a three- or four-person cell in the workshop.[59] A ten-person cell under the direction of Luo Renyi was set up in the Eleventh High School in Anyang. (It was through an introduction by Luo, a teacher at the school, that Yang Jieren came into contact with Guominjun officers.)[60] In the Liuhegou mines, the party recruited twenty members (including alternates) into three cells, one each for water pump workers, boiler workers, and mechanics.[61] This indicates that party organizers were mostly successful with skilled workers. The party was able to build these cells only because it had secured the support of the Guominjun through Guomindang members. Liu Shouzhong, a Guomindang Central Executive Committee member, served as the liaison between the Communists and the Guominjun. The Guominjun commanders were all tolerant of, if not sympathetic toward, Communist activities in the area. Moreover, the mayor of Anyang, a Mr. Zhang, was a Guomindang member, although a "rightist." When Yang Jieren set up Guomindang headquarters in the city, all the so-called Guomindang members were either Communists or student "leftists." The Communists were operating in a very friendly environment.[62]

At the plant level, leadership was composed of student activists and rank-and-file laborers, all natives. One or several party cells usually directed the operation. The front organization was the labor union headed by plant workers themselves. A typical example was the Huaxin Textile Labor Union in Weihui county, where the Communists also operated in an amiable environment: the regional military commander, Zheng Sicheng, was a pro-Communist who gave workers the right to assemble. In 1925 the party sent two members, Gao Feng and Chen Jiuding, to organize a labor movement in the factory. They joined the plant as janitor and cart-pusher and within a couple of months had formed a number of party cells. With these as their bases, they moved to form a labor union in the summer of 1925. Leadership in the union was controlled by both Communists and non-Communists. The 1,700 members paid a day's wages each month as dues. These funds were used to create a recreation club, and it was in this club that the Communists extended their network of contacts. Young workers became prime targets for recruitment into the Communist Youth League.[63] Only after they had infiltrated the plant and had the union solidly under their control could the Communists mobilize the laborers in a strike.

Although plant units were normally under the supervision of local-level leaders, who in turn reported to the provincial party, some units, due either to their special location or to the significance of the industry, were directly under Beijing's control. One such case was the Jiaozuo mining industry, which embraced both the British-dominated Peking Syndicate Collieries and the native Zhongyuan mines and had a large number of workers. The adjoining Daoqing rail line, the transport system for the coal produced in the area, formed part of the mining complex. Jiaozuo, due to its unique position, was treated as a special zone by the party, and was directly supervised by Beijing.

The significance of Jiaozuo is indicated by the number of high-level ex-provincial leaders the party poured into the locality. The entire top leadership of the Jiaozuo local party (*diwei*) were outsiders, mostly from Hubei and Hunan.[64] All were intellectuals and veterans of labor movements. Liu Changyan, the party secretary and a former student at the Labor University in Moscow, had lengthy experience organizing labor on the Jing-Sui line in Zhangjiakou as well as in the Anyuan mines. Transferred with him from Zhangjiakou was He Zhizheng, the technical secretary and a former organizer of the Jing-Sui line recreation club. Also from the Anyuan mines in Hunan was Zhu Jintang, an alternate member of the Fourth Central Committee of the CCP. Another party secretary, Luo Siwei, was a student at the Peking Syndicate Mining University who had been active in antiforeign and peasant movements before becoming a labor organizer. Others, like Yang Tianran and Gong Yiqing, were students assigned to work on the youth and peasants in the greater Jiaozuo area. The lower-level leadership consisted of local college and elementary school students; only the plant-level leadership was made up mostly of laborers.[65] Some of the student leaders were ex-provincials; the plant leaders were natives.

We can reconstruct the process of party building and mobilization in the Jiaozuo area from the participants' recollections. As with the rebuilding of the Anyang center, the party commenced with the rehabilitation of a rail line, and in late 1924, the first group of activists—She Liya, Yun Long, Liu Changyan, and Gong Yiqing—was sent to the Daoqing railway.[66] Yun Long, the head of the Daoqing Railway Labor Union in 1923, resumed his post after the rehabilitation. The Communists seized control of the railway with ease because the superintendent of the Daoqing line, Jiao Yitang, was a Guomindang member. Moreover, She Liya, the special emissary appointed by the All-China Railwaymen's General Union to take charge of the Jiaozuo labor movement, was in love with Jiao's daughter and later married her. On top of that, the Guominjun brigade commander stationed at Jiaozuo, Shi Kexuan, was also a CCP member. Such relations gave She complete freedom to operate in the area.[67]

With the rail line securely under its control, the party set out in early 1925 to establish local parties and unions. Communist leaders brought with them a letter from Guomindang headquarters in Zhengzhou requesting local commanders and the county government to provide their activists with protection should they run into trouble.[68] These labor agitators were mostly urban elite in intellectual outfits—white gown, top hat, and a briefcase, as one worker described Luo Siwei, the head of the group. They were ill at ease in the mines and seldom mixed with local workers. In fact, Luo devoted most of his time to soliciting financial support from local businessmen.[69] They did come to the mines occasionally to talk to the laborers, and in a short time were able to form a local party and a Communist Youth League in the area.

Much of the grass-roots mobilization was done by local students. In fact, when the ex-provincial leaders first came to the area, they resided with students in the dormitory at the Mining University until the GMD headquarters was created in August 1925. The Communists made the best use of the May 30th Movement, which greatly aroused the students and enabled Communist leaders to recruit party members and channel the students' energy into antiforeign and labor movements. It also allowed them to form a party cell in the university. Amid boycotts, strikes, and rallies, the youths integrated themselves into a student union. The hard-core radicals organized themselves into a "revolutionary youth corps." The establishment of the Society for the Support of the Shanghai Incident and the subsequent movement for donations in support of the Shanghai strikers brought students out of their classrooms and into the streets, the countryside, the mines, and the factories to agitate. In a populist movement, students set up night schools and literacy classes for workers, using local temples as classrooms. Embedded in their teachings were heavy doses of propaganda, xenophobic attacks on foreigners for their criminal activities in the raid on Beijing during the Boxer Uprising, stories about the brave actions of their fellow workers in other towns in the May 30th strikes, and also some fundamental knowledge of unionism.[70]

Using their labor recruits as intermediaries, the Communists penetrated the mines.[71] By June they had set up a miners' union in the Peking Syndicate Collieries. Its members were predominantly permanent workers—administrative staff, electricians, and handymen. The Communists also successfully organized foreigners' household servants into a union. The chefs were first to join, and they contributed generously to the strike fund.[72] These unions were still underground organizations. Party members were carefully screened for political reliability. Candidates had to be introduced by a member, who acted as a guarantor, and their names were sent to Beijing for approval. Undoubtedly, workers must have realized some benefits in joining the party. According to one miner, they heard that by becoming members they would get a chance to be sent to Guangzhou to "study."

The fund-raising campaign gave the Communists the opportunity to extend their influence into the local bank, which handled all remissions of strike funds to Shanghai. Three party members worked among the staff in the Jiaozuo bank, which was in fact one of the Communists' operational centers.[73] By June 1925, the Communists had secured a solid base in the area, with party cells in the railway, the schools, and the mines. The Zhengzhou party branch sent top leaders to the field to make sure that the basic groundwork had been laid.[74] It was at that point that the party felt ready to launch a general strike in the area.

Strike Activity: Communist Strategies

The Henan strikes started off as a political protest. The cause of the stoppage was related to the strikers' working conditions but also had a wider political relevance—the May 30th Incident in Shanghai. The clash between demonstrating students and the British police in Shanghai's International Settlement on May 30, 1925, resulted in the killing of nine students and serious injury to many others, and touched off a nationwide demonstration and labor strikes. The movement rapidly spread to Henan. In June, students and businessmen organized rallies and boycotts of foreign goods in all central cities. A Society for the Support of the Shanghai Incident was set up in every major city in the province to raise funds to support the striking workers in Shanghai. Locally, the Communists exploited the movement to build up their power and to seize control of the labor movement.

It is important to note that labor strikes did not erupt in Henan until the beginning of July, after all the groundwork had been laid. One participant suggested that the party deliberately timed the outbreak to coincide with the founding date of the Chinese Communist Party.[75] Foreign industrial establishments, in particular the British-controlled Peking Syndicate Collieries, were the first targets of hostility. In Jiaozuo in Qinyang County, students at the Peking Syndicate Mining University took the lead in organizing citizens' rallies, some attended by the military. In early June, the party had assigned four provincial-level leaders to Jiaozuo to direct the movement.[76] The Jiaozuo Society for the Support of the Shanghai Incident was created in mid-June. An 80-person student vanguard called the Revolutionary Youth Detachment was set up. Two meetings were held to plot the course of the labor movement, one in the Young Men's Association of the Catholic church, the other at Fu Lun Elementary School.

The Communists' strategy was to bring the Peking Syndicate Collieries to a complete halt, and their tactic was to drive foreigners out of the area. They therefore called a servants' strike first, in which 200 members of the Employees' Union—chefs, interpreters, gardeners, and maids who provided domestic service to foreigners—walked off their jobs. Food and water supplies were cut off, forcing 40 foreign employees of the mines to leave for Beijing. Then on July 8, 600 miners and 2,000 students met in a local temple to plan the miners' strike, which they called the following day. To consolidate their forces, miners' and chefs' unions were immediately created.[77] Later, the Jiaozuo General Union, which incorporated the Daoqing union and the Employees' Union, was formed. The General Union then presented Peking Syndicate management with 22 demands. At this point, the party felt it necessary to strengthen leadership by assigning more high-level leaders to the locality, and five more labor veterans arrived in Jiaozuo to supervise the strike activity.[78]

An immediate problem confronting the Communists was the means of support of thousands of striking workers. There were 10,000 miners in the Peking Syndicate Collieries, but many drifted back to the countryside in the summer; only 4,000 remained at work. Of these, 2,300 participated in the strike. The Communists were able to place 500 of them in the Zhongyuan mines. The company only agreed to take in these workers because it had profited from the Peking Syndicate strike. Consumers increasingly turned to the Zhongyuan mines as a source of coal, thus causing them to boost production.[79] Later, through the intercession of the mayor of Qinyang, another 1,000 miners were taken up by the indigenous Liuhegou mines. The remaining 800 strikers had to be sent home and paid out of the strike fund. The miners joined the strike with the understanding that it was a government-sponsored activity and that they would receive C$7.50 a month during the work stoppage, double their normal wages of C$2.00 to C$3.00 a month. The money was said to have come out of a government workers' reserve fund.[80]

The party took steps to find other means of financial support to prolong the strike. It organized two "Donation Drive Propaganda Teams" to go around the province raising money.[81] Posing as Guomindang members, the team workers wore shirts with the Guomindang flag on the front and back. They raised C$20,000 for the cause. These propaganda teams, traveling from one urban center to another, also served as liaisons within the network. They secured support from government officials, participated in local strikes, and coordinated activities within the area.

To ensure that no workers entered the mines and no vendors supplied foreigners with food, the party organized 120 miners into a workers' picket. They were subdivided into twelve ten-man teams, all carrying clubs and swords, and charged with the responsibilities of maintaining security, keeping an eye on the foreigners, and patrolling the mines.[82]

The management responded immediately by sending its manager to the mines to negotiate. Because the military had already abided by the treaty by making sure that foreign lives and property were protected, the foreigners had no cause for protest. They only requested that domestic service be restored and pump workers remain at work so that the mines would not be inundated by water, thus ruining the entire mining operation. At first they tried to replace workers with those from other mines, but the Communists blocked their attempt. The only recourse left for the mine managers was to use diplomatic means to exert pressure on Duan Qirui's executive government to intercede on their behalf. But Governor Yue Weijun, who was still committed to the alliance with the Guomindang and was seeking military assistance from the Soviet Union, backed the strikers. Yue argued that since foreign lives and property were not in jeopardy, no damage had been done. The central government sent mediator Li Shi, interpreter for the Foreign Affairs Bureau, to talk with the management and a delegation of workers. The military and the county mayor also acted as go-betweens. The process dragged on until March 1926, when an agreement was reached that recognized the union. Management agreed to pay C$25,700 in reparations for wages lost in the strike. The company also promised to give workers a pay increase, set up a night school, improve the contract labor system, and institute such benefits as accident compensation and travel expenses for ex-provincial workers. With government and military support, the Peking Syndicate strike had lasted eight months.[83]

The party was not content with organizing labor strikes in foreign-dominated enterprises; it wanted to extend the movement to Chinese-owned industries. Three sympathetic strikes, two in the mines and one on the railroad, were called in July and August 1925, after the Peking Syndicate shutdown had become effective. Even though the Chinese-owned Zhongyuan and Liuhegou mines had been helpful in the movement, absorbing a large band of striking miners from the Peking Syndicate Collieries, the party must have thought that it had better seize control of the labor movement, in native as well as foreign-owned industries, while its relations with the military government still permitted it to do so. Moving into a Chinese-owned enterprise, however, raised a different set of problems.

Encouraged by the success of the Peking Syndicate strike, the party began to transfer some of the labor activists to the Zhongyuan mines.[84] Luo Zhanglong, leader of the Beijing-Hankou Railway General Union, assured the miners that they would receive pay amounting to C$7 a month plus subsidies during the stoppage. The strike, he said, had the blessings of the government. He intimidated nonparticipants by warning them that the Xiuwu county government would have them arrested if they refused to join. The Communists set up two branch unions in the

Zhongyuan mines, and most of the mechanics became members. They presented management with seven demands, giving them 24 hours to respond. Since all major company business had to go through the Tianjin headquarters, local management had no authority to give the union an answer on such short notice. A strike was called on August 9, 1925. Management, however, retaliated with its own weapons. The company promised to give workers a pay raise if they resisted the influx of Peking Syndicate workers. Pump and boiler operators refused to strike. A clash broke out between the Peking Syndicate strikers and the union pickets on one side and the nonparticipating workers and the security force on the other. This time Governor Yue took a hard line, appointing three special emissaries to deal with the incident. But in the end, Yue yielded, and the strikers got their demands.[85]

In the Liuhegou strike, the Communists won the support of local commander Gong Haiting. Luo Renyi, the Communist leader, convinced the troops that they would realize no gain by suppressing the strike and should instead use the opportunity to seize the coal from the mine and sell it in the local market to bring in additional income. Thus when the Communists called a strike in the fall, the troops did not interfere, and the Communists easily won their demands.[86] A Daoqing railway strike was also staged in support of the Peking Syndicate strike. The strike was settled in March 1926, when the Peking Syndicate strike came to an end.[87]

The Communists carefully coordinated two textile strikes in central Henan to coincide with the miners' strikes in the north. These were the Yufeng strike in Zhengzhou and the Weihui textile strike. The Yufeng strike was directed by the provincial party in Zhengzhou, using the labor activists on the Beijing-Hankou line. In the spring of 1925, the party had infiltrated the Yufeng Textile Factory with four members, two women who joined as textile workers and two former Beijing-Hankou workers ordered by the party to organize a union in the plant.[88] With a wave of labor strikes sweeping China after the May 30th Incident, the Communists seized the opportunity to build up a union in the factory. As in the case of the coal industry, the closing of textile mills in Shanghai sharply increased the demand for cotton yarns in Henan. To increase production, Yufeng management hired several hundred workers from Anyang. These workers received a high wage, which greatly offended local workers.[89] The company also took precautions to stop the spread of labor strikes by replacing radical workers, and it did away with holiday pay, bonuses, and travel expenses for foremen and mechanics.[90] As a result, all the foremen and mechanics joined the union.

Top leaders in Zhengzhou had a meeting to plan the Yufeng strike.

Present were Party Secretary Wang Ruofei, veteran labor leaders Li Zhenying and Zhang Kundi, Mikhail Borodin, and possibly Li Dazhao, who was in Henan negotiating with Yue Weijun at the time.[91] Because the Yufeng union was weak, the party used the more organized Beijing-Hankou railway workers as its fighting force. A Beijing-Hankou "dare-to-die" corps was formed to back the textile workers, and a sympathy strike was called on August 5, 1925. Yufeng management was presented with twelve demands and given 48 hours to respond. A strike committee was then created among the workers. The committee used its "Youth Corps" and pickets to inform all factory workers that they were receiving donations from Shanghai, Guangzhou, and Hankou. All striking workers were guaranteed C$1 a day. With 5,000 workers on their payroll, the committee said the strike fund could last six months.

Yufeng management fought back with its own weapons. Mu Ouchu, the manager, came to Zhengzhou and struck a deal with Yue Weijun. The company agreed to "contribute" to Yue's military expenses and build barracks for his soldiers in return for a crackdown on the dissidents. Yue then outlawed the Beijing-Hankou union and closed down the Communist publication *The Revolutionary Army*. The Zhengzhou police sent secret agents and local militia to track down instigators. The company fired sixteen activists from their jobs but failed to buy over the union leaders. Management hired several hundred hoodlums to beat up the unionists. They also formed a company-sponsored union called the Order Preservation Association to lead 3,000 workers in the fight. Carrying yellow flags and wearing arm bands, these company-controlled workers demanded the right to work. The Communists held an emergency meeting and decided on a confrontational approach. They sent several hundred Beijing-Hankou "dare-to-dies" and Youth Corps members and 1,000 pickets bearing knives and clubs into the factory to drive out the company-approved unionists. The police moved in to quell the unrest, which resulted in 2 dead and 70 injured (including Communist labor leaders Li Zhenying and Liu Wensong). Union funds amounting to C$1,700 disappeared during the conflict.[92]

The strike committee immediately issued a message denouncing the plant manager, and ordered workers to form an armed picket to protect the strike committee. The party ordered a Beijing-Hankou engineer to drive his locomotive to the front gate of the factory and blow its whistle in protest. It also organized a widely publicized memorial service for the two workers killed in the incident. The service was attended by thousands of students and workers and the caskets were carried down the street by students. What finally brought Yue Weijun and the Yufeng manager to their knees was the "urgent order" issued by the

Beijing-Hankou union to all of its workers to stop transporting coal and yarn to the factory and fabric out of it. At this point, the merchants' association and civic leaders mediated. The police backed down and returned the union sign, which they had seized during the conflict. Realizing that business could not go on without the transport system, management finally acceded to all sixteen demands, thus ending the eighteen-day strike.

The Weihui labor movement was not as dramatic as the one at Yufeng. A Communist-dominated union existed in April 1925, but the company managed to buy over the union secretary and set up its own recreation club for workers. Those who joined the club were promised a pay raise.[93] When management heard that a strike was about to be called, they ordered that the union be dissolved and workers join the club instead. The Communists, however, had the backing of local military commander Zheng Sicheng. They responded by calling in troops to disperse the club members. The subsequent conflict between club members and soldiers ended in ten wounded and the death of Mr. Zhou, the recreation club leader. Commander Zheng then assigned 500 soldiers to protect the union. The Weihui union was thus secured.[94]

A Pilot Peasant Movement in Youth Village

While the May 30th Movement is usually perceived by historians as essentially a Communist-instigated urban proletarian movement, in the suburban countryside in Xihua county the antiforeign struggle attracted a sizable number of peasants. Surprisingly, the Xihua boycott in Youth Village (*qingnian cun*) was organized in the name of a peasant organization, the Central Plain Peasant Association (*Zhongyuan nongmin xiehui*). Youth Village was a suburban village located 35 *li* (16 kilometers) east of the Yancheng county Beijing-Hankou rail station. The area was under the protection of Fan Zhongxiu, the Guomindang commander who was a follower of Sun Yatsen and a supporter of the southern revolution.[95] Under Fan's protection, this region became an ideal place for Communist mobilization.

Originally known as Xiaowu Ying, Youth Village had been dramatically transformed in the early Republican period by Wang Gongbi, a native villager and a 1911 revolutionary. Wang was a student who had returned from Japan and devoted seven years after the 1911 Revolution to changing the countryside. He used Youth Village as an experimental station for his modernization project called "New Village Life." Under his leadership, the village built a public school and published a local magazine, *The Green Field*. Other civic organizations sprang into existence.[96] Wang also set up the Central Plain Peasant Association and the Village Autonomous Association. The village was later presented as a model for rural modernization.[97]

When news of the May 30th Incident reached Youth Village, local students were swiftly drawn into the antiforeign movement. They fanned out into the countryside, propagating their cause among the peasants. It is amazing that local peasants responded positively. Because they had been using imported yarns for their textile production, Xihua peasants had already been drawn into the global market. The boycott of foreign goods undoubtedly affected their lives. The lack of concrete evidence available at this time prevents us from knowing exactly how the students secured the peasants' support, but it seems that the activists might have bought off the peasants with the C$100,000 "war fund" (*zhanfei*) they had received from Kaifeng.[98] Consequently, despite the busy harvest season, tens of thousands of rural cultivators urged the Peasant Association to hold an emergency meeting.

The meeting brought together peasant representatives and primary school activists from nearby towns and villages. The Central Plain Peasant Association, acting as the leading organization, issued a telegram in support of the Shanghai compatriots. Following in the footsteps of other Henan cities, the Peasant Association endorsed a boycott of foreign goods and passed a resolution calling for the formation of a "Volunteer Corps," which was to be made up of local militia and merchant corps from the area. Funding for the Volunteer Corps was to come from a new surcharge on land taxes. Later, the Volunteer Corps was renamed the "Student Army" (*xuesheng jun*), and a Mr. Ding, a graduate of the Japanese Military Officers Academy, was hired as its trainer.[99]

Though the boycott was a brief phenomenon, the Xihua incident can be regarded as a Communist pilot project for peasant mobilization. The peasant-based revolution in China can be traced to this period of urban insurrections. The urban-rural linkage was established right from the outset. The early mobilization in Xihua gave the county added significance. After the May 30th Movement, it became a stronghold for Communist activities. As we shall see in Chapter 5, in the resistance war period Xihua would become an established Communist base from which the Communist Party in Henan would draw resources to rebuild the movement and launch the social revolution.

Conclusion

I have demonstrated that the labor movement in Henan was successful in this period not simply because society was strained, which heightened the impulse toward antisocial behavior. Admittedly, economic and social injustice in the workplace were real and were frequently exploited by the Communists to mobilize workers in violent industrial protests. But socioeconomic forces alone cannot explain the timing and the magnitude of the May 30th strike wave. Nor can they explain why the Peking Syndicate miners' strike lasted eight months, while the strike by Beijing-Hankou railway workers in February 1923 was put down by the military in days.

As pointed out, the political factor, or party politics, determined the timing, form, and success of the movement. It was the Guomindang-Guominjun alliance and the understanding between the Guominjun and the Soviet Union that provided the Communists the opportunity to move back into the province and rebuild their party structure and the trade unions. It was the support of the military that gave them the chance to make political advances in the workplace and to build up the power needed to confront management without being turned aside by the police or troops. It was also government consent that enabled the party to collect enough strike funds to sustain the movement; without adequate financial resources, the strikes could never have gotten off the ground. A tolerant government thus greatly cuts the cost of and facilitates collective actions.

For collective actions to be successful, strong leadership and effective organizations are required. In terms of manpower, the party had redirected a large group of highly experienced labor veterans from other provinces into Henan. This injection of outside labor leaders into the movement is in sharp contrast to the predominantly native leadership group which we later find in the Red Spears movement. Such action, in a way, reflects the importance the party placed on labor insurrections at the time, even in a relatively remote area like Henan. Considering the little time they had, the Communists' effort in setting up a network capable of mobilizing and integrating so many people in a movement should be considered a great success. Based on the more organized railway unions, Communist activists stretched out to form satellite parties and branch unions in nearby areas. Internal links were provided by provincial leaders touring the localities to inspect, supervise, and direct the activities. During the protests, the party constantly reinforced local organizations by a downward transfer of higher-level leaders. Protest actions were very well integrated. The Yufeng workers would never have been able to withstand management's assaults without the party's mobilized support of the Beijing-Hankou railway union.

The Communist labor organizers were most successful in mobilizing the skilled workers in the mining industry. Many of the labor activists at the plant level in the Liuhegou mines were pump workers, boiler workers, and mechanics. In the Peking Syndicate Collieries, the miners' union was set up among the permanent workers: administrative staff, electricians, and handymen. In the Zhongyuan mines, again, a branch union was established among the mechanics. It was with the more educated workers that the May Fourth intellectuals found the most affinity. The educational background of these workers made them more receptive to nationalist and socialist propaganda.[100] By contrast, outside labor agitators such as Luo Siwei were ill at ease with the unskilled workers, and many probably did not speak the local dialects. At this point, lack of materials does not permit us to fully explain the workers' motivations and aspirations, but many of them were obviously driven to participate not only by socioeconomic injustice in the workplace, but more so by the nationalist sentiment that surged forth in the May 30th period. The key process in the mobilization, as both the Anyang and Jiaozuo movements indicate, was to work through teachers and students in local schools.

The party was skillful in seizing the opportunity of the May 30th Movement to extend its influence into the schools and factories. The Peking Syndicate strike received nationwide support from intellectual, business, and military circles. Native merchants, aroused by a sense of nationalism and moved by self-interest, lent their support. But the Communist strategy went too far in moving too quickly into indigenous enterprises. The Communists wanted to make the most of their cordial relations with the military to introduce social reforms in native industry while they still could. But their confrontational approach backfired. They lost the support of the indigenous merchants, and increasingly came into conflict with the military. For a time, Yue Weijun yielded to their demands. But later events (which will be treated in the next chapter) show that once Yue received his arms shipment from the Soviet Union, he did not hesitate to adopt a harsh policy toward these Communist radicals. Yue broke up their unions and outlawed their members, driving them underground. Their existence, as well as the success of their movement, depended very much on the tolerant attitude of the Guominjun military government.

CHAPTER 2

Mobilizing the Sectarians: The Communists and the Red Spears

The Communists' second revolutionary mobilization was strikingly different from the first. This time, cadres were instructed to mobilize a sectarian group—the Red Spears—in the Nationalist Revolution. Between 1926 and 1927, the party ordered a large number of cadres to return to their hometowns in Henan. Their goal was to instigate a rural revolution and to pave the way for the coming Northern Expedition. According to Communist historians, the movement was a resounding success. Penetrating deeply into the countryside, these revolutionaries succeeded in recruiting about one million peasants into peasant associations. Cadres were also able to reorganize the local Red Spears sectarians into peasant self-defense armies, which, according to party historians, were used as the Communist fighting force in the countryside.

When Nationalist troops approached the area, thousands of peasants rose up in revolt. They resisted paying taxes to the warlord government and joined the Communists in the redistribution of gentry property. Indeed, a social revolution was in the making in the broad countryside. Active peasant participation, Marxist historians argue, was crucial for the success of the Nationalist Revolution. During the fighting, they say, peasants voluntarily gave the soldiers food, assisted in the transportation of military materiel, gathered military intelligence, and served the army as guides. Peasant revolts behind enemy lines, they contend, hastened the collapse of the Fengtian Army, which eventually brought the Northern Expedition to a successful conclusion.[1]

But scholars studying millenarian movements have repeatedly pointed out that transforming sectarians into a revolutionary force is never a simple task. First, sectarians are dominated by a specific religious world view. Their religion is apocalyptic and predicts the imminent disaster associated with the turning of the kalpa.[2] It preaches salvation for the whole group but emphasizes the believers' active role in cataclysmic events. Sectarians' religious beliefs sanction the use of magical power. Because of their specific world view, sectarians are often regarded by revolutionary intellectuals as superstitious; there is always an intellectual gap between urban-oriented, modernly educated revolutionary intellectuals and superstitious, rural-bound sectarians.

Second, sectarian divisions have always presented revolutionaries with a major problem. Sectarians are invariably involved in bitter disputes over competing ideologies. Protracted ideological feuds are not only destructive, but they harden these religious groups into separate political-ideological entities. Moreover, Chinese sectaries practiced different schools of martial arts and martial arts rivalry often kept them apart. Martial arts groups seldom possess an organizational structure that gives them unity.[3] They are loose, kinship- or community-based organizations integrated by teacher-student relations and often characterized by a very weak vertical linkage. Although charismatic leadership of sectarians produces group cohesion, it invariably gives rise to sectarian divisions. Revolutionaries have to find a way to weld these divisive religious groups together before they can be used as a revolutionary force.

Third, in order to use sectarians as a revolutionary force, revolutionaries have to wrest them from the control of the rural gentry. Given the kinship and community basis of these groupings, local gentry, as leaders of the kin organizations and local community, have undisputed control over the sectaries. Rural elites frequently regard sect power as a political instrument for personal gain. Religious sects are bonded by a patron-client relationship. Sectarian groups are invariably closed organizations and it is almost impossible for revolutionaries to claim the obedience of sectarian adherents without some sort of acquiescence from gentry sectarian chieftains.

Fourth, revolutionaries are confronted with the problem that sectarian affairs are usually localistic. Their normal activities include defending their sect belief, participating in local power politics, and occasionally rebelling in response to the turn of the kalpa. To be sure, major economic dislocation or the trauma of colonial occupation have historically transformed millenarianism into major religious movements with mass appeal. Confronted with subsistence problems or outside threat, sectaries have sometimes gravitated into larger groupings for the purpose of collective defense. But such social clusters, although covering a wider area, remain very loosely integrated. Their mentality is still parochially focused. To successfully absorb these groups into a revolutionary movement requires introducing sectarian leaders to modern revolutionary politics at the national level. It also requires giving the diffused groupings a hierarchical organizational framework, and it requires constant negotiations with the rural elite to secure their allegiance.

There are a number of studies of the Red Spears, for instance, the works of Dai Xuanzhi and Baba Takeshi, that emphasize their loose organizational structure and religious beliefs. Our limited knowledge of these groups, mainly of Red Spears organized publicly by the rural elite, comes from newspaper reports. So far, we know little about Communist activities in the Red Spears movement. We do not know why these sectarians suddenly sprang to life in 1924, even though Red Spears are known to have existed as early as the 1911 Revolution. Political instability, exorbitant taxes, and rampant banditry, often cited as the root causes of their dramatic growth, were an integral part of the Chinese rural landscape before 1924. We have little explanation of why these groups varied from area to area. It would be interesting to look into the theory, proposed by Elizabeth Perry, that the Red Spears were basically "protective" groups organized by local elite for the purpose of local defense against military excesses and banditry.[4]

How did the Communists compete with the rural elite for control of these powerful sects? How did the Communists infiltrate these organizations? How did they draw these fractious groups into an integrated movement? Did they encounter any problems in their interaction with the sectarians? Was the movement a resounding success, as Communist historians claim? What role did the movement play in the Communist revolution?

Political Disintegration and Problems of Insecurity

During the warlord period, Henan increasingly disintegrated into a fragmented society. The province was successively occupied by various warlord factions, each of whose leaders controlled a personal army. These included Zhang Zhenfang's Henan Army (*Yu jun*), Liu Zhenhua's Pacifying the Song Army (*Zhen Song jun*), Zhao Ti's Resolute Army (*Yi jun*), his brother Zhao Jie's Magnificent Army (*Hong jun*), Wu Peifu's Zhili Army, and Hu Jingyi's (later Yue Weijun's) National Army (Guominjun). The ever-growing provincial military forces made increasing claims on local resources. Large segments of the provincial budget were allocated to support the military establishment and the internecine war. In 1923, for instance, 84 percent of the provincial budget went to military expenditure. This figure was only surpassed by those of two other provinces, Sichuan (88 percent) and Hubei (94 percent).[5]

The year 1924 was a significant point of departure for Henan. The province had enjoyed a degree of political stability under Wu Peifu's rule, but with Wu's defeat in the Second Zhili-Fengtian War, political disintegration in Henan increased sharply. Subsequent rulers spent most of their energy building up their military power. Hu Jingyi, the Guominjun victor in 1924, doubled the size of his Shaanxi forces within a year by taking over defeated soldiers. His successor, Yue Weijun, rapidly expanded the National Army into five divisions, and by the summer of 1925, into eleven divisions. Under Yue's rule, southeastern Henan alone had to support 200,000 soldiers.[6] The situation further deteriorated with the collapse of the Guominjun and the return of Wu Peifu. By that time, Henan was completely fragmented into a mosaic of military bases dominated by bands of undisciplined soldiers.

The problems stemmed not only from the enormous size but also the heterogenous nature of these forces. The Guominjun soldiers were mostly outsiders from Shaanxi. In 1926, Wu Peifu returned to the province with a very different army, a highly mixed bag composed of his own Third Division of the Zhili Army, some troops he brought from Hubei, and the Guominjun who had defected to his camp during the war.[7] The ex-provincial troops, known to the natives as "guest armies" (*kejun*), had little feeling for the civilians. Their primary objective was to extract as much as possible, as fast as possible, from the civilian population under their control.

No army can be fully effective without adequate and regular military provisions. All warlord armies lived off the land and used coercion to make their claims. Militarists frequently taxed people in advance. In March 1927, Jin Yun'e, then the commander in southern Henan, gave the local residents a month to pay their 1930 land taxes. If residents had already paid taxes for that year, they were required to pay taxes for the following year. If the local headmen, who were responsible for the collection, failed to come up with 60 percent of the tax money within a month, they were court-martialed. Jin also sent a battalion to the countryside to "assist" the headmen in tax collection and law enforcement.[8] To ensure that non-combatants "contributed" fully to sustain the war, militarists often made sure they completely dominated the area. In the seven years of "bandit suppression" in Runan, Tian Weiqin personally appointed the mayor and the heads of all the tax bureaus in the county.[9]

Tensions always ran high when troops came to the countryside to requisition food and labor from the people. In May 1926, Ren Yingqi used his troops to coerce a peasant association in Shangcheng county to "contribute" to his war chest. To avoid bloodshed, the peasant association dispatched three representatives to negotiate with the army in the Temple of the God of War, only to have them detained by the troops. The soldiers agreed to release the negotiators and leave the village upon receiving C$500 and five guns from the villagers. But they came back the following day to pillage, their attack resulting in 76 dead, 6 wounded, and 20 houses burned down.[10]

It was the multiplicity of small encounters—the assaults on towns and villages by bands of unruly soldiers—that formed the most common and most unpleasant side of warfare. Battles, which could last only a couple of days or as long as a month, often caused heavy casualties: thousands of people were killed and hundreds of thousands of dollars of property damage was done. An eyewitness gave a vivid account of the devastating effect of these raids. "Within five *li* on both sides of the Beijing-Hankou railroad," he says, "villages were deserted. Not a sign of life could be found. Houses stood there without doors; household belongings were all gone."[11]

Resentment against the soldiers was strong. Community-military conflicts often involved the rural elite, who were constantly looking for ways to settle disputes and protect their communities. An examination of the civil war in two counties best illustrates the point. Tian Weiqin had been stationing his army in Runan county since 1921. Conflicts between troops and the local community did not occur until the defeat of the Zhili Army in 1924. Desperately in need of weapons, Tian looked to the local militia for the replacement of firearms lost in the war. With the county mayor's support, he ordered the militia to assemble at the Northern Gate, in an attempt to have them disarmed. The plot was uncovered by the militia commander, who immediately disbanded his forces. The incident almost brought the troops and the militia into direct armed conflict.

Unable to obtain arms from the militia, Tian looked for an alternative way to build up his military power. He reorganized local bandits into his army. To support his troops, Tian sent soldiers to the countryside to demand labor service and military supplies from the people. In the spring of 1926, when the Northern Expeditionary Army reached Runan, Tian defected to the south. But the alliance was merely a temporary measure to stop the southern advance. Conflict soon broke out between his bandit chiefs and the National Revolutionary Army. Tian then occupied the county town and put up a line of defense along an embankment, while the National Revolutionary Army attacked from surrounding villages. For more than ten days the southern forces bombarded the county seat with heavy artillery. The city was completely cut off from the outside. Tian's army ordered the citizens to take turns supplying food. Unable to take the city, the southern army finally moved out of the area.

After the war, the immediate issue confronting Tian was how to obtain an adequate food supply for his army. Villages with a strong Red Spears defense were in a position to oppose the incessant army demands. Tian's troops were therefore forced to turn to militarily weak non–Red Spears villages for supplies. The army depleted an area within a twenty-*li* radius of grain. Fighting between local communities and the military over the scarce food supply brought existing tensions to a boiling point, and local elites were forced to step in to find a peaceful solution. To avoid a mutiny and to raise the necessary provisions for the troops, an "Army-Citizen Peace Preservation Association" was formed by a few retired army men and local gentry. The association also bought firearms and put together a militia to defend the city against bandit attacks. Internecine wars and their attendant problems of insecurity thus led to militarization of local communities.

A similar episode of military abuse can be found in Xinyang. In this southern county located on the Beijing-Hankou railroad, military disruption was practically a way of life. Conflicts between local communities and the army went back to the 1911 Revolution, when Yuan Shikai brought his Beiyang troops south to defend the faltering Qing dynasty from attack by revolutionary forces. As soon as they stepped off the train in their retreat from Hankou into Henan, Yuan's First Division plundered the countryside in the border counties of Xinyang and Luoshan in Henan and Xiaowei in Hubei.

However, it was Li Chun's Fifth and Sixth Divisions, which were stationed at the railroad town of Willow Forest (Liulin), that did the most damage. To obtain military provisions, the Fifth Division attacked the Fuo Family Stockade. Unable to take the heavily defended fortress, Li's troops plundered three surrounding villages and kidnapped eighteen gentry instead. A few soldiers were killed in the skirmishes, and, using the army casualties as a pretext, Li ordered the arrest of two local notables. Local residents raised 150 strings of cash and paid off the army. Finding this the most effective means of raising funds, Li coerced the prefect to put ten more gentry under arrest. In the countryside, soldiers also kidnapped local magnates for ransom. Residents fled the area by the thousands, thus missing the sowing season. The incident was temporarily settled after the Xinyang Autonomous Society and Xinyang residents in Shanghai strongly protested to Yuan Shikai and local people paid the soldiers another 2,000 strings of cash.

Although a settlement was reached with the Fifth Division, the Sixth Division used the same incident to blackmail the local gentry and merchants. To prevent looting, the local elite bought off the army with several thousand silver "honorary medals." In the following year, the Sixth Division again tried to appropriate 7,000 strings of cash from opium fines deposited in the county public funds bureau. This time the town council put up a loud protest and the attempt failed.

Military appropriations became even more frequent in subsequent years. In the anti-Yuan campaign of 1916, the army forced local gentry to buy C$80,000 in "military provision notes." After Yuan's forces collapsed, defeated soldiers poured into Xinyang from Hunan. The local gentry had to reorganize the defeated soldiers into the local army to avoid disruption. In 1917 when Duan Qirui passed through Xinyang, the county took out C$600 for "entertainment expenses." Duan never got off the train, but his troops went to the countryside to requisition fodder, eggs, and fish from the people.

Competition among rival armies for provisions always caused the most serious disruption in rural areas. For instance, in 1919, there were two armies—the Eighth Mixed Brigade, or "host army," and the Sixth Regiment, or "guest army"—stationed in Xinyang. A tacit understanding had been reached between them that the host army would control the county seat and the guest army the nearby railroad station. But the guest army could not get much money out of the rail station and army pay was eight months in arrears. On the evening of April 3, 1919, the guest army mutinied. Soldiers looted the missionary school, the military granary, the post office, and the rail station, and set fire to houses. Unable to capture the city, which was strongly defended by the host army, the mutinous soldiers pillaged the countryside, particularly the area near the South Gate. Some members of the host army came out of the city for a piece of the action and joined in the plundering. The next morning, the mutinous guest army troops returned to the area, this time playing the "peacekeeping force," firing their guns all the way. Incredibly, when local organizations protested to the president, the local *daotai* received presidential instructions asking the gentry to donate C$10,000 to reward the soldiers who did not take part in the mutiny. The president did not discipline his troops; the only action he took was to give the victims C$10,000 out of his treasury.[12]

When the 1918 Zhili-Anfu War broke out, the local gentry tried frantically to mediate between the opposing military factions. The defeated Anfu troops finally agreed to lay down their arms and be reorganized into the Zhili forces after the county government promised to give them C$200,000 in "reorganization fees." Obviously, it was the gentry who came up with the money.[13]

The fighting between the Guominjun and Wu Peifu in 1925 was another devastating experience for Xinyang citizens. The battle lasted a month, with Wu's troops continuously bombarding the city and Guominjun troops fighting pitched battles within the city walls. An eyewitness gives an unpleasant account of the civil war: trenches were dug inside the county seat; the city wall was full of holes; houses were torn down; furniture was used for heating material. Faced by mass starvation among the populace, the Red Cross and local gentry set up soup kitchens in the city. The place was swamped with soldiers.

During the Northern Expedition, strategically located Xinyang again became a bone of contention for the military. There were 100,000 soldiers in the county seat alone. The main conflict, again, was between the city and the rail station forces. But small armed bands fanned out into the countryside, claiming tiny territories as their military bases and creating complete chaos. One newspaper observed, "Daily items are difficult to obtain. Damp firewood costs over one hundred coppers. Lumber is requisitioned by the troops for heating and cooking. In the town of Minggang, business came to a halt after armies looted stores for grain. One army seized the grain from merchant A; then sold it to merchant B. Another army moved in, seized it again from Merchant B and sold it to merchant C."[14]

Breakdown of the Officially Sponsored Defense Structure

Disruption of the countryside might have been greatly minimized if the government and officially sponsored community defense structures had been strong and intact, but during the warlord period this was not the case. The militarists' interference in local government resulted in a systematic breakdown of local government security systems as well as officially sponsored community defense structures. Military forces created by local governments and communities were frequently commandeered by warlord armies.

The basic concepts of mutual security come from the Confucian sage Mencius, who taught country folk to collectively assist and protect each other. The idea of collective defense had always been present in Chinese society. Actual local security systems, however, were not activated until residents were confronted with a threat of violence from war, government tax collectors, or banditry. In Henan, a county collective defense system was created by Mao Chanxi, the superintendent of the Henan militia, during the Taiping period. The policy called for the creation of five separate militia units in each county for the purpose of defending the county seat and other towns.

While the local government focused on the defense of administrative and urban centers, local gentry were charged with the responsibility of protecting the broad countryside. Rural elites were instructed to construct stockades for community defense, usually with themselves as stockade heads (*zhai chang*). In the late Qing, a tight defense network was thus formed in Henan, one that proved highly effective in the provincial defense against Nian assaults. The quest for security, on the other hand, had given rural elites an opportunity to build up power in their communities.[15] Although military drills were seldom conducted once the threat of violence disappeared with the suppression of the Nian and the Taiping by the Qing government, this community defense structure lasted until the 1911 Revolution.

As political instability increased during the 1911 Revolution, local leaders immediately revitalized the defunct defense system. Local authorities set up a city defense bureau (*chengfang ju*), which oversaw an armed force of around 100 men. When order was restored with the creation of the republic, the police took over the function of social control. The new police system did not differ much from the old defense structure of the Taiping period. The county was sectored into four districts (*qu*)—north, south, east, and west—with the county seat as the center. Each district had its own police force.

The county police, the principal county defense force, underwent various stages of reorganization and changed its name several times, but basically remained the same.[16] The force consisted of roughly 200 men, divided into three squads. Funding for the force came from local taxes, salt surcharges, or the combined land-poll tax. For various reasons, the county police force was always short-lived. The 100-man guard squad in Xinyang, for instance, came into existence with initial funding obtained through the sale of railway bonds. Subsequent support for the force was financed by salt surcharges. However, two months after its formation, the force had to be reduced by half for lack of funds. It went through further attrition in 1917. Down to 40 men, the county police force was incorporated into a patrol regiment in 1918.[17]

In Runan county there was a protection regiment, which consisted of three militia squads headed by elected community leaders. When Anfu warlord Zhao Ti became governor, his brother Zhao Jie took over the 200 men and expanded the regiment into a 500-man patrol. In 1918, Zhao Jie became commander of the patrol forces in the ten counties in southeastern Henan. But his forces vanished with the defeat of the Anfu clique in the Zhili-Anfu War of that year.[18] Such examples indicate that county seat security systems often collapsed for lack of funds or because the fortune of their patron(s) took a turn for the worse in this highly unstable civil war era.

With the collapse of the county police and the patrol regiment, county security began to fall back on subcounty defense systems, namely those at the district (*qu*) and neighborhood (*bao*) levels. In 1920, the household clearance movement divided the county into five defense districts, each centered around a township (*zhen*). By 1922, the neighborhood or standard household system (*bao*) gradually emerged as the basic unit of local defense. In Zhengyang county in May 1923, for instance, local gentry in the southern district built a county militia in response to rampant banditry. A meeting of the 44 constituent villages of the *bao* was called for the purpose of electing a militia head (*tuanzong*) and a superintendent (*baodong*) to serve as joint commanders of the force. Funds were allocated to purchase more arms to beef up the militia. The district militia (*qu tuan*) was subdivided into a number of branches (*zhi tuan*) based in market towns (mostly in the *dian*, or inns). These lower-order community defense units in Henan's southeastern counties were made up of traditional rural "crop-watching societies" (*shouwang she*).[19] The two-tiered defense structure based on the *qu* and the *bao* formed optimal basic fighting units and was similar to the Red Spears structure discussed later in this chapter. This subcounty defense system was the most efficient way for a county to mobilize manpower and resources in times of crisis, especially if the county government defense had already disappeared.

By 1925, even the officially sponsored district militia had broken down. Local militia were takeover targets of the ever-expanding armies. For instance, after returning to southeastern Henan, the defeated Guominjun seized the weapons of the Runan militia, thus dissolving the county's officially sponsored defense structure. In Zhengyang county, Yuan Ying incorporated the district and branch militia into his army. Lacking any type of defense against the approaching Northern Expedition, rural elites hastily put up "reserve forces" (*houbei mintuan*) to maintain some sort of order in the countryside. By this time, any semblance of an officially sponsored subcounty defense system was gone, leaving a vacuum in the countryside to be filled only by the Red Spears—the private defense forces organized by the local gentry, the bandits, and the military commanders.[20]

Private Defense: Red Spears Sectarians

The origin of the Red Spears is still very murky. Further studies have to be done before we will have a clear knowledge of their origin. Most sources agree that they were descendants of the Eight Trigrams (the White Lotus tradition); some literature, however, indicates a relation to the Boxers, particularly the Big Swords. The Eight Trigrams underwent a dramatic transformation over the years after their rebellion in 1813.[21] Their descendants can be divided into two groups, those who retained their sectarian beliefs and those who were heavily influenced by the Elder Brother Society (the Heaven and Earth, *tian di hui*, tradition) when the Taiping swept through the area along the Yellow River.[22]

One source makes a clear distinction between large and small sects (*da xiao dao hui*, such as the Yellow Way Society, *huang dao hui*) and the Red Spears, which it insists was a secret society–like organization.[23] The sectarians, it argues, appeared before the Elder Brother Society, while the Red Spears came afterward. The sacrificial attendants the Red Spears worshipped were markedly different from those of the religious sects.[24] Moreover, the Red Spears had a different set of heavenly officials, such as "defenders of the faith" (*hu fa*) and "celestial disciplinary investigators" (*dutian jiucha shi*). Another account shows two separate trajectories: a branch of the White Lotus (the secret society type) transformed itself into the Boxers, then into the Benevolent and Righteous Society (*ren yi hui*), and again into various forms of Red Spears; the other, more religious, branch turned itself into the Red Lantern (*hong deng zhao*), then into the Iron Pass (*tie guan zhao*), and finally into the Heavenly Gate Society (*tian men hui*) and the Temple Way Society (*miao dao hui*).[25]

Although the Red Spears might have been remotely related to the White Lotus and the Heaven and Earth Society, they were unmistakably the direct descendants of the Boxers.[26] Most claimed that their teachers came from Caozhou prefecture, around the north of the old Yellow River in southwest Shandong province.[27] The movement in Henan had its beginning in Shangqiu county, just south of the old Yellow River and across from Caozhou.

The Red Spears were highly mixed groups, differentiated by color into Red, Yellow, Green, and White Spears, and by trigrams into *li*, *kan*, *qian*, and so forth. In the main, they can be put into two major categories. The first is made up of the Big Red Spears (*da hong xue*) or the Traditional School (*lao pai* or *lao xue*). Rituals of the traditional school were simple and consisted of praying, incense burning, calling deities down from their abodes, and meditating with legs crossed, all done at night and in remote areas. The Big Red Spears received their power of invulnerability from a rhymed magic formula (*jue*), which they recited before their patron deity every night. They were meditationists. The school is said to have descended from the *li* sect, probably the group dominated by the Gao family in Shangqiu county in the early Qing period. Because the Big Red Spears usually performed their rituals in private, which made them less visible, the school attracted few members.

The second category is made up of the Little Red Spears (*xiao hong *xue*) and the Middle Red Spears (*zhong hong xue*), also known as the New School (*xin pai*). The Little and Middle Red Spears were definitely related to the Big Swords, who were practitioners of Armor of the Golden Bell, also known as the Iron Shirts.[28] They relied on charm swallowing and incantation to produce the power of invulnerability. They were martial artists and practiced breathing exercises and body pounding with bricks and swords to augment their physical strength. This school had rigid disciplinary codes that prohibited rape, arson, murder, and robbery. Members were reported to belong to the *kan* sect, probably the descendants of Lin Qing's Flowery Splendor sect. Since they were more open, performing martial arts exercises in public, the New School was more visible and had a larger following.[29] Unlike Joseph Esherick's findings that, in Shandong, only one school of Boxers predominated in a single area, in Henan, the Big and Little Red Spears coexisted in the same areas, for example in Luoyang city.

In the late 1920s, the Red Spears formed the basic community defense structure in Henan. The smallest unit was a chapter (a hall, *tang*; a school, *xue*; or a society, *hui*), which was often based in a village. Every village household (no exceptions for rich families) was mandated to give an able male member between the ages of 12 and 45 to the chapter. Members were required to provide their own weaponry, usually a spear or a sword. Other large expenses, such as the purchase of firearms or the manufacture of cannon, usually came from donations or extra levies allotted to landowners. Shrines and ancestral or religious temples frequently served as chapter headquarters. A chapter was headed by a chief (*xuezhang* or *huizhang*), a position invariably held by local notables. Within the chapter, Red Spears were grouped into platoons (*pai*) or household squads (*pai hu dui*) of ten persons each, a replica of the existing decimal units in the standard household structure. Chapters then came together to form larger units: a battalion (*ying*) and a regiment (*tuan*). The regiment, several hundred men strong and large enough to defend from a few to dozens of villages, seems to have been the largest optimal unit. Occasionally, in a conflict with an army unit several times larger, a number of regiments might temporarily join in a coalition (*zong tuan*), but beyond the optimal unit of the regiment, group linkage was somewhat tenuous. In times of conflict, a Red Spears coalition might, for better cohesion, give itself a military-style structure. The structure usually consisted of an army headquarters headed by a military commissioner (*tu ban*) or commander in chief (*zong siling*) with the assistance of a chief of staff (*can mou*) and a secretary (*shuji*).[30]

A regiment operated like a small government. Functionally it was divided into two sections, civil (*wen*) and military (*wu*). The civil section took care of the day-to-day operations of the organization. It managed the chapter's finance, handled local litigation, and acted as custodian of documents. The military section oversaw all martial arts training.[31] The usual procedure for creating a chapter was for a local magnate to donate money and make the ancestral temple or some other religious institution available as the chapter's headquarters. The next step was to hire a martial arts teacher (*laoshi*) from a neighboring village to train the members. The practice of recruiting teachers from adjacent villages created a tight defense network, cemented by teacher-disciple and disciple-disciple relationships, which ensured instant mobilization of tens of villages in times of crisis.[32] In fact, martial arts masters usually extended their control to surrounding villages (to scores of villages whose combined size roughly equalled that of a regiment) simply by placing their disciples as first teaching-brothers (*da shixiong*) in nearby village chapters. The first teaching-brother was normally the military and religious head of the group. In matters such as religious sacrifice, charm writing, and spell incantation, he was assisted by a second teaching-brother (*er shixiong*) and a third teaching-brother (*san shixiong*).[33]

At the top of the organization was the patron deity (*shen*). The Red Spears had a whole pantheon of popular deities drawn from Confucianism, Daoism, Buddhism, and from folklore such as the *Enfeoffment of the Gods* (*fengshen yanyi*), the *Romance of the Three Kingdoms* (*san guo yanyi*), and the *Journey to the West* (*xi you ji*). Some deities, such as the Jade Emperor (*yu huang*) and Great Unity (*tai yi*), were worshipped for their supreme divine power. Others, like the God of War (*Guangong*), Goddess of Mercy (*Guanyin*), and God of Literature (*wenzhang dijun*), supposedly could provide members with specific assistance on critical occasions. Certain deities were classified as "protective deities," for instance the Four Diamond Kings of Heaven, the Snorter and Blower who guard the gates of the Buddhist temple, and the Monkey and Pigsy, protectors of the pilgrim monk Xuan Zhuang. They were usually invoked for their power to provide security. This "protective" tradition of the Red Spears clearly excluded heroes from the social banditry tradition. It is important to note that the folk heroes in the popular novel *The Water Margin*, frequently mentioned in secret society literature, are conspicuously absent from the Red Spears pantheon of patron deities.[34]

Bandit/Militarist–Dominated Red Spears in the Mountains of Western Henan

Although all Red Spears groups were community defense organizations, there was a marked difference between those operating in the mountains of western Henan and those operating in the floodplain in the eastern part of the province. Most of the western Henan Red Spears were controlled by bandits and militarists, while the ones in the east remained in the hands of community elites.

The Red Spears around Luoyang in western Henan were practitioners of Armor of the Golden Bell, or Iron Shirts. They were known locally as "hard stomachs" (*ying du*) or "hard beans" (*ying dou*). These Red Spears, descended from the Big Swords tradition, emphasized external physical fitness. They also had a set of invulnerability rituals. The group frequently identified themselves with the *li* trigram. Their patriarch (*zushi*) was a descendent of the Gao family in Shangqiu in eastern Henan. Their "spiritual teacher" (*shenshi*) had reportedly come from Nine Dragon Mountain (probably in Guangdong).[35] The group first appeared in 1917 as a low-level, loosely organized self-defense force made up of ten-man platoons. Prior to 1924, the area had no Red Spears structure above that of the platoon.[36] Ambitious Red Spears chiefs occasionally banded together and exercised influence over several platoons, but they were quickly broken up by the repressive power of the government.[37] However, after 1924, the Red Spears no longer consisted solely of small units.

With the collapse of Wu Peifu's relatively stable rule in Henan after Feng Yuxiang's coup, and the subsequent military conflicts between Wu's remnant forces and the Guominjun, western Henan was thrown into complete turmoil. Wu's associate Han Yukun's resistance to the southward movement of the Guominjun greatly intensified the military conflicts in the Zhengzhou-Luoyang area. Determined to carve out a base in western Henan, Han rapidly built up power by taking over Wu's defeated troops and by extensively recruiting bandits into his army. However, between February and March 1925, Hu Jingyi successfully wrested west Henan from Han. Ashamed of having been driven out of Luoyang, Han took his own life. His bandit troops scattered all over west Henan, preying on local citizens. Repeated takeovers of Luoyang and nearby railroad towns by different military factions subjected local residents to constant pillaging by undisciplined troops. To avoid further looting, shopkeepers in Luoyang city put out window signs saying "Shops are empty due to recent raids" or "Already raided by armies several times."[38]

There was another problem—the undisciplined guest armies. Hu Jingyi's Second Guominjun Army was composed of men from Shaanxi province. As outsiders, these soldiers had little feeling for the Henanese. The quality of the Guominjun was greatly diluted as a result of its rapid expansion after the 1924 war. At the time of the coup, Hu commanded only one division and two mixed brigades. Wu's fall gave him the chance to absorb defeated soldiers into his army. But it was his successor Yue Weijun who expanded the Guominjun fivefold, from 40,000 to 200,000 men in a year, by sponging up all the available local armed forces—disbanded soldiers, subcounty militia, and bandits. From their stations at strategic towns on the Beijing-Hankou and Longhai railroads, Yue's forces fanned out to the countryside, competing with local residents for the scarce resources of food and weapons.[39]

Local residents responded to the military threat by organizing Red Spears defense organizations. The Red Spears movement in western Henan was particularly active in the railroad counties of Luoyang, Xin'an, Mianchi, Yanshi, Menjin, and, to a limited extent, Lingbao. For example, all 1,300 villages in Luoyang were reported to have formed individual Red Spears chapters. The total Red Spears membership in Luoyang alone was 20,000.[40]

The Red Spears in western Henan were a very mixed lot. Leadership of these groups remained in the hands of local magnates, mostly former soldiers, social bandits, and military puppets. After Han Yukun's death, his troops became Red Spears. Some officers joined forces with other Red Spears organizations to resist the Guominjun. In an era of political turmoil, army men were eagerly sought after by the Red Spears for their organizational and fighting skills. Arms-bearing soldiers could bolster a chapter's firepower. But Han's troops were originally part of the Pacification Army (*zhen Song jun*), a group of social bandits (*dao ke*, or swordsmen) who, under Wang Tianzong's leadership, had turned revolutionary in 1911. This branch of the Red Spears had a long history of banditry.

He Fengming, for example, a Red Spears chief of the North Kiln Village in northern Luoyang, was a former officer in the Pacification Army. Most of his Red Spears were soldiers. He built up a Red Spears network by supplying related chapters with thousands of hand grenades he received from a fellow Pacification Army officer in Shanxi.[41] He also had connections with Wang Weizhou, an affiliate of the Pacification Army and the head of another Red Spears network located near the East Gate of Luoyang. Wang had under his control seven battalions of Red Spears in the city and six more chapters in the suburbs. Unable to destroy these Red Spears and eager to minimize their opposition, the Guominjun resorted to legitimizing these groups by incorporating them into local militia.[42]

Sun Dianying was another bandit/military Red Spears chief. Sun was a petty officer in the Pacification Army who made use of the Red Spears to achieve personal power. First he found a way to become the protégé of a prominent gentry figure in Yiyang county who was leader of a 500,000-man Red Spears network. Then he moved in with the gentry figure's family and took up martial arts training with a Red Spears master. After infiltrating the group, he used the Red Spears to run a narcotics business, then used his drug profits to purchase firearms and make himself a company commander. In the 1924 civil war, his Red Spears looted the city of Luoyang. They captured two counties for a short while and Sun declared himself head of the Eighteenth Route Army.[43] He was later appointed brigade commander of Song county by the Guominjun. Reportedly, his martial arts teacher, while possessed by the spirit of the Monkey, predicted that someday Sun would become an emperor. The local people, including some gentry, believed the story, and many sold their belongings and joined his group. Some even offered to marry their daughters to Sun to secure a brighter future.[44]

Parochialism allowed many former Pacification Army officers, who were mostly Henanese, to channel anti-Shaanxi feelings and mobilize local residents and Red Spears to resist paying taxes to outsiders. When the Guominjun came to the villages to get provisions, they often encountered intense hostility from the local people, and in many instances troops were disarmed by the Red Spears.[45] Wu Peifu, who sought to reestablish control of Henan, encouraged these anti-Guominjun feelings by negotiating with his former subordinates and occasionally supplying them with arms. The officers looked to Zhang Zhigong, a Pacification Army commander and a native of western Henan, for leadership. When Wu Peifu made a comeback in 1926, Red Spears in west Henan poured from the countryside by the tens of thousands to join in the attacks on the retreating Guominjun. As many as 140,000 guns fell into the hands of the Red Spears. With these firearms in their possession, large and small Red Spears chapters proliferated in the area. Most of these groups had only a few hundred men under their direct control, but they had the capability to mobilize several thousand men from affiliated chapters in concerted action.[46]

Once the Zhili clique was in power and its leader Zhang Zhigong was named military commissioner of Luoyang, Red Spears chiefs were promoted to military office. Zhang also ordered his police chief to launch a campaign to create more Red Spears chapters in the greater Luoyang area. As part of a lawful local defense system and with more firearms, the Red Spears began to compete with the military commissioner for badly needed local resources. Like other militarists before him, Zhang rapidly expanded his 2,000-man force into an oversized army of 40,000. The exorbitant taxes he levied on the people (five times a year) again touched off a wave of conflicts between the Red Spears and his troops.[47] Zhang's officers, many of whom were Red Spears chiefs themselves, were sharply divided over the question of whether to suppress these tax revolts, usually with the ex-provincials for and the natives against. But the recurring armed conflicts between the army and sectarians forced Zhang to move against the Red Spears, breaking their power. Many Red Spears leaders were either outlawed or executed, their strongholds in the villages destroyed. Some sought refuge on the south side of the Yi River, away from Zhang's government in Luoyang. The Red Spears movement in west Henan lost its momentum and sharply declined.[48]

Elite-Dominated Red Spears in the East Henan Floodplain

The Red Spears in eastern Henan differed markedly from their counterparts in west Henan. They were obviously an integral part of the traditional community defense system. These groups were organized strictly under the standard household (*baojia*) system. The territorial base that each network controlled corresponded neatly with a sub-county administrative unit. In Queshan county, for instance, the Red Spears were divided into the Red, Yellow, Green, White, and Black Spears. The Red Spears, the dominant group in the southeast, had 100,000 men and 200 guns, while the Yellow Spears, who occupied the northern part of the county, numbered 40,000 with 100 guns. A mixture of various sectarians coexisted in the west of the county. Their organizational structure was like that of the standard household system. They were commonly known as "plated-household squads" (*pai hu dui*).[49] The basic unit, similar to that of the *baojia* system, was the "plate" (*pai*) of ten to twenty men.[50] Ten plates were grouped into a *jia*, three *jia* into a branch squad (*zhi dui*), and three branch squads into a squad (*dui*). The *bao*, the basic local administrative unit, had under its control one to two squads, depending on the population of the area under its jurisdiction.[51] In turn, three *bao* were grouped into a regiment (*tuan*).

The county was divided into four routes (*lu*)—north, east, south, and west—corresponding roughly to the four subcounty administrative districts. The number of regiments in each route varied in accordance with the number of *bao* in that particular district. Each route was under a commander general (*zong zhi hui*), probably the same as the *tuanzong*, the commander of the regiment coalition.[52] In some areas, such as Shangcai county, stockades became the rallying points for the Red Spears defense. The stockade defense system had a long history in this county, since it was located on the path connecting the bandits' lairs in west Henan with their targets in northern Anhui. Bandits passed through the county several times a year, and therefore local militarization was strong.[53] The basic Red Spears unit was again the chapter (*hui*), which embraced one to several villages. These chapters usually revolved around a stockade that commanded an armed force of a thousand men (equivalent to the size of a large bandit gang), enough to provide protection for 10 to 30 villages.

Red Spear leaders in eastern Henan were drawn mostly from the less powerful members of prominent gentry families. Wu Tingbi, for example, head of the Green Spears in the Bai Gui Temple Stockade, was a member of a prominent gentry family (*shuxiang jia zi*). He had two regiments, about 1,000 men, directly under his command. Wu had little education but was immensely popular among local residents because of his "virile and knight-errant character." He also headed a five-stockade coalition, which gave him authority over 10,000 men.[54]

Another example is Liu Boxun, the famous Red Spears coalition chief in eastern Henan. Liu was a member of a prominent clan in Tongxu county. The Liu clan, based in Four Towers, an urban center on a major roadway, was a powerful force in the second district in the eastern part of the county.[55] In the Republican period, clan members had under their control fifteen towns and the surrounding villages in the northern and eastern parts of the county. Typical of powerful clans in China, the Lius produced a large number of degree holders and government officials. The clan reportedly first attained prominence in the Yuan dynasty, when Liu Xing won a presented-scholar (*jinshi*) degree. It subsequently produced two more *jinshi* in the Ming-Qing period, and in the Republican era, a clan member was elected county assemblyman.[56]

Clan members were also educators who contributed generously to the education of minorities in Hubei. The clan raised funds to set up the Number Five County Primary School in Four Towers and clansmen successfully served as school headmasters.[57] Clansmen excelled in the military field too. They held low-ranking provincial military posts in the Qing and Republican periods.[58] As local notables, the Lius were involved in community defense. When the *baowei tuan*, the local militia, was formed in 1915, the Lius took over central and eastern district commands for a few years, thus consolidating their power in these areas and paving the way for Liu Boxun to become the Red Spears' head.[59]

Liu Boxun was a native of Liuguai village and came from the lesser Liu lineage, a "petty landlord family," to use the Communist term. He was a self-taught man who had only a few months of formal education but developed an interest in veterinary science and yin-yang philosophy. He was also a healer. He often mediated in clan disputes and was extremely generous to kinsmen in times of need.[60] He was reportedly a Boxer follower. The Red Spears chapter, known as the Liu regiment, was set up by him in 1923 in his hometown and belonged to the *kan* trigram and the Little Red Spears tradition. Directly under his control were three networks of Red Spears, all centered in market towns: the Four Towers, which included his village, Liuguai; Changzhi, in the north; and Liuying, east of the county seat.[61]

Contrary to what Elizabeth Perry has stated in her work, these Red Spears were not only territorially based but also lineage-dominated groups.[62] In Four Towers, for example, leadership rested with the most senior member of the lineage, Liu Heshan, who was the nominal coalition chief (*tuan zong*) of the network. As he was too old to lead the troops in fighting, actual leadership was taken up by his two sons, Liu Jiran and Liu Yuanping. Liu Jiran, the commander of a 4,000-man regiment, was a traditional soldier; his brother Liu Yuanping, leader of another regiment the same size, was one of the founders of the Number Five County Primary School. This lineage commanded a force of 8,000 men and 100 guns.[63] But Liu Boxun's influence was not restricted to his own county. He was the head of an intercounty coalition of several regiments, all lineage-based and bearing their clans' surnames and centered in market towns.[64] By 1924, Liu Boxun's power covered an area roughly 80 *li* (29 miles) wide. Aside from the three networks directly under his control, he had indirect authority over 27 regiments in neighboring counties (14 in Qixian and 13 in Suixian), an influence that could not escape the attention of military leaders like Wu Peifu.

During his conflict with the Guominjun, Wu sent his lieutenant to seek Liu's support, promising him a military title afterward. As a result, the Red Spears in eastern Henan were particularly active in the anti-Guominjun campaign. After Wu became the ruler in Henan, Liu put in a request to have his Red Spears reorganized into the army. Wu went back on his word and refused. After that, conflicts between Liu's Red Spears and Wu's troops occurred frequently in the area. Wu finally ordered his armies to crack down on Liu's men, resulting in the bloody massacre of Red Spears in fourteen villages. Wu's suppression effectively broke Liu's power in the region.[65] But it gave the Chinese Communists an opportunity to turn the aggrieved Red Spears forces into self-defense armies and to use them in the Nationalist Revolution.

Indigenous Leadership and Communist Networks

As demonstrated in Chapter 1, it was the coalition among the Chinese Communists, the Guominjun, and the Soviet Union that gave the Communists the chance to build up their power in Henan. During the May 30th Movement, under Guominjun patronage both Communist power and labor movements grew dramatically in the province. In the aftermath of May 30th, Communist-Guominjun relationships remained amiable for a couple more months. Apparently impressed by Yue's public support of the May 30th Movement, and in response to a request made by Soviet adviser V. K. Putna, the Russians decided to extend military assistance to Yue. On June 21, 1925, a group of 43 Soviet advisers, headed by intelligence chief G. B. Skalov (Sinani) and known as the Kaifeng group, arrived in Kaifeng. Lapin (Seifulin), the Soviet military attaché in Beijing, served Yue as chief of staff. A military school with 2,400 students was set up. The Guomindang also cemented its relations with the Guominjun commander by sending a number of Whampao graduates to Henan to build up Yue's army.[66] These officers were mostly Shanxi natives. Among them were Xu Xiangqian, who became Yue's staff officer in the military training school, and Yu Youren, the Guomindang veteran who served as Yue's adviser.[67]

But neither the Soviet advisers nor the Communists had much control over Yue's actions. Yue's only ambition was to extend his power into the neighboring provinces of Shandong, Hubei, Hebei, and Shanxi. To dissuade him from such aggressive actions, Li Dazhao made a trip to Kaifeng in the summer of 1925. While still waiting for Soviet arms, Yue verbally acceded to Li's request. He even appeased the Communists by extending them the privilege of moving freely along the Beijing-Hankou railroad. On the other hand, he was secretly negotiating with his former boss, Wu Peifu, at Rooster Mountain (Jigong shan).[68] By August 1925, Yue had reached an agreement with Hubei, and in September, arms from Xiao Yaonan, Wu's associate, came in. When the Soviet shipment of 1,500 rifles and 900,600 cartridges finally arrived in Kaifeng in November 1925, Yue had no further reason to placate the Communists. He ordered the police to "look out for Soviet propaganda" and to destroy all Communist headquarters.[69]

Yet for roughly a year, between December 1924 and November 1925, the Communists had a free hand in building power and mobilizing sectarians in the countryside. Early in January 1925, the Fourth National Congress of the CCP adopted a policy of mass movement, directing its members to go to the countryside to mobilize rural cultivators for insurrections. However, it was not until October 1925 that the party began to pay much attention to the peasant movement. Peasants were urged to join in the revolution. In "A Letter to the Peasants," the party called upon cultivators to form peasant associations and to join peasant self-defense armies. To train more peasant activists for the movement, the Guangzhou Peasant Training Institute broadened its base to enroll peasant leaders from provinces other than Guangdong in its fifth class.[70] Li Dazhao also issued a directive telling cadres that mobilizing peasants behind enemy lines would greatly enhance the Communist position in the coming revolution. To implement Li's directive, Wang Ruofei, then secretary of the Henan-Shaanxi Regional Committee, held a special meeting to discuss the party's peasant policy. During this period, Communists were very active organizing peasant associations and creating Red Spears networks in eastern Henan.[71]

The Zheng-Xing-Mi Network

It was the May 30th Movement that gave the party an opportunity to spread its influence to the countryside. It is not difficult to understand that the incipient Red Spears movement was located in the countryside surrounding Zhengzhou, the railroad town where the Communists had the strongest influence. In May 1925, as a supplement to the labor movement, Xiao Rengu, a Whampao Military Academy graduate, was instructed by the party to proceed to Henan to create a peasant movement.[72] Simultaneously, Li Dazhao ordered nine additional Communists to use their covers as Beijing-Hankou railroad workers and Guominjun administrators to conduct rural surveys and organize peasants near the railroad.[73] Apparently with the help of the Guominjun, in a brief period of five months the Communists were able to form 10 regional and 93 village peasant associations in the three counties of Zhengzhou, Xingyang, and Mixian (see Map 2). The Zheng-Xing-Mi peasant movement was nothing but an extension of the Zhengzhou labor movement. In Zhengzhou, the railroad and factory activists were all seasonal workers who moved constantly between the city and the countryside and served as liaisons between the Communists and the peasant masses.[74] These worker-activists conducted propaganda sessions in eating places and at temple fairs. To attract the peasants they set up reading classes, evening schools, and associations for women. The movement was reported to be a success until it was destroyed by Wu Peifu upon his return to Henan in late 1926. At one time, the Communist leaders Dai Peiyuan and Hu Lun were called "super county mayors" by local residents. In Xingyang alone, peasant association membership totaled 20,000, the majority of whom were said to be Red Spears sectarians.[75]

Let us take a close look at the Xingyang movement. When Communist leader Zhang Jifan made an investigative tour of the county in December 1925, he found a very active peasant movement there. There were already one county- and six district-level peasant associations in Xingyang (total membership was 2,000 households). According to Zhang, peasants participated "self-consciously" in the defense move-

Map 2. Henan counties.

ment. The Red Spears had already been reorganized into the peasant self-defense army. There were four Communist cadres overseeing the county movement, and another two in Shuangliuguo township.[76]

Shuangliuguo township. The county peasant association was located in Shuangliuguo township. Below the county level was a district (*qu*) peasant association, which oversaw 50 "young peasants" (*qing nong*) in five village associations. The Communist Youth League had five members, among them three peasants. The party's focus was on influencing young people. Cadres had set up a variety of educational institutions in town: two peasant schools (with 100 poor peasant children, said to be dressed in tattered clothes), a night school for workers and peasants (40 students), a youth department (20 to 30 members), and various literacy classes. The Communists had infiltrated the straw hat factory and recruited 60 members there. Two teachers and many students from the township elementary school were sympathetic to the movement.[77]

Zhang Jifan found the town's peasant movement very loosely organized. Peasants usually lacked organizational concepts. Most of the party members were students, and very "bookish" (*shusheng qi*). Zhang discovered that the villages around Shuangliugou were still very much under the traditional dominance of the rural patriarchal system (*zhongfa ji*), but that generational gaps and conflicts were beginning to emerge. Zhang criticized the cadres for promoting "purely pedantic activities" and suggested they organize more recreational activities instead. One way to gain access to village society, he noted, was for the Communists to serve as intermediaries between the young and the old. He urged cadres to set up "honor-parents societies" (*kenqin hui*) to bring the generations together. By fostering the traditional Confucian ideal of respect for the aged, the party hoped the movement might gain acceptance by the rural elite and by senior citizens in these conservative villages.[78]

Shuimo village. Below the county committee in Shuangliuguo was the district structure in Shuimo village. The Shuimo district committee and the district peasant association were set up by Tang Shikui. Tang was a native of Hebei who was introduced by the Baoding party branch to Zhang Zhaofeng, a CCP member in charge of a Guominjun regiment in Zhengzhou. Tang went to Zhengzhou, where his first assignment was to be editor of a small paper in the party propaganda section in Luoyang. In July 1925, he was transferred to Xingyang county to work on the peasant movement. His area of operation, a district of some 20 to 30 *li*, was centered at Shuimo village. The village inhabitants were predominantly members of the Tian clan, so to cover himself, Tang changed his name to Tian Zhengyi (Upright Tian). Probably because of an introduction from the county mayor (a GMD member), Tang was well received by the village head, Zhang Peize. He took up residence in a cave. Tang's tactic for conducting propaganda was to choose a certain location, play a record of revolutionary songs to attract a crowd, and then preach to the villagers the ideas of warlord and imperialist oppression. Communist propaganda also emphasized unity and organized tax resistance.[79]

However, the concept of imperialism was foreign to the illiterate peasants. Warlord oppression became an immediate concern only when soldiers came to the countryside to plunder the villages. To organize a peasant movement in an apolitical and conservative village was immensely difficult. The night school and literacy classes the Communists set up did attract some peasant youths who were eager to learn and get ahead, but what really impressed them, according to one peasant activist, Zhang Mashuan, was the singing of revolutionary songs.[80] Because of this unusual appeal, Communists organized the peasant youth into Young Pioneers and conducted a singing competition in the Patriarch Temple in neighboring Shuangliuguo township. The party recruited a large number of peasants into the peasant association this way. Through peasant members who had connections with the local Red Spears, Dai Peiyuan, the peasant leader in Xingyang, established contacts with the sectarians.[81] Chapter by chapter, the Communists extended their influence into these Red Spears organizations. Playing on the problems of military disruption and insecurity, the Communists were able to convince the elites of the necessity of organizing these sectarian groups into the Communist-dominated self-defense armies.[82]

The Qi-Sui Network

In the fall of 1925, following the party's success in Zhengzhou, Xiao Rengu was instructed by the regional committee to use the Zhengzhou experience to extend the peasant movement to nearby Qi and Sui (Qixian and Suixian) counties. A group of Henanese studying in Kaifeng, including Wu Zhipu and Zhang Haifeng, was chosen to assist Xiao in the movement. They were ordered to return home to Qi county and to infiltrate the village Red Spears by becoming the sectarians' sworn brothers.[83]

All these students were natives of Qi county. Their friendship went back to their days of study at the Mengs' private academy. Many of them were active county reformers and some were members of the local Social Science Study Group. All of them later studied in county agricultural schools and then in high schools in Kaifeng. Thus these students formed a very cohesive group, their ties cemented by longtime school relations.[84] In Chinese society, where interpersonal bonds always played an important role, all particularistic relations, such as kinship, territorial, and classmate ties, were essential elements in the building of an emergent revolutionary movement.

The headquarters of the first party branch was located in a member's home in Qi county. There were two other centers of operation: a house in the salt-retailing district, which was semipublic and served as a contact point, reading room, and school; and a grain warehouse, completely public, which was used as living quarters for visiting cadres. The basic tasks of the student group were to infiltrate local schools, set up literacy classes, and recruit peasants. They were also involved in mass movements, and took part, for instance, in denouncing landlords at public meetings in the City God Temple and organizing student demonstrations. Government crackdowns forced them to relocate their headquarters twice, first to Fu market town on the south side of the city and then to the Song Stockade at the remote county border.[85]

A subnetwork was also created in neighboring Sui county. As early as 1925, a Communist by the name of Guo Xiaotang had built a party cell in this county. Guo was an educator and a classmate of the Qi county group. Through Guo, a link was established between the network and subnetwork in the two counties. The Sui subnetwork leadership was drawn from students at the county normal school. Their party headquarters was located in a sock factory that was set up by the students. In the spring of 1927, the party appointed Yu Xiumin, a graduate of Zhongzhou University, to be the head. Upon arrival, Yu upgraded the cell into a party branch and placed it first under the Qi county party in Fu market town and later directly under the provincial party. The group's contact point was Zhongzhou University in Kaifeng.[86]

Yu Xiumin, though a Henanese, was not a native of Sui county. He came from Xiping county in central Henan. As an outsider, Yu had to rely on Sui natives to gain a foothold in the county. Through a recommendation from a Communist Party member in the sock factory, he secured the post of school inspector on the county board of education, a powerful position that gave him the chance to influence county schools. Like the Qi county activists, he also set up literacy classes and night schools to attract a following.[87]

Gaining access to local schools only gave the Communists the opportunity to recruit radical students as leaders; it did little to promote a peasant movement. The party's urgent task at this time was to infiltrate the local Red Spears. The objective was to mobilize these sectarians and make use of their armed forces in the coming Nationalist Revolution. In order to achieve this goal, Yu had to move out of his urban environment and take up residence in the countryside. He therefore stayed in the house of a fellow Communist, a native of Guo River Village. As the name indicates, Guo River was a monoclan village, and in order to keep under cover and to have a chance to mingle with the clansmen, Yu changed his name to Guo Tinghe.[88]

In two months, Yu was able to set up a Sui county subnetwork with eight operation centers. Of these, only the headquarters in the sock factory was in the county seat; the rest were scattered over various county districts. Five of these centers can be clearly identified as Red

Spear centers, each embracing 20 to 30 villages. Most of the centers were located in a central market town (*zhen*) or a standard market town (*ji*), or in a fortified tower (*lou*). Thus, the early peasant movement was not exactly a rural movement in the strict sense of the term, but rather a suburban peasant movement directed from urban centers. Urban ties and influence were essential in launching the peasant movement in the suburban countryside.

The support of the Red Spears was secured through friendship and school relations. For example, Miao Zesheng, leader of the Miao Tower Red Spears, was won over through his father Miao Tiefeng, a county school teacher who was introduced to Yu by a Communist in the sock factory. Through Miao Zesheng, Yu extended his social contacts to the Red Spears chiefs in Tu Tower and Ma Village, targeting them along with Miao Tower because these three chapters had previously cooperated in a tax resistance movement. Two nephews of Tu Yuheng, the head of the Red Spears at Tu Tower and a *xiucai* (degree holder), had been Yu's classmates at Zhongzhou University. Ma Jixun, the Red Spears chief in Ma Village, was a salt merchant and a former commander of Feng Yuxiang's. He was won over to the revolutionary cause by Miao Zesheng because his father, a degree holder and a Guomindang member, had been imprisoned by a warlord. Altogether, these Red Spears leaders commanded a force of 20,000 to 30,000 men covering 80 villages in the southern and western parts of the county.[89]

The use of indigenous leadership was absolutely crucial in building an emergent revolutionary structure in the countryside. As most of the Red Spears were under the patronage of the local gentry, rural elite support was indispensable in the recruitment of these sectarian groups. Since villages in eastern Henan were either monoclan villages or communities dominated by a few powerful kinship groups, these villages were mostly closed corporate societies. The only way for outside cadres to infiltrate the area, establish contacts with the rural elites, and wrest the Red Spears from gentry control was for the party to utilize the social ties of native students to gain access to the communities. As we have seen, the Qi-Sui Communist network was essentially set up with extensive use of these social ties.

The Queshan and Xinyang Networks

The networks in Queshan and Xinyang counties were not set up until late 1926, after the Northern Expedition had begun. The basic objective of the Queshan-Xinyang peasant movement was to make the best possible use of the peasants as insurgent forces to pave the way for the Northern Expeditionary Army to move into Henan. The Guomindang launched the Northern Expedition in May 1926, and five months later captured the city of Wuchang. A month before the fall of Wuchang, the party had sent Li Mingqi, a Whampao graduate, to Queshan county to make initial contact with local youths. Li, however, stayed in the county only twenty days before other duties called him away. In October 1926, a group of native students was sent back to Queshan to continue Li's work. Under Zhang Jiaduo, the leader, a special party branch was set up in Zhumadian, a town on the Beijing-Hankou railroad.[90] Zhang was soon replaced by Lin Zhuangzhi, a banker from the northern mining town of Jiaozuo. After that, the secretary of the party branch was always an outsider from another county.[91]

Below the party secretary, the second leadership tier was composed of natives, eight Kaifeng students who were ordered by the party to go home to participate in the revolution.[92] These native students were instrumental in securing the support of the Red Spears in their own neighborhoods (*bao*). Liu Jianzhao, for instance, was responsible for winning the support of Zhang Lishan, his relative and head of the Red Spears in Liu Town (Liu Dian) in Number Five *bao* in the east of the county. Zhang was an easy target. He was a graduate of the county normal school and a classmate of Li Zeqing, a fellow Communist leader.[93] Through Zhang, the Communists later linked up with other Red Spears chapters.[94] According to a Northern Expeditionary Army report, this network comprised 100,000 peasants, most of them reorganized from the local Red Spears. Under direct Communist command were 20,000 Red Spears, 10,000 of whom were controlled by Zhang Lishan, the Communists' most important ally.[95]

Below the Queshan network were two subnetworks: the Runan subnetwork, located right outside the county seat, and a subnetwork in Suiping county. The Runan subnetwork was a newly established and temporary institution, but it already had an elaborate structure featuring seven executives and two supervisors. Most of the executive positions were held by students from either Zhongzhou University or the Number Six Provincial High School. The county party supervised seven district parties (*qu dangbu*), which in turn oversaw three to six subdistrict parties (*qu fenbu*). There were 300 party members in the county (including 7 or 8 females); of these, 200 were students, 30 to 40 were elementary school teachers, 20 to 30 were peasants, and 4 or 5 were workers. The party was practically a party of intellectuals, most of whom joined the movement at the height of the Northern Expedition in April and May 1927.

Since the party had only a brief history in this county, the Communists encountered numerous obstacles in their work, particularly in winning the support of the Red Spears. Most of these sectarians were very much under the gentry's control. Local Red Spears did join the Communists in attacking the Guominjun, and later Wu Peifu. But they did so only to augment their own firepower. Runan Red Spears were ready to seize firearms from anyone, warlords as well as Communists. The Communists, in fact, said that the Red Spears were "gun crazy."[96] They found these sectarian groups to be so weak and so loosely organized that they were repeatedly defeated by local bandits. Red Spears under the control of powerful gentry often stayed away from the Communist movement. Party control of the Red Spears was extremely weak; the Communists only succeeded in recruiting as allies some Red Spears chapters in Sandy River Mouth in the eastern part of the county. These Red Spears were later reorganized into voluntary mutual aid squads (*yi zhu dui*).[97]

The so-called Suiping subnetwork was even weaker. It was nothing but a youth association hastily reorganized into a party organization after the outbreak of the Northern Expedition. When southern forces reached the county, the party was still being formed.[98]

On the other hand, the Xinyang network had a longer history and an elaborate structure. Xinyang city was a major railroad center situated at the Hubei-Henan border. It was the first city in Henan the Northern Expeditionary Army had to capture in its northward drive to power. The Xinyang Communist Party was formed in 1925, during the May 30th Movement. It expanded into a large structure supervising 10 districts, 47 subdistricts, and 3 independent subdistricts. The party's authority extended over two Communist operations in the railroad towns of Minggang and Liulin. It also oversaw four nearby counties: Luoshan, Huangchuan, Xixian, and Shangcheng. In 1927, it had 560 members, 12 percent of them female. Only 50 percent of the members were intellectuals (not very different from the Runan subnetwork), 30 percent were workers and peasants, and 8 percent were merchants. The party had under its control 33 peasant and merchant associations.[99]

The party started infiltrating the Red Spears in the summer of 1926. Flying the Guomindang flag, the Communists made much headway in the county. Wu Peifu's conflicts with the Red Spears helped drive sectarians into the Communists' arms. By June 1926, the Communists had reorganized 10,000 Red Spears into a peasant self-defense army, which was then divided into two regiments, north and south. Other chapters refused to join the self-defense army but were recruited as allies and designated as "separate detachments" (*beidong dui*).[100]

Red Spears under direct Communist control fell into two distinct categories: the core groups and the affiliates. Within the core groups, the leaders were all CCP members, either Communists who joined the

Red Spears as sworn brothers or Red Spears chiefs who were invited to join the party.[101] The affiliates were mostly gentry-dominated Red Spears sympathetic to the Guomindang revolutionary cause. They were ready to fight the warlords but refused to be party members. The Xinyang party made good use of the United Front tactic, approved by the Wuhan government, to recruit these Red Spear leaders. In September 1926, it set up an organization called the General Headquarters of Henan Peasant Self-Defense Regiments for that purpose. Altogether, seventeen Red Spears coalitions (*tuan zong*) were recruited as affiliates.[102] By early 1927, the Communists estimated that the General Headquarters had under its direct command 25,000 Red Spears, with the capability of mobilizing an additional 20,000 men. In April 1927, with their influence growing, the Communists decided to create a command center to integrate these sectarian forces. A "Coalition of Armed Organizations in Southwest Xinyang" was set up to coordinate the 40 Red Spears chapters in the region.[103] The Communists succeeded in recruiting only some Red Spears in some localities. In Minggang, for instance, there were two regiments of Red Spears, a northern and a southern regiment, and the party was able to secure only the southern regiment. The northern regiment, which had few weapons but was numerically more powerful, had always been under gentry control and continued to oppose the Communists. Party influence was strong only in the second and third districts in the county.[104]

Thus, on the eve of the Nationalist Revolution, the Communists were able to make good use of the Guomindang-Guominjun alliance to win over the support of some "progressive" gentry and to infiltrate the Red Spears sectaries. The number of sectarians the party claimed to have under its control looked formidable, yet the loyalty of these groups was tenuous. Although the party succeeded in gaining a foothold in the countryside by forming tactical alliance with the rural elites, Communist influence over the local gentry was very weak. The gentry joined the movement simply as a direct response to the military disruption in the countryside and out of sympathy for the Guomindang revolutionary cause. However, the only Red Spears the Communists had tight control over were the core groups, whose leaders were mostly party members. The affiliated groups and other unaffiliated Red Spears always stayed on the periphery. Their allegiance was with the Guomindang, not the Communists. This uncertain loyalty accounts for the fact that, during the revolution, when relations between the CCP and GMD went sour, a split occurred among the local elites. In the next chapter, we shall see that many of the Red Spears leaders went over to the Guomindang side and heeded Nationalist calls for a purge of Communist influence in rural communities.

Sectarians and the Nationalist Revolution

Party Policies and Integration of Red Spears Networks

As mentioned, the Communist Party began to realize the power of the Henan peasant movement only after its initial success in the Zheng-Xing-Mi area. Li Dazhao was the first Communist leader who called the party's attention to the peasantry. Drawing on surveys conducted by Communist rural activists in the area, on December 30, 1925, Li Dazhao published an article in *Political Life* (*Zhengzhi shenghuo*) in which he underscored the bankruptcy of the countryside and repeated Sun Yatsen's call for equalization of landownership.[105]

The first apologist for the Red Spears was Chen Duxiu, the co-founder of the Chinese Communist Party. In an article entitled "Red Spears and Chinese peasant uprisings" (*Hongqiang hui yu Zhongguo nongming baodong*), Chen criticized the current intellectual stereotype of the Red Spears as "conservative" and "superstitious" groups, capable of "barbaric" and "destructive" actions only. The Red Spears, he contended, were not bandits. They were "armed defense forces," traditional antimilitary, anticorruption, anti-banditry dissent groups engaged in tax and rent resistance activities. The Red Spears, he said, were peasants and small landholders; only on rare occasions did they mingle with bandits and militarists. The Red Spears movement, he argued, was part of a century-long Chinese dissent tradition going back to the Boxers, the Taipings, and the Yellow Turbans.[106] Chen Yun, another Communist leader, also wrote about the Red Spears Movement. Like other forms of rural protest in China, he warned, the Red Spears movement might appear feeble, but it was really "a mighty force mobilized by revolutionary consciousness."[107]

But it was Li Dazhao who gave the Red Spears the strongest support. Writing in *Political Life* on August 8, 1926, Li reaffirmed Chen Duxiu's statement that Red Spears were not bandits but local self-defense forces. The Red Spears in Shangdong, Henan, and Shaanxi, he maintained, were products of warlordism and imperialism. They appeared to be superstitious only because they believed in the yin-yang and five elements concepts and in practices such as charm writing and incantation. However, they were not secret organizations, but public-minded civic groups. Most of the time, Li argued, their headquarters were built in public places, such as local temples, county schools, and public institutions, and they provided public services such as city patrols and traveler protection for residents.

In the article, Li explained to his readers the seemingly eccentric behavior of these sectarians. The Red Spears were xenophobic, he explained apologetically, because they had little understanding of the imperialists. They were always looking for a "true lord" (*zhen zhu*) because they longed for peace and security. They did not know, however, that only mass politics could put an end to the current political chaos. To make up for military weakness and primitive weaponry, they were forced to turn to superstitious beliefs and practices. Li was, however, very much impressed by the sectarians' brute power, which, he said, had already wiped out the Second Guominjun in Henan and another warlord, Liu Zhenhua, in Shaanxi. But he warned that such community-based forces were powerful only in their native places. Once uprooted from the peasant base and reorganized in warlord armies to fight in other places, they would immediately lose their military effectiveness and would collapse like any other warlord forces.

Li somehow equated the Red Spears' parochial feelings (*xiangtu guan nian*) with class consciousness. He urged the Communists to use this consciousness (in his words, the ties to fellow peasants in a particular locality) to wrest the sectarians from the military and to urge them to return home. Li was aware that localism might lead to factionalism. He therefore told the Communists to help the peasants overcome their narrow-minded local sentiments, bridge the gaps between these groups, and organize them into a cohesive force. Employing a populist tone, he called upon the Communist youth to go to the countryside to transform these "traditional" Red Spears into modern self-defense forces, and turn the rural crop-watching societies into "democratic" peasant associations.[108]

In March 1926, to prepare the Communists for the rural revolution, the Henan-Shaanxi Regional Committee sent 29 Henanese to Mao Zedong's Peasant Training Institute in Guangzhou for training.[109] The Peasant Institute also broadened its student body by enrolling students from provinces other than Guangdong in its sixth class. Cadres from Hubei, Henan, and Jiangxi, provinces right on the route of the Northern Expedition, were given special preparation for launching a social revolution in those areas. Of the 29 Henanese attending the Peasant Institute, 2 were workers, 3 were peasants, and the rest were elementary and middle school students. They spent thirteen weeks in Guangzhou, taking 25 short courses. At the end of their study, the Henan students visited Haifeng and Shaoguan to observe firsthand the peasant movement in action before heading back to their home province in October 1926.[110]

In July 1926, the Nationalist government launched its Northern Expedition against the warlords from Guangzhou, and on July 11, the

National Revolutionary Army took Changsha, the capital of Hunan. By October 10, the Nationalists had occupied the walled city of Wuchang. The Nationalist government was then formally transferred to Wuhan. Wu Peifu's army collapsed and the Zhili warlord quickly retreated to Henan. Realizing this was the perfect chance to expand his power, Chang Zuolin decided to send 100,000 troops across the Yellow River into Henan. Wu's troops under Jin Yun'e put up a defense along the Longhai railway. But the two months of fighting ended with Jin's defeat and with Fengtian troops rolling down the Beijing-Hankou railroad into central Henan, where they posed an immediate threat to the Guomindang government in Wuhan. For the Wuhan government, Henan province thus became a strategically extremely significant center for the "anti-Fengtian campaign" (*fan Feng zhanzheng*). The Nationalists had to make use of all available forces in the province for Henan's revolutionary struggle against the Manchurian warlord.

From July 12 to July 18, 1926, the CCP Central Committee held its second enlarged plenum and adopted a comprehensive set of resolutions for the promotion of mass movement in the Henan, Hebei, and Shandong areas. It called upon the Communists to use the United Front for mass recruitment of workers, peasants, merchants, women, students, and militarists. It acknowledged that the Red Spears might have been dominated by "evil gentry," "local bullies," or even by "a large number of vagabonds," but repeating the arguments put forth by Chen Duxiu and Li Dazhao, it insisted that Red Spears were essentially "primitive self-defense organizations composed of middle and petty peasants." It urged cadres to go to the countryside to recruit Red Spears into peasant armed forces and to use them to create peasant associations.

The party then issued directives on how to bring these fractious Red Spears together into a cohesive fighting force. It called on the Communists to set up a secret communication center as the command post. According to the directive, the communication center should always remain under direct Communist control, and would serve as the principal organ for information sharing and mutual assistance. After setting up the communication center, the cadres should convene a conference to bring the Red Spears representatives together to formulate a political platform. The platform should emphasize self-defense against banditry and opposition to warlords and corrupt officials.[111] The party's objective, it said, was to integrate and transform these "products of warlord politics" into a major force for the Nationalist Revolution.[112]

In late October and early November, the Henan-Shaanxi Regional Committee began to implement the order by first calling 57 Communist cadres from fifteen counties for a meeting. The goal was to work out an overall strategy for reorganizing the Red Spears into peasant associations. At the meeting, cadres reviewed the political and economic situation in the province and discussed such problems as organization, propaganda, and mobilization. Thus the movement went through the first stage of integration at the local level. In order to bring about integration at the national level, which would put the Henan movement in line with the nationwide movement, the Regional Committee sent Xiao Rengu, the director of peasant associations, and Tang Shaoyu, a CCP member and the Guomindang Party Secretary in Zhengzhou, to attend the Second Conference of Peasant Representatives in Guangdong.[113]

The Communist Party and the Wuhan government also wanted to make sure that rival Red Spears groups from Henan's networks and subnetworks would come together as a cohesive force in the revolution. To achieve this goal, two conferences were held in Wuhan. The first was the Peasant Representatives Conference, which was designed to bring the cadres together. At this conference, Mao Zedong met with Communist peasant leaders from the five regions (east, west, north, south, and central) in Henan, and together they drew up a plan for concerted action.[114] The other, more important, conference was the six-day (March 15–21, 1927) Conference of the Representatives of Henan Armed Peasants. At this conference, pro-Guomindang Red Spears chiefs were invited to meet with high-level Guomindang and Communist leaders. The conference was attended by 800 delegates, of whom 69 represented 45 counties in Henan. The Henan delegates were said to represent 400,000 "armed peasants," that is, Red Spears, in their province.[115]

At the conference, local leaders took turns reporting on peasant conditions in their respective provinces. Zheng Zhenyu, an executive committee member of the Henan Communist Party representing that province, gave a lengthy report on the conditions of peasants and Red Spears in Henan. According to him, 150,000 Henan peasants were ready to take part in the revolution. He said that groups of 30,000 to 100,000 Red Spears were already organized into self-defense armies and integrated locally under a command center called the "joint office" (*lianhe banshi chu*).[116] Henan's regional leaders then gave detailed reports on the peasants in their respective areas. At the end of the conference, the delegates drew up a manifesto and the text of a telegram denouncing Manchurian warlord Zhang Zuolin. They also voted on and passed three documents: a Resolution on the Organization of Peasant Associations in Henan and two outlines, one on the organization of and the other on the establishment of a Temporary Executive Committee of the Peasant Self-Defense Armies. Xiao Rengu was elected head of the Temporary

Executive Committee. The conference brought the Red Spears chiefs and the Wuhan government together. Legitimized by the Guomindang and fully integrated under Xiao's Temporary Executive Committee, the Red Spears were now ready to be used as local insurrection forces in the Nationalist Revolution.[117]

Revolutionary Uprisings

Although the party was rather successful in integrating the Red Spears networks in the Wuhan conference, cadres still found it very difficult to work with the chiefs, let alone to control them. Zhou Enlai had given specific instructions to Communist leaders to carefully plan all rural uprisings to time with the arrival of Northern Expeditionary forces. But carrying out Zhou's instructions was not that simple. Many Red Spears chiefs were genuinely committed to assisting the Guomindang in driving both the Fengtian and Zhili warlords out of their communities; however, they had little understanding of Communist military tactics or of the theory of struggle. Nor did they have the patience to wait for instructions to move into action. Since warlord armies invariably obtained their provisions from the people, conflicts between local residents and militarists were inevitable and frequent. Local armed forces were always ready to jump into action whenever the military stepped into their territory. The Communists repeatedly argued with Red Spears chiefs that their parochial protests must be carefully integrated into the nationwide movement, and the time must be ripe before they made any moves, but the Red Spears simply took this as a sign of weakness and boasted that they were always strong enough to take independent action.[118]

While the Wuhan government was still debating whether to move ahead with the northern drive, the Henan situation became highly critical. In March, a clash broke out between Red Spears and local garrison troops who had antagonized the sectarians. Without consulting the Communists, the Red Spears hastily decided to permanently rid themselves of this military menace by directly assaulting the armies at their post. Because the party immediately sent a cadre to plead earnestly with the sectarians, and because the Xinyang prefect promised to wire Wu Peifu and request that the Zhili leader discipline his troops, the conflict was narrowly averted. But the local situation was highly explosive, and the party decided to call an emergency meeting to find a solution to such impetuous Red Spears actions.

Cadres attending the meeting were completely at a loss and hopelessly divided over what course of action the party should take. Some argued that since the masses had been energized, the party should seize the opportunity and lead then into action. However, most cadres realized that, without the solid backing of the Northern Expeditionary Army, a takeover of the county seat, which they were certain the Red Spears would attempt, could be suicidal. Such an action would only give the military an excuse to retaliate. But at that critical juncture, communication with Wuhan was temporary disrupted by a rail transport and postal service stoppage caused by the fighting. The Queshan branch therefore sent cadre Zhang Shaozeng to Wuhan for instructions. Unfortunately, Zheng was injured in an accident, so Lin Zhuangzhi, the party branch secretary, made the trip. In Wuhan, Lin learned that the Guomindang had already decided to move into Henan. He was told to go back to his province immediately to prepare the Red Spears for action.[119]

Back in Queshan, Lin called an urgent meeting to draw up slogans to be used in the uprising, to decide on the targets of attack, to organize an armed demonstration (*liang pai*) by the Red Spears at the temple fair, and to make a revolutionary banner.[120] On April 3, amidst the operatic performances that were a traditional way of mobilizing Red Spears for action, 20,000 Red Spears, armed with swords, spears, guns, and cannon, gathered at a stadium. When Mayor Wang Shaoqu, a Guomindang member, came to the stadium to mediate, he was arrested on the spot. Wang was released upon promising to abolish some taxes, stop labor conscription, release prisoners, and hand over four prominent gentry for punishment. But once released and back in the city, Mayor Wang opted to fight rather than yield to the rebels' demands. The party then ordered an attack on the city and called upon Red Spears in neighboring counties to join in the assault.[121] Fifty thousand Red Spears, divided into ten routes according to their respective localities, converged on the city. At the time, most of the garrison troops were away in Xinyang, and the remaining government forces fled the city. Two hundred soldiers were killed by the Red Spears. The rebels easily captured the Queshan county seat, and the mayor, and scores of county notables, were arrested.[122]

By April 1927, the Nationalist Revolution had taken an unexpected turn. Personally leading a segment of the National Revolutionary Army up another route northward through Jiangxi province, Chiang Kaishek took the city of Nanchang on November 8, 1926, and by March 22, 1927, his troops had entered Shanghai. As a measure to curb Communist influence, on April 12, Chiang carried out an anti-Communist coup in Shanghai and a massive purge against the CCP in the southeast provinces. He also set up a rival government in Nanjing, while the national government in Wuhan remained under Wang Jingwei's control. A split thus occurred between the Wuhan and Nanjing Guomindang.

After holding a Fifth Congress in Hankou, Chen Duxiu reaffirmed the continuation of the United Front policy with the left-wing GMD under the leadership of Wang Jingwei, a policy adopted by Moscow in the Eighth Plenum of the Executive Committee of the Comintern, and denounced Chiang's anti-Communist moves in Shanghai and Nanjing.

By mid-April, with the Communists reaffirming their support of the GMD, the Wuhan government decided to resume the Northern Expedition. The National Revolutionary Army and the Fengtian troops engaged in battles in Siping, Shangcai, and Linying counties in central Henan. Defeated by the Nationalists, the Fengtian troops scrambled to retreat across the Yellow River to North China. At the same time, Feng Yuxiang, who had recently returned from the Soviet Union and announced his support of the southern government, brought his Guominjun troops from northwest China along the Longhai railroad into Henan.

Once the Wuhan government sent advance units of the Northern Expeditionary Army into Henan, the Communists immediately mobilized 10,000 peasants and Red Spears to welcome the army at Liulin. At both Liulin and Zhumadian, the two Communist operation centers, the party organized soldier-civilian get-togethers, reported to have been attended by thousands of residents. On April 17, 1927, a peasant representatives meeting was called in Xinyang, where 125 delegates gathered to pass a "Resolution on the Peasant Associations and Peasant Self-Defense Armies." These delegates began to form a temporary county government. They discussed politics, the local economy, and education.[123] A five-man committee was elected to run the county. As a means of centralizing and controlling local armed forces, steps were taken to wrest the Red Spears from the gentry. A "Temporary Committee of Henan Armed Peasants" was formed to reorganize the Red Spears into self-defense armies. Communists trained in special courses were ordered to gather at Xinyang to be sent to the countryside to do rural work.[124]

One should not construe this rapid seizure of county seats and the reported outpouring of residents to welcome the troops as unqualified support for the revolution. The besieging of county towns by thousands of rebels was a familiar sight in traditional peasant uprisings in rural China. It did not take the Communists much of an effort to accomplish this. There was a rebellious impulse among local residents because of the continuous military disruption in the countryside. A close examination of field reports filed by the Northern Expeditionary Army tells a different story. These accounts clearly demonstrate that rural mass mobilization was no easy task for the party. "The Red Spears in Queshan," one report observes, "are mostly uneducated men. They show no outward sympathy toward the revolution. They are indifferent toward our actions."[125] "The power of the reactionaries are strong," another report states. "We are short of funds and few members have a good knowledge of party affairs. The parties are very loose; few cadres attend meetings. Among the problems we confront are carelessness and lack of discipline."[126] Speaking of the Zhumadian Communist Party, a report noted, "Although the party has one district and four subdistrict headquarters in the area, most of the 70 party members congregate in one part of town. Very few peasants join the party."[127] "Most of the party members are Christians. They are naive and lack the basic knowledge of running the party."[128] "In Runan county," a report points out, "mass activities are still under the control of the landlords and local bullies. The masses were very courteous to the revolutionary army but they do not give us much help, not to mention material support. . . . There are many big landlords in Runan, who have the lives of the peasants tightly controlled in their hands. Some are puppets of the warlords."[129]

In some places, gentry-dominated Red Spears even opposed the revolutionary armies. An example of this is the so-called Liulin Incident, which was engineered after Chiang Kaishek's purge of the CCP and the split between the left and right Guomindang. A couple of Red Spear chieftains at Liulin were angered by Communist mistreatment of the gentry during the social revolution in Xinyang. In addition, a few of their leaders had been arrested by the left Wuhan government in Hankou. So these anti-Communist Red Spears leaders mobilized thousands of followers to destroy the railroad, an action intended to delay the Nationalist drive northward.

Initially the Communists tried to avoid a direct confrontation and negotiated with the opposition. But when the Red Spears ranks began to swell because of their alliance with the Manchurian army, the Communists/left Guomindang decided to suppress the uprising by force. But much damage had already been done during the incident; telephone lines were down and rail transport near the Li Family Stockade came to a complete standstill for three days. In order to prevent the rest of the Red Spears from joining the rebels, Tang Shengzhi, then commander of the left Guomindang, seized control of these groups and reorganized them into "volunteer squads" (*yiyong dui*). In other areas, the rebellious Red Spears seized cartloads of grain from the revolutionary army and raided the Xinyang railroad station.[130]

During the revolution, the Communists and the Wuhan government did seize the chance to mobilize the masses in the countryside. They created a number of organizations to achieve that goal. First, a propaganda squad known as the "Representatives of the Nationalist Government for Consoling the Military and Civilians in Henan" was set up and dispatched to Henan. This team left Wuhan on April 1 with three trunks of propaganda materials, 968 dozen biscuits, and 50 cartons of cigarettes.[131] Upon arriving at Liulin, these oral agitators fanned out to the countryside, telling local residents success stories of the Northern Expedition and of the "imminent" collapse of the Fengtian troops, and trying to convince the people that they could play an important role in the revolution.[132]

Second, the general political department of the National Revolutionary Army also did some propaganda work. The political department was charged with the responsibility of calling mass meetings. The party affairs section of the department usually worked with local party members to agitate and mobilize the people in the countryside. They traveled in their own special propaganda train. Both the general headquarters and the political affairs department of the National Revolutionary Army conducted social surveys along the Beijing-Hankou railroad. They gathered data on the Red Spears, party activities, local organizations, monetary and educational affairs, and local living conditions. The organization section of the political department set up mass associations and reorganized Red Spears and Boxers into self-defense armies. They made "progressive" gentry and elementary school teachers their targets.[133]

At every stop, propaganda brigades left the train and broke up into functional teams conducting such party activities as social surveys, editorial work, accounting, recreational propaganda, and military propaganda. Most of these propagandists were southerners, outsiders to the Henanese. They did not make much headway at the outset. Most of them did not speak the local dialects. They reported that they found the masses conservative and indifferent, "so used to warlord oppression and profoundly under the influence of reactionary propaganda." There was also the usual cultural gap between the illiterate peasantry and the urban students. To these intellectuals, the masses were "too simple-minded and never question the feudal authority." They found that the only way to penetrate the countryside was to make use of local cadres. The department therefore set up an Institute of Party Doctrine to give local cadres—mainly peasant association leaders, Red Spears chiefs, and students—some basic knowledge of Marxist ideology. Afterward these ideologically correct cadres were enrolled in crash courses in propaganda training sessions. Once they had received the proper ideological and practical training, they served as liaisons between the Hankou intellectuals and the country folk.[134]

The most powerful propaganda machine, however, was the War Zone Peasant Movement Committee, headed by Deng Yanda. The committee was organized in Wuhan on April 28, 1927, and moved to Henan on May 5, 1927. According to committee members, they had little knowledge of rural mobilization and came to the province with no concrete plans. The committee itself was made up of various groups. The main body followed the armies in their northward drive up the Beijing-Hankou railroad. At every stop, the committee left behind a few party members who would serve as a core group taking charge of mobilization work in that particular locality.

Upon its arrival in Zhumadian, for instance, the War Zone Peasant Movement Committee immediately took over the peasant movement from the General Political Department of the army. Like the General Political Department, the committee divided itself into three functional sections: organization, propaganda, and training. The organization section set up peasant associations, party headquarters, and volunteer squads. The propaganda section, as the title indicates, propagated in the countryside, distributing leaflets, giving speeches, and organizing get-togethers with rural citizens. The training section organized peasant training institutes. Eight such institutes were set up at various stations on the Beijing-Hankou railroad. In Zhumadian, for example, a Political and Military Training Institute for the Peasant Self-Defense Army was formed which recruited 100 young peasants and Red Spears from the adjoining counties of Queshan, Runan, and Suiping. Funding for the institute (C$1,000) came directly from the Guomindang. In two weeks of training at the institute, local activists were taught the basics of the Guomindang, some theory of revolution, and knowledge of how to organize a self-defense army.[135]

The War Zone Peasant Movement Committee was the main organization that set up the infrastructure for the revolution. In mid-June, when the revolutionary army reached the Zhengzhou area, the committee was abolished. After the fall of Queshan, Wuhan dispatched Communists Yu Shude and Hu Lun to the area to set up a new government structure.[136] The new government was called the Security Committee of Queshan, and it carried out a number of social reforms. (1) It abolished some taxes, confiscated the property of four powerful gentry figures, distributed grain to the poor, and released prisoners. (2) It set up a patrol force to provide basic security for the city. This 200-man patrol would replace the existing Red Spears and peasant armies, which the party ordered to disband and return to their villages. (3) It linked up with the Northern Expeditionary Army in Liulin and received 300 silver dollars from the Guomindang. (4) It reorganized the Red Spears groups into security brigades (*zhian da dui*). It also mobilized students, workers, and Red Spears to support the revolutionary armies; for example, local citizens helped gather military intelligence, served as guides, and provided labor for the transport of military equipment. (5) The new government set up a library and a bookstore for propaganda purposes.[137]

While the Queshan government is described in Communist literature today as "the earliest peasant-worker county government in Henan," this fragile government structure only lasted a short while and collapsed in June 1927, when the CCP-GMD split occurred in Wuhan.[138] Alarmed by the "leftist excess" in the mass movement, Wuhan general Tang Shengzhi declared his intention of "saving China from Communism." An anti-Communist movement known as the "Horse Day" massacre was staged in the Wuhan area. Communist leaders were arrested and killed. When the Indian Comintern leader M. N. Roy, after appealing to Moscow for instruction, showed Wang Jingwei Stalin's famous telegram calling for the punishment of the culprits in the massacre, the Wuhan GMD decided to sever relations with the CCP. Negotiations were carried out with Chiang Kaishek in June, and the Communists in Wuhan were ordered to renounce their affiliation, thus outlawing the CCP and making it an underground organization.

On June 6, the Henan GMD, threatened by the local social reforms, issued an order to stop all mass movements and subsequently arrested 300 Communist leaders. The split also dealt a blow to the Red Spears movement. The pro-Guomindang Red Spears, who had supported the Communists, swiftly changed sides and brought their troops back to retake the city. Unable to fight the Guomindang forces, Communist leaders left the city and sought refuge in the countryside. Before they finally dispersed, twenty Communist cadres and Red Spears chiefs went through a solemn ritual ceremony in a Christian church, a practice common among Red Spears in times of crisis, in which they swore to uphold the cause and to remain faithful as brothers till death.[139]

In northern Henan, the Communists had the same experience of only briefly controlling power. On May 24, 1927, 10,000 Red Spears, secretly organized into self-defense armies by Communists Xiao Rengu and Wu Zhipu, surged toward the Qi county seat. Most of the regular Fengtian troops had moved away to guard the major railroad town, leaving a vacuum in the county seat, which was defended only by a local militia. The 10,000 Red Spears rebels easily captured the town. In neighboring Sui county, the remains of the Manchurian army quickly fled the area after they saw propaganda leaflets put up by the Communists announcing the approach of southern troops. Using the Red Spears as their instrument of power, the Communists captured four county seats in the greater Kaifeng area (those in Qixian, Suixian, Tongxu, and Chenliu counties) with very little resistance. Like their southern comrades, they set up a security committee to oversee county affairs. They also initiated social reform by disarming the local militia, confiscating the property of the rich, executing a couple of corrupt officials, and abolishing a few taxes.[140]

But after that, bad news came. They learned that the National Revolutionary Army had taken Kaifeng city and had already returned to the south. Instead of coming to assist them in setting up a new government, the Wuhan government had handed the territory over to Guominjun general Feng Yuxiang. With the Communist Party in complete disorder after the split, the cadres received no direct instructions from the regional committee and were completely at a loss. Finding themselves unable to maintain a huge force of 10,000 Red Spears without adequate military supplies, and with the harvest waiting for the peasants in the countryside, the cadres had to order the Red Spears to disperse. Wu Zhipu, their leader, suddenly received unsigned instructions telling him to leave the city at once and seek refuge in a rural area. Later he found out that there was an open split within the party and that some of the Red Spears' activities were regarded by high-ranking party cadres as harmful to the party's relations with the Guomindang. Wu and Xiao Rengu were singled out as scapegoats, and Wu was expelled from the party; Xiao was allowed to retain his party membership but was put under observation. The brief mass movement in Henan came to a tragic end.[141]

Conclusion

Except for the small pilot project in Xihua county mentioned in the previous chapter, the Red Spears movement was the Communists' first experience at organizing a large-scale peasant movement in Henan. The Red Spears sectarians were essentially kinship- and community-based self-defense forces created by rural elites in response to rampant banditry and military extractions. The sudden outburst of these groups in the post-1924 Zhili-Fengtian War period was a result of increasing rural disruption caused by internal warfare. Severe internal conflicts and social stress activated the local sectarian movement. After 1924, warlord politics, political instability, and dislocation grew not only in scope, but also in intensity. The size of the armies in Henan expanded greatly as the constant factional strife between Wu Peifu's Zhili clique and the Guominjun lead to social dislocation in the countryside. The increasing claims of guest armies on the scarce resources of localities generated high tension between warlord troops and local residents in the villages, and particularly pitted natives against outsiders.

In the early Republican period, social order in the countryside was effectively maintained by county armed forces, notably the county police, with the support of state-sponsored militia, which were usually under the dominance of the rural gentry elite. The need to expand warlord armies after 1924 increasingly led to the collapse of these forces. Both the county police and the state-sponsored militia were repeatedly reorganized into warlord armies, their firearms seized by garrison troops. The resulting vacuum in the countryside was filled by privately sponsored self-defense groups—the Red Spears—the only means of physical protection. The collapse of county-level armed forces thus resulted in an intense grass-roots militarization of the countryside.

The provincial power crisis created by warlord factional rivalry also permitted ambitious rural power holders to participate in regional power politics. In turn, this led to another outburst of Red Spears energy. In the political disputes between Wu Peifu and the Guominjun, Wu skillfully utilized local Red Spears to gain power, supplying them with arms and promising to reorganize them into his army. Wu's political game activated the Red Spears sectarian groups on the Beijing-Hankou and the Longhai railways. These were areas where heavy fighting was concentrated, and it was with the military assistance of the Red Spears that Wu was able to decimate the Guominjun forces in eastern Henan. In the aftermath of the war, Wu's subordinates used the same tactic to create sectarians en masse and to build up their power.

Communist revolutionary action was also responsible for this sudden increase in Red Spears activity. It was the tacit understanding between the Chinese Communists and Hu Jingyi in late 1924, and later Yue Weijun's tolerant attitude, that gave the CCP an opportunity to mobilize these sectarian forces. The Communists exploited economic grievances and mass recruited Red Spears in antitax protests and subsequently in the Nationalist Revolution. The sudden transformation of these otherwise passive sectarians into militant, violent political groups cannot simply be explained by the survival strategies these peasants adopted in addressing the questions of state claims and military threats. The Red Spears movement was not simply a spontaneous and reactive movement. The movement assumed the magnitude and intensity it did only because the Communists exploited local antitax and anti-warlord sentiment in order to actively mobilize and form a common bond with the villagers against Wu Peifu, and also because some sectarian groups were also manipulated by warlord power contenders as pawns in the game of power politics.

Lacking the modern weaponry necessary to fight the well-trained, well-equipped warlord forces, these private self-defense groups had to fall back on the two essential elements of primitive combat: the masses of illiterate peasants, and the sheer willpower to do battle. They drew their magical power from a curious mixture of the Eight Trigrams, Daoism, the yin and yang school, popular novels, and local folklore. Like the Boxers in the late Qing, they relied on martial arts exercises to strengthen the body and on invulnerability rituals to bolster fighting will. The Red Spears sectarians can be differentiated into two distinct groups: the meditationists of the Big Red Spears and the martial artists of the Little and Middle Red Spears. But the basic difference is between the bandit/military–dominated Red Spears who roamed the hilly areas in western Henan and the community-based, gentry-led Red Spears in the eastern floodplain. As far as the Red Spears in west Henan are concerned, the demarcation between their "predatory" and "protective" activities was extremely fuzzy. Some were genuinely "protective" groups, anti-bandit and anti-warlord; others were made use of by militarists and bandits as instruments in their quest for political power. The eastern Red Spears, essentially community-based, were more anti-warlord.

Structurally, the western Red Spears were organized into platoons in the form of a pseudo-army, while their eastern cousins had a closer resemblance to the local decimal *baojia* system, usually organized as household squads. This variation clearly reflected the marked ecological differences between the underdeveloped and bandit-infested west and the relatively more developed east. The Red Spears were dispersed and fragmented groups, often involved in sect disputes. They were bound as clients to their patrons, usually the most prominent elite in the locality. Within the basic village defense unit, there was a strong bond between patron and peasant clients. Such unit solidarity was based on the peasants' need for protection, which only the gentry patron had the means to provide. Once the group was formed, it was reinforced by a stable teacher-disciple or disciple-disciple relationship.

This collection of isolated units sometimes coalesced into larger units. The optimal cohesive Red Spears organization was a regiment, which would be composed of about a thousand sectarians and spread over dozens of villages or one district. Beyond the regimental level, vertical linkage gradually broke down. In times of crisis, sectarian gentry sometimes came together to build larger political organizations and more powerful movements. They shared a common interest in local security and mutual defense. This kind of coalition was integrated purely by weak personal bonds. These were loose confederations, temporarily brought together by a number of gentry commanders who used the sectarian organizations to acquire wealth and power. These gentry commanders, however, were fierce contenders for power, and power conflicts eventually pulled these coalitions apart.

In the beginning, the Communists simply treated the Red Spears movement as nothing but a rural extension of the labor movement they had organized in the cities as part of the May 30th Movement. But with the success of the Zheng-Xing-Mi movement, the party found the sectarians to be a potent force. Red Spears could be skillfully mobilized to stir up troubles behind enemy lines and help make way for southern forces to move into Henan during the Nationalist Revolution. The party therefore began to integrate the sectarian movement into the revolution.

The location of Red Spears networks reflected this revolutionary strategy. The Communists were particularly active in organizing the sectarians along the Beijing-Hankou and Longhai railroads, the lines of troop movement in the revolution. Leadership factors also dictated the whereabouts of these movements. Building sectarian networks required the use of indigenous leaders who had access to rural areas and the necessary local contacts for recruitment of Red Spears patrons. Radical students who studied in Kaifeng and Xinyang were ideal for the task, and early Red Spears networks were invariably built in the areas adjacent to these urban centers. The Red Spears movement was essentially a suburban movement.

The movement began to gather momentum with the approaching Nationalist Revolution. Prior to the Northern Expedition, the party sent radical students back to their native counties to secure the support of local Red Spear chiefs. By extensively using territorial, kinship, and school ties, the Communists gradually built up the sectarian networks. They seldom challenged the religious belief and practices of these sectarians. Communist cadres infiltrated Red Spears organizations by becoming sworn brothers. In such cases, the Communists were absorbed by the sectarian groups.

Red Spears leaders were also invited to join the Communist Party. In joining the movement, these gentry members were motivated by opportunism and power. With the help of the sectarian chieftains, the Communists extended their contacts, drew other Red Spears groups in as allies, and gradually expanded their coalition. Similar to the gentry sectarian network, Communist sectarian networks lacked any tight organizational structure. These networks usually consisted of a small cohesive core group dominated either by Communist leaders or "progressive" Red Spears chiefs. On the outside was a peripheral group whose loyalty to the revolutionary cause remained highly dubious.

Given the fact that these territorially based groups were tightly controlled by the rural gentry, the Communists had to incorporate them en bloc. As the gentry and peasants were solidly bound by patron-client relations, the party found it very difficult to pull gentry leaders and their followers apart. In absorbing these sectarian groups into the Communist-led self-defense armies, the Communists only linked up with the gentry at the top. They were unable to subvert the peasant base of these groups. The party made little effort to develop direct linkage with the rank-and-file sectarians. But this approach presented the party with major problems after the CCP-GMD split, when pro-Guomindang Red Spears left the Communists en masse. By enlisting the support of gentry leaders, the Communists were presiding over a very loose military confederation. The size of the groups on paper was very impressive, but the revolutionary commitment of the peripheral affiliates was highly questionable.

The majority of the Red Spears leaders regarded their joint venture with the Communists as a defensive action against warlord oppression, not as offensive action in a social revolution. Yet the party had little choice but to make the Red Spears its allies. Lacking manpower and material resources in the early stage of the revolution, the only way it could create instant military power was by taking over these existing defense structures in their entirety. The result was impressive. The tactic enabled the party to mobilize tens of thousands of peasant followers into collective violent action in a matter of months. One must also bear in mind that the Communists were flying the Guomindang flag in their recruitment of Red Spears chiefs. These chieftains were not joining a Communist social revolution but a Guomindang national movement. Their targets of hostility were the warlords, not the exploitative gentry. When the Communists launched the social revolution and directed their targets at the local gentry, many of them Guomindang members, Red Spears chiefs immediately severed the Communist link and supported the Guomindang in a brutal repression of the Communist movement.

Mobilizing Red Spears in tax or rent resistance was a relatively simple task because there were always legitimate economic grievances in the countryside. But coordinating parochial dissent with a nationwide revolutionary movement was a different matter. To a certain extent, the Communists succeeded in coordinating these separate sectarian groups by providing them with a higher-level framework. Isolated networks were brought together in the Conference of the Representatives of Henan Armed Peasants, and a secret communications center was created to coordinate these groups on a national scale. The sectarian movement was thus integrated into a modern revolutionary movement.

However, there were severe limits in using sectarian groups in a modern revolution. Red Spears chiefs were invariably ambitious men seeking personal wealth and power. Conflicts with the warlords brought the Communists and Red Spears together, but these firebrands were always ready to spring into action when soldiers stepped into their territory, and the Communists could never control the Red Spears' independent course of action. Even though tens of thousands of Red Spears were supposedly under Communist command and some were even recruited into the self-defense armies, the majority of these groups were actually outside the Communist realm of control and still firmly in the hands of the local gentry. Those groups under Communist influence remained the minority.

Moreover, Communist political disputes with Chiang Kaishek, and later with the left Guomindang, greatly complicated the matter. After the split, the Nationalists formed an alternate power center claiming the loyalty of the Red Spears chieftains. The chiefs could either take a neutral stand or join the GMD. The party's last-minute decision to put a lid on the mass movement in order to avoid confrontation with the left GMD spelled disaster for the movement as a whole and created much confusion. Under Communist leadership, sectarian groups captured county towns only to find themselves stranded without military reinforcements because of the split. Later, when Feng Yuxiang lent his support to Chiang, he was rewarded with the governorship of Henan. The Guominjun moved into the area and immediately outlawed the Red Spears. Most of the sectarians were reorganized into local militias and the Red Spears sectarian movement thus collapsed.

The Red Spears movement was not a "resounding success," as Communist historians have claimed. Early Communist success was abruptly terminated by the CCP-GMD split. At the outset, the movement enjoyed some degree of success because it formed part of the Guomindang-led Nationalist Revolution; in the Northern Expedition, we see high turnouts of 30 to 40 Red Spears chapters for a single protest. This is in contrast with the few chapters the Communists were able to mobilize after the split in the urban insurrections of 1927 and 1928. But as Communist historians have correctly indicated, the Red Spears did pave the way for the National Revolutionary Army to move into North China and bring the revolution to a successful conclusion. Although at this point the party did not have plans for a comprehensive social revolution, it did briefly initiate some social reforms at the county level. The Red Spears movement therefore can be considered a success, but only a limited one.

Is there continuity between this movement and the later Communist revolution? Elizabeth Perry sees no continuity between the two movements. She points out that the method of social mobilization the Communists used and the modes of collective violence they engaged in during the war period were not the same as those used during the Northern Expedition.[142] This is very true, since the Communists were operating in an entirely different political and social environment during the wartime period. It was absolutely essential for them to adapt their revolutionary strategies and tactics to the new environment. In fact, their mobilization tactics, as following chapters will demonstrate, varied from period to period and underwent a gradual transformation.

Despite the changes, we do detect some continuity between the Red Spears movement and the Communist revolution. A revolution takes time to build and early movements lay the groundwork for subsequent activities. Each movement, whether a success or a failure, invariably forms part of the valuable revolutionary experience. The peasant self-defense armies created in this period became the core fighting force in the Eyuwan period and were later incorporated in the New Fourth Army. The networks built in the Nationalist Revolution survived underground and were rehabilitated by the party in wartime to form the Sui-Qi-Tai and the Yuwansu anti-Japanese bases. The student and Red Spears leaders trained in both the sixth class of the Peasant Institute and in the two-week short courses later formed the backbone of the revolutionary cadres in the Sino-Japanese War. In terms of leadership and location, there is definite continuity between the early movement and the subsequent revolution. In terms of mobilization, the Communists learned from the Red Spears experience and modified their tactics. We can say there were both continuity and change.

CHAPTER 3

Penetrating Settled Peasant Communities: The Case of Eyuwan

After the CCP-GMD split, the Communists lost their foothold in urban centers and had to seek refuge in the countryside. Unlike during the May 30th Movement or the Northern Expedition, Communist cadres now had to direct the revolution from rural areas; it became a peasant-based revolution. One perplexing question that confronts all students of peasant-based revolution is, How do revolutionaries penetrate settled peasant communities, which normally are directly or indirectly under the dominance of the rural elite? Answering this question is crucial to an understanding of the Chinese Communist revolution. Both Barrington Moore and Theda Skocpol have repeatedly underscored the preponderant position of the Chinese gentry in rural communities, which, they assert, acted as a constraint to peasant mobilization.[1] In Qing and Republican China, gentry power in rural areas was omnipotent. Economically, the gentry were holders of large estates and thus formed the wealthiest segment of the rural population. Politically, because of their many ties with the state, they often served as brokers between the government and the local people. Socially, they always served as overseers of rural affairs. They were judicial arbiters of local disputes, managers of public works and welfare activities, and guardians of local customs and moral teachings.

The gentry and peasantry were frequently bound by a shared identity. They were members of the same kinship organizations and the same residential communities. They participated jointly in religious/sectarian activities. In times of political turmoil, the gentry-peasant bond was further reinforced by problems of insecurity. The gentry's function in local defense was indispensable to the maintenance of social order in the countryside. Both gentry and peasants participated in the local militia. Local gentry put up money and peasants provided manpower for the construction and repair of rural fortifications. Rural defense units were frequently an outgrowth of the prevalent kinship and religious/sectarian structures, in which gentry leadership had always been dominant. Such structures often gave the gentry enormous power and tightly cemented the gentry-peasant relationship, particularly during the unstable warlord period when security problems were so urgent. The gentry and peasants developed a mutually dependent relationship, which, it would seem, no Communist appeal could pull apart.

Given the gentry's preponderant position in the countryside, how did the revolutionaries gain access to and seize power in these settled rural communities? This chapter examines Communist activities in the Eyuwan base in the late 1920s and early 1930s.[2] It seeks to find out whether the Dabie Mountains, where the Eyuwan base was located, were, as in the writings of Eric Wolf, the kind of "peripheral geographical location" that provides Communist rebels with tactical advantages in mobilizing the peasantry.[3] If we assume gentry power to be a decisive factor in facilitating or inhibiting grass-roots mobilization, an examination of the composition of the gentry class and its repressive power in this mountainous region will certainly further our understanding of peasant-based revolution. Finally, it would be interesting to find out which tactics Communists employed in rebuilding their armed forces, and the difficulties they encountered in implementing radical land reform.

Marginal Geographical Location: Three Ecological Zones

Scholars studying revolutions often emphasize "marginal geographical locations" as ideal places for staging peasant-based revolution. In mountainous locations where state control is minimal, revolutionaries often have tactical advantages. It is in these remote areas that one finds the wide economic disparity between agrarian overlords and cultivators that generates intense rural tensions. It is also in these marginal areas that revolutionaries can evade state repressive power by hiding out in "defensible mountainous redoubts" or by moving across provinces and seeking refuge in a slightly less hostile political environment.

The Hubei-Henan section of the Eyuwan revolutionary base, located at the very heart of the Dabie Mountains in the southeastern part of Henan, is often cited as one such "marginal geographical location" (see Map 3). Rising 2,756 feet high, the Dabie Mountains, together with the Tongbai Mountains, form an east-west barrier between Hubei and Henan provinces. The area is a watershed for both the Yangzi and the Huai rivers. This region is not exactly remote. The land, well watered by

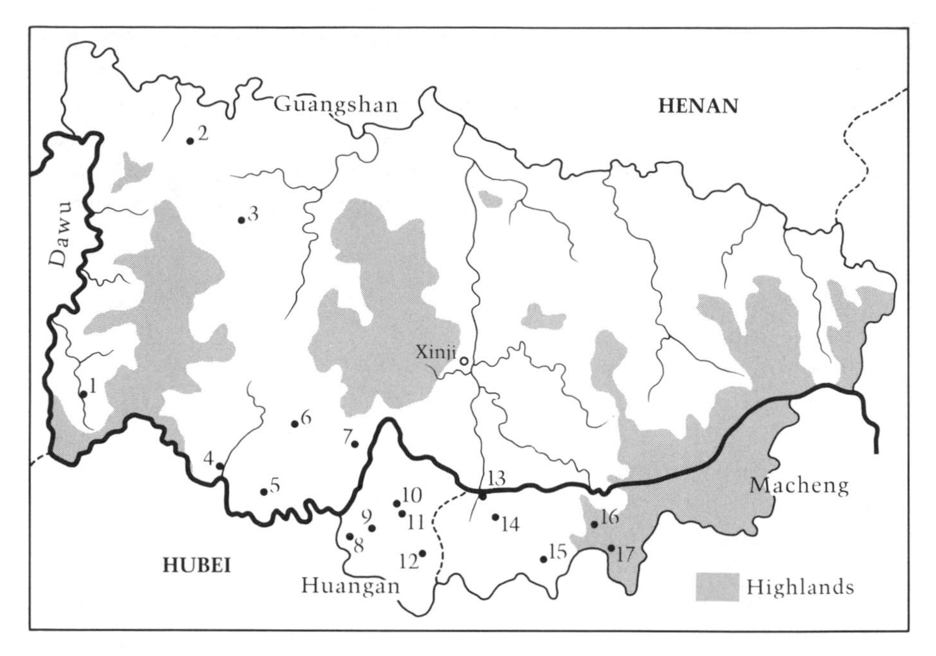

Map 3. Eyuwan border base, Henan-Hubei section. 1, Kafang; 2, Yudian; 3, Yanggaoshan; 4, Panwan; 5, Henanwan; 6, Beihujia; 7, Wangwan; 8, Huanggufan; 9, Sijiaocaomen; 10, Jianhe; 11, Zhengbian; 12, Fangwan; 13, Sidian; 14, Miaowa; 15, Wanglou; 16, Cangzigang; 17, Songwa.

mountain streams, is very productive and provides a variety of local products, including rice, wheat, oil, tea, herbs, bamboo, and lumber. The mountains themselves are rich in minerals, marble, and crystals. Since the establishment of the People's Republic, this section of the Eyuwan base has been made into a new county called Xinxian (New county), which takes in a large portion of Guangshan in Henan and small segments of Huangan and Macheng counties in Hubei.[4]

In the 1930s, southeastern Henan was, on the whole, commercially very active. Trading in all sorts of food grains and cottage industry commodities took place there. Merchants made good use of the Huai River, shipping their goods either upstream to Zhoujiakou, a major trading center in eastern Henan, or downstream via Zhenjiang to Shanghai. An alternate route was to ship products to Xinyang by barge, and then to Hankou or points north by rail. Guangshan, the Communist revolution center, was a rich county. Despite a temporary setback in the 1920s, in the 1930s there were still a Christian church, three agricultural schools, a textile factory, and a number of well-maintained stores in the county town. Its agricultural produce, mainly rice, beans, and sesame seeds, went by barge to Xinyang and then to Hankou and Shanghai by rail. Guangshan wholesaled 50,000 *jin* of raw cotton, 3,000 bolts of cotton fabric, and 100,000 *jin* of peas annually.[5]

Agriculturally, the region was predominantly an area of irrigated wet rice cultivation, markedly distinct from the dry wheat farmland in the rest of the province. The average household landholding was very small but the fertility of the soil helped make up for this. Roughly 60 percent of farm households were either landless tenants or owners of ten *mu* or less, a farm size considered to be on the verge of, if not below, the poverty line. The GMD-sponsored Rural Revival Committee reported 60 percent tenancy (pure tenants plus part owner/part tenants) in this area.[6] Compared with the north, where tenancy rates were in the single digits or the teens, southeastern Henan had a decidedly high tenancy rate. Large estates were characteristic of the region. Official gentry, for example, frequently possessed several tens of thousands of *mu* of top-grade land.[7] According to one survey, fixed rent in kind (*ding'e gu zu*) was the prevalent form of payment in the irrigated rice-growing area in southeastern Henan.[8] Obviously both forms of rental arrangement, fixed rent and sharecropping, existed in this region. Rental arrangements varied from county to county and sometimes from village to village. Unfortunately, we do not have exact figures on their distribution. In Xinyang county, for instance, fixed rent was predominant in the suburban area. Peasants were allowed to switch to sharecropping only in times of natural disaster. Yet in Zhongshan Inn, a market town located a short distance from the county seat, sharecropping was the prevalent rental arrangement.[9] For the area as a whole, rents were roughly between 40 and 50 percent of the yield. Leases were mostly three-year short-term contracts that required a deposit. As in other areas, tenants were obliged to perform labor services or to bring gifts to landlords throughout the year, especially on festive occasions.[10] All the objective conditions conducive to a revolution—scarcity of cropland, concentration of landownership, and disparity of income differentials—were present in the Dabie mountain region.

A study of Guangshan county, where the Communist headquarters was located, illustrates the particular socioeconomic setting in which the Communists launched their social revolution. Guangshan was divided ecologically into two zones: rice paddies in the south and wheat farms in the north. Ninety-nine percent of its households were farmers. Each household always had one or two itinerant merchant family members peddling grain or poultry in adjoining market towns. According to the local gazetteer, the majority of inhabitants were said to lead a comfortable life. Twenty percent of households were of the landlord class, with most of these landed gentry having holdings of less than 100 *mu*, a few with several hundred *mu*, and only two or three with a few thousand *mu*. The 1930 Chinese Communist survey found only six landlords in Xinji, the county seat, one in each of the four wards and two in the town. Landlords made up only 1 percent of the Jianhe population but owned 80 percent of the cultivated land.[11]

Seventy percent of the households in Guangshan were tenants; 2 percent were agricultural laborers; 4 percent were part owner/part tenants, another 4 percent owner-cultivators.[12] The sharecropping arrangement between landlord and tenant was usually 40:60, occasionally 50:50, often with some provision for crop failures. Landlords did not participate in cultivation but usually provided tenants with seed. Leases were signed before a witness and required a deposit, usually calculated as a percentage of the annual rent, payable in cash, and returnable without interest at the end of the tenure. There were the usual two types of rent arrangements in the county, fixed rent, where the landlord's share was determined before harvest, and unfixed rent, where the landlord's actual share was determined after harvest.[13] In the second arrangement, tenants were required to give the landlord a banquet, at which he would inspect the crop and negotiate the amount of grain to be turned over to him. Subsidiary crops (tea, lumber, fodder, oil, iron, cotton, beans, etc.) customarily went to the tenants. Tenants also had obligations to perform labor and make gifts of farm produce to landlords.[14] The landlord seldom rescinded the lease unless he was seriously offended, but a tenant's right could be reinstated after an apology. In fact, tenants seemed to hold a permanent cultivation right, working the same plot of land year after year even if it changed hands several times.[15]

While the Henan-Hubei border area has always been cited as the ideal "peripheral mountainous region" for a revolution, the Eyuwan revolutionary base was not an undifferentiated, remote region completely shielded from exogenous market forces. First, the Henan-Hubei segment of the Eyuwan base was not infested with bandits and smugglers, it was a region of settled peasant communities. Second, the area was not ecologically homogeneous. Socioeconomic conditions in the northern highlands and the southern flatlands differed markedly, and each, as will be shown later, had a different impact on the Communist mobilization.

In the 1930s, Communist rural mobilizers usually differentiated among three ecological zones in the region: the north, the middle, and the south. They indicated clearly that the north and the middle actually belonged in one zone. According to them, the ecological zones varied in the following ways.

The Northern Zone

Located in rugged terrain in the heart of the Dabie Mountains, the northern zone was a depressed peripheral highland marked by an acute shortage of arable land. In the midst of the mountains, old forms of social arrangement remained intact. In this type of depressed agrarian community, impoverished peasants were highly dependent on landlords for access to cultivable land, farmsteads to live on, and even for agricultural implements. In the north, ownership of land was highly concentrated. Any agricultural surplus usually went for the upkeep of the landlord's luxurious lifestyle. The exploitation of the peasantry by landlords often generated a great deal of agrarian tension. Northern highland peasants, the Communists observed, were working in a serf system (*nongnu zhidu*), always within the power domain of the overlords.

The Middle Zone

In the middle section, landownership was relatively less concentrated. There were fewer large landholders; most proprietors were rich peasants and smallholders. Peasants had easy access to land, and rent was usually a sharecropping arrangement, 50:50 in kind. Tenants provided the seed and agricultural implements. Unlike northern peasants, those in the middle zone did bring in a good income, although much of that went for urban goods, leaving very little for savings. Peasants in the middle zone were less dependent and living standards were higher. The north and the middle zones differed in some ways, but there were also similarities between them. In both zones, peasants had tenuous ties to the market, except as consumers. Land rent was the principal form of income for the landlords. Old institutional and social arrangements remained intact, and the traditional traits of agrarian communities were preserved.

The Southern Zone

The southern lowlands were distinctively different from the other two zones. Because of its propinquity to Wuhan, the regional market, the south had undergone a capitalist transformation. The agrarian classes, both gentry and peasants, were greatly commercialized. Large numbers of peasants had been drawn into the market to trade local products. Even though there was a dense population and a high concentration of landownership in the area, there was apparently enough land for all cultivators, since many peasants gave up farming and turned to trade. Because the majority of the landed elite actively engaged in commerce, they hired wage laborers to cultivate their land. The marked difference between these landlords and those in the north was that southern landlords were landlord-merchants and therefore less dependent on land rent for income. Drawn by market forces, peasant proprietors also became very enterprising. They earned a combined income from various economic activities, including agriculture, trade, and work in the landlords' stores. Commercialization in the lowland area thus brought in a new class of agrarian elite, a wealthy urban-oriented peasantry.

Agrarian class relations in the southern lowland also underwent fundamental changes. A strong personal tie developed between landed merchants and landless peasants, a new form of relationship based upon mutual dependence and reciprocity. Landed merchants, who spent most of their time in the cities, often relied on peasants to collect rents for them. In return, they willingly provided enterprising peasants with low-interest credit with which to start their own businesses. Because wealthy landlords and enterprising peasants were busy doing business, they relied on hired laborers to cultivate their farms. This led to an increase in farm wages, which brought about a higher living standard for agricultural laborers. The result of capitalism was a relatively strong alignment of the upper and lower agrarian classes and an easing of social tensions in the entire southern region. Although capitalism frequently increases the number of farm laborers with no claims on land as landholding becomes more commercialized and concentrated, usually resulting in a polarization of the landed and landless, it seems that the problem of access to land is also mitigated by high farm wages. Our findings confirm Linda Arrigo's argument that there is less social inequality in more commercialized regions.[16]

A close look at Macheng county may give us a better understanding of the regional variation and socioeconomic transformation of the area. Typical of the region, the northern and southern zones of this county differed from one another immensely in topography, economic production, social composition, and rural livelihoods. There were few landlords in the northern highlands, most with holdings of less than 300 *mu*. In the wet rice irrigation lowlands of the South, landlordism was more prominent, and many landholders had 1,000 *mu* of land.[17] A holder of 400 *mu* was considered only a middle landlord in the south but a big landlord in the north. Petty landlords, several times the number in the north, proliferated in the south. Southern middle peasants, who always generated a surplus income, had enough money to hire farmhands to do the cultivation; their lifestyle was similar to that of rich peasants in the north. On the other hand, middle peasants in the north had barely enough to eat. Poor peasants in the south, albeit subservient to landlords, always had enough food on the table because rent was low and payments were few. According to a Communist survey, even lowland hired farmhands earned better wages than private teachers in the north.[18]

Landlordism alone cannot be used to indicate rural exploitation; one should look at the social relationships in a particular locality. Despite the small number of landlords in the north, rural relations in the highlands were extremely exploitative. Strongly dependent on land rent as their only source of income, highland landlords were forced to make larger claims on tenants' production (normally two-thirds of the crop in kind, plus other "gifts" of non-staple grains). Rescinding of land contracts was not infrequent. Although highland landlords did give tenants a rent reduction in times of economic adversity, poor tenants were required to show gratitude by giving their master a banquet.[19] All of this indicates that traditional forms of socioeconomic relationships were very much preserved in the north. Communist cadres found these traditional agrarian communities highly conducive to social revolution. Northern peasants were not only willing to participate in agrarian protests, they even actively sought Communist help in rural self-defense and land redistribution.

The southern agrarian society, on the other hand, had been transformed by market forces, and rural feudal authority had been greatly undermined by the market. Because they had easy access to the metropolis of Hankou, landlord-traders were always away from home doing business. These absentee landlords entrusted their families and property to hired farmhands (*gu nong*, or hired labor), who were frequently regarded by the landlords' family members as substitute heads of household.[20] Some farmhands even had an affair with the landlord's wife or daughter while the master was away. Communist revolutionaries found that this bond between lowland peasants and their masters made peasant mobilization immensely difficult, if not impossible. In southern Huangan, for instance, landlord-merchants voluntarily gave tenants rent or interest reductions. Southern landlord-merchants sometimes negated the Communist land program by temporarily exempting their tenants from rent payment.[21] Very few southern peasants were truly revolutionary, the Communists reported.[22]

Different class interests in the north and south also produced different landlord behavior in response to Communist revolutionary offensives. Since lowland landlords did not rely solely on land rent for a living, they had a better understanding of peasant economic hardships. They objected to the hard-line policy of repression advocated by highland landlords and preferred to win peasants over with material benefits. Many therefore refused to finance or participate in the northern programs of rural suppression (*qingxiang*). A couple of lowland landlords were locked up by the authorities for noncompliance.[23] Northern landholders, highly dependent on land income, felt seriously threatened by the Communist land program. Should the Communists take away their landholding, they would lose their political and economic power. They believed they were under attack and strongly supported the Guomindang policy of repression.

The southern landlord-entrepreneurs, on the other hand, could live on their commercial profits and hold out in the urban centers until the movement blew over.[24] These two groups of rural elites thus differed sharply over the question of how urgent it was for the government to invade and recover Communist-occupied areas. The southern gentry merchants favored a gradual approach (*huan gong*) that would not alienate the peasants. The northern landed gentry (those in northern Huangan, northern Macheng, and southern Guangshan) insisted on an immediate invasion and speedy recovery of their economic base.[25]

We have found that north/south socioeconomic variations led to a very different response to the Communist stimulus by the rural elites and the peasantry. In the economically depressed north, conservative rural elites put up strong resistance against Communist encroachment, while impoverished peasants welcomed the Communist revolution. The reverse was true in the south, where relatively well-off peasants who had been drawn into the market were indifferent to Communist appeals. The urban-based gentry merchants, more interested in commerce than land, were more sympathetic toward both the plight of the peasants and the Communist revolutionary cause.

Such variations compelled the Communists to adopt different peasant mobilization tactics in the two divergent ecological areas. In the northern highlands, where the party did penetrate the countryside, the Communists used class differences to mobilize the cultivators. They set up peasant committees to recruit peasants. A hierarchy of township and district committees was formed to take charge of grass-roots mobilization.[26] In the southern lowlands, especially in suburban areas, where both party influence and peasant response were weak, the Communist tactic was to work with landlords and rich peasant elites, and through prevalent peasant organizations.

The peasant organizations they penetrated, known in Communist terms as "grey organizations," included the "Double Ninth Festival Society" (*chongyang hui*), the blood-oath "Fraternal Society" (*xiongdi hui*), the "Martial Arts Society" (*quanshu hui*) and the "Percussion Society" (*luogu hui*).[27] In the south, the party exercised great caution and adopted a nonantagonistic approach. Cadres were strictly forbidden to mention the term "revolution." If they wanted to launch a land reform, they were instructed to do so through a third party with non-Communist members. Only when objective conditions clearly allowed it and class conflicts were sharp were they permitted to lead southern peasants in turning these "grey organizations" into peasant committees. And only in special cases when class conflicts were approaching an explosion were Communists given permission to organize peasants into clandestine dissident groups.[28]

Political Power Crisis and Differentiation of Gentry Elites

In *States and Social Revolutions*, Theda Skocpol states that "the Chinese peasants were, in the normal scheme of things, not in a structural position to revolt collectively and autonomously against the landed gentry." In order for a peasant revolution to occur, she argues, the Communists had to first destroy the gentry's strong socioeconomic base and undermine its leadership in the community. In contrast to the French and Russian cases, she points out, the Chinese gentry, though vulnerable, was much more entrenched locally after the collapse of the old regime. To effectively mobilize Chinese peasants in a revolution required displacing the gentry at the local level.[29] We will not be able to fully understand the peasant-based revolution in China without having first examined the regional political power crisis that caused a rapidly changing local power structure at that particular historic time.

In the late 1920s and early 1930s, Henan was engulfed in a bitter power struggle between national leader Chiang Kaishek and regional warlord Feng Yuxiang, a struggle that gave rise to a regional power crisis in the province. After his Nationalist army occupied the capital at Kaifeng on June 1, 1927, Feng held a conference in Zhengzhou with delegates from the Wuhan government. Fearful of an attack on Wuhan by Chiang Kaishek, Wang Jingwei ordered the National Revolutionary Army to return to Hubei, leaving the defense of North China to the Guominjun. Feng was also given control of Henan, in return for a promise to restrict Communist influence in the province. Feng, however, was determined to bring the Nanjing and Wuhan governments together so that they could jointly finish the Northern Expedition. Between June 19 and June 21, Feng and Chiang Kaishek conferred in Xuzhou (Jiangsu), after which they proclaimed their determination to oppose the Communists and complete the Northern Expedition. Feng then took independent action to rid Henan of Communist influence, ordering 240 Communists working in his army and local government to leave the province.

Following the fierce suppression of the Communists by the Wuhan government on July 15, and with the Communist threat rising in Nanchang and warlord Sun Chuanfang attacking Nanjing, both the Nanjing and Wuhan governments found it politically necessary to come to a reconciliation. At the end of August, after a conference, Nanjing and Wuhan merged again to form one government. With the Guomindang reunited, the Nationalist Revolutionary Army launched its second Northern Expedition. By mid-June 1928, National Revolutionary forces had taken Beijing and the Northern Expedition was completed.

But power conflicts between Feng Yuxiang and Chiang Kaishek began to emerge in the aftermath of the Northern Expedition. First, Chiang denied Feng control of Hebei province, which included the lucrative port of Tianjin that Feng coveted. Instead, he was only given control of the city of Beiping (renamed from Beijing in the Nationalist period) and the tax bureau in that city, which gave the Guominjun leader an income of merely C$200,000.[30] Income derived from his territorial bases in Shandong, Henan, Shaanxi, and Gansu provinces was woefully inadequate for the support of his huge army of 200,000 men. Second, in a move to undermine the military power of the warlords, Chiang called a conference to disband the troops. The disagreement between Chiang and the provincial warlords over this issue led to increased tension between Nanjing and regional warlord power holders.

Conflict between Chiang Kaishek and the Guangxi clique under Li Zhongren and Bai Chongxi erupted in March 1929. To break Guangxi power in central China, Chiang personally led a punitive military campaign against the southwestern warlords. By early May, Guangxi military power had collapsed in Hunan and Hubei provinces. Sympathetic toward the Guangxi clique, Feng was prepared to launch an assault of Nationalist troops from southern Henan. The plan, however, was thwarted by the defection to the Nationalist camp of over 100,000 of his troops, led by several of his generals, including Han Fuju and Shi Yousan.

Enmity between Feng and Chiang finally led to direct military clashes in October 1929. This time Feng had the backing of Shanxi warlord Yan Xishan, but by the end of November Chiang's forces were winning the battle around Luoyang, forcing Feng to retreat to Shanzhou in western Henan. Threatened by the approaching Nationalist troops, Yan and Feng joined forces with GMD leader Wang Jingwei and the Guangxi military faction in an attempt to destroy Chiang's power. The subsequent civil war, which occurred in the later part of 1930 and was commonly referred to as the *Zhongyuan dazhan* (Zhongyuan campaign), was fought in Henan, Shandong, and Shanxi provinces.

Feng's army moved rapidly down the Beiping-Hankou railroad and then eastward along the Longhai railway, dealing a crushing defeat to the Nationalist troops along the rail lines. The Guangxi clique simultaneously moved into Hunan to threaten the Nationalist flank. On June 26, Yan Xishan's forces successfully took the city of Jinan (Shandong). In mid-July, Wang Jingwei, Feng Yuxiang, and Yan Xishan gathered at Beiping for an "enlarged conference" in an attempt to organize an alternative to Chiang Kaishek's national government in Nanjing. But by August, Chiang's forces had retaken Jinan and Yan was forced to retreat to his home province of Shanxi. With the support of Manchurian "Young Marshal" Zhang Xueliang, who had been brought over by Chiang, Nanjing was making rapid progress in the battlefield. The anti-Chiang front began to collapse. In October 1930, with the recovery of Kaifeng and Zhengzhou and the capture of Luoyang, Chiang was able to bring his campaign against Feng Yuxiang and Yan Xishan to a successful conclusion.[31] But two years of internecine warfare in the Henan-Hubei area not only provided the Communists with the perfect political opportunity to create the Eyuwan border base in the southeastern corner of the province, a region relatively free of state political interference, it also created a high degree of differentiation among the gentry elites, who by siding with various power factions were invariably drawn into the political dispute.

Chronic civil war at the national level had the effect of redefining the local power structure at the county and subcounty levels. In the 1920s and 1930s, the counties in Republican China had two distinct levels of authority. The county administration was nominally under the state but was actually dominated by whichever warlord happened to be stationed in the area. County government was nothing but an instrument used by these regional military groupings to extract resources from rural communities in order to sustain the war. Subcounty-level authority, however, remained firmly in the hands of the rural elites. Subcounty administrative positions, from the district (*qu*) and subdistricts down to the *baojia* standard household system, were controlled by rural elites, mostly the landed gentry and rich peasants.[32]

In the Republican period, the landed gentry in the Hubei-Henan border area were highly differentiated. Communists working in the area usually categorized them by their economic power:

1. Rural bosses, (*da haoshen dizhu*, or big despotic gentry landlords) were those county and subcounty bureaucrats, militia commanders, and tax agents who owned large estates. Their number varied from

place to place. Rural bosses were not determined strictly by the size of their landholding. The owner of a medium-sized piece of property of several hundred *mu* could be designated a rural boss by the Communists if he happened to be the predominant power holder and/or tax agent in that particular locality.

2. Medium-sized landlords were smaller holders who often served as commanders of the state-sponsored village-clearing squads (*qingxiang tuan*). These landlords usually assisted state troops in the repression of Communists.

3. Petty landlords were the small holders who, according to the Communists, were supporting the revolution.[33]

The Communist use of property size as the criterion for differentiation of rural elites does not, however, give a clear picture of the rural gentry class. The Henan and Hubei landed gentry should be differentiated into the following two distinct groups: rural bosses (*jiu haoshen dizhu*, or the traditional landed gentry), and urban-based reformist gentry. This is a close parallel to the highland/lowland division discussed previously. These two groups of gentry differed markedly not only in their economic activities, but also in their political/ideological leanings. The upland traditional rural bosses were allies of local warlord Ren Yingqi. The reformist commercial landlords, more urban-oriented and modern-minded, were mostly left-wing GMD and supporters of the Communist cause at the time of the first CCP-GMD United Front. Some were associates of Feng Yuxiang, the famous modern-minded Christian general of the Guominjun, who cooperated with the Communists in the May 30th Movement and in the Northern Expedition.[34]

Post–Northern Expedition politics greatly complicated the political environment in Henan and Hubei and led to a reshuffling of elite alignments. National and regional power politics helped to completely redefine community power in the countryside. For a brief period after the CCP-GMD split, when the left and right GMD made up their differences and reunited under one party, and when Feng Yuxiang, as governor of Henan, supported Chiang Kaishek's anti-CCP policy, rural elites in Henan were temporarily united under the joint leadership of Chiang Kaishek and Feng Yuxiang. Together they launched an attack against the Communists in Henan and Hubei. But in the early 1930s, with the breakdown of talks over troop disbandment at the national level and a civil war between Chiang Kaishek on the one side and Feng Yuxiang, Yan Xishan, and Wang Jingwei on the other, the region suddenly experienced a political power crisis at the county level.

Locally, a corresponding split occurred between the respective gentry clients of Chiang and Feng. Conservative rural bosses supported

Chiang Kaishek because of the Nationalist militant policy of eliminating Communist influence from the area and thus stabilizing the power of the conservative gentry. Local Guominjun commanders, who had earlier worked with the CCP in the May 30th Movement, and the reformist urban-oriented gentry, who supported Feng Yuxiang, began to show sympathy for and to lean toward the Communists.

In the aftermath of the civil war, the region also saw competition between these two groups of rural elites for dominance of rural administration. Formerly, conflict had been minimized because there was a general consensus among the rural elites, and Guominjun commanders and conservative elites worked smoothly together. The reformist elites were busy with business in the urban centers, and usually refrained from involvement in local politics. Traditional rural bosses acted as the sole dominant force in rural administration. With the defeat of Feng Yuxiang, the political picture changed. The Guominjun commanders and the left GMD were removed from power. They therefore joined hands with the reorganizationists (*gaizu pai*) and other anti-Chiang reformists. As an out-group, they tried to recover their power base. This power crisis brought traditional and liberal elites into direct armed confrontation at the local level. They fought over control of the county militia and the tax revenues. Some did try to resolve their differences by legal means, but everyone realized that the only way to stay in power was to build up an armed force. Each gentry faction hastily created its own blood-oath fraternity or Red Spears group to use as an instrument of violence. Such efforts furthered the process of rural militarization and led to a proliferation of privately owned armed forces in each locality.

There was a frantic race among these power holders to procure weaponry from the cities. The liberal gentry, who possessed more resources because of their commercial activities, used agricultural products to trade for arms from the urban centers. Those who lacked material resources abducted women from Communist bases and sold them for weapons. Every group made the best use of whatever armed forces were under its influence (village militia, bandits, Red Spears, and other community defense groups) to extract resources from the people solely to procure arms. Some did it with the blessing of the county authority; others did it completely on their own. When rural bosses used administrative authority, and occasionally brute force, to coerce petty gentry into subscribing to their military endeavors, many rural elites defiantly refused to comply and put up strong resistance. During the 1930s, the countryside in Henan was completely engulfed in endless violence and quarrels among armed gentry groups.[35]

Most of the time, the rural gentry was pulled apart by parochial interests and divided along geographic lines into blocs of regional power. Gentry militia in Luoshan county, for instance, reportedly refused to help the Guangshan gentry when it was under attack by the Communists. Gentry-dominated village-clearing squads and merchant corps were organized strictly along community lines and supported by community resources.[36] Some of these community forces had been infiltrated by the Communists at the time of the Northern Expedition and therefore refused to participate in attacks on the CCP.[37] It was the dissension within the gentry class that gave the Communists a chance to seek out individual members for support.[38]

Conservative rural bosses were generally targets of attack by the Communists. Usually there were one or two rural bosses in every section (*fang*) of a village.[39] Common defense interests often brought together several rural bosses from counties in adjoining provinces. These rural magnates formed power coalitions[40] through marriage or other personal ties, their power blocs consisting mostly of clan bands of several thousand men.[41] But rural bosses were in a delicate political position. As power brokers, they were sandwiched between ruler and ruled. As government tax collectors, they were frequently attacked by villagers in tax resistance movements. Most of them were in charge of local security and were required to raise money for upkeep of the local militia and for construction and repairs of local fortifications.

Even though rural residents did not object to gentry leadership in building a strong defense system in times of increasing political instability, taxing people always offered opportunities for greed and corruption. When rural bosses lined their pockets and shifted the tax burden onto the peasants, social class tensions began to build. With competition for local resources increasing among the power blocs, rural bosses, who relied on land rent for a living and therefore had much to lose in a social revolution, did not hesitate to use force to extract money and manpower from locals so they could effectively defend their power bases.[42] Heads of dominant lineages sometimes exercised clan authority to compel minor and weak lineages to contribute to war chests.[43] Many minor lineages probably yielded to such authority; some, however, resented such high-handed actions. Lineage rivalries in the countryside thus offered Communists a golden opportunity to manipulate minor lineages and to vie for power.

Elite Repressive Power

With the central power becoming weaker, violence in the countryside became rampant. Old forms of social control based on garrison troops and county militia disintegrated as these armed forces were gradually commandeered by regional warlords. To protect their families and property from marauding armies and roving bandits, local magnates created private armies and turned their residences into armed fortifications. Practically every local community had its own military establishment. Local community defense organizations came in various forms: private clan bands, blood-oath fraternities such as the Red Spears, public militia, anti-Communist squads, and merchant corps.

The most pervasive form of armed defense was the clan bands. As clan heads, the dominant gentry were charged with the duty of protecting the clan from outside attacks. Using the clan regulations (*jia gui*) and prohibitions (*jin lu*), the gentry had the authority to order kinsmen to join clan bands. In this way, the entire clan was turned into a corporate kinship defense community under gentry leadership. In Huangan, for instance, the majority of gentry-controlled armies were nothing but clan bands.[44] Some units were later sanctioned by the government and even reorganized into state-sponsored village-clearing squads. Other militias also received government funding once they promised to help the authorities fight the Communists.[45]

The Red Spears, another form of community defense, were most prominent in the three Henan counties of Luoshan, Guangshan, and Shangcheng. As we saw in the previous chapter, these sectarian groups were created in the post–1924 period mainly as a "protective" type of community defense. Most of these forces were under gentry dominance. In the post–Northern Expedition period, some of these groups had gravitated toward the Communists. But the gentry, who sided with the GMD, often employed Red Spears to rid their communities of Communist instigators. Armed rivalry between gentry- and Communist-dominated Red Spears remained a fixture in the Hubei-Henan border area.[46]

Red Spears defense structures proliferated all over the Henan-Hubei border. In the eastern section of Macheng county (Hubei) alone, there were 300 chapters of Red Spears. In Yellow Earth Mount, for example, every villager was a Red Spears member. In a community of only fifteen square kilometers near the town of Yan Family River, there was an array of 40 Red Spears units composed of 5,000 villagers.[47] According to a Communist account, the gentry urged villagers "to join these invincible organizations to protect their own lives and those of their families from attack by the Communist Party and those pantless Communists."[48] Most sectarians were either hired farmhands or long-term wage laborers. Sometimes shopkeepers were forced by their bosses to take up martial arts. With the emergence of the Communist movement in the early 1930s, Red Spears militarization greatly intensified. In Macheng, practically every wealthy household had its own Red Spears chapter. As the movement spread, these chapters were integrated hierarchically into Red Spears networks with the martial arts masters as the links. Later, when the commander agreed to fight against the Communists, the chapter received firearms from the county authority.[49]

Local gentry also had under their control the state-sponsored militia (*mintuan*). The militia were semiofficial and semiprivate armed forces. Most of them were originally privately owned Red Spears groups that were reorganized into militia after Feng Yuxiang, during his governorship, outlawed all sectarians. The majority of the forces were still in private hands. Some were officially incorporated into the county militia system; others were temporarily affiliated with the GMD garrison troops (*jingbei dui*) stationed in nearby cities.[50]

Aside from these forces, the gentry also had under their command two other kinds of anti-Communist organizations: the village pacts (*lianzhuang hui*) and the Communist Elimination Society (*zhan gong hui*). The village pact dates back to the late Qing period, when the government ordered villages to integrate themselves into pacts and put up a common defense against the Taiping and Nian rebels. In the 1930s, the GMD reactivated and actively promoted these structures as a form of anti-Communist community defense. Whenever the GMD recovered a peasant community from the Communists, the government would issue orders to reorganize the Communist-formed peasant associations into village pacts. Later, when groups of villages were reorganized under a Communist Elimination Society, village pacts were used for Communist repression.[51]

In urban centers, the commercial gentry had their own instrument of social control: the merchant corps. The rank-and-file members of the merchant corps were mostly tenant farmers. According to the Communists, these peasants were more sympathetic toward the Communists, but reluctant to join the movement for fear of government reprisal. They therefore stayed on the sidelines.[52]

No matter what name or form they took—Red Spears, Big Swords, the Communist Elimination Society, village-clearing squads, military squads (*bianlian dui*), or militia—these community defense units were very similar in structure and membership. All were clientele-serving groups banded together by kin, martial arts, sectarian, and community ties. Members were drawn mostly from clansmen, sectarians, secret society members, village thugs, bandits and, above all, ordinary peasants. These patron-client bands were organized hierarchically into regiments and squads (*zhituan* and *zhidui*). Each possessed a few guns. The defense communities seem to have been market communities centered around the stockade (*zhai*), market town (*ji*), or township (*zhen*). Like the Red Spears mentioned before, gentry patrons usually donated a site (an ancestral temple or a stockade) and gave the group money for initial arms procurement, while the peasant clients, including some displaced farmers, provided the basic fighting force.

Rural militarization in the 1930s usually took on a cellular structure. Military bands formed cells fifteen *li* (seven and a half kilometers) apart. These cells were then integrated into two or three regional military networks within a county. The networks were dominated by a couple of powerful gentry, typically men with some military skills and connections with the GMD.[53] Many networks were incorporated into the state repressive mechanism, usually the Communist Elimination Society or Autonomous Self-Protection Regiment (*zizhi baowei tuan*).

It was these corporate gentry-controlled defense forces that posed the greatest threat to the Communist movement. Even if the gentry in an area were sharply divided and highly suspicious of each other, they were forced to stay together in the face of Communist violence and land reform. For the local people, these units provided community security. Villagers and urban dwellers were more than willing to subscribe to such common defense needs.[54] As an inducement to peasant participation, gentry patrons sometimes allowed villagers to share 30 percent of the loot taken in retaliatory raids against Communist-controlled villages. In some villages, liberal patrons urged landowning gentry to collect only 40 percent of the rent and to give captured land to land-short peasants. Such actions turned these patron-client military networks into powerful and solid repressive blocs.

Some networks crumbled under Communist attack. But the gentry would only temporarily flee the area, hold out in nearby fortified towns, wait for the Communists to move out, and then return. Others left the countryside for the county town, gathered enough men to build a militia, formed an alliance with the GMD garrison army, and attacked the Communists to recover their base. Yet political disputes among the gentry greatly intensified the process of fragmentation of local power in an area. The countryside was eventually turned into a collection of small-scale military strongholds. Military groups were always fighting against each other. It was this fragmentation of gentry power that allowed the Communists to penetrate the settled rural communities in Henan and Hubei.[55]

Indigenous Leadership and Penetration of Rural Communities

Villages that shared an identity, closed rural communities, and the preponderant sociopolitical position of the local gentry made Communist penetration of rural communities very difficult, if not impossible. Initial rural mobilizers, therefore, had to be drawn from indigenous members of the communities that the Communists wished to penetrate, preferably from progressive members of the gentry class. Apparently it was unwise for the Communists to recruit mobilizers from the traditional landed gentry or rural bosses, who often served as state agents and were therefore regarded by the people as oppressors. Hence, rural mobilizers had to come from the liberal segment of the gentry class, like the sons of "petty gentry" who studied in the city and were exposed to liberal ideas. These indigenous liberal gentry members often played the role of seeders. They were the ideal Communist mobilizers. Their families were powerful in the countryside and often controlled the military and financial resources needed by the Communists for the revolution, and they had connections with other gentry families. They could also be used to maintain sustained contact with rural cultivators.

In interviews, Zheng Weisan, a rural mobilizer in the Eyuwan border base, repeatedly underscored the significance of "revolutionary intellectuals" (*geming zhishi fenzi*) as the determining factor for the location and ultimate success of the Communist revolution.[56] Although Eyuwan was "marginally" located on the mountainous provincial border, its accessibility to the major political and cultural metropolis of Wuhan should not be overlooked. Educational institutions in Wuhan were actively recruiting students, mostly sons of liberal gentry, from northeastern Hubei and southern Henan. Much credit should be given to Dong Biwu, an early Communist organizer, for setting up a Communist high school in Wuhan, which eventually became the center for recruiting Communist revolutionaries for the entire region. Through his efforts alone, seven students from Huangan, four from Macheng, one from Luotian, and one from Xiaowei joined the Communist Party.

These students were greatly radicalized by the antiforeign sentiment of the May 30th Movement. Some later went to Beiping and Japan to study and were recruited by the party as core leaders in the Eyuwan area. During the Northern Expedition, they were ordered to return home. They took up teaching in their home counties and used their teaching positions to recruit student activists into the party.[57] It was these teacher-student networks, built during the Nationalist Revolution, that formed the basis for Communist rural mobilization in the 1930s.

Early Communist rural mobilization tactics focused on the creation of their own kinship defense forces as instruments of power seizure. Cadres were instructed to use the village (rather than the neighborhood pact, or the *lianbao*, which was later used in the Sino-Japanese

War) as primary mobilization units.[58] Indigenous Communist leaders were told to use their social ties to build a revolutionary organization. The basic tactic was to "hold rap sessions, contact relatives, and make friends" (*tan tian, chuan qinqi,* and *jiao pengyou*).[59]

An examination of the clan defense structure created by Wu Huanxian in his hometown at Cao Gate may give us an idea of the process of early grass-roots mobilization. Wu belonged to a gentry family at Cao Gate. He received an education in the county professional school in Macheng, where he was recruited by the Wuhan CCP into the Workers' Mobilization Institute. Even before he was a party member, Wu had actively organized local youths in rural self-defense. With this experience in rural mobilization, he was sent by the party to organize the Red Spears in his hometown. Using the threat of banditry in the area, Wu successfully persuaded his uncle, clan head Wu Weigan, to donate a building and other clan resources for the creation of a lineage-based Red Spears chapter. He shared power with his uncle by appointing Wu Weigan's son (his cousin) to be the Red Spears "boss" (*xuedong*). As the "boss," his cousin was the administrative head of the group and in charge of the chapter's finances. Wu himself commanded the force, serving as its military chief (*xuezhang*). The Red Spears fighters were mostly clansmen and tenant farmers. In this setup, the financial resources and weapons were still in the hands of the powerful lineages within the clan, who maintained tight control of the force. Only when the village was actually under bandit attack did Wu have a chance to wrest control of the armed forces from his wealthy clansmen. Timid and unwilling to go into combat, the powerful lineages gave up their arms and agreed to give Wu all necessary funds provided he took up the actual fighting.[60]

After gaining control of the chapter, Wu used both his position as Red Spears chief and the political turmoil in the area to persuade other groups to participate in a joint defense network. The purpose was to form a defense structure which hopefully would later be taken over by the party. He therefore infiltrated neighboring groups in the region by extensively recruiting local youths into the party and then using them in similar fashion as seeders in their own kinship defense units. The Communists then concentrated on village schools as recruiting grounds for mobilizers.[61] The prevalence of monoclan villages in the area dictated that initial Communist rural mobilization had to target the clans. Of the thirteen Communist-dominated defense groups listed by the party in the area, at least seven were lineage-based organizations.[62] Each of these defense units consisted of a hundred to a few hundred men. By using school ties, Wu Huanxian was able to pull together an armed network of seven villages on the Henan-Hubei border. When the CCP later reorganized the lineage-based defense organizations into peasant associations, the leadership of the associations remained very much in the hands of powerful clan members, mostly landlords and rich peasants.[63]

Communist rural mobilization was greatly facilitated by extensive use of kin and community ties. Because the peasants' primordial loyalty was directed toward kinship and community groups, such tactics allowed Communists to win the trust of the peasants, who otherwise would have been apprehensive about joining a Communist movement. To the peasants, these radical students were respected kin leaders. The proliferation of radical intellectuals in the Eyuwan border base, which was facilitated by its proximity to Wuhan, enabled the party to move swiftly and rebuild the movement in a different location after the original site had been destroyed by government repression. The rebuilding of a new base in Fodder Hill Neighborhood (Chaishan bao) after the party had been crushed by GMD armies in Huangan and Macheng counties, for instance, was only possible because the party had previously sent two students back home to start a clandestine structure in Fodder Hill.[64] The use of indigenous students was very crucial to the creation, expansion, and sustenance of the Communist rural movement.

Subversion of Elite Sectarian Defense Structures

The 1927 CCP-GMD split put an end to the brief cooperation between the Communists and the local gentry. It terminated the joint effort to build Red Spears defense forces in the countryside. The gentry, who sided with the emerging GMD after the split, turned their Red Spears against the Communists. In Huangpo and Xiaowei counties, gentry Red Spears put together a joint force and attacked the Communists. Backed by GMD troops, these local armies pillaged and destroyed the Communist bases. Armed violence between the gentry and Communist Red Spears became a constant phenomenon in rural areas.

The Communist Party was acutely aware of the importance of wresting control of the Red Spears from the gentry. In order to dominate the countryside, they needed military power. Red Spears were armed forces, prevalent and readily available in rural areas. Cadres admitted that mistakes made in Red Spears mobilization in the Northern Expedition had been very costly to the movement. But they believed they had learned their lessons. Despite the advantage of instant power building, the tactic of taking over the Red Spears en bloc by simply recruiting the gentry at the top had inherent weaknesses. Vacillating gentry made control of these forces highly unreliable. In times of political adversity, the gentry, who often sided with the government, disengaged themselves from and did not hesitate to use the sectarian forces to suppress the Communists.

The Communists faced a dilemma. They could not afford to ignore such a formidable rural force as the Red Spears. Moreover, Marxist ideology preaches that the Communist Party is a party of the masses, and therefore it was obliged to lead the peasant masses fighting for justice in the countryside. Since the rank-and-file Red Spears were peasants, who, according to Communist reasoning, were simply forced by the gentry to oppose the Communists, it was the party's duty to win them over "by threat or by material inducements." Therefore the party was forced to redefine its tactics toward the sectarians. Cadres were required to clearly distinguish between the broad peasant masses and the gentry leaders. They were told to isolate the leaders at the top, subvert the group, and bring the peasant followers over to the Communist cause. However, such tactics raised a basic problem. Rural Communist mobilizers were well aware of the strong ties between gentry patrons and client peasants within the groups. They knew it was no easy task to divide Red Spears leaders from their followers.[65] In the case of the Benevolent and Righteous Societies, a local variation of the Red Spears, peasants were not coerced into opposing the Communists. They joined the sect of their own free will, which made it virtually impossible to pull the ordinary members away from the gentry leaders.[66]

At the Second Joint Conference of Northeastern Hubei Counties, the party finally worked out a new resolution on Red Spears mobilization. The new tactics called for extensive use of written propaganda, recruitment of "teachers" and rural leaders, use of personal ties to gain direct access to the masses, employment of Communist armed forces to lead sympathetic Red Spears in economic struggles, and creation of dissent among rival Red Spears groups.[67]

Communists later reported that they implemented the new formula in a number of ways. When dealing with peasant followers, the Communists focused on tactics of political indoctrination and material trade-offs. Communists deliberately captured large groups of Red Spears peasants for propaganda purposes. Some captives were released immediately, while others were detained for prolonged political indoctrination. If a whole family was captured, the head of the household was allowed to go while the rest of the family stayed behind. The Communists then gave the peasants grain, clothing, and other items in an attempt to buy them over. The party also used peasants who fled the GMD area as propagandists among their fellow agriculturalists. Cadres were given strict orders never to kill a peasant Red Spear. After capturing a Red Spear village, their duty was to "console" and not to exterminate these sectarians.

It was only after the sectarians had developed sympathy toward the movement that the party proceeded to the second step, that of transforming them into an effective fighting force directed against other Red Spears sects. The problem was to find a way to overcome peasant timidity toward the gentry-led Red Spears, who they had been led to believe were invulnerable to bullets. In order to break the concept of invulnerability and instill confidence in the peasants, the Communists made sure that their fighters were the first to kill in battle. They lengthened their spears to three and a third meters, which allowed peasant soldiers to reach out and make a hard jab at their opponents. The tactic worked, and sectarian forces killed thousands of rival Red Spears. From then on, peasants called the new weapons "dragon spears." In every battle, the party also employed a skilled marksman to gun down martial arts "teachers," to demonstrate that these divine commanders were no longer invincible. Such military tactics frequently led to a speedy collapse of enemy forces and greatly boosted peasant morale.[68] To avoid offending followers, the party also altered its previous slogan "Kill the Red Spears" to "Kill the Red Spears teachers," targeting the leaders rather than the entire group. In return for their support, the Communists allowed the peasants to keep the weapons they captured. They knew that possessing guns gave the peasants not only a sense of security but also power.

In contrast to the accommodative policy used during the Northern Expedition, Communist strategy toward Red Spears elites in the Nationalist period was more confrontational. Cadres were urged to use all available means to forge alignments with and thus neutralize gentry leaders. If they failed to do so, they were instructed to detain or kill the leaders if necessary. However, the party also understood the strong influence the gentry exercised in local communities. Harming the gentry physically could only alienate the people and produce adverse political effects. Hence, Communist Party policy strictly prohibited the killing of popular Red Spears chiefs. Should cadres find it absolutely necessary to execute a sectarian leader, they were required to explain their actions clearly to Red Spears followers afterward.

Instead of extermination, the Communist Party favored the tactic of dividing the gentry. If conditions permitted, cadres were told to buy them over and use them as propagandists in the GMD areas. They were not allowed to divide the rank-and-file Red Spears members. Communist policy denounced only the leaders, not the organization. Cadres were not allowed to annihilate sectarian forces in areas where the gentry were divided, but were instead instructed to look for opportunities to win over rival groups. Even if attacked by the sectarians, they were told to defend themselves rather than take offensive action. The basic aims were to neutralize these forces, to skillfully manipulate them for propaganda purposes, and to wrest these forces over from the other side rather than to decimate them by military action.[69]

Since the Red Spears were so popular among the peasantry in the region, the Communists were forced to retain them as auxiliary forces in the soviet period. In the Huangan Soviet area, for instance, rural defense units were named Self-Defense Squads (a Communist designation for reorganized Red Spears) instead of Red Guards (*chiwei dui*), the name normally used for auxiliary forces in soviet areas. Because of the peasants' strong attachment to these forces, the Huangan Soviet government even actively promoted the creation of Red Spears armies as a way of gaining public support.[70] The best-known sectarian units, extolled by the Communists in their literature, were the three chapters of Red Spears the party created in southern Guangshan to seize power. In its own words, the party was able to "stage a revolution with three chapters of Red Spears" (*san tang hongxue gao geming*). The Red Spears movement was so prevalent in Guangshan that the Eyuwan Soviet government, in order to claim authority over other Red Spears in southern Henan, named its military headquarters in Guangshan the "Southern Henan Red Spears Command Headquarters" (*Yunan hongxue silingbu*) instead of the "Red Spears Joint Administrative Office" (*hongxue lianhe banshi chu*).[71] Many of these Red Spears units were reorganized into the Red Army and later, in the Sino-Japanese War period, into the New Fourth Army. The Red Spears thus became part of the main fighting force in the Communist revolution.[72]

Forms of Contention: The Initial Phase

In Chinese society, social cleavages seldom ran along class lines. The two main rural classes—gentry and peasants—shared a common identity in kinship group and residential community. In order to penetrate a settled community, the Communists had to veil their class struggles in terms of weak lineages versus powerful lineages, emergent liberal gentry versus established rural bosses, and disadvantaged communities versus privileged communities. It was by exploiting these cleavages that the Communists conducted their social revolution in the countryside.

Even though the Communists designated all gentry targets generically as "despotic landlords" (*eba dizhu*), a close examination of these rural elites shows that they fell into the following two categories:

1. Powerful clan elites in charge of clan estates (*gongtian*). These powerful clan elites were often accused by weak lineages of abusing their power and dominating clan affairs. One particular grievance was over the right to use sacrificial land. Friction over the use of corporate clan land in the village of God of Mercy Bridge gave Communists the chance to bring down clan leader Fang Xiaoting. Afterward, the insurgents took over the ancestral temple, symbol of gentry authority, and seized clan property. Most of the clashes the Communists instigated in Macheng in June 1929 were directed toward the ten most powerful lineages in the area.

2. Government tax collectors (*huishou*) and militia heads. Wu Weicun of Arrow River, for instance, was accused by the Communists of pocketing tax money and misappropriating military provisions. After being tried by clan members in the ancestral temple, Wu was convicted of corruption and later executed. Other targets were officials and guards in the salt tax booths. In the Republican period, tax bureaus had increasingly become symbols of bureaucratic gentry power and government oppression. In tax resistance struggles, Communists frequently led villagers in attacks on guards posted by the government along the Henan-Hubei border to crack down on interprovincial salt smuggling.[73]

Outwardly, the Communists seldom gave local people the impression that they were promoting a class war. In Fodder Hill, for example, the party instructed cadres to avoid mentioning the class line. Class attacks were generally restricted to a couple of evil rural bosses. The party slogan was "We don't execute gentry who are not evil and landlords who are not tyrannical." Most of the time, the party's principal objective was to seize control of the clan bands. The Communists were perpetually embroiled in factious clan feuds at the village level. In Big Zhu Family Village, for instance, Communists sided with Zhu Xiangzhou, a petty gentry member and holder of 30 *shi* of land, in his dispute with two other powerful clans, the Wus and the Chens. The Communists forged an alliance with Wu Wenli, a member of the weak lineage in the Wu clan, and used his Red Spears to attack the dominant lineages of the Wu and Chen clans. The collective violence the party engaged in, as we have seen, was mostly traditional kinship and community feuds.[74]

Yet, in times of subsistence crises such as droughts and famines, Communists had a chance to mobilize peasants along class lines, mostly in food seizures or "grain borrowings," as they called these activities.[75] When the Communists were driven out of their base and deprived of a means of support, they frequently resorted to red social banditry (robbing the rich and giving to the poor) as a way of survival. Generally they conducted their predatory activities in locations where state and gentry control was weak. Food seizures were carried out at night to avoid direct clashes with the local militia and government troops, of whom timid peasants were afraid. Frequently, under the direction of ten or so armed Communist secret agents (*tewu yuan*), a small band of impoverished villagers or a chapter of Red Spears would descend on public and private granaries at night and seize grain for distribution. In times of hardship, such activities attracted a large number of peasants. Communists reportedly led 8,000 peasants in a raid against twenty granaries in Xiaowei county in Hubei province.[76]

In desperate situations, the party sometimes resorted to terrorism and assassination. At one time, five Communist guerrillas assassinated a gentry member in broad daylight and at night put up a poster denouncing his wrongdoings. But this mode of violence—what Zhang Guotao refers to as "guerrilla habits"—was counterproductive.[77] It forced otherwise rival gentry into a temporary coalition against the Communists. In reprisal, gentry members, usually aided by state troops, led the Red Spears in ravaging Communist bases. Gentry repressions were highly effective in most cases. The gentry murdered villagers by the hundreds, greatly eroding peasant morale and eventually putting a halt to the Communist peasant movement.[78] Although party policy publicly advocated the use of the so-called "five forms of resistance" (resistance to rent, taxes, grain, debt, and non-staple crop payment), Communist field cadres knew very well that it was impossible to use economic grievances alone to mobilize the peasants. In practically every struggle, they found that at the outset or immediately afterward, the economic struggle gave way to a power struggle in the form of clan vendettas or political feuds between rural bosses and the liberal gentry.[79]

Rich Peasant Policy: Marxist Vision and Practical Reality

The rural mobilization tactics the Communists employed at the start of the movement—recruitment of indigenous students as seeders, use of personal ties to gain access to communities, exploitation of cleavages between commercial landlords/rich peasants and beaucratic rural bosses, and infiltration of prevalent social organizations—are double-edged swords. These tactics facilitated rural mobilization, enabling Communists to penetrate deeply into the rural communities and seize local armed forces and gain power. But the involvement of reformist gentry and liberal rich peasants in the revolution often severely limited the possibility of real change. The Communists quickly realized the limitations once they carried out a land reform.

The indigenous cadres who recruited liberal gentry and rich peasants tended to leave these rural elites in power in the Communist organizations. Cadres and rural elites were bound by strong personal ties, which in some ways constrained the implementation of radical programs that were pernicious to gentry interests. Consequently, Communists had to refrain from mentioning the term "revolution" in areas of strong gentry influence.[80] Even in Huangan and Macheng, the very core areas of the Communist revolution, cadres showed little interest in land reform. Their excuse was that the peasant masses still lacked a basic understanding of these radical changes. Thus, seven months after the Communist takeover, Macheng county had not undergone a land repartition, and in other places land reallotment was nothing but a piecemeal operation. The Communists still resorted to red social banditry as their main tactic for mobilizing the peasantry.[81]

In Guangshan, a county firmly under Red Army control, resistance to land redistribution was stiff. Red Army cadets were originally recruited from the Red Spears. They were inextricably linked to the gentry patrons in these sectarian organizations, and turned out to be the principal opponents of land reform. They argued that the landlords and rich peasants had contributed immensely to the revolution by participating in economic struggles against tax collectors. Redistributing their land in a social revolution would surely drive them over to the "reactionary" camp.[82] Furthermore, since these cadres were busy fighting the Guomindang, they had neither the time nor the intention to put the reform into action. For them, the easiest way to circumvent party policies was to redistribute only those properties left behind by absentee landlords.[83]

The contradiction between the practical need for enlisting elite support and the vision of launching a social revolution is revealed in inner party disputes over the central question of "rich peasant policy" (*funong luxian*). To maintain a cordial relationship with rural elites so that the party could use their armed forces to gain power, indigenous cadres were required to adopt a conciliatory attitude toward landlords and rich peasants. Kinship relations, which formed the very basis for building early rebel organizations, also dictated that cadres refrain from taking radical measures against their wealthy kinsmen.

In order to gain control over non-soviet areas, some cadres felt they had to take a moderate approach. Since the party had gained only a foothold in these areas, landlords and rich peasants were still very powerful. If the Communists were to extend their influence, they believed it was imperative for the party to befriend the rich peasants and limit its political and economic struggles strictly to the landlords. In this way they would not make too many enemies. Hence, in non-soviet areas, Communist propaganda explicitly portrayed rich peasants as one of the "oppressed" classes. Cadres were prohibited from using force to make heavy demands on rich peasants; instead, the party emphasized persuading them to voluntarily reduce rent and interest. Communist laws strictly forbade rich peasants' exporting grain to the cities. In return, rich peasants were allowed to join peasant committees, though they did not have the right to be elected committee executives. Only those who maintained strong ties with the landlords or who were powerful in the village were placed under close observation. Only in soviet areas where Communists had complete dominance did cadres redistribute excess village land. Even in these areas, confiscation was restricted to the properties of the rural bosses and "reactionary rich peasants." Rich peasants sympathetic to the revolution were given voting rights.[84]

Indigenous leaders used the moderate approach to mobilize local citizens until 1929. In the early 1930s, with the arrival of extralocal Communist leaders who had no attachment to the community, the party policy on land reform and rich peasants took a dramatic change. These newly arrived Communist fundamentalists came to the area with a mission not only to wage a class war against rural elites but also to alter the very social fabric of the countryside. Extralocal party leaders shared no common identity with community elites. To them, only poor peasants and wage laborers could form the "rural foundation of the Chinese Communist Party." The peasant committee, they insisted, should be composed only of rural craftsmen. They fervently believed it was their duty to employ all propaganda tools, verbal and written, to promote land reform. According to the Resolution on Peasant Mobilization adopted by the Second Joint Conference of Northeastern Hubei Counties, land reform was to be sold to the peasants in a nice package that included anti-imperialism and the formation of a soviet government.[85]

After three executive committee meetings, the Eyuwan party decided to reformulate and radicalize the land reform program. The new policy was to "use the agricultural laborers as the base. Form a solid alliance with the poor peasants. Stabilize the middle peasants. Shake up and eliminate the rich peasants." Politically, the new program called for the discharge of rich peasants from all Communist mass organizations, including the Red Guards, Youth Vanguard (*shaonian xianfeng dui*), and Children's Corps (*tongzi tuan*). Women of rich peasant background were excluded from participation in the Female Job Improvement Society (*funu zhiye gaijin she*). Economically, the reformulated policy urged the adoption of a progressive tax structure to weaken rich peasants. It also aimed at placing a heavy financial burden on rich peasants by forcing them to give up surplus grain and involving them in costly projects such as famine relief and provisioning of the Red Army. Rich peasants became the major targets of Communist impositions (*zhengfa*). The basic objective was to extract as much from them as possible. Ideologically, the new policy intensified the political indoctrination of rich peasants.[86] At one time, some Communist fanatics even advocated "killing the rich peasants and overthrowing the middle peasants" (*sha funong fan zhongnong*), a radical policy squelched by Nie Hongjun, the director of the political department of the 27th Red Army.[87]

However, this radical new policy had never been implemented universally. The power of the landlords and rich peasants could not be obliterated so easily. Rich peasants had local connections and were able to hold on to their leadership positions in mass organizations, even in Communist-controlled areas. To avoid confiscation of their property, rich peasants denied their status; cadres accorded their rich peasant relatives protection, claiming that their kinsmen were no obstacles to the revolution. In the commercialized southern lowland, the need for the Communists to work through existing organizations in order to reach the peasants provided rich peasants with a haven and the necessary shield to defend themselves against Communist persecution. Rich peasants always dominated the mass organizations in the south. It was almost impossible for the Communists to challenge their power in these institutions. Many cadres simply refused to implement the policy of targeting rich peasants. A Communist report accused indigenous cadres in the two districts (*qu*) in Huangan county of "not paying attention to the new policy, still following the old mode of struggle against the village bosses and leaving rich peasants untouched."[88] In some cases, the report says, cadres simply made a lot of noise about the "reactionary nature of the rich peasants" without actually pressing home their attack.

The Communists encountered other obstacles in implementing the "rich peasant policy." One of them was confusion over the classification of rich peasant status. There was little consensus among the cadres, even at the top, about the exact status of the "rich peasant" or "middle peasant." Party policy defined rich peasants as those "who had a surplus," but it was difficult for field cadres to know what "surplus" meant. Consequently, middle peasants with some surplus grain were classified as rich peasants. One cadre even confiscated cash belonging to a street vendor, accusing him of being a rich peasant. Such radical actions created panic all over the countryside. Peasant women cried when they were called rich peasants. To avoid being classified as such, many cultivators hid their money and refused to work. Rumors went around villages that the party was first struggling against rich peasants, would then target petty rich peasants, and so on, all the way down the line to poor peasants. The new policy posed a particular threat to middle peasants, who believed they were next in line. Fearful of being designated rich peasants, middle peasants simply stopped producing.

Once peasant masses were aroused in a class war, it was hard to keep them under control. Struggles often soured relationships and turned the countryside upside down. In Macheng, for instance, middle and poor peasants severed ties with rich peasant relatives. Some accused rich peasants of spying so that they could seize their property and food. Others took the opportunity to become vindictive and humiliated rich peasants by forcing them to carry sedan chairs or stretchers. A few hired farmhands even coerced rich peasant widows into marrying them.

The Communists found that implementing the new policy also produced unintended and undesirable outcomes. In Macheng, cadres strictly followed the policy and focused most of their energy on attacking rich peasants, completely forgetting the village bosses.[89] In some areas, cadres abused their power so much that the party was forced to order a halt to all forms of confiscation.[90] Cadres took the order to be an end to the rich peasant policy. On the other hand, although party policy explicitly forbade indiscriminate killing, cadres sometimes misconstrued the new policy to mean a physical elimination of rich peasants, and they pitied and tried to protect them. Party policy in fact only required rich peasants to engage in manual labor and contribute to the revolution.[91]

Such abuses and confusion obviously generated intense debate within the party. Some cadres argued strongly that support from middle peasants was essential to the success of the movement, and that the rich peasant policy had frightened middle peasants and thus eroded their support. Others contended that the party should not sacrifice the welfare of poor peasants and wage laborers, the social base of the movement, in order to appeal to middle peasants. The cadres finally agreed that the middle peasants' support was crucial because, after the completion of land reform, the majority of poor peasants and wage laborers would have become middle peasants.

The radical version of the rich peasant policy, in fact, had never been fully enforced. Rich peasants retained substantial political power in Communist organizations; their properties were seldom taken away. They still dominated the local armed forces, even the Red Guards. The implementation of the rich peasant policy clearly demonstrated the social constraints to radical changes. The Communists had initially built their movement on the basis of clan loyalty. Indigenous cadres had to work closely with liberal rich peasants, and frequently gentry, in their own community to build an emergent revolutionary structure. In this process of party building, large numbers of rich peasants and gentry were recruited into the movement. They were given dominant positions in both the party and mass organizations. It would be extremely difficult for the party to later take that power away from them.[92]

The radical Communist policy, on the other hand, had greatly alienated rural elites and eradicated their support. A large number of rich peasants defected to the Nationalist side; others worked with other Communist enemies to subvert the revolution. Those who remained in soviet areas employed a variety of tactics to bring chaos to the border bases.

First, landlords and rich peasants competed with the Communists for the support of middle and poor peasants by cancelling debts and offering loans. Some voluntarily transferred part of their property to the soviet government and declared that the social revolution had been accomplished. Second, as long as they were in control of the peasant associations, rich peasant leaders could change or reinterpret policies in order to pit peasants against the government. For instance, acting in an official capacity, some rich peasant cadres coerced middle and poor peasants into giving the government money and materials. Others deliberately classified middle and poor peasants as rich peasants so as to incite them to protest against the new regulations. In a district in Huangan, rich peasants executed the head of the peasant association, falsely charging him with rape. In another case, when the soviet government instructed the local party to implement new progressive taxes in the villages, the rich peasants in charge ordered other peasants to hand over their grain stock, keeping only two *shi* and seven *dou* of grain apiece for their own consumption.

Third, rich peasants spread rumors and created confusion among the uneducated cultivators. They intimidated middle and poor peasants by spreading rumors of the imminent return of GMD forces. They urged panicky peasants to flee the area and burn their grain stock, although there was no apparent threat of an enemy attack. Some secretly used their kinship and community ties to carry out "antirevolutionary activities" in the "white zone" (i.e., the GMD-controlled region, as opposed to the Communist-controlled "red zone" and the contested "grey zone"). Others refused to flee and were the first to welcome the enemy when GMD forces arrived. Many rich peasants defected and organized militias for the GMD and frequently assisted Nationalist troops in suppressing the soviet areas. Some found their way into the Red Army through personal connections and then used the army to oppose the class struggle directed against them and members of their families.[93]

Conclusion

Our findings caution us from accepting the idea that the Communists were able to sustain the revolution in the 1930s only by operating in inaccessible areas in marginal geographical locations. This chapter illustrates that Eyuwan was far from being a totally "remote border area," at least on the Henan-Hubei border. The revolutionary base, in fact, consisted of a remote and a relatively commercialized section. The Communists were able to mobilize the people in both sections effectively, poor peasants in the depressed section in the north and liberal elites in the commercialized section in the south.

The communities the Communists worked with in this area were mostly settled peasant communities. Contrary to our preconceived idea, their revolutionary recruits were not "peasants who had been displaced into illegal activities."[94] They were not déclassé elements such as bandits, ex-soldiers, and smugglers.[95] Soldiers in the First Division of the Red Army of the Henan-Hubei soviet were mostly settled peasants who had strong ties to local clans and residential communities. Many had elite backgrounds, having come from local gentry and rich peasants.[96] It seems that the use of peripheral mountain redoubts as bases of operation was more characteristic of the post-1934 period, when the Chinese Communists were driven from their bases and were out of power.

Even though the border areas in which the Communists operated were normally beyond the reach of state control, these communities were very much under the tight control of local gentry and rich peasants. One cannot deny that marginal geographical locations possess revolutionary potential (such as that caused by social tensions derived from exploitative landlords and problems of access to land); the real tactical advantage the Communists had, however, did not come so much from geographical location as from the very fragmentary nature of local society in that particular region. It was the local political factor that enhanced the chances of the Communist mobilization. The internecine wars between regional warlords in the 1920s, and between the Guominjun and Chiang Kaishek in the early 1930s, radically transformed local communities into a matrix of armed defense collectives. Regional warfare also broadly redefined social relationships in the area.

Members of these defense communities were closely bound to the gentry, who commanded the instruments of coercion and the headed defense networks. Problems of security thus created a dependency between the gentry and the peasants, a bond that Communist revolutionaries found extremely difficult to destroy. To a certain extent, this community loyalty dictated that the Communists use indigenous leaders to penetrate local areas.

On the other hand, once admitted to the political arena, these collective defense communities competed with each other for political advancement. It was the national power struggle between Chiang Kaishek and the Guominjun that produced differentiation of the gentry class and resulted in a dispersal of authority in rural areas. In turn, local competition among the militarists who controlled the communities generated a political power crisis in the countryside. The penetration of market forces into the southern lowland brought a new group of liberal gentry into power. Sharp political rivalry between urban-oriented gentry and traditional rural bosses gave the Communists the opportunity to penetrate the countryside and draw the liberal gentry into the revolution. The Communists were operating in a rural setting where the gentry was predominant but hopelessly divided. It was local politics that facilitated rural penetration.

James Polachek has shown us the tactics Communists employed to infiltrate the countryside in the Jiangxi Soviet.[97] The Jiangxi Communists exploited the basic contradiction between upland ethnic minorities and lowland clan villages to gain access to rural areas. The party manipulated the clans and blood-oath fraternities to build up military power. In the Eyuwan revolutionary base, Communists adopted a variant of these tactics. With few initial resources, cadres were invariably forced to use existing local defense forces to build their military power. Communist-influenced students used their kinship ties and military and organizational know-how to assist their own clans in creating armed bands and Red Spears armies for community defense. When the opportunity came, they wrested these forces from clan control. They also exploited the differences in local defense needs of the upland and lowland gentry to make peace with southern liberal gentry. In this way, the party gradually built up military and organizational resources.

Revolutionary tactics frequently produced unintended results. Using indigenous leaders and working through prevalent social organizations set severe limits to the possibility of real reform. There is an inherent weakness in using indigenous cadres in rural mobilization. Working with the elites ultimately created a tight bond between cadres and elites, who came to share a common personal interest. Cadres who made use of local institutions to gain power were obliged to protect the local elites they had recruited in the class struggle. Kinship and community loyalty placed restraints on the revolution. This accounts for the strong resistance we find to land reform. It is also the reason behind the heated debate over the "rich peasant policy." When extralocal leaders later used party authority to enforce the radical program, it generated internal party conflict. By implementing a radical land program, the party also lost the backing of the gentry and the rich peasants, important support groups in the early stage of the movement. These rural elites eventually turned against the party and subverted the Communist movement. The tactic of working with rural elites through prevalent social organizations and the Marxist ideal of championing rural economic justice through seizing and redistributing the wealth of the same elites were incompatible.

CHAPTER 4

Peasant Mentality and Ideological Constraints: The Case of Eyuwan

In *Political Order in Changing Society*, Samuel Huntington calls our attention to the typical dual image of the peasantry.[1] Peasants, he says, are sometimes negatively regarded as a highly conservative force wedded to local traditions, religious institutions, and the community, and therefore resistant to outside agents of change. On the other hand, they are also positively perceived as a highly revolutionary force. Frantz Fanon called them "the revolutionary proletariat of our times."[2] Peasants can become militant when provoked and are capable of seizing land from landlords. Some are even ready to overthrow the traditional agrarian order and set up a new social and political system. How do we reconcile these two very different perceptions? Are peasants conservative and reactionary, or progressive and revolutionary?

Peasants are also characterized as backward, illiterate, culturally traditional, communalistic, organic, and politically apathetic.[3] All of these indicate that peasants have a different mentality than the rest of society, one that often serves as a constraint to peasant revolutions. These problems are further aggravated by the vast social distance between urban-oriented revolutionaries and rural peasantry. The two social groups have conflicting goals. Peasants usually work for immediate, concrete, and personal interests, while the actions of revolutionaries are governed by ideals and visions. Revolutionary intellectuals often work with abstract principles. The two groups speak distinctly different languages. The mistrust and misunderstanding between them often limit any effective rural mobilization.[4]

It is not surprising, therefore, that efforts to arouse the peasants often meet with apathy and indifference, and hence enjoy little success. Rural reformers often meet resistance to changes in the countryside. Some of these obstacles are structural; others are ideological. Political apathy is common in the countryside. Particularistic power relations give rise to clientelist politics. A narrow focus on local issues often prevents peasants from comprehending issues beyond those of their village and community.[5] Peasants are said to be the least aware and worst organized group in society. All these factors caused Karl Marx to characterize peasants as "a sack of potatoes."[6]

Undoubtedly, Communists have been able to forge alliances with politically motivated peasants. But these alliances have been few and fleeting, lasting only as long as government political tolerance allowed. This chapter looks at the interaction between revolutionary intellectuals and rural dwellers, and at how the peasant mentality restrains the revolutionary process. By studying the interaction between peasants and revolutionaries, we hope to have a better understanding of peasant motivation and the constraints that peasant values have had on political participation.

Paternal Authority and Peasant Participation in the Soviet Government

The Communist government was initially set up by Communist forces after they occupied Fodder Hill in the southern section of Guangshan county. In the summer of 1928, Communist guerrilla forces drove away some opposing gentry in the area and neutralized others by using United Front tactics. Once the powerful landed gentry and neighborhood heads (*dibao*) had fled, the lesser gentry, lacking the power to fight the Communists, opted to compromise with the CCP. They agreed to subject themselves to Communist rule for the time being. As demonstrated in the previous chapter, by playing the commercial against the traditional gentry, the Communists were able to secure the support of the lesser gentry-merchants. Such tactics allowed the movement to slowly spread from south to north in the Eyuwan area.

The Communist movement in Eyuwan began in the spring of 1929 with a mere 200 members. By October of that year, it had grown to include 1,000 cadres, 30,000 peasants in peasant associations, and 20,000 rural laborers in the armed forces. With the GMD forces held down and preoccupied by the civil war against Feng Yuxiang and Yan Xishan, the Communists swiftly seized the opportunity to consolidate their power in the area. By mid-1932, the CCP in Henan claimed to control eighteen district (*qu*) soviets in Guangshan county, which were subdivided into 197 subdistrict (*xiang*) soviets.[7] The Guangshan soviet was further segmented into a core and a periphery.[8]

A district soviet commonly oversaw from only a few to as many as ten subdistrict soviets. The *xiang* soviet, the lowest administrative unit, had two organs under it: a committee for the implementation of land reform, and the Red Guards for community defense. The headquarters of the soviets were normally located either in local and ancestral temples or, if they were the headquarters of the local Red Spears, in the mansions of gentry whom the Communists had driven out or neutralized.[9] The Communists usually used special "work committees" (*gongwei*) and "work teams" (*gongzuo zu*) to infiltrate rural areas. These units were composed of politically motivated cadres drawn from established bases in Huangan, Macheng, and southern and central parts of Guangshan. Cadres used personal kinship and friendship ties to make contacts. As rural relationships were mostly dyadic, only these tactics permitted them to make contacts and expand their influence. Some cadres took up lowly professions as peddlers, fortune-tellers, and long-term agricultural laborers in order to gain access to peasant circles.[10] Most of them were sent directly to the villages by the county soviets to mobilize peasants for land reform or to get them to join the Red Guards.

Theoretically, soviets were created by elections. First, a representative assembly was set up, and it in turn created a preparatory committee. Representatives were elected according to a fixed quota: one candidate for every 150 residents at the township level, one for every 500 at the district level, and one for every 5,000 at the county level. Two-fifths of the representatives had to be workers and three-fifths peasants. One-fourth had to be female. The elected candidates were nominated by the party at one level and approved by the party at the next higher level. The election usually resulted in a hired farmhand as soviet chairman, while members of the committees were mostly peasants and workers.

Although the party intended to recruit only the underprivileged classes into local government, it was not able to prevent some unintended outcomes. The CCP failed to rid the local government of local elite influence. Since the Communists depended heavily on indigenous leaders to start the movements, and since Eyuwan villages were either monoclan or dominated by a few powerful clans, official positions in some soviets were invariably controlled, directly or indirectly, by clan members. These representatives might have come from worker or peasant backgrounds, but they were invariably members of dominant clans, which were dominated by clan elites.[11]

Even though the Communists wanted the government to consist of workers and peasants and even passed regulations specifically stating that only two Communist cadres could be on the soviet committee, the end result of every election was that the entire committee was composed of Communist cadres. Since active cadres usually worked in the party, inactive cadres were often elected to the soviet committees. One report criticized both the soviet government and the executive committee of the peasant association, saying that these Communist organizations were completely dominated by rich peasants.[12] The soviet government could not function independently as a government organ; it depended heavily on, and was dominated by, the party.

These problems stemmed from the peasants' traditional respect for authority. Traditional rural authority was always paternalistic; patriarchal families and lineage organizations dominated the countryside, and the authority of the father and clan elders always prevailed. The young and the underprivileged usually adopted a submissive attitude.[13] Respect for higher authority was ingrained in the peasant mind. Peasants seldom made independent decisions, except in minor agrarian matters, and many remained submissive to and dependent on the clan. This respect and dependence were carried over to the Communist Party.

On the other hand, once in power, peasant cadres expected others to follow their orders absolutely, just as children strictly obeyed their parents. They were so used to a rigid superior-subordinate relationship that they believed others should respect and fear their authority too. Thus, as He Yulin, a Special Committee member in eastern Hubei, stated in a report to Party Central, "A notice on discipline issued by the Special Committee usually carried a few orders but the tone was that of lecturing someone for their wrongdoing. Comrades were ordered to abide strictly by the rules. Then the order was followed by a long list of penalties, both heavy and light, for anyone who defied them: a warning for minor offenses, dismissal from office, or execution of offenders and family members for serious transgressions. When low-ranking cadres received the notice, they had it posted on their doors (not realizing that it was a secret internal document). Those who read the notice were so frightened their tongues hung out. Cadres thus adopted a policy of inaction for fear of defying any of the orders."[14] Reports show that peasant cadres did execute a large number of people. The party referred to such actions as "red terrorism" (*chise kongbu zhuyi*).[15] Fearful of punishment if anything they did went wrong, low-ranking cadres chose to exercise great caution and refused to make or carry out major decisions, simply performing their duties mechanically instead.

This gave rise to a patriarchal authority structure, often dominated by a couple of powerful leaders, within the Soviet government. Since to oppose official views was frequently branded as "disruptive," "strong-willed," or being "on bad terms because of difference of opinion" (*nao yijian*), few subordinates ventured to articulate their viewpoints in party meetings.[16] Decisions made by the county party secretary became ironclad laws, mechanically obeyed by all subordinates. There was no initiative at lower levels of government.

To show off their authority, cadres often openly discredited their opponents in meetings in order to shut them up. The social and intellectual distance between Communist elites and rural peasants also kept cadres apart. High-ranking urban-educated cadres often looked down on low-ranking peasant cadres as being "stupid." After making a couple of mistakes and being publicly censured, frightened peasant cadres kept their opinions to themselves. The result was a perpetuation of traditional patriarchal political authority. The party ended up running everything in the county. Subcounty party branches became dependent on the party at county and regional levels. The party found it very difficult to recruit nonelite cadres.[17]

The political process in peasant society was characterized by personalism and the patron-client relationship. Local politics were essentially personalistic, often run by a couple of members of the elite acting as authority figures. This attitude was criticized by the party as "heroism" (*yingxiong shi de haozhao*), the worship of authority figures. But in rural society, peasants were usually members of well-defined territorial and kinship groups commonly dominated by a few authoritarian figures. "Following the heroic commands" of a few was part of peasant culture. The Communists found it extremely difficult to change this mentality. In order to accommodate peasant hero worship (actually, respect for authority), the party was forced to recruit respectable members of the local elite as Communist leaders. Such actions further perpetuated the traditional paternalistic political structure. As a result, the party seldom held meetings. Government affairs were run by a few patrons at the top, and most of the elections were fakes. Party resolutions were frequently ignored.[18]

The party found peasant cadres very money-minded. After all, peasants lived in a society where people performing services were paid or rewarded. Peasants were always thinking of their immediate personal interests, including how to meet their living expenses. Before taking up an assignment, peasant cadres often bargained with their superiors for a pay raise. The regular cost of living for a cadre was C$10 to C$11 a month, but district cadres sometimes used their authority to raise their allowance for living expenses to C$70 a month.

Many high-ranking peasant cadres maintained very wasteful lifestyles. Some, for instance, ate a chicken at every meal. Others carried a fountain pen in their pocket, or wore a watch as a status symbol, even though they might be completely illiterate or unable to tell time.

In peasant culture watches and fountain pens conferred prestige. These items distinguished them from other country folk. Peasants were highly rank-conscious. Red Army officers went around the border base carrying a flashlight and a rifle and followed by an orderly, despite the fact that it was perfectly safe to walk around the Communist-occupied area. All this behavior was rooted in traditional peasant values: a desire for material benefits, social prestige, and the status symbols associated with political power and authority. Although the party repeatedly denounced such behavior as a "mercenary style of revolution" (*guyong shi de geming*) or a "decadent" (*fuhua*) lifestyle, there was little it could do to change the peasant mentality.[19]

Peasants had little sense of what the soviet government meant to them. Many were excited by its founding and made it a festive occasion. At the founding ceremony, peasants presented the new government with tablets bearing horizontal inscriptions of praise and good wishes (*bian*), as well as slaughtered animals. The founding ceremony was usually attended by thousands of villagers. Many peasants took pride in their government and boasted of their soviet to peasants in other soviet areas. But their understanding of the soviet government was superficial. Cadres simply followed orders perfunctorily. Others were so busy romancing their fellow cadres that they had no time to carry out their duties. As mentioned, peasants were used to paternalistic government; participation in the political process was completely alien to them. They were too timid to criticize the government. They had been taught that the government was always right. If something did go wrong, they believed it was the fault of low-ranking officials who had abused their power. High-ranking officials, they insisted, had no knowledge of such wrongdoing.

In 1930 Zeng Zhongsheng, secretary of the Special Committee, reported that the soviets were plagued by corruption, the domineering attitude of cadres, and bureaucratic tendencies. Some cadres defected to the Nationalist side; others were the first to flee when GMD troops approached their area. Though Zeng indicated that such tendencies were not pervasive, in July 1930 the party found it imperative to conduct a screening of the entire soviet structure. Many cadres were deprived of their party membership, and others faced severe penalties. But this action put the party in a bind: after purging its membership, it was short of experienced leaders. The party did recruit new cadres, but the new recruits were mostly poor peasants and wage laborers. They were illiterate and lacked any broad social contacts in the villages, factors that greatly limited Communist revolutionary activities. But the party policy was ideologically committed to putting poor peasants and wage laborers in leadership roles. The only way out of the predicament, the party reasoned, was to provide illiterate peasants with a thorough education.[20]

Peasant Leaders and Ideological Constraints

In the latter part of the Eyuwan period, after it had eliminated many of the landed elite and some of the rich peasants from power, the Communist Party increasingly recruited members and low-level leadership from the peasantry. Unfortunately, information on the social composition of the entire Eyuwan party leadership is not available at this time. However, we are told that virtually all the leaders in the party command center at Fodder Hill were of peasant origin.[21] Except at the county and district levels, all party branch leaders in Macheng were peasants.[22] The Communists reported that over half of the party branches in Huangan county held regular meetings. In these meetings, cadres seldom discussed Marxist principles but instead focused on simple and concrete matters that peasants understood, such as reconnaissance, membership recruitment, the killing of counterrevolutionaries, and the setting up of peasant associations. To the romantic revolutionaries at higher levels, these low-ranking peasant cadres had little political understanding.

Low-level peasant leaders always equated party success with military conquest. They were familiar with this form of collective violence from traditional peasant uprisings. The peasants' knowledge was conditioned by past experience. Translated into modern politics, party success meant the ability of the Red Army to take over county seats, the ultimate target in traditional rebellions. Very few peasants understood the underlying meaning of land reform; many were governed by the simple egalitarian concept of equal division of land among all residents.[23]

Since peasant leaders equated party achievement with military success, cadres devoted much of their attention to random acts of violence. The party denounced actions such as pillaging, burning, and killing (*shao sha zhuyi*), but as Eric Hobsbawn has indicated, "social banditry" had traditionally been a form of peasant expression against injustice in preindustrial and pre-capitalist societies.[24] To many peasant cadres, social banditry involved actions which the peasants wanted. It was a lot simpler for them to seize the grain and belongings of opposing gentry than to propagate and mobilize the peasants in the "white areas" of contested border zones. But this behavior always resulted in a great deal of destruction and was highly disruptive to the countryside. In conflicts with rival Red Spears, for instance, party cadres believed it was normal to kill hundreds of peasants. The party severely criticized these activities, saying that such actions would eventually divorce the party from the masses.[25]

According to Communist reports, the cadres also lacked discipline. The party rule forbidding smoking was never observed. Cadres' love lives frequently interfered with their work.[26] In an effort to improve leadership, the party organized short-term training courses for peasant cadres. In the fall of 1929, the party conducted a careful screening of its membership in order to rid itself of "undesirable elements."[27] The result was that by eliminating many peasant cadres and leaving leadership in the hands of student intellectuals it became an elite party at high levels. Out of the 150 cadres at the district level, 80 percent were intellectuals. There were only two peasant and worker leaders in the party at the county level.[28]

Parochialism (*difang zhuyi*) was another obstacle the Communist movement had to overcome. Since the party depended so much on indigenous leaders in the initial stages of the movement, the majority of cadres were drawn from local elites. In 1929, 80 percent of the cadres in the Hubei-Henan section of the Eyuwan base were Huangan natives. In the Huangan party, everyone was a native.[29] This gave rise to strong localistic feelings. Understandably, local cadres had a narrow focus on the needs and problems of their particular locality, and one county would often refuse to help another. Should a neighboring county ask for assistance, leaders would simply send over a few unreliable cadres. The Red Army was also very localized. Red Army troops stationed in one county refused to come to the aid of other counties, usually using the excuse of a lack of funds. A further problem with local people in the party was that nepotism became common in all local administrations.[30]

Parochialism, Communist reports reveal, became so intense that it impeded the development of the revolutionary movement. Since kinship and territorial social cohesion were an integral part of peasant culture, village settlements were perceived by local residents as well-defined, solid communal units, frequently antagonistic toward each other. Clan feuds and territorial conflicts between communities were common in the Chinese local scene. Cadres who embraced these values always looked out for and acted in the interests of their own communities.

Cadres usually took the easy path in the revolution. Since it took less effort to mobilize peasants in the "centrally administered areas" (*zhongxin diqu*), areas defended by the Red Army, cadres often put off expansion to highly contested white zones. When the white zones asked for assistance, the centrally administered areas generally gave them financial assistance only, rarely manpower.[31] In one case, when the party did send two cadres to the white zone on the Beiping-Hankou railroad, one cadre fled back to his native county while the other stayed but refused to work.[32] Communist documents also show that Red Army troops refused to risk fighting guerrilla wars in the white zones. Instead they remained in the red zones, where they could lead quiet and tranquil lives, with local residents serving them as sentries.[33] The immediate interest of these cadres was mobilizing the Red Army to procure enough firearms so that they could set up a secure base in the Dabie Mountains. The security of their own community was their primary concern. It was difficult for cadres to see beyond the immediate environment of their villages and communities. Parochial feelings segmented the Eyuwan base into communitarian units, each fighting for its own immediate interests.[34]

Another problem the Communist revolutionaries encountered in grass-roots mobilization was peasant illiteracy. The problem became more acute after the establishment of the Eyuwan Soviet government. The party policy of mass recruitment of peasants into the soviet resulted in a party membership consisting overwhelmingly of peasants. Of the 10,000 party members in this period, 80 percent were of poor peasant or wage laborer origin. Peasant leaders dominated the lower levels of the Communist structure. There were few literate cadres at the party branch level, and most cadres at the district level could not even read a notice. Illiterate peasants frequently lacked a firm commitment to the revolution. Many were unreliable and defected to the enemy. According to party reports, policy decisions were made by the traditional elites (*jiu fenzi*), whom the party viewed as being completely divorced from the peasant masses. Party documents repeatedly expressed the hope that under party politicization programs illiterate peasants would eventually obtain adequate training to be able to perform party functions.[35]

Peasant illiteracy produced many problems. Illiterate peasants lacked a basic knowledge of the Communist system of government. Many thought that by becoming members of peasant associations they had joined the Communist Party. Peasants did identify with the Communists and often referred to the CCP as "our party." If they found out they had not been asked to attend a party meeting, they became furious and accused cadres of treating them like "reactionaries." Many truly believed that the party was on their side; others had heard that "Communists were their good friends." Communist struggles against tax collectors and oppressive landlords apparently appealed to some peasants. But most rural cultivators thought it was too risky for them to personally take part in political struggles, which they believed should be left to the cadres. Peasant timidity and its free-rider mentality often became major problems in the class struggle.

Peasant folk culture abounds with heroes who right wrongs and fight to gain social and economic justice for the downtrodden. The moral views of peasants were often derived from folk tales and theatrical performances of popular novels such as *The Water Margin*. Their perception of Communist leaders was that they were social bandits or "benevolent robbers." To many peasants, Communist revolutionaries were rebels who had committed crimes and were forced to take up arms against the political authority. Others thought that Communist cadres achieved their official status through the traditional civil service examination. In the eyes of the peasants, these were the usual paths up the social ladder, one illegitimate, the other legitimate. To peasants in the remote areas of Guangshan county, the Communist Party was simply trying to set up a "new dynasty" (*da jiangshan*). As portrayed in folklore, they formed the broad masses of *laobaixing* who assisted the party in effecting dynastic change.

In areas where the Communists did not have tight political control, the peasants' image of the party was that of a knight-errant (*xiayi*). In contrast, peasants who had been heavily influenced by GMD indoctrination considered the Communists "bandits" seeking a windfall profit. Action (*gen*) was what the peasants were looking for; for them the party's role was to attack village bosses, GMD-controlled militia (*qingxiang tuan*), and local brigands. Revolution meant military action conducted by the Red Army and Red Guards. Many regarded the approach of GMD armies as a revolutionary high tide. Only by defeating the GMD and forcing its armies to retreat could the Communists achieve revolutionary success in the eyes of the peasants.[36]

Some peasants could not even distinguish between the GMD and the Communists. Some insisted that there was another Communist Party in the city promoting class struggle against village bosses. Typical of these were rural cultivators whose thinking was governed by a belief in magic. To them, Communist leaders seemed to possess some sort of mystical, magical power. Wu Guanghao, the head of the guerrilla fighters, was said to be the personification of a star. Other Communist leaders were said to possess certain superhuman qualities, such as the ability to see on a pitch-dark night, or the ability to walk 320 *li* (160 kilometers) in a day. Some peasants did not know what the soviet government was. They thought "Soviet" must be the name of a town. Nevertheless, peasants were extremely hospitable to the Red Army because Communist soldiers usually paid for their room and board.[37]

Impetuosity, or what the Communists called "putschism" (*mang-dong zhuyi*), was another problem that came with peasant mobilization. Impetuous and rash actions in combat were common in traditional collective violence. Timid and weak peasants always believed in the omnipotence of the Mauser pistol; to them, power came from the man and his gun. A peasant Red Guard once said, "Who needs the party. If we had a hundred men like me, I am sure we could march all the way to Wuhan."[38] Peasants had faith only in the armed forces. They believed the role of the Red Army was to overthrow gentry landlords. Such heavy emphasis on military power made it difficult for the Communists to introduce peasants to other revolutionary concepts, such as those of peasant organization and peasant political power.[39] As the protracted conflicts with the GMD continued, peasant soldiers sometimes tired of fighting and developed a defeatist attitude, saying if they were going to die in battle anyway, why not have some fun in the meantime. Communist revolutionaries pointed out that such defeatism presented major problems in peasant mobilization.[40]

Revolutionaries found that the most effective means of peasant mobilization was "guerrilla warfare," which meant leading peasants in grain seizures. Such actions addressed a basic need of the peasants. After defeating the local gentry in battle, the party normally led poor peasants in opening local granaries for food distribution. However, grain seizures, although highly appealing to peasants, invariably produced unintended adverse results. They often involved much killing and pillaging. Grain seizure might appeal to poor peasants in one locality, but random violence and killing destroyed villages in other localities and drove settled peasants to the gentry side. Such actions frequently forced the gentry to institute some sort of social reform or to create a Red Spears chapter to defend the community against future Communist attacks. Random violence in fact promoted community cohesion by rallying peasants to the gentry. It also polarized local communities and made it impossible for the Communists to expand their movement.

The cultural distance between urban-based Communist intellectuals and rural cadres became an acute problem in the soviet period. Since low-level rural cadres were peasants, they had little understanding of or respect for orders issued by the Central Committee. Peasant leaders often looked upon party directives as something produced by an urban environment and completely divorced from the needs of peasants in backward northeastern Hubei and southern Henan. When peasant cadres were criticized by their superiors for such thinking, their reaction usually was, "If you say it is peasant mentality, let it be peasant mentality."[41]

Peasants and Land Reform

As Howard Newby has pointed out, land as a factor of production has always been decisive in subsistence and near-subsistence economies.[42] The structure of power in agricultural communities is shaped by the structure of landholding. Access to and control over land is a crucial source of power in agricultural societies. Power politics in rural areas is often dominated by disputes over the control of property. Since land is fixed in quantity and cannot be increased in the short term, only a redistribution of existing holdings can allow the poor better access to land. It was therefore natural for the Chinese Communists, who championed the political and economic interests of the underprivileged, to launch a program to redistribute landholding for the benefit of poor peasants and wage laborers.

The success of land reform, however, depends on a number of factors: the urgency of the peasants' need to gain land, the comprehension and miscomprehension of policymakers, their forms of intervention, and the inherent conflicts between the goals envisioned by idealistic revolutionaries and the concrete concerns of peasants over material conditions such as land tenure, interest payment, and taxes. It also depends on the objective social conditions under which policy is implemented.

The First Stage

Land reform, or the "land revolution" (*tudi geming*), as the Communists called it, was a lengthy and complex process involving several stages. The formative stage commenced with the Communists gaining a foothold in Fodder Hill in the fall of 1928 and ended with the party's passage of the May 1929 "Temporary Land Law" (*linshi tudi zhenggang*). Although party policy explicitly stated that cadres were to lead peasants in struggles to achieve certain objectives—to struggle against rent, interest, and tax payments, to "attack the local tyrants" (*da tuhao*), and to redistribute land to the poor—the Communist Party apparently did not have enough time or power to implement all aspects of the policy. Both the party and the "worker-peasant army" were very much preoccupied with fighting guerrilla wars in order to get enough food to sustain themselves. Their primary objective was not social reform but the consolidation of power around the military stronghold at Fodder Hill.

Without adequate military power to control the area and enforce land policy, the party sustained the movement by simply recruiting peasants through what it called the "popular [*pingmin shi*] revolutionary tactic." This meant employing the easy-to-conduct tactic of provoking peasants to protest against payments of rent, crops, taxes, loans, and tax surcharges (the "five protests"). In some areas, such as New county, party policy demanded the seizure of all properties belonging to "the evil gentry and the reactionaries" as well as the fertile landholdings of rich peasants. But this policy was seldom enforced. Instead the party adopted a simplified formula: "Whoever farms the land takes in the harvested crop" (*shei zhong shei shou*).[43]

The simplified formula had a number of weaknesses. It affected tenant land only. Land without tenants remained untouched and very much in the landlords' possession. The policy also had little impact on the commercialized and land-short southern sections of Huangan and Macheng counties. In areas that had been penetrated by market forces, the majority of holdings remained in the hands of landlord-merchants. These enterprising commercial gentry seldom had tenants on their land; practically all the land was cultivated by hired labor. Therefore little of this land was confiscated and redistributed.[44] Moreover, the simplified formula only gave peasants the right to use the land; it did not transfer ownership to them. Effective implementation of land policy required a certain degree of control over the area which the party lacked in the initial period.

The Second Stage

With the military success of the spring of 1929 and the creation of a county party in Xinji (today the county seat of Xinxian), the Communists were able to begin to seriously implement the land reform program. First, the party recruited several hundred highly motivated cadres from the poor central and northern parts of the county as core reform agents. These cadres were given careful training and then sent back to their native villages to carry out the program.[45] The Hubei-Henan border revolutionary committee then drew up a couple of land reform guidelines, which were enacted into the Temporary Land Law. In the winter of 1929, the "Detailed Regulations of the Land Law" (*Eyu bian geming weiyuanhui tudi zhenggang shishi xize*) was also passed. The obvious overriding goal of these laws was to use land in exchange for peasant political support.

As in all social revolutions, it took time to overcome inertia. At the start, land redistribution was only carried out in a couple of neighborhoods (*bao*) near the Communist headquarters at Fodder Hill. These neighborhoods served as a testing ground.[46] They were directly under Communist control, making it easier to implement land reform. Under the new law, leased land was immediately transferred to the tenants.

Landholdings were taken from the gentry and redistributed to landless or unemployed peasants and to veteran soldiers. The Temporary Land Law still represented only mild reform; rich peasants were allowed to keep their landholdings and "middle and small merchants" their money. However, at the end of the year, with the base securely under Communist control, the Detailed Regulations took another step toward land revolution. The new law called for redistribution, without compensation, of not only all land belonging to "the evil gentry, landlords, and reactionaries," but also of property owned by civic institutions such as lineages, monasteries, churches, and other public and official organizations. The stated party policy was to "rely on the poor peasants, unite the middle peasants, limit the rich peasants, and attack the landlords."[47]

Government cadres and a land committee were to be in charge of the actual repartition. The reform was to be conducted in a democratic fashion. The size of the holding each household would receive was to be decided publicly in a "peasant representatives meeting" (*nongmin daibiao dahui*). The unit of redistribution was the village, the basic unit for the Red Spears and local militia. Each village formed its own land committee, composed of the village head and seven to nine poor peasants and wage laborers drawn from the work committee.[48]

The actual reform involved several processes. First, the party had to strip rural elites of their political and economic power. Wealthy and powerful gentry were singled out for attack. They were humiliated in public meetings and paraded through the streets, and a few were publicly executed. All land deeds, loan contracts, and account books in their possession were systematically destroyed. Afterward, the party took a population census and a land survey. Particular attention was given to land quality and distance from irrigation ditches. The survey was followed by a class identification. Rural households were broken down into five standard categories: landlords, rich peasants, middle peasants, poor peasants, and wage laborers. Class identification was theoretically based on the extent of one's possessions and the "degree of exploitation" used to generate one's income.[49] At the end, landlords and rich peasants were dispossessed of their land and it was redistributed.

Although the principle of "completely equal distribution" (*tongyi daluan pingfen*) was to be universally adhered to, the actual method of class identification and distribution varied from place to place in accordance with local needs and customs. In general, peasants were given a unit of land between one and three *dou* (half to one and a half *mu*) in size. The amount, size, and location(s) of the holdings each household received after redistribution were clearly marked on and demarcated by signposts erected by work teams. Property ownership was later legally confirmed by deeds issued to individual owners by the soviet government.

The second stage of the land reform program seems comprehensive, but actual implementation was not as systematic as planned. As in all rural transformation, there were always problems of corruption, inconsistency of policies, local variations and adaptations, and cases of peasant resistance to change. The report filed by the Hubei-Henan border revolutionary committee gives us a picture of land reform that because of these problems was carried out in a rather haphazard way:

> Under the rule of the Huangan peasant government, the party began to promote an empty land reform slogan. At that time, cadres were too busy burning, killing, and taking flight, they did not have time to implement the land policy. Later, when the party came to power after the success of the Huangan-Macheng revolution, some of the evil gentry and most of the reactionaries had already fled the area, giving the authorities a chance to implement the reform. The new government, however, failed to systematically carry out the land program. Some land, nevertheless, was seized from the evil gentry and the reactionaries and given to the peasants in a sentimental fashion. The peasant association was then placed in charge of rent collection (and there was a slight reduction of rent).
>
> It was not until the revolutionary committee was finally established that a more thorough policy of redistribution of land was carried out. The results of land redistribution are as follow: From the rural surveys, the soviet government drew up a chart of those who needed land and those who had excess land. Land was then redistributed strictly according to the basic principle of non-infringement on the land of owner-cultivators. In some areas, redistribution was carried out by the *xiang* [subdistrict] soviets; in others, under the supervision of the *qu* [district] soviets. There was surplus land in some subdistricts, while others had a shortage. Some villages voluntarily shared their land with neighboring villages; others, however, steadfastly held on to their property. To achieve equity among the villages, the soviet government then devised a plan to relocate peasants in land-short villages to neighboring villages, but most of the cultivators refused to be relocated. In some areas, excess land was not redistributed but instead placed under the soviet government for collective cultivation. In certain villages, fistfights and quarreling occurred over the question of equitable redistribution.
>
> Land was occasionally given to individuals because of personal connections, and there were cases of "chicken dinner"–style redistribution [that is, after peasants had invited cadres to a chicken dinner, they received a piece of fertile property]. Some peasants, on the other hand, insisted on redistributing the land themselves without cadre interference [a protest to the "chicken dinner"–style distribution]. Certain regions had to go through a second redistribution because villagers found the first redistribution to be

> unsatisfactory. Land redistributed to cadres and to families of Red Army soldiers was usually placed under "substitute cultivation"; in some cases it was not. Some cadres and Red Army soldiers were not given enough assistance in cultivation. On the whole, wage laborers received a great deal of land and, consequently, their number was greatly reduced. Some rich peasants voluntarily gave up their excess land for repartition, others refused to do so. In some instances the authorities had to coerce rich peasants to give up their property, but in other cases cadres made use of their authority to protect rich peasants and rebuked the peasants. Occasionally, cadres refused to go work in areas bordering the "red" and "white" zones, and the peasants therefore took up the task of redistributing the land themselves. In certain areas it was the peasants who urged the cadres to redistribute the land, only to be told that the authorities had no intention of doing so until the autumn harvest.
>
> As a result of this, the revolutionary committee issued a directive warning the cadres of these mistakes. But the prevalence of rich peasant ideology (the majority of cadres in the soviet government and most of the executive members in the peasant committees were rich peasants) plus feudal sentiment made it impossible for the party to promptly solve all these problems.[50]

Moreover, not all districts undertook land reform, and those that did used a variety of processes. Some districts, for instance those in southern Guangshan, did go through redistribution.[51] An examination of land reform in these centrally administered districts helps illustrate the various redistribution processes.

In Arrow River (Jianhe), residents first conducted a class identification, in which villagers were ranked by the size of their holding and the type of "exploitative activities" (leasing land, employing wage laborers, or lending money) they engaged in.[52] Afterward, all village holdings were pooled and divided equally among the entire population.

Villagers in Cao Gate (Caomen) adopted a different procedure. First, the party set aside "public lands" for the government and the Red Army, to ensure they would have the means to support themselves. Since government officials and Red Army soldiers could not cultivate their land because of their work, all "public lands" were to be farmed by substitute cultivation. Through a system of "allotment" (*tanpai*), labor gangs were drawn from among the peasants to assist the army and the government in cultivation. They were paid for their services from the harvest. The remaining land was then redistributed in equal shares among the population. The quality of the land was taken into consideration. Each individual received an average of about two *dou*, or about one *mu*, of land. Landlords and rich peasants received allotments that were slightly smaller than average and of inferior quality.

The basic redistribution principle in Fodder Hill was to preserve the holdings of the middle peasants as far as possible, and to give poor peasants land from the rich. In this town, each individual received three *dou* of land.[53] In some villages, forage lands were also redistributed. As a standard practice, special considerations were accorded Red Army households; to induce people to join the army, families of Red Army members were given slightly larger and more fertile pieces of land.[54]

Since the army was the main beneficiary of the land revolution, Red Army soldiers, no matter where they went, were committed to propagating for the land program and arousing their fellow peasants to rise up against the gentry. Yet despite all this propaganda, the most effective mobilization tactic at the time, the Communists reported, was not land reform but grain seizure. As Daniel Little has indicated, reverse-stratified projects were difficult to achieve without strong support and shared moral commitment.[55] For the timid peasants, it was better to seize the landlord's grain in the confusion of an assault than to attack the same landlord publicly in struggle meetings in order to seize his land afterwards. Peasants participating in grain seizures did not have to worry about landlord reprisal. Communist guerrilla fighters had great success in leading hungry peasants in attacks against the wealthy gentry and in the seizure of grain stocks for distribution.[56] Only in areas where the Communists had complete control did land reform enjoy marked success. (In New county, for instance, 500 villages underwent land redistribution.)[57]

In fact, the second stage of land reform was marked by a series of compromises and accommodations, particularly between southern pro-Communist gentry and middle peasants. The party was very careful not to alienate the commercial gentry in the south. The Detailed Regulations specifically provided that "members of reactionary families not engaging in any kind of reactionary activities are entitled to a piece of land." Property belonging to non-reactionary gentry who had fled the area because of warfare was to be placed under the custody of the village peasant association and released to the rightful owners upon their return. The policy also protected the privileges of the middle peasants. Their holdings in villages other than the one in which they resided were to be redistributed, but the proprietors were to be compensated, as far as possible, by their own villages.[58]

The Third Stage

The third stage consisted of radical land reform. It began in 1930 with the implementation of the Li Lisan line.[59] The radical policy was actually put into action by Zhang Guotao and his Communist fundamentalists in 1931. This stage coincided with the establishment of the Eyuwan Soviet government; it came to an end with the collapse of that government in October 1934.

When they arrived at Eyuwan, Zhang Guotao and his associates annulled the previous reforms. Denouncing prior practices, these radical reformers insisted that "benefits from the land revolution, which the wage laborers, poor peasants, middle peasants, and workers were entitled to, had been stolen by the evil gentry, big landlords, and rich peasants." Zhang called for complete negation of the former policies, which he called the "rich peasant policy." The hard-liners ordered a complete redistribution of all landholding. Under the radical new policy, not only land but draft animals, agricultural implements, and the houses of landlords and rich peasants were to be redistributed. The new policy proclaimed that the party would continue reforms until the rich peasants were "swept out of the door."[60] Middle peasants were urged to hand over their land for repartition. Those who refused and insisted that previous redistributions had been fair were singled out as class enemies at mass meetings.[61] Under the new regulations, landlords were denied the right to own land; rich peasants were allowed a piece of barren land, provided they did the cultivation themselves. All villages, regardless of whether they had or had not gone through land redistribution before, were to redivide the land according to a new formula based on population and labor.

This radical policy generated stiff opposition from indigenous cadres, who argued that the new policy deprived landlords and rich peasants of the basic means of support. They also pointed out that land redistribution at spring planting would greatly affect production efficiency. This generated a heated intra-party debate over the new policy. Because of strong local opposition, the drastic new measures were not universally applied. The policy had little success, particularly in the commercialized South; for instance, only 93 villages in the southern part of Guangshan underwent the "sweeping" land reform.[62] In 1931, even in the very core Communist areas, such as Bowstring East, Bowstring South, and Bowstring West (Xian dong, Xian nan, Xian xi) in Guangshan county, and Purple Cloud (Ziyun) and Horse-riding (Chengma) in Huangan and Macheng counties, peasants only went through the second stage of the land reform and never the third radical stage.[63]

Judging from the reports, it seems that the radical land reform was ill conceived and ill structured. The earlier Li Lisan version was based on the assumption that each cultivator required a minimum of two to two and a half *dou* of land to obtain a minimum standard of subsistence. Peasants were thus given that amount of land. Certificates of users' rights were issued to the peasants by the soviet government. The rest of the land was then collectively pooled into state farms (*nongchang*). The rationale behind the state farm program was based on two basic Marxist concepts: eventual nationalization of all farmland by the state, and the need to speed up social change through collective production. All property, including mountains, fish ponds, and bamboo groves, should therefore be collectively owned, not redistributed to individual peasants.

The Eyuwan Special Committee passed a resolution to decide on the number of state farms each county should build: five for Huangan, three each for Macheng, Huangpi, and Guangshan, and one for Luoshan. Each state farm was to be no smaller than twenty *shi*. The farms could only be established in centrally administered regions (*lao qu*) where the Communists exercised complete political control. The new policy meant that in core areas where peasants had just completed the second stage of land redistribution, land was once again taken away from them to be made into state farms.

The re-pooling of land under the radical policy was highly disruptive for peasants in the core areas. The Long Stream (Changcong) state farm in Tan River Dam is an example. The village traditionally had about 100 households. The renewed land reform drove away more than twenty wealthy families, and the remaining families were relocated to make way for the new state farm. The state farm was of considerable size, occupying 80 *shi* of mostly fertile village farmland. Attached to it was a ranch. The farm was cultivated by 40 peasants with ten draft animals. Within the state farm structure there were an administration, a labor union, a party branch, a branch of the Communist Youth League, and a self-defense force.[64] The state farm thus served as a political, economic, and defense unit combined.

State farm productivity was usually very low. Since the government, not the peasants, owned the state farms, peasants had no incentive to work hard to increase production. They viewed the land reform as a measure benefiting the soviet government rather than the individual cultivator. It promoted the public good but had little to do with the peasants' concerns. Since the new policy relocated peasant families at quite a distance from state farms, it took them more time to get to work. Since peasants had no incentive to do so, they did not even bother to show up for work.

The reorganization and rescheduling of farm activities also disrupted the peasants' way of life. The smallholder peasant farm had traditionally been a family enterprise. Peasants were used to working with immediate family members and occasionally a couple of kinfolk, who might help out in peak farming seasons. Grouping all peasant households into large collective units for "joint cultivation" (*gong geng*) alienated the peasants. Moreover, forcing them to share food from a common kitchen disrupted their daily routine, something the Communists would find to be a major problem in the Great Leap period. The "rich peasant policy" was also psychologically damaging. It created anxiety among the peasants, some of whom dared not bring in the harvest from their fields for fear of being designated "rich peasants" and therefore class enemies. The "substitute cultivation" system also turned out to be an added burden for the peasants: so many cadres required peasants to cultivate their land for them that peasants generally shunned the system as nothing but traditional corvée labor.[65]

In the spring of 1931, the Eyuwan Soviet area was struck by a serious famine. The state farm projects had to be dismantled and all joint and substitute cultivation was abolished. Farmlands, fish ponds, and mountain lands were returned to the peasants. Peasants once again resented the disruption. "When the government relocated the peasants to make way for the state farms, they were unhappy about it but they dared not say anything," one report stated. "They were really angry this time when asked to move back to their farms. Many said the party had gone mad. The revolution, the peasants insisted, was a revolt against the peasants." Since state farms were generally set up in core Communist areas where peasants were supposed to be highly motivated to undertake collective political action, such back-and-forth changes in land policy and the attendant disruption of farm life greatly alienated cultivators. It also dampened their political incentive, which the Communists were trying very hard to cultivate in order to make the revolution a truly peasant-based movement.[66]

Peasants often possess a sense of simple, but relative, equalitarianism. To them, equality is calculated on the basis of the individual: each individual is entitled to his or her due share of land. This is the reason Eyuwan peasants first requested that land be redistributed on an individual basis. But the peasant concept of equity and that of the party rarely agreed. The party viewed equity from the Marxist standpoint, as determined by the needs and productive capability of each peasant household. Radical land reform policy based on this view required that local parties make a detailed survey of the number of individuals in the community and their needs, and of the productive capability of all households.

Information about the quality and quantity of land in the area as well as the number of landless peasants had to be gathered. The subdistrict and district administrations were charged with doing this. With the help of the village land committee, village and district authorities then assembled the peasants to decide on the procedure for and method of recruiting leaders to carry out the land redistribution. As clearly stipulated in the Detailed Regulations of the Land Law, land was to be distributed first to the landless and land-short peasants, to soldiers and officers of the Red Army, to retired soldiers and family members of revolutionary functionaries, and to the aged, the disabled, the destitute, and widows and widowers.[67]

The actual land repartition was a lengthy and arduous process that seldom worked out as planned. The government did conduct detailed surveys of all excess land and identified those in need of farmland, and surplus land was redistributed to the poor and landless. In some areas, reallotment was carried out by the soviet government, not by the village land committee. In others, the government acted as supervisor of the process. But complete equity, the party found out, was hard to achieve. The amount of excess land varied from village to village, and in some villages even after all the hilly lands were redistributed there was still a shortage.

To ensure equity not only among households but among villages, the soviet government would redistribute land among villages or relocate peasant households to neighboring land-abundant villages. But repossession of land and relocation of households always generated resentment and resistance, partly because of peasants' strong localistic feelings and partly because of their unwillingness to take risks in a completely new environment. Peasants commonly opted for a smaller piece of land in a crowded village rather than moving to a new locality. Kinship and Red Spears self-defense units often solidified Eyuwan villages into cohesive territorial units. The traditional peasant values of the dyadic relationship, kinship ties, territorial attachment, and fear of the uncertain all ran counter to the party ideal of village equality. Land reform created so many community disputes and fistfights over land that some cadres, finding it impossible to cope with these conflicts, completely ignored party instructions and went for what they believed to be a simple solution in terms of organization, namely putting all excess land under joint cultivation instead of redistributing it according to the principle of equalitarianism.

Some rich peasants did voluntarily give up their surplus land; others did so under coercion. Hired farmhands, in particular, faced a dilemma. Everyone wanted land, but cultivation required more than a piece of soil. It took seeds, farm tools, and at least some capital, which all farmhands lacked. On the other hand, if they refused the land and continued to work as wage laborers, there was no guarantee that they would find employment the following year, and they would still be without their own land to fall back on. The party discouraged agricultural laborers from seeking land and instead encouraged them to fight for higher wages. The policy thus went against the rationale behind land reform, which was to give land to the underprivileged landless class. This party action also defeated the original purpose of the reform, to put an end to land tenancy and the exploitation of wage laborers. Landless workers could not reap the profits of radical reform.

In certain villages, land reform was delayed until the villages were recovered by the Guomindang. Peasants in these areas never had the chance to experience reform. In other areas, repeated complaints from villagers forced the soviet government to redistribute the land anew. In areas over which the Communists had only weak control (for example in the contested grey zones), land redistribution was left pretty much to local residents, with little or no party intervention. In some villages, peasants actually asked for a redistribution but Communists cadres were lazy or had no interest in implementing the reform. In localities where the reform was carried out, those hired farmhands who dared to accept some land benefited most from the process. Cadres and Red Army soldiers also benefited from the reform. But corruption, personal feelings, and abuses of power often entered into the picture. (Villagers were reported to have been given better land after bribing cadres with a chicken.)[68]

Zeng Zhongsheng, the secretary of the Eyuwan Special Committee, gives the reasons why, despite all these constraints, the land reform program did enjoy success in some areas of Eyuwan. According to Zeng, years of violence had effectively depopulated the region to the extent that access to land was no longer a problem. Some people died in the fighting; others were dislocated by civil war. An estimated 7,000 peasants had joined the Red Army and were away from home. Poor peasants, afraid of being designated rich peasants, refused to accept too much land. Hired farmhands, desirous of being regarded as "proletarians," sometimes handed the redistributed land back to the government. Only a small group of agricultural wage laborers who feared unemployment in the immediate future asked for land. The soviet government was able to pool unclaimed surplus land into state farms.[69]

Peasant Support for the Red Army and the Party-Army Relationship

In spite of the limited success of land reform, peasant support for the Red Army was enthusiastic. The Eyuwan Red Army was composed of three separate divisions corresponding roughly to the three subbases of the border region. More research has to be done before we can have a better knowledge of the development of this army, but we do know that the Eyuwan Red Army had multiple origins. The First Division, stationed in the Huangan-Macheng subbase, originally evolved from the peasant self-defense army, the sectarian armed forces organized by Wu Xianxuan at the time of the Northern Expedition. After the CCP-GMD split in 1927, this division became the party's main fighting force. The First Division included some soldiers who had mutinied. The Second Division, which was made up of defected county militia in Shangcheng, was a result of the Communist military subversion program (*jun yun*). This division included a large number (40 percent) of bandits. According to the Communists, it was "a feudal mix" of neighborhood units, clan bands, and bandit gangs. The Third Division was a spin-off from the Second Division. Similar to its parent, it was composed of peasant fighters along with bandits and sectarians such as the Big Swords. The First Division was the purest; the Second and Third divisions (the Second Division in particular) were looked upon by Eyuwan residents as nothing but bandit gangs. It was the Second and Third divisions that practiced random violence and predatory activities. Soldiers in these two divisions had no interest in fighting a guerrilla war and were particularly resentful of the condescending and paternalistic attitudes of the First Division.[70]

Civil wars and guerrilla fighting gave the Red Army the opportunity to expand. For instance, it took in a large number of defeated soldiers and seized a lot of weapons in Hubei during Chiang Kaishek's Guangxi military conflict.[71] It also absorbed some soldiers during the guerrilla war in southwest Henan, where it defeated the local militia and caused the defection of some enemy troops.[72] By the time the three divisions were reorganized into the First Red Army in March 1930, the total number of soldiers in the Eyuwan army had swollen to 2,100.[73]

Yet it was the Zhongyuan Campaign, the civil war fought between Chiang Kaishek and Feng Yuxiang in Henan, Shandong, Shanxi, and Shaanxi, that enabled the Red Army to achieve phenomenal growth. As Communist forces were victorious on the battlefield and the Eyuwan border base became larger and larger, the Red Army captured more and more arms and increasing numbers of peasants enlisted in the army. In the recovery of Jinjia zhai in May 1930, for example, the Red Army seized 1,000 weapons from its opponents. In the celebration that followed, 270 men joined the army. By now the troops were better armed, with such heavy weapons as machine guns and mortars captured from the enemy, a big contrast to the simple swords, spears, staffs, and few guns they had owned before.[74] There was also a change in the type of warfare they fought. Instead of roaming the countryside and ambushing or launching sudden attacks on their enemy as in guerrilla and mobile warfare, thus overcoming only the local militia based in market towns, by mid-1930 they were fighting battles of annihilation, besieging county seats, and eliminating entire divisions of regular GMD army.[75] At the same time, the army exploded in size. By November 1931, when the army was reorganized into the Fourth Front Red Army, it was a sizable force of 30,000 men. At the height of its power in June 1932, the main force of the Eyuwan Red Army numbered 45,000 men, with a subsidiary force (mainly local militia) of 200,000.[76]

The Red Army was made up mostly of peasants. For instance, in 1929 (the only year for which we have figures on its social composition), of the 397 men in the 31st Division, 75 percent were peasants, 15 percent workers, and 10 percent students. The majority (70 percent) of commanders were intellectuals, some of whom had formerly served in the GMD armies.[77] Because the Red Army was mainly a peasant army, it maintained a very cordial relationship with the peasant population in the countryside, even in areas not under direct Communist occupation. There is every indication that peasant support for the Red Army was connected to the land program. Despite all its shortcomings, the policy of giving Red Army families more fertile land and of helping them with "substitute cultivation" served as a strong incentive for peasants to join the armed forces. As the Red Army was made up essentially of local peasants, villagers understandably looked upon the Red Army as their own. No matter where the army went, residents always gave the soldiers a hearty welcome, and some citizens even gave soldiers gifts. Since the soviet government insisted that soldiers pay for their room and board, the presence of the Red Army never became a burden to local citizens. Local people only complained that they had to give the army too much conscript labor for transporting wounded and war materiel.

Women were ardent supporters of the Red Army. They became the army's principal advocates, propagating its cause among captives and defected soldiers. This was due to personal reasons: members of their family or other kinsmen were in the army. Women complained about the food hospitals gave injured soldiers, and frequently brought them home-cooked meals. Some even gave wounded soldiers money to buy their own food. Women wanted Red Army soldiers to sing and play games with them, or talk to them in the assembly. In view of such support, the soviet government made the best use of these friendly groups of women as propagandists by organizing them into "Red Army expansion committees."[78] There was another reason country folk were so supportive of the armed forces: the Red Army gave them military protection. The army defended the area against attacks by the GMD and warlord troops, which had reportedly destroyed the homes of 30,000 residents in the area.[79] Thus, the Red Army was fondly looked upon as a local security force. Peasants gladly gave soldiers food and gifts to entice them to remain in the area and protect them.

The party-army relationship, on the other hand, was highly strained. Red Army soldiers strongly resented the party's "excessively" harsh treatment of rich peasants. Rich peasants normally had connections in the Red Army, people who came to their protection in times of political persecution. The party and army were divided over other issues as well. The party viewed illiterate peasant soldiers as too trustful by nature, and accused the army of failing to prevent enemy infiltration, particularly by the reorganizationists. When the party showed the army concrete evidence of enemy penetration, the army often refused to take action. Red Army leaders, on the other hand, said that party leadership was paranoiac, and insisted that even if the army was infiltrated by the enemy, these perpetrators could easily be won over with the right dose of ideological education. Party cadres reacted by denouncing the Red Army for its "rightist" leanings, saying the army not only harbored counterrevolutionaries and reactionaries but ignored mass works. The Red Army in turn accused cadres of indiscriminate killing (some of the Red Army leaders had been purged and executed by Zhang Guotao and the hard-liners). Cadres, however, insisted the accusation was completely irresponsible. Relations between the party and the army eventually deteriorated to the point that when the party ordered the army to move to the Yangzi, the army disobeyed the order, instead moving troops back to the Beiping-Hankou railroad.[80]

Zhang Guotao and his associates also denounced the army policy of seizing guns. Since there were "undesirable elements," such as bandits, in the army, the army obviously engaged in all kinds of predatory activities. Under Zhang Guotao's leadership, the party was determined to eliminate pillaging and indiscriminate killing. But when the Red Army captured a "reactionary" gentry member, the party, determined to go against the upper classes, ordered his execution. The army instead only fined him and then let him go. Red Army soldiers had little knowledge of party building and of Communist ideology and failed to understand the role of the party in the revolution. They regarded the soviet government as the fruit which grew out of the hardships they endured on the battlefront. The party leadership had greatly benefited from this fighting and now enjoyed a comfortable, combat-free lifestyle in the peaceful inner base.

Because of the hardships the army had endured, soldiers felt they were entitled to have all their needs met, including the need for lodging or military supplies. They felt the soviet government should always be at their service. When cadres were unable to fulfill their needs, soldiers scolded them or even beat them up. Seldom did the Red Army consult the soviet government on its military operations. Most of their requests were issued in the form of a command. Political cadres were highly resentful of the army's authoritarian attitude, but there was little they could do to change peasant mentality. The only recourse open to them was to avoid the soldiers when they came to the base and hope that by giving them a Marxist education, these uncouth peasants would someday be transformed into Communist revolutionaries.[81]

Effects of Political Repression

Peasant willingness to participate in revolution is directly related to state power, government tolerance, and political repression. Charles Tilly has said that government repression at the nadir of a revolution can raise the cost of social mobilization by jailing and executing leaders, disrupting organizations, making communications difficult, and freezing the resources of opposition groups.[82] Severe government repression can crush the opposition or temporarily brake the movement. On the other hand, a weak state frequently results in rebel strength. There are also limits to the employment of violence in blunting revolutionary movements. Without exception, violence leads to massive dislocation of citizens, and displaced citizens, out of anger and desperation, are more disposed to join the rebels. In the case of Eyuwan, state repression deprived the Communists of needed resources and caused disruption and internal confusion.

Protracted conflicts between the Communists and the local gentry brought instability to the Eyuwan countryside. Fighting repeatedly created a no-man's-land in the border areas between the white and red zones. To set up a buffer between themselves and the Communists, the gentry often used village-clearing squads to clear the border areas. The Nationalists sometimes resettled as many as 3,000 villagers in the white zone in a single move. Warfare had effectively destroyed a broad area between the Communist base and the GMD-controlled zone.

War had an even more devastating impact on the soviet area. It brought chaos to the Communist base. Thirty thousand homeless peasants drifted into the base, creating a major refugee problem for the soviet government. Constant plundering of the base by Nationalist troops reduced the Communists' food supply. Without adequate food to support the refugee population, the soviet government was forced to ask refugees to return to the border area. Yet peasants were very afraid of the village-clearing squads. They knew that these militia, as well as the Nationalist forces, would soon return and attack the villages again. They preferred to stay in the relatively safe Communist base, but without adequate food and shelter, many eventually died of starvation and exposure to the cold weather. Others pleaded earnestly with the Communist government to send troops to recover their hometowns.[83]

Extermination campaigns were even more damaging. Between 1930 and 1934, the GMD conducted five extermination campaigns against the Eyuwan base.[84] Because Chiang was busy fighting Feng Yuxiang, Yan Xishan, and Wang Jingwei in the civil war, the Nationalists did not have much time or energy to fight the Communists. Therefore the first two encirclement campaigns were undertaken by a second-rate force, a combination of GMD troops supported by warlord armies and village-clearing squads. These forces were what the Communists termed "sundry armies" (*zapai jun*), very mixed and inferior. They were obviously no match for highly motivated Communist guerrilla fighters. Consequently, the first two extermination campaigns had no marked success. Instead, these campaigns gave the Communists the opportunity to consolidate their power in the region.

Still, these campaigns had some disastrous effects, both materially and psychologically, on the peasants in the Communist base. In the first campaign, with the warlord armies approaching, the Communists swiftly ordered an evacuation of the area. Enemy forces set fire to villages and executed the remaining residents, sparing only the aged and disabled. The village-clearing squads then led local clan bands (*bianlian dui*), the harvest committee (*ge gu weiyuanhui*), and displaced peasants from the refugee society in seizing the crops. The Communists and the villagers who had taken to the hills were forced to subsist on wild vegetables. Cadres and peasants lost all their strength after a long period on this inadequate diet. They could not do anything except sit under trees, their knapsacks on their backs. The Communists reported that a sense of terror reigned over the entire area. Fortunately, the GMD troops, after destroying everything in the area, did not have the means to stay there long. The enemy finally retreated, and cadres and peasants slowly made their way back to the base.

By the second campaign, the Nationalists had learned that it would be impossible to bring the area under control using only military force. Random killings only drove peasants to the Communist side. They therefore tried another tactic. This time they forced people into defense organizations such as the Communist Elimination Society, village pacts, and the Red Spears. Such measures had better results. Peasants, thinking they no longer could depend on the Communists for protection, halfheartedly joined these organizations. Those who were strongly committed to the revolutionary cause sought refuge in the Communist base.

The second campaign dislocated another 100,000 peasants. But the civil war forced Chiang Kaishek to pull his troops out of Eyuwan and thus gave the Communists breathing space. With the GMD forces away, refugees gradually drifted back to their home villages. Many found their homes destroyed by the fighting and their belongings gone. Intermittent localized conflicts still erupted. If the Red Army left the area temporarily to fight a guerrilla war, gentry-commanded militia came in for a raid. Usually a couple of gentry-dominated villages formed an alliance in a concerted effort to invade the Communist base. To create a diversion, these gentry members ordered local forces and refugee societies to plunder villages near the base. They simultaneously made a direct thrust at Communist-controlled territories, burning and killing indiscriminately and causing a great deal of damage.

After capturing a village, as mentioned earlier, the Nationalists immediately reorganized citizens into local defense organizations. Playing on the peasants' need for security and protection, the GMD hoped to exercise some sort of control over local residents. The Nationalist government badly needed these local militia as auxiliary forces to fight against the Communists. Like the Communists, the Nationalists exploited the acute food shortage in the countryside by mobilizing peasants in food raids against the Communist base. This tactic frequently worked and enabled the Nationalists to rally peasants to their side. Grain seizures conducted by both sides increasingly polarized local communities. Opposing villages, gravitating toward either the CCP or the GMD, were locked in incessant bitter conflicts.[85] Cycles of violence went on continuously in the countryside.

Endless conflict made the food problem more acute. Fighting produced tens of thousands of dislocated peasants who drifted into the Communist base area and relied on the Communist government for food. Wailing old men and children became a familiar and demoralizing sight in the area. With the incessant civil war, the number of wounded and sick continued to mount. Moreover, the Red Army, which was usually self-sufficient when it came to food because of its raiding of the white zone, was forced to stay in the base because of a GMD blockade. The sudden increase in people dependent on the soviet government for food created complete chaos in the Communist area.

Although the Communists were relatively successful fighting the first two extermination campaigns, and even captured some badly needed arms from the enemy, violence successively depleted the base of its food supply.[86] The loss of a Communist village frequently meant the loss of tens of thousands of *dan* of grain. The ill-conceived policy of state farms had robbed peasants of their incentive to produce, so they expended only the effort required to grow just enough food to meet the immediate needs of their families. Some even refused to harvest such valuable mountain crops as catalpa wood for the market. Peasant apathy and low productivity eventually led to a shortage in the Communist base of practically all basic items such as salt, vegetables, fabric, and paper.

The Communists tried to solve the problem by actively involving everyone in the base in some sort of activity. The answer, they believed, lay in active mobilization and effective organization. The party therefore set up an organization committee to handle mobilization. To get idle persons off the streets, the party employed the elderly and children as sentries and as transport laborers on the battlefront. They were also asked to produce straw sandals and gather firewood. Women were organized into propaganda, intelligence, and clothes-washing squads. Able-bodied males were urged to join the Red Army. Politically motivated peasants were given a Marxist education and then sent back to the white zone as spies.

To ease the food supply problem within the base, the soviet government instituted a "grain-borrowing" program in which it borrowed grain from those who had a surplus and guaranteed to pay it back after the situation improved. However, this program was met with strong resistance locally, partly because of the universal shortage of grain in the base area and partly because of the unpopularity of the "grain imposition" the party had forced on rich peasants before and which had created panic throughout the countryside. The only solution left for the Communists was to attack GMD-controlled villages for grain or to mobilize local people to seize gentry grain. The Red Army therefore led bands of hungry peasants in attacks on gentry families. After distributing some of the loot, first to soldiers and then to poor peasants, the rest of the grain was transported back to the soviet area for refugee relief.[87]

Although the Communists were able to fight off the inferior forces used in previous campaigns, the fifth encirclement campaign, which Chiang launched against the Eyuwan base in April 1934, was decisive. The Communists faced not a weak state but a unified government determined to use all its means to repress the Communist movement. With the civil war over, Chiang was in a position to devote all his energy to eliminating Communist influence in the area. In February 1933, he had set up a headquarters in Nanchang to direct military campaigns against the Communists. The Nationalists surrounded the Eyuwan base with blockhouses so as to stifle the Communists out of existence. Unable to fight against an overwhelmingly superior force, in mid-November 1934, the party finally decided to abandon the base. Leaving behind a couple of highly committed cadres and 1,300 troops to continue an underground movement while waiting for the next opportunity to resurrect the revolution, the rest of the cadres and the 25th Red Army, consisting of 2,980 men, broke out of the encirclement and left the area on the Long March to Yan'an. Communist resistance in the Eyuwan regional base temporarily came to an end.

Conclusion

Peasants are both conservative and revolutionary. The dual image of the peasantry is a true one. Peasants are illiterate, tradition-bound, communistic, and sometimes politically apathetic. The values peasants hold come out of the work settings and communities in which they live. Dominated by kinship, patriarchal families, religious sects, and small-scale farming, social relationships in agrarian settings are mostly paternalistic, clientelist, and personal. Peasants have social obligations to the clan, community, and friends. Their actions are not governed simply by immediate personal interests; their actions are social actions regulated by social obligations. It is perfectly natural therefore for native cadres to help relatives and friends in times of trouble. A parochial outlook and a strong territorial attachment are common in rural areas.

Peasant mentalities are often shaped by past experiences, personal contacts, and knowledge acquired from folktales and theatrical performances. Their world is one of strict superior-subordinate relationships. They are used to having people in higher stations make decisions for them. Peasants develop a respect for and a dependence on authority. In mobilizing the Eyuwan area, the Communists discovered a pattern of deference among peasants. Respect for authority led them to accept their lowly position and to submit themselves to higher authorities. Just as persons in higher stations lorded it over them, peasants believed it was normal for them to lord it over those in lower positions. Those values and behaviors of peasant culture often portrayed by social scientists, such as hero worship, impetuosity, material-mindedness, a mystical-magical outlook, and a simple concept of equality, were found by the Communists in the Eyuwan peasantry. These values and behavior, the Communists learned, greatly constrained peasant mobilization.

On the other hand, if the right leadership is given the chance to provide incentives, peasants can be revolutionary. But mobilizing peasants is not a matter of simply exchanging material benefits for political support. To be sure, subsistence matters, such as access to arable land and reduction in rent and taxes, are pressing peasant concerns. Peasants do see chances to enhance their welfare. Our findings bear this out. When peasants were offered the privilege of obtaining more fertile land and getting assistance, through the system of substitute cultivation, in return for enlisting in the Red Army, many joined. Members of their families, particularly women, were supportive of the army because of these privileges. As Forrest Colburn has observed, "If peasants are conscious and rational decision makers, clear-cut benefits must be provided when they are asked to change their behavior."[88] Peasants always pursue their own interests.

Yet the success of a social revolution is not determined simply by peasants' needs; it is also determined by how a social program is implemented. Elites often set goals that are different from those of peasants. Erroneous policies can stifle peasant incentive and make peasants unreceptive to revolutionary appeals. The Chinese peasants were often criticized by cadres as being politically apathetic. Theoretically, land reform should have served as a positive incentive for land-hungry peasants to support the revolution. But the program was hampered by faulty radical ideals, and its implementation suffered because of internal party conflicts and external constraints.

Peasants were confused by the Communists' constant shifting of policies (instituting and later abolishing state farms, for instance), which severely disrupted their daily farming routine. In the end, peasants came to view the reform as beneficial to the government rather than to poor cultivators, and they rejected it. Some problems stemmed from the peasants' cultural and social environment. Peasants lived in small communities composed of people of recognized social and cultural affinities. They shared a common identity expressed in dialect, kinship, and neighborhood. Local loyalties were strong, and peasants found it unreasonable to ask them to leave their communities. These are some of the reasons behind the failure of peasants to respond positively to the new economic opportunities offered them. Social and cultural constraints often made it difficult for the peasants to take advantage of reform; erroneous government policies frequently killed peasant commitment to change.

WARTIME MOBILIZATION

CHAPTER 5

Coalition Politics and Movement Revitalization

There is a general consensus among historians that the Sino-Japanese War completely transformed the revolution. International war not only gave the Communist movement new impetus, it made the revolution possible. "Without the international conflict that engulfed China," Tetsuya Kataoka maintains, "the revolution could not have taken place."[1] Chalmers Johnson also points out that the prewar Communist movement was a failure and the Communists were unable to obtain peasant support through their land programs. But the war changed all that. International military conflict created a more fluid and much more dynamic political situation in China and provided the Communists with a unique revolutionary setting. Communist wartime mobilization was radically different from the prewar mobilization.[2]

There is no denying that the international conflict breathed new life into the revolutionary movement. Henan CCP membership statistics clearly prove this. One sees a phenomenal surge in Communist membership during the early war period. In 1928, the Henan Communist Party had about 3,000 members. By 1931, party membership had decreased slightly to 2,200. The Red Fourth Army in Henan, however, had 30,000 soldiers. With the success of Guomindang "bandit suppression" campaigns, the Communist movement was practically driven out of existence. It became essentially a clandestine movement. Communist cadres went underground and lost all contact with Party Central. On the eve of the Sino-Japanese War, Communist Party membership in Henan was down to 96. But with the outbreak of hostilities in 1937, we see a dramatic turnaround. Membership increased tenfold, to around 1,000. By November 1939, it had surged to 16,000 (northern Henan not included).[3] This phenomenal upswing in membership is a clear indication of the Communists' resurgence as a national power.

But party membership was not the only area that underwent dramatic change. The party also drastically altered its revolutionary strategy in the resistance war. The war offered new political opportunities and allowed the Communists to set up territorial bases behind Japanese lines. It gave them the chance to capitalize on the issue of national survival and to appeal patriotically to intellectuals. The threat of foreign invasion provided the Communists with a receptive audience for their political appeals. To broaden its popular support, the party abandoned its radical prewar land redistribution program and instead adopted moderate policies such as rent and interest reduction, tax reform, and an agricultural production drive.

International war frequently leads to the emergence of a political power crisis favorable to national revolution, and such was the case in China. First, foreign war helped undermine state power, which increased rebel strength. The Guomindang lost its nationalist credentials because of its unwillingness to fight the Japanese in North China. The Communists never ceased to capitalize on the evils of foreign encroachment and to cultivate the image that they were the true defenders of the nation. The party conducted a nationwide campaign in which it appealed to all classes to support the war effort. Second, with state control weakened, the political situation became extremely fluid. The opposition was weak and disorganized. Political relations and loyalty collapsed. Old political alignments came to an end and gave way to new regional security arrangements. The party benefited greatly from this change in the political balance of power. In short, the war produced a power vacuum in the county government apparatus and a more favorable political situation that permitted the Communists to revitalize their revolutionary movement.

The New Operational Environment: A Highly Fragmented and Militarized Society

In order to understand how the Communists seized the opportunity to revitalize the movement, it is necessary to take a look at the new political environment in which they were operating. In wartime, Henan was in a state of anarchy. Local society was increasingly militarized and highly fragmented. Military commanders who shared common political interests settled old disputes and forged new tactical alliances. The Nationalists' loose hold on these regional military commanders in wartime offered both the Japanese and the Communists a chance to work out special arrangements with them. New political clusters came into existence. Let us examine the collapse of the GMD armies in the face of Japanese invasion and the subsequent political structural transformation in eastern Henan at that time.

After the outbreak of the Marco Polo Bridge Incident, fighting began between the GMD and Japanese forces, the start of a protracted war between China and Japan. Unable to stem the advance of invading Japanese troops, the Nationalist armies retreated southward along the Beiping-Hankou railway, allowing the North China front to collapse. Japanese forces moved deeper into North China, taking the cities of Beiping and Tianjin. From their bases in the urban centers, the Japanese armies pushed southward along three railway lines, the Ping-Sui (Beiping-Guisui), the Ping-Han (Beiping-Hankou), and the Jinpu (Tianjin-Pukou). Around August 1937, Japanese troops were rolling down the Beiping-Hankou railroad. On September 24, they captured the city of Baoding (Hebei). Anyang fell on November 4. By mid-November 1937, Japanese forces had taken over many urban centers in North China. Henan, still under Nationalist rule, was instantly turned into an immediate rear area of Japanese-occupied North China and a front line for central China, a buffer zone separating the Japanese from Wuhan and the Communist border region in the northwest. Strategically, Henan became the key link between the northern and southern battlefields.

Between November 1937 and October 1938, the Nationalists put up such a weak defense that most of the time it collapsed. In early November 1937, for instance, when Japanese troops occupied the railroad station at Anyang and launched an attack on northern Henan, GMD troops under Song Jieyuan and Wan Fulin simply retreated. The Japanese then captured the rail center of Xinxiang, just north of the Yellow River. Fearful that the Japanese would use the tactic of "fighting a quick battle to force a quick decision" (*suzhan sujue*) to move swiftly down the Beiping-Hankou railroad and take Zhengzhou, Chiang Kaishek blew up the Yellow River bridge. Unable to cross the river, Japanese armies then proceeded westward along the Daoqing railway. By February 1938, all territory north of the Yellow River had fallen into Japanese hands.

Taking another route, Japanese forces continued their southward attack along the Jinpu railway into Shandong. Jinan fell on December 25, 1937. Between March and April 1938, Guomindang forces fought bravely, defeating the Japanese in the famous battle of Tai'erchuang in southern Shandong. But the Japanese simply brought in more troops from northern and central China to converge at Xuzhou. Guomindang forces were forced to give up that city on May 19, 1938. The battlefield then shifted to eastern Henan as Japanese troops advanced along the Longhai railroad to assault GMD troops in Lanfeng in eastern Henan. When the major east Henan city of Shangqiu fell on May 26, Chiang Kaishek decided to give up eastern Henan and made a hasty

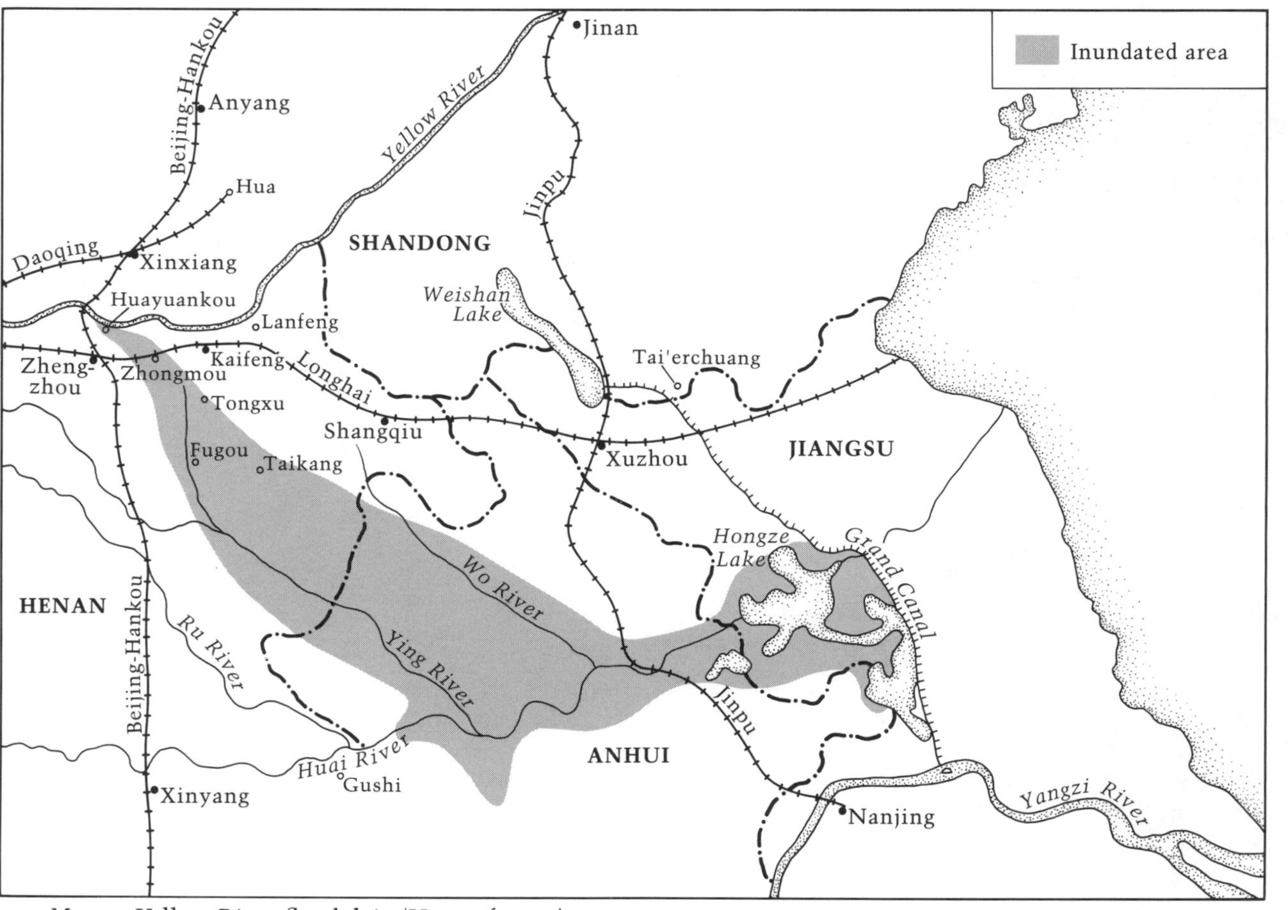

Map 4. Yellow River floodplain (Huang fan qu).

retreat to the west. Japanese troops, however, were advancing so fast along the Longhai railroad that Chiang felt he would not be able to complete his retreat in time, and he therefore ordered that the Yellow River dike be broken to stall the Japanese advance. The floodwater from the Yellow River gushed down the Jialu River and inundated eastern Henan and western Anhui, creating a floodplain that separated the Japanese in the east from GMD troops in the west.

Their progress blocked by the floodplain, Japanese troops then moved through eastern and then southeastern Henan toward the metropolis of Wuhan. Nationalist forces put up an effective defense at Fujin Mountain in Gushi county in September. Japanese troops then captured Xinyang, the Beiping-Hankou railway town in south Henan. The Nationalists retreated westward to Nanyang. The Japanese divided their forces into two armies, one moving down the Beiping-Hankou railroad toward Wuhan, the other pressing toward the city of Macheng in Hubei province. Wuhan finally fell on October 25, 1938. Thus, within roughly a year, Japanese forces were able to take over 50 counties in Henan. The territory occupied by Japan included the area north of the Yellow River, the region east of the Jialu River, and all of southeastern Henan. GMD rule was restricted to the area south of the Yellow River, west of the Jialu River, and north of the Huai River. For the next six years, the two powers fought each other across a narrow strip of the Yellow River floodplain referred to by the Communists as the Rivereast (see Map 4).[4]

The collapse of GMD power and the Japanese occupation of eastern Henan completely altered the politics and economy of the region. Protracted fighting heightened the sense of insecurity already threatening local residents. Flood, war, and a depressed economy displaced tens of thousands of rural cultivators, who either drifted into the ever-expanding armies or simply took to the hills and became bandits. The collapse of social controls also let loose local brigands, both predatory and social. Notorious outlaws such as Wang Zini, Sun Dianying, Wang Mao, and Cui Huashan ravaged the eastern Henan countryside. Constant military disruption made matters worse as the Japanese armies, their puppet forces, and Nationalist troops repeatedly raided the countryside for the conscript labor and food they so badly needed to sustain the war.

The war period also saw increasing militarization at the local level. After the collapse of the GMD armies in Xuzhou, defeated Nationalist commanders stayed behind in the province, many carving out territorial bases for themselves in the localities. Militarists formerly associated with Feng Yuxiang in the Northwest Army (*Xibei jun*) quickly seized on the war as a golden opportunity to entrench themselves in the countryside and attempt to regain power.[5] Local gentry also based themselves in towns and put up so-called anti-Japanese defense forces for protection. From these urban centers, they rallied neighboring villages together to compete with other groups of villages for power. Eastern Henan was thus broken up into a mosaic of military fiefdoms, somewhat like the "feudalism of decay" Karl Polanyi describes.[6] The region was filled with self-appointed military commanders (*tuanzhang* and *siling*), whom the Communists called "kings of the wasteland" (*caotou wang*). Many militarists acted independently. Some coalesced into the Japanese or Nationalist forces. Others supported the revolution and sided with the Communist Party. As political fortunes changed, commanders came and went. A constant reshuffling of alignments was the order of the day, and everything depended on who was in power and who was not.

The war created a tri-polar structure in the area, centered upon the Japanese, the Guomindang, and the Communists. Regional politics gradually revolved around this structure. Local militarists and armed gentry made themselves the political clients of these national power groupings. A look at the armed forces in the region immediately reveals the anarchy and political turmoil in Henan at the time. It was by careful political manipulation in this chaotic environment that the Communists gradually built their way back to power.

The Japanese and Their Collaborators

Stalled after the Nationalists broke the Yellow River dikes, Japanese troops occupied all major rail stations and urban centers on both sides of the new Yellow River.[7] They also took over the county seats.[8] Japanese forces in eastern Henan numbered roughly 17,000, all of them well equipped and very mobile. These forces were normally broken up into smaller armed units, with about 1,000 men garrisoning the major railroad city of Shangqiu on the Longhai line. About 200 men were placed in county towns, and between a few dozen and 100 soldiers guarded the minor rail stations and rural townships (see Table 5.1; unfortunately, only the information for 1941 is currently available).

The Japanese occupied the area with the support of Chinese collaborators. With the expansion of the war in China into a Pacific war in 1941, Japanese forces were spread thin in the China theater, and the Japanese were forced to recruit local forces to do the fighting for them. It was Japanese policy to accept anyone who was willing to join their side, be they Nationalists, Communists, independent militarists, or local bandits. The puppet troops recruited by the Japanese in eastern He-

TABLE 5.1
Japanese Armed Forces in the Yuwansu Area, 1941

Area	Troops
Kaifeng	35th Division
Shangqiu	5,000 soldiers
Xuzhou	17th & 67th divisions
Huaiyang-Zhoukou	1,000 soldiers
Bengbu	13th Independent Brigade

SOURCE: Wang Feixiao, "Kang Ri zhanzheng shiqi Yuwansu qu de wei wan wuzhuang budui gaikuang" (A survey of Japanese, puppet, and GMD troops in Yuwansu during the Sino-Japanese War), Aug. 24, 1983. *P:Shangqiu* 2: 141.

TABLE 5.2
Military Collaborators with Japan, 1941

Officer	Area	Troops	Social background/Military affiliation
Sun Liangcheng	Kaifeng Dongming Bagongqiao	13,000	High-ranking officer in Northwest Army, deputy commander of Nationalist Army
Pang Bingxuan	same as above	12,000	Officer in Northwest Army, defected to the Nationalists after Feng Yuxiang's fall from power; later ordered by Chiang to defect to the Japanese
Zhang Lanfeng	Yuwansu	50,000	Officer in Northwest Army
Hao Pengju	Xuzhou	12,000	
Dou Guangdian	SW Xuzhou	3,000	

SOURCE: Wang Feixiao (see Table 5.1), 142–44.
NOTE: The total number of puppet troops given in the source is 94,000. The breakdowns by troop are rough estimates (and total only 90,000).

nan at that time numbered 94,000 (see Table 5.2). Except for Peng Bingxuan, Chiang Kaishek's protégé who defected to the Japanese side, the puppets were mostly out-of-power military commanders who had had conflicts with Chiang or his associates. Many were Northwest Army generals and former subordinates of Feng Yuxiang, including Zhang Lanfeng, a powerful anti-Communist general who vowed to "put the New Fourth Army out of business." The puppet forces were far from a homogeneous group. Zhang had strong disagreements with his Japanese bosses, and there was also dissension among his own troops. Together, these disparate forces formed part of the Japanese regular armies (*zhenggui jun*).[9]

The puppet commanders looked out for their own personal interests. They welcomed collaboration with the Japanese as a means of gaining or regaining political power. Many of them were fence sitters. Given the strong anti-Japanese sentiment in the area, very few puppets were willing to lean all the way to the Japanese side. Some would have genuinely preferred to be on the Nationalist side but found the Guomindang an unreliable ally. They were unable to get adequate protection from the Nationalists against Japanese attacks. Nevertheless, many still professed loyalty to the GMD and kept up their Nationalist contacts. Most defected to the Nationalist side after the war. The majority of puppets were definitely anti-Communist, but few had the military strength to independently take on the Communist armies.

The Nationalists

The leading commander of the Nationalist forces in eastern Henan was Tang Enbo. Initially he had 100,000 soldiers under him; by the end of the war, the number had diminished to about 50,000. Most of these forces came from the "inner circle" (*di xi*, or the stem) of Chiang Kai-shek's army (see Table 5.3). They often traded intelligence with Japanese collaborators, including Zhang Lanfeng. There were occasional skirmishes between Nationalists and Japanese troops. But the Nationalists' primary objective was the elimination of Communist influence in the area. The GMD conducted four major offensives against the Eighth Route and New Fourth armies in the Sino-Japanese War period.[10]

Local Military Forces

War and the decay of central authority set off centrifugal forces in the area. As violence intensified, petty military officers, powerful gentry, GMD secret agents, and bandits created all kinds of localized war bands (*difang jun*) in the region for the purposes of protection and building power. They originated mostly from county defense forces, bandit gangs, and gentry militia. The tri-polar struggle among the Japanese, Nationalists, and Communists greatly transformed local power in eastern Henan, which was increasingly fragmented into clusters of power holders who acted as clients to one of these national power centers.

Communist sources identify 45 local military commanders in the triangular region marked by the metropolises of Kaifeng, Shangqiu, and Zhoukou in eastern Henan in addition to those sympathetic to the Communists. Twelve of them rallied to the Japanese as "puppet armies," or *difang weijun*. Thirty-three were Nationalist affiliates (*difang wanjun* or *tuwan*, literally, local "reactionary" armies). These militarists commanded minor forces ranging from a few hundred to 5,000 men. They dominated a small base, often carved out of a section of a

TABLE 5.3
Officers in Nationalist Army, 1941

Officer	Area	Social background/Military affiliation
Tang Enbo	Linquan	Commander in chief of border area
Li Xianzhou	E Linquan	"Stem," Commander of 92nd Army
He Zhugou	Shenqiu	2nd Cavalry
Wang Yuwen	Jieshou	"Stem," Commander of 28th Army
Cao Fulin	Shangqiu	Commander of 55th Army
Sun Xiangxuan	N Shangqiu	Commander of 20th Army

SOURCE: Wang Feixiao (see Table 5.1), 146.

county, a segment of an inland waterway (such as the Yellow River or the Sha River), or a border area between several counties.

The pro-Japanese local military forces were commonly known as the Anti-Communist Peace and National Salvation Army (*fangong heping jiuguo jun*). Their commanders were mostly puppets and warlords (see Table 5.4). These troops were normally stationed at small towns flanking Japanese strongholds. Led by Japanese troops, they emerged from their bases to terrorize the countryside in "mop-up" campaigns (*saodang*, or blanket destruction campaigns).[11] There were some gentry forces on the Japanese side, mainly private gentry security forces whose interest was to protect their families and properties. The majority of them were militarily very weak and disorganized. They were reluctant to move in offensives against the Communists unless coerced by the Japanese. The stockades they constructed were usually located near Communist bases and posed a direct threat to Communist forces.[12] There were some bandits among the Japanese collaborators. Pro-Japanese bandit chief Song Anjie, for instance, commanded a force of 100 plainclothesmen. He hated the Communists and vehemently denounced the Communist land reform program. He boasted about his power, and to demonstrate that he was not afraid of the Communists, even pulled down his stockade.

Yet one can hardly make a distinction between pro-Japanese and pro-GMD local military forces. Their commanders switched sides frequently. This was particularly true after the outbreak of the war in the Pacific when the Japanese, desperately in need of armed forces to defend the area, actively recruited local pro-Nationalist commanders. The Nationalists took advantage of Japanese desperation and adopted a policy of following a "crooked path to national salvation" (*quxian jiuguo*). Guomindang commanders (such as Hou Dianqing and Ma Haichuan; see Table 5.4) were encouraged to defect to the Japanese side and to subvert the Japanese armies. County defense commanders and bandit

TABLE 5.4
Local Collaborators with Japan, 1941

Commander	Area	Troops	Social background/Military affiliation
Ma Decheng	Taikang	800	
Wang Jinxuan	Qixian	2,500	Bandit, reorganized and later killed by Zhang Lanfeng
Hou Dianqing	Chenliu	500	Pro-Nationalist, defected to the Japanese
Meng Zhaohua	Suixian	1,000	
Zhu Guangren	Minquan	600	County defense, pro-CCP
Zhang Shaoru	Kaocheng	800	Special CCP member
Liu Zigu	Ningling	600	County defense
Qi Yanxuan	Xiayi	400	County defense
Wang Lanjiang	Luyi	700	Subordinate of Zhang Lanfeng
Meng Heting	Haoxian	600	Former follower of Wu Peifu, Haoxian gentry, staff member of Zhang Lanfeng
Dou Dianchen	Yongcheng	800	County defense
Ma Haichuan	Xuxian	800	Nationalist military, defected to the Japanese

SOURCE: Wang Feixiao (see Table 5.1), 144–46.

chiefs gladly complied with the GMD order and used collaboration with the Japanese, now legitimized by the Nationalist government, as a channel for political advancement. Many served as clients and auxiliary forces (*yubei dui*) of Zhang Lanfeng, the most powerful Japanese puppet. They shared military intelligence with the GMD and also among themselves. Although decidedly anti-Communist, many avoided direct confrontations with Communist forces if possible. Some even leaned toward the Communists. Among them were a "special CCP member" and a pro-Communist general.[13] But for these commanders, the main concern was preservation of their power.

The pro-Nationalist local military forces numbered about 57,000 (see Table 5.5), and were a highly heterogeneous group. The majority were commanded by local gentry or county mayors who supported the Nationalist cause because of the brutal Japanese occupation. Some had been ordered by the GMD to build an armed force to ward off Japanese attacks. Others were military commanders recruited by the GMD as "Special District Commissioners" or "Commanders of Peace Preservation Squads" (*bao'an dui* or *da dui*). These militarists were all clients of three Nationalist generals, He Yinqin, Liu Zhi, and Hu Zongnan. Some had connections with the Blueshirts, the CC Clique, or the Nationalist intelligence service.[14] Most of them were die-hard pro-Nationalists.

Within the pro-Nationalist local military forces were bandits, drug smugglers, and drug pushers. Numerically, these bands (a thousand to a few thousand strong) were larger than the pro-Japanese local military

TABLE 5.5
Nationalist-Affiliated Local Armed Forces, 1941

Commander	Area	Troops	Social background/Military affiliation
Chen Youxin	E of flood area	3,000	Graduate of Whampao & Japanese Military Officers Academy, He Yingqin's client
Feng Shouqing	SSE Huaiyang, N of Yellow R.	3,500	Peddler, bandit, defected to Japanese, killed by Cao Fulin
Chen Tao	?	1,200	Bandit, Hu Zongnan's client, defected to Japanese, killed by Nationalists 1947
Yu Bolong	W Huaiyang	500	Gentry, die-hard Nationalist
Zhang Guorong	N Huaiyang	500	Nationalist *baoan da dui*, killed by CCP 1944
Zhang Gongda	Rivereast	2,000	Killed by CCP 1944
Gao Lantian	Huaiyang Taikang Xihua	1,000	Weakened after defeat by CCP
Guo Xinbao	W, S, & SE Taikang	400	Local gentry and county major
Wei Binfang	W & NW Taikang	1,000	Nationalist "special commissioner," assassinated by Nationalist secret agent in dispute over business deal, troops disbanded
Jiang Tingyan	W Yellow R. Taikang	1,200	Bandit, drug addict, defected to Zhang Lanfeng
Cao Shiyi	Weishi Weichuan Tongxu	3,500	Bandit, connected to Wei Binfang
Ma Fengluo	Kaifeng Minchuan	1,200	Affiliated with Blueshirts, bodyguard of a Minchuan gentry, Liu Zhi's client, defeated by CCP
Zhang Shengtai	Minchuan	5,000	Connected with Nationalist secret agent
Liu Jidong	NE Ningling Caoxian	400	Nationalist-appointed mayor of Ningling
Shi Fuqi	Minchuan Shangqiu Caoxian	1,200	
Sun Xingzhai	SE Caoxian N Shangqiu Yucheng	3,000	*bao'an siling*, pro-Japanese
Liu Yueting	NW Yucheng	500	Defected to Sun Liangcheng
Jiang Jiabin	N Xiayi W Dangshan E Yucheng	5,000	Pro-CCP, defected to CCP 1946
Geng Yunzhai	Xiaoxian Suxian Yongcheng	3,000	Former CCP officer, 1940 defected to Nationalists, causing a split among his officers
Wu Xinrong	?	?	Infiltrated by and defected to CCP camp 1944
Ma Haichuan	S Suxian	1,000	Defected to Japanese 1943
Liu Ziren	Shangqiu Haoxian	3,000	former CCP officer, defected to Zhang Lanfeng
Li Guangming	E Xiayi	1,200	Originally under Li Ziren, a fence sitter

Continued

TABLE 5.5
(continued)

Commander	Area	Troops	Social background/Military affiliation
Liu Ruiqi	E Dangshan	2,000	Weakened by CCP after 1944
Wang Chuanshou	E Xiaoxian	2,000	Killed by New Fourth Army 1944
Han Qingshan	S Suxian	1,000	Eliminated by CCP 1944
Pan ?	N Fei R.	800	Defeated by CCP 1941
Jiang Xinliang	Shangqiu Haoxian Woyang	1,200	Connected with secret agent in CC Clique
Jiang Xinchun	same as above	3,000	Client of Zhang Lanfeng, defected to Nationalists 1944
Zhang Zhaogang	S Xiayi	1,000	Bandit, defeated by New Fourth Army
Yan Jingben	Shangqiu	300	Head of *bao'an tuan* 1945
Chen Chunyi	N Sha R.	2,000	Drug pusher
Zhao Jiesan	N Sha R.	1,200	Followers were beggars, drug pushers; killed by subordinates

SOURCE: Wang Feixiao (see Table 5.1), 148–52.

forces, but they were inferior in quality, having been hastily put together for the sole purpose of common defense. Rivalries and defections always set them apart. Many could not stand their ground against the attacks of better-trained and well-disciplined Communist troops and were easily beaten by the guerrilla fighters. But the commanders of these groups were local people with strong roots in the villages. To them, defeat by the Communists meant only a temporary setback. They could never be eliminated completely. Somehow, they would resurrect their armies in some form, somewhere. Many operated in county border areas and could simply flee across the county in times of adversity. The Communists were never sure of their true political identity; as they observed, these men often operated in the image of a "trinity of a pro-Japanese, a pro-Nationalist, and a pure bandit commander."

Among the local military forces were also some remnants of warlord armies, which the Communists called *zapai jun*, or inferior sundry troops. Most of them were in some way associated with Feng Yuxiang's Northwest Army. These officers commanded great respect locally and had strong personal ties with the local gentry. With the collapse of GMD rule in the area, and with the Japanese bogged down in battle in Wuhan, they became the *tu huangdi*, or "local Emperor." Many appointed themselves county mayors or special commissioners. They became the de facto power holders in the localities. Altogether, they controlled a force of 10,000 men and their power extended over four or five counties.

These local military forces commonly clustered in temporary alliances. Shifting political alignment was a common phenomenon. A group commanded by Geng Yunzhai, for instance, had formerly been an ally of the Communists. Geng had three detachments, led by Liu Ziren, Wu Xinrong, and Ma Haichuan. In late 1940, the group defected to the GMD. After Geng's death, they split up. Wu Xinrong later died and his band, taken over by his younger brother Wu Xinyuan, rejoined the Communists in the autumn of 1944. Ma Haichuan, on the other hand, defected to the Japanese. Liu Ziren became an ally of Japanese puppet Zhang Lanfeng.

Community Armed Forces

In eastern Henan, community armed forces existed in a variety of forms. The majority of them were descended from the warlord period and had undergone a transformation during Nationalist rule. Although still not very well trained, these forces were definitely better armed than the Red Spears examined in previous chapters. They fought with rifles and machine guns rather than the swords and spears used in the Northern Expedition. Local militarization had intensified in the Nationalist period. Chronic civil war in Henan (the Guangxi revolt and then the conflict between Chiang Kaishek and Feng Yuxiang) led to a proliferation of modern firearms and defeated soldiers in the countryside. The following are several types of community armed forces common in Henan in the wartime period.[15]

Gentry-dominated "house-watching squads." These squads (*kanjia dui*) were family-centered clan bands organized by gentry who remained in the area after the Japanese invasion. Sometimes known as "wealthy household squads" (*fuhu tuan*), these clan bands were under the supervision of the heads of the neighborhood pact (*lianbao zhuren*), who were frequently urban gentry themselves. These squads were composed predominately of peasants, either agricultural tenants or local Red Spears. Their primary function was self-protection and particularly protection of the landlord's family and properties. These security forces could hardly be distinguished from the traditional Red Spears sectarians or village pacts (*lianzhuang hui*). In fact, Communist sources indicate that Red Spears were often incorporated into the "house-watching squads."[16] Their political allegiance varied from group to group. Many were pro-Nationalist.[17] Some supported the Communists.[18] Others made a truce with the puppets and, occasionally, supported the Japanese collaborators in their fight against Communist guerrillas. Few had enough military strength to resist the Japanese forces independently, so they cooperated with the GMD or the Communists.[19]

Anti-Japanese guerrilla squads. The anti-Japanese guerrilla squads (*kang Ri youji dui*) can be divided into two types: those organized by Communists or pro-Communist intellectuals, and those commanded by the local gentry and bandits. The gentry commanders, or *siling*, used the anti-Japanese guerrilla squads for the dual purposes of protection against Japanese attack and power building. The squad was the coercive instrument used by gentry to create a base of their own, to seize weapons from other anti-Japanese guerrilla squads, and to extract resources from the locals.[20]

A survey of community forces in the Kaifeng area gives us some idea of the nature of these gentry-dominated anti-Japanese squads. In Fugou, Taikang, Tongxu, and Qixian counties, they were known as "Guerrilla Squads for Resisting the Japanese and Removing the Puppets" (*kang chu youji dui*). The commanders were army men, semi-intellectuals, bandits, and sectarian leaders.[21] Many were low-ranking army officers who had formerly served under Feng Yuxiang.[22] Some, like the group that Huang Xiangbin commanded, were purely clan bands.[23] As Zhang Zhonghang, an organizer of Huang's forces recalls, most of the anti-Japanese guerrilla forces were remnants of former gentry-commanded Red Spears, only this time armed with handguns and rifles instead of swords and spears. Squads varied in size from 1,000 to 2,000 men, and were frequently subdivided into bands of 100. They ambushed the Japanese in the cotton fields, and sometimes a team of three or four individuals would plant bombs at enemy bases. They turned to the GMD for help if they encountered a major Japanese attack of 2,000 to 3,000 soldiers. Due to their close affiliation with the GMD, many were incorporated into Nationalist "Peace Preservation Squads" (*bao'an dui*).[24]

Some groups, however, joined the puppet troops.[25] Others disintegrated when soldiers fled the area during the flood. The majority were based in market towns and pulled surrounding villages together into a defense network. Frequently, they started off with a couple of hundred men and grew to about a thousand after defeating Japanese troops or local bandits. Victory in battle gave them respectability as defense leaders and often attracted nearby villages into the defense network. But they remained mainly community-based and community-financed groups which lost their effectiveness when removed from their native areas. As mobile troops, they were frequently defeated by the Japanese.[26] They were valuable only as militia for local defense.

Joint defense battalions. The joint defense battalions can also be divided into two types: those controlled by bandits and those controlled by gentry. The bandit-controlled battalions were called "joint defense squads" (*lianfang dui*). These squads often came together to form a confederation ten times the size of the anti-Japanese guerrilla squads. In eastern Henan, the defense squads were armed with machine guns.[27] Socially, they were slightly different from ordinary bandits. There were a large number of escaped convicts within their ranks. Each battalion occupied a base, from which it then moved out to kidnap and plunder in the surrounding countryside. Squad members were active not only at night but also in the daytime, and many were looking for personal vengeance.[28]

The gentry also brought villages together and formed their own joint defense battalions (*lianfang dadui*) for protecting villages and crops. In this case the joint defense battalions were purely local militia, not very different from the village pacts (*lianzhuang hui*). As in all community forces, each village remained a basic unit, commanding a platoon (*fendui*) that was subdivided into squads (*ban*). The militia were financed by local residents, regardless of their economic status. Each militiaman, or house-watcher, as they were sometimes known, was given six *liang* (300 grams) of rice a day. Like the members of village pacts, villagers pledged not to assist enemies and to come to each other's aid in case of an attack.[29]

Thus, in wartime, the Communists were operating in a very different sociopolitical environment. Foreign invasion, decay of central authority, local political instability, rampant banditry and outlawry all contributed to the emergence of new political arrangements in eastern Henan. In response to urgent problems of insecurity, numerous large and small armed forces sprang into action. We find not only a proliferation of armed forces but also an increasing atomization of these groups. Most of the units were a few hundred to a couple thousand men strong. Many were hastily assembled either for community protection or personal aggrandizement. The quality of troops was very low and many were undisciplined. These military units were too weak to challenge the Communists independently. The power gap and resource differential between the Communists and their opponents narrowed considerably, making it easier for the better-trained and more motivated Communist guerrillas to defeat these sundry forces.

With the Nationalists tied up in international conflict, the balance of power slowly shifted in favor of the Communists. Competition among the Japanese, the GMD, and the Communists for the support of these local armed forces made personal loyalty and military alignments extremely fluid. Fragmentation of armed groups, shifting coalitions, and factional rivalries offered the Communists the opportunity to subvert these forces and bring them into tactical coalitions. Because of the highly unstable political situation, local gentry had to turn to anyone who could give them physical protection. Civil disorder therefore allowed the Communists to capitalize on their military and organizational skills and draw gentry into local defense alliances. The Sino-Japanese War, marked by regional political instability and an urgent need for physical security, thus created a new political order that opened the way for the Communists to consolidate power.

Rebuilding Party Organizations

Although the Sino-Japanese War has been viewed as the catalyst for the revolution because it contributed to political breakdown and the emergence of a revolutionary crisis, favorable sociopolitical conditions alone do not make revolutions. To make a revolution, political contenders have to build coherent organizations. They have to recruit and train leaders, form alliances with other power holders, devise tactics to neutralize and co-opt enemies, and propagate their beliefs among and mobilize the people. Revolutionaries have to seize new opportunities as soon as they appear.

At the outbreak of the war, the Chinese Communist movement was already an experienced revolutionary force which had survived the ups and downs of sixteen years of political struggle. The Communists immediately made use of the war to rebuild the movement. The wartime revolutionary movement went through three distinct phases of transformation: rapid rehabilitation and expansion (from the outbreak of war on July 7, 1937, to the winter of 1939), retreat (from GMD repression in the winter of 1939 to the spring of 1944), and consolidation of power (from the Japanese offensive in the spring of 1944 to the end of the war in September 1945). In each of these phases, the party flexibly altered its strategies to respond to new challenges.

In order to revitalize the movement, the first task the Communists had to undertake was to rebuild the defunct party, the nerve center of the movement. The party had had the foresight to predict that the war would bring Japanese troops south into central China. The war, if they had predicted correctly, would create a vacuum in Henan, giving the party a golden opportunity to rebuild in the area. The Communists made sure that the party would be in place to compete for power should that happen. Prior to the outbreak of war, the Central Committee, then in Yan'an, dispatched Zhu Lizhi, a veteran in coalition politics and white zone work, to Henan.[30] He was instructed to gather all remnant forces in the province in order to rebuild the party and other mass organizations. Soon after his arrival in Henan in September 1937, Zhu rehabilitated the underground party in Kaifeng. He also built up local party structures in other parts of the province.[31]

The party did not use the village as the basic unit of mobilization, as it had in the Northern Expedition. With society increasingly fragmented at the local level, the size of the mobilization units also went through a process of atomization. Party branches, the lowest unit for grass-roots mobilization, were set up within the neighborhood pacts (*lian bao*). To centralize the movement, counties were grouped into administrative territories with one centrally administered county (*zhongxin xian*) overseeing the revolutionary movement in that particular area.[32] A mid-1940 figure shows that, on paper, the Communists had 610 party branches. Out of these, only 150 were in actual operation, 150 to 200 existed in name only, and the rest were still being formed. In contrast to the Eyuwan period, in the early stage of rehabilitation the majority of party branches were led by proletarians and student intellectuals, not peasants. Party organizations were often set up among postmen and railway workers. Others were placed in local educational institutions. Communists reported very few purely peasant party branches. Peasant organizations were usually attached to the party structures in schools.[33]

Cadre Training and Student Leadership

The party also devoted much attention to leadership training. As early as July 1937, well before the Communists rehabilitated their party in Henan, two cadres were directed by Party Central to set up membership and cadre training classes in western Henan and Shaanxi.[34] In November 1938, when the Central Plain Bureau (Zhongyuan ju) was created under the leadership of Liu Shaoqi in Zhugou in Queshan county in southern Henan, the party made a systematic effort to train cadres for the area. All sorts of party schools, cadre training classes, and military training squads were set up. Roughly 2,000 party members went through these training programs. Other training classes were established within the armies. Courses varied in length from a few days to a month. The instruction was relatively brief, but these cadres later became core leaders in party branches and political commissars in the army.[35]

Students were vital materiel for all social movements. Revolutionary activities could not be expanded without the mainstay of strong student leadership, which was also crucial in building an incipient party structure. The Communists' initial tactic was to base themselves in elementary and high schools. Using these institutions as basic mobilization centers, they recruited patriotic students into work teams used to penetrate the countryside. The outbreak of war saw an exodus of students from Japanese-occupied areas. The party immediately seized the opportunity to recruit them into the movement. On March 15, 1938, the Central Committee passed a resolution calling for massive membership recruitment in Henan. Within six months, thanks to the war, provincial membership increased eightfold, from 1,000 to 8,000. Many new recruits undoubtedly were students dislocated by the war. As a result of this active recruitment, in 1940, the Henan Communist Party was composed mostly of students and peasants. Within the party membership, 40 percent were intellectuals, 48 percent peasants, 9 percent landlord-merchants, and only 3 percent workers or wage laborers.[36]

The party could never have achieved such a membership increase if students had not been disillusioned with GMD war efforts. The Nationalists had lost their credibility among students because of the Japanese invasion and Communist denunciation of GMD inaction. The war also greatly undermined GMD social control at the local level. Henan had traditionally been under the influence of the CC Clique and the Revival Society (*Fuxing she*). In ten years of GMD rule, student leaders and heads of the neighborhood pacts had joined the Revival Society, voluntarily or under duress, and thus the organization was 100,000 members strong; even the Henan CC Clique claimed a membership of 70,000. The collapse of GMD armies in the face of the Japanese invasion was accompanied by student desertion from these organizations. The CC Clique and the Revival Society were eventually closed down.[37]

The war also radicalized student intellectuals. After two crackdowns by the GMD at the outbreak of the war, membership in the National Liberation Vanguard of China, a front organization for the Communist Youth League, had dwindled to a mere 120 men. The disruptive Sino-Japanese War swiftly changed that situation. Displaced students from Beiping and Tianjin continuously drifted into Henan. The party immediately created recruitment centers to enlist these intellectuals in the revolution. An array of National Salvation Societies sprang up across the province. Veteran student organizers, such as Wu Zhipu (the Red Spears organizer in the Nationalist Revolution) and Guo Xiaotang (the December Ninth student leader), actively mobilized the students and channeled their energy into all kinds of populist movements.

Under the patriotic banner of the Anti-Japanese National Salvation Movement, these dislocated youths were organized into theatrical troupes and choral groups for spreading propaganda in the countryside. Another forum created by the Communists for rural propaganda was the Henan Wartime Educational Work Promotion Squad (commonly known as the Wartime Educational Squad, the *zhan jiao tuan*). The ability of these student squads to move around and set up branches in rural areas without GMD interference greatly facilitated grass-roots mass mobilization. Students also became more politically aware and articulate. Thus it was the political fluidity of wartime and the loosening of social control as a result of a weak state that allowed the revolutionary movement to penetrate deep into the villages.[38]

Students were employing the same tactic of rural mobilization they acquired in the December Ninth Movement. The theatrical performances, skits, and emotionally charged speeches, however, had more of an impact on the students than on the peasantry. The flood of patriotic publications such as *The Great Era* and *The Wartime Students* and the myriad organizations students formed at the county level gave them a collective identity. The party also organized elementary and middle school students in military drills, so as to provide them with basic military training. According to Zhu Lizhi, the provincial party secretary, there were 74 youth organizations in Henan (excluding those in the guerrilla zone) with a total membership of 17,000. Of these, 44 youth organizations with 10,000 members (59 percent of the total) were directly under Communist control. The National Liberation Vanguard was revived in a couple of counties in eastern Henan. In Xihua county alone (where the Communists organized their pilot peasant movement during the May 30th Movement), it had 20,000 members.

Students from different localities and diverse social backgrounds added a new dimension to the movement. They not only served as intermediaries between the party and local power holders, they also became active peasant mobilizers in the countryside. As Zhu Lizhi points out, the student movement could never have caught on had it not been for the tolerance of the GMD government, particularly the political department of the GMD First War Zone. Given the nationalistic sentiment of the time, the GMD could do nothing but legitimize the patriotic student movement. Zhu also indicates that since these organizations were under GMD patronage, they were vulnerable to demobilization and co-optation when the GMD regained control of the areas.[39] But by that time, it was too late. The Communists had gained considerable strength and many students were strongly committed to the revolutionary cause.

Party Building in Southern Henan

To sustain the revolution, the Communists had to maintain staying power at the grass-roots level. This meant that the party had to create a network of viable party organizations at the county and subcounty levels. Party branches were crucial in guerrilla warfare; they also served as local centers of resource mobilization. It was through these branches that the Communists gathered military supplies and intelligence information and recruited manpower for the guerrilla armies. Let us examine the tactics the CCP employed in setting up local party organizations in southern Henan.

Reinvigorating traditionally party-controlled centers. One of the tactics of power building was to reinvigorate strong party-influenced centers. The rebuilding of the party in Queshan was an example. The Queshan district party was located at Pointed Hill (Jianding shan qu) on the border between Queshan and Xinyang counties, in a hilly region where Communists had been mobilizing the peasants for revolution since the Northern Expedition. It was here that cadres had led peasants in tax and rent resistance movements in the 1930s, when many urban operations had come to an end as a result of the GMD crackdown. Situated in rugged terrain, the area was "politically unstable," a land of bandits. Since it was located in a remote area at a distance from the main rail center of Xinyang, Pointed Hill was not occupied by Japanese troops. For these reasons, and given the previous contacts they had built in the area, it was relatively easy for the Communists to reestablish political control here.

The party center was a semipublic organization. Communist cadres dominated most of the official subcounty positions in the *lianbao*, the *bao*, and the *jia*. From Pointed Hill, the party stretched out to establish branches in nearby towns (*zhen*). Total party membership in the district was 500, half peasants and half young intellectuals. Eighty party members were organized into a security force. Since Communist influence in the area had been traditionally strong, the Communists did not have to dominate all leadership positions. Instead they let local people hold some community positions, although the CCP insisted that they be "democratically elected."

The Communists skillfully exploited local defense needs to strike a compromise with the Guomindang county mayor. In return for a free hand to operate in the area, the CCP agreed to reorganize its troops into a county "Forward Thrust Squad" (*tingjin dui*) and help build up this armed force. With the county backing them, they ordered the gentry to give up their guns. Later, more firearms were obtained through seizures in anti-bandit campaigns conducted jointly by the party and the gentry. The Communists also tried their best to recruit disbanded soldiers. The tactic of working with the existing government gave the Communists several advantages. First, the Communists did not have to pay taxes, and the money saved could be used for other purposes. Second, helping local people conduct bandit suppressions bolstered the Communist image as a protector and gave the locality political stability. Third, by giving guerrilla training classes, the party successfully recruited 300 guerrilla fighters into the New Fourth Army.

Using indigenous Communist elites. Communist activities in Tan Family River (Tanjia he) are a typical example of how the Communists used indigenous elites in party building. Tan Family River was a town located south of the county seat of Xinyang, close to the strategic transport line of the Beiping-Hankou railroad. It was one of the revolutionary centers where Communists had been successful in mobilizing several thousand people in the Nationalist Revolution. The party was able to stage a peasant uprising in the 1930s under the leadership of three student activists—Ren Ziheng and Zhang Yusheng of Tan Family River, and Zhou Yingqu of the neighboring town of West Double River (Shuangxi he). Although the rebellion was crushed, clandestine movement was thus built in the area and groundwork laid for the future. The failure of the 1930 uprising and subsequent government repression forced the three leaders to leave town for a couple of years, but in 1935 they drifted back. Completely out of touch with the party because of GMD political repression, these Communist leaders took cover by operating a sock factory in town. They were able to escape government detection because all three came from elite local families with strong ties to town notables. They operated clandestinely as respectable local businessmen.

Japanese aggression gave the three a chance to rebuild the movement. With the threat of war looming, Sun Lianzhong, the GMD military commander in southern Xinyang, set up a military training course to recruit townspeople to participate in local self-defense. Ren, Zhang, and Zhou immediately seized the opportunity to infiltrate the program. They recruited young students and formed a core group. Their plan was to later disengage these students from the defense program and reorganize them into the Eighth Route Army. Soon Sun Lianzhong's warlord army moved out of Tan Family River, and a student propaganda team from the Communist-run "South Henan Citizens' Mobilization Directing Section" came to town. Ren, Zhang, and Zhou then reestablished contact with the Communists and reapplied for party membership. A party branch was later set up among these student fighters. Instead of joining the Eighth Route Army as previously planned, the party instructed the group to stay behind and carry on the anti-Japanese guerrilla war in the strategic Tan Family River location.[40]

Using peasants. Although there were few purely peasant party branches set up by the Communists, the CCP did occasionally use peasants to set up these low-level organizations. The Li New Shop party branch is an example.

The Li New Shop party branch was located at a major town 30 *li* northwest of the railroad center of Minggang. When Japanese troops invaded and occupied the town, all landlords and their bullies fled the area. Only local peasants remained. Since the town was under repeated Japanese attacks, the timid peasants refused to fill such community positions as heads of *bao* and *jia*. The Communists immediately stepped in to fill the vacuum. In order to gain the peasants' confidence, the Communists helped the existing GMD-sponsored Anti-Japanese Village Protection Society (*kang Ri baoxiang hui*), now controlled by the peasants, raise a guerrilla force.

The party branch later created in this town was purely a peasant organization: all eighteen members were peasants. The party secretary was a "middle peasant" who had acquired some military knowledge during his capture by the Red Army. Unlike in other party organizations, there were no fees for joining. Whenever they could afford it, peasants donated a few coppers to the party. The basic function of this branch was local security—keeping night watches, posting sentries, and gathering intelligence. The party also conducted tax resistance movements. Using the Anti-Japanese Village Protection Society, the party led peasants in collective bargaining with county authorities over allotted taxes. Under Communist leadership, local peasants frequently drove tax collectors out of their villages.

Using urban students. We have very little information on this tactic except that pertaining to the Zhugou Street Youth Armed Party Branch. This party branch consisted of a small force of 30 persons armed with twenty guns. Their main activity was bandit suppression. The party was controlled by urban students who were said to be well trained and very reliable.

Success in rural mobilization and building party branches depended on a number of factors: proper timing, effective leadership, and the right choice of localities. The Communists reported that mobilization had to be done prior to a Japanese attack, when there was a lot of fear among area residents. There was another chance for them to mobilize, right after the Japanese retreated and before local power holders took over, or before the Guomindang returned to the area. The normal tactic was to exploit the problems of local insecurity and to offer local residents the military and organizational skills they needed to create local security forces. But the Communists also learned from their previous experience with the Red Spears that they could not leave these armed forces in the control of the gentry or local residents. Once the armed forces were formed, the party had to swiftly disengage them from the area so that they would not be co-opted by the GMD. The Communists could not hide these forces from the Nationalists.

As the Communists learned from the Northern Expedition, indigenous leadership was crucial to party building. Natives not only had contacts, they were well acquainted with local conditions. In times of political adversity, indigenous party leaders knew where to hide and how to preserve party organizations. But the party knew that it had to be very scrupulous in recruitment. Unlike the en bloc incorporation of military forces used in the Northern Expedition, new party policies emphasized reorganizing and retraining newly recruited armies, not simply taking them over. The Communists also put more stress on getting rid of the "undesirable elements" in their party and military organizations.[41]

Coalition Politics

Coalition, as Sidney Ulmer notes, is "an alliance among individuals or groups with diverse long-range goals. As a consequence, coalitions are temporary and means-oriented. They not only lack agreement on values, but tacit neutrality on matters beyond the immediate aims is necessary for stability."[42] Coalitions are not value-based. Participants are often motivated by power considerations. This describes most of the coalitions the Communists formed with local power holders in wartime. Many were short-lived and "means-oriented."

Weak military commanders and rural elites did not have the ability to withstand Japanese attacks, but forming a coalition with the Communists could keep them in power. Wartime coalitions were based principally on strategic considerations. These alliances were formed mainly for collective security reasons. The goal was a common defense against the enemy. In coming together in a temporary political arrangement, coalition members hoped that, at least for the moment, differences among them could be minimized and they might be able to pool their resources for political gain. Invariably, this kind of arrangement could only be temporary, since it was nothing but an emergency measure and a momentary convenience.

It was war and political conflict that brought together these strange bedfellows, the Communists and the local commanders. By playing coalition politics, the Communist Party was given a chance to expand and consolidate its power. Local power holders gained a friend instead of an enemy. They received some military support, valuable in case of Japanese attack. The payoff for these out-of-power groups was security and, perhaps, power gain. To understand the coalition politics at work, let us examine how coalitions were formed and what payoffs the players obtained in this political power game.

Threatened by Japanese attacks and under pressure from the rising nationalistic sentiment in the country, Chiang Kaishek was forced to take serious steps to negotiate with the Communists for a workable united front against the Japanese. This gave the Communists a legal status to operate within the province. Direct negotiations between the two parties began at the local level. On July 28, 1937, Gao Jingting, political commissar of the 28th Army of Eyuwan border base, and He Yaobang, secretary of the Communist Anhui-Hubei Special Committee, began talks with Guomindang representative Liu Kang. After seven days of negotiation, they reached an agreement for cooperation. In September, Zhu Rui, a leader of the Eighth Route Army, working with Li Shizhang, a GMD official in the First War Zone, set up a "Committee for Mass Mobilization to Resist the Japanese in Northern Henan." And in October, under the newly formed CCP-GMD United Front, the Red Army in Hunan, Jiangxi, Henan, and Anhui was reorganized into the New Fourth Army and nominally placed under GMD command. After that Liu Zhi, head of the Guomindang troops in Henan, began to adopt a more tolerant attitude toward the Communists in the area.

Separate negotiations were undertaken at various localities. In southern Henan, for instance, the Communist leader of the "People's Independent Regiment for Resisting Japanese in Southern Henan" obtained from Zhou Junming, a GMD representative, legal status and financial support for his independent regiment.[43] In October 1937, after intense bargaining, the Eighth Route Army secured the right to set up a liaison office within the GMD First War Zone in Xinxiang county. In December, at the Henan-Hubei border, CCP United Front leader Liu Zihou negotiated with the local GMD official and worked out an agreement for cooperation with Zhang Fang, the local military leader in that region. By January 1928, the CCP-GMD United Front was more or less in place. High-ranking military leaders such as Zhu De, Peng Dehui, Lin Biao, Liu Bocheng, and He Long joined Chiang Kaishek on January 15 for a First and Second War Zone conference in Luoyang. In February, the Communists succeeded in obtaining from Cheng Qian, the GMD governor of Henan, a promise of noninterference in Communist activities in the province in return for Communist assistance in work with the masses. Cheng's secretary Li Shizhang invited the Communists to join him in his political training department in the First War Zone.[44] It was only in this congenial atmosphere of political cooperation, compromise, nationalism, and solidarity against the Japanese invaders that

Communist leaders and local power holders were able to successfully use coalition politics to regain power.[45]

The Sino-Japanese War completely transformed local society in Henan. Powerful gentry who had the means to move to major cities like Wuhan or Luoyang departed with their private armed forces. Left behind were the lesser gentry and retired military commanders, who continued to take up residence in the villages. Some of them were intellectually progressive, and they looked to the CCP as the party that might lead them in a protracted war against the Japanese. Others were forced to make some kind of defense arrangements with the CCP out of sheer need for an armed force to ward off Japanese attacks. Many county mayors had no choice; they were charged with the duty of defending the area under their control, and the Communists could provide the organizational as well as the military skills required for local defense.

Thanks to the chronic political instability in the area, rural elites had no difficulty whatsoever in gathering a few hundred to a thousand men and arming them with both modern and old-fashioned weaponry. What they badly needed was someone to organize and give these peasants rudimentary military training. The Communists were willing to move into the area and fill the gap. Partly because of their nationalistic commitment, and partly because it was a chance to instantly build power by establishing a guerrilla base behind Japanese lines, the Communists did not hesitate to seize the opportunity to lead local people in the fight against the Japanese. After GMD authorities had fled the area, many local leaders approached the CCP and asked for help in setting up military training classes.[46] The Communists used a variety of tactics to form coalitions with local elites. According to Communist documents, there were two types of coalition politics: upper- and lower-level coalitions (*shangceng tongzhan* and *xiaceng tongzhan*, or upper- and lower-level united fronts). The upper-level coalition aimed mainly at political targets such as Guomindang officials, regional military commanders, and county mayors. Lower-level coalition politics involved securing support from bandits, sectarians, and community defense forces. Let us first examine upper-level coalition politics.

Working Through Existing Authority in Xihua County

Xihua county was situated on the Jialu River in the east Henan plain, on the transport artery linking the agriculturally productive northern Anhui and eastern Henan regions with the GMD-controlled area. Nearby was the bustling town of Zhoukou. The Xihua county seat was also a commercially active city of 700 households. Communist influence had traditionally been strong in this county and dated back to the May 30th Movement, when the party set up a pilot agrarian program in the area (see Chapter 1). In subsequent years, despite repeated GMD crackdowns, the party retained its contacts and recruited a local commander, Hu Xiaochu, into the party. During the civil war between Chiang Kaishek and Feng Yuxiang, Hu bought firearms from deserters and built up a personal armed force. Later, using Hu's native Three Mount Village (Sangang cun) as a stronghold, the Communists created a special committee and built a party branch in the area to oversee the Xihua-Huaiyang-Fugou border base.

The outbreak of war gave the party a chance to rebuild its influence in the county. The party called upon cadres to use the United Front to recruit "local elites, youthful students, progressive teachers, and enlightened gentry." The main targets, according to the report, were non-GMD military commanders and old-fashioned politicians. These out-of-power commanders and politicians were opponents of the GMD. Some were wanted by Nationalist authorities; most were seeking a chance to strengthen their power.[47] As was typical of the Communists, the party began by infiltrating local schools and using them as mobilization centers. In this case it was the Communist-run Puli School in Three Mount Village. With the support of Wang Qimei, the school headmaster and a CCP member, the party set up an "Anti-Japanese National Salvation Training Class," which then served as a rallying point for all "progressive" forces in the area.[48]

Guomindang defeat in Xuzhou and Huaiyang immediately posed a problem to all local power holders. If they were to remain in power, they had to find a way to strengthen local defenses against imminent Japanese attack. In view of the Japanese menace and local anti-Japanese sentiment, Liu Woqing, a GMD-appointed special commissioner in the Seventh War Zone in Huaiyang and a patriot, strongly supported the Communist call for a United Front. Liu was impressed by the Communist student defense mobilization program, and dispatched 100 students from the Huaiyang Higher Normal School to participate in the Communists' "National Salvation" training project. With Liu's support, the Communists built a 300-man all-student army for the defense of the county.

Impressed by the Communists' skill at county defense building, Mayor Chu Bo of Xihua county also solicited Communist help. The CCP then moved the headquarters of the "National Salvation" training program from its original site in a village school to a city temple in Xihua. The Communists also introduced their defense program to neighboring Huaiyang and Fugou counties. Mayor Chu created a political department to oversee county defense and appointed two Communist political commissars to the neighborhood pacts (*lianbao chu*) to supervise subcounty programs. After Mayor Chu joined the Communist Party, he replaced all district heads with Communist cadres. The neighborhood pacts also went through similar changes and were headed either by party members or by "progressives."

The county, now dominated by the Communists, ordered local residents to join the defense forces and deliver any arms in their possession to district headquarters. The government threatened to imprison landlords who refused to part with their weapons. Landlords who possessed no firearms were required to contribute cash. Fighting men were drawn from the peasantry, particularly from the dislocated flood victims. The county defense force, called the "self-defense army," consisted of 4,000 men divided into three detachments, all under Mayor Chu's command. At the subcounty level, each district had a detachment of 500 to 1,000 men, with the district head acting as captain.[49]

Cooperation between the Communists and Chu enabled the party to control the county. The CCP was able to dominate the political department overseeing county defense and to supply defense forces with advisers and political commissars. Shen Dongping, a veteran Communist activist, became the mayor's chief of staff.[50] The party slowly extended its influence over these forces by cultivating personal ties with local commanders, but the combination was tenuous and relations between the Communists and the commanders were uncomfortable. Military commanders were apprehensive of the CCP. They trusted only the military cadres, not the political commissars. This gave rise to continual intra-party conflicts. The political commissars always gave in to the wishes of the commanders, despite repeated reproaches by the party.

As long as they dominated local defense, the Communists had no difficulty securing military provisions from the people. These were usually obtained through a regular system of allotment (*tanpai*) from the county down to the districts and neighborhood pacts. Contributions invariably came from rich gentry households. Manpower for the forces was provided by the young peasantry; 80 percent of defense force members were aged 20 to 25. The Communists had learned a painful lesson from their earlier mistake of recruiting old-style soldiers, hoodlums, and former military commanders, many of whom later defected. This time they carefully avoided that error. Although local commanders in Xihua county were more reliable, party influence in the military depended highly on cordiality and personal ties between cadres and officers. Party control was strong in the first detachment, a force of 1,400 men, 340 (24 percent) of whom were party members, while in the 2nd detachment, in which soldiers were mixed, party influence was rather weak.[51]

There are advantages and drawbacks to forming coalitions with local power holders and using community forces. For the Communists, working with local power holders solved the immediate problem of financial support for their forces: they could tap local resources. It also gave the army legitimacy. But there were constraints to incorporating community forces in the revolutionary movement. Local forces had strong parochial attachments and personal ties. It was very difficult for the party to turn such troops into a mobile army. In July 1938, when the CCP mobilized troops in the Eastern Expedition, some peasant soldiers deserted the army and returned to their home villages. The CCP then chose some of the more dedicated soldiers in these forces, disengaged them from the locality, and reorganized them into regular Communist armies; the rest stayed in the county and were used purely for community defense.[52]

Since the coalitions the Communists formed with local commanders were means-oriented, these forces were highly susceptible to enemy co-optation. The Communists tried their best to build personal ties with the commanders and treated their forces as ally armies, but for these commanders the primary consideration was power. Once the army was formed, the GMD immediately co-opted it and ordered that the force be reorganized into the Seventh Route Army. The Nationalists dismantled the *tanpai* system, depriving troops of local funding, and financed the army with GMD funds and gentry contributions. The force was also given a new commander, Pang Guojun, a protégé of Chiang Kaishek's and a member of the Whampao clique.

The Communists, on the other hand, skillfully exploited the GMD co-optation policy and used it as a threat to drive a wedge between local leaders and the Nationalists. Warning the military commanders of the possibility of being taken over by the GMD, the Communists persuaded some pro-Communist officers to disengage themselves and join the New Fourth Army. Two detachments eventually left Xihua county and joined Peng Xuefeng, the commander of the New Fourth Army. The party also employed these forces to set up new bases in other areas. After GMD-CCP relations deteriorated, the party, with tacit support from one of the local commanders, ordered Wang Qimei, a detachment commander in the self-defense army, to proceed with some of his troops to northwestern Xihua to create a new center inside a stockade. In a couple of months, Wang built up a tiny force of 160 men. With 60 party members in the force, he set up two party branches in the area.[53] Similar efforts were undertaken by Wei Fenglou, a district head in Xihua who brought his force to Fugou and assumed the office of mayor in that forsaken county.[54]

Although the Communists were using a tactic somewhat similar to the one they had employed in the Northern Expedition period, namely working with local elites and military commanders in building up party military power, this time they did not simply incorporate forces en bloc. Instead of helping local power holders build community forces and then leaving them in their hands, the Communists infiltrated these forces, recruited the dedicated soldiers to form a core, and disengaged this core and used it to build party centers in other areas. Such tactics were possible because patriotic commanders had lost faith in the GMD as a national defender against Japanese aggression, and because the Communists seized the opportunity to offer their services in local defense building. In this way, the Communists gradually built up their own military force and consolidated their power in the area.

Neutralizing Enemies in Zhugou County

Another power-building tactic the Communists used was neutralizing their enemies, as they did in Zhugou. Zhugou was a stockade town of 4,000 households located 64 *li* west of Queshan county in southern Henan. The town, as indicated in Chapter 2, was one of the earliest centers of Communist peasant mobilization during the Northern Expedition. It was in Zhugou that the Communist Party claimed to have set up its "earliest county-level worker-peasant revolutionary authority" in Henan.[55] During the subsequent Nationalist crackdown, Communist forces here managed to survive by conducting a guerrilla war in the hilly region at the Hubei-Henan border.

With the heightening of nationalistic sentiment after the outbreak of the Sino-Japanese War, the Communists renamed their guerrilla force the "South Henan Anti-Japanese Independent Regiment." Sensing that the Communists were becoming more and more powerful in the region, the GMD tried to restrict their activities in the county and put pressure on them to be reorganized into the Nationalist army. A warlord also wanted to absorb the Communist unit into his forces. But an understanding between the CCP and GMD was reached that led to the reorganization of the Communist units into the New Fourth Army. The South Henan Anti-Japanese Independent Regiment thus gained legitimate status and survived as an independent Communist-controlled anti-Japanese resistance force.

In the spring of 1938, the party decided to rebuild the base in Zhugou, which, they believed, was strategically important as a "midway station" between central China and Yan'an. The party therefore ordered Peng Xuefeng, Zhang Zhen, and a group of cadres from Henan and Shandong to proceed to Zhugou with rifle and assault units. At the same time, a group of Wuhan cadres was dispatched to Zhugou by Zhou Enlai and Ye Jianying, chief of staff of the Eighth Route Army. Upon arrival, these cadres immediately took steps to build the party's military power. The party came to an agreement with some area bandits, but had them disbanded later because of lack of discipline. At this point, the Communists were militarily very weak. Their small 600-man force was always vulnerable to GMD and warlord attack. The party had to shift its headquarters constantly to avoid being destroyed by enemy forces.

The Second United Front, however, gave the CCP political legitimacy and a chance to expand. The party capitalized on that and set up a command center in Zhugou to fight against the Japanese. It then consolidated power by sending troops to drive out opposing forces in the nearby countryside. With their enemies out of the way, the party moved its headquarters into town. It then turned Zhugou into the main operation center in Henan. It was in this "Little Yan'an" that cadres were trained and the Communist army was built. The party injected a large number of outside leaders into the area, including Red Army commanders, graduates from Kangda and Shaangong cadre schools, and high-ranking cadres from Wuhan.

In Zhugou, the Communists recruited local leaders and sent them to Kangda for training. Others were enrolled in local short-term cadre training classes. In its brief existence in Zhugou, the party trained 3,000 cadres and recruited 2,200 party members, mostly dislocated students from nearby metropolises. Under Peng Xuefeng's leadership, the CCP greatly expanded the New Fourth Army. It recruited, trained, and dispatched 2,000 military cadres and seven military units to other areas to set up Communist bases. These units later formed the Second, Fourth, and Fifth divisions of the New Fourth Army, the core units that brought the Communists to power. In January 1939, Liu Shaoqi and his Central Plain Bureau (*Zhongyuan ju*) were relocated to Zhugou. Zhugou then became the command center for the entire Communist operation in central China.[56]

Survival of Zhugou as a command center depended very much on how skillfully the Communists played coalition politics to neutralize their enemies. There were many power holders, both friends and foes, in the area. They could generally be divided into three groups: the pro-Guomindang diehards (known to the Communists as "the headstrong," *wangu pai*); the neutralists (or *zhongli pai*, the "fence sitters"), who supported the CCP when they ran into trouble with the GMD; and the "progressives" (*jinbu*), the pro-Communists. The diehards and the neutralists were those with real coercive power in the area. The pro-CCP "progressive" elites were militarily weak but commanded a great deal of respect in the localities. The party's policy was to exploit the rivalry among these leaders and divide them. The basic tactic was to support the neutralists and "progressives" in local elections. Once they were in a position of power at the county and subcounty levels, the party could join them in the fight against the pro-Guomindang diehards and Japanese puppets.[57]

To play the game of coalition politics, the party created a United Front Committee, which focused on seeking the support of out-of-power military commanders. The United Front Committee was headed by Peng Xuefeng, who was assisted by Liu Guanyi and Wang Enjiu.[58] These cadres were connected in one way or another with Feng Yuxiang's Northwest Army. Peng Xuefeng, for instance, graduated from the officers' academy in Nanyuan under the Northwest Army. His uncle, Peng Yuting, was a Northwest Army commander. Peng Xuefeng was a native of Zhenping county in southwest Henan, and therefore was able to use both his army and community ties (*tongxiang*) to contact local commanders. Liu Guanyi served in the Chahar liaison bureau (*lianluo ju*) at the time Feng and his Northwest Army were stationed in that area. Wang Enjiu was originally a major in the Northwest Army and joined the party in 1936. Thus all these cadres had personal ties to Northwest Army commanders, which proved an important asset in the game of coalition politics.

Thus it is not surprising that the party was particularly successful in forging coalitions with the commanders of the Northwest Army. Party allies included Zhang Zhenjiang, special commissioner of the Eighth District in Runan county, and Liu Ruming, a garrison commander stationed near Biyang county.[59] All were former Northwest Army officers who had been defeated by Chiang Kaishek in the 1930 civil war. For these commanders, maintaining neutrality freed them from the Communist menace. Instead of fighting each other, they could make better use of their resources against the Japanese. In the cooperative arrangement, the CCP promised to help them militarily should they confront a Japanese or GMD attack. Both the CCP and the local commanders were motivated by strategic considerations when they joined the coalition.

A look at the coalition between the Communists and Zhou Fucheng might help illustrate the bargaining process and the payoff for both parties. In early 1937, the CCP formed a coalition with Zhou Fucheng, a commander in the Manchurian army (Dongbei jun). In the aftermath of the Xi'an Incident, Zhang Xueliang, the head of the Manchurian army, was imprisoned by Chiang. Zhang's troops were demobilized and scattered all over China. Zhou Fucheng, a subordinate of Zhang's, was sent by Chiang to Biyang county on the Hubei-Henan border to suppress the Communist "revolt." Chiang's tactic was to kill two birds with one stone. In a protracted war between Zhou's army and the Communists, Chiang hoped that both sides would suffer heavy losses.

An opportunity for negotiation between Zhou and the Communists arose when the brother of a Communist cadre was mistaken for a bandit and captured by one of Zhou's officers. When tortured by the soldiers, the captive cried out that Red Army soldiers were not afraid to die. The officer, because of his anti-Chiang and anti-Japanese feelings, had been looking for a chance to contact the Communists. Hearing that cry, the officer thought the captive must be a Communist. He had the captive released and asked him to serve as liaison to the Communists. The CCP and Zhou Fucheng eventually came to an understanding, both sides agreeing to aid each other in case of an attack by another army. The Manchurian officer promised to support the Red Army with arms and ammunition, and to supply intelligence information on GMD forces. He also agreed to protect the lives and properties of the citizens. In return, the Communists allowed the flow of food into the Biyang county seat, which immediately solved the army's problem of military provisions. The accord proved to be vital for Communist survival in the area. Later, one of Zhou's regiments defected to the Nationalists and was ordered by Chiang to move against the CCP. Zhou informed the Communists, who immediately took to the hills, thus escaping attack and preserving their strength for other battles.[60] The agreement was basically an exchange of food for protection. It worked only because the Manchurian army was anti-Chiang, a result of his slow action against the Japanese invasion. For Zhou it paid off to work with the Communists, as there was no other way he could obtain the food needed to support his troops.

Grass-Roots Coalition

For the Communists, grass-roots-level coalition (or *xiaceng tongzhan*, lower-level united front) meant penetrating rural settlements through the manipulation and infiltration of community defenses. As outlined by the party, infiltrating local communities involved a number of procedures:

1. Actively recruiting and training bandit chiefs, popular peasants, low administrative officials, and anti-Japanese activists as leaders.

2. Infiltrating the two tiers of local defense systems, the regular

forces (*changbei dui*) and the reserves (*houbei dui*). The tactic was to use the military training program to enlist county support. After convincing the county authority of the need for the program, the party reasoned, Communists should have no problem penetrating these forces. These community forces, composed mostly of rural peasants, did not need highly qualified military cadres. The basic issue was one of gaining control. The party suggested that cadres infiltrate these forces and create party branches or four-man cells. As for the reserves, which were made up mostly of peasants, the cadres should set up a peasant party branch to oversee mobilization and basic military training within each unit.

3. Competing actively for subcounty administrative positions such as county deputy commander, district head, brigade chief, neighborhood pact (*lianbao*) head, and deputy of the neighborhood forces.

4. Competing for leadership in community defense organizations such as village protection societies, old-fashioned gun squads (*tuqiang hui*), house-watching squads, and village pacts (*lianzhuang hui*).

5. Infiltrating the private armies of landlords and merchants. Most of the time these elites possessed a few hundred guns and badly needed people to man their forces.

6. Urging party cadres who came from elite families to organize and seize control of their private clan bands.

Chronic instability, the proliferation of competing armed forces, and the desperate need for manpower and military skills at the local level provided the party the chance to use community defense building as their tactic for grass-roots penetration.[61] Let us look at some examples of grass-roots mobilization the party undertook in eastern Henan during the war period.

Disarming and Reeducating Bandits

At the outset, a weak Communist Party had to utilize all available instruments of violence to build up its military strength. One of these readily available instruments was the local bandits, and the Central Committee therefore issued a directive forbidding the physical elimination of bandit gangs. Instead, it emphasized winning over and transforming these brigands. Such policy made much sense especially in the Tongbai Mountains in southern Henan. It was virtually impossible for the Communists to defeat and eliminate the 10,000 major and minor bandits operating in the region. Moreover, this accommodative policy fit right into the party guideline of abandoning its former tactic of "isolationism." Cadres were now ordered to practice coalition politics at all levels.

The policy also carried a Marxist overtone. The CCP was supposed to be a champion of the oppressed classes. According to the Communists, bandits were often driven into outlawry by poverty and oppression. In the romantic tradition of *bi shang Liangshan* expressed in *The Water Margin*, corrupt officials and poverty had forced these oppressed country folk to "take to the hills" and become rebels. Hence, the party was obliged to formulate a policy for "recruiting the bandits" into the revolutionary movement. This bandit policy was called *feiyun*, bandit mobilization. Communist guerrillas were specifically told to work out a truce of mutual nonaggression with bandit gangs if these vowed not to harbor hostility toward the Communists. If bandits should mistakenly wander into the Communist base area, they would be informed of the Communist policy. If they apologized, they would be allowed to leave without harm.[62]

In the Tongbai Mountains, where Communists and bandits frequently operated in the same area, mutual nonaggression was absolutely necessary.[63] Direct confrontation was tactically impracticable, for the bandit forces were normally a couple of hundred to a thousand men strong, several times more powerful than the Communist troops. Moreover, in areas of political instability, peasants commonly spent the nights in fortified stockades in the mountains, which became ideal targets for bandit attacks. Local people also had to work out arrangements with bandits to achieve some sort of order in the area, and it made sense for a weak Communist power to seek compromise with these brigands too. The party ordered cadres to close their eyes to bandit activities, as long as these were not carried out in Communist areas of operation. Gradually, local bandits learned to avoid the Communist bases.[64] Some bandit groups were won over by the Communists and joined the revolutionary camp. In such cases, they were immediately reorganized into Communist-controlled independent regiments.[65]

Occasionally, the party won bandits over and then disarmed them. This tactic was applied to two bandit gangs—headed by An Kexing and Duan Qixiang—in southern Henan. Members of these gangs had prior connections with guerrilla fighters led by Communist Zhou Junming. Zhou commanded a battalion which the party wished to expand into a regiment. But soldiers for the new regiment had to come from some existing armed groups, so Zhou negotiated with and brought over these two bandit groups from the southwest Tongbai Mountains. The bandits were reorganized into two Communist regiments, each with about 800 men. An and Duan were specifically ordered to station themselves in a village close to the Communist headquarters in Zhugou, so that the party could keep an eye on them. The Communists, however, had no way of preventing them from pillaging the countryside. Such predatory activities were to a certain extent necessary, because the party lacked adequate resources to support the new regiments.

To prevent plundering, the party finally decided to have these bandit forces disarmed. The Communists tricked the bandit officers by inviting them to a get-together in the Temple of the God of War. Communist forces then suddenly moved in and disarmed them. But the party took great care to explain the move to the rest of the bandit leaders. Each leader was later given C$5 and sent home. Most of the peasant soldiers, on the other hand, were retained and reorganized into local defense forces. A clear distinction was made between the bandit chiefs (*touzi*), professional brigands (*guanfei*), and bandit followers (*feizhong*). Party bandit policy underscored reeducation and transformation. The party assigned two experienced military commanders from Yan'an to make sure that peasant bandits received a thorough reeducation.[66] The New Fourth Army also issued a public statement carefully explaining its actions to the citizens.[67]

Sometimes, pro-Communist neighborhood pact heads (*lianbao zhuren*) were used to win the bandits over. The party frequently presented itself as a champion of the *Liangshan* tradition of the code of brotherhood. It adhered strictly to bandit ethics of personal loyalty. The party practiced only social banditry by robbing the rich and the bullies.[68] Co-opted bandit forces were often used to eliminate military rivals.[69] But bandit policy was employed by the CCP solely as a quick means of building power when the party was weak. Once the party became strong, the Communists frequently allied with other local armed forces to eliminate the bandits, thus promoting a different image of themselves, that of protector of citizens. It was the confidence and cooperation of ordinary citizens, not bandits, that was the primary party goal.[70] Wen Minsheng, head of the political department in the south Henan independent regiment, proudly pointed out that although Communist guerrillas had been operating for a long time in the bandit lair in the Tongbai Mountains, the 400-man Communist squad was practically free of bandit elements.[71]

Incorporating Community Forces

The community forces the CCP targeted were mainly the Red Spears (*hongqiang hui*) and the village pacts (*lianzhuang hui*).

As indicated in Chapter 2, Red Spears sectarians were pervasive in Henan. Although banned by Feng Yuxiang when he was provincial governor, these groups did not disappear. Many were reorganized into militia according to government regulations; others survived clandestinely and took a different name. During wartime, these community forces became the party's prime mobilization targets. Party policy at the time emphasized the use of all available armed forces to rebuild Communist military power, and the Red Spears offered the best instrument for power building. The pervasive and popular Red Spears, the party maintained, were a "latent" political force. The party admitted that they were relatively primitive; still, these community self-defense groups had always opposed official corruption and banditry. Peng Xuefeng, commander of the Fourth Division of the New Fourth Army, issued instructions to cadres telling them to ignore the Red Spears' "superstitious rituals" and regard them instead as "popular, heroic armed forces" ideal for mobilization against Japanese attack.[72] Moreover, the Communist Party looked upon securing Red Spear support as a crucial part of mass mobilization in guerrilla warfare. The tactic preempted the Japanese and their collaborators and prevented them from using these forces against the Communists. Working closely with these local forces eased tensions and prevented conflicts between Communist forces and the rural population.[73]

In July 1937, in a work plan for the creation of guerrilla forces, the provincial committee ordered local cadres to set up a training unit (*jiaodao dui*). Within this unit, a special training class (*te xun ban*) was established for the specific task of mobilizing Red and Yellow Spears.[74] But according to Wu Zhipu, a veteran Communist Red Spears mobilizer in the Northern Expedition, the Communists had learned a painful lesson from the previous sectarian mobilization. This time, they made absolutely sure that leadership of the sectarian forces was wrested from the hands of warlord officers and defeated soldiers and placed firmly in those of politically motivated teachers and students.[75] But to infiltrate and win over the Red Spears leadership, they still had to follow the traditional sectarian ritual of becoming "sworn brothers" (*bai bazi*) in Red Spears fraternities.[76] In some cases, the party deliberately diluted the social base of these sectarian societies by broadly recruiting all kinds of peasants, young and old. The Red Spears chapter was then reorganized and renamed the "Elder and Younger Brother Society" (*lao shao xiongdi hui*).[77] The purpose was to undermine the religious aspects of these sectarian groups and replace them with the popular peasant value of brotherhood.

Village pacts were another target of Communist mobilization. Working with village pacts, the party argued, served two important purposes. By replacing the local government with a village pact, the Communists could restructure local authority. Controlling the pacts also gave the Communists the means to mobilize and arm the masses.[78]

But the party realized that there were limits to such mobilization. Most village pacts were hastily put together or resurrected from the past for the single overriding purpose of local defense, particularly against banditry; they were "too primitive and lacked a tight organizational structure. Villagers seldom had nationalistic sentiment."[79] Yet because of the urgent need for local defense, community forces were pervasive and constituted the most readily available armed forces. The Communist army in Huaiyang, for instance, worked out a defense agreement with a village pact in neighboring Taikang county to jointly protect themselves against puppet troops and local bandits.[80] As will be shown in the next chapter, the party used village pact mobilization extensively in building and expanding the border base in eastern Henan.

Students and Grass-Roots Mobilization in the Sui-Qi-Tai Border Base

As shown in Chapter 2, the Communists actively mobilized peasants in Suixian, Qixian, and Taikang counties in the Northern Expedition period. A solid foundation was laid for future Communist activity in eastern Henan. At the onset of the Sino-Japanese War, the party promptly ordered populist leader Wu Zhipu back to the area to rebuild the base. Wu was an active organizer of the Red Spears in Qi county. He was commonly known as the "teacher" (*xiansheng*) and "commander" (*shizhang*) of the Red Spears in the area. Both of these were respectful sectarian leadership titles. In the repression period of the 1930s, party structure in the three counties had been systematically destroyed by the GMD. The movement survived only as an underground operation. To rebuild the Communist movement from the grass-roots level, Wu relied heavily on dedicated students (particularly the December Niners) in the Datong and Sui county middle schools.

The Communists made the best possible use of the prevailing anti-Japanese sentiment to arouse and train students as local mobilizers. The program in Sui county is a good example. When Japanese forces were about to cut off communication on the Longhai railroad and push toward Shangqiu, an urban center in east Henan, the Communists played on the threat of war to rally village school teachers and students to their side. With the support of the county mayor, they set up a mobilization committee (*dongyuan weiyuanhui*) and a cadre training class to recruit and educate rural intelligentsia in national politics, mobilization tactics, and guerrilla warfare.

The program was only for one week of training, and served more as a rallying point to achieve mass support than as actual basic training in resistance. After taking the course, the politicized students were broken up into cells and sent to the countryside as rural mobilizers. The party divided the county into eight sections, each to be penetrated by a mobile propaganda team. The propaganda teams were hierarchically integrated by a liaison network. Before moving into the countryside, students were armed with an arsenal of government propaganda literature denouncing corruption and urging villagers to support the anti-Japanese forces.

The propagandists had learned their lessons in the December Ninth student movement in 1936. They knew that political language and lofty ideas such as national salvation were too vague and had little appeal to rural cultivators. Instead, they played on the issues of war and suffering to convert the discontented masses to their political purposes. They used stories of Japanese atrocities in the occupied areas to foment a sense of fear in the agrarian population. They emphasized the heavy extraction of money and labor by the Japanese, and the tremendous economic burden the people would have to bear should the villages be occupied by Japanese armies.

From past rural mobilization, students had learned that fear could create frustration among the peasantry, but that it could also lead to withdrawal. Peasants usually accepted it as their fate that they should suffer, believing that simple folks like themselves had no way of altering the course of their misfortune. Students therefore used the peasants' fear of the Japanese and their sense of insecurity to generate a positive and active rural movement. They told the peasants that the only way to stand against Japanese attack was to unite and organize. They cited the concrete example of residents in the First War Zone, who came together to form a defense unit before the Japanese invasion and finally brought peace to their area. They also told the peasants that defense was a legitimate government program. Since local defense had traditionally been part of rural life, something the peasants could relate to, rural cultivators had no difficulty accepting the Communists' plan.[81]

By unleashing the fear of war, radicalized students could take over leadership in the self-defense program and thus gain access to the village pacts. And it was from these community defense forces that Wu raised the first three military detachments for the party's army. As has happened during the Northern Expedition period, party military building grew out of the incorporation of community armed forces. But this time, leadership in these detachments was controlled by Communist-trained student activists. Although the rank-and-file soldiers were mostly peasants and Red Spears, they were relatively better trained and definitely better armed. The First Detachment, for example, consisted of 370 fighting men armed with 300 rifles, a machine gun, and 30 handguns.

Aside from absorbing village pact defense units, Wu Zhipu also built up the party's military strength by incorporating other military units. He took over a 40-man unit after the defeat of the GMD army.[82] Firearms and ammunition were obtained in guerrilla fighting, either by ambushing Japanese soldiers who came to villages to get provisions from peasants, or by attacking weak puppet forces in the area.[83] By August 1938, Wu claimed to have raised an army of 4,000 men. But his army was really very mixed and only loosely organized. Only a fourth of the soldiers were said to be reliable.[84] In fact, his army consisted of two very different units: a core of community forces led by dedicated students, and defeated soldiers and other units as affiliates. According to Peng Xuefeng, the commander of the New Fourth Army, Wu's was a regiment (*dadui*) "in name only. As for the quality of the troops, it is pathetic."[85]

The fact that Communist armies were able to score victories over the combined forces of bandits and gentry-led community units in this period can only be explained by a number of factors: the atomization of these troops, factional rivalry among local forces, and the guerrilla warfare the Communists had perfected in the past decade of GMD repression. Victories on the battlefield enabled the Communists to instill confidence in and win the trust of the local populace. The flexible United Front policy adopted in this period gave the party legitimacy and allowed the Communists to form alliances with any local elite willing to collaborate. Wu boldly used the call for national unity to drive a wedge between "progressives" and the die-hard GMD.[86] By playing coalition politics and dividing local elites, the Communists were able to subvert the social base of the GMD at the grass-roots level.

Infiltrating Defense Positions in Queshan County

Another method of mobilization the Communists employed was to gain a foothold in certain villages, using them as a power base to compete for county defense positions, and then to use these county-level positions to infiltrate downward into other villages. Let us trace how the Communists used this bottom-up and top-down method of mobilization in Queshan county. The Communists had been very active in organizing peasants in rural uprisings in Queshan during the Northern Expedition. But in the 1930s, Communist power in this county dramatically declined as a result of GMD repression. Only a small band of Communist guerrillas operated clandestinely in the area. At the outbreak of the war, native cadres were ordered to go back to Queshan to reinvigorate the defunct party and mobilize the people. Party building was a lengthy process. It began with the rehabilitation of the "centrally-administered district," the third county district, where the Communists traditionally had strong political influence.

As in the Northern Expedition period, cadres were first sent back to their home villages to create clan bands. These clan bands were then integrated into village pacts. The Communists used the same traditional method to mobilize villagers in self-defense. In Big Cao Village, for instance, at the sound of a cannon, villagers assembled at Locust Tree Temple for military drills. The Communists gained a foothold in the area, dominating a market town (Xinan) and two villages (Big Cao and Big Zhao).[87] To give these groups nationalistic appeal, the party renamed the village pacts Anti-Japanese Village Protection Societies.

Using these community forces as a springboard, cadres then competed for higher-level county defense positions. For instance, Zhao Jinxian, a cadre and native of Big Zhao village, was appointed head of the county police. Zhao was able to secure that post because of his personal tie with the county mayor—both had served previously under Feng Yuxiang.[88] Using his position as police chief, Zhao tactically placed Communist cadres in subcounty defense positions. These cadres in turn infiltrated community defenses through their control of local security programs such as the "County Cadre Training Class" and the "Wartime Service Squad." From these programs, the party recruited politically motivated young men and placed them in leadership positions in neighborhood pacts. Through this trickle-down tactic, the Communists slowly extended their influence throughout the county, finally dominating 41 out of the 57 county neighborhood pacts.[89] Through these community defense organizations, the Communists came into contact with the civilian population and continued to conduct subversive activities. But the party always carefully separated its public and clandestine activities. There was no horizontal linkage between the two. Coordination was managed vertically, through party members serving in legitimate positions as GMD-appointed county and district officials.

Japanese aggression gave the Communists a chance to expand their military power. When Japanese troops were approaching Minggang on the Beiping-Hankou railway, Communist subcounty officials led civilians in a frantic effort to expand the defense system. Because of the threat of imminent war, response to the recruitment program was very positive. The Communists were able to recruit 50 men in a day. A variety of community forces were then integrated into a regular force called "The Queshan County People's Anti-Japanese Guerrilla Squad." The squad was headed by a Red Army officer who answered directly to the county party secretary. After the Japanese occupied Minggang and the mayor fled the county, Zhao Jinxian revealed his Communist identity. He then combined his police force with the Guerrilla Squad to form a 300-man, 350-gun guerrilla army. The force was now a professional army consisting of dedicated young students and dislocated peasants. The majority of them were party members and under 40 years of age. Zhao quickly disengaged this newly created guerrilla force from the county and reorganized into the New Fourth Army to prevent it from being exterminated by the Japanese or reorganized by the Nationalists. The Communists had successfully transformed these immobile community forces into a mobile army.[90]

The Limits of Coalition Politics: The Geng-Wu-Liu Revolt

Even though the Communists were successful practitioners of coalition politics and skillful in the use of United Front tactics, there were limits to practicing this game. Coalition partners were frequently hastily recruited and often made strange bedfellows. Cohesion of a particular coalition depended highly on political gains and mutual profitability for the participating parties. Coalition cohesion is usually strong in times of uncertainty, or when the enemy is weak. In times of adversity, or when the enemy is militarily and politically strong, partners tend to break away from a coalition. The revolt of three coalition partners—Geng Yunzhai, Wu Xinrong, and Liu Ziren—is a good example of this tendency.

Geng Yunzhai, a Xiao county (Anhui) native, was a graduate of the Wuhan branch of the Whampao Military Academy and a former CCP member who left the party during the Nationalist period. After the outbreak of the Sino-Japanese War, Geng gathered a small guerrilla unit in eastern Henan and made himself a commander in the resistance war against the Japanese. Wu Xinrong, also a Xiao county native, was a landlord who controlled a local armed force. He was also a mayor and had jurisdiction over the counties of Xiayi, Yongcheng (both in Henan), and Dangshan (Anhui). Liu Ziren, a native of Yongcheng county (Henan), was an old-style army commander. These three local power holders were recruited into the Communist camp at the beginning of the Sino-Japanese War through coalition politics. Their armed forces were reorganized into the Communist army.[91] Liu's forces, in particular, were transformed by the party into an integral part of the New Fourth Army. Twenty percent of the soldiers in Liu's army were party members, and the majority of officers above the rank of company commander were directly recruited from and trained by the Red Army.

The so-called Geng-Wu-Liu revolt occurred in late 1940, at a time when the Communist Eyuwan border base was under heavy attack by Nationalist and Japanese forces. The Communist Party decided to strengthen its army by reorganizing part of Geng Yunzhai's troops into the Eighth Route Army under Peng Xuefeng. Peng was then ordered to take the newly reorganized force to the upper Huai River. The party then appointed Geng "Border Area Peace Preservation Commander" (*bianqu baoan siling*), putting him in charge of rear area defense. Geng, apparently unhappy about the loss of some of his troops, viewed the party's decision as a demotion.[92] In early December 1940, accusing his superior of using repressive measures against him, Geng left his post without authorization and joined forces with his friend Wu Xinrong in northern Xiao county. Fearful of a defection by Geng and Wu, Peng Xuefeng decided to put an end to any such plan by ordering Liu Ziren to go to Xiao county and have Geng and Wu arrested, and to use force if necessary to bring them back to the border area for trial. The main Communist army was fighting in the upper Huai area, and the party lacked the necessary forces to make the arrest itself, so it had to fall back on the local power holder. However, the Communists believed Liu to be reliable enough to do the job for them. Since Liu's troops had been reorganized by the Red Army and many of his soldiers were party members, the party probably thought that this was the only armed force that could take on the task. Some cadres, pointing out the connection between the three officers, strongly objected to the move. They insisted that the party could not depend on Liu because he was only an affiliate member (*tebie dangyuan*), not a full-fledged member, and because Liu and Geng were fellow Xiao countians and neighbors. Army leader Wu Zhipu came up with an alternative solution to the problem. The party, he suggested, should try negotiation first, instructing Liu Ziren to invite the two commanders over for dinner; should negotiation fail, Wu would, with the assistance of Liu, personally make the arrest.

But Liu had no intention of being part of this Communist intrigue. He not only informed Geng and Wu of the party plan but also arrested the guards Wu Zhipu sent to help carry out the plan. Liu was an old-fashioned army officer; it would have been absolutely unthinkable for him to betray his friends and arrest his fellow county natives. Moreover, the conflict between the party and these coalition officers occurred at a time when the Communists were under attack by the Guomindang troops in the area. Observing the increased weakening of the Communist armies, Liu probably thought it was time for him to break away. He therefore repeatedly urged Geng and Wu to join him in a revolt against the Communist Party. It was only because of intense pleading from some Communist cadres that Geng and Wu finally decided to resolve the problem through peaceful means. The two officers agreed to hold a talk with the party in Honghe market town. The Communists let them leave the coalition peacefully, but subsequent conflicts between the party and these officers broke out in early 1941. With the assistance of local armed forces under their control, Liu, Geng, and Wu launched an attack on Communist Party organizations and peasant associations in the Henan-Anhui-Jiangsu border area, imprisoning many Communist activists and seizing their arms. Later, with the assistance of Nationalist troops, they also attacked the Communist base in Yongcheng county, killing 80 cadres and Red Army soldiers and arresting 100 Communist members. After the purge of Communists in their areas, the three officers announced their defection to the Nationalist camp; their armies were then reorganized by Tang Enbo into the Guomindang National Revolutionary Army. As a result of the Geng-Wu-Liu revolt, the Communists lost a large stretch of territory at the Yuwansu border area.[93]

Conclusion

It was during the Sino-Japanese War that the Communists began to revitalize their revolutionary movement. By skillfully playing the game of coalition politics, the party took steps to rebuild its bases and to consolidate its power in eastern Henan. Japanese imperialistic intrusion into China offered the Communists a new political opportunity. The war eroded Guomindang state power, changed the political balance, and created a political vacuum in the region. Under these favorable conditions, the Communists identified themselves with the nationalistic cause and issued a patriotic appeal to the people. Military defeats and the threat of invasion forced local power holders to seriously reevaluate security problems. The Japanese threat made the Guomindang more vulnerable. The Nationalists were forced to come to a truce with the Communists. Using the newly created Second United Front, the Communists forged new security arrangements with regional and local power holders.

In wartime, the Communist Party operated in an entirely different political environment. War, banditry, and social disorder had turned the region into a state of anarchy. The game of coalition politics analyzed in this chapter was played out in the floodplain, where both the GMD and the Japanese were relatively weak. Moreover, the countryside in this area was highly militarized, and Henan society hopelessly fragmented. Regional alliances lost cohesion. Rival commanders and community militarists were increasingly willing to come to a tactical compromise with any military faction for personal ends, either to preserve power or simply to survive. These militarists gravitated into military camps revolving around the three factions that offered them physical protection. Thus they became Japanese, Nationalist, or Communist clients.

With increasing political instability and rural militarization, large and small armed forces under all kinds of military designations proliferated in the countryside. The war splintered regional military groups, and local armed forces became atomized. The size of these local units varied from a couple of hundred soldiers to a few thousand men. These minor forces did not possess enough military power to challenge the Communist guerrillas. The opposition was too weak and disorganized to fight independently. Neither did they have sufficient military strength to defend themselves against Japanese attacks. In this new political game, all the players were of more or less equal weight. It was the inability of any local power holder to survive without entering into special military arrangements with other power holders that gave the Communists the chance to draw them into tactical revolutionary alliances.

In the main, the power holders who entered into coalitions with the Communists were invariably out-groups who used the coalition to stay in or to gain power. Each was guided by a set of interests. The Communists usually forged political alliances with groups who opposed or had an ambivalent relationship with the state. Among them were a few Guomindang-commissioned guerrilla armies, warlords (in particular, former commanders of the Northwest Army), and county mayors who were charged with the duties of local defense and bandit suppression. These allies were less weighty players in the political game. To them, compromising with the Communists was a practical necessity. It was impossible for them to confront a number of foes at the same time. Tactical compromise allowed both parties to maintain peace and to combine resources to fight their common enemies.

Coalition politics would not have been possible if the Communists had not worked out the national-level United Front with the Guomindang. Coalition politics was practiced in a wave of military-political compromises at both national and local levels immediately after the outbreak of the war, the Communists on one side and GMD officers and local power holders on the other. The Second United Front legitimized the political game. By cooperating with the Communists, local power holders did not have to worry about GMD reprisal. The majority of these cooperative arrangements were based primarily on collective security. The Communists offered local commanders, rural elites, and village headmen their military and organization skills and, more importantly, their willingness to fight the Japanese invaders, the kind of assistance community leaders needed to raise and train a self-defense force. By providing protection to villages, the party once again secured the opportunity to penetrate settled peasant communities. It was an exchange of Communist military-organizational skills and physical protection for community financial and political support.

The process of rebuilding the bases bears a clear resemblance to the mode of revolutionary mobilization the Communists employed in the Northern Expedition. Indigenous leadership figured prominently in the rebuilding of bases. Personal relationships and diplomacy were widely used in building power. Veteran native revolutionaries such as Wu Zhipu, Peng Xuefeng, and Guo Xiotang were sent back to their home counties to revitalize the defunct movement after the Xi'an incident and particularly after the outbreak of war. Using tactics typical of the revolutionary movement, Communists infiltrated schools and recruited patriotic students as rural mobilizers. Personal, territorial, and school ties were used extensively to forge new alliances and cooperation. The longtime relationship between the Communists and the Guominjun (now the Northwest Army), which dated back to the May 30th Movement of 1925, became the foundation of many cooperative projects. As in the Eyuwan mobilization, in some cases clan bands formed the basis of incipient Communist power.

There were various methods of jump-starting the movement: the party reinvigorated clandestine cells and activities in traditionally Communist-controlled areas (for instance, in Pointed Hill); it made use of its guerrilla force to take over an area and neutralize the enemies (for example, in Zhugou); it actively sought compromise with out-of-power commanders and worked through existing authorities (for instance, in Xihua and Huaiyang).

But the war provided the Communists with added advantages. International war and the Yellow River flood produced anarchy, disruption, and dislocation. The large number of patriotic students, disillusioned with the Guomindang and displaced by war, provided a dynamic aspect of mobilization. And the party repeatedly identified its cause with national interests, calling upon patriotic students to resist Japanese aggression. In the early war period, the Communists went all out in a campaign to recruit and train progressive intellectuals. Eventually, these radicalized educated recruits formed the core leadership in the party, the army, and in rural mobilization. In the countryside, disaffected gentry, who were critical of the Guomindang war effort and worried about the threat of war and increasing instability in rural areas, came out to support Communist calls for a united front against Japan. Undoubtedly, part of the reason for the Communists' success at wartime mobilization was their nationalistic appeal to the elite.

The devastating war also displaced peasants, who became increasingly disposed toward the Communist cause. The Communists relied on existing armed forces to build up their military power, but unlike the en bloc incorporation tactic adopted previously, they now disengaged reliable core units of newly created forces from the localities and reorganized them into the New Fourth Army. Wartime dislocation enabled the Communists to turn these traditionally parochial and immobile community forces into mobile revolutionary armies. Those units not incorporated into the regular armies remained as instruments of community defense.

The coalition politics the Communists played consisted of both top-down and bottom-up strategies. The top-down strategy involved making tactical compromises with local commanders in order to neutralize them. It also meant collaborating with local authorities, such as special commissioners and county mayors, in building defense programs. There is no doubt that local connections, elite contacts, and superior weaponry also worked for the GMD. However, many of these collaborators were attracted to the Communist camp because of their long-standing animosity toward the GMD (the Northwest generals, for example, who saw the war as a chance to break away from Nationalist control and gain military independence) and a sudden loss of faith in Nationalist military capability as they witnessed the collapse of GMD armies when Japanese troops swept through eastern Henan. The Japanese invasion clearly created panic in the countryside. The support of these local power holders thus enabled the Communists to gradually gain control over county and subcounty defense positions.

The bottom-up strategy entailed incorporating and reorganizing bandit groups and infiltrating community defense networks such as the Red Spears, local militia, and village pacts. Invariably, the basis of cooperation was local security and the chance to gain power. The Communists offered military training courses, such as the Anti-Japanese National Salvation training classes or the Student Defense Mobilization Program, to local militarists and rural communities. County forces were designated nationalistically as "anti-Japanese guerrilla squads." These tactics were specially designed to give Communist programs the broadest nationalistic appeal possible.

The benefits for the Communist Party were many. Playing coalition politics gave the Communists a breathing space in which to regroup forces and rebuild power. By forming tactical alliances with disaffected militarists and local authorities, the Communists gained a chance to penetrate the countryside, infiltrate community defense networks, initiate structural changes, and seize political power. Defense programs allowed them to effectively mobilize rural communities in revolution. By diplomatic maneuvering, or what the Communists termed "making friends," the party neutralized foes who otherwise might have been harmful to Communist base building. It also helped defray the expenses of creating military forces. Cooperative security arrangements brought with them arms and ammunition from allies, and other benefits such as military intelligence and support. All these were vital for rebuilding a revolutionary structure. They were also crucial for the very survival of the movement.

Maintaining a coalition depended on a number of factors: the imminence of the Japanese threat as perceived by local power holders, friendly relations between the CCP and the GMD, which formed the legitimate basis for the alliances, and GMD tolerance for Communist expansion. Local coalitions were means-oriented. The collective security the CCP promoted was based purely on a coincidence of interests. It was a momentary convenience for the two parties. The Communists did face intense GMD competition in this political game. After they helped local power holders create and build up community armed forces, the Nationalists immediately offered these commanders military titles and weaponry in a move to co-opt them into the GMD armies (for instance, the GMD co-optation of local armies in Xihua into the Seventh Route Army). The Communists also had to compete with GMD gentry in local elections in Zhugou. As the Geng-Wu-Liu revolt demonstrates, in times of adversity, local power holders did not hesitate to disengage themselves from the Communists and move into the Nationalist camp. Even though the United Front did not last because of the irreconcilable differences between the CCP and the GMD, the Communists still made good use of this brief period of friendliness to rebuild their power. Within a year or so, they had created a number of permanent bases in the Huai basin. It was in these relatively stable base areas that the Communists launched their social revolution. In some places, relations with local militarists went sour and ended with the collapse of the United Front, but in areas where party influence had traditionally been strong, collective security arrangements were long lasting.

CHAPTER 6

War and Rural Mobilization: The Rivereast Floodplain

An understanding of war is central to an understanding of revolution. Warfare has often contributed to the emergence of revolutionary crisis. Foreign invasions always create policy differences and cause internal divisions between decision makers. Defeat in war is a powerful precipitant of revolution, which invariably undermines existing political authority and transforms long-standing social and political relations. War triggers internal upheaval, creates a fluid society, and becomes a catalyst for revolutionary change.[1]

Warfare frequently produces various conditions conducive to major structural change. First, warfare is highly disruptive. It destroys lives and causes major economic dislocation. Transportation comes to a standstill. Regions, sometimes an entire nation, sink into anarchy. Undisciplined troops create tremendous social disorder. Armed bands of marauders plunder the countryside. Crops are destroyed by fighting, and production declines. With prolonged disturbance, violence and terrorism become a way of life for civilians. Brutal and savage repressions sometimes become pervasive. The displaced victims of pillagers are often compelled to join the conflict, either as soldiers or as bandits. Warfare invariably shatters rural political and economic structures and sets afoot fundamental changes.

Second, warfare is costly. Noncombatants always bear much of the brunt of war. Paying for war becomes the immediate problem of citizens. The ever-growing demands of the military result in larger and larger claims on the resources of civilians. Some armies simply live off the land. Moreover, there is always the enticement of the spoils of war: the opportunity to rob and pillage with impunity is always present, and militarists are always ready to seize the chance for immediate personal gain. Others resort to overly burdensome taxation. Outrageous military requisitions are frequently levied on the people to pay for local garrison troops, invariably resulting in military-civilian conflict. War often strains local resources, creates much discontent with the troops, and perpetuates political instability.

Third, violation of security by the military raises the problem of physical protection of civilians. As a result, warfare frequently facilitates rural mobilization for self-defense and offers the mobilizers a chance to reach out to villages to activate the elites and the peasantry in defense programs. Poorly defended civilians somehow have to find the means to defend their families and property against undisciplined troops and bandits. The threat of attack usually gives rise to a sense of cohesion, a common commitment by people to work collectively to defend themselves. The normal response of disgruntled citizens to the unstable wartime environment is to raise funds to develop effective defensive systems. In most cases, rural elites provide strong leadership, actively mobilizing popular support for projects of community protection. Thus war often leads to the birth and later proliferation of grassroots military establishments. War is such a unifying force in channeling people's energy toward the problems of coping with instability that it would be interesting to find out how communities and communal institutions are transformed by the requirements of war.

Fourth, foreign intrusion, aside from its destructive effects, often produces a surge of nationalistic sentiment. Fear of imperialism always results in the development of a national consciousness among intellectuals, who are determined to drive out the foreign power and put an end to foreign domination. Nationalism is an important asset for revolutionary changes in the countryside, too. Terrorism and wholesale destruction by foreign troops affect all classes of citizens. Both rural elites and common folk suffer under foreign occupation, making it easy for revolutionaries or other patriotic leaders to seize on the problem of insecurity and mobilize people in local defense programs. In a foreign war, all classes of citizens are susceptible to patriotic and political appeals.

In his study of the Sino-Japanese War, Chalmers Johnson argues that the Japanese invasion of China caused a nationalistic awakening not only of the intellectuals but also of the masses of peasants in the countryside.[2] Ruthless suppression of rural areas by the Japanese had dramatically transformed the peasantry. To cope with pervasive mass destruction and anarchy, peasants welcomed Communist leadership in organizing resistance to the invaders. Peasants were more receptive to Communist political appeals in a wartime setting. Unlike the prewar Communist mobilization, which failed to mobilize the peasantry by economic and class interests, as Johnson points out, wartime mobilization was based on the mutual interest of the party and the masses in fighting a common enemy—the Japanese. Johnson sees the war as having uprooted the peasantry, broken the hold of parochialism, and introduced them to the nation.

What kind of impact did the Sino-Japanese War have on the peasants? How did the Communists mobilize the peasants in wartime? How did the peasants respond to Communist defense mobilization? Did they exhibit a clear sense of nationalism? All these questions are essential to our understanding of peasant-based revolution in China. In this chapter, we analyze the Rivereast base in eastern Henan, which had been the Sui-Qi-Tai base in the Northern Expedition period. Within this triangular base, enclosed by two Japanese strongholds (Kaifeng and Shangqiu) and the Yellow River, peasants experienced flood, drought, and famine. It was also the scene of constant fighting, first against the Guomindang and then against the Japanese. The Communists did not have a firm grip on the area until late 1944. Unlike other established Communist bases, in which the party exercised control and could use economic appeals to mobilize the peasantry, Communist economic reconstruction came very late to the Rivereast area, due to the fighting there, and it had a limited effect. Essentially, the party pulled the movement together through an elaborate war mobilization effort. It is in this specific war-devastated area that we will examine Communist mobilization and test Johnson's theory of "peasant nationalism."[3]

Brutal Repression and Disastrous Flood

During the war, the Communists operated in a harsh environment in this area: eastern Henan was a land of fear, filled with the disruption of war and brutal Japanese repression. The rapid advance of Japanese troops into northern and central China was marked by destruction in urban centers and dislocation of the urban population. The cities were constantly under Japanese air raid, transport lines were destroyed, and trade and commerce often came to a standstill. The Japanese occupation created an exodus of urban residents, particularly the rich and wealthy, who left the cities and took refuge in the countryside. Urban schools were closed and moved to local towns (*zhen*) or to market towns (*ji*). In many counties, mayors retreated from the county seats with their militia and put up a resistance fight in the countryside.[4] The Japanese occupied only the urban areas, while the countryside became an area of resistance.

The war had a strong negative psychological impact on local residents. Stories of Japanese atrocities were all too familiar to citizens in the war zone. Newspapers daily carried accounts of Japanese brutality, and news of indiscriminate killings and rapes by the Japanese military traveled fast and wide in the countryside.[5] The accounts included many bizarre stories, like that of an herb doctor in Xunxian who was beheaded by a Japanese soldier and whose head was later dragged down the street by a dog.[6] Innocent civilians were buried alive and others were crippled by torture.[7] In Suixian, a Japanese soldier chased a woman down a rice field and attempted to rape her. When the woman resisted, the soldier had her killed, then cut off her breasts and hung them over the city gate. Many women, young and old, were said to have been gang raped by troops.[8] In Zhuxian zhen, a town south of Kaifeng, Japanese troops rounded up 30 women. After raping them, the soldiers sold them as prostitutes to a military brothel. Many women were reported to have committed suicide after being molested. Others were left lying dead on the road, often completely naked.

In a recently published gazetteer, an eyewitness recounts a story of the Japanese massacre of villagers.[9] On June 12, 1938, 100 Japanese soldiers marched into Old South Gate Village in Shangqiu county with the purpose of rounding up guerrillas known to them as the "beard-men," or *huzi*. They immediately slaughtered 70 to 80 villagers. Both the dying and the dead were dumped into a dung pit. The soldiers then set the bodies ablaze with gasoline. Villagers, the eyewitness says, could hear fellow countrymen screaming as they burned to death. Afterward, Japanese troops conducted a house-to-house search for the guerrillas. Some fighters were found and were executed on the spot. A woman and her one-year-old were drowned by the soldiers. The Japanese then set fire to farmhouses, and local residents saw a nineteen-year-old burn to death. Three hundred houses were destroyed in the raid. Of the 380 villagers, 100 were killed, among them an 80-year-old man and several babies. The raid turned the village into a complete ghost town. Most of the surviving residents fled, and the village farmlands lay completely wasted.[10]

Such stories often terrified otherwise complacent residents in the countryside. Japanese brutality did cow some of them into submission; a few villagers even turned "traitor" (*hanjian*) by working for the Japanese. But others, outraged by the horrible acts they witnessed and influenced by nationalistic sentiment, joined the resistance forces. Rural intellectuals and *baojia* heads were inordinately active. Some were particularly responsive to Communist appeals because they were frequent targets of Japanese repression. Japanese colonial authorities often used rural elites as instruments of economic extraction. Those who refused to cooperate with Japanese demands were often executed on the spot. Local administrators and *bao* heads frequently became victims of Japanese repression.[11] Many subcounty functionaries died heroically, defending their native towns and villages. Some sacrificed themselves by refusing to comply with outrageous Japanese demands.

In Yucheng county, an unyielding county director of education died nailed to the wall by the Japanese. Six heads of neighborhood pacts were killed at one time. A *bao* head in Zhuxian zhen was shot after he refused to bring the Japanese soldiers 30 women.[12] Another *bao* head was held by the Japanese for ransom. When he failed to raise the stipulated ransom money, he was burned alive.[13] Japanese troops usually resorted to extreme violence after suffering defeat at the hands of resistance fighters. Frequently, they returned to a battle site with more troops and demolished the opposing village, destroying all the houses and killing everybody in sight. Families of the *bao* and *jia* heads were particular targets for revenge, for the Japanese were convinced that no rural resistance could ever be mounted without the sanction of these subcounty administrators.[14]

But what alienated elite and peasants most was Japanese economic extraction from the countryside. It drove many into the arms of either the Nationalists or the Communists. To finance the war, the Japanese had to exercise complete control over the economy. They created huge development companies, like the North China Development Company and its affiliated North China Comprehensive Investigation and Research Company, to manage all transport facilities, including railways, roads, and inland waterways, for both freight and passenger traffic. Out of the 97 "military-dominated" factories under Japanese control, 14 were located in Henan. Major industries such as electricity, flour, tobacco, matches, cement, and chemicals were under Japanese control. Both the Mitsui and the Mitsubishi companies were ordered to collect food grain for export to Japan.[15] Indigenous enterprises crumbled under Japanese rule.

At the rural level, the Japanese competed with citizens for increasingly scarce resources. The Japanese designated 26 counties in Henan as key grain-producing areas. Compulsory grain delivery to the government at depressed prices was carried out by a system known as *paigou*, or "purchase by allotment." Under this system, neighborhoods were used as basic units of economic extraction. A neighborhood was given quotas in cash, livestock, and grain. Neighborhood heads were responsible for raising the designated amounts. A partial account of Japanese extraction from one county in the second half of 1944 gives the following figures: 660 tons of wheat, 1,400 tons of animal feed, 10,080 tons of fodder, 68,000 timber logs, 65,000 sleepers, and 20 tons of pig and wrought iron. Such huge amounts of coerced extraction frequently generated local resentment, particularly in the depressed flood area.[16] Neighborhoods banded together to resist the levies. It is no accident that in the war period, neighborhoods (*bao*) or neighborhood pacts (*lianbao*), rather than villages, became the primary units of rural Communist anti-Japanese mobilization.

Another source of rural grievance were the cooperatives. Under Japanese rule, the rural economy was dominated by a hierarchy of cooperatives and granaries. These cooperatives collected produce from the countryside and then, through a strict rationing system, distributed such daily necessities as grain, kerosene, and matches back to the peasants.[17] In some areas a system was established for exchanging farm produce for other needed items, such as salt for soybean oil.[18] Rigid price controls on principal agricultural commodities like grain and cotton drove small traders out of business.[19] Even larger enterprises crumbled under heavy tax burdens.[20] The Japanese frequently used the Peace Preservation Association to extract materials and labor from the people. Local communities were forced into service groups to perform fund-raising, fodder gathering, grain collecting, conscript labor, intelligence work, and local armed forces duty.[21]

Much of the discontent was over labor conscription. The endless need for manpower in fighting and construction compelled the Japanese to use excessive coercion to obtain labor. Young men in their twenties were ordered to join the Japanese "Peace Army" (*Heping jun*).[22] Others were shipped to Manchuria as laborers.[23] Recruitment expenses were often borne by village residents through a variety of garrison surcharges and local surtaxes.[24] It was not uncommon for ten to twenty Japanese soldiers to enter a village and round up all able-bodied youths for defense of a stockade or repair work on the Yellow River embankment. Conscripts were required to provide their own food, equipment, and even bedding.[25]

The Japanese employed several unconventional methods of labor recruitment. In Anyang, Japanese plainclothesmen made sudden raids on theaters and rounded up several hundred audience members, among them women and children. In 1944, with the outbreak of the Pacific war, the Japanese were desperately short of labor. They drew up a plan to recruit 1.8 million men, 100,000 of whom were to be sent to Japan. In order to meet the quota, Japanese troops started intercepting trains and seizing passengers. At one time 6,000 conscripts were forcibly recruited and locked up in a train to be sent north on the Beiping-Hankou railroad. Many died of suffocation in the railcars and never reached their destination.[26]

Japanese aggression in China and its penetration to the subcounty level alienated many community elites, in particular heads of districts, towns, local townships, and neighborhood pacts and neighborhoods. Compulsory delivery of commodities was levied by neighborhood.[27] Rich households were frequent targets of cash extraction. The wealthy were ordered to come up with large sums of money and many were brutally beaten or executed for not paying up. In one instance, an entire business community was locked up by Japanese troops until members agreed to pay the taxes imposed on them.[28] In eastern Henan, rich households were required to give up a third of their grain supply and deliver their beans to Japanese authorities for half the market price.[29] During the flood, property owners, mostly local magnates, were asked to contribute (4 *jin* of grain per *mu* of land) to the public granary for relief. In order to save time, the Japanese ordered property holders to make a three-year donation at once.[30]

No matter how savage Japanese repression was or how heavy economic extraction was, it is unthinkable that individual peasants could systematically articulate their nationalistic sentiment. Those who were personally or whose families were directly affected by Japanese oppression might have independently perceived the Japanese as their foreign enemy. Some might have harbored hatred for the Japanese and a resentment of the random acts of violence, but that does not mean that they had the nation clearly in mind. Anti-Japanese nationalism, articulated as a group sentiment, was first espoused by rural elites and then quickly copied by the peasantry. Brutal Japanese repression, especially that directed against elites, angered rural leaders and turned them against the invaders. Since most of them were community leaders, it was inevitable that they would use the collective community institutions under their control, such as the clan bands and village or neighborhood pacts, as an anti-Japanese forum. And it was through the involvement in these anti-Japanese community institutions that peasants began to acquire and express anti-Japanese nationalistic feelings.

The Guomindang Blunder

Japanese brutality would not necessarily have driven the people into the Communist camp had it not been for the blunders the GMD made during the war. If Japanese brutality alienated and stirred up nationalistic sentiment among local citizens, this would normally cause them to rally to the Nationalist government. However, Guomindang credibility was greatly tarnished when the Nationalist government, in an effort to halt the Japanese advance and to make a hasty retreat to

Luoyang, broke the Yellow River dike, allowing floodwaters to inundate the Huai basin. The initial plan was simply to break a section of the dike at Zhoukou in Zhongmou county, which would have limited the amount of flood damage. But the scheme failed because silt blocked the water flow and resealed the opening in a matter of two hours. The government then activated its contingency plan and on June 9, 1938, bombarded the dike at Garden Opening (Huayuan kou). This time the plan succeeded and floodwater surged down the Jialu River, along the old course of the Yellow River in Anhui, and then into the Huai River, causing that waterway to overflow its banks. The Nationalists did achieve their objective of delaying the Japanese move down the Beiping-Hankou railroad to join southern forces in an attack on Wuhan, which was especially important because Japanese forces had already taken the rail junction at Xuzhou on May 19. Breaking the dike gave the Nationalist government time to regroup its army, but it created a man-made catastrophe for the people in the Huai area.

Floodwater inundated the entire 2,000 *li* of land stretching from Kaifeng to Hongze Lake. The flood affected 44 urban centers and counties, 20 in Henan, 18 in Anhui, and 6 in Jiangsu. It destroyed 844,259 *ching* of farmland, roughly half the arable land in the provinces of Henan, Anhui, and Jiangsu. The flood killed 893,303 persons, rendered 4 million homeless, and wiped out 3,500 towns and villages. It caused untold suffering and inflicted immeasurable damage to livestock and property. According to government statistics, every day there was a total of at least 10,000 new victims seeking relief at the cities of Zhoukou, Xuchang, Luohe, and Zhengzhou.[31] Even though the Nationalists did set up a government relief committee to take care of relief work and to transport flood victims to southwestern Henan and as far as Shaanxi province, the magnitude of the damage can clearly be seen in the precipitous drop in the population of the twenty Henan counties ravaged by flood and famine.[32] In the ten-year period between 1936 and 1946, total population in those counties fell by over 1.25 million, a drop of almost 19 percent, at an annual decrease of roughly 2 percent.[33] Subsequent flooding and famine further compounded the misery and increased the toll. The flood victims, the homeless, and those on the brink of starvation must have been the main recruits into the Communist revolutionary movement.[34]

A recently published local gazetteer provides a vivid picture of the devastation the flood caused in the Fugou area. The floodwater reached that county right in the middle of the summer harvest. Early wheat was already in but late wheat was just being harvested. The approaching flood created panic in the area. Local residents scrambled to gather their belongings (food grain, livestock, and clothing) and retreated to the nearby fortress or high ground. However, the flood hit many completely unprepared. Their property was swept away. Thousands of citizens took refuge at the county seat, filling up the temples and spilling out into the streets. The number of flood victims swelled to 10,000 in a couple of days and immediately exhausted all the resources of the government relief committee.

Unable to obtain relief in Fugou, flood victims began a mass migration to Xinjiang province. Able-bodied males were fortunate to find jobs as farmhands in distant provinces. But many were forced to leave their children and elders behind as beggars. Those who thought they were lucky in reaching high ground in time to escape the flood saw their possessions go up in smoke during a couple of accidental fires. Cholera took many lives (38 in the town of Lutan alone). It was not until 1939, after Wei Fenglou, the Communist-appointed mayor, mobilized the local people and rebuilt the western dike that some sort of normalcy returned to the county. After that, flood victims slowly drifted back to their home villages.[35] In Shenqiu county, citizens fought the flood by building a dike. But the hastily constructed structure could not contain the floodwater, which overflowed the banks every year, forcing local residents to make annual repairs. Between 1940 and 1942, the river gradually shifted its course to the north, which required the building of another dike. The flood cost the villages millions of dollars in property damage and flood control measures.[36] Undoubtedly the people blamed the Nationalists for their misery. All this made the villagers in this particular region more disposed toward the Communist revolution. It was in the Yellow River inundated area (*huangfan qu*) that the Communists' anti-Japanese Yuwansu border base sprang into existence.[37]

Guerrilla Warfare

Unlike other bases in which the Communists' main focus was on social revolution and reconstruction, in Yuwansu, particularly at the Henan-Anhui border, it was warfare that held the revolutionary movement together. From mid-1940 until the end of the Sino-Japanese War, the Yuwansu Communist Party spent most of its energy conducting wars, both against the Japanese and the Nationalists. High-ranking cadres such as Deng Zihui, the political commissar of the Fourth Division of the New Fourth Army, had repeatedly emphasized the significance of fighting. In a talk given to other high-level cadres in 1943, Deng said that the cadres had three basic responsibilities: fighting, food production, and training. Yet among them, Deng continued, fighting a war was the primary duty.

"Military victory," Deng said, "would give us the opportunity to further expand. In victory, all our problems will be solved. Just like once you chop open a bamboo, it will split all the way down. Defeat in war, on the other hand, means that our problems will never go away." The Yuwansu base, he insisted, differed immensely from the Shan-Gan-Ning (Shaanxi-Gansu-Ningxia) border base. In Shan-Gan-Ning, everything hinged on revolutionary reconstruction, but in Yuwansu, "warfare formed the key link." Deng then summed up his speech by saying, "Everything should be geared to military victory. Everything should revolve around warfare. Everything should adapt to the environment and needs of war. To stray away from war and simply talk about production and training is a grave mistake."[38] Fighting a successful guerrilla war thus became the primary function for the cadres in this area.

Guerrilla warfare was initially formulated by Mao as a military means of handling the GMD campaigns launched in the 1930s. But this type of warfare was later refined by other Communist commanders. During the Sino-Japanese War, guerrilla warfare came to be widely employed as the main form of combat. In Yuwansu, this form of warfare was skillfully adapted and refined by Peng Xuefeng, a commander of the New Fourth Army. Peng's version was known as "plain guerrilla warfare" (*pingyuan youji zhan*) and was adapted for fighting in a floodplain. In the beginning, cadres were highly doubtful that this type of warfare, which was originally designed for fighting in the mountains, could be used in the plain. Unlike mountain fighting, in which soldiers could easily seek cover in the trees, hiding was practically impossible in the floodplain, cadres contended. Peng, however, argued that fighting a guerrilla war in the plain was not only possible but that there were real advantages there. First, the plain was more productive than the mountains, which made it easier for troops to obtain military provisions. Second, guerrillas could take advantage of other natural environments for cover, such as forests, villages, brooks, ragweed, rice fields, earth mounds, and the curtain of tall green crops.[39]

In his 1943 lecture to the training units, Peng Xuefeng gave an outline of what he called the plain guerrilla tactics. They were a repertoire of military maneuvers designed to overcome an overwhelmingly superior enemy force. Soldiers were told to practice attacking in short and swift thrusts, breaking up and reassembling for concerted attacks, deception, and confusing the enemy by going around in circles.[40] The plain tactics also emphasized the use of long-range raids (*banns*), night attacks (*yeti*), and ambushes (*fiji*). Fighting a plain guerrilla war, Peng said, called for flexibility, bravery, resolution, endurance, sacrifice, and a willingness to take chances.

Guerrilla warfare, according to Peng, also required building a solid social base in the countryside. "The enemies are the city gods," he quoted a local folk song, "but we are the village deities." Guerrilla warfare, he insisted, must be grounded in the villages and must have broad mass support. Concerted attacks by regular armies, for example, had to be carefully coordinated with local militia, which could be employed as auxiliary forces to pin down the enemy. Guerrillas needed a good knowledge of enemy troop movements and a familiarity with the terrain and even with weather conditions. All this information could only be provided by local residents. The swift movement of guerrilla fighters (who could cover 100–200 *li* a day), the absolute secrecy of their whereabouts, the need for a place to assemble, to conceal forces, to shelter the sick and the wounded, all required that guerrilla fighters develop good relations with local people. Therefore, mass mobilization, Peng said, was very much a part of this type of warfare.[41]

But all this is true in theory only. Actual guerrilla fighting in the inhospitable floodplain in Yuwansu was an entirely different matter. The Communists fought two major wars in the 1940s, a three-month war against the Guomindang in 1941 and a 33-day war against the Japanese in 1943. Let us examine these two wars and Communist guerrilla warfare in action.

Fighting the Nationalists

Rapprochement between the Nationalists and the Communists lasted only very briefly. Cordial relations soon degenerated into an uneasy armed truce. By mid-1940, skirmishes between the two forces began to occur in northern Jiangsu. Chiang Kaishek's plan was to drive the New Fourth Army out of central China all the way north of the Yellow River, where the Communist forces would directly face Japanese attack. In August, Chiang therefore used his Guangxi-affiliated troops to encircle the Communists in the Huai basin. He also managed to get some Communist warlord allies to defect. In early 1941, after the GMD success in the "Southern Anhui Incident" (Wannan shibian), Chiang employed his forces to clear the western section of the Tianjin-Pukou railroad—that is, the Yuwansu border base—of Communist influence.[42] The military power he deployed—regular GMD armies, local militia, and defected warlord troops—was seven times stronger than the New Fourth Army. All of a sudden, Communist troops faced a precarious situation. At the same time, the Japanese launched a mop-up campaign against both the CCP and the GMD. It was under these ominous conditions that the Communists had to defend themselves against Nationalist attack.[43]

The GMD offensive was directed by Li Zhongren. Central China was marked out into four war zones: central Hubei, Huainan, Huaibei, and Xiangxi. Altogether, the Nationalists mobilized a total of 30 divisions and 200,000 men in the campaign. The Huaibei campaign, the one under study here, was headed by General Tang Enbo. Huaibei was subdivided into three "bandit clearance" zones.[44] In this "anti-GMD struggle" (*fan wan douzheng*), the CCP faced an overwhelmingly powerful army, one that was well trained and well armed and backed by defected warlord armies, local militia, and bandit forces.

Fighting the powerful GMD army was more complicated than Peng Xuefeng's "plain guerrilla warfare" made it out to be. The GMD army was composed of a variety of forces. The most powerful was He Zhuguo and Ma Biao's cavalry, which was highly mobile and effective in flatland fighting. The Communists avoided it by all possible means. They were not even strong enough to confront the Nationalist main armies, especially those led by Tang Enbo and Li Binxian. The party therefore ordered the New Fourth Army to engage these troops in protracted fighting using both guerrilla and mobile warfare techniques, depending on the circumstances. The Communist tactic was to concentrate on soft targets—the weak warlords and subcounty armed forces. The party's instructions were to eliminate these weak forces.

Although the party did not have enough military strength to combat the GMD armies on the battlefield, the Communists were determined to win the war on the political front. They combined military and political means to counter the GMD offensive. The party used local elections to place their "progressive gentry" in subcounty official positions. The objective was to prevent anti-Communist forces from seizing power at the local level. Simultaneously, the party drummed up a populist campaign to "detain, force out, intimidate, and settle accounts" with any gentry who went against them. The Communists also conducted an extensive patriotic campaign to discredit the GMD for not fighting the Japanese. Fortunately for the CCP, its appeal fell on fertile soil. After the GMD launched its offensive against the CCP in Yuwansu, the Japanese immediately took the opportunity to move in and conducted a mop-up campaign in Henan. In half a month, Japanese troops scored a number of victories and expanded their dominance over 14 more counties, forcing the GMD to retreat. Guomindang credibility took a nosedive, particularly in the eyes of intellectuals.

But credibility aside, the GMD had definite advantages over the

Communists. Not only were they ten times more powerful militarily, the GMD armies had been seasoned by four years of fighting against the Japanese. They also enjoyed some topographical advantages. For instance, they could make a swift thrust at the Communists and quickly retreat across the Yellow River. The CCP guerrillas, on the other hand, were confined to a narrow corridor of 50 by 200 *li*, sandwiched between the GMD and the Japanese. This strictly limited their troop mobility. The fact that the tiny strip of land the Communists controlled was too small to produce enough food to provide for a large armed force became a major problem for the Communist army.

Guerrilla tactics called for breaking up the army into smaller units to confuse and distract the enemy, yet when Communist troops did that, the GMD employed its cavalry to hunt them down individually in the flatland. Backed up against the Japanese strongholds, Communist troops were cornered and had no place to go. The Nationalists were able to use their large army effectively to engage the Communists in a "rotation warfare" (*chelun zhan*). Various GMD units took turns chasing the Communist troops and keeping them constantly on the move to wear them out. The GMD also enjoyed the support of defected warlords, who provided them with good knowledge of the terrain as well as of Communist methods of military operation. Occasionally, Communist coalition politics failed to achieve the desired results. In the eyes of some local gentry, the GMD remained the legitimate government. Moreover, GMD secret agents continuously employed the threat of political reprisal against local residents to prevent them from joining the New Fourth Army. They also told the gentry that Communist land reform would destroy their class economically and eliminate them physically.[45]

In countering the GMD offensive, the Communists were basically fighting a defensive war. As Peng Xuefeng and Deng Zihui's report indicates, the Communists had tremendous difficulties maintaining a guerrilla war against the Japanese and a mobile war against the GMD at the same time. They had to move their troops rapidly among enemy strongholds. In fact, the Communists found themselves in a very awkward position politically, victims of their own coalition politics. In order to survive and preserve their base, they were forced to fight the GMD armies, yet they could ill afford to antagonize the GMD military commanders, some of whom, they realized, could one day be won over by United Front tactics. Shortage of food presented another serious problem. The famine made it impossible to support a large force, say two regiments. With the motorized Japanese mop-up and the GMD cavalry charges working against them, the only way for the Communists to survive was to flee the area. Yet some of them did not even have enough time to do that. Others did, but returned because they found it impossible to fight a guerrilla war in unfamiliar terrain.

It was easy for military strategists to say that Communist troops should break up and reassemble for concerted attacks in guerrilla and mobile warfare, but in real fighting, coordination of troop movements always presented a problem. Cadres sometimes ignored orders to break up and flee, instead engaging in concerted attacks (for instance, in the Bangu Inn and Wan Tower battles). Sometimes the main force was ordered to close in for an attack but failed to do so. In a battle at Zhang Stockade, a small unit miscalculated enemy strength and attacked a GMD-occupied town. The unit was completely decimated by enemy forces. In another instance, after winning a battle, troops failed to leave the area "in big strides" (*da tabu*) and were crushed by GMD cavalry. In these cases, the Communists reported suffering heavy losses.[46]

Fighting a guerrilla war, as theory indicated, depended on accurate military intelligence about the enemy. But in the floodplain, where everything was in a constant state of flux, it was practically impossible to obtain that kind of precise intelligence information. Even if information got through by telegraph, the fluidity of enemy troop movements made it useless by the time it arrived. Everything depended ultimately on the mobility, resoluteness, expediency, and flexibility of individual units. Some forms of guerrilla tactics—surprise attacks, for instance—worked very well in plain warfare. The Ma Family Tower battle was a victory because the GMD never anticipated a Communist assault on a freezing, stormy night. The Communists lost four soldiers in the deadly cold. They learned that they had to catch the enemy off guard. Ninety percent of all night assaults they conducted were successful, and were carried out with little or no casualties. They also found that GMD forces dared not attack them if they hid behind Japanese strongholds.[47]

Chen Yi has said that the Fourth Division of the New Fourth Army fought mechanically. The troops were prepared for victories, but defeats often found them in "a complete mess." They never learned to back up a mobile war with guerrilla war. They lacked the ability to coordinate six or seven regiments in a concerted attack. The fighting was done mostly by the regular army because local forces were too weak. When the main force was at the front fighting the GMD armies and the Nationalists sent auxiliary forces to disrupt the Communist base, local cadres were at a loss as to how to handle the situation. Military cadres often found guerrilla and mobile warfare confusing.[48]

The counteroffensive against the GMD was a dismal failure on the whole, in spite of the fact that Peng Xuefeng insisted it was an important learning experience for the troops.[49] A number of factors worked against the Communists. They were operating in terrain enclosed by the Wo River on one side and Japanese strongholds on the other. This made troop dispersal extremely difficult. Moreover, they were confronting two strong enemies: the GMD cavalry and Japanese troops equipped with motor vehicles. Military provisions were hard to come by after the flood and the famine. The GMD "rotation warfare" wore them out and wasted much of their ammunition.[50] They suffered heavy casualties in several battles (Banbi Inn, Lo market town, and Daxiao ying market town). In the Wan Tower campaign, an entire Communist regiment was obliterated by GMD forces.

Military defeats forced the party to decide to move out of the area. Leaving behind a small force to carry on a clandestine movement, the regular army fled across the Tianjin-Pukou railroad and set up a new base (the Suwan base, examined in the next chapter) around Hongze Lake in the Huaibei area.[51] Defeat was very costly to the Communists. Deng Zihui reported that Communist troops in the area were greatly reduced and their morale was very low. The main force fled the area, and local militia either disbanded, fled, or defected. The army lost many of its firearms in the fighting. The border base was taken over by the Japanese, their collaborators, and the GMD; the Communist Party was completely destroyed. Local cadres who had not already left the area were arrested and killed by the Nationalists. Many of the so-called neutral elements, sympathizers whose relations the party had been cultivating for three years, swiftly changed sides and became enemies. Communist influence among the local people was greatly diminished. By retreating from the area, the party was able to save the cadres and preserve their main forces. The revolutionary movement in eastern Henan was temporarily put on hold. It survived as an underground movement and was only revitalized at the end of the war (see Chapter 9).[52]

Fighting the Japanese

The Japanese used two types of warfare against the Communists: mop-ups and "nibbling" wars. The mop-up campaign, usually accomplished with scorched-earth tactics, was a brutal and debilitating attack aimed at blanket destruction of enemy territories. It was a quick way of eliminating the military threat of the enemy. "Nibbling" warfare, on the other hand, was a slow encroachment on and then annexation of enemy territories. Japanese troops extended their power over enemy soil in piecemeal fashion by building a network of strongholds linked by transport lines. Their goal was to dissect the Communist base and take it over bit by bit, fragmenting the enemy's power and reducing its fighting capability. The two types of warfare complemented each other. After crippling opponents with "nibbling" warfare, the Japanese could drive home all-out mop-up attacks. The Japanese army therefore used these two strategies alternately in dealing with the Communists.

In November 1942, the Japanese launched a massive mop-up campaign against the Communists at the Henan-Anhui border. The campaign was a reprisal for the Communists' Hundred Regiments Offensive. In August 1940, the Communist Party had mobilized 300,000 soldiers in 105 regiments to attack the rail lines and strongholds occupied by Japanese troops in northern China. In that three-month offensive, the Eighth Route Army was able to inflict real damage on the Japanese, particularly on the railroads. Following the shock of the Hundred Regiments Offensive, from mid-1941 the North China Area Army, under the command of General Okamura, implemented scorched-earth tactics against Communist guerrilla bases in North China. The November 1942 Henan-Anhui offensive was part of the Japanese reprisal.[53] The military power the Japanese deployed in the mop-up was awesome: 7,000 infantry, 600 cavalry, 2 tanks, 120 armored cars, 19 boats, and 8 airplanes, all backed by various puppet forces. The campaign lasted 37 days and was planned very carefully. As early as October, the Japanese army had slowly begun encroaching on Communist territories. They first sent out a group of secret agents disguised as refugees, famine victims, peddlers, street singers, and prostitutes to scout the Communist base for intelligence. These agents infiltrated Communist schools and recruitment centers, offering C$5 for Communist newspapers. In some areas they used sex to ensnare soldiers.[54]

The Japanese strategy in the November attack was to converge on the Communists' centrally administered area. It was typical conventional warfare: driving straight into the base and employing cavalry to seek out the main Communist forces. Afterward, the Japanese army broke up into smaller units, converging on county and subcounty towns and engaging in sectional assaults. The cavalry and puppet forces were used mainly to distract the Communists, while regular Japanese troops and mechanized units encircled the base and closed in for a sudden and violent attack.

The Communists were well prepared for the Japanese mop-up. At the Second Huaibei Border Local Consultative Conference, Peng Xuefeng had warned cadres of the approaching Japanese campaign. By this time, Communist troops had been fighting GMD forces for sixteen months since the 1941 defeat, and had dramatically improved their ability in both guerrilla and mobile warfare. With constant training in daytime combat, they gradually mastered the technique of storming military fortresses. They had also acquired good knowledge of enemy military positions and strength.[55] When the mop-up finally came, Communist troops were ready. Their basic tactic was to avoid direct confrontation with the regular Japanese army. In order to do so, they broke out of the encirclement, removed their main forces from the attack, and left a small detachment behind to engage and pin down the enemy. Then, using both the main and local regular forces, the Communists conducted flanking and rear operations against the enemy. Whenever the Japanese tried to set up forts and communication lines, the Communists moved in and systematically destroyed weak targets in the outer defense line so that the enemy could not gain a foothold in the area.

Another effective tactic was to deny the Japanese troops the basic resource needed to sustain a protracted war—food. Cadres actively mobilized local citizens to evacuate the area. As they retreated, the Communists cleared the villages of all food grain and destroyed the roads.[56] The Japanese were forced to bring grain in on pack animals and ox-drawn carts. This greatly complicated logistics and burdened the troops with a considerably heavier military load. Hampered by bad roads, Japanese troop movement was severely delayed. All this was designed to prevent the Japanese from prolonging their stay in the area. The Japanese army could obtain food by plundering neighboring villages, but such predatory activities would only infuriate the civilian population and stiffen resistance, ultimately making conquest and control of the area much more costly and difficult. Japanese troops did fine-comb the area, but with the guerrillas already removed from the base, they usually closed in on empty space. Eventually, they had to pull their troops out.

To forestall Communist attacks, the Japanese had taken the tightest security precautions and heavily protected their garrison posts. Barracks were connected by trenches and guarded from watchtowers. Military strongholds were secured by several rings of outer trenches, barbed wire, logs, and reeds. Another outer ring of defense was created with puppet troops. As they were under constant military threat from the Communists, the Japanese army further tightened security measures by imposing a night curfew. The curfew in fact created a physical separation between strongholds, cutting off all possible contacts at night. The fortifications were turned into isolated islands, making it easier for Communist troops to take them out one by one. A stronghold under attack at night seldom received reinforcement from another stronghold. Mistrust between the Japanese and their collaborators made the Communist assault even easier. The two enemies carefully guarded against each other. When the Communists attacked one unit, the other units remained onlookers, sometimes even taking pleasure in the other's misfortune.

On the whole, Communist night assaults were highly effective. They were carefully coordinated by the party, with plainclothesmen serving as secret agents on the inside. Although the Japanese possessed heavy artillery, which would normally deter Communist attacks, this machinery was rendered utterly ineffective at night. By the time the Japanese spotted Communist fighters, the invaders were already too close for the artillery barrages to be effective. Communist soldiers then attacked the Japanese with hand grenades and set fire to barracks to flush out Japanese soldiers. Night attacks always put the Japanese in a completely defensive position. The party seldom launched an offensive until the Japanese had comfortably settled in their strongholds. Then Communist troops began coordinated assaults, starting with outlying strongholds. Isolating these fortresses one by one, the troops closed in, put up a blockade, cut off supply lines, and then took these bastions.[57]

Mass Mobilization in Mop-up Campaigns

As Peng Xuefeng told soldiers, guerrilla warfare required building a solid social base in the countryside. Successful counteroffensives against Japanese mop-ups depended very much on Communist ability to mobilize people at the village level. Wen Minsheng, head of the political department in the South Henan Anti-Japanese Independent Regiment, also emphasized that close cooperation with local party branches was absolutely essential for the survival of the army.[58] Peng Xuefeng also stated that a well-organized mass movement—one that included coordinating the fight with local militia, clearing fields, ferreting out spies, and disrupting communication lines—was the "decisive factor in breaking up the Japanese mop-up attacks."[59] But how did the Communists actually implement this plan?

Coordinating the Fight with Local Militia

One of the difficulties in conducting a mass-based campaign was coordination between the regular army and local armed forces. Unfortunately, not every cadre was convinced of the importance of local militarization. Some doubted whether there was really any need for militarization in a relatively peaceful centrally administered district within the Communist base. In its directives, however, the party always emphasized the crucial role of local militia. It outlined several distinct advantages of employing these militia in fighting. Local residents, it said, were always well informed about enemy troop movements. If the people identified the war as their war, the power of the masses could be limitless. Moreover, in terms of military strategy, militia forces formed small targets that were less vulnerable to enemy attack. With some coordination, these forces could be broken up and reassembled quickly. They could get close to and break away from the enemy without much attention. They were ideal material for guerrilla warfare. The most important ingredients in employing these troops were effective leadership and smooth coordination.

The party therefore adopted a couple of measures to solve these problems. To ensure smooth coordination, regular armies were instructed to work out a set of clear signals with self-defense squads. Once local forces pinned down the enemy in a fight, main forces would immediately be signaled to attack the rear and flanks of the enemy. Alternately, part of the regular army would be disguised as plainclothesmen and would mix with the self-defense squads. Under favorable military conditions, these regular soldiers would lead locals in encircling and assaulting the enemy. To instill confidence in the militia, the main force was to send one or two machine gunners or a couple of experienced target shooters, and, if need be, army officers, to lead local forces in combat. The party had acquired this practice in the Eyuwan period (see Chapter 3), when they used skillful target shooters to embolden Red Spears sectarians. Communist directives always underscored the significance of regular army leadership in local wars.

Local militia were always on alert. The party made sure that these forces were constantly combat-ready by mobilizing them in troop movements with the main force for a day or two, even in peacetime. Afterward, the militiamen were rewarded with public commendations or with supplies such as hand grenades and cases of cartridges. Peng Xuefeng told the main army that they had the duty to cultivate the militia as "apprentices."

But the success of mass mobilization depended on making the war a people's war, something local residents could relate to, so that they would not flee in a Japanese mop-up. To accomplish this, the party played on territorial attachment, community loyalty, and the people's need for physical protection. Exploiting parochial sentiment and the necessity of protecting families and property, cadres stressed "resisting the Japanese on the spot; fight a guerrilla war on the spot." The party promoted the localistic slogan "Natives of the county do not leave the county, fellows of the same district remain in their district, and fellow villagers in their villages."[60] To foster territorial attachment, militia commanders were recruited locally; military units were called by the commander's name in order to promote personal loyalty. All these measures were designed to provide troops with a sense of personal and territorial identification. According to Peng Xuefeng, the party wanted to make the militia an integral part of the masses, "inseparable as their flesh and blood."[61]

Emptying Houses and Clearing Fields

Since no combined Communist forces, main or local, could withstand the attack of the overwhelmingly powerful Japanese armies, the key to success was to organize the populace to flee. The Communist term for this was *paofan*, or "run for shelter under enemy attack." But fleeing the enemy was not a simple matter. There were always citizens who took chances, who were convinced the enemy would not attack and therefore refused to leave. Peasants who did flee sometimes headed directly toward the enemy. Although the Communists conducted evacuation exercises in peacetime, Japanese attacks always threw the population into complete disarray. Disoriented peasants huddled in large groups with their livestock and household belongings, forming an ideal predatory target for the enemy. Instead of immediately seeking shelter close by, they fled ten to twenty *li* from home. The first flight from the Japanese cost the peasants dearly; the party estimated they suffered a loss of C$22 million.[62] The party had to retrain peasants to scatter in small groups and to seek hiding places immediately. In times of emergency, all able-bodied males were ordered to leave home and sleep in caves or in the fields. They were required to sleep in groups and post sentries to watch for Japanese troops at night.

To minimize losses, cadres actively mobilized civilians to evacuate and clear the area of everything, or "to empty the houses and clear the fields" (*kongshe qingye*). The response to the Japanese, "burn all, kill all, and loot all" tactic was to "remove everything, evacuate everybody, and hide everything." This called for a detailed evacuation plan. The first item to be removed was food grain, the very lifeblood of invading troops. All grain stocks were taken from urban centers and from near major roadways and hidden in remote villages. The grain was usually buried in holes in the ground or hidden in walls in small bundles mixed with sand, making it difficult for the Japanese to burn and too heavy for the enemy to carry away. In the event that some grain was captured by the enemy, local militia, with the help of the main force, would intercept and recover it. The militia normally avoided the Japanese troops and instead attacked and frightened away the porters and animal pullers. Since Japanese soldiers could not carry the heavy loads themselves, they usually discarded the cargo. After the Japanese army departed, local people retrieved the grain.[63]

The Communists also instructed local residents to plaster their walls to prevent them from being completely burned down by the enemy. All combustible materials such as lumber, fodder, and furniture were systematically removed. The wok and the stone mill, the two utensils essential for making a meal, were hidden (the Japanese did not carry their own). Total destruction applied also to stockades, bridges, temples, even convents. The Communists realized that thorough destruction depended on the completely voluntary acquiescence of the populace. No amount of coercion could do the job. The party therefore took great care to explain to residents that all the Japanese could do to them was burn down their houses. But if they destroyed everything and denied the enemy food and water, in the end, the Japanese troops would have to leave.[64]

Security and Counterespionage Work

Communist success in countering the mop-ups owed much to the party's cooperation with local residents in evolving a system of intelligence gathering, and in taking precautions to prevent enemy infiltration. The Communists made each village an intelligence unit responsible for gathering information within a twenty-*li* area. Information was channeled upward through the district to the county, and then circulated by the party among various defense units. Using the traditional concept of the village pact (*lianzhuang hui*), the Communists integrated communities into a common defense and intelligence-sharing network.

To prevent enemy infiltration, Communist troops worked out a set of precise signals with villagers. Before Communist armies arrived at a village, a plainclothesman, usually bearing a hoe or a wooden plow (depending on the established signal), would enter the village and establish contact. Reviving the standard signals of traditional community defense, the Communists often used smoke, fire, a horn, or a gong to alert neighboring villages to impending enemy attack. This security system helped ferret out some Japanese spies, but the system suffered as a result of Communist coalition politics. During the Second United Front period, as a gesture of friendliness the Communists had several times released the spies captured by their armies. Many of these later turned out to be working for the Japanese. With increased intelligence gathering by the Japanese during the mop-up campaign, the party was forced to tighten the security system. It began to check all passersby for identification and to issue passes to travelers.

Road Destruction

Guerrilla fighting included systematic destruction of roadways to deter Japanese attacks. The success of this project was due partly to Communist organizational skill, but mostly to the Japanese threat. Local residents seldom heeded Communist calls for road destruction and usually adopted a tactic of false compliance. But once Japanese troops reached an area, communities suddenly sprang into action, and villagers actively assisted the Communists. In Huaisi, for instance, the county claimed to have mobilized 5,080 villagers and 25,394 road destroyers with its "road destruction committee." At the sound of a wooden block or a gong, local residents would march off in teams to pull up the roads. They often worked at night or after the enemy had left the area. In one month, these villagers had destroyed 7,000 *li* of roads.[65]

Peng Xuefeng pointed out that war created the most favorable conditions for mobilizing and educating the masses. "In a month of fighting, the masses have learned more than in the entire last year," he noted. "It was the wave of nationalistic struggles that carried every kind of mass work to such a high level. The fighting fettle has not subsided yet. The urgent task now is for the masses of workers and the Communist Party to strike while the iron is hot, to organize, to channel their energy in the right direction so that we can build the masses into a strong force. Indeed, it was the enemy who gave us such favorable conditions for organizing and educating the masses."[66]

A Case Study of Guerrilla Warfare: Rivereast

The counteroffensives against the Guomindang and the Japanese discussed above were short-term warfare. The GMD offensive lasted three months, and the Japanese mop-up was only a 33-day affair. Although Communist success in resisting the Japanese mop-up changed their image and boosted army morale, one military victory was certainly not enough to change the peasants' disposition toward the revolution. Peasant support for the Communist cause came from the party's skillful management of the day-to-day menace of war in the countryside. The problems of wartime insecurity affected the daily lives of the ordinary people and became their primary concern. It was the military and organizational assistance the party gave local citizens in helping them handle these problems that finally drew rural people to the Communist side. Only by examining wartime party-peasant interaction at the village level and by finding out how the Communists handled the war menace can we understand the method the CCP used to forge an alliance with the rural people. Communist activities in war-ridden Rivereast in the eastern Henan floodplain illustrate the Communist war mobilization efforts.

The Rivereast border base was originally known as the Sui-Qi-Tai area. Located at the border of Suixian, Qixian, and Taikang counties in east Henan, the base had been a Communist Red Spears mobilization region since the Northern Expeditionary period. As mentioned in Chapter 5, after the outbreak of the Sino-Japanese War, the party sent Red Spears mobilizer Wu Zhipu back home to Qixian to mobilize his fellow villagers to fight the Japanese. After recruiting a small force from the area, Wu left the base and joined Peng Xuefeng in the Eastern Expedition to consolidate Communist power in eastern Henan. Wu took with him "three detachments," leaving behind a small militia under the command of Communist leaders Ma Qinghua and Wang Jiefu.[67]

Ma and Wang continued to build the movement by creating a community defense program and drawing local notables into the defense forces. Chronic political instability in the area and deep concerns for physical safety enabled the party to integrate twenty villages in a militia known as the "Combined Regiment for Sui-Qi-Tai Anti-Japanese Self-Defense." Both Ma and Wang were killed in battle, and another local cadre, Han Dasheng, took over and in early 1940 reorganized the regiment into the "Sui-Qi Independent Regiment." After that, the Sui-Qi Independent Regiment formed the principal guerrilla force protecting the area, and kept the movement alive in this base.[68]

With the breakup of the CCP-GMD United Front in early 1941, Nationalist troops invaded the area. In order to preserve its armed forces, the party ordered the Sui-Qi Independent Regiment to pull out of the area and join the New Fourth Army at the Henan-Anhui border. Guomindang troops then occupied much of the base. The Communists lost their leader Han Dasheng in battle. To rebuild the base, the party had to create another armed force. It therefore combined a tiny force from nearby Huaiyang county with whatever local militia remained in the area to form a new unit called the Rivereast Independent Regiment (*Shuidong duli tuan*). Using this newly formed regiment, the CCP created a base in the inundated plain in the northwestern part of Taikang county. From this "water base" (*shuishang jidi*), the Communists rebuilt the movement by organizing another community defense project, known as the Rivereast Collective Defense (*Shuidong lianfang*). By integrating various flood-devastated communities into the defense program, the Communists not only sustained the revolution but also consolidated and expanded their power in the region.

In 1942 and 1943, the Rivereast base experienced the most devastating flood and famine in the history of the area. After the floodwater receded a drought occurred, followed by a plague. During this period of natural calamity, many people died of starvation. Communist soldiers and local peasants often subsisted on yams, cotton seeds, and wild vegetables. Tens of thousands of villagers fled the area. In Banmunan, 82 of the 110 families in the village vanished, all of their members dead of starvation. Cannibalism and the sale of young girls were widely practiced.[69] In order to survive, Communist troops organized hungry peasants in food raids on Japanese areas. Since many landholders had fled the area because of the flood and the land had little value, the party successfully implemented a program of land buy-back. The party also carried out an equitable tax reform. In January 1943, for administrative purposes, the base was incorporated into the Ji-Lu-Yu (Hebei-Shandong-Henan) anti-Japanese base. From then on, this floodplain base was known as "Rivereast" (*Shuidong*) because of its location just south of the Longhai railroad, on the east side of the new Yellow River. This base, essentially in the same area as the Sui-Qi-Tai base of the Northern Expedition, was sandwiched between the Japanese urban strongholds of Kaifeng and Shangqiu.

By the time the base was incorporated into the Ji-Lu-Yu region, Rivereast consisted of five small pockets of resistance, all located at county borders (southern Qixian, Qi-Tong-Chen, Kai-Qi-Tong, Sui-Tai, and northeastern Qi). The Communists controlled 850 villages, including the core (279 villages) and the periphery (571 villages). The Japanese and their puppets, on the other hand, had 166 strongholds in the region.[70] The main Communist force in Rivereast consisted of a small 1,254-man independent regiment, supported by a local militia of 682 men. Each pocket maintained a tiny armed squad, ranging from 60 to 250 men. The Japanese force in the region was also small, only 399 soldiers, but it was backed by 6,592 puppet troops.[71]

Rivereast was strategically very significant because it was located near the Beiping-Hankou and Longhai railroads. Hence, the base posed a direct threat to the Japanese-dominated transport systems. It had always been regarded by the Communists as "a dagger in the enemy's heart." Rivereast served as a bridge between the Communist bases in northern and central China, and the party therefore spent a great deal of energy and manpower preserving the base. More than 5,000 Communist guerrilla fighters sacrificed their lives defending this area. In order to maintain control of this strategic "bridge" during the civil war, the party committed seven divisions to and fought four major battles in Rivereast.[72]

The Communist armies were operating in very inhospitable terrain, but that gave them some tactical advantages. The northern part of Qi county was mostly desert and woods. The woods made guerrilla fighting possible. In the Yellow River floodplain in the south, inundation posed tremendous obstacles for conventional warfare, which helped deter enemy attacks. The rest of the area was nothing but stretches of flatland dissected by numerous small streams. For the Communist guerrillas, there were no places to hide.

Collective Defense as a Mobilization Tactic

It was in this economically depressed and inhospitable terrain that the Communists successfully sustained a revolution. They preserved the base as the strategic bridge between north and central China. But how did they manage to survive under such adverse conditions, and what mode of mobilization did they employ to get the people in the area to commit themselves to the revolution? Sun Weihe, a Communist rural mobilizer, left behind a diary that covers the short time span of a month and a half in late 1942. Although brief, this diary gives us a very clear picture of Communist mass mobilization at the subcounty level.

Sun Weihe was a Communist military commander in Shandong. In late 1942, the party transferred him to Rivereast as a deputy of the Collective Defense Office, a county-level mobilization organization. In September, Sun left Shandong and proceeded to eastern Henan. He did not arrive in Rivereast until November 20. During his one and a half month stay in Henan, Sun was all over the place, constantly moving with guerrilla forces and shifting his headquarters. In that short period he passed through 32 places, including two stockades and a township (*zhen*). He and his troops mostly stayed a day in one place; they sometimes passed through several villages in a day, but seldom spent more than four days in a single area. Through Sun's keen observations, we gain invaluable knowledge of the environment in which the Communists operated and of the methods and communal institutions they used to involve country folk in the revolution.

Sun's diary clearly demonstrates that it was the political instability and high anxiety of wartime that gave the Communists the opportunity to penetrate Rivereast villages. The places Sun passed through were utterly depressed, completely ruined by flood and fighting. For instance, an old woman in Yellow Mount Village in northern Qi county told Sun that rural villagers constantly lived under the threat of violence, from the Japanese in daytime and from bandits at night. Most of the village leaders, the *bao* heads in particular, had died in the fighting. Left behind in the 20 to 30 households in the village were only the elderly and children. Although wheat was ready for harvest, villagers had neither the manpower nor the courage to take it in. People were so fearful of troops that they went into hiding. When Sun walked into a previously bustling village like Xuhu zhuang, he found it a complete ghost town, with all the doors sealed by plaster. The wealthiest had moved away; the poor had fled the famine. Only the middle peasants, who had some means of support and a strong attachment to their property, stayed behind. Of the original 100 residences, only 30 still had survivors living in them.

It was the military raids conducted by GMD-appointed "special commissioners" (*zhuanyuan*), Sun pointed out, that inflicted the greatest damage in the countryside. These "special commissioners" were mostly warlords and bandits, the real power holders in the countryside. They were the local guerrilla forces commissioned by the Guomindang to do regional fighting. These power holders usually based themselves in a township (*zhen*) or a subdistrict (*xiang*), from which they fanned out to pillage the countryside. "Special commissioners" sent fear throughout rural areas. These predators took not only grain, livestock, and wine, but also daily necessities such as vegetable oil, soybeans, and villagers' personal belongings. Their indiscriminate looting stripped villages of everything, even the very shoes and clothes village children were wearing. No families, not even those regimental commanders, were spared in such raids.

When Sun asked an elderly lady why she did not cover her head with a towel in the cold October weather, the old woman replied that the towel had been taken away from her by the soldiers. Village women found that the best way to stop a child from crying was to tell him that a "special commissioner" was coming.[73] Another old woman, Sun reported, turned stone white, completely stupefied and trembling with fear, when she was told that GMD troops were approaching. In Mud Wall Village, to pretend that the village was deserted, all villagers went inside and escaped out their back doors. Residents of Yu Town told Sun that commissioners' armies had raided the town seven times. A *bao* head told Sun that Ma Village was saved by the New Fourth Army, which had helped them eliminate 22 bandits. Sun also reported that wealthy residents at Gaoyan had gathered all their food and belongings and taken refuge inside a stockade. But then the stockade became the favorite target of soldiers. The "special commissioner" sent his troops to raid the place, and they took everything. The wealthy folks found themselves stranded inside the stronghold without food, and were completely at a loss.

This military disruption gave the Communists the chance to build their power in the countryside. Sun reported that Communist revolutionary appeals often fell on fertile soil in the most disrupted areas. Villagers in these areas begged the party to help them build up local defenses, offering Communist soldiers food, shelter, and money to entice them to stay.[74] The Communists seized the chance to promote the idea of "collective defense" (*lianfang*) wherever they went. Yet the new Communist "collective defense" was not very different from the traditional village pact system of community defense, or the *lianzhuang hui*, a concept dating back to the Nian Rebellion period.

As in the past, the party had to work closely with existing community elites, both the gentry and the *baojia* heads, to set up a defense system. Cadres went from village to village inviting local elites to village pact meetings. In these meetings, the Communists carefully explained to rural leaders and villagers the urgency of the situation and the basic mechanics of collective defense: protection of families and common defense against bandits, warlord armies, and "traitors." The villagers then took a vow to clear their own area of "bad elements" and pledged to help each other in times of enemy attack.

The Communists then helped these villages set up "house-watching squads" (*kanjia dui*), the basic defense units. For easy identification, and to avoid attracting GMD attention, these units were known by their leaders' names or by territorial designations.[75] Normally, 30 villages came together to form a pact, which commanded a militia of 600 men (roughly 20 per village), a force large enough to withstand an average warlord army. These village pacts were then integrated into a common defense network under the direction of the Communist-dominated Collective Defense Office (*lianfang banshichu*). Below the Collective Defense Office, the party set up a hierarchy of central branches (*zhongxin hui*) and local branches (*fen hui*) as network links in towns and villages. Sun's diary shows that collective defense as a form of rural mobilization caught on quickly in this area. Sun reported that one stormy night, 600 delegates from 30 villages braved the wind and rain to attend a village pact meeting.

It was through the community defense program that the Communists could legitimately claim local resources for the revolution. The communities agreed that the cost of defense would be borne equally by all residents. Defense funding was provided by taxes collected under the traditional "equal allotment" (*tanpai*) system. Communist cadres usually worked closely with heads of the *lianbao*, *bao*, and *jia* to devise an equitable way of levying taxes. This new system gradually replaced the old disorganized and often-abused *paifan* method. The new system, once accepted by all local citizens, was then institutionalized. When a Communist unit moved into an area, its members used predetermined passwords to gain entry to a village.[76] Then the army located the guide or contact man (*loa xiang*, or fellow countryman). The unit was broken up and soldiers lodged with the peasants, usually three or four soldiers to a family. If it was a very large army, two villages would share the responsibility. The high expenses of supporting troops came out of local taxes. At the end of 1942, after a meeting of six neighborhood pacts, the Communists had worked out with community leaders a reasonable and equitably integrated tax-grain program for the support of collective defense in the area.

Collective defense was used not only for protecting communities; it was often employed by the Communists to organize neighborhoods to raid other communities for food. Communist troops frequently led hundreds of villagers in grain seizures in GMD-dominated areas. At one time, they intercepted 30 cartloads of grain a "special commissioner" had seized from a neighboring village. After retaining part of it, the party distributed the rest through the neighborhood pact. After a military victory, when morale was high, the Communists often propagated their ideas among the local populace. On such occasions they also held public trials of bandits or corrupt officials.

By addressing local needs for collective security, the Communists succeeded in subverting the GMD social base in the countryside and in building strong popular support, mobilizing rural residents to commit themselves to the Communist cause, and sustaining the revolution in the area. In villages that belonged to their defense network, Communist troops were able to move around freely. The party could effectively mobilize villagers to gather intelligence and to care for the sick and wounded. In these villages, they could lawfully claim peasants' agricultural surplus as military provisions (this was always done in the name of community defense).[77] Villages that refused to participate in collective defense often lost out and were raided by the enemy.[78] Despite this, the Communists were not always successful in getting villages to join the defense program. In Daxing zhuang, a prosperous village located near the main roadway, the Communist appeal for common defense elicited little response, despite strong local anti-Japanese feelings. At times, effective Nationalist propaganda completely negated Communist appeals. In some cases, cadre misconduct, such as beating villagers or seizing items like oil and salt from peasants, alienated the people.[79] On the whole, when the defense program was in place, villagers benefited collectively from a relatively peaceful environment. Guomindang-affiliated warlord armies usually avoided confronting Communist troops and seldom attacked these villages.

The community defense program thus became a very popular and effective grass-roots mobilization tactic, particularly in the war-ravaged Rivereast area.[80] Sun Weihe concluded his diary by pointing out the effect of the program in transforming Communist power in the area at the end of 1942. "The nature of our work has changed," he wrote, "from simply fighting military battles to actually seizing political power, from being led to leading the people, and from having no administrative responsibilities to taking charge of villages." The defense program had dramatically changed the revolutionary movement, from simply fighting guerrilla wars to ruling the area. Collective security enabled the party to build its political authority and to anchor it deeply in the countryside, which eventually became the very engine that propelled the Communists to national power.

Problems of Fighting a War in Rivereast

Despite their success in mass mobilization through collective defense, fighting a war in an area of flood and famine presented the Communist Party with tremendous difficulties, ranging from an inadequate food supply to dampened army morale and problems of recruiting and training cadres. The Rivereast Independent Regiment left behind two reports (1943 and 1944) that give us some idea of the overwhelming problems the Communists faced at the time.

In 1943, the Communists had 1,936 soldiers in their regiment in Rivereast (1,254 in the main force and 682 in the local forces). The army operated in 571 villages in the area. The Japanese, on the other hand, occupied 166 strongholds and had an army of 6,991 men, 399 Japanese and 6,592 puppet soldiers. (Figures on the GMD forces are unavailable.) The Japanese and their puppet forces possessed three times the military power of the Communists. Skirmishes between the Communists and the Japanese or GMD occurred frequently. The Rivereast Independent Regiment is reported to have conducted 276 battles in 1943. They killed 1,023 enemy soldiers and captured a great deal of firearms and ammunition. The Communists themselves suffered 260 casualties. The guerrilla combat took various forms: offensives, minor encounters, surprise attacks, defensive moves, enemy attacks, ambushes, pursuit attacks, and interceptions. The majority of encounters were either offensives, surprise attacks, or defensive moves.[81] The standard tactics adopted by the Independent Regiment were concerted attacks against the GMD and dispersal of the regiment in Japanese mop-ups.

The Communist movement, however, was severely hampered by flood and famine. The 1942 drought had seriously damaged crops and produced a great famine in Rivereast in 1943. Many people died of starvation, and bodies littered the area. Even the rich, such as owners of 200 *mu* of land, had problems surviving. In some villages, peasants fled the famine in groups, seriously reducing the tax base for the Communists.

Economic misery hit the Communists, too. Depleted of its food resources, the army stopped paying the soldiers. Cadres and soldiers barely survived on yam leaves, wheat bran, and seedlings. Each soldier was given a ration of four *liang* (200 grams) of grain every other day. Peanut cakes were reportedly considered a gourmet food. Cadres caught eating a steamed bun (*wowotou*) faced severe criticism by the party in struggle sessions. Even high-ranking officers had to subsist on yams. Many starved to death. Commanders were forced to sell their horses, and daily necessities such as oil and salt, to pay the peasants to keep the grass-roots United Front alive.[82] And Communist troops devoted all their energy to one activity and one activity alone: finding food. Usually it was obtained through predatory activities, such as raiding GMD-occupied areas (*zhengliang*, as the Communists called it). Even food raids, though, were becoming increasingly difficult to conduct. In the beginning, a platoon of soldiers could raise enough food for a company. But with increased security in enemy zones, the party now had to mobilize as many as 1,000 men in each food raid. For the moment all other activities came to a complete halt.

Another urgent task for Communist troops was providing peasants with adequate protection against enemy attacks during harvest. This was usually achieved by launching preemptive strikes against the enemy to cripple its forces before they could seize the crops.[83] In 1943, the Communists conducted two successful strikes against local pro-GMD forces to protect their crops. One battle lasted only three hours before the pro-GMD troops fled. The GMD learned from the mistake and adopted a different approach. In the second encounter, the Nationalists deployed 1,500 men to capture a town and set up a stronghold. They then dug trenches and made preparations for war. The CCP were too busy harvesting and ignored these enemy activities. The GMD forces then emerged from their stronghold and attacked, but the Communists somehow managed to defeat the invaders, reducing the enemy forces by a third.

Out of desperation, in October 1943, GMD-appointed "special commissioners" again resorted to their usual defense tactic and broke the dikes. This tactic always worked. Floodwater gushed out of the Yellow River banks and washed away two insurgents' pockets, forcing the Communists to evacuate and resettle peasants in the centrally administered area. The main force was ordered by the party to move to dry land in northern Qi county. One company was left behind to rebuild the dikes and continue the mobilization. Another unit was told to seek high ground and set up temporary posts on any spot they could find. GMD dike breaking was highly damaging to the revolutionary movement; the flood reduced the Communist base practically by half. But such rash actions also tarnished the GMD image. Flood victims, antagonized by such actions and dislocated by the flood, became more committed to the Communist revolutionary cause. Even under these adverse conditions, in 1943 the Communists were able to recruit 226 more men into their militia and to obtain 79 more guns.[84]

The Japanese launched three offensives against the Communist base during this time. The first was a motorized attack. Fortunately, Communist troops managed to break the encirclement and flee, but they lost their leader, Tang Kewei, who jumped off a cliff when chased by the Japanese troops. The May Japanese offensive was conducted by 1,000 Japanese and puppet troops, both infantry and cavalry. The invading army suddenly doubled its size when a pro-GMD army defected to the Japanese. With this strong combined force, the Japanese seized a large section of Communist territory and set up 30 strongholds there. The offensive reduced the Communist base by a third. Afterward, the invading Japanese army backed up its effort with a "nibbling campaign."

The October mop-up was different from the previous two. It began a couple of weeks before the actual attack, with a rumor campaign and some feints by the Japanese. Then the Japanese launched a concerted attack from an entirely different direction. Unable to fight 900 men and 27 motor vehicles, the only choice for the Communists was to break out of the encirclement. The Communist army was saved by a lack of coordination between Japanese punitive forces and their puppet garrison troops. After the puppet forces were defeated by the Communists, they refused to engage in any more battles. The Japanese occupied the area for a month or so. But in December, the puppet troops moved out of the area to fight in the north. Without the backing of these troops, the Japanese forces could not stay on forever. They soon moved out of the area and the Communist forces instantly moved back in, eliminated the remaining weak puppet troops, and started rebuilding their bases.

Although Communist troops successfully evaded and survived the Japanese mop-ups, repeated shrinkage of the base eroded the Communists' means of support. Troops were forced to live off local people. "The people are our natural providers," the Independent Regiment report states. "A brave man with a gun can get food wherever he goes."[85] This is how the Communists described the *paifan* system of receiving handouts from peasants. Acute food shortage during the spring famine of 1943 made the party abandon any coordinated measures and adopt a laissez-faire policy of raising troop provisions. Commanders were individually responsible for feeding their own units. During the first six months of 1943, the stated party policy was "random collection and centralized distribution," the purpose of which was to have at least some form of centralized food distribution for the army, regardless of where and how commanders obtained their provisions. But the practice reportedly ended up as "random collection and individual consumption," that is, every man for himself. It was only after the fall harvest, when the food shortage eased a bit, that the Communists could set up an office and began to centralize army provisions.

Food was not the only visible shortage. In an economically depressed floodplain with hardly any factories, the army found it extremely difficult to obtain a regular supply of uniforms. Soldiers rarely got one basic uniform a year, not to mention underclothing, socks, or padded cotton vests. Soldiers were seen wearing their quilted uniforms in the summer heat because that was the only clothing in their possession. Military provisions and supplies could sometimes be obtained from other sources: friendly allies, gentry contributions, fines on "evil landlords," and captured puppet troops. Even with that, the army always lacked something. Under these harsh conditions, soldiers continually had to make do, for instance using bayonets as kitchen knives and cotton jackets as saddles. There were reports of waste and corruption. Commanders and soldiers were repeatedly criticized by the party for their "bad guerrilla behavior" (*youji xiqi*).[86]

Famine, military defeats, and repeated evacuations greatly dampened army morale. Continuous combat made soldiers mechanical and numb and often created chaos and confusion. Commanders were sometimes unable to decide whether to fight or to run. According to the 1943 Independent Regiment report, 80 percent of the fighting lacked any sort of plan.[87] One intoxicated commander gave the order for an attack of the GMD. In the typical Red Spears style of fighting, another commander bared his shoulders, shouted abuse at his enemy, and then led the soldiers in a charge. Troops often drifted freely and aimlessly, according to the report. They became so used to orders to seek cover that they completely forgot their duty to fight and recover the base. The segmented nature of the base made military coordination difficult and bred what the Communists called "unitism" (separatism). Each Communist base acted as if it were an isolated resistance area fighting its own separate war. On the whole, the regular army did most of the fighting. Local militia were mostly ineffective and often suffered heavy losses in battle.

Army coordination under such conditions was practically impossible. With the party driven out of its base, and with the constant breakup and reassembling of troops characteristic of a guerrilla war, liaison work and the chain of command were thrown into complete disorder. In the first seven months of fighting in 1943, there were actually two command centers. Southern Qi county received orders from the Collective Defense Office (*lianban*), while northern Qi county was under the command of the First Battalion. The party soon realized that unless it created a clear structure of authority and set up liaison points, this state of confusion was likely to persist. However, it was not until July that the party was able to integrate its bases and come up with a command structure. In the new system, leadership still rested with the regiment. A hierarchy of liaison centers was established to hold the base together: a central station (*zhongzhan*) for the entire Rivereast border area, and a branch station (*zhizhan*) for each pocket (north Qi county, west Qi county, and so forth), which in turn oversaw a number of substations (*fenzhan*). After the floodwater receded, a new string of branch stations was set up along the river. Even so, cadres were still confused. For instance, a branch station liaison man, who was supposed to be a secret agent, exposed himself by publicly organizing a Collective Defense Office, and was later arrested by a Japanese puppet.[88]

Hasty and indiscriminate recruitment of cadres in wartime severely undermined the quality of the army and the caliber of the cadres themselves. The Communists listed a number of frequently committed offenses: beating and scolding people, requesting leave to go home, saying things in an irresponsible manner, exhibiting strong familial attachment, being corrupt or politically unreliable, defecting, getting married without informing the party, and executing people without party permission.[89] These cadres were highly mixed, mostly middle-aged natives recruited after the outbreak of the Sino-Japanese War. Many had received little or no education or training; others had enough education to be able to read a newspaper. Even though 84 percent were Communist members and many reportedly had strong faith in the party, economic hardship and practical reality in times of war and famine forced them to look out for the interests of themselves and their families first.[90] For many, the immediate problem was survival. Desperate for food, a cadre in southern Qi county slaughtered a peasant's draft animal. Many bargained with the party for money and other material benefits before taking on a task.[91]

Political instability and constant troop movement made military training and reorganization an immensely difficult task. Guerrilla fighting required that the army to be broken up into small units of no more than 150 men. These tiny companies and battalions were scattered all over the place and seldom had the opportunity to come together for reorganization. During the spring famine, practical necessity forced these troops to spend all their time and energy finding food. Soldiers normally slept in the daytime and raided enemy strongholds at night. The army was constantly on the move, which made training impossible. The party realized that soldiers could take on training only after the basic problem of the food shortage had been solved, so it ordered units to concentrate on food raids one week and spend the next in training. Short-term drills were given in deserted areas, with the units taking turns.

After the autumn harvest, the situation began to change. The problem of provisions eased slightly. Soldiers then gathered for training in the basics of guerrilla fighting, such as wheat-field and village combat. But changing peasant soldiers was no easy task. Impetuosity and romanticism were deeply ingrained in the minds of these guerrilla fighters. Peasants were convinced that they only needed courage and determination to be good guerrillas. Many therefore refused to participate in training, and the party had to exert its authority and sometimes use coercion to get them to accept military training.[92]

Revolutionary Transformation: From Guerrilla Base to Anti-Japanese Resistance Base

Despite the fact that their base was greatly reduced by the Japanese mop-up and the GMD-made flood in 1943, Communist influence did not subside in the area. Of the 571 villages under their control, the Communists reported losing only 19 (16 where they had regular military operations and 3 where they had smaller operations). They clearly still maintained a strong influence in the villages. Their armed forces actually increased by 12 percent. In the following year, the Communists were able to convert Rivereast from a guerrilla base (*youji genjudi*) into an anti-Japanese resistance base (*kang Ri genjudi*). The regular army nearly doubled its size, from 1,936 in 1943 to 3,728 in 1944. The base itself expanded to embrace neighboring Ningling, Zhecheng, and Shangqiu counties. The total number of villages under Communist dominance was 815, and by August, Communist governments were established in seven counties. By the end of the year the area had been stabilized politically.[93] What caused the turnaround? The transformation was brought about partly by the changing international situation and partly by effective Communist grass-roots mobilization.

But in the beginning of 1944, the military situation in Rivereast remained extremely tense. The much-reduced Communist base was sandwiched between two roadways dotted with Japanese strongholds.

The Japanese made another effort to rid the area of Communist influence once and for all, ordering puppet troops to attack the Communists and clear them out of Qi county. Intense fighting ensued. In January alone, there were 27 clashes between the Communists and Japanese-affiliated forces. Simultaneously, GMD armies plundered the area. These offensives caused heavy damage to key Communist base areas, and many villages were completely deserted. Some GMD armies made a pact with Japanese puppet Meng Zhaohua and planned a joint attack on the Communists. Faced with the prospect of an attack by a more powerful force, both the party and the military reportedly went into a panic.[94]

But, by early spring, both the international and national situations had shifted in favor of the Communists. The Japanese had expanded the Sino-Japanese War into a Pacific war. In April, they had mobilized 50,000 men in the Zhongyuan Campaign against the GMD. The withdrawal of Japanese troops from eastern Henan completely redefined the military situation there. It instantly lifted the military pressure on the Communists. By then, most of the puppet troops had retreated. Those that remained lacked the military capability to defend themselves and thus became "soft targets" for Communist attacks. Timid and frightened, these sundry forces joined in alliances and held tenaciously to their strongholds.

Without Japanese military backup, these local commanders lost their soul. Many lacked confidence and the will to fight. Some puppets, including Meng Zhaohua, became inactive. Meng decided to delay his attack until "the sorghum is in" in autumn.[95] Another puppet, Zhang Lanfeng, became completely immobilized; his military organization, hampered by internal dissension, began to disintegrate. Puppet bandits like Song Anjie only made a lot of noise. Song reportedly forbade villagers to conduct "Communist activities" within 30 *li* of his base, but he did nothing to prevent or punish such activity. All these commanders had one thing in common: without the Japanese armies, they were incapable of dealing with the Communists militarily. Once the Communists defeated one party in a puppet alliance, the rest would flee and the pact would fall apart.

Taking advantage of the vacuum created by the Japanese retreat, the party instructed all Communist forces to make a concerted effort to recover the strongholds taken away by puppet forces.[96] Accordingly, the Communist army changed its tactic to a more aggressive one of offensive warfare against the puppets and annihilation of pro-GMD forces.[97] In a summer offensive, Communist troops captured seven strongholds.

The battle against Meng Zhaohua was a resounding victory and brought about a complete turnaround in the military situation in the area. Lacking armed men after the Japanese pullout, Meng, as mentioned, put off his assault. In autumn, he finally assembled a medley of local troops from the counties of Suixian, Qixian, and Taikang and launched an attack against the Communists. But these heterogeneous armed groups not only distrusted each other, they had never fought together. The Communists accurately predicted that reinforcement from the Japanese in Shangqiu was not likely to come because Suixian was 100 *li* away. The party decided to fight, and it won. The battle lasted only one day. The Communists captured quite a few arms, including a cannon. They then used this newly acquired firepower to eliminate other pro-GMD and puppet forces in the area.[98]

Military success on the battlefield did not alone drastically transform the Communist image in the eyes of the peasantry. It was in common defense against enemy grain raids (*qiangliang*) that the Communists built the long-lasting relationship between the party and the peasants that eventually formed a solid base for the Communist triumph in this area. In the "Chronology of Major Events of the Rivereast Independent Regiment in 1944," the Communists listed fourteen major grain raid defense operations undertaken with villagers.[99] In one instance, on January 27, a GMD-affiliated army (*tuwan*, or local "reactionary" force) led by Zhang Guorong launched three grain raids on He Village. He was repelled by the Taikang Communist forces. Most of the time, Communist troops successfully helped residents defend their locality against invaders. Sometimes they were unsuccessful. On October 13, Suixian puppet troops managed to capture 20,000 *jin* of grain in one raid against a village. But through such collective defense operations, the party won the support of and tightly cemented its relations with peasant villagers.

Conducting operations against enemy grain raids allowed the Communists to gradually perfect their tactics of grass-roots mobilization. First, the Communist Party set up mobilizing teams called "military work teams" to penetrate enemy-occupied areas, using the flood grain raids to arouse anti-GMD and anti-puppet sentiment among the local people. Second, through trial and error, the CCP acquired a good knowledge of enemy troop movement in grain raids. For instance, puppet troops had been leaving their stronghold in Fu market town in Qi county daily to seize peasants' grain. The Communists carefully analyzed their activities and mobilized three companies to ambush them. They finally annihilated them at Song Jitun. In Yu town, a very productive wheat area, the Communists mobilized two crack troops to help peasants defend the area against Japanese grain raids.

The Communist Party achieved a number of goals through these operations. Collective defense not only gave the peasants badly needed protection against enemy menace, but also safeguarded Communist resources necessary for sustaining the revolution.[100] Common defense also allowed the Communists to broadly expand their influence in enemy-occupied zones. Although Japanese puppets continuously used mop-ups and grain raids to deprive the Communists of resources, and continued to pressure cadres to defect by threatening their families with reprisal, the Communists combatted these puppet actions by actively using the issue of common defense to mobilize peasants in village pacts and by holding "anti-bully" campaigns against Japanese collaborators.

These grain raid resistance operations were carefully coordinated by the party and included Communist propaganda and production campaigns. Immediately following a successful operation, the party initiated a propaganda drive to "settle accounts with those who exploited the people" (the party conducted such an "account-settling" campaign after Meng Zhaohua was defeated by the Sui-Qi-Tai forces). After the flood receded, the "military work teams" called on flood victims to return to their home villages and begin spring planting "so that their land would not be taken away by the puppet troops and offered to Japan." As an inducement for peasants to return, Communists loaned seed grain (probably seized in anti–grain raid actions) to the cultivators. The loan program greatly cemented relations between the party and flood victims, and in turn strengthened the collective defense movement. By promoting collective security and production, the Communists created solid village communities committed to the revolutionary cause. Gradually, puppet troops, such as those in Longqu and Gaoxian, found themselves unable to raid communities for provisions because of strong local resistance; they eventually gave up and moved out of the area. Communist propaganda was so effective that when Rivereast was invaded by locusts from the GMD-occupied area west of the Yellow River, peasants blamed the Nationalists for the natural disaster.

At the end of 1944, the party further integrated the programs for local defense and agricultural production. Soldiers and peasants were instructed to form mutual aid teams to increase production and to fight. The party popularized the saying "While puppet battalion commanders watch the show, Communist battalion commanders plow the land." The party also drummed up support for fighting and farm production in a popular song:

Desolate village after desolate village
We fight and open up land
Give us a home by leveling the field
And prosperity by reclaiming wasteland
Weightier than Mount Tai the New Fourth's task must be
Comparable to King Yu's accomplishment in those days,
the army's achievement is.[101]

With a friendly party-peasant relationship and the enthusiasm to produce and fight, the Communists succeeded in mobilizing peasants to bring 10,000 *mu* of land into production. It was by depriving the puppets of food resources through effective anti–grain raid operations, Communist reports insisted, that the revolutionary outcome was ultimately determined. Without adequate food to support their troops, puppet forces were unable to expand.[102] And it was the shift in the international situation that directly altered the power balance between the Communists and their enemies, giving them the chance to seize power in the area.

War, Political Appeal, and Peasant Organization in Rural Mobilization

Let us come back to Johnson's theory of "peasant nationalism." Peasants are involved in revolutions neither because of a desire for a new national society nor because they are influenced by radical visions. Most peasants are indifferent to political debate and nationalistic issues that do not affect them directly. They participate in revolutions because of concrete and immediate goals. Then how did the Chinese peasants transcend preoccupation with agricultural labor, parochialism, and platitudes to become involved in the fate of the nation? Does Johnson's functional approach to nationalism explain the shift? Did the peasants respond to Communist appeals because Communist "organizational activities structured the peasants' response to the war in a nationalistic fashion"?[103]

There is no doubt that the revolution the Communists promoted was both a nationalist and a social revolution. In mobilizing the peasant masses, the party placed equal emphasis on nationalistic and economic appeals. In his report on the work with the masses, Communist mobilizer Wu Zhipu stated, "When we mobilize the masses, no doubt we have to have the national interests in mind, but we also have to have class interests in mind."[104] With this statement, Wu urged cadres to combine national and class interests in grass-roots mobilization. For the peasantry, the two were inextricably linked. When Wu spoke of national interests that affected the lives of the peasantry, he was referring to the potent threat of war, the problems of political instability, and the economic hardship associated with the Japanese invasion. Japanese aggression was always accompanied by a violation of peasants' physical security; the ferocity of its violence and severity of its destruction had tremendous impact on peasants' lives. Japanese imperialism caused a major dislocation of the peasantry that resulted in the creation of a large body of free-floating peasants, many of whom eventually drifted into the Communist camp. Social and economic disruption provided the Communists with the political opportunity to mobilize peasants to defend themselves against the Japanese terror.

It is possible to argue that the brutal Japanese occupation of the region and their harsh reprisals against the peasantry precluded any peasant accommodation with the Japanese, as Johnson has contended. But the peasants had another political alternative: siding with the legitimate Nationalist authorities. The reason for the peasants' unwillingness to seek accommodation with the GMD can only be explained by the boisterous behavior of GMD allies, in particular the GMD-commissioned warlord and bandit guerrilla forces. For the peasantry, the GMD image was greatly tarnished, not so much by their policy of "waiting in preparation" for the Japanese invasion, but, more importantly, by the flooding they produced and the unruly behavior and predatory activities associated with their affiliated forces.

The Communists did their best to capitalize on Guomindang behavior. They blamed the GMD for the breakdown of the United Front and the resulting skirmishes, and also for turning its guns against its own people. The party portrayed the Nationalist government as capitulationist. Communist propaganda campaigns frequently tied Japanese imperialists and undisciplined GMD troops together as China's twin evils, the same way that they had simultaneously denounced warlordism and imperialism in an earlier period. In their propaganda, Communist troops claimed they were "determined to drive away the Japanese bandits and the puppets, those who burned, killed, kidnapped, and plundered the people, and to clear out the warlord armies and local bandits so as to swiftly establish an anti-Japanese political authority in the area." They portrayed themselves as defenders of the peasantry against the evils of GMD armies and foreign invaders. Defeating GMD guerrilla forces was nationalistically linked with defending peasants against Japanese invaders.

How did the peasants make the transition from traditional local politics to modern national politics? According to Johnson, peasants became functionally nationalistic through participation in the fight against the Japanese. Peasants were willing to commit themselves to a nationalist movement only when that movement addressed their immediate and concrete interests. Eugene Weber has observed, "The peasants lent an ear when things plainly affected their own lives."[105] Chinese peasants were able to rise above their limited interests to a new political horizon, and to embrace nationalistic feeling, only when national interests and their personal interests happened to converge.

In eastern Henan and Rivereast, the coincidence of national and individual interests frequently revolved around a common concern about external threat and collective security, both at the national and personal levels. The Communists addressed peasant security concerns by helping them evolve a collective defense against any parties, be they Japanese, puppets, or GMD-affiliated troops, who made outrageous claims on peasant production and destroyed the families and property of rural cultivators. The Communists unceasingly propagated the problems associated with war and Japanese aggression, such as wartime anarchy, rural violence, the brutality of Japanese reprisals, outlawry, execution of *bao* heads, heavy extraction from the people, as a means to mobilize the peasants in collective defense. Their propaganda constantly contrasted the behavior of GMD and Japanese armies with that of disciplined Communist troops. They repeatedly claimed that in the eyes of the peasantry, they were the "most civilized troops under heaven."

In their propaganda in eastern Henan, the party never ceased to use such concepts as collective security, family loyalty, and community attachment to appeal to the peasantry. One piece of propaganda literature stressed self-reliance: "It is better to rely on yourself than on heaven and earth. Organize self-defense corps; arm and protect your hometown."[106] In an open letter to the Yuwansu people in 1944, the New Fourth Army appealed to peasants: "Today, the Yuwansu border area is the rear area of the rear area. In order to achieve our goals, we have to mobilize everyone to set up our own armed forces and our own organizations. With the help of the regular armies, we can create our own local self-defense. We can organize our own militia. Join the armies. Our goal is to protect our families, our hometown, and our nation. Consolidate the rear area and help out on the front line."[107]

In this letter, the Communists tried to help peasants transcend the locality and relate to a broader unit, the nation. By pointing out that the function of physical protection must be extended from the microcosm of the family, to the intermediate unit of one's home territory, and finally to the macrocosm of the nation state, the party assisted peasants in rising above the limits of their parochial feelings. Local self-defense was intimately connected with the broader function of civilian-military cooperation in the resistance war against Japan. Thus the Communists used external threats to arouse nationalistic feeling among the peasantry.[108] But one should not, as Johnson has done, over-romanticize the response of the peasants to the Communists' nationalistic appeals. Whatever national concepts the peasants might have acquired during the war, they were extremely limited. It was a rudimentary ideological expression based on the concept of common opposition to a foreign foe. On the other hand, there is no doubt that the Communists did use political appeals effectively to mobilize the peasantry.

But do peasants have the organizational capacity for collective action? Which communal institutions in Chinese peasant society gave the peasants their organizational strength? Which did the Communists tap for collective revolutionary action? In eastern Henan, it was those community institutions such as clan bands, village pacts, and neighborhood pacts that served as the organizational basis for peasant collective action.[109] These were the institutions traditionally used by Chinese rebels to mobilize peasants to challenge state power. The Communists used the same institutions as the basis for uniting peasants for self-defense.

There was usually a considerable degree of community solidarity in Chinese villages. The village had always been a collective unit sharing certain communal tasks such as famine relief, water control, and crop watching. Villagers were also obligated to collectively defend their community against bandits, warlord armies, and tax collectors. Communal units such as *bao* and *jia* were traditional official tax units, corporately liable for delivery of cash and grain to the government. When the Japanese designated the neighborhood pacts as tax units during the war, they made this community institution the ideal collective unit for Communist mobilization, directed this time not toward the state, but toward the foreign intruders.

The basic framework for collective action had always been present in Chinese village communities. What the CCP provided were leadership and coordination. The heightened sense of insecurity and external threats gave the Communists the chance to activate these collective institutions. The party simply organized them into effective military units under the collective defense program. In the revolution, these solid community institutions were not used for opposition to landlords or to fight for class interests. Rural elites and ordinary peasantry acted collectively to pursue common interests. Community institutions were employed by the Communists mostly as organized political and military forces for power building and power seizure.

Even though the Communists were able to tap communal institutions and to mobilize the masses in collective defense, fighting two major enemies with overwhelming military superiority at the same time undoubtedly brought severe damage to Communist armies and confusion to Communist bases. The GMD enjoyed several political and tactical advantages over the Communists: numerical strength, better equipment, favorable terrain, and the image of legitimacy. The Communists were in fact fighting with one hand tied behind their backs, because the Communist Party emphasized the United Front and winning the support of "middle-of-the-roaders" in the GMD and Japanese armies. Enemy repression also effectively denied the Communists vital food resources and caused chaos and confusion among the troops, making military coordination virtually impossible.

Yet it is surprising how resilient and resourceful the Communists were in the face of such odds. By using local security concerns to build a sturdy social base, the Communists became well entrenched in the countryside and maintained staying power in the villages. They skillfully employed the guerrilla elusion tactics of "running and hiding" to avoid being decimated by superior enemy forces. Most of the time they emerged from battle largely unharmed. Their enemies usually failed to destroy the Communist fighting capability. And the Communists frequently adapted and survived by fighting inconclusive wars. They conducted defensive operations and conserved their resources. They avoided major engagements and used surprise counterattacks on soft targets. They effectively used mass evacuation and blanket destruction to deny the enemy of resources. They disrupted enemy supply lines to prevent a prolonged enemy stay.

Once the enemy left an area, the Communists immediately organized peasants to move back and rebuild the villages. The relationship between the party and the peasantry was based on defense cooperation. Japanese atrocities and the brutal occupation never broke the people's will. Instead, the Japanese occupation generated rage and village cohesion and stiffened local resistance. Peasants refused to close ranks with the Nationalists because of the poor discipline of GMD-affiliated guerrilla forces and their widespread abuse of power. Under Communist leadership, villagers acted collectively to address the problems of rural insecurity. And as Daniel Little has pointed out, collective defense is a clear example of a nonexcludable public good.[110] It gave the communities under attack a shared interest. Collective defense provided the Communists with the framework for rural collective action.

CHAPTER 7

Revolutionary Reconstruction: The Huaibei Lake Area

Revolution is not merely a process of destruction or dismantling of an outdated system. A revolution also involves rebuilding and reconstruction. For the Communists, two monumental tasks of the revolution in Huaibei were alleviating poverty in the region and rebuilding it economically. This required channeling the energy of as many people as possible into revitalizing the regional economy, reclaiming land, building irrigation facilities, and mobilizing the peasants to produce. This also meant that the revolutionaries had to address rural social and economic problems and give peasants the right incentives to commit themselves to revolutionary tasks. The revolutionaries therefore had to enact tax schemes to considerably lighten the peasants' burden and to eliminate the great income gap between rich and poor. In doing so, they were forced to go against certain class interests and to destroy the economic power of the rural upper class.

Another task the Communists faced was reintegrating and rebuilding the communities socially. Social reforms pitted class against class, and sometimes worked against integrative goals. Current studies of peasant-based revolution in China have often focused too much attention on party's class conflict policies.[1] Yet, in order to involve all agrarian classes and communities in the collective rebuilding of the economy, the Communists had to bring classes to a compromise and to organize isolated and sometimes rival communities in working for a common goal. Through accommodation and arbitration, the party, acting as a mediator, persuaded divergent parties and groups to participate collectively. It had to define collective goals and mediate between groups separated by vested interests. In this way, it could reduce the social forces that obstructed change. It had to persuade divided communities that the Communist-inspired program would bring benefits to all concerned. The party had to be an agent for change and a force for integration. It was by welding together the elements of a diffuse society that the Communists created power and established a legitimate political authority for themselves at the local level. It was only after the Huaibei base had been sufficiently consolidated, with the Communists firmly in control, that the party was able to move more in the direction of class-based policies. In a peasant-based revolution, the Communists had to play two distinct and yet complementary roles, those of social revolutionary and social harmonizer. In this chapter, we examine the Communist effort in revolutionary reconstruction of the Huaibei lake area.[2]

Ecological Conditions

The Huaibei base (also known as the Huaibei Suwan or Wan dongbei border base) was located south of the Longhai railroad, east of the Grand Canal, north of the Huai River and west of the Tianjin-Pukou (Jinpu) railroad along the border of Jiangsu and Anhui provinces (see Map 5). It was a segment of the larger Communist Yuwansu (Henan-Anhui-Jiangsu) anti-Japanese base. The base was enclosed by three Japanese strongholds—Huaiyin, Tongshan, and Bengbu. Watered by the Huai River, the base was a relatively fertile lake area, rich in soybeans, mung beans, peanuts, cotton, and sesame seeds. Its forests supplied lumber. Hongze Lake yielded reeds, fish, lotus roots and seeds, gorgon fruit, and daylilies. These were the main exports from the area. The base had once been an important salt trading center and the main salt supply routes for three regions—northeastern Anhui, central Hubei, and western Henan—all passed through the border base. But the salt trade, together with its distribution points, had been destroyed by the Japanese troops. The legitimate salt industry, which had once provided a profitable livelihood for the peasantry, was extinct.[3] As in all border regions, salt smuggling had always been and continued to be a lucrative trade for rural cultivators and a problem for local government.[4]

Although a productive area on the whole, the region was far from uniform. Certain sections were ravaged by flooding from the Yellow and Huai rivers. According to Communist statistics, seven of the eight Communist-controlled counties suffered from constant flooding. The total inundated area in 1944 was 15,492 *qing*.[5] The whole base was dissected by numerous small streams. The majority of properties were covered by floodwater when the GMD broke the Yellow River dike. Siyang, a county bordering on Hongze Lake, flooded "nine out of every ten years." In 1942, the Communist government found that over 30 percent of the population in this area was on the verge of starvation.[6]

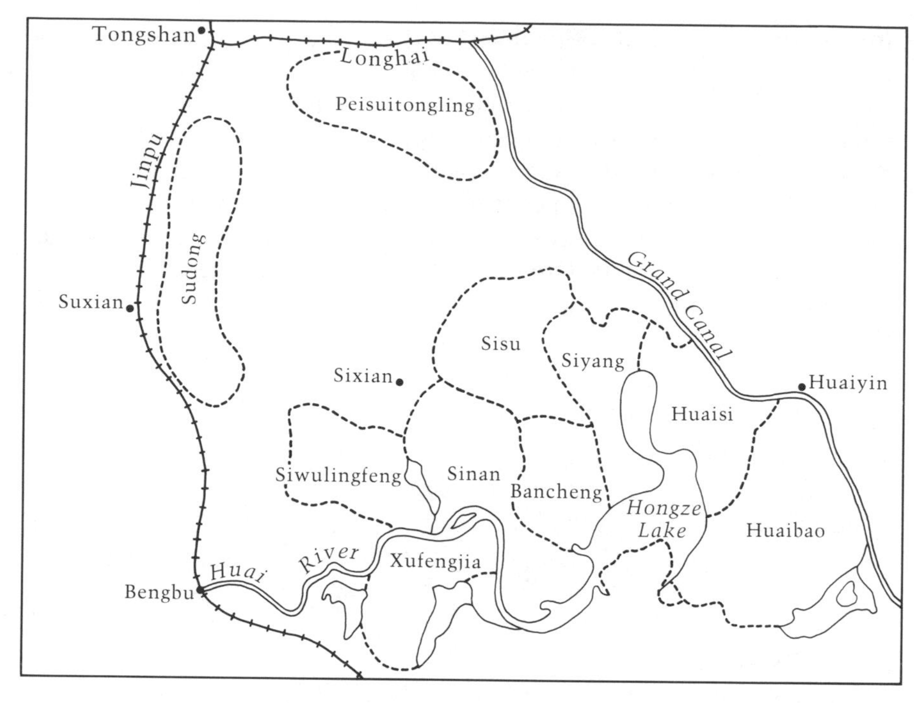

Map 5. Huaibei Suwan border base.

The CCP found flooding the most pressing problem they confronted in Huaibei. A November 1941 party survey of six subdistricts (*xiang*) and directly administered districts (*zhishu qu*) indicated that lakeside land accounted for two-thirds of the 310,000 *mu* of arable land in the 43 neighborhoods (*bao*) of the base. Most of this land was under water. Wastelands and grasslands were also pervasive in the Hongze Lake area. Only about a third of the cultivable acreage was planted in autumn crops.[7] Uncultivated land could be divided into two types: "virgin wasteland" (*shenghuang*) and "abandoned cultivable land" (*shuhuang*). This uncultivated property was owned either by the government and other public institutions or by individual landowners.[8]

So much uncultivated land was tempting, and wealthy landlords often extended their holdings by encroaching on public property.[9] The landlords' income, however, fluctuated tremendously from year to year because of flooding. Lakeside properties did not guarantee a constant high yield. When the land was inundated, "wealthy household" (*da hu*) incomes were sometimes sharply reduced to the level of middle peasants.[10] On the other hand, although this was generally a flood-prone area, property located only a short distance from the lake was often struck by another form of natural disaster—drought. The persistent drought in Sisu county, for instance, turned the area into vast stretches of sandy mounds. Productivity dropped precipitously, by 50 percent.[11]

In the region as a whole, less than 4 percent of residents were landlords. Some of these owned huge tracts of land.[12] Most of the population consisted of middle and poor peasants, with only a few wage laborers (see Table 7.1). Most peasants were owner-cultivators. Tenancy was not common, though relatively more common than in northern Henan (see Table 7.2). Available data indicate that there was no shortage of land (which does not necessarily mean there was easy access to land) or of draft animals. For the area as a whole, per capita availability of land was eight *mu*, which is a rather high figure considering that the average for Henan was two *mu*. On the average, half the households owned an ox, a donkey, and a pig.[13] But aggregate data can be deceiving. Many of the computed landholdings (roughly 24 percent of the area's farmland) were submerged under floodwater (see Table 7.3). In Xufengjia and Hongze counties, 56.5 and 96.2 percent of the land, respectively, was submerged.

As in other Yuwansu areas, tenancy arrangements varied according to the quality of the soil and whether or not the landlord provided seed, agricultural implements, or fertilizer to the cultivator.[14] Tenancy came in two forms: sharecropping and fixed rent. The ratio for dividing crops varied from 50:50 to 40:60 to 30:70 (owner:cultivator), depending on locality and on custom. In some areas, fodder, animal dung, and other subsidiary crops were also divided by landlords and tenants according to local custom.[15] A different rate was used for land on which vegetables were grown, but information on the exact ratio is not available. Reeds gathered by peasants were usually divided between the contractors (*baoren*) and the cutters (*gecao ren*).[16] As in other areas, common tenant practices included giving obligatory gifts to landlords at New Year's and

TABLE 7.1
Social Composition in the Suwan Border Area, 1941

Class	Percent	Class	Percent
Landlord	3.6%	Poor peasant	39.9%
Rich peasant	11.8	Wage laborer	5.1
Middle peasant	35.8	Others	3.8

SOURCE: Zhao Min, "Huaibei Suwan bianqu xingzheng gongshu zhishu qu ershi wu tian de liangshi gongzuo zongjie" (A comprehensive report submitted by the administrative office of the Suwan border base in the Huaibei region of 25 days of tax grain work in the directly administered area), Nov. 1, 1941. *P:Anhui* 2: 30.

NOTE: The area consisted of 6 administrative villages divided into 43 *bao* and 368 *jia*, with 8,969 households and a population of 46,327.

other holidays and inviting landlords to a requisite post-harvest banquet (*fenchang jiu*), at which the parties sat down and haggled over their share of the crop. Such tenancy arrangements do not seem outrageously exploitative compared to the crushing rent systems in some areas of Henan province.[17]

The main source of social tension in the area was land, in particular lake and beach properties that lacked precise property demarcations. Powerful households, often with the connivance of a local authority, encroached on public and private waterfront land. Gentry members bribed government officials and obtained deeds to take over peasant-reclaimed lakeside lands. Deceitful gentry, using the pretext of bringing waterlogged land under cultivation, deliberately drew up vague property lines in their title deeds. Very often, property lines were ambiguously put down as "to the middle of the lake" (*huxin weijie*), "as far as the eye can see" (*yi wang zhi di*), or "land with a water reflection" (*shuiying di*).[18]

The Communists found that the public beaches in Huaisi county, the reed beaches in Hongze county, and the 240 bays on both sides of the An River in Siyang and Sinan counties were the most contentious spots.[19] In these counties, government courts were commonly overloaded with cases of lakeside property disputes. As long as ownership was pending in court, landowners usually put off cultivating the land. Property disputes therefore contributed to the pervasiveness of wasteland in the region. Neither were tenant farmers, desperately in need of land, able to rent farmland from landowners. If the land was already under cultivation, peasants usually put off applying fertilizer as long as

TABLE 7.2
Social Composition in Hualianjing Village, 1944

Class	Number	Percent
Landlord	4	3.8%
Rich peasant	1	1
Poor peasant/ wage laborer	6	5.8
Tenant		26.9
Middle peasant	13	
Poor peasant	15	
Owner-cultivator		62.5
Middle peasant	24	
Poor peasant	41	

SOURCE: "Huaibei bianqu jianzu zengzi shengli gei jieceng shenghuo shangsheng" (The victory of rent reduction, wage increase, and increase of living standard of various classes in the Hubei border area), Jan. 22, 1944. *P:Anhui* 2: 182.

NOTE: The village was located in Bancheng district, Sinan county, Anhui.

TABLE 7.3
Area of Suwan Affected by Flood, 1943

County	Total land (*mu*)	Affected land (*mu*)	Percent
Huaibao	1,424,496	280,000	19.7%
Huaisi	1,290,635	216,000	16.7
Siyang	729,813	280,000	38.4
Sinan	1,459,927	350,000	24.0
Siwulingfeng	1,396,200	220,000	15.8
Xufengjia	424,677	240,000	56.5
Hongze	25,151	24,200	96.2
TOTAL	6,750,899	1,610,200	23.9

SOURCE: Liu Chongguang, "Huaibei Suwan bianqu yijiu sisan nian de shengchan jianshe zongjie" (A summary of production and reconstruction in the Suwan border base in Huaibei in 1943), Nov. 5, 1944. *P:Anhui* 2: 251.

NOTE: The material for Hongze was obtained from the mayor. The figures are estimates. (There is a miscalculation of totals in the original chart.)

the property was under dispute.[20] There was an additional problem: Disputes over the use of water drove people into solid, contentious communities. Lakeside residents often acted as cohesive groups fighting for collective water rights. Intercommunity disputes were frequent. Downstream communities strongly resisted upstream waterworks because they feared such supposedly constructive projects might cut off their water supply and render their soil unproductive.[21]

There was no doubt that the Communists were operating in a land of rural misery. Lakeside flood victims often lived in abject poverty. The poor included fishermen, shrimpers, and reed cutters. Reed-cutter households were particularly pervasive in this region; one estimate put the number of peasants dependent on reed cutting for a living at 100,000.[22] In certain areas, such as Daxin in the Banchengnan district, all of the villagers were reed cutters. The poor also included peasants who grew white potatoes, radishes, and buckwheat and those who collected animal dung.[23] Rural poverty and outlawry often went hand in hand. Siyang county, for instance, was reported to be a place of "barren land and poor people" (*di ji min pin*), a place well beyond the reach of political authority.[24] Brigands roamed freely in the five districts in Sidong county, although these outlaws only came together in small bands and presented little or no problem for Communist authorities. In the couple of years since they had come to power, the Communists had been able to destroy 79 bands and to clear 2,300 brigands out of the area.[25]

Building a Base

The ability to acquire an autonomous territorial base was the basic requirement for rural mobilization and agrarian reform. A stable base not only provided some degree of security, a basic condition for any social-revolutionary operation, it also gave the movement a territory from which revolutionaries could gather the manpower, grain, and tax revenues needed to sustain the revolution. Only in a relatively secure base could the Communists effectively conduct mass politics, introduce social programs to secure peasant loyalty and commitment, develop the rural economy, rebuild village institutions, and consolidate their power. One of these bases was located at the border of Jiangsu and Anhui provinces.

The Suwan (Jiangsu-Anhui) or Wan dongbei (northern Anhui) base was set up by the Communists in early 1940. That year, the Nationalists launched an offensive against the New Fourth Army in an attempt to drive them out of central China and all the way to the northern bank of the Yellow River. Simultaneously, in a move to weaken Communist influence in the area, the Japanese and their puppet troops mounted an attack on the Communists from the western part of the Tianjin-Pukou railroad. Facing imminent attacks from two superior armies, the party decided to preserve its main forces by moving them out of the Luxi area (west of the Tianjin-Pukou railroad) into northeastern Anhui province (Wan dongbei). In eastern Henan (the Rivereast area), the remaining regular armies were told by the party to combine with local forces, put up resistance, and carry on a clandestine movement against the enemies.

After having regrouped and held a brief party conference at Renhuo market town, the Communists decided to settle around Hongze Lake in northeastern Anhui province. Typical of Communist strategy at that time was the party's successful utilization of elite coalition politics to gain a foothold in the area. Their target was Sheng Zijin, a graduate of the Whampao Military Academy and a former Communist Party member. Arrested by the GMD, he was later released and then defected to the Nationalist side. When hostilities against the Japanese broke out, Sheng was appointed by Chiang as "special commissioner" of northeastern Anhui province. At the time, the Nationalists had adopted a policy of employing auxiliary warlord forces as guerrilla fighters against the Japanese invaders. But in the process of building his base, Sheng became entangled in a power struggle with warlords of the Guangxi clique in the area. He was desperately looking for an ally and for the military assistance he needed to stay in power. This gave the Communists an ideal opportunity to use their standard coalition politics to draw Sheng into some kind of nonaggression pact.

After a period of negotiation, the CCP and Sheng achieved a mutual understanding. The Communists agreed to use the Eighth Route Army to help Sheng drive out his enemies and stabilize his rule in the region.

In return, Sheng promised not only to let both the Eighth Route and the New Fourth Armies operate in his base area but guaranteed the Communist troops a C$10,000 a month subsidy.[26] It was under these conditions of minimum security and a cordial political atmosphere that the CCP was able to set up the new base—the Suwan Border Area of Huaibei Region (Huaibei Suwan bianqu)—in the Hongze Lake region. The base, as part of the Yuwansu (Henan-Anhui-Jiangsu) anti-Japanese border base, operated under the leadership of Deng Zihui, who headed the Northeastern Administrative Office (later renamed the Huaibei Administrative Office). In this rather bleak lakeside region, the Communists gradually consolidated their political power, pushed for socioeconomic reforms, and successfully reintegrated local communities into the revolution.[27]

Set up in March 1940, the Suwan border base originally consisted of eleven anti-Japanese resistance pockets. In October 1940, these isolated pockets were integrated and put under the control of an administrative office.[28] When the CCP first captured the area, they had to rebuild the base and the local government from scratch. The party had very few resources. The C$15,000 left behind by former local authorities was not even enough to support several thousand soldiers in the New Fourth Army, not to mention several thousand local administrative functionaries. Soldiers were said to have subsisted on sorghum buns and water, sometimes going without salt for several days. The sole source of income was the party's economic guerrilla warfare, namely robbing and taxing the rich in the puppet areas.

The political alliance with Sheng Zijin, however, yielded a tax base with which the Communists could sustain the revolutionary movement. The alliance gave the party two sources of income: commercial taxes (mostly transit taxes) and land taxes. Under the pretext of collective defense, Sheng Zijin gave the Communists permission to set up checkpoints along all major trade routes in order to collect transit taxes on local exports of grain, livestock, and poultry and imports of fabric, cotton yarn, and metals. This revenue became the party's most reliable source of income. But the ability to collect these taxes depended on the effectiveness of patrolling the border and on the elimination of salt smuggling. By November 1941, a network of checkpoints had been set up by the party in all major market towns to prevent the smuggling of grain and salt.[29] Following the establishment of the administrative office, a clear separation of base and county fiscal policy was put into place. Commodity transit taxes, the salt tax, surcharges, and half of the land taxes and title fees were allocated to army and administrative expenses, with the rest of the taxes, brokers' license fees, slaughter taxes, wine and tobacco taxes, and the remaining land taxes and title fees going directly to the county coffers.

In the early stage of base building, from 1940 to late 1942, the Communists made few inroads in the villages. In this period, repressive GMD forces in Jiangsu effectively blockaded the base. The border base was reported to be short of everything. Local inhabitants were uncertain of the New Fourth Army's ability to fight the enemies and thought Communist authority could collapse any day. This uncertainty made support for the CCP lukewarm at best. The party was unable to get its production drive off the ground. When the CCP promoted a slogan of a 10 percent increase in productivity, peasants took the production drive as another state measure to extract more labor from the people.

The party later employed all sorts of economic leveling devices to appeal to the peasantry: "equitable taxation" (*heli fudan*), wage increases, and rent and interest reduction. It also ordered government units at all levels to produce vegetables and livestock for their own consumption. At the same time, by carrying out the "crack troops and simplified administration" program, it streamlined the government and reduced its functionaries by 72 percent, thus substantially cutting government expenses.[30] Cadres also set up cooperatives and began engaging in local trading. But most of these trade agencies either crumbled due to corruption or were destroyed by enemy attacks.

It was not until 1943, with the conclusion of the 33-day Japanese mop-up campaign, that the area first achieved a sense of security. With a relatively stable base area, the party changed its role and its image. The Communist movement was no longer perceived as simply a force of destruction; the party took on the task of nation building and became a force of construction. Both the Central Committee in Yan'an and the Central Plain Bureau ordered cadres to devote full attention to production, prompting the Suwan Communists to launch a production drive.[31] In the rest of the chapter, let us examine the Communist efforts at revolutionary reconstruction in the area.

Equitable Taxation

Revolutionary reconstruction involved introducing social reform and economic programs and required the Communists to actively mobilize the masses to participate collectively in these programs. One of the reforms the Communists initiated was an equitable tax system. Unfair and burdensome taxation had been one of the major grievances in the area. It was not only the large amounts but the myriad kinds of taxes peasants had to pay that accounted for the misery in the countryside. Another source of social tension was the unfair way the tax burden was distributed among various groups of taxpayers through the *tanpai* or "compulsory allotment" system. Although the *tanpai* system, which was based on one's landholding, was supposed to be fair, the system was much abused by the rich and powerful, who used their political influence to shift the tax burden to the rural poor. The system ended up "taxing those who had little or no land heavily." Therefore, an immediate task for the Communists, who professed to champion economic justice in the countryside, was to evolve an equitable tax system that would alleviate the suffering of impoverished peasants.[32]

To a certain extent, creating a fair system of taxation was a practical necessity. The Communists' ability to sustain themselves in combat depended very much on their ability to extract enough resources, particularly food grain, from the local people. Military expenses (including food) constituted about 75 percent of the Communists' budget. There were tens of thousands of military personnel and administrative officials to be fed in the border base area.[33] The enemy blockade cut off all outside supplies. The Japanese also adopted a policy of "using combat to support combat," which involved using their armed forces to obtain food supplies from the Communist-dominated countryside.[34] The sustenance of the revolution depended heavily on Communist self-sufficiency in food, which in turn relied on the creation of a tax system fair enough to induce peasants to pay taxes. Right from the beginning, the urgency of creating a tax base to sustain the fighting dictated that Communist cadres focus their energy on tax reform.

The Communists adopted a number of measures to change the existing tax system. First, given the difficulties of obtaining grain in times of war, land taxes were collected in kind instead of in cash.[35] Second, the Communists abolished the *tanpai* system and instituted a new progressive tax system. The fundamental principle behind the new system was that every household and locality had to pay a fair share of local taxes based on income. The household still formed the basic unit of taxation. Starting from August 1941, an individual whose income was less than three *dou* of grain a year was exempt from all taxation. The government also did away with other minor taxes and surcharges. Only land taxes, title fees, brokers' license fees, salt taxes, transit taxes, slaughter taxes, and wine and tobacco taxes were retained. The abolition of salt surcharges was particularly important to the local economy. It turned the base into a very active salt-trading region.

Taxes were levied progressively, according to productivity and ability to pay. Rural households were divided into four categories:

1. Upper-class households: roughly 20 percent of all households in the locality. These included wealthy gentry, rich peasants, and merchants. The tax rate was 12 percent of their income.

2. Middle-class households: 40 percent of all households. These were mostly owner-cultivators. Their tax rate was 8 percent.

3. Lower-class households: 10 percent of all households. These were part owner/part tenants. Their tax rate was 5 percent.

4. The extreme poor: no more than 15 percent of all households. These low-income households were completely exempt from tax payments.

The Communist policy restricted the number of tax exemptions so as not to place an unfair burden on certain categories of taxpayer. Special privileges were accorded servicemen's dependents; households of revolutionary martyrs received a three-year tax exemption; other military households and government functionaries obtained a reduction in taxes.[36] Tax reductions and special allowances were made for emergency situations such as crop losses due to natural disasters or soil infertility. Taxes were usually levied on principal crops, for instance sorghum in the Huaibei area, and non-staples such as beans. The types and the proportion of crops to be paid to the government were worked out in accordance with local productivity.[37] People were not required to pay taxes in wheat, which was considered a high-quality, easily marketed grain. The policy was designed to show rural people that government troops and functionaries were required to consume coarse grains and to maintain a living standard similar to that of ordinary peasants.

In order to minimize the traditional conflicts between government tax collectors and taxpayers, the Communists instituted a hierarchy of tax organs, from the village all the way up to the county, as centers of tax collection. The exact amount of the tax payment and the distribution of the tax burden were not, as in the past, arbitrarily decided by county mayors or district heads, but were to be worked out consensually by a tax grain mobilization committee composed of government officials, local assemblymen, members of the Peasant Famine Relief Association (*nongjiu hui*), the local military, and five to fifteen local notables. The committee was responsible for collecting taxes, conducting local surveys, mobilizing people to propagate the program, and, after tax collection, for the storage and transportation of the grain.

At the outset, neighborhoods (*bao*) formed the basic administrative unit, each headed by a cadre experienced in finance. But this decentralization produced very poor results, so the larger administrative unit of the *xiang* was then designated the basic unit. The exact amount of taxes to be paid by each household was decided in a public neighborhood meeting.[38] The month between September 16 and October 15 was designated as tax collection month. The Communists employed "shock brigades" (*tuji dui*), groups of three to four tax collectors, to insure that taxes were promptly collected. Each subdistrict was to raise three to four of these shock brigades, which were charged with the responsibility of bringing in the government revenue on time.[39]

The new tax system was designed to make sure that taxes were promptly collected to finance the revolution, and that the tax burden was equitably distributed over the entire rural population. To ease social tension in the countryside, the government made sure that the traditional practice of the rich of shifting their tax burden onto the shoulders of the poor was discontinued. The Communists also took away the tax authority of the county mayors and *bao* heads, which had been the main source of tax abuse and rural grievance in the past. The new system was based on a consensus in which all segments of rural society, including the landed gentry, had a voice. Although it was undoubtedly part of the class struggle, the Communists did not want to antagonize the upper landed classes, who might then put up stiff resistance against Communist rule. The Communist authorities carefully prescribed the exact tax percentage for each class. Taxes were proportionately fixed so that there would be no reverse discrimination with the upper landed classes bearing an unfair share of the tax burden.

Rural Land Survey

Effective implementation of an equitable tax system required good knowledge of the population size and the landownership system in the area. A population census therefore had to be taken, and a property appraisal was needed before neighborhoods could make a final decision on the amount of taxes each individual household was required to pay. Accurate land data was used to refute false claims from certain localities that they were unfairly overtaxed. Correct assessments expedited tax collection and minimized disputes. The party ordered all cadres, government functionaries, local citizens, and soldiers to participate collectively in land surveys and tax collections. The government realized that tax collection consumed a great deal of time and manpower. This was made worse by the widespread confusion that usually forced Communist authorities to employ thousands of cadres and spend several months each year in tax grain collection. An accurate land survey and a proper register of property could save time and manpower, clarify field boundaries, settle disputes, confirm property rights, obtain population figures for tax assessment, and create an equitable tax system.

As stated before, without clear landownership rights, peasants were unlikely to bring wasteland under cultivation. Since the new tax system was not based solely on property ownership but also on actual income in terms of crop yield, an accurate survey of land productivity was absolutely crucial to its successful implementation. Another immediate objective of the land survey was to return land and beaches (public and private) unlawfully encroached upon by powerful gentry members to the rightful owners. The land survey could also help track down and penalize tax evaders. Cadres were instructed to focus on two troublesome areas: the quality and productivity of the sandy mound land (*sa gang di*), and the lake/beach land disputes (*hu tan di*). They were told to ignore all minor land disputes, for example those along boundaries, walls, ditches, and within residential properties, and to tackle only land disputes dating back to the beginning of the Republican period.

But the land survey was a formidable task. It involved several thousand surveyors and took a couple of months to complete. Though the party tried its best to oversee and coordinate all aspects of the program, the actual surveys were undertaken by the cross-class village and *xiang* assessment committees made up of reputable gentry, intellectuals, workers, and peasants. Disputes were settled, if possible, either by "mass organizations" (*qunzhong tuanti*, such as peasant associations) or the assessment committee. Only when these organs were unable to resolve a conflict did the case go to court. Appraisal results did have to be approved by the village council.[40]

As expected, the Communist land survey did not receive enthusiastic support from all local inhabitants. Generally, local citizens' perception of government land surveys was that they meant higher taxation. Moreover, anyone mistakenly underreporting productivity usually faced a heavy penalty. New titles also cost money. For the peasants, all this surveying, spot-checking, and rechecking was immensely troublesome and disrupting to their daily farming routine. Most of them held the resigned belief that, as the underprivileged class, they would have to bear a heavy tax burden anyway.[41] Filing a report on their holdings presented several practical difficulties for them. For one thing, there were not enough wooden land-measuring devices (*gong*) to go around.[42] Peasants were told to substitute rope on a sunny day and reed stalks on a wet day (as ropes could shrink in wet weather). But even if illiterate peasants were able to locate the boundaries of and accurately measure their land, they had absolutely no way of calculating and recording the information. The Communists therefore had to mobilize schoolteachers to help them finish the job.[43]

A close look at the land survey in Ever Victory subdistrict (Changsheng xiang, which consisted of several natural villages) illustrates the practical problems the Communists confronted. At the outset, local cadres thought they could copy the successful experience of a nearby district, Yanfu qu. The basic land survey unit there was the village, each of which organized its own surveying team. The model, however, was inapplicable in Ever Victory because of the dispersed nature of its landholdings—the holdings of a household were usually scattered over several villages within the *xiang*.[44] A village-based survey team would not be able to check landholdings in neighboring villages. The village as a corporate entity always resented outside interference and infringements such as the Communist land survey. The Communists therefore had to group several villages together into a larger unit, called a "joint neighbor land survey team" (*lianlin xiaozu*), to perform the task. This Communist tactic reminds us of the traditional method of adjudicating interfamilial and inter-village disputes by using ad hoc arbitration committees. After the survey, the categorization of land was carefully worked out by the cadres and the people in public meetings, taking into careful consideration the opinions of respected individuals who served as advisers and mediators and of such civic groups as mutual aid teams and the old peasant associations. Class identification was arrived at by consensual group decision.

By openly posting the survey results, the party obtained feedback from the public that allowed it to correct injustices and track down tax evaders. Afterwards, proprietors brought their deeds in for verification and adjustment. The Communists found that the most troublesome spots were lakeside villages. Proprietors tended to conceal holdings as property boundaries frequently shifted because of flooding. This made it immensely difficult to tell who owned what. Sometimes it was the cadres who made mistakes, under-classifying certain holdings, but subsequent spot-checking (*fucha*) corrected these. The Communists made sure that the project was open to criticism, revision, and reconsideration. In the end, only one household in the entire subdistrict was penalized for tax evasion.

The Communists, like other rural workers, found peasant indifference the most difficult obstacle to overcome. Peasants' passive attitudes often stemmed from the fact that many regarded land surveys as a serious disruption of their daily routine. When surveyors came to the countryside and beat gongs to gather the peasants, many simply ignored the call, since they knew that the surveyors had to come to them eventually anyway. Yet the party realized that no accurate survey could be accomplished without the peasants' intimate knowledge of local landholdings. The only way to get their active participation was to demonstrate to peasants that it would be in their interest to join the survey.

To do this, the joint neighbor land survey team arbitrarily fixed a date for all land reregistration. Nonparticipating proprietors who suffered losses due to errors had no recourse for adjustment. Nonparticipants could also be heavily fined should discrepancies be found in the reports they filed. By linking the land survey to the peasants' concrete interests, and by applying the threat of a penalty, the Communists finally induced the peasants to participate. And it was only through active peasant participation that the party was finally able to track down land concealment and prosecute tax evaders, particularly cadre evaders. The Communists were convinced that the effectiveness of the land survey depended on whether people felt that the project was intimately their own, not something simply devised and operated by outsiders. Although there were nineteen outside organizers, most land disputes were settled internally with the help of indigenous leaders.[45]

To be fair was not easy. There were practical difficulties. As in the Eyuwan land reform in the 1930s, proper classification of households into rigid upper, middle, and lower categories posed enormous problems. Intentionally or unintentionally, the rich were sometimes undertaxed and the poor overtaxed. In some cases an entire village or *xiang* was undertaxed.[46] Occasionally, cadres mechanically stuck to the regulations without bothering to perform the survey, the property appraisal, or the productivity assessment. Some lazy cadres adopted a laissez-faire attitude and left the survey and the classification to the *bao* heads. Others simply followed suggestions from the *baojia* heads and forced upper-class households to pay 50 percent of their income in taxes. In one case, cadres forcibly decreed that village residents were to pay their taxes in equal portions of "large and small sorghums" (*da xiao shushu*), without bothering to find out that the entire crop of large sorghum in that area had been swept away by floodwater. The assessment of a merchant's income presented additional problems. Their incomes varied immensely, depending on whether they were managers of large business enterprises or owners of barber shops.[47]

Insufficient preparation frequently caused delays, mostly due to time spent ironing out differences in class struggle meetings. For instance, in an impoverished area inhabited mostly by poor fishermen and fodder collectors, the Communists mechanically followed orders and without prior investigation classified 15 percent of the population as "poor households," while the rest, mainly dirt-poor peasants, were grouped into the middle or rich peasant categories.[48] Such actions generated intense conflict in public neighborhood meetings.

In Guiren township, many of the poor manure collectors and fishermen, traditionally exempted from taxation, were included for the first time as taxpayers. Sometimes cadres found land surveys too troublesome a task and simply went back to the traditional *tanpai* system of tax assessment. Others ignored party regulations and employed stopgap measures, such as jacking up tax rates and overassessing peasants' yields to insure fulfillment of the government's tax quota. In one newly developed subdistrict, Communist cadres, in order to fulfill the tax quota, overvalued the white potatoes produced by flood victims.[49] The main concern for these cadres, as the Communists reported, was how to bring in tax revenue as quickly as possible. Few understood that it would require careful planning and coordination to make the project work. Many local cadres were governed by parochial feelings and made decisions favoring their own neighborhoods and villages.[50] Some cadres used their position and personal influence to obtain benefits for their families and friends. Neighborhood cadres and *bao* heads underclassified themselves as rural poor.[51] There were of course cases of corruption and abuses of power. Occasionally, cadres threatened the poor and forced payment from them.[52]

The equitable tax system was designed to alleviate economic injustices in the countryside, but the system would not work without some degree of backing or cooperation from the landed upper classes. Through personal contacts, cadres assiduously cultivated relations with local elites. They appealed to the upper classes in patriotic terms and persistently reasoned with them about the need for the government to obtain adequate tax revenue to sustain the battle against the Japanese invaders. The government assured the rich that they were required only to pay their fair share and that the new tax system would not overburden them. Past social revolutionary experience clearly demonstrated to the party that radical Communist policies like the Eyuwan land reform in the 1930s only antagonized rural elites and turned them into political adversaries, giving them a chance to spread rumors and create panic among rich and middle peasants.[53] Instead of coercing rural elites into compliance, the Communists used persuasion. The party capitalized fully on the sense of local insecurity and reasoned with the gentry that it was in their best interest to pay taxes to support the anti-Japanese Communist government.

A gentry member in the town of Shuanggou, though supportive of the Communist resistance effort, strongly protested against the tax rate (only 10 percent of his total income) and demanded a tax reduction. Cadres patiently argued with him that it was absolutely necessary for the Red Army to collect taxes in order to obtain provisions needed to survive. Like the GMD and Japanese troops, they explained, Communists could use force to get what they wanted from the people, but they preferred not to. On the other hand, without adequate provisions and means of survival, Communist forces would have to pull out of the area, leaving all citizens, including the gentry, vulnerable to local bandits and Japanese attacks. The government could also leave it to the gentry itself to raise provisions for the troops, but, the cadres insisted, the area would then be embroiled in unending disputes over the lack of an equitable tax standard, and in the end, the government would never be able to obtain the revenue it needed to function.

The Communists always tied tax payment to the immediate concrete interests of the rich, namely the protection of the lives and property of their families. They played upon both patriotic feelings and concerns about local security to convince rural elites that Communist armed protection was crucial to creating political stability in the locality and vital to their personal survival. They pointed out that armed protection was a collective good that benefited not only the rural poor but also the landed upper classes, but that it had its cost, too, and required their sacrifice and cooperation. Elite concessions were obtained through nationalistic appeals and Communist provision of physical protection.[54]

To secure the support of the rich, the Communists allowed the gentry to participate in the decision-making process. They were well represented in such organizations as the "Committee for Favored Treatment of Servicemen's Families" (*you kang hui*) and the "Mediation Committee to Resolve Conflicts in Neighborhood Assemblies." Along with party members and peasants, local gentry also formed the tripartite leadership of the local power structure. The gentry were urged to assume not only their traditional leadership roles in relief and water conservancy but new roles in propaganda and production. They were frequently consulted by the Communists in local matters. In short, it was a policy of patriotism, moderation, and constant consultation that ultimately won the support of rural elites for the revolution.[55]

A look at tax collection in Zhushu qu, a directly administered district, may help demonstrate the dynamics and the difficulties of implementing an equitable tax system. The Zhushu district was composed of six subdistricts (*xiang*) divided into 43 neighborhoods (*bao*). Located in a lakeside area, two-thirds of the land was unproductive, consisting either of wasteland or land inundated by floodwater. The remaining third was under cultivation, with an average productive capacity of 30 *jin* per *mu*. The Communists, after taking control of the district, immediately mobilized local assemblymen and gentry into a "tax grain work squad" to survey the land and collect taxes. The squad was reported to have conducted 174 preliminary, sampling, and rechecking surveys. The basic tax unit was the neighborhood. Each neighborhood went through at least four or five and sometimes as many as seven or eight surveys. The entire process of land surveying and tax collection was completed within 25 days. During that time, local residents spent roughly five days in public meetings.

To be sure, reports do indicate that cadres sometimes mistreated and mishandled rural elites. The party referred to and harshly criticized such actions as a divisive "leftist" tendency. According to one report, cadres took various unlawful measures to extract as many resources as possible from the gentry: forcing rich households to give them room and board in times of famine (*chi dahu*), overassessing the productivity of their land in order to force the upper classes to pay more, severely fining the rich, and forcing the gentry to pay a business tax for the surplus grain in their reserves, which, the cadres insisted, would be sold by the gentry eventually.[56] But these problems were quickly corrected.

The implementation of an equitable tax system served a number of economic and political purposes. It was not designed simply to correct economic disparity and to alleviate rural misery. It was a mechanism employed by the party to insure that people paid their taxes on time so that the Communist command had adequate resources to finance the war. The party also used it as a means to reshape the local power structure. In the 25 days of rural mobilization, the Communists reelected a third of the *bao* and a fifth of the *jia* heads, thus giving them tighter control over the countryside. In conjunction with this, the party revitalized the local militia (the self-defense squad) and mobilized the peasants in production programs such as autumn planting. The equitable tax system should be seen as part of a rural reconstruction package the party sold to local people. The program not only energized the peasants but also the elites. It brought these two usually rival classes together to participate collectively in rural revolutionary reconstruction. Whether out of patriotism or concern for private security, the local gentry made concessions to the Communists. And as a result of rural mobilization, both rural elites and the peasantry were increasingly politicized.[57]

Land Reclamation

Land surveys and an equitable tax system were corrective measures aimed at bringing some degree of economic justice to the countryside and providing revenue for the Communist coffers. But to win the support of the people, the party had to show that communism was a constructive force that would help rebuild the countryside. By reclaiming land, the party hoped to expand cultivable acreage and increase agricultural productivity.

The pervasiveness of wasteland in the area prompted the Communists to initiate massive efforts to mobilize peasants to reclaim land, particularly the swampland around Hongze Lake in Huaibao, Huaisi, and Sinan counties. The party started with a land survey to detail precisely the amount of uncultivated land in the region. A reclamation committee (*kenzhi weiyuanhui*) was set up under the administrative office (*xingzheng gongshu*) to oversee the operation. The Communists then ordered all public organizations and local citizens to reregister their uncultivated land. They found a sizable amount of unused acreage. The 1942 Siyang county land survey, for instance, put the total uncultivated area at 11,000 *mu*, 63 percent of which was private land and 37 percent of which was public property. The survey also found that 69 percent was virgin wasteland and 31 percent abandoned cultivable land. Along the An River in Siyang county, the survey found that 60 to 70 percent of public wasteland had fallen into private hands because of gradual gentry encroachment.[58]

To encourage peasants to reclaim land, the Communist government provided certain material incentives. Those reclaiming abandoned cultivable land (*shuhuang*) enjoyed a year of rent and tax exemptions. Peasants reclaiming virgin wasteland (*shenghuang*) automatically received permanent cultivation rights, three years of free rent, five years of tax exemption, and a rent ceiling not to exceed 30 percent of the land's future yield.[59] The Communists also made all wasteland, public as well as private, available for peasant reclamation.[60] Both the reclamation committee and the Peasant Famine Relief Association (*nongjiu hui*) actively recruited local people as land reclaimers. Public wastelands were made available to poor peasants, refugees, and servicemen's families for reclamation. The government also made special efforts to provide reclaimers with farmsteads, agricultural implements, and seed. To induce outsiders to participate, immigrants and refugees were given similar privileges to those of native peasants. In some areas local authorities even extended additional incentives to outsiders to attract them to the Communist base.

But in a region of land shortage, servicemen's families were given the first right to reclaim land. For privately owned wasteland, landholders were given a deadline by which the land was to have been reclaimed. If owners had no intention of doing this, or if they failed to do so, the government would recruit peasants to bring the land under cultivation. The original proprietor still owned the reclaimed land, but the reclaimer enjoyed permanent tenancy rights. The Communists also simplified the procedure of reclamation. Reclaimers could directly apply to the owner, or in the event the owner was an absentee landlord, they could approach the government. Anyone who reclaimed more than twenty *mu* of land or who assisted the government in recruiting immigrants as reclaimers was rewarded.[61] When the land was brought under cultivation, peasants qualified to apply for a government grain subsidy to finance construction of an embankment that would protect their newly acquired property from future flooding.[62]

The Communist policy of tax exemption and free rent attracted many poor peasants to the land reclamation program. According to available data, Huaibei peasants brought a total of 74,021 *mu* of wasteland under cultivation by 1944. The Communist government spent roughly C$485,000 on financial aid, mostly for the collective purchase of draft animals.

A program like this always produced some unexpected problems. Occasionally, peasants brought a piece of land under cultivation and enjoyed a good harvest the first year. But the following autumn their crops would be washed away by a flood, thus severely dampening their enthusiasm for further land reclamation. Some cadres were looking for a quick fix for the economy; for example, cadres in Siyang county hastily recruited landlords and rich peasants to reclaim land, even though the party ordered them to use the middle and poor peasants as the backbone of the land reclamation program. Wealthy landholders sometimes received financial aid from the government because cadres misinterpreted the concept of equality to mean an "equal chance for every citizen [to obtain government help]." In some cases, poor peasants misused their government subsidy to purchase personal items rather than the seeds, draft animals, and agricultural implements for which the subsidy was intended. Others used government money to acquire a piece of property. Some peasants cheated the government: instead of reclaiming land, they simply turned over part of the soil along the property line, reported to the government that the land had been brought under cultivation, and applied for government funds.[63] In this way, they were able to acquire a piece of property and enjoy the privileges of landownership without doing the necessary work.

Despite all these problems, the reclamation project did produce desirable results. It repopulated the previously desolate and inundated Communist base. There was a continuous flow of peasant migrants into the Communist-administered counties in the Hongze Lake region. In some counties, the number of households doubled after the program was instituted.[64] The land reclamation project brought an additional eight to ten households to each of the villages in the region. Indeed, there was a movement for peasants in eastern Henan and southern Shandong to "migrate southward to Sizhou" (Sixian), an area formerly considered by local people to be a bandit lair marked by extreme poverty and a depressed economy.[65]

Hydraulic Engineering

Another Communist-inspired project to boost agricultural production was hydraulic engineering. Chronic flooding of the Huaibei area affected all citizens, elite as well as peasants, and flood control was traditionally a communal project. Rural elites provided leadership, and peasants basic manpower. It was a cross-class collective action that integrated communities and promoted social cohesion. The Communists realized that party involvement in such a project would allow them to penetrate villages, foster a better understanding of the revolution, and strengthen the political alliance between the Communist government and the people. The collective participation of peasants in such a community-wide project would also heighten mass enthusiasm and retain peasant loyalty. From an economic standpoint, hydraulic engineering was a practical necessity, a prerequisite for rebuilding rural agriculture.

As early as 1941, after gaining a toehold in the area, the Communists embarked on a couple of waterworks projects. All three waterways in the region—the An, Sui, and Li rivers—urgently needed work.[66] The party created a waterworks committee (*shuili weiyuanhui*) and charged it with the task of mass mobilization. Major engineering works were to be handled separately by an engineering section. To broaden its appeal to residents, the waterworks committee was deliberately structured to represent all segments of society. Since water control was a multi-county project, members of the committee were drawn from several counties. County representatives were asked by the party to submit waterworks proposals for their respective localities to the committee.[67]

The party was convinced that for the project to be successful, elite participation and support were absolutely essential. Rural elites were recruited into leadership positions based on the highly publicized party policy of a "three-thirds system." According to the formula, only a third of local leadership positions were to be filled by party members; the rest were to be made up of local elites and peasants, in this case "progressive gentry" and "middle [i.e., neutral] elements."[68] Under the principle of "democratic centralism," the party had the right to make all final decisions, but Communist cadres were told to always look for local initiatives and to secure mass participation. Elite suggestions had to be taken into consideration. If there were differences of opinion, cadres were instructed to be patient and to use persuasion, not coercion, to bring the opposition around.[69]

Hydraulic engineering was a very labor-intensive and time-consuming undertaking.[70] The first dredging of 30 *li* of the An River, for instance, took 4,000 workers one month to complete. But the benefit to the area, as well as to the party, was immense. The project brought 3,240 *qing* of land under cultivation.[71] As a result of improved irrigation, according to a 1944 report, the amount of arable land in Huaisi county doubled. In Sinan county, agricultural productivity increased by a third.[72] Yet the project also produced an unintended negative result. Local elites, instead of the rural poor, were the principal beneficiaries of the project: most of the reclaimed land fell into the hands of the powerful gentry.[73] But hydraulic engineering greatly enhanced the image of the Communist government. After the project was completed, citizens expressed a growing trust in the Communist authorities. The residents' reactions were highly favorable: "Only a Communist democratic government would do such a good deed," "The traditional government wouldn't bother with such things," and "The new democratic government did do some good things for us ordinary citizens." The hydraulic engineering project also provided a valuable education for cadres and involved them in production work.[74]

Hydraulic engineering required technical and management skills as well as detailed planning. Research had to be done to determine the rate and velocity of the flow of water, the length of the route, and the width and depth of the riverbed. Calculations had to be made on the amount of dirt required, the wages workers would be paid, and the amount of food needed for the laborers. A miscalculation could spell disaster. In the areas of coordination and technical expertise, Communist leadership was essential. Still, not all water control projects were successful. Two rivers overflowed right after dredging as a result of a lack of planning and an inadequate survey.[75]

For the Communists, providing the necessary technical and management skills for the project was simple. The basic problem was how to levy taxes for the project equitably from various rural communities in a way that would not generate community conflict. Chinese riverine communities had traditionally solidified into cellular structures characterized by intra-community cohesion and intercommunity rivalries. In Guangdong province, it was not uncommon for rural kin-based communities to engage in armed violence over irrigation rights. In Huaibei, lakeside communities were similarly solidified into corporate communal entities. But the basic line of conflict in this area was between upstream and downstream settlements. Like the Cantonese, these solid communities did not hesitate to band together to fight for their collective rights and interests. In the An River project, for instance, the basic cleavage was between the downstream flood-prone communities in Sishu and Sinan counties, which benefited immensely from the project and obviously favored dredging the river, and the upstream communities in Siyang county, which stood little to gain and were therefore strongly opposed to the project.

The party had to be particularly careful in assessing the burden each community had to bear. Special attention had to be paid to both the overall need for the plan and to specific community interests. In fact, the party's role was to be the mediator. The party accurately calculated the type and amount of benefits each community and each household would reap from the project and assessed the tax burden accordingly. Rural communities were differentiated into "direct beneficiaries" and "indirect beneficiaries" depending on the seriousness of their former flood problems. The distinction between these two types of beneficiaries within a village (Pan Village, for example) was based on whether a certain household had been a flood victim before. Those that had been were "direct beneficiaries," the rest were "indirect beneficiaries." The party made sure that non-victim households were required to bear part of the expense of the project, though at a lower rate. The ratio of tax burden between direct and indirect beneficiaries was 7:3. However, to avoid putting a crushing burden on flood-prone communities, the party set a tax ceiling for these communities of no more than a third of total community income.[76]

In assessing the tax burden, the party also gave special attention to the ability of various classes to pay for the project. Landlords and tenants were asked to pay their fair share and ratios were determined according to the type of land and the kind of tenancy arrangement. Private owners of land were required to shoulder 80 percent and tenants 20 percent of the tax burden. If the land were rescinded within a year, it was mandatory for the proprietor to reimburse tenants for two-thirds of the taxes they had paid, one-third if the rescission occurred within two years. The ratio for publicly owned land was also 80:20. Permanent tenants shared the tax equally with their landlords. In the case of pawned land, the pawnbroker's tax burden was two-thirds for a one-year redemption, one-half for a two-year, and one-third for a three-year.[77]

By 1942, the party had completed the necessary survey work on the An River project. It estimated that a 130-*li* embankment had to be constructed, which would require 28,900 cubic meters of earth. The project would eventually benefit 354,000 *mu* of arable land.[78] The execution of the project required careful coordination; timing was a crucial factor. First, the project could not be carried out in the rain. Yet right after the rainy season, the peasants had to begin planting, which would consume all available rural labor. The party therefore decided that water control work would commence in the slack season in late winter, around the fifth of the first lunar month. It figured that at that time, even the poorest peasants still had sufficient grain in reserve to tide them over to the next harvest. The project had to be completed ten days before the Qingming festival, which coincided roughly with spring planting activities. Once the spring planting began, all peasants had to return to their fields, leaving any remaining work undone.[79]

Another major problem was labor recruitment for the project, since peasants traditionally shunned corvée labor. The Communists had to be very careful that labor conscription did not become a divisive issue in rural communities. In Stonetown Neighborhood, the project generated a great deal of opposition simply because cadres went back to the traditional *tanpai* system of raising funds and manpower. Under the old allotment system, landless laborers were also required to shoulder part of the labor cost. In Pan Village Neighborhood, the Communists adopted a different formula. The labor cost was shared equally by all villagers, while property owners were required to pay extra for food expenses. Property owners, who were mostly landlords and rich peasants, complained bitterly that they were doubly taxed. In their own words, they were "beaten and then tortured."[80] The wage laborers, who possessed no property and therefore received no visible benefit from the hydraulic engineering project, were asked to provide labor. Like the property owners, they protested.

The government could not afford to pay high wages for the labor it needed because that would have placed too heavy a burden on property owners; on the other hand, if wages were too low, the Communists would have a hard time recruiting labor. Confronted with this problem, they elected to tax residents and hire the labor through a workfare system. But the workfare system produced its own problems. Attracted by good wages, large numbers of peasants applied for work.[81] Labor gangs stepped in, took over as contractors, and ran the project. Since wages were paid by the amount of work performed, hooligans tried to create more work for themselves by forcing people to let them dredge their ponds. The local gentry and peasants had to guard their ponds at night. Many blamed the party and the project for the problem, and it gave landlords and rich peasants the kind of ammunition they needed to fire at the party. Instead of helping them increase agricultural productivity, the upper classes complained, communist policies actually reduced the area to a land of poverty.[82]

Poor wage laborers were a highly unreliable work force. The primary concern of these peasants were the lives and property of their families. If a dike broke while they were at work, instead of trying to stop the flood they fled the site and headed home to save their families and their belongings. Cadres had to threaten to kill anyone deserting a site in order to stop the flight. Only force brought them back to work.[83]

In spite of all these problems and failings, the hydraulic engineering project received strong local support. According to Communist statistics, using the workfare program the Communists dredged 106 rivers and 786 ponds in two months. The villagers also built 6 embankments. The project cost the government C$1.5 million and 13.5 million *jin* of grain, but the government estimated that total grain production increased by 361,702 *shi*. The project benefited 25,437 *qing* of land, roughly a third of total arable land in the area.[84]

Spring Planting

As with the hydraulic engineering project, the success of the spring planting program depended very much on the government providing initiative and effective leadership. The urgent task for cadres was to get the peasants to plant early, to plow deeply, and to grow not only staple crops but also non-staple crops such as squash and vegetables. Peasants were encouraged to produce more commercial crops. In traditional cotton-growing areas, the government plan called for an allocation of at least 7 percent of total acreage to cotton production, and in non-cotton-growing areas, an allocation of 3 percent. Each village was asked to plant 2,000 to 5,000 trees. To stimulate cottage industry, the government brought in spinning and weaving machines and distributed them to peasants. In addition, the Communists developed a livestock industry in the area.

The government itself set an example. The party ordered all administrative and military personnel in the base (with the exception of guerrilla areas) to participate in agricultural production. Each soldier was required to produce half a *dan* of grain, 3 melons, and 100 *jin* of vegetables, and to plant 5 trees. The program produced enough vegetables to satisfy government consumption needs for two months. The army, for example the troops stationed in Pancheng county, was largely self-sufficient in grain and vegetables. The program not only cut government expenses, it allowed the Communists to make use of part of their tax revenue to encourage peasant participation in production projects.

The party was able to set aside 1,000 *shi* of small sorghum and 40,000 *jin* of bean cakes as interest-free loans for poor peasants. Since grain was crucial to survival and production, the party prohibited all grain exports from the area and mobilized gentry to voluntarily loan peasants seed grains.[85]

To mobilize the peasants in the program, the Communists conducted a production campaign, bombarding rural cultivators with all sorts of easy-to-remember propaganda slogans. The following were some of the highly popular slogans promoted by the party in the Jiangsu-Anhui border base:

1. Step up spring planting so you won't have to worry about hunger and cold.
2. Grow more staple grains; grow more squash and vegetables.
3. Grow more cotton and you will be able to wear a new padded jacket in the winter.
4. Put a grain of millet in the soil in the spring; harvest 10,000 grains in the autumn.
5. Speed up production; improve your livelihood.
6. Increase production; reduce your tax burden.
7. Increase production; fight a protracted war against Japan.
8. Don't waste an inch of land.[86]

These slogans were designed to whip up peasant enthusiasm for the production drive. The messages were: produce enough to ensure an adequate food supply in times of hardship; producing more guarantees a better standard of living; production is patriotic. Unfortunately, there is no information available on how effective the slogans were and what impact they had on the peasantry.

Let us look at the Communist attempt to mobilize the peasants for spring planting in Siyang county. Siyang was a marginal area located on the edge of Hongze Lake, a remote place known to be "well beyond the reach of the whip" (*bianchang moji*). Typical of the area, the county suffered chronic problems of flooding, poverty, and lawlessness. At any given time, 30 percent of the population was reported to be on the brink of starvation. In order to mobilize the local people in a production drive, the Communists actively sought the help of local gentry, whose support they believed to be crucial to the smooth execution of the program. On New Year's eve, the Communists hosted a banquet for schoolteachers, local gentry, government functionaries, peasants, and civic and professional groups in the area. Together they drew up a plan for spring planting. The Communists hoped to make the spring planting program a true collective effort.

The Communist government set up a hierarchy (county, neighborhood, and village) of production and famine relief committees as its agent for local mobilization. The duty of the production and famine relief committees was to oversee and coordinate the four basic functions of agricultural loans, propaganda, production, and spring planting. Each neighborhood (the basic production unit) was given a seed grain quota to be raised from wealthy households. Large neighborhoods were told to raise fifteen *shi* of grain, medium neighborhoods ten *shi*, and small neighborhoods five *shi*.

There was always a labor shortage for spring planting, so the government had to mobilize the non-agrarian population to help. The new production teams were essentially recruited from nonagricultural laborers, fishermen, and salt peddlers. As the data indicate, the Communists were fairly successful in their production efforts. In the central administrative subdistrict (*zhishu xiang*), an area under tight Communist control, the party was reported to have raised 95 *shi* of grain and C$1,439 for spring planting. Three hundred and eighty-three persons joined the production team, which was then subdivided into 64 small work units. The production team was then employed in such projects as reclaiming and cultivating wasteland, constructing irrigation works, and assisting soldiers' families in cultivation. The government also launched a program to get government functionaries and ordinary citizens to plant trees, and set aside a date for that purpose. The entire production agenda was said to have been accomplished within a month.[87]

Rural mobilization was never as easy as rural planners expected it to be. In some areas, government reports indicated that production and famine relief committees were nothing but empty structures. Rich households sometimes resisted loaning the government grain. Corruption was reported in certain neighborhoods. Although the tree-planting movement received popular support, local peasants carried out the order mechanically. Substitute cultivation was performed mostly for combatants' families and very seldom for poor peasants, thus defeating the original purpose of the plan, which had aimed at helping the poor also.

Despite its problems, the mobilization for spring planting, as the data mentioned indicate, received a high degree of rural support. Local people in this economically impoverished and war-ravaged area had every reason to support a production project. Producing adequate food for survival during a subsistence crisis was a primary rural concern and a collective interest that cut across class lines. The program was carried out effectively, with the collaboration of the government, the gentry, and the local peasantry. The cadres provided leadership, planning, and management skills, the gentry donated some of their resources as initial funding, and the peasants supplied the necessary labor to make the project work. In the process, the Communists effectively penetrated the rural communities, consolidating their power in the villages. Cadre involvement in production work was accompanied by a gradual transformation of the sociopolitical structure. Cadres dominated the local government, tax loopholes were tightened, the power of the local gentry was undermined, and elites and peasants were successfully mobilized in collective self-defense. These were various segments of a concerted effort by the party to reintegrate and reconstruct the countryside. They represented the Communists' monumental effort to build a nation, block by block, from the bottom up.[88]

Community Integration and Collective Participation

The basic prerequisite for revolutionary reconstruction was the development of an autonomous territorial base. As Theda Skocpol points out, "The Chinese revolution as a whole took place under the military and administrative 'umbrella' provided by the party's control of its base area."[89] It was in the border base area, which provided some degree of autonomy and security, that the party was able to create an effective administrative structure, carry out social and economic reforms, develop a mass following, and mobililze the masses to revitalize the economy.

As we have seen, it was after the Communists had skillfully used coalition politics to create a relatively secure Huaibei Suwan border base that they began to build rural institutions, secure a strong mass base, and launch various revolutionary programs. In turn, the successful execution of both the redistributive and constructive revolutionary programs enabled the party to augment the human and material resources necessary for the struggle. In the process of revolutionary reconstruction, the party penetrated rural settlements, secured the support of the local elite whose political and economic power had been significantly undermined by the war, reshaped the sociopolitical structure of the village, expanded and consolidated its power, and built up its relations with the peasantry and secured their loyalty. It was through the use of coalition politics and through social revolution in the countryside that the party gained power.

There is no doubt that the revolution in China was a peasant-based social revolution. Factors such as the subsistence crisis created by war and natural disaster, rural poverty, and class relationships played an important role in the revolution. By redistributing rural income through clarification of landownership rights, progressive tax policies, and rent reduction, the party unleashed social forces that enabled them to mobilize the masses of peasants in a collective struggle with traditional elites. Through social leveling, the party, with the support of the peasant masses, was able to gradually chip away some of the elite's economic privileges and political power. After elite power in the countryside had been somewhat weakened by international war and social leveling, the party could proceed to solicit elite compliance, to reorganize rural communities, and to strengthen the political alliance between itself and the peasantry. On the other hand, the party also realized that elite power, albeit weakened, was still very much entrenched in the countryside. In dealing with the local elite, it had to adopt a dual tactic of struggle and compromise.

Because of their rigid Marxist attitudes, Chinese Communists overemphasize class terms in explaining their triumph. The party was riding class conflict to power, and Chinese peasants heeded Communist appeals and responded actively, and at times voluntarily, to Communist calls for the correction of socioeconomic injustices in the countryside. There was no doubt that rural misery and peasant discontent formed part of the picture. Programs such as rent reduction, debt cancellation, and forced seizure of grain from the rich for distribution to the poor had their economic appeal, but such redistributive programs were socially divisive and had a negative impact on certain poorer segments of the peasant population. But the wartime social programs were of a different nature than the radical land reform of the 1930s. They were mostly moderate and relatively nonconfrontational reforms. Some of these programs (such as rent and interest reduction) had been initiated by the Nationalist government in Zhejiang and Jiangsu and might have been acceptable to some patriotic and reformist elites. Such programs were less divisive and disruptive and more attuned to the overall United Front policy advocated by the Communist Party.

Governed by the Marxist ideology of class struggle, Communist literature has often lost sight of the fact that social reforms sometimes served as an integrative force in rebuilding the nation. Revolutionary reconstruction was facilitated by eliminating some of the socioeconomic injustice embedded in the system. But reconstructing society and building a nation also involved drawing various classes and communities together in a concerted effort to remold and rebuild the economy and the local political structure. The party needed the support of both rural classes: the elites, who provided leadership and controlled local resources, and the peasantry, whose manpower and support formed the bedrock of all revolutionary programs. Only after undermining the will and minimizing the capacity of rural elites to organize internal resistance against them could the Communists make their reforms work. The acquiescence and cooperation, even halfhearted, of the rural upper classes were essential for the success of Communist social reform programs.

In the process of reconstruction, the party worked incessantly to secure elite support and participation for its programs. The local gentry were allowed a role in decision making. Friendly persuasion, rather than coercion, was used whenever possible. But Communist rural mobilization was made a lot easier by the fact that gentry power in the countryside had been considerably undermined by the war. The powerful gentry had fled to find refuge in urban centers. Those lesser gentry, commonly known as the "middle elements" or "progressive gentry," who remained behind often found their vested interests rapidly eroded by increasing political instability and the dislocations of war. A fear of Japanese attacks, of GMD military reprisals, and of banditry left them little choice except to cooperate, albeit passively and halfheartedly, with the Communists both in bringing some sort of order back to the area and in restoring the depressed economy. The wartime weakening of elite power rendered the countryside permeable to Communist influence. The rural upper classes were in no position to pose a significant challenge to Communist power. Rural elite cooperation can be explained by a number of factors. Some elite joined the revolution in order to retain power; they saw participation as a chance for upward mobility. Others perceived it as an opportunity for private economic gain, for instance in the land reclamation program. Still others were motivated by the fear of a common enemy, the Japanese, and by a desire for physical protection.

As Quincy Wright has stated, "In times of great emergency such as war, when the objectives of a society's policy—defeat of the enemy—are clear and unquestioned, the integrating influence of administration reaches a maximum."[90] After the gentry was substantially weakened, elite opinions became malleable and revolutionary reconstruction possible. The mobilization and transformation of the countryside could only be achieved with some degree of elite collaboration. Spring planting, for example, would have been impossible, or would only have been achieved with much difficulty, if the wealthy gentry had not been persuaded by the party to give up part of their grain as seed for the program.

The party did not simply act as a mediator between the various rural classes; its economic programs served to integrate communities. Previously isolated and contentious villages were brought together to resolve their differences and work collectively for their common interests. The urgency of such problems as political instability, floods, and subsistence crises allowed the party to ask communities for cooperation. Serving as an agent for change, the party provided initiative, direction, and leadership, but its most significant contribution was arbitration. The planning and execution of programs could only be accomplished through accommodation and community consensus. The party was able to break the barrier of isolation and traditional parochialism.

Although redistributive programs (the progressive tax system) were community-divisive, many of the production projects, such as land reclamation, hydraulic engineering, and spring planting, were community-integrative. Projects such as water control had traditionally been collective programs involving the entire community. By getting rural communities to work together in these enterprises, the Communists made them feel that the projects were their own, not simply something devised by outsiders. In an article on "resistance to social change," Goodwin Watson points out that only programs adopted by consensual group decision with provision for feedback and revision and reconsideration can minimize opposition and facilitate change.[91] Many of the economic programs the Communists promoted in Huaibei were based on this principle.

In the process of transforming the countryside, the Communists were building new social and political institutions. The authority of county mayors and district heads, offices normally dominated by the upper classes, had greatly diminished. Decision making fell into the hands of newly formed multi-class committees, such as the tax grain mobilization committee and the Peasant Famine Relief Association, or inter-village functional groups, such as joint neighborhood land survey teams and the waterworks committee. By involving themselves in production work, the Communists acquired the opportunity to effectively change rural sociopolitical structure. The neighborhood still remained the basic unit of production, propaganda, and collective defense. But above the *bao*, the power structure in the countryside was dramatically transformed, integrated by a hierarchy of cross-class functional committees reaching from the *bao* to the village and the county. Decision making, mass mobilization, and economic transformation were achieved through these committees under the leadership of the Communist Party.

The shift of the peasant masses from passivity and indifference to collective participation in Communist programs cannot be explained solely by their concrete private interests. There is no doubt that equitable taxation, easy access to land, and the tax exemptions in the land reclamation program directly addressed the immediate personal interests of the peasants. We have demonstrated that the peasants were willing to participate in the land survey because nonparticipation would put them in a disadvantageous position. The free ride problem was thus eliminated. Peasant involvement was also governed by the fact that some of these projects were collective; water conservancy had traditionally been a communal project that involved both the elite and the peasantry. Spring planting was collectively planned and executed with the financial assistance of the rural elites. In this way the peasants were assured of its success and its benefits were visible.

Peasant cooperation also hinged on the peasants' growing acceptance of the Communist Party as a legitimate authority. Forming an alliance with the GMD "special commissioner" Sheng Zijin, the party endowed itself with political legitimacy. This image was further enhanced by the Communist success in defending the area against Japanese attacks and introducing a certain degree of political stability. The support of the gentry in production projects bolstered that image even further. Moreover, all these reform projects were backed by the full weight of the Communist government. It was not simply perceived as an agent of surplus exaction and an instrument of social control; it had taken up the traditional gentry role as the leader in rural mobilization and transformation.

Peasants have always been characterized as a social entity of comparatively low "classness."[92] Even when they feel exploited, it is very doubtful they will perceive class issues and come together in class action to correct the unjust situation. Other factors can inhibit peasant class action as well. Their isolation as small producers, the looseness of peasant organizations, the often opposing interests among peasants, the vertical linkage to patrons, and peasants' loyalty to cross-class organizations such as kinship and religious organizations, village, and community, all serve to inhibit collective class action. The Communists were able to heighten the class consciousness of the peasantry because of a number of objective conditions. The breakdown of gentry authority in wartime enabled the party to undermine the vertical link between the rural elite and peasants and establish a horizontal link among the peasants as a class. The new Communist power structure effectively eliminated the brokerage function of the local gentry and significantly undermined the traditional client relationship in the countryside, which had formed the primary obstacle to the Communist attempt to penetrate settled peasant communities discussed in Chapter 3. In times of national and subsistence crisis, and in areas where Communist power was entrenched and strong, chances for class and collective political actions under party leadership increased sharply. The Communist Party relentlessly propagated among the peasants and educated them in class interests.

The transformation of the peasantry was achieved through collective participation and collective action. Participation in the struggle and in revolutionary reconstruction brought the peasants into "public arenas."[93] Peasants were mobilized to join mass organizations, such as the Poor Peasants Credit Bureau (*pinmin jie dai suo*), the Peasant Famine Relief Association (*nongjiu hui*), self-defense squads (*ziwei dui*), and cooperatives. They participated in public neighborhood meetings to decide on household classification and tax payment. Many became low-level administrators in the Communist government. Middle and poor peasants formed half of the leadership at the subdistrict level, and about two-thirds at the neighborhood level.

In the early stages of the revolution, the party led the peasants in food seizures, thus fighting for their private interests. In the period of reconstruction, peasants were mobilized by the cadres, under party leadership, to come together and work for collective and class interests. Eugene Weber says about the transformation of the French peasants, "The transition from traditional local politics to modern national politics took place when individuals and groups shifted from indifference to participation because they perceived that they were involved in the nation."[94]

CHAPTER 8

Structural Constraints: The Taihang Mountains

Social Exchange Theory

In studying peasant revolutions, political scientists often use social exchange theory as an analytical concept for explaining peasant political motivation and peasant participation in revolutionary movements.[1] In spite of its individualistic tendency to focus on a dyadic and face-to-face relationship, social exchange theory is indeed a very powerful paradigm. It concentrates on political interaction and individual behavior and is rooted in economic factors. According to the theory, the input of support can only be understood through careful analysis of social exchanges based on material incentives. It assumes that political actors, as economic beings, always make rational choices in the pursuit of self-interest. Samuel Popkin, for instance, perceives peasants as rational decision makers motivated by concrete interests, and as always seeking to maximize personal and family welfare. Human behavior is often governed by the law of rewards and punishments and the calculus of costs and benefits. Interacting individuals are seen as trying to satisfy their needs and maximize their rewards. The theory also uses a stimulus/response process as the conceptual device for understanding political actions.[2] In studying peasant revolutionary actions, therefore, one should focus on incentives, deterrents, and the process of social exchange.

Jeffrey Race indicates that exchange theory is particularly useful in analyzing an emergent structure. It was through the direct exchange of land, protection, and social mobility for cooperation, compliance, and legitimacy that the Communists established their emergent structure in rural areas.[3] Joel Migdal also contends that peasants are induced to participate in political revolutions by awards and sanctions, not by frustration arising from deprivation. Peasant actions vary tremen-

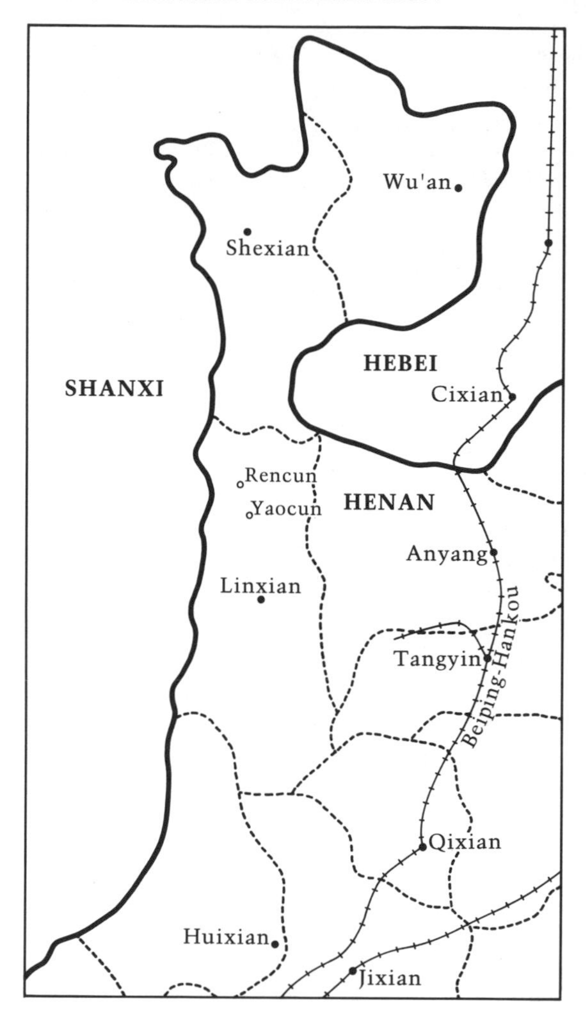

Map 6. The Taihang military zone: area under the administration of the third prefectural commissioner's office.

dously. Peasants usually accommodate the demands of the government, and they are capable of switching from radical revolutionaries to reactionaries. Peasant participation in a revolutionary movement varies, going through stages from low to high. Whether revolutionaries can get peasants to join their side depends on how successful they are in using material incentives to win peasants' trust.

According to Migdal, revolutionaries can sustain peasant participation only by organizing them, institutionalizing social exchange, and routinizing peasant behavior and actions. "This comes about," he observes, "in a process of social exchange, in which peasant support and participation are trade-offs initially for individual rewards. . . . Revolutionaries must provide rewards and sanctions that can overcome the costs and risks to the peasant of participating."[4] This theory can be tested by looking at the interaction and exchange processes between the Chinese Communists and peasants in the Taihang region of northern China. The Taihang is an area well known for its subsistence economy and the extreme economic hardship it suffered at the time of the Communist revolution.

The Chinese Communists penetrated the Taihang region as early as 1925. Initially, the movement was based in the cities, but the Communists gradually fanned out into the countryside. When the Nationalists seized the area after the Northern Expedition, the Communists were driven out of the urban centers. Later, intense state repression almost destroyed the movement.[5] However, at the outbreak of the Sino-Japanese War in 1937, the CCP made a dramatic comeback. The Second United Front provided the party with another political opportunity. The Communists successfully traded military support for peace with GMD-affiliated warlord armies. Communist military commanders, many of whom had graduated from the same military academies as the warlords, used their social ties to approach the warlords about possible alliances.

They helped the warlords set up military training classes so they could defend themselves against the Japanese. In return, the warlords allowed the Eighth Route Army to move into northern Henan and build up an "Anti-Japanese Democratic Government" in Xiuwu county during the summer of 1938. The growing conflicts between the GMD and CCP in the early 1940s eventually put an end to the temporary alliances. The Xiuwu government also collapsed. Meanwhile, the Eighth Route Army had built up its military strength and had captured Ren Village in northern Lin county. The party then turned the village into its headquarters, around which a guerrilla base was set up behind Japanese lines. For the next two years, the Communists continuously fought both the GMD and the Japanese.

In 1942, the party greatly broadened its social base by appealing directly to peasants for support. They did so through income redistribution and a rent and interest reduction movement. With the Eighth Route Army securely entrenched in the area, the party directed the northern Henan military command to consolidate its power in the area. Gradually, the army transformed the guerrilla base into what was commonly referred to as the "Anti-Japanese Democratic Base." Communist influence then slowly expanded to the rest of Lin county. The CCP tried to build its resources by actively engaging the peasant masses in production drives in early 1944. At the same time, the party led local peasants in a class struggle against landlords while also conducting a series of reforms. It distributed famine relief to the poor, reeducated cadres, and rectified the party. In May 1944, it vigorously mobilized peasants to collectively combat the locusts swarming over the region. A couple of months later, it deepened the rent-reduction movement.[6]

This chapter focuses on the three types of interaction the Communists had with local residents in the Taihang region. We concern ourselves first with the start-up process in the countryside and the question of gaining power in a predominantly gentry-controlled rural area. The Communists had virtually nothing to start with except a few idealistic and dedicated student activists. How did they seize power? How did they undermine gentry authority in the countryside? What did they have to offer local people to get them to come over to their side?

Next, after having established their authority in the villages, how did the Communists redistribute rural income? Was rent reduction an effective inducement for securing popular peasant support? Here we have to look at the social conditions within which the exchange with the peasantry took place. Socioeconomic conditions such as land tenure arrangements, rural class relationships, and the particular exploitative nature of the rent system are the crucial factors affecting the three-way relationship among the Communists, the gentry, and the peasants.

The last section concentrates on the goods and services the Communists provided peasants in order to obtain legitimacy for their authority and to mobilize rural cultivators to generate new resources to sustain the revolution. In this section, we look at the problems the Communists encountered in winning compliance and cooperation. During its rule, the party mobilized the peasants in a variety of programs. By carefully examining a few of those programs in detail, we hope to have a better understanding of peasant motivation and response to the complex process of party-peasant revolutionary exchange.

Emergent Structure and Power: Village Struggle in Houjiao

To seize power in a village is never easy. Revolutionaries who move into a village are invariably confronted with a shortage of manpower and a scarcity of material resources. The only option open to them is to make the best use of whatever human and material resources they find in the area. These include agrarian elites, whose support is crucial for any restructuring of power in a village. But elite co-optation always presents problems. Village power holders tend not to be cooperative. Some rural elites may choose to accommodate the new authority temporarily, waiting to see which way the wind blows; others offer out-

TABLE 8.1
Class Structure in Houjiao Village, 1944

Class	Households		Population		Land owned		PHAL	PCAL
	No.	Pct.	No.	Pct.	*Mu*	Pct.	(*mu*)	(*mu*)
LL	4	1.4	9	0.7	42.1	2.8	10.5	4.7
RP	19	6.6	104	8.3	118.0	7.8	6.2	1.1
MP	131	45.8	560	44.8	924.6	60.9	7.1	1.7
PP	120	42.0	490	39.2	431.8	28.5	3.6	0.9
WL			88	7.0				
M	12	4.2						
TOTAL	286	100	1,251	100	1,516.5	100		

SOURCE: *P:JJLY-CJ* 3: 514, appendix 2.
ABBREVIATIONS: LL, landlord; RP, rich peasant; MP, middle peasant; PP, poor peasant; WL, wage laborer; M, merchant; PHAL, per household availability of land; PCAL, per capita availability of land.
NOTE: There might be some double-counting of households in the table. Some of the merchant households might have been included in other classes, giving a total of 286 households rather than the 279 cited in the report.

right resistance. Undermining the power of traditional village elites frequently involves political intrigue and skill at forming alliances.

Aside from appeasing the elites, revolutionaries also have to build a mass base in the area. This requires them to move into the countryside and organize peasants into peasant associations. But popular mass support is not easy to obtain; it hinges on what tangible rewards the revolutionaries have to offer. Without bringing down village power holders, and without seizing the elite's resources, the revolutionaries will have nothing to exchange with the peasants. The first stage of the revolutionary process entails building an emergent local political structure, and this invariably causes a village struggle. To illustrate this process, let us examine the power struggle in Houjiao Village in Lin county in northern Henan. In this case study, we hope to find out how the revolutionaries, with very little to start with, built up power at the grass-roots level.

Houjiao was a typical North China village. According to a Communist survey, in 1944 the village consisted of 279 households with a population of 1,205. Only 35.3 percent of the population (425 persons aged 18–45) were engaged in agriculture. Total acreage was 1,621 *mu*, 5.8 *mu* per household or 1.3 *mu* per capita.[7] If we only include cultivators in this calculation, there were 3.8 *mu* of land available for every active agrarian laborer. The important point is that peasants in Houjiao had easy access to land.

One thing stands out about the social structure in Houjiao: the number of landlords, household and individual, was very small (see Table 8.1). The proportion (2.8 percent) of land they owned was diminutive. In fact, according to a Communist report, most were landlords "in name only." The majority of them were widows and single persons who were forced to rent out their land simply because they lacked sufficient manpower to cultivate the fields. The largest landholder in the village owned only 26 *mu* (62 percent of the total land held by the landlord class). But landlord households as a class possessed roughly three times as much land as the poor peasants, indicating that some sort of income inequity did exist in the community. Still, when compared with figures from other areas of Henan, these statistics lead us to conclude that class differentiation in Houjiao was not wide, and class conflict was not intense.[8]

Village social harmony stemmed from the fact that Houjiao was predominately a monoclan village. Of the 279 households in the village, 270 shared the surname Fu. Corporate kinship, with its internal mechanism of economic leveling, must have had an impact on class structure and the mode of conflict resolution in the village. It is clear that material conditions in the village did not seem very conducive to class struggle, and one can assume that the Communists would have found it difficult to use land as a material inducement for peasant support in this particular village.

The patriarchal power structure in a village is an important factor in analyzing revolutionary struggles. Patriarchy often acts as a structural constraint to revolutionary movement. North China villages were often dominated by patron-client groups. Members of these groups shared certain social identities—kinship, religion, community and rural residence. The bond between patrons and clients was very strong, and patrons often had a combination of clan, religious, and political power. One can assume that in a predominantly monoclan village like Houjiao, village power was in the hands of the dominant clan. However, Chinese clans do not always act as a cohesive group. Cleavages do exist among lineages. Moreover, religious sects, such as the Heavenly Gate Society, were pervasive in the northern part of Henan.[9] The fragmented nature of these sectarian groups, which were usually divided by chapter (centered at the community-based religious altar, or *tan*), and also by their own particular school of martial arts, divided village society along religious/martial arts lines, offering revolutionaries a chance to manipulate rival village factions in their quest for power.

There were two dominant religious sects in Houjiao Village, the Great Immortal Sect (Daxian dao) and the Sage Sect (Sheng dao), both variants of the Heavenly Gate Society. Sect power and community power (*she*) overlapped; community leaders (*she shou*) were often sect leaders. Sect leaders also held administrative positions, such as those of village head (*cunzhang*) or village secretary (*shuji*). And if the sect leader did not personally serve in such a capacity, his protégés always did. The village power structure and sectarian/political groupings thus overlapped.

Socioeconomic forces such as the introduction of modern education into the village, the expansion of the link between the village and global markets, and the political crisis during the Northern Expedition greatly reshaped the village power structure and reshuffled alignments in the 1920s and 1930s. By the time the Communists arrived in the area, there were three dominant sectarian/political factions in Houjiao Village:

1. The Three Little Bands (*san xiao gu*), a new intellectual faction headed by Fu Yuwen. The Three Little Bands controlled 69 households in the village. Its leader was Fu Yuwen, a new intellectual. Fu was reported by the Communists to have come from a rich middle peasant family. He taught at the village primary school and served concurrently as acting district head (*daili quzhang*) in the village. His followers were mostly his primary school students. Extremely shrewd politically, Fu commanded great respect in the community and was considered by the Communists to be the most powerful man in the village. He was also a GMD ally and therefore did not hesitate to sabotage Communist activities if he could. On the other hand, he also supported the Japanese puppets in the area. Because of his immense prestige in the community and his scholarly standing, the intellectual faction was considered by villagers to be the legitimate communal authority, or the "orthodox faction" (*zhengtong pai*).[10]

2. The Five Big Bands (*wu da gu*), the commercial faction headed by Fu Riwang and his cousin Fu Baowang. This faction, composed of 110 village households, was a commercial grouping under the leadership of Fu Riwang, a gentry merchant. An illiterate, a holder of over twenty *mu* of land (probably the largest holder mentioned before), and a "very money-minded usurer," Fu Riwang controlled most of the village's commercial activity. His main business was a village store that sold mountain products, but his financial network reached as far away as Tianjin. He had also established connections with Japanese puppets in the southern part of the county. His cousin, Fu Baowang, a former deputy village head and owner of ten *mu* of land, was his business partner and spokesman. This faction was referred to by the villagers as the "hooligan faction" (*liumeng pai*).[11]

3. The Forty-eight Schools (*sishi ba men*), Fu Penghua's martial arts fraternity. The Forty-eight Schools initially consisted of 60 households but lost four households when their members fled to Shanxi province. At one time this martial arts fraternity was the most powerful faction in the village, and was supported by the Three Little Bands in a feud with

the Five Big Bands. But the Heavenly Gate outburst in 1927 during the Northern Expedition brought about a factional realignment in the village. The Three Small Bands, under the rising star of Fu Yuwen and his students, successfully forged an alliance with the Five Big Bands, and together these two factions dominated village affairs. The Forty-eight Schools went into a decline. Its leader Fu Penghua was 35 years old and a holder of twelve *mu* of land. According to a Communist report, Fu, typical of martial arts masters, was a brave man who often fought for social and economic justice in the village. But the Communists also discovered that he engaged in bribery and often oppressed the people. As an out-of-power group, the Forty-eight Schools gave the Communists strong support in hopes of regaining power.[12]

When the Communists first moved into Houjiao, they controlled the village administration but not the village itself. The power structure in the village remained intact, with the intellectual and commercial factions in complete control. To seize power in the village, the Communists had to ally themselves with some of the rural elites. The party's initial recruits were mostly men of dubious character, for instance Fu Penghua, for whom supporting the Communist authorities was the best chance to regain power. Another ally was Fu Kuanyu, a martial arts teacher in the Great Immortal Sect and the brother-in-law of Wang Zhenguo, a Japanese collaborator. Fu Kuanyu was a typical fence sitter, a man of many faces. He curried the favor of the Communists, acted as a political spokesman for the intellectual faction, and, at the same time actively sought accommodation with the Japanese. Also among the Communist recruits was Fu Kuanyou, a tricky man and a corrupt former village head. According to the Communists, Fu Kuanyou was a lackey of the intellectual and commercial factions. But he was also an ardent supporter of the CCP, and provided the cadres with badly needed protection during the Japanese mop-up campaign.

The party had only two peasant recruits. Fu Yutang was an insidious rich middle peasant, the brother of Fu Yuwen, head of the intellectual faction. Fu Liuhe, the only poor peasant recruit, was owner-cultivator of two *mu* of land. He had reportedly been "oppressed" by the Forty-eight Schools, turned revolutionary, and become an activist in village mass movements.[13] In spite of the obvious unreliability of these characters, the party found that it had to settle for whomever was willing to support it. The CCP needed manpower and local support to build an emergent village structure. For the recruits, supporting the Communists offered the opportunity of upward mobility in the party hierarchy. In the case of the Forty-eight Schools, it meant regaining power in the village. It was essentially a tactic of the weak combining forces to attain political power.

The Communists hoped to use anticorruption as the issue to set in motion a class struggle in the village. The party predicted that the matter would assuredly draw broad support from the masses. But it backfired. The intellectual faction, the party's principal opponent, immediately seized on the issue and discredited the Communists' leading supporter. Fu Yuwen, head of the intellectual faction, accused Fu Kuanyou, the Communist protector, of embezzling C$550 and 140 *jin* of millet during his tenure as head of the village. The intellectual faction hoped to use the corruption issue to manipulate public opinion and deal the CCP a heavy political blow, thus drawing villagers away from the Communists. But Fu Yuwen and the intellectuals also wanted to end the movement as quickly as possible, knowing all too well that if they let it drag on, sooner or later they themselves would become the target of attack. They pressured the Communists to promptly call an anticorruption meeting to single out Fu Kuanyou for punishment.

The party's strategy was to postpone the struggle meeting until it had sufficient time to build up mass support. In order to strengthen its position, the CCP sent cadres to the countryside to mobilize three groups of villagers: impoverished mountain households, peasant activists it had already recruited, and those who were forced to pay unfair taxes. The party used tax reduction to gain peasant support. It also skillfully shifted the target of attack from Fu Kuanyou to Fu Baowang, Fu Kuanyou's patron and the leader of the commercial faction. The Communist argument was that the root of the corruption problems lay not with Fu Kuanyou, but elsewhere. They maintained that it was not the small fish (their supporter) but the big fish (the commercial faction) that the people should target. The party promoted a number of slogans to support its case. "To pull out a creeping plant," one slogan contended, "one has to search for its roots." "To deal with the wolf, one must kill the tiger first," another pointed out.[14] Secretly, the Communists urged their protector to admit his wrongdoing. They also instigated their peasant follower Fu Yutang to openly accuse Fu Baowang of corruption. Initially, however, Fu Kuanyou stubbornly refused to admit his errors at the public struggle meeting, and Fu Yutang refused to go against his kinsman.

The Communists finally persuaded Fu Kuanyou to admit his mistakes at a second struggle meeting. With the case of their own supporter out of the way, the party could now focus its energy on attacking the commercial faction. Fu Baowang steadfastly insisted that he and his faction had done nothing wrong. In the struggle meeting, he arrogantly reprimanded the villagers for accusing him of crimes. Public attention was now focused on him; apparently angered by his arrogance, villagers demanded that his financial accounts be audited by a committee. A committee was set up and spent seven days on the accounts. A follow-up hearing was held. The Communists thought the evidence of corruption and tax evasion they had gathered from the commercial faction's financial statements would be the kind of material they could use to mobilize local residents for an attack on the faction, but they were dead wrong. The villagers had no interest in these issues.

However, by sheer luck, during the course of questioning, the Communists hit upon an entirely different issue. Apparently, in his many business transactions, Fu Baowang had sold the Japanese puppets some firearms. The Communists immediately seized upon the matter and had Fu Baowang arrested and fined. The movement against Japanese collaborators somehow caught on. Through heavy fining of these collaborators, the party slowly built up its financial resources. Chalmers Johnson is not altogether wrong; the party did use political appeals to mobilize the peasantry. The Houjiao case clearly demonstrates that the Chinese Communists did successfully exploit nationalistic anti-Japanese sentiment in the villages to mobilize peasants in the revolution.[15]

With the head of the commercial faction in prison and financially crippled, the Communists then moved to bring down the intellectual faction. This time they made sure they had enough mass support before moving against Fu Yuwen, the most powerful and respected intellectual gentry member in the village. The Communists traded C$1,500, 200 *jin* of grain, and 56 *mu* of land that they had collected in fines to the peasants for participation in the movement. The beneficiaries were organized into a 140-man peasant association and a 30-man militia. To make sure the peasants stayed in the movement, the party stipulated that only members of the peasant association were allowed to join the cooperative, the organ that distributed the rewards. With a group of peasants and a militia behind them, the Communists then launched an anti-traitor movement to bring down Fu Yuwen. Using informants who accused Fu Yuwen of supporting the Japanese peace preservation movement, they persuaded villagers to destroy their most powerful community leader.

With opposing factions shattered and the village firmly under its control, the party broadened its reform programs from selectively benefiting individuals by rewarding them with money, grain, and land to collectively benefiting all villagers by granting interest reductions and introducing progressive taxation. The party initially reduced village taxes by 20 percent, and then conducted a village-wide rent and interest reduction campaign. But it found class benefits alone were not enough to mobilize the peasantry; interest and rent reductions were simply not the main concerns of the majority of villagers. Because of the pervasiveness of owner-cultivators in the village, only four households benefited from this movement. The party found itself still relying heavily on the anti-Japanese collaboration movement to mobilize rural residents.[16] However, with the party securely in power, the Communists could use fine and tax money to promote other programs to build their authority. For instance, they twice dispensed relief loans to villagers. In this way, they were able to enlarge the peasant association to 160 men. The entire village struggle took two months and six days.[17]

The Houjiao Village struggle illustrates that rural revolution is a tortuous political process. To build a revolutionary structure requires the utilization of existing human and material resources, of which revolutionaries always have a limited supply in the beginning. Village factional disputes can sometimes provide an opportunity for recruiting and manipulating out-of-power elites in order to gain power. Winning the peasants' confidence is usually a difficult and unpredictable process. Revolutionaries can proceed to mobilize the peasantry only if they offer tangible rewards for trade-offs. Very often, the material benefits that the revolutionaries can offer are not those the peasants prefer. And political intrigue and social reforms can backfire.

However, the resources gathered in political struggles can be effectively used to buy peasants' support through selective rewards. By means of social exchange, the Communists won over the elites and the peasants and gradually built an emergent structure. Only after having undermined local power holders, having seized their resources, and having built a revolutionary structure can revolutionaries proceed to institute programs to correct social and economic injustices. During the process, revolutionaries must continually routinize peasant behavior and slowly transform the movement into an institutionalized revolutionary struggle.

Redistribution Programs

Scholars studying peasant-based revolutions often postulate that at the initial stage of a revolutionary movement, redistribution of wealth and income among social groups is a useful, and may be the only, means of getting the exchange process going.[18] A shortage of material resources, they insist, does not inhibit revolutionaries in making effective exchanges with deprived groups. Revolutionaries can simply redivide the fixed quantity of wealth and direct a larger portion to the underprivileged. The frequently cited examples of this kind of redistributive exchange are land reform, rent and interest reduction, and progressive taxation. Such programs, scholars argue, enable revolutionaries to utilize existing resources to establish an exchange relationship with those at the bottom of the social ladder, particularly at the incipient stage, when the revolutionaries have little else to offer. To find out how redistributive exchanges worked for the Communists, we will look at one of the programs—rent reduction—that they instituted in the Taihang region. But it is impossible to fully comprehend the workings of Communist rent reduction without a clear knowledge of the prevalent social structure, land tenure arrangements, and class exploitation in the area. Social structure and social relationships often serve as constraining factors that limit the actors' behavior.

Social Structure and Relationships in the Taihang Area

Our data is drawn from the Fifth Special District (*di wu zhuanshu*) of the Taihang military region of the Jin-Ji-Lu-Yu (Shanxi-Hebei-Shandong-Henan) anti-Japanese base. The district was composed of portions of four counties: Shexian, Ciwu (Hebei), Linbei (northern Lin county), and Anyang. In the 1940s, the Fifth Special District was considered by the Communists to be one of the important centers in the Jin-Ji-Lu-Yu border region.

On the whole, the Fifth Special District was a depressed area. The more fertile part, located near the Beiping-Hankou railway, was controlled by the Japanese. Within the area under Communist control, the wetland segment of She county was relatively productive; the rest of the land was nothing but rugged terrain. There was an acute shortage of arable cropland in the area. It was reportedly normal for peasants to subsist on "grain for half a year, and on a mix of brans and vegetables for the other half."[19] The Japanese mop-up campaigns and the ensuing 1942–43 drought completely devastated the region and created one of the most widespread famines in its history. In the spring of 1944, swarms of locusts rendered 70 percent of the land unproductive. As a result, tens of thousands of people perished in the famine; survivors had to subsist on wild vegetables. Most local residents were dependent on the government for relief. The Taihang region experienced a major subsistence crisis in wartime.

Poverty was a common denominator in the region as a whole, but land productivity varied widely from area to area. A Communist survey divided the district into four economic zones; the real dividing line,

TABLE 8.2
Landownership in Northern Henan, by Percent of Households, 1934

County	> 100 *mu*	51–100 *mu*	31–50 *mu*	11–30 *mu*	1–10 *mu*	Landless
Linxian	0.9%	21.7%	4.2%	15.4%	63.6%	2.1%
Shexian	0	0.05	2.5	36.9	50.3	10.2
Wu'an	1.3	4.7	9.9	15.9	49.2	19.1

SOURCE: Zhao Jinsan 1934: 13560–62.

however, was between the plain and the mountains. Rural income was derived mainly from agriculture. In the Communist-designated First Zone, for instance, farming accounted for 86.9 percent of rural income. However, in the mountain zone (in She county), a sizable portion of rural income (24 percent) came from mountain products (*shan huo*), which included lumber, walnuts, persimmons, pears, apples, hot peppers, and hemp. Contrary to the usual perception, the mountains, which covered most of the area, were more prosperous than the plain. The only exception was the section where the Shanxi, Hebei, and Henan borders came together. There, in the most remote part of the mountains, life was extremely difficult. In this area, which was well beyond government control, the only state function was annual tax collection. Here, local residents were said to live on bran and wild vegetables for three-quarters of the year. The Communists reported that if the people had rice for their meal, one could count the number of grains in it. Still, except for this very remote section, the mountain zone produced an annual agricultural surplus of 15–27 percent.[20] This percentage is taken from May 1945 statistics, however, after the Communists had economically transformed the area.

There were hardly any commercial or handicraft activities in the area before the Communist takeover. Some wine making, tobacco growing, and papermaking existed in She county. Typical peasant cottage industries such as spinning and weaving, vegetable oil extraction, livestock raising, and transport work predominated in the rest of the area. Domestic industry, however, represented only a minor part of peasant income.[21]

In 1943, the per capita availability of land in the area was 1.6 *mu*, slightly below the provincial average of 2 *mu* (or 10.5 *mu* per household).[22] After the Communists had reclaimed the land, its per capita availability went up somewhat to 2.29 *mu* (ranging from 1.76 *mu* in She county to 3.04 *mu* in Anyang), close to the provincial average.[23] Most of the property owners were smallholders. The data gathered by the GMD in 1934 (see Table 8.2) indicate that the majority of peasant households owned 1–10 *mu* of land.[24] The table also shows a low concentration of landownership. The highest percentage of households owning more than 100 *mu* was 1.3 percent, in Wu'an county. In She county, no household owned more than 100 *mu* of land and only 0.05 percent of households owned 51–100 *mu*.

Landlordism was seldom a prominent feature in the wheat-growing area in the north, in contrast to the rice paddies in southern Henan. A survey of Ren and Xifeng villages in northern Lin county shows a low percentage of landlordism in both (Tables 8.3 and 8.4). In Ren village, landlords (2.5 percent of village households) owned only 4.1 percent of village land, while in Xifeng, the 1.7 percent of households classified as landlords (including managerial landlords, who invested in and managed the land instead of simply renting it out) held 5.8 percent of village land.

Most of the peasants were owner-cultivators. Even the extremely poor owned some land (for instance in Ren village). In Xifeng village, tenants constituted only 2.4 percent of households and 3.1 percent of the village population. This is supported by GMD data from 1935, which give the proportion of tenants plus landless wage laborers as 8.8 percent (see Table 8.5). However, the disparity of household income among the classes was noticeably wide. In Ren village, landlord household income was nearly 7 times that of the extreme poor; in Xifeng village, it was almost 25 times that of the tenants. This large income gap between rich and poor might have led the Communists to believe that income redistribution through rent reduction could be used as a material benefit in an exchange to gain peasant support.

The Communists' socioeconomic data on Linbei (the northern part of Lin county, where the CCP had its headquarters) is even more revealing. Linbei was located at the foot of the Taihang Mountains in the southern part of the Jin-Ji-Lu-Yu base. West of the county were the mountains, and the Zhang River was to the north. The county, covered

TABLE 8.3
Land and Income Distribution in Ren Village, by Class, 1944

Class	Households (pct.)	Population (pct.)	Land owned (pct.)	Income per household in *shi* of grain a yr.
Landlord	2.5%	1.9%	4.1%	29.1
Rich peasant	10.5	11.0	20.0	29.0
Middle peasant	30.1	33.0	38.3	17.8
Poor peasant	23.7	26.5	21.3	10.9
Extremely poor peasant	31.0	27.3	15.1	4.3
Other	2.2	0.4	1.2	10.5

SOURCE: *P:JJLY-CJ* 3: 364.
NOTE: Income based on total of cereal production, mountain products, handicrafts, trade, and other.

TABLE 8.4
Land and Income Distribution in Xifeng Village, by Class, 1944

Class	Households (pct.)	Population (pct.)	Land owned (pct.)	Income per household in *shi* of grain a yr.
Landlord	0.4%	0.3%	1.6%	39.2
Managerial landlord	1.3	1.2	4.2	28.6
Rich peasant	4.5	6.2	11.0	24.8
Upper middle peasant	7.1	9.9	13.8	18.2
Middle middle peasant	13.6	18.4	22.7	14.8
Lower middle peasant	25.8	26.9	29.3	9.4
Poor peasant	44.4	33.8	21.2	4.2
Tenant	2.4	3.1	0.2	1.6

SOURCE: *P:JJLY-CJ* 3: 368–75.

TABLE 8.5
Types of Peasants in Northern Henan, 1935

Type of peasant	Anyang	Shexian	Linxian	Wu'an
Owner-cultivator				
Households	44.5%	69.4%	79.2%	61.6%
Individuals	42.8	60.9	83.5	59.0
Part owner/part tenant				
Households	43.0	20.0	8.9	22.2
Individuals	45.7	24.4	7.6	25.8
Tenant				
Households	8.5	10.0	5.7	8.9
Individuals	7.5	14.5	5.3	9.2
Wage laborer				
Households	4.0	0.6	6.1	7.3
Individuals	4.0	0.3	3.5	6.0

SOURCE: Henan sheng tongji xuehui et al., *Minguo shiqi Henan sheng tongji ziliao* (Henan statistical materials: The Republican period), 1986 1: 151.

with graded but well-irrigated fields, was situated in very rugged terrain. When the 1941 survey was taken, Linbei had 147 natural villages, grouped into 73 administrative units. Typical of residents of the northern counties, the Linbei people did not have sufficient land for cultivation and county economic performance was poor. The per capita availability of land was only 1 *mu*, and per capita productivity of grain 1.5 *shi*. Local authorities were forced to import 100,000 *shi* of grain a year from neighboring Shanxi province to feed the population. The labor force, mostly cultivator-traders, was highly mobile, and capable males often sought employment in the Japanese-occupied cities. In Dongzhi, for instance, 23 percent of the 400 residents (70 percent of able male laborers) left the village for the urban centers. As a result, seven- or eight-year-old children, most of whom never went to school, had to work in the fields. The standard of living was extremely low. Except for a few wealthy merchants, villagers normally subsisted on carrots and bran for half the year.[25]

The rentier-renter relationship was highly exploitative, as Ralph Thaxton has amply illustrated in his works on this area.[26] Rent, usually collected in midsummer, constituted 50 percent of the yield in fertile lands and 66.6 percent in less fertile lands, in good years. Most rents were fixed and payable partly in wheat and rice, depending on the needs of the rentiers. Abject poverty, according to the Communists, forced rentiers to collect even nickels and dimes. The tenants, not the landlords, paid the taxes and were obligated to provide free labor service to the landlords in times of need. Leases were long, sometimes five years, which gave some protection to tenants. But because of the land shortage, the slightest infraction by the tenant could cause the landlord to rescind his land. In fact, it was clearly stipulated in many land leases that "the landlord has absolute rights to rescind the land at any time without any objection from the tenant."[27]

Tenancy in Linbei, however, was somewhat distinctive. The majority of rentiers were poor "widowers, widows, orphans, and singles" (the *guan-gua-gu-du*), similar to those in Houjiao Village described earlier. These households were forced by a lack of labor to rent their land.[28] The shortage of labor was caused by the flight of workers to nearby cities, which offered attractive employment opportunities. The renters in this county were therefore not poor peasants or the landless, as one might expect, but middle and sometimes rich peasants.[29] The exploiters were the poor, the exploited the rich. Such a peculiar relationship, as we shall see, had a major impact on the Communist rent reduction program.

The county's tenanted land consisted of two types, grain land and radish land. The grain land could be broken down into drylands and rice paddies. Conforming to the national pattern, rentiers of rice land were mostly wealthy landlords, while rentiers of drylands were largely middle and poor peasants. Table 8.6 shows a higher concentration of landownership in the rice-producing paddies than in the wheat-producing drylands.

Tenancy in radish-growing areas was highly exploitative. The majority of leases were short-term and of unfixed tenure; land was rented out for a season and would then lie fallow for the remainder of the year. Tenanted lands were often fragmented into tiny scattered strips. For example, in one village, 22 rentiers leased a total of 80.4 *mu* of land to 169 tenants. Yet radish land was highly productive and attracted a large number of rich and middle peasant renters despite the very high rent.[30]

TABLE 8.6
Social Composition of Rentiers and Renters in Linbei, by Household, 1944

	Rentier			Renter			
Class	No. of households	Amount of land (*mu*)	Tax burden	RP	MP	PP	Total
			WETLAND				
LL	2	70.0	Tenant		12	2	14
RP	1	4.5	Tenant			2	2
UMP	1	7.5	Tenant		3		3
TOTAL	4	82.0			15	4	19
			DRYLAND				
LL	1	4.5	50:50	1		1	2
RP	1	1.8				1	1
MP	3	7.0	Tenant		2	7	9
PP	4	6.4	Tenant		3	7	10
TOTAL	9	19.7		1	5	16	22

SOURCE: *P:JJLY-CJ* 3: 501.
ABBREVIATIONS: LL, landlord; RP, rich peasant; UMP, upper middle peasant; MP, middle peasant; PP, poor peasant.

What we find in Linbei, and in northern Henan in general, is a wartime subsistence economy in which economic distress and severe dislocation were predominant. In that type of economy, one is likely to assume that the scarcity of cropland and the exploitative rent system in the area were exactly the kind of economic explosives the Communists were looking for in peasant mobilization. Operating in this kind of depressed and exploitative economy, the Communists could effectively use land redistribution and rent reduction as material incentives to recruit peasants into the revolution. However, despite such a depressed agrarian situation, North China as a whole was characterized by a low tenancy rate and a low concentration of landownership. In some areas, one cannot even find a landlord. Moreover, local land arrangements, as demonstrated in the Linbei data, sometimes can be very peculiar. In the case of Linbei, the landlords (or rentiers, for they were not landlords in the usual sense) were poor "widowers, widows, orphans, and singles," typically the sort of people the Communists were trying to help. The rentiers, on the other hand, were the relatively rich and middle peasants, or the large landholders. As we will find out, this peculiar social arrangement served as a structural constraint on the Communist rent reduction movement.

The Rent Reduction Movement

The Communist revolutionaries were visionaries. To them, mobilizing the peasants in a rent reduction movement was not simply using concrete rewards in exchange for peasants' political support and participation. Their overarching goal, as defined by Mao in his June 1, 1943, directive on the "mass line," was to learn from the masses what they wanted, put their ideas into action, and eventually transform their consciousness. This involved "taking the ideas from the masses, propagating them until the masses embraced them as their own and putting them into practice." It was only after the masses were sufficiently awakened to their needs and the Communists had won their confidence that cadres could put their programs into action.[31] To learn from the masses and to arouse their consciousness, the party adopted a number of revolutionary tactics, most of which were later employed in the land reform movement of the 1950s.

Venting one's grievances. Cadres were instructed to seek out the most oppressed tenants in a village and to urge them to vent their grievances (*suku*) so that they could use these as examples to draw a class line between landlords and tenants. They were told to warn the peasants that the landlords were politically very powerful. The only way the peasants could win the struggle was to augment their collective strength by coming to each other's assistance. In other words, cadres were instructed to promote class solidarity.

Settling accounts. Cadres were to demonstrate to peasants how landlords took advantage of them by "settling accounts" (*suanzhang*), actually calculating for peasants the amount landlords gained from their exploitative actions.

Explaining government legislation to peasants. Communists cadres were told to explain carefully to tenant peasants the new government legislation, underscoring the fact that the Communist Anti-Japanese Democratic Government was set up to work for their welfare. The cadres were to highlight the differences between the new Communist government and former warlord authorities.

Face-to-face and group discussions. Cadres were instructed to seek out active peasants for face-to-face discussion and to recruit them into the movement. They were also told to hold small group discussions and tenants' meetings to arouse the peasants. In the tenants' meetings, the revolutionaries were to use local cadres who had influence in the village to head the discussion. The party hoped that their influence in the community could put pressure on the gentry to agree to reduce the land rent and to sign long-term leases. They were also instructed to focus the discussions on the landlords' arguments and use those arguments to demonstrate to the peasantry the gentry's evil mentality and exploitative schemes.

How effective were these revolutionary tactics? Did they transform the peasant class consciousness? The results were mixed. The dyadic contacts adopted by the party at Yaocun, the village where Ralph Thaxton conducted a social survey, had only limited success.[32] Few peasants poured out their grievances, but the party did manage to recruit a couple of peasant activists. On the whole, the Communists failed to mobilize the peasant masses. Because of the low tenancy rate in the area, peasants regarded tenants' grievances as isolated individual problems. In group discussions, if cadres illustrated their points with concrete problems (as in Chengbei and Beiling villages), the peasants understood their arguments and the Communists obtained results. Once they moved from concrete incidents to more ideological topics, the peasants were completely at a loss. Many cultivators found these meetings a nuisance. The most effective method the Communists found was to focus the discussion on landlords' arguments. In this way, the cadres could use concrete examples to highlight class differences.[33]

The party's goal was to instill a sense of "historical class self-awareness" (*lishi jieji zijue*) or "emancipating consciousness" (*fanshen zijue*) in the peasantry. Through long-term education of the peasants in class differences, the party hoped to drive a wedge between landlords and peasants and to mobilize aggrieved cultivators in a rural class struggle. However, the peasant response was essentially one of passivity. Party programs often ran into the obstacles of timidity and traditional servility. Some Communist tactics went against established rural customs and usages. North Henan tenants were so accustomed to the prevalent rent system that many believed it was unreasonable (*likui*) to require landlords to reduce rents. Some tenants insisted that such actions went against their conscience, even though cadres showed them the new government legislation which required landlords to lower rents, thus demonstrating that the landlords had been taking advantage of their ignorance. The peasants still remained essentially indifferent. One peasant told a cadre, "If you insist that I should ask him to reduce the rent, well, I will do it. But it still weighs on my conscience." Another tenant apologized to a landlord, saying "I never asked for a rent reduction. The cadres ordered me to do so. So, let's reduce the rent. You know very well that tenants have the obligation to pay rent anyway."[34] Communist rural mobilizers often complained in their reports that although peasants were outwardly complying with orders, they were secretly still paying the same rent. Their apparent agreement was only a show. The peasants, the Communists said, were simply following orders mechanically in the class conflict, and had little understanding of the meaning of class struggle. One peasant even told a cadre that he was "struggling for the government." In spite of the misery they had to endure in wartime, most peasants did not display the kind of moral outrage portrayed by moral economists. It seems that it was apathy and passivity rather than moral anger and revolutionary fervor that the Communists encountered in northern Henan's rural communities.

In their reports, Communist mobilizers tried to rationalize the peasants' passive behavior. They stated that the peasants were indifferent to Communist programs because these cultivators had no leaders of their own, except for the Communist cadres, who might be there only temporarily. Peasants were not sure if the Communists were there to stay. Most of them were only looking for immediate economic gain; no one wanted to take on political responsibility. This explained why no peasants wanted to be elected village head after a successful political struggle. The peasants realized that once Communist troops moved out of the area, the traditional political order would return and gentry power would again become predominant. Only in a few instances, when the peasants backed one another and were confident of a successful political outcome, did they become bold enough to refuse rent payment to landlords. In one case, a tenant fearlessly threatened his landlord, saying, "You told me, 'Wait till the Eighth Route Army leaves town, then I will come back for the rent.' Well, let me tell you. I will pay the rent only after the Eighth Route Army has left town." Another peasant bickered with his landlord over the rent payment, saying that he was abiding by government regulations. But these were very rare cases, the Communists reported.[35]

The Communists realized that the best way to secure peasant support was through an exchange of economic benefits with the peasantry. But at the same time, they were moved by lofty Marxist ideals to go beyond a simple reliance on material incentives to mobilize the peasants. They wanted to educate rural cultivators and arouse their consciousness through the process of class struggle. To their disappointment, they found that the class struggle was often bogged down by peasant economic interests, or what they referred to as "peasant economism" (*nongmin jingji zhuyi*). It seemed that the peasants were energized by one thing and one thing only—private economic benefits. The Communist tactic of settling accounts did arouse some peasants, but only those who had something to gain from rent refunds. In the class struggle, the peasants usually focused on one thing: coercing landlords to give up their grain stocks for redistribution. Nothing else mattered.

The struggle meeting in Swallow Ravine (Yanyu) village was a good example. When a particular landlord opened his mouth in the meeting, the peasants immediately shut him up, accusing him of making a show of his authority. Trying to avoid a conflict, the landlord then became very courteous, but the peasants accused him of "smiling and grimacing" (*xipi xiaolian*). The landlord then bowed his head and dared not utter a word. The peasants again chided him, this time for "pretending to be a dead dog." The struggle promptly ended after the landlord agreed to give up 100 *shi* of grain for redistribution. The Communists insisted that they wanted all struggles to be "a struggle for reason." Nevertheless, it was not reason but concrete material benefits that guided peasant behavior, and most of the time it was coercion and not reasoning that eventually forced landlords to yield to peasants' demands.

The party hoped that by continually educating peasants about class relationships and clearly informing them of new Communist legislation the peasants would eventually be awakened and would rise up on their own in the struggle against their class enemies. What they did not anticipate was the highly dependent nature of the peasant mentality. Tenant farmers, so accustomed to deferring to the gentry and local authority, simply asked the Anti-Japanese Democratic Government to take responsibility and make decisions for them (*zuozhu*). Class struggle was frequently a "government-run" business (*guanban*). If the cadres did not take control of and manage the struggle, all class struggle sessions would simply degenerate into mob contentions, with local thugs taking over and using brute force to extract things from anybody and everybody, including the middle peasants, the very agrarian class with which the party sought to ally.

The preponderance of gentry power and the skillful tactics gentry used often severely limited Communist-peasant exchanges. To confront the Communist assault, the gentry adopted soft- and hard-line tactics. Some gentry, the so-called progressives, for instance, readily admitted their mistakes in struggle sessions and vowed that in future they would abide by the new Communist legislation. Such tactics prevented tenants from denouncing them. Many gentry were very courteous. A common tactic was to flee the area once the struggle began and to return to the village only when it was over. The politically powerful but economically weak gentry tended to support the Communist policy of economic redistribution, as they had much to gain and little to lose. But all rural elites were frightened at the thought of class struggle. Many made "donations" to Communist relief programs to demonstrate their "progressiveness" and to prevent a class attack. The "evil" ones intimidated peasants and bribed cadres (giving the cadres gifts, agreeing to make them their adopted sons, and offering their daughters to them in marriage).

Another tactic the gentry used was to spread rumors about a "change of heaven" by intimidating the peasantry with the overwhelming military superiority of the Nationalist forces and by predicting an imminent return of Nationalist rule. Playing on the peasants' superstitious mentality, some gentry convinced peasants that rural sufferings, although deplorable, were a matter of fate. The only way to alleviate such misery, they said, was to make religious offerings to the deities in the village temples. Some used cadres' mistakes to divide the party and the masses. Others talked about a landlord alliance to quell the movement and threatened peasants into submissiveness. The Communists found it extremely difficult to undermine the authority of the rural gentry. The best they could do, they reported, was to replace one opposing elite faction with another that was slightly more sympathetic to the revolutionary cause. They found that extracting material from rural elites to satisfy the needs of peasants was one thing; overturning the traditional feudal order in the villages was an entirely different matter.

Part of the problem stemmed from the ignorance and the inefficiency of low-level party leadership. The party repeatedly issued directives to educate the cadres in the basics of rent reduction, and guidelines were clearly spelled out in county-wide cadre conferences. But many cadres accepted these directives only halfheartedly. Some of them found the "mass line" too abstract to understand. Others insisted that the landlord-tenant dispute was not the principal contradiction in the countryside. Without a rent reduction campaign, they argued, they could still effectively mobilize the peasantry. Instead of following the party goal of channeling peasants' energy into rent reduction, many cadres directed it to the anticorruption and anti-bully movements.

Apparently, it took less effort to fine corrupt gentry than to institute a rent reduction. Moreover, heavy fines enabled cadres to extract more material to exchange with peasants. Even in areas where rent reduction movements had already been started, the idea of immediate concrete gains through direct extraction by fining led cadres to call off rent reduction and launch the anticorruption and anti-bully movements instead. Some even used these campaigns to reap a windfall profit for themselves. As the focus of class struggle was on fines and heavy extractions, struggle sessions were relegated to show only. Struggle meetings often ended abruptly after a couple of gentry were arrested and fined. The peasants were seldom mobilized, one report complained, and cadres did not understand the real meaning of rural contradictions. Without clear direction, class struggles often degenerated into chaos. In Ren village, for instance, villagers were robbed. In East Mount village, groups of villagers scrambled to seize landlords' firearms. In Yaocun, corruption became so widespread that nine cadres were eventually prosecuted by the Communist government.[36]

Communist reports were highly critical of cadres for having "leftist" tendencies or being overzealous in mass movements. These leftist cadres reportedly believed that it was more rewarding to mobilize the masses to attack landlords than to mobilize the peasants to join the army. Class conflict brought the masses concrete material benefits, and anticorruption and anti-bully campaigns in particular provided maximum rewards. Cadres were therefore convinced that it was better to be "left" than "right." The leftist tendency, they explained to the party, meant taking care of the needs of the peasantry. As a result, their policy was that to mobilize was better than not to mobilize. The leftists always worked on a policy of extracting the maximum from landlords. This tendency, a report noted, accounted for much of the excessive peasant behavior referred to as "peasant economism." On the other hand, some cadres suffered from a "rightist" tendency. They held a conviction that it was impossible to mobilize the peasants. They either completely ignored party instructions or adopted a laissez-faire attitude and left class struggle to the masses.[37]

In summarizing half a year of class struggle, one report had this to say:

> On the whole, the struggles in the past half a year did accomplish something. But there were also major shortcomings. The people in Linbei did not have a clear understanding of the true nature of the land policy and the real meaning of class struggle. The county leadership was not always in agreement. The cadres failed to combine class struggle with revolutionary works. Some of them struggled for the sake of struggle; for others, it was merely carrying out their duty. At least half of the cadres never participated in any struggle. There was a lack of control in the leadership. Some cadres lacked discipline, became idle, and did not spend much time organizing the masses. The lower-level party organizations were out of line with the upper-level party organizations. Cadres disagreed among themselves and formed factions, thus greatly complicating the mass movement. At the lower level of the party, we find a laissez-faire attitude and a lack of discipline and, at the upper level, bureaucratism. All these mistakes severely hindered the development of the mass struggle in Linbei. Many cadres ignored the main objective and failed to unite the classes. They only engaged in foolhardy and reckless actions.[38]

How successful was the rent reduction movement in Linbei? Party statistical data indicate that the rent reduction was successfully carried out in only 12 (5.5 percent) of the 218 villages the Communists in-

TABLE 8.7
Effectiveness of Reform Movements in Linbei, by Type of Village, 1944

Movements	Number of villages	Percent
Rent reduction[a]		
Type A	12	5.5%
Type B	29	13.3
Rent reduction, anti-bully, debt clearance[b]		
Type C	36	16.5
Type D	41	18.8
Type E	30	13.8
No mobilization	70	32.1
TOTAL	218	100 %

SOURCE: *P:JJLY-CJ* 3: 428.

[a]Type A: peasantry successfully mobilized in rent reduction; party branches, peasant associations, local militia, and Communist authority established. Type B: rent reduction partially successful; government managed most movements.

[b]Type C: movement focused mainly on tenancy problems, but was poorly carried out. Type D: Mainly anti-bully movements. Type E: Slightly affected by the movement; some problems solved, but little mobilization in the area.

tended to mobilize (see Table 8.7). Over 30 percent of the villages were not ever mobilized. In many villages, the target of attack was only local bullies, not the gentry. Reports stated that the movements were poorly carried out and frequently divorced from the masses. Party cadres simply bestowed land on peasants as favors (*enci*) and ran the whole movement without consulting the peasants, although the overriding objective, as clearly stated in all party directives, was for the party to lead the masses to struggle for their own rights.

An analysis of 50 mass struggles that the party conducted in Lin county in the latter part of 1944 shows the same limited results. The movement affected 36 villages in that county, with a total participation of 5,000 people. The largest number of participants in any single struggle was 270 persons, the smallest 30. Of the 50 struggles, only 5 (10 percent) resulted in rent reductions. The rest of the struggles revolved around other issues: anticorruption (13), unfair taxation (13), loan payment clearance (3), wage increases (3), anti–feudal society (1), anti-bully (8), anti–secret agents (2), and others (2). Figures on the attack targets in 33 struggles involving 3,209 participants show only 47 persons were under attack, an average of slightly over 1 person per struggle, which demonstrates that the scope of the attacks was very restricted. The majority of the attack targets were, obviously, landlords (including managerial landlords) and rich merchants (usually moneylenders), but the movement also affected a number of rich middle peasants and middle peasants. Many of the targets were GMD members or *baojia* headmen, the traditional power holders in rural society.[39]

Did the mass movement alter the social structure in the countryside? Were the underprivileged classes (the poor and dirt-poor peasants) better off after the struggle? Did the movement undermine the economic power of the landholders? Statistics from two villages, Nanlingyang and Langlei, both in Lin county, provide us with answers (see Table 8.8). The figures show that the landlord class (both ordinary and managerial landlords) was greatly reduced, in number of households as well as people. This may be a direct result of landlords fleeing the area. There was also a reduction in the number of households and individuals in the underprivileged classes. There was a corresponding bulging of the rich and middle peasant classes, an indication that some of the underprivileged peasants might have moved up to become middle peasants.

In terms of economic gains for the poor, the supposed leveling effect of the mass movement is not very noticeable. Managerial landlords evidently lost a sizable amount of land in the struggles, but ordinary landlords actually gained land in the process. Not only did the percentage of land they owned as a class increase, but also the per household and per capita availability of land. The mass struggles apparently did not prevent the landed upper classes from using political instability to acquire more land. But, as we have seen, many of them did suffer considerable losses in the struggle. Landlords were coerced into giving up the grain stocks, and, in areas where the rent reduction movements

TABLE 8.8
Class Structure, Population, and Landownership in Linbei, Before and After the Reform Movements

	Pct. of households		Pct. of population		Pct. of land owned		PHAL (*mu*)		PCAL (*mu*)	
Class	B	A	B	A	B	A	B	A	B	A
LL	1.1	0.5	2.9	0.8	2.9	4.1	28.0	32.2	2.8	10.7
ML	2.3	1.6	3.4	2.1	12.4	3.9	56.3	21.4	10.2	3.8
RP	4.0	4.9	7.3	6.6	9.8	16.4	26.1	25.0	3.8	5.1
MP	45.8	51.6	50.8	57.8	53.1	45.9	12.2	6.6	2.9	1.6
PP	41.5	38.9	32.0	31.3	21.5	29.5	5.4	5.6	1.9	2.0
EP	4.4	2.3	3.6	1.4	0.2	0.2	0.4	0.7	0.1	0.3

SOURCE: *P:JJLY-CJ* 3: 425.
ABBREVIATIONS: B, before; A, after; LL, landlord; ML, managerial landlord; RP, rich peasant; MP, middle peasant; PP, poor peasant; EP, extremely poor peasant; PHAL, per household availability of land; PCAL, per capita availability of land.
NOTE: The data come from Nanlingyang and Langlei villages in Linbei. The table compares 1944 (before the mass movements) with 1945 (after the movements). Computational errors in the original data have been corrected.

TABLE 8.9
Socioeconomic Change in Jiabi in Ciwu County, 1942–44

Class	1942	1943	1944	Change
Changes in household distribution (%), by class				
Landlord	4.0%	3.4%	2.6%	−1.4%
Rich peasant	2.3	2.7	3.0	+0.7
Rich middle peasant	2.3	4.7	5.1	+2.8
Middle peasant	28.5	39.2	44.9	+16.4
Poor peasant	54.6	46.2	42.2	−12.4
Landless peasant	6.4	2.7	0.5	−5.9
Petty trader	1.4	1.0	1.6	+0.2
Handicraftsman	0.4	0.1	0	−0.4
No. of households	692	775	779	+87
Changes in population (%), by class				
Landlord	3.9%	3.0%	2.2%	−1.7%
Rich peasant	3.7	3.7	4.5	+0.8
Rich middle peasant	3.0	7.2	7.2	+4.2
Middle peasant	29.4	40.0	43.8	+14.4
Poor peasant	54.9	43.2	40.6	−14.3
Landless peasant	3.9	1.7	0.4	−3.5
Petty trader	0.9	1.0	1.3	+0.4
Handicraftsman	0.4	0.1	0	−0.4
Population	3,246	3,204	2,937	−309
Changes in landownership (%), by class				
Landlord	16.2%	10.8%	7.2%	−9.0%
Rich peasant	9.0	7.6	9.7	+0.7
Rich middle peasant	6.2	11.5	11.9	+5.7
Middle peasant	42.9	46.3	49.6	+6.7
Poor peasant	25.6	23.6	21.5	−4.1
Landless peasant	0	0	0	0
Petty trader	0.1	0.2	0.1	0
Handicraftsman	0	0	0	0
Total land (*mu*)	5,173	6,746	6,798	+1,625
Changes in per household availability of land (in mu), by class				
Landlord	29.9	28.1	24.4	−5.5
Rich peasant	29.1	24.4	28.6	−0.5
Rich middle peasant	20.0	21.5	20.1	+0.1
Middle peasant	11.3	10.3	9.6	−1.7
Poor peasant	3.5	4.4	4.5	+1.0
Landless peasant	0	0	0	0
Petty trader	0.6	1.7	0.7	+0.1
Handicraftsman	0	0	0	0
Changes in per capita availability of land (in mu), by class				
Landlord	6.5	7.5	7.5	+1.0
Rich peasant	3.9	4.3	4.9	+1.0
Rich middle peasant	3.4	3.4	3.8	+0.4
Middle peasant	2.3	2.4	2.6	+0.3
Poor peasant	0.7	1.1	1.2	+0.5
Landless peasant	0	0	0	0
Petty trader	0.2	0.4	0.2	0
Handicraftsman	0	0	0	0

SOURCE: *P:JJLY-CJ* 3: 137–39.

succeeded, into reducing the land rent. The poor and extremely poor peasants did benefit materially, but gained very little in terms of land. The most profitable reward peasants received usually came from the grain redistributions of the anticorruption and anti-bully campaigns. For instance, statistics are available for 326 cases handled by the Communists in 29 village struggles in the Sixth District of Lin county.[40] In only 93 cases (29 percent) involving 310 *mu* of land did rent reductions take place. But through fines, local peasants obtained 580 *shi* of grain, C$184,790, 24 houses, and 7 guns.[41] These figures confirm the fact that the most rewards in the class struggle came from fines.

Similar results were found in Ciwu county. The Communists conducted a detailed survey of a typical village, Jiabi, in the northern part of Ciwu, in 1942 and 1944, the two years when rent reduction movements were being carried out in the area (see Table 8.9). As a class, the size of the population and the holdings of landlords diminished. The per capita availability of land increased for all classes, including landlords and rich peasants. This might have resulted from the land reclamation program initiated by the Communists, which augmented total acreage by 1,625 *mu*. But if we look at the changes in the per capita availability of land, surprisingly, it was the landlords and rich peasants who came out slightly ahead. This might be the result of a drop in the total number of individual landlords and rich peasants as a consequence of some having fled the war; those who stayed behind were perhaps able to take advantage of the situation to acquire more land. In terms of landownership, it seems that it was not the poor peasants or the landless but the rich peasants, rich middle peasants, and middle peasants who were the beneficiaries of Communist reform.

In areas where rent reduction was successful, for instance, the Sixth District of Lin county, there was a marked change in the socioeconomic status of tenants. Data from the 411 tenant households in the twenty villages there indicate that 20 of the 57 extremely poor households became poor peasants, and 42 of the 225 poor peasant households moved up to be middle peasants. Initially, there were only 3 rich peasant households; after the movement, 29 more were added.[42] But as stated before, the scope of the rent reduction movement was extremely limited. Only in areas where the movement was completely carried through did underprivileged classes make some gains.

Our findings demonstrate that the Communist rent reduction movement was not a simple formula of an exchange of rent reductions for peasant support and involvement in the revolutionary movement. The social exchange process was highly constrained by the existing social structure and relationships in the area. On the surface, the abject poverty in the countryside in northern Henan and the exploitative nature of the landlord-tenant relationship portrayed by Ralph Thaxton should have served to facilitate the exchange between the Communists and local peasants. In a way, one can even use the term "immoral" to describe the subsistence-oriented economy in the area.[43] But the small size of the landlord class, the lack of a concentration of landownership, and the distinctive nature of landlordism in this area (the poor exploiting the rich) served to block a meaningful social exchange.

Communist cadres found it less complicated to direct the peasants' energy toward anticorruption and anti-bully movements than toward the rent reduction program. They found it much simpler to aim their attacks at a couple of corrupt officials and village bosses, to appropriate materials from these people, and to trade these resources for peasant support than to mobilize the peasantry to fight for rent reductions. The existing social structure and social relationships in the area give us a clue to understanding the poor peasants' failure to heed the Communist calls to refuse rent payments to landlords. Most of the rentiers, like the tenants themselves, belonged to the underprivileged classes. Peasants therefore looked for tangible rewards such as grain, cash, and other material benefits in the struggle. It was material rewards, not political consciousness or political responsibility, that the poor sought. It was not moral outrage or moral consensus that motivated them to take action. The exchange between the Communists and the peasants was hampered by a number of factors: the traditional passivity of the peasantry, the predominant power position of local gentry, and the idealistic program implemented by inexperienced low-level cadres. All these objective and subjective factors inhibited the exchange process. They also account for the limited success of the Communist rent reduction movement. Rent reduction was not enough of a motivating force to get peasants to participate in class struggle. The scope of the attack was too restricted and the payoff too small. The only redistributive program that really worked was a siphoning off of some surplus grain, cash, and firearms from one or two local despots and corrupt officials for distribution to the underprivileged. In view of the limited success of the redistributive program, the Communists had to institute other programs to attract peasants into the revolutionary movement.

Famine Relief and Production Programs

The legitimacy of Communist rule in the countryside depended on winning the confidence of the peasantry. This involved providing the goods and services rural elite patrons had traditionally offered peasants. According to James Scott and Benedict Kerkvliet, the established patron-to-client flow in traditional rural society includes physical protection, access to arable land, provision of seeds and implements, the guarantee of a subsistence livelihood, and the giving of food and loans to cultivators in times of economic distress.[44] But in wartime, the Communist revolutionaries had to do more. Resources were scarce, and if the Communists wanted to provide these goods and services to cultivators, they had to increase resources through production. By mobilizing peasants in production drives, routinizing their behavior, and gradually building stable reciprocal exchange relationships, the party won the trust of the peasantry. It was by playing the role of the rural elite and by institutionalizing and routinizing their relationship with the peasants that the Communists ensured their authority would be regarded by the peasantry as legitimate. Communist revolutionaries thus had to be agents of community integration and state builders. Next we find out how the Communists promoted and institutionalized their rural programs, and we then examine party-peasant interaction.

Famine Relief

One of the traditional roles of the gentry was the dispensation of relief to local people in times of such crises as crop failure, drought, or war. The Communists' deep concern for the welfare of the peasants, particularly in times of suffering, prompted them to institute a crisis-mitigating relief program immediately after seizing power. The famine in northern Henan in 1943 was particularly severe. In disaster areas under Communist control, there was a 22 to 38 percent drop in village population.[45] War and famine together created so many social problems that the Communists sometimes found them almost impossible to handle.

In Lu Stockade village (Lu zhai) for instance, of the 703 village households, 82 fled the famine and 87 of those remaining were totally dependent on the Communist government for relief. During the famine, 9 children in the village were sold, 18 girls were given to wealthy families as child brides, and out of desperation, 1 villager joined the Buddhist monastery. There were originally 20 beggars in the village; 23 more were added to their ranks. Twenty-seven households were forced to marry off their daughters and six couples filed for divorce. Many senior citizens died and 130 villagers had swollen faces from subsisting on scholar-tree leaves (*huai ye*). The village was pillaged again and again by bandits. The situation further deteriorated because of a devastating Japanese mop-up campaign. During the attack, the village lost 150 *shi* of grain and 234 able males, who had failed to flee the area, were captured by Japanese troops. Even the wealthy households could not get food. Survival became the major problem confronting villagers. As a result, the Communist court was clogged with cases of personal dispute, divorce, and coerced marriage. The CCP was able to cope with problems of such magnitude only because it had anticipated a protracted war with the Japanese and had stored some grain. The entire government grain stock (war grain, grain earmarked for combatants' families, grain gathered by the Village Relief Committee and confiscated in village struggles, grain "donated" by the gentry, and credit grain) was immediately distributed by the Communists to provide relief.

It was through programs such as this that the party began to organize the peasants and to build the institutions and reciprocal exchange relationships that eventually won the peasants over. In order to distribute grain equitably, peasants were ordered to form committees to assess the degree of hardship of each recipient. Relief households were graded by their needs. Neighborhoods (*lu*, or lane neighborhood, literally the gate entrance to an alley) constituted the basic famine assessment units, and neighborhood households elected their leaders and held relief fund distribution meetings. Villagers were required to oversee each other's conduct and expose cases of misappropriation and misuse of funds, for example, for such unnecessary items as clothing in times of starvation and struggle for survival. Peasant communities were mobilized as collective units. These communities not only acquired organizational skill in the process, but the mobilization and institution building became a revolutionary educational experience for both cadres and villagers. Famine relief also promoted village integration; when the Communists ordered villages that had escaped disaster to loan grain and money to famine-stricken villages, peasant associations from these villages cooperated with each other to solve the famine problem.[46]

The famine relief project was not carried out without problems. Peasant self-interest and greed frequently entered into the picture. For instance, peasants who had two *shi* of grain and who were considered to be rather well off in times of famine went around begging. Landless peasants often seized this opportunity to acquire land, as the price had declined to very low levels. Some peasants used all their cash and grain savings to purchase a piece of land and afterward went to the government for relief. The "grain borrowing" movement created a great deal of social disruption. Even though the party had cautiously instructed cadres to use grain borrowing as a last resort because of its disruptive effect, the acute food shortage and widespread rural suffering left the government with no choice.

Most of the time, cadres had to coerce the gentry to loan the government grain. In one district, party cadres conducted a house-to-house search for food, forcing villagers to open their cellars for inspection. Grain holders were then offered the options of selling, donating, or loaning their grain to the government. In some areas, to put pressure on the gentry to give up their grain, cadres organized demonstrations to denounce landlords for hoarding grain. They promoted slogans such as "Those who refuse to loan the government grain are traitors." Some cadres even used local thugs and sectarians from the Heavenly Gate Society to accomplish their task. These ruffians marched into a landlord's house, made themselves a hearty meal, and then seized the landlord's grain stock, keeping some of it for private use before handing the rest over to the government. The Communists reported that such actions were highly damaging and condemned these "excesses" as "subjective" and "isolationist."[47]

In order to minimize rural instability and to limit the scope of attack, the party reformulated its grain policy. New regulations permitted each household to possess two *shi* of grain for private consumption. Local governments were allowed to "borrow" only 20 percent of the surplus grain in each locality, 30 percent of the grain stock of landlords and rich peasant households and 10 percent of the stock of the rest of the village households. The new regulations also urged cadres to seek support from the "progressive" gentry. They were required to involve the peasants in all grain-borrowing decisions and to debate all problems in peasant associations. Cadres were ordered to use social pressure rather than brute force, to encourage interfamily borrowing, and to get relatives and neighbors to pressure the gentry to give up their grain.[48]

Production Drives

The debilitating wartime famine made the party realize that unless it organized the peasants in a production drive, they were not going to be able to provide the people with their daily necessities and to guarantee them a subsistence livelihood. In 1944, the party therefore promoted three projects to increase production—spring vegetable cultivation, spinning and weaving, and mutual aid teams for labor exchange. Party policies, no matter how beneficial they were to rural residents, had to overcome the basic problem of peasant resistance to change.

In mid-March 1944, the CCP called upon peasants to begin growing vegetables. The policy planned for production of 200 *jin* of vegetables per person. The party had carefully studied the project and had propagated it widely among the peasants in the "winter schools," (*dongxue*). The initial negative responses from the peasants were "It's useless. April is too late for growing vegetables." "We have no seeds nor the manpower. Even if we had the manpower, we have no money for the seeds." "We have no land to spare for vegetables."[49] Such reactions were typical of the peasants' way of expressing their aversion to innovations.

To solve the critical problem of seeds, the party purchased vegetable seeds through peasant cooperatives and local stores and also obtained seed loans from rich households in the village. They then distributed the seeds to the peasants. To make sure that the project was understood by the cultivators, cadres carried out a house-by-house promotion, carefully explaining the government policy to the peasants. But even with such active promotional efforts, the result was highly disappointing. In the First District in Linbei, only five of the twelve villages in the government plan fulfilled their quotas. The party later found out the reasons for the failure. Even the cadres had been skeptical about the plan and their main concern had been simply fulfilling the government quota. The peasants argued that vegetable cultivation took up arable land, which might delay or interfere with autumn wheat planting. Some peasants ignored the order and grew cotton instead, expecting the cash crop to bring in a higher profit. Others reported to the government that their land was already under vegetables, but in fact they had only plowed the fields in preparation for the autumn wheat planting. In April, the government conducted three inspections of 28 households in Ren village and found that only 10.89 *mu* of the reported 12.6 *mu* of land were cultivated with vegetables. Moreover, it was the middle peasants, not the poor peasants, who followed government orders, because they were the cultivators who had the seeds and the land.[50] The poor peasants were prevented from participating by the high cost and risk, despite the fact that the project was intended to bring more food to their dining table.[51]

Another Communist project was organizing women in the villages to form spinning and weaving teams. The goal of the government was to organize 8,000 women in each county into such teams. Participation in the project was completely voluntary and these teams were organized on the traditional principle of a rural labor exchange. The household formed the basic unit of exchange. The teams were subdivided into spinning and weaving sections and freely exchanged labor among themselves. The spinners obtained cotton from the government or from rural cooperatives and then received grain for the finished product. The rule was to return one *jin* of cotton fabric for every two *jin* of raw cotton.

The project ran into obstacles right from the start. Either because of the inferior quality of the cotton the spinners received or because of their poor technical skill, few peasants were able to produce the required amount of fabric per unit of cotton. Their finished product was usually two to three *liang* short of the quota. Unable to obtain their wages, many quit the project. Poor peasants, more vulnerable to such losses, did not even dare to participate.

Official bureaucratism and cadre ineptitude sometimes were the reasons for the failure. Peasants were cheated by store owners who gave them inferior cotton. There was also a lack of coordination between the government and the cotton stores. Frequently, the stores did not have enough cotton in stock to satisfy the demand of spinners. In certain areas, it was lack of organization that destroyed the project. Cadres thought that their job was done once they had given out the cotton. Instead of vigorously overseeing the project, as they should have done, they simply sat back and waited for the finished product. In other areas, favoritism ruined the plan. Cadres recruited only fellow villagers, usually excluding from the project women without connections. In some places, cooperatives found it too burdensome to be in charge of the project, so in these villages, there was always a surplus of cotton and the spinning and weaving movement was nothing but a formality. Occasionally, women lost interest in the job when the government paid them in non-staple instead of staple grain. Some spinners found out that they had been cheated by the stores and they in turn cheated the government by spraying the fabric with water to increase its weight. Some women participated involuntarily, in the belief that the project was traditional corvée labor, and designated their product as "corvée clothes" (*zhichai bu*).

In certain areas, the spinning and weaving project was used by the government as a workfare program for rural famine relief. But lack of planning spelled trouble for the Communist authorities. Before the Japanese mop-up campaign, there was an ample supply of cotton and a demand for spinners. The program therefore worked smoothly at the outset. But the war created a large number of workfare applicants, and the government suddenly found its cotton in short supply and a clamor among victims for relief. The workfare program was originally designed to benefit famine victims only, but non-victims, mostly rich peasants, rich middle peasants, and middle peasants, somehow found a way to become beneficiaries of the project.[52] Some cadres made a windfall profit from the project. For example, two village representatives were reported to have received 42 *jin* of cotton for the project from the government, with an advance wage payment of 63 *jin* of wheat. Instead of giving the cotton to members of their families to spin and weave, they devised a scheme to make a profit. First, they processed the wheat into 47 *jin* of flour for sale in the local market. With the money obtained from the sale, they bought cotton fabric to return to the government. In this transaction, they made a net profit of C$61, plus the 42 *jin* of cotton they had initially received from the government.[53]

The project, however, was not a total failure. It was successful in at least one area, Linbei. Its success there stemmed from effective organization and cadre assertiveness. As in other areas, the project ran into some difficulties at the beginning because of favoritism, but the problem was swiftly corrected in a party meeting. Afterward, cadres carefully sought out active women to help them promote the program. They also issued an order that no one was allowed to participate without first joining the mutual aid team. Problems of coordination were carefully worked out by team members and the party made sure that all cadres were involved in the project. As a result, around 30 to 40 percent of the county women, about 8,300, participated in the program. The Communists reported that after the project went into effect in April 1944, social problems such as robbery and divorce virtually disappeared in the area. Women took pride in being the breadwinners in their families, and formed their own guard unit to protect the area from enemy raids.[54]

Another service the Communists provided was the organization of mutual aid teams. One objective factor contributing to the success of this project was the critical shortage of manpower and draft animals in the countryside because of the war. In Linbei, for instance, most of the able-bodied males left for the cities in search of urban employment. Women who remained in the county thus became the work force there. Sometimes, in border areas devastated by the war and in famine-stricken regions, entire villages were composed only of women, children, and the elderly. In these areas, women commonly constituted the main source of recruits for the mutual aid teams.

Two years of famine had created an acute labor shortage in the countryside over the entire region. Table 8.10 demonstrates the dramatic reduction in households, manpower, and draft animals in several villages in Ciwu county. There was a 13–35 percent drop in manpower

TABLE 8.10
Change in Manpower and Draft Animals in Ciwu County, 1941–44

Village	Year	Land (*mu*)	Households	Pop.	Manpower	Animals
Manjiancheng	1941	1,244	782	1,364	323	86
	1944	958	205	693	209	19
Baitu	1941	4,421	924	3,941		262
	1944	4,334	768	3,085		61
Chishang	1941	1,389	207	846	228	70
	1944	1,331	174	744	199	35

SOURCE: *P:JJLY-CJ* 3: 84.

TABLE 8.11
Mutual Aid Teams in Ten Villages in the Sixth District of She County, 1945

Village	Households	Manpower	Participants	Percentage
Taihua	236	249	80	33%
Guanfang	165	158	150	95
Dongda	533	435	81	19
Houyan	164	152	152	100
Qianyan	238	147	117	91
Dougong	197	179	166	92
Xida	330	249	110	44
Lingdi	458	439	89	20
Dongjiao	251	241	76	32
Songjia	123	130	42	32

SOURCE: *P:JJLY-CJ* 3: 171.

and a 50–78 percent decrease in the number of draft animals in this county.

In the villages in She county, there was an average of less than one labor power per household (see Table 8.11). The shortage of draft animals was even more severe. Animals either died or were consumed by residents during the war or the famine.[55] Such shortages made it absolutely essential for the remaining population to cooperate with each other in the basic struggle for survival. This made mutual aid teams particularly attractive to the peasants.

The Communist survey showed that 20 percent of the labor force in She county joined the mutual aid teams. But data for the Sixth District in She county (Table 8.11) disclose that several villages had over 90 percent participation. Acute labor shortage in those localities undoubtedly account for such a high rate of participation.

In Linbei, peasant involvement in mutual aid ranged from 6 percent to 80 percent of the village population, depending on the effectiveness of Communist leadership. At the outset, villagers were highly skeptical of the program. They were not at all convinced of the collective payoffs spelled out by the Communist authorities. In Xida village, five of the sixteen mutual aid teams collapsed within a month. Peasants again perceived all government projects as imposed corvée labor. Their attitude was usually one of indifference: "It doesn't make any difference if we have a mutual aid team or not." "Since it is a government project, let us just go through the motion."[56] The traditional negative image the peasants had of the government as tax collector and labor recruiter accounted for their indifferent reaction.

Some villages in She county that achieved over 90 percent peasant participation (Houyan and Guanfang) owed much of their success to effective Communist leadership. Cadres spent a great deal of time in dyadic contact with peasant activists, convincing them to take a lead in the project. The movement only began to catch on when peasants actually saw the payoffs from working together, especially in the land reclamation project. Cadres repeatedly underscored the completely voluntary nature of participation. Anyone could drop out at any time. The Communists also provided the vital service of drawing up labor schedules for the peasantry, and daily activities were clearly written down on a blackboard. In Guanfang village, cadres used both persuasion and coercion to get mutual aid teams started. The project caught on only after the cadres launched a production drive to increase output and organized public meetings to extol the laborers as heroes. At times, a symbolic reward seemed to be as good an incentive as material gain.

In other areas, the project was a complete failure. In Taicang village, there was too much resistance from the inhabitants. The cultivators found it too troublesome to work together in a mutual aid team; the traditional household labor unit provided much more freedom. Some peasants contended that their land was too tiny and too fragmented to require any mutual aid. Illiterate peasants also had tremendous difficulty calculating what they thought would be a fair exchange. Should a day's work by a draft animal be exchanged for two manpower days or 30 *jin* of fodder? What if a labor-short household could not return the labor in the future? The problem of equitable labor exchange, as the Communists also found in the 1950 reforms, was not easy to solve. Organizing peasants in collective units requires clear direction, effective planning, and dedicated leadership.[57]

In border areas between the Communist bases and enemy zones, mutual aid became a practical necessity. Peasants needed all the manpower they could get to rush in the harvest before it was seized by enemy troops. The Communists usually provided military protection for the harvesters. In these areas, there was immense social pressure for every villager to participate in collective projects. Sanctions against nonparticipants were intense, and villagers often identified "those joining mutual aid teams as progressive and others backward." Such pressure forced even landlords and rich peasants to participate, at least temporarily. In a collaborative effort, villagers were usually able to get the harvest in ahead of schedule.[58]

Mutual aid and labor exchange came in several forms:

1. Temporary mutual aid teams (*linshi xing huzhu zu*) consisted of large groups of 200–300 persons who temporarily joined forces to reclaim wasteland. The group jointly cultivated the reclaimed land and shared the harvest. Sometimes they reclaimed marshes and later divided the land according to the amount of labor each individual had contributed.

2. Labor exchange teams (*bogong zu*) consisted of three to five persons who voluntarily came together for short-term labor exchange. They also engaged in reclamation projects. Rich and middle peasants were permitted to hire labor substitutes to do their work.

3. Contract labor teams (*baogong dui*) were normally small teams of ten people headed by foremen. Team members jointly cultivated fields. In their spare time, they earned extra income by working on projects such as dike construction.

Some teams did not divide their profits, instead using them to buy grain, which was stored in a common granary as insurance for future famines. Some used their profit for capital investment, for instance, a draft animal for the group. Most of these teams were formed by the government but did not begin to function properly until cadres actively helped them organize their activities. Active Communist leadership was vital for the operation and peasant activists, extolled as "labor heroes," were crucial in holding the teams together.[59]

Revival of the Silk Industry

Another project the party promoted was the revival of a defunct cottage industry: sericulture. The silk industry had a long history in Linbei (mostly in Hecao village), dating back to the middle of the Ming dynasty. In the olden days, well-known "Hecao silk" was marketed as far away as Beiping, Tianjin, and Xuzhou. The industry reached its peak in the Qing dynasty. During the Daoguang period (1821–50) of the Qing, residents of Lin county cleared the land and planted mulberry trees on the western slopes of the Taihang Mountains. At that time, practically all the households in the area were involved in some aspect of silk production.

In the beginning, the industry confined itself to silk production and silk reeling. It was not until a Nanhuang villager by the name of Zhang Taobao acquired the weaving technique from Shandong that silk weaving began to appear in the area. At one time, it was reported that there were as many as 300 silk weaving machines in Linbei. By 1889, silk stores began to spring up in nearby market towns, six in Yaocun and four in Rencun, with a combined capital investment of a million taels of silver. Even small retail stores in sixteen villages on the western slopes had a combined investment of 180,000 taels. The major marketing center of Yaocun alone was said to have sold eight million cocoons a year to seven counties in the provinces of Henan, Hebei, and Shanxi.[60] Villagers were able to derive half their autumn income from the silk trade; silk reeling was customarily referred to by villagers as "*ban ge qiu*," or "half an autumn." Unfortunately, like all other handicraft industries in China, silk production collapsed in the early Republican period. The price of silk went up for a brief period in 1920–22, but the import of rayon in 1927 brought the industry to an abrupt end.[61] After that, only a small quantity of inferior silk was produced, mostly for local consumption.

The Eighth Route Army arrived in Linbei in the winter of 1938. The troops brought with them a sense of security the area had not enjoyed since the outbreak of the war. In the same year, a village girl caught three silkworms in the Taihang Mountains. Peasant rumors had it that the Eighth Route Army had brought salvation to Hecao in the form of a silkworm deity. The silk industry was temporarily revived in 1939, but badly damaged by the civil war and by the drought the following year. In 1941, with the Communist government vigorously campaigning to revive the trade, silk reeling and weaving again took on new life and gradually became the major industry in the region.

Since silk reeling and weaving could be practiced by residents within the 50-*li* production area on the western slopes of the Taihang Mountains, and since it brought additional income to an estimated 8,700 peasants in 110 natural villages in the area, the party energetically promoted its revival. Though a lucrative business, silk production required heavy capital outlay. In times of famine and economic crisis, villagers could ill afford to spend money on such a risky business. After having given it up for seventeen years, peasants had no faith in its success, and the Communists had to find a way to instill confidence in the industry in villagers.

The CCP found the answer in government-sponsored cooperatives. The cooperatives (for instance, those formed in the three villages of Hecai, Ximanzhan, and Xixiangping) consisted of two types. Peasants could join long-term cooperatives at C$50 a share. By the spring of 1944, 1,800 households had joined these co-ops, which had combined capital of C$57,000. There were also short-term cooperatives. These were set up only in the spring and autumn, the peak silkworm-raising seasons. Each short-term co-op share went for 10 *jin* of millet or 200 coppers. Shareholders received their dividends in late summer and winter, and also had the privilege of obtaining credit from the cooperatives. Unlike other programs, the silk industry benefited the poor. The majority of shareholders were middle and poor peasants; only 10.4 percent were rich peasants, and apparently there were no landlord shareholders.[62] Women also participated in the program. Fifty-nine women reportedly bought 35 autumn shares.

What the project received from the party was organizational skill. The cooperatives had five publicly elected officials who performed various services. Cooperatives were normally divided into two sections, the mountain silkworm section and the consumer management section. The consumer management section provided the services of purchasing and retailing daily items for local residents. The silkworm section, on the other hand, focused on production, working closely with representatives from the silk farms (*canchang*). Because the industry had been dead for almost twenty years, few villagers knew the silk production technique. Those who had practiced the trade before were now mostly middle-aged men. The government employed all of them as silk masters (*canguan*), who managed silk farms and coached apprentices.

The cooperatives also served as employment agencies. They hired all silkworm farmers, offering them a daily wage of 1.4 *jin* of millet, plus a group share of 20 percent of the cocoons they gathered. This generous offer attracted the underprivileged classes and, as a result, only 25 percent of silk farmers had a rich peasant background. The majority were middle or poor peasants. Each silk farm was managed by a leader known as "*ling'e*" (literally "moth manager"), whose duties included running the day-to-day affairs of the farm and calling a team meeting every 40 days. Cadre overseers received no salary, but under the "labor compensation subsidy system" (*jintie choulao zhidu*) received 20 percent of the profit. Cooperatives usually cleared their accounts every six months and paid dividends to investors. Silk farmers could also obtain a second income by gathering such mountain products as cranberries, red peppers, medicinal herbs, and tea, or by hunting rabbits and squirrels. Since the nearest market town was located quite a distance from the western slopes, cooperatives also served as marketing centers for the farmers. Under the co-op was a transport team of 500 men, which performed the service of acquiring such consumer items as salt, oil, matches, and cigarettes for the villagers. The co-ops formed the center of activity for the villages.

As with the other projects, cooperatives also suffered problems. Communist reports indicated that many teams were mere formalities. Extremely poor peasants had no money to buy co-op shares and they were left out of the project. The accounting system was sometimes chaotic, and few cadres had adequate training in accounting. Some Communist officials were corrupt and most had no business knowledge. Sometimes there was a lack of coordination between cooperatives and local stores and the co-ops were unable to sell the mountain products.[63] In spite of all these shortcomings, the Communists reported that the silk industry was an immense success. It benefited a large number of peasants, including the poor. Those who lacked the financial resources to become shareholders could participate in the program as cocoon collectors, which gave them an additional income. The cooperatives helped promote village solidarity, rallying residents to work collectively in production. The co-ops also replaced traditional kinship organizations as the source of economic benefits and credit for the agrarian poor, and they provided the marketing service farmers needed. Moreover, cooperatives eliminated traditional "bosses" (*dongjia*) from the rural handicraft industry. It is not surprising that cooperatives were highly popular in the Taihang region.

Conclusion

This study of the Taihang region clearly demonstrates that the Communist revolution in this mountainous area was a very different political process from the one presented by Ralph Thaxton in his work on the area. It was far from being a self-generated revolution determined by peasant moral outrage at the hardship suffered in an "unjust" economy. No one denies that socioeconomic grievances, particularly when aggravated by war and famine, could produce peasant revolutionary potential in the countryside. But the crucial question is, How did the revolutionaries translate this potential into revolutionary action? It was not only rural discontent and peasant rebelliousness and enthusiasm but also the purposeful actions taken by Communist revolutionaries in organizing, institutionalizing, routinizing, and sustaining peasant actions and behavior that made the revolution a success.

Our data on the Taihang area show no dearth of economic exploitation and rural distress during the anti-Japanese war period. But the Taihang economy was not always below the subsistence level or without a surplus. Whatever economic hardship the peasants endured did not seem to produce a moral outrage in the countryside that energized dissident peasants into rebellious actions. What we do find is peasant unresponsiveness to such programs as the rent reduction movement, even though the program was specially designed to correct a social injustice under which they suffered. The particular social context in the Taihang, that is, the low tenancy rate in the region and the distinctive nature of Taihang landlordism, somehow negated the effectiveness of the program. In studying the Chinese revolution, students should refrain from romanticizing the peasantry and overemphasizing the inner dynamics of the peasant class. One should focus instead on the creative and adaptive roles of the Chinese Communist Party and the complexity of the problems of rural social mobilization.

How effective an analytical device is social exchange theory for the study of peasant-based revolutions? There is no doubt that exchange theory is a more useful analytical tool than the idea of a romantic peasant "moral economy." However, as critics of the theory have pointed out, social exchange has its limitations too. It is only a special theory, David Easton argues, that explains the motivational basis of political support.[64] It assumes that an exchange of material and psychological benefits is sufficient to understand the basis of support. However, the theory overlooks the structural context of interaction and the way in which each social situation to some degree constrains the actions of the individual. Our findings clearly illustrate that social arrangements in the Taihang acted as a constraint on peasant behavior in the rent reduction movement. The acute shortage of labor, on the other hand, facilitated peasant participation in mutual aid teams in certain areas. Peasant commitment is not so simple an equation of exchange of tangible personal gains for political support. Social exchanges must be analyzed within the social context.

The social exchange theory is an effective tool for probing individual motivations. Motivation, however, is only part of social interaction. What is more dynamic is the interaction itself.[65] What fascinates us most about Communist revolutionary activities in China are the varying impacts of Communist policies on the peasantry and the complex interaction between the cadres and rural residents. It would be more productive to look closely at the revolutionary process and interactions, for instance, party tactics (organizing, indoctrinating, coordinating and maneuvering, and institution building), peasant responses and feedback (unresponsiveness, accommodation, and overreaction), and subsequent adaptation and reformulation of policies (the switch from rent reduction to the anti–Japanese collaborator movement in the village struggle in Houjiao).

What we have found in this study of the Taihang is that Communist revolutionary success varied from program to program and from place to place. Certain programs, such as famine relief and the revival of the silk industry, were well received by the peasantry. Others, such as spinning and weaving and mutual aid, worked in certain localities but not in others. The effectiveness of peasant mobilization seems to be determined by certain structural conditions. This leads us to conclude that it is not sufficient to use a behavioral approach (such as exchange theory or social interaction theory) alone to analyze peasant mobilization. In studying peasant-based revolutions, one has to combine both the behavioral approach and a social-structural approach.

CHAPTER 9

Mobilizing to Take Over the Cities

As the Sino-Japanese War drew to a close, the Communist Party began to plan its eventual return to the cities. Moving into the cities was not a simple matter. After the Communists had been driven out of the cities at the end of the Northern Expedition, they had had to adopt a vastly different strategy and operate in an entirely different environment. The Communist rural-based guerrilla operations of the 1930s and 1940s were designed to mass-mobilize the peasants in order to combat enemies in the countryside. The attitudes and work styles of Maoist rural strategies were totally incompatible with an urban environment. By the end of the Sino-Japanese War, the cadres were somewhat out of touch with the urban centers. But protracted absence from the cities did not mean that the Communists had completely neglected the urban centers. The cities had always remained an indispensable source of manpower for the revolution, the place from which the party recruited its leaders, especially student intellectuals and "progressive" elements. Cities had been power centers where enemy troops congregated, and where the Communists could subvert enemy forces in their attempts to build the party's military power (*junyun*). For the Communists, a final victory in the revolution depended on the successful encircling and taking over of the cities. But the final stage of the revolution was not merely "a final showdown through direct military confrontation."[1] Moving into the cities involved breaking the enemy's repressive capacity in the urban centers. The Communists had to infiltrate urban enemy forces. The subversion of urban forces was achieved through intensive political negotiations with enemy officers and through securing troop defections. It involved alliance building and a step-by-step extension of Communist influence in the cities. Taking over cities was a slow process of infiltrating and gradually gobbling up low-level urban centers before finally converging on the major cities. It required gathering sufficient resources before mounting the final major military campaign. All of this took time to accomplish. Although the Communist revolutionary focus had shifted to rural mobilization in the war period, political negotiations with enemy forces and attempts to subvert the enemy army had always gone on in the cities. In fact, they formed an integral and indispensable part of the Communist war effort. During the civil war period, such operations were greatly intensified and systematized by the party so as to prepare for the final showdown.

Rapid Military and Political Development

The takeover of the cities was achieved during a period of rapid military and political development, a period of military expansion, retreat, and recovery. Toward the end of the Sino-Japanese War, the political situation in Henan was shifting in favor of the Communists. The expansion of the China war into a Pacific war had greatly weakened the Japanese forces. In April 1944, defending itself against Guomindang attacks, Japan launched a preemptive offensive against the GMD troops in Henan. It deployed 97,000 troops in an all-out attack on the GMD in western and southwestern Henan. By May 25, the 200,000-man GMD force had crumbled. The so-called Henan Campaign came to an end. After giving up Zhengzhou, Xuchang, Luoyang, and 35 other cities, the Nationalists retreated from central, southern, and western Henan to Funiu Mountain in the southwestern corner of the province. That gave the CCP the chance to expand rapidly into the newly Japanese-occupied areas. Japanese troops were spread thin within the province, occupying only major cities and transport lines.

As early as May 11, 1944, Party Central had directed Communists in various base areas to expand into the newly occupied area. High-ranking cadres such as Liu Shaoqi, Zhu Rui, Peng Xuefeng, and Li Xiannian were sent to Henan to strengthen the leadership. The party was determined to transform the province into a pivot for the anti-Japanese resistance war in central China. In July, the Eighth Route Army moved out of the Taihang area into western Henan and created a new Communist base there. As shown in the previous chapter, the Ji-Lu-Yu armies assisted local forces in the Sui-Qi-Tai area in reinvigorating the Rivereast base. At the same time, the Fourth Division of the New Fourth Army moved westward from the Yuwansu base and recovered some of the areas east of the new Yellow River. The Fifth Division of the New Fourth Army moved up the Beiping-Hankou railroad to rebuild the bases in central and southern Henan. The basic CCP policy was to take advantage of the rapid disintegration of the GMD forces and the inability of the Japanese to control the countryside in order to expand and regain power behind enemy lines.[2]

Although the Communists had a perfect chance to expand because of the Japanese attack and the resulting collapse of the GMD forces, the CCP did not have enough time to consolidate its power in these bases. The Sino-Japanese War ended with the Japanese surrender on August 15, 1945; the Nationalists instantly moved out of their base at Funiu Mountain to compete with the Communists for control of formerly Japanese-occupied land. In late August and early October, the Guomindang gathered a huge army of 100,000 men and moved against the Communists in western, eastern, and northern Henan. In a short time, Nationalist troops were able to recover western and central Henan as well as the areas west of the new Yellow River. They effectively cut off the Communist armies in Henan from those in northern and eastern China. But it was at exactly this time that many local commanders, who had been cultivated by the CCP in their army subversion movement, defected to the Communist camp.

In late October, the Eighth Route Army and some local Communist forces retreated to southwest Henan and set up a "Central Plain Liberated Area" (*zhongyuan jiefang qu*) centered at Tongbai county. During the first half of 1946, amidst intense peace negotiations between the Nationalists and Communists, Guomindang troops continued to expand and retake much of the territory in Henan, closing in on the Communist Central Plain Liberated Area. To prevent themselves from being defeated by the overwhelmingly superior GMD forces, Communist troops in the liberated area in southwest Henan broke the encirclement (known as *zhongyuan tuwei*) in June 1946 and fled to the area around the borders of Henan, Shaanxi, and western Hubei, as well as to the Anhui-Jiangsu border area. Even though the Nationalists were able to take over additional areas in northern and eastern Henan, the Communists were successful in recovering their "old base" in Eyuwan.[3]

But the CCP had always considered Henan the key area in the liberation of central China and the bridge between the northern and central war zones. Hence, Party Central decided that it was essential for the Communists to recover this key province. In the latter part of 1947, it changed course: instead of simply conducting defensive moves to protect its position in the peace negotiations, the party threw much of its military power into the province and launched an all-out offensive against the GMD. The military strategy was to deploy several crack troops in Shandong, northern Henan, and on the Anhui-Jiangsu border to converge on Henan. On June 30, 1947, moving out of southwestern Shandong, the 130,000-man Jin-Ji-Lu-Yu field army of Liu Bocheng and

Deng Xiaoping crossed the Yellow River into Henan. After defeating the Nationalist troops, Liu and Deng brought the army down the floodplain in eastern Henan and into the Dabie Mountains in the southeastern section of the province. In August 1947, Chen Geng and Xie Fuzhi led the Taiyue segment of the Jin-Ji-Lu-Yu field army down through northern Henan and into the western part of the province. Moving along the Longhai railroad, the Chen-Xie army pushed the Nationalist forces back into Shaanxi, thus threatening the city of Sian. This military success enabled the CCP to set up a Henan-Shaanxi-Hubei liberated area based on Funiu Mountain in west Henan. In September, Chen Yi and Su Yu brought their East China Field Army to fight the Guomindang troops in the Yuwansu area. By October, they had captured 24 cities and had extended the Yuwansu base, bringing it into direct contact with the Communist base in the Dabie Mountains in southeastern Henan. By late 1947, the combined Communist forces had been able to clear the province of much of the Nationalist influence. Guomindang power was restricted to a number of cities and a few military centers along the Beiping-Hankou and Longhai railroads.

In this rapid political and military development the Communists successfully subverted enemy forces, mobilized civilians in land reform and military campaigns, and gradually took over operations in the urban centers. But the work of mobilizing to take over the cities was by no means easy. Let us take a look at what they did and how they overcame their difficulties.

Subverting Enemy Forces

A look at the "urban work" discussed at the 1945 cadre conference might give us some idea of the kind of urban strategy the CCP was devising at that time. After having been driven out of the cities and having worked in rural areas with a guerrilla strategy for a protracted period, some Communists cadres had doubts about whether they were fit to go back to work in the cities. Marxist ideologues, in particular, had an outright disdain for decadent urban life-styles and contended that they, as rural mobilizers, were completely unsuitable for urban work. Others foresaw insurmountable obstacles in urban operations: the lack of urban social ties after a long period of intense focus on rural areas, the enemy's superior military strength, and the competent Japanese and GMD intelligence that might make repression effective.

Other cadres vehemently argued that city work was paramount. They insisted that at the final stage of the revolution, it was as important as, if not more important than, rural base work. Deng Zihui, the political commissar of the New Fourth Army, strongly justified with both ideological and practical arguments the urgent need for urban work. From a Marxist point of view, cities were the fortresses of the proletariat, he said. In a proletarian revolution, urban workers should assume the leadership, and the party had the duty to mobilize these workers.

From a practical viewpoint, controlling the cities would enable the party to correct unfair commodity exchanges between the cities and the countryside. Although self-sufficient in food grains, the rural bases were still heavily dependent on the cities for industrial commodities. Peasants were unfairly forced to pay inordinately high prices for these industrial products, for example, ten *dan* of grain for a bolt of cloth. From a strategic point of view, liberating the cities was a coordinated effort of external attack and internal insurgency. It would be necessary to infiltrate the cities so as to be able to back up the external attacks. Without the subversion work of Communist agents prior to the attack, the party would never be able to consolidate its power in the urban centers, and the military takeover would only degenerate into prolonged political chaos.[4]

The party, however, was convinced that political and military developments were working in its favor. Not only the "upper bourgeois" and the middle elements, but also the "bad elements" had lost faith in the GMD. The balance of power had dramatically shifted against the Guomindang. With their relatively stable rural bases and the increasingly powerful Communist army behind them, Communist agents were in a unique position to set up diplomatic contacts, raise funds for the army, and persuade fence sitters to defect in preparation for the coming conflict.

The primary objective of urban work, according to a party directive, was to subvert and engineer the defection of the puppet armies. The basic Communist strategy of skillfully playing the political coalition game at both the upper and lower levels still applied. The essential goal of the cadres' work was to seek the cooperation of petty officers and common soldiers through low-level coalition politics. But the party warned that this tactic would be effective only if backed by support from high-ranking officers. The party had learned from past experience that the support of high-ranking puppet officers could be temporary and based purely on immediate interests. But it insisted that this support was vital to the movement since it would serve as a shield for lower-level coalition work. The two levels of work, according to the party, had to complement each other. The central strategy for taking over the cities, the party repeatedly emphasized, was *liying waihe*, "collaboration from within with forces attacking from outside."[5]

Neutralizing High-Ranking Officers

The party understood very well that most high-ranking puppet officers were highly unreliable adventurers. That, however, did not prevent them from negotiating intensively with these militarists. The neutrality of these officers was critical for the survival of the Communist bases. Forming tactical alliances with puppet army officers also prevented them from combining with the GMD. The party had in fact actively pursued a policy of political negotiations with puppet officers since as early as 1940. The primary target was Zhang Lanfeng, the most powerful puppet commander in the region, whose influence extended over all of eastern Henan and the railroad city of Shangqiu.

Zhang Lanfeng was a native of Zhecheng county in eastern Henan. In 1921, Zhang joined the Guominjun and was sent by then commander Feng Yuxiang to study at the Japanese Military Officers Academy. Right from the beginning, he was intimately associated with these two major military forces, Feng's Guominjun (later the Northwest Army) and the Japanese military. After returning from Japan, he was made an artillery regiment commander, and later headmaster of the Northwest Military Officers' Academy. In that capacity, Zhang built a group following among his students. With the collapse of Feng's power after his revolt against Chiang Kaishek in 1930, Zhang deserted the Guominjun and allied himself with Chiang Kaishek.

Zhang later made a brief trip back to Japan, but soon returned to join Song Jieyuan, Feng's former subordinate and then commander of the Beiping-Tianjin region, as Song's chief of staff for the 143rd Division. With the outbreak of the Sino-Japanese War, Zhang returned to his native county of Zhecheng. When it was conquered by the Japanese, Zhang became a Japanese collaborator. He received two appointments from the foreign invaders, as "East Henan Pacification Commissioner" and "Commander of the Communist Extermination Forces." Basing himself in the railroad metropolis of Shangqiu, Zhang extensively recruited gentry-controlled militia and bandit forces in order to build his power. He eventually commanded a formidable force of 18,000 men.[6]

Zhang's political background clearly revealed that he had four basic social ties: his local ties in Zhecheng county, his military ties with Feng's Guominjun and later with the Northwest Army (*xibei jun*), his teacher-student ties at the Northwest Military Academy, and his tie to Chiang Kaishek. The army under his command reflected all these social ties.

Zhang's army was divided into four military factions:

1. The Nationalist faction was composed mainly of former officers of the Nationalist 26th Route Army who had defected to Zhang's camp

at the beginning of 1941. This military clique was extremely powerful and many of its members had originally been Zhang's colleagues in the Nationalist government. By the latter part of 1943, this faction controlled two army divisions, the Fourteenth and the Eighteenth.

2. The Native (Zhecheng) faction consisted mostly of local gentry forces plus a powerful bandit gang. This military grouping was tightly bound to Zhang by territorial ties, and its members were considered by him to be his most reliable troops.

3. The Northwest military faction consisted of 150 former students of Zhang's, most of them above the rank of major. These officers had the strong backing of Zhang's wife, Zhang Zhilan.

4. The Third Route military faction comprised former subordinates of Han Fuju, the governor of Shandong and a former subordinate of Feng Yuxiang. This clique had some power and Yang Shusan, their principal commander, controlled the Seventeenth Division.[7]

Zhang's army was a heterogenous group, and at times the rivalries within it were severe. Yet one should not overemphasize the political and military divisions among its commanders. There were some overlapping ties and interests. Some members of the Nationalist and Native cliques were also former commanders in Feng's Northwest Army. Many had been elbowed out by Chiang Kaishek and harbored ill will toward the Nationalist leader. Others had been members of the CCP when the Communists and the Guominjun had collaborated during the late 1920s. The defection of these Communist affiliates to Zhang's camp was encouraged by the party as a temporary measure to avoid Nationalist retribution and crackdowns. Within Zhang's formidable army, many low-ranking officers were wavering elements, ideal material for Communist subversion. The heterogeneous and fragmented nature of Zhang's troops made subversion much easier for the Communists.

Social ties and urban roots were absolutely essential for infiltrating and subverting enemy armies. But social contacts could not be set up overnight. It took a long time to cultivate relationships. As early as September 1941, the Communist Party had institutions in place in eastern Henan to work on army subversion. Various agencies (the party's city work department, the army's enemy work department, and the enemy work sections in various counties) were created by the party specifically to perform this task.

Army infiltration work was rendered a lot easier as the war drew to a close and the military situation radically changed. By June 1944, the Central Committee had issued an urban work directive ordering Communist armies to converge on cities and transportation lines. In the fall of 1944, the political situation changed dramatically when the New

Fourth Army successfully recovered the area west of the Tianjin-Pukou railroad. The puppets sensed that the CCP was emerging as the new center of strength in the region. Cracks began to develop in the puppet military structure, political divisions deepened and shifts of loyalty occurred. The Nationalists also seized on this opportunity and competed with the Communists for Zhang's support. In a move to woo Zhang, Chiang Kaishek appointed him commander of the Third Route Army. Zhang, however, was a veteran of this kind of political game, and knew very well that his former association with the Guominjun would work against him. He hesitated.

The Communists took this opportunity to formulate two distinct tactics for subverting Zhang's army: direct negotiations with Zhang himself, to obtain his neutrality, which would guarantee security for the rural bases and serve as a cover for the Communists' lower-level subversion work; and subverting the army at the base.

Direct contact with Zhang began in the autumn of 1944, when the party dispatched two cadres, Li Subo[8] and Miao Zesheng,[9] to Zhang's headquarters in Shangqiu for negotiations. Once again, the party skillfully used its social ties to make contact. The negotiations were arranged by two reputable local gentry members, the headmaster of the Zhecheng First High School and Zhang's uncle, both of whom had Communist connections. Zhang often denied that he was a traitor collaborating with the Japanese simply for private gain. He contended that siding with the Japanese was a "curvilinear way" of saving the nation (*quxian jiuguo*). Zhang was therefore always willing to talk with anybody else who was trying to save the nation. There was always a practical reason behind his talks with the Communists: in order to avoid a direct military confrontation with the growing Communist power, Zhang had to agree to a truce with the CCP.

Zhang therefore sent two of his officers, Wang Jixian and Du Xinmin, to negotiate directly with the Eighth Route and New Fourth armies. In the second round of negotiations, Zhang's representatives reached an agreement with the Communists. Zhang pledged to retreat and to refrain from encroaching on the Communist bases in eastern Henan. He also promised the Communists protection within his territories and intelligence on GMD troop movements. We have no information on what the Communists gave Zhang in return; probably the same thing. After this, the Communists tried hard to get Zhang to defect so that his troops could be reorganized into the Communist army, but Zhang, who had always wavered between the GMD and the Communists, refused. Finally, in early 1947, Zhang was ordered by Chiang Kaishek to reinforce GMD troops in Shandong province. He carried out that order and was defeated by the Communist army, led by Liu Bocheng and Deng Xiaoping.[10]

As the party expected, political negotiations with high-ranking officers such as Zhang Lanfeng were just a stopgap measure to neutralize enemy forces. The tactic temporarily eased tension between the Communists and the puppet troops and helped them avoid direct armed confrontation. But more importantly, a temporary alliance at the top often provided the Communists with a cover for direct negotiations with low-ranking officers at the bottom. It was the alliances between the party and these petty officers, and their subsequent defections, that led to the eventual disintegration of Zhang's once formidable puppet army.

Recruiting Low-Ranking Officers

Charles Tilly notes that the Chinese revolution was a periphery-in process.[11] This is true if we consider the Communist revolution as a gradual encroachment upon the city from the countryside. The takeover of the city, however, was both a periphery-in and a middle-down process. While part of the tactic was to negotiate with top military officials in order to defuse tension and obtain their neutrality, another was to subvert the puppet army at its very base. By winning the support of petty officers and engineering defections, the Communists took over the outlying, lower-order central places before converging on the central metropolis of Shangqiu, Zhang Lanfeng's power center. Only by infiltrating and generating an internal disintegration (*wajie*, in Communist terms) of the puppet forces could the Communists initiate their final move toward the central city.

Infiltrating the army took two different routes. The first was reestablishing relations with military officers who had formerly been party members and who were sympathetic toward the Communist cause. The second was to sow dissension among low-ranking enemy officers.

Reestablishing relations with pro-Communist officers. Among Zhang's commander were a number of pro-Communist officers, including Du Xinmin, Wei Fenglou, Wang Jixian, and Cheng Peizhao, all of whom had former connections with the CCP. The infiltration of Du Xinmin's Eighteenth Division is a good illustration of the process of reestablishing relations with these officers. Du Xinmin was a native of Fengyang county in Anhui province. He had joined Feng Yuxiang's army in Beijing in 1923. Du was exposed to Communist influence during the Northern Expedition, when Feng and the Communists collaborated in the Nationalist Revolution. After Feng's forces were crushed by Chiang

Kaishek in 1930, Du's troops were reorganized into Chiang's 26th Route Army under the command of Sun Lianzhong. Du later rejoined Feng under the so-called Anti-Japanese Allied Army. In March 1939, he became a Communist Party member. He was accused of being a Communist and was arrested the following year by Sun Lianzhong. Without enough evidence to convict him, Sun finally let him go.

Du proceeded to Shangqiu at the end of 1940 and used his connections as a former subordinate of Feng to secure the position of commander of the training regiment in Zhang Lanfeng's army. At the time, Zhang was desperately looking for men to rebuild his army because 17,000 of his troops had defected to the Nationalist side. Du's entry into the army came at the right time. His position as head of the training regiment enabled him to extend his political influence among young cadets, many of whom later joined his Eighteenth Division as petty officers.

Du reestablished contact with the Communists in early 1941, when the Rivereast Communist Party began an extensive program to subvert Zhang's army and sent its agent Wang Feixiao, a former soldier in the Northwest Army, to Shangqiu.[12] The party's subversion tactic included several concrete steps:

> Communist agents start off with infiltration of the army training units and recruitment of military students as cadres. The next step is for these pro-Communist cadres to gain military power by becoming officers in the army. These pro-Communist officers then strengthen the Communist influence in the military units under their command by eliminating all anti-Communist elements and by absorbing more pro-Communist elements into their units. They then build up their military power, maintain their cover for as long as possible, and wait for the right moment to defect to the Communist side.[13]

As a former Communist Party member and the head of the training unit in Zhang's army, Du Xinmin was the ideal candidate to implement the party's army subversion plan. Using the training unit as a launching pad, Du gradually transformed it into three platoons and began propagating Marxist ideas among the young cadets. He greatly impressed Zhang with his vigorous training program and soon won his superior's confidence. He then extended his influence by placing his students in other platoons and companies as petty officers. In June 1942, Du reapplied and once again became a member of the Chinese Communist Party.

Having gained Zhang's confidence, and with strong support from his student officers, Du won the position of commander of the Eighteenth Division in March 1944. Zhang then ordered the division to station itself in Zhengcheng city (Yongcheng county) at the Henan-Anhui border. Zhengcheng was located some distance from Shangqiu, away from Zhang's command center and right across the provincial border from the Communist Huaibei Suwan base. Hence, Du not only obtained control of a military division, but his troops were located in an ideal place, one where he could establish direct contact with the Communists without his superior's notice.

But the Eighteenth Division was under the watchful eyes of the Japanese and GMD secret agents. Du and the Communists had to get rid of these agents. First, they managed to get the Japanese agent addicted to opium. When the Japanese army found out, it transferred him to another unit. Du then encouraged the GMD agent to smuggle salt, a lucrative business at that time. After making a large profit, the agent voluntarily left the division to devote full time to his commercial enterprise.[14] By promoting and transferring other anti-Communist officers out of his division and replacing them with his pro-Communist student officers, Du slowly transformed his division into a pro-Communist unit. Party branches were eventually set up within the division, and the Communist Party dispatched a large number of cadres to plan Du's eventual defection with him. Meanwhile, Du won Zhang's favor by giving his superior 300,000 *jin* of wheat, which other army officers refused to do.

After the Japanese surrender in September 1945, the party believed it was time for Du to defect and join the New Fourth Army. The date for the "uprising" was set for the mid-autumn festival. The basic tactic was the same: "internal insurgency coordinated with external attack." The defection, however, required not only Du's support, but that of his subordinate officers. Of the three regimental commanders in the Eighteenth Division, one was a party member and another supported the Communist cause. Han, the third commander, was a landlord and was naturally apprehensive of the Communists. But, through personal relations and diplomacy, Han was assured by Du of his position after the defection and was thus neutralized.

There was one remaining obstacle: Du's anti-Communist deputy commander, Liu Wenyao. To get rid of him, Du gave Liu C$100,000 and ordered him to return to Shangqiu to spend the holiday season with his mother. To prevent reprisals by Zhang, Du asked his two sons, who were attending school in Shangqiu, to come home to Zhengcheng for the holidays. After Liu left the area, the New Fourth Army encircled and took over the city of Zhengcheng. Du revealed his Communist ties to the public and defected to the Communist side.[15] Using similar tactics, the Communists secured the defection of three more of Zhang's divisions, which together accounted for 13,700 of Zhang's soldiers.[16]

Sowing dissension among low-ranking officers. Another army subversion tactic the Communists employed was to use the power conflicts within Zhang's fractious army to stir discord and bring about internal disintegration. The main objective was to undermine Zhang's military position. The two targets of Communist subversion were Yang Shusen, who was from Zhang's home county, and Wang Jinxuan, a bandit chief.

Yang Shusen had joined Han Fuqu's army in 1917, when Han was commander of the GMD Third Route Army in Shandong, and was later promoted to regiment commander. After the Zhecheng county seat was taken by the Japanese, Yang brought together a number of bandit squads to form a 1,000-man guerrilla force under his command. In the latter part of 1938, his force was reorganized by Zhang into the "Communist Extermination Army." Yang was considered the head of the native faction within Zhang's military clique.

In pursuing his political interest, Yang had apparently alienated many officers within the Nationalist faction, particularly Chen Fumin, Liu Qinchu, Huang Xiufu, and Zhang Zhilan, all defectors from the GMD 26th Route Army. The Native and Nationalist factions were, in fact, engaged in keen competition for power. Yang, as a native officer slowly rising through the ranks, resented the sudden climb to power of these newly defected officers from the GMD camp. He disdained all former Northwest officers and refused to accept any of them in his Seventeenth Division.

The better-educated commanders of the Nationalist faction looked down on Yang as "an illiterate soldier who knew nothing about military campaigns." They thought that Yang was unworthy of his military position. The bone of contention was the position of commander of the First Army, which both Yang and Chen Fumin coveted. This gave Du Xinmin the chance to capitalize on the personal conflicts and sow dissension between the two camps. Du supported Chen of the Nationalist faction for the command. He warned that Yang was a recalcitrant commander who was greedy for power and who maintained close connections with the GMD (through subordinates in Han Fuqu's army). Du predicted that eventually Zhang would have difficulty controlling him (*wei da bu diao*) and that one day Yang would break away and form his own power center. Yang's personal conflicts with Zhang's uncle and wife further strained his relations with his superior.

Zhang, siding with Du and the Nationalist faction, finally decided to resolve these personal conflicts by using the traditional method of "taking away someone's power by promoting him to a sinecure office" (*ming sheng an jiang*) to undermine Yang's military power. Zhang had Yang transferred to Shangqiu and made him commander of the First Army, overseeing the Seventeenth and Eighteenth (Du Xinmin's) divisions. In fact, the "promotion" gave Yang only nominal authority over the two divisions. He was deprived of any actual military command. By transferring Yang to Shangqiu, Zhang was actually putting him in his military headquarters in order to supervise him.

Yang understood that this move would deprive him of his military power, so he set three conditions for accepting the post: he should be made concurrent commander of the Seventeenth Division, which would give him actual military power; Du Xinmin's Eighteenth Division was to be transferred to the Luyi-Huaiyang area, where it would be directly under his supervision; and he would be allowed to stay in Luyi and to set up a new army headquarters there. Du indicated to his superior that such a counteroffer was a clear sign of Yang's insubordination, and to other commanders, Du strongly argued that Yang's three conditions and insubordination would eventually lead him to break away and join the Guomindang. So in late May, 1944, Zhang summoned Yang to his house on a pretext so that he could order one of his commanders to have Yang arrested and killed.[17]

The elimination of bandit chief Wang Jinxuan involved several stages of political intrigue: infiltration, isolation, political maneuvering, and finally, takeover. Wang Jinxuan was a native of Shawo village, located on the border between Qixian and Tongxu counties. He was a pill peddler and a bandit chief. With 2,000 men under his command, and some connections with the Japanese, Wang was recruited by Zhang to be commander of the 55th Regiment of the Fourteenth Division. The 55th Regiment was very well armed, and was reported to be the best of Zhang's forces. Wang also commanded an unofficial regiment. But from the time that Wang and Zhang joined forces, their relationship was a power game to see which of them would take over the other.

The party assigned the job of subverting Wang's regiment to Chen Fumin, Du Xinmin's intimate friend and fellow Northwest Army commander. The first step was to infiltrate Wang's forces by making faithful Communist cadres petty officers in the 55th Regiment. These cadres then used their Northwest connections to recruit other petty officers to their cause. The next step was to isolate and separate the 55th from other regiments in the Fourteenth Division by transferring the other regiments to the Haoxian-Woyang area. Then, claiming that the 55th Regiment had "placed too great a burden on the people," Chen had

Wang and his regiment uprooted from their bandit lair in Qixian and transferred back to Shangqiu for close supervision.

Wang realized that he was isolated and immediately struck up a friendship with the guard unit in Shangqiu by giving the soldiers watches. Both Chen and Du reported to Zhang that Wang's bribing of the guards was the first sign of rebellion. Zhang, Chen, and Du then began a series of political maneuvers to get rid of Wang. In the spring of 1942, Zhang ordered Wang to Nanjing for "further training" at the Nanjing Officers' Academy. Once Wang left the city, Zhang immediately had Wang's cavalry company and rifle units reorganized into a division under his direct control. When Wang got the news of Zhang's action and rushed back to Shangqiu, Zhang had him assassinated in the rail station. Du and Chen then sent troops to Shawo, Wang's lair, to clean up the rest of the bandits and to seize their ammunition and property. By eliminating Wang's forces, Du not only destroyed a powerful military opponent, he increased his firepower by capturing the bandits' arms and ammunition.[18]

The move to take over the cities was not simply "positional warfare." It involved the skillful use of Communist military subversion tactics, or *junyun*, to disable the enemy. The objective was to sow dissension and stir up animosity among enemy officers. As Deng Zihui has told us, army subversion consisted of two parts: continuous negotiations with Zhang Lanfeng at the top to obtain his neutrality which would provide a cover for low-level subversion work, and playing on the distrust and suspicion among his officers to stir discord within and to fragment his camp.

The fact that Zhang was a former officer in the Northwest Army made Communist army subversion work much easier. Some of his officers were former Communist members or sympathetic toward the Communist cause because of the Communist-Guominjun collaboration in the Northern Expedition period, and the party was in a position to exploit such personal ties to gain access to Zhang's army. Officers such as Du Xinmin, Wang Jixian, and Wei Fenglou, all CCP sympathizers, were employed by the party as subversive agents. The tactic was to play on differences between the elite units (the 26th Route faction and the Northwest Army group) and the plebeian units (represented by the bandit and semi-bandit troops in the Native faction). By exploiting the internal feuds and the competition for power among the various cliques in Zhang's army, the Communists successfully stirred dissension within his troops and undermined his power. Only after Zhang's military structure was greatly weakened by internal dissension and defection and was on the verge of disintegration could the Communist troops move in to capture the cities.

Provoking the Peasants: Last-Minute Land Reform

The end of the Sino-Japanese War gave the Communists an opportunity to stage another social revolution in the countryside. As the Eighth Route and New Fourth armies made headway on the battlefield, the party was formulating a revolutionary social policy for the newly liberated rural area, the *xinqu*. The objectives were to extract more resources from the rich to sustain the war, to tighten control over the area, and to use land reform as an exchange for peasant support in the recently liberated areas.

As always, addressing the peasants' land problems was a central objective in the Communist social revolution. In late 1945, the party urged all cadres to "freely mobilize the masses in the newly occupied areas" in rent and interest reduction and wage increase movements.[19] This was soon followed by a call to seize land from "traitors" and redistribute it to soldiers' families, activists, and poor peasants.[20] But this hard-line policy was not strictly followed. At the outset, the Communist policy toward landlords in the postwar period, at least in the Taihang and Ji-Lu-Yu (Hebei-Shandong-Henan) areas, was the same moderate policy enacted during the Sino-Japanese War. It called only for a reduction of rent and interest payments. Although local cadres were ordered to fight for higher wages for hired farmhands and income increases for tenant farmers, the party still generally adhered to the United Front tactic and followed a nonconfrontational policy toward the rural upper classes.[21]

As military conflicts between the CCP and the GMD sharpened in the so-called Second Encirclement and Suppression Campaigns (*weijiao*), the CCP clearly felt that there was a greater military threat than before from GMD armies and a subversion threat from pro-GMD gentry. As military conflicts became more intense, so did the radicalism of land reform. In May 1946, after a high-level party conference, the Central China Bureau issued a new land policy. The "May Fourth directive," as it was known, abandoned the moderate rent and interest reduction and opted for radical land reform measures in the newly liberated areas. All twenty counties in the northern and eastern Henan liberated areas were ordered to carry out the land reform program.[22] The reform slogan was "Land to the tillers," an echo of Sun Yatsen's social theme, apparently chosen to influence and appeal to GMD intellectuals.[23] According to the directive, the new land reform program was to be completed by the end of the year.

The new program called for the confiscation of the holdings of all "traitors" without reservation. Peasants were to be mobilized to "settle accounts" with landlords, now defined as traitors, wealthy gentry, tyrants, and usurers. Rural struggles were to focus on issues such as rent and interest payments, exploitation, unfair taxation, land infringement, racketeering, and unjust appropriation of peasant land and property. Each natural village (*cun*) and subdistrict (*xiang*) was to form a unit and conduct its own rural struggle. Per capita availability of land was to be calculated and excess land recorded. Thorough investigation into concealed holdings was to be undertaken. The policy did allow landlords to retain a piece of land to maintain a livelihood. After setting aside a portion of the confiscated land for rural welfare and education, the rest was to be redistributed to land-short peasants.

The new policy strictly forbade cadre infringement on the rights of the middle peasants, who were regarded as allies of the rural poor. Rich peasants were protected and their holdings were to be left intact. They were required to reduce rents only if they were unjustly high. The party instructed cadres to carry out the struggle in an orderly and democratic way, through mass discussion and public debates. The party was convinced that the land reform program would heighten the fighting morale of the peasants, the main force in the war of liberation. Local cadres were urged to bring poor peasants, tenants, wage laborers, and activists, all of whom benefited from the reform, into politics. The Communists predicted that this exchange of land for political support would bring 5 to 10 percent of the rural population into the people's army. The party called upon cadres to "boldly recruit hired farmhands, tenants, poor peasants, and activists into the party, to double and triple party membership."[24]

But implementing the policy locally was a very different matter from designing the policy. When the Yuwansu party received the land reform directive from the Central Bureau, there was a great deal of confusion among local cadres. They could not come to an agreement on the criteria for land redistribution. Should emphasis be placed on revolutionary contributions or on social equality? One line suggested that land should be redistributed according to degree of economic hardship and contribution to the revolutionary movement. The principal beneficiaries of this would be tenants, cadres, and activists (those who joined the peasant association). The other suggestion was for a simple "fair, reasonable, and equitable redistribution" (*gongping heli de pingjun fenpei*), one that would be highly favorable to the rural poor.

When the question was referred to the Central Bureau, the party sided with the radical faction. It gave cadres a free hand in peasant mobilization and in armed struggles against landlords. The implementation of the land reform, it reemphasized, was to be based on the principle of "land to the tillers." Local cadres were instructed to adhere to "equal redistribution" and "overall leveling." But they were also asked to consult constantly with the middle peasants. The party condemned the traditional practice of allowing landlords to keep a piece of land double the size of the peasants' holdings. The new policy required that should cadres wish to give any land to the "progressive" and military gentry, even just enough to provide them a living, they first had to obtain the approval of at least 90 percent of the local peasantry. The basic party policy was a "thorough pursuit" of the landowning classes. Local cadres were instructed to give the "drowning dog a thorough beating."[25]

For the time being, the hard-liners had the upper hand. The party launched a "Peasant Emancipation and Investigation Movement" (*nongmin fanshen da jiancha yundong*) in the Yuwansu border area. The provincial party refused to accept the preliminary result of the first wave of land redistribution. It insisted that landlords still possessed more land than ordinary peasants.[26] It ordered cadres to put aside all considerations and feelings for the landlords and actively mobilize peasants to confront the landed upper classes "face-to-face." The correct way of conducting rural struggles, the party said, was to have the class-conscious peasants launch the movement themselves, without any interference from the party leadership. Peasants were urged to thoroughly investigate landlords' estates and other possessions. In the Emancipation and Investigation Movement, cadres were told to pay special attention to concealment of land by landlords and to find ways to eliminate the peasant illusion of the beneficial role of landed upper classes. They were to make sure that grass-roots peasant organizations were made up only of wage laborers, poor peasants, and middle peasants, and that the class struggle and land redistribution were not carried out perfunctorily.[27]

By mid-1947, conflicts between the GMD and the CCP had greatly intensified. Under the command of Liu Bocheng and Deng Xiaoping, Communist armies had crossed the Yellow River in a southward thrust into central China. The party was particularly concerned about gathering sufficient resources to support the coming military campaigns. Between October 2 and December 26, the Jin-Ji-Lu-Yu Central Bureau assembled all cadres above the county level for a conference. The primary objectives were to deepen the land reform program and to rectify the party. Because of the approaching conflict, the party was anxious to purge itself of all cadres embracing a "landlord–rich peasant ideology."[28]

In January 1948, the party adopted an even more vigorous and radical approach. Imminent military conflicts forced the CCP to reformulate and broaden its policy so as to further the war effort. The land reform program now emphasized not only land redistribution and increased production to provide economic resources to support the Communist armies, but also the gaining of political control at the local level. The party was determined to break the landlords' power locally so that it could seize their military forces and economic resources and tighten its control over rural areas. The goal was a complete political and economic dominance of the countryside in preparation for war.

Land reform, the new directive said, was to be accomplished politically, through elimination of the gentry's repressive power and a restructuring of local authority. Economically, it would be accompanied by famine relief and increased production to improve the peasants' livelihood. Cadres were given permission to use coercion to enforce the policy. Paramilitary units, like the "armed land reform squads" (*wuzhuang tugai dui*), were organized locally to give cadres and the rural poor the necessary coercive power to challenge the landlords. In areas not directly under Communist control, troops were deployed to enforce the changes. The destruction of gentry power in the countryside was crucial to the CCP. If the land reform was to be successful, food and agrarian capital had to be extracted from the rural upper classes and given to the poor. Gentry repressive power (*dizhu wuzhuang*), the bulwark of their authority, had to be dismantled by the armed land reform squads. The *baojia* system, the century-old village power structure, had to be replaced by poor peasant corps and peoples' committees.

But the Communists also drew lessons from their previous attempts at social revolution. They knew that elite power had been deeply entrenched in the countryside, particularly after the GMD had revitalized the *baojia* system, and that it would not be easy to uproot. Under Nationalist rule, most of the village and *bao* heads were drawn from the rich and middle peasants. Some were recruited from groups of local thugs. All these lesser elites had been given proper training in intelligence gathering. Many of the *bao* heads were directly controlled by landlords and local bullies. Though the big landlords and local bullies had fled after the Communist takeover, the remaining petty landlords and rich peasants would not hesitate to use the community armed forces under their command to defend their political positions and economic interests. Moreover, GMD secret agents had penetrated deeply and were still very active in the villages.

The party therefore drew up a step-by-step plan to undermine gentry power in the countryside. The land reform movement was to be carried out in two stages. In the first stage, the attack was to be confined to landlords (not rich peasants), with the big landlords as the main target. The tactic was to neutralize the middle peasants and, if necessary, get the support of small landlords in the assault on the big landlords and their bullies. Land and movable property belonging to landlords were to be redistributed to poor peasants according to the principle of "leveling" (*tianping*). The party hoped that land redistribution would heighten the class consciousness of poor peasants. With the peasants sufficiently aroused, the land reform program would then proceed to the more radical stage. At this second stage, poor peasants would be mobilized for an all-out social revolution: they would search landlords' houses for concealed belongings, conduct class identification, and carry out a thorough and equal redistribution of land and property.[29]

The radical policy stipulated that this time leadership of the reform was to be in the hands of poor peasants and wage laborers. Past experience had shown that peasant associations had always been dominated by middle peasants, local hooligans, and even rich peasants. Poor peasants seldom became leaders of the rural revolution. In this reform, the party therefore called for the creation of a new revolutionary organization: the Poor Peasant Corps (*pinnong tuan*). The second stage of the land reform, the party insisted, should be carried out by peasant activists under the direction of the Poor Peasant Corps. Cadres were instructed to mobilize the rural poor as leaders of the revolution.

Some experienced cadres had serious doubts about the effectiveness of poor peasant leadership. They argued that peasants, intimidated by GMD reprisals, had been pathetically apolitical in past reforms. They also warned that land reform could bring undesirable outcomes. For example, it could temporarily disrupt the rural economy. But many Marxist ideologues contended that land reform would definitely be successful if it were run jointly by the class-conscious rural poor in the Poor Peasant Corps and by the elected peasant committees (*nongmin weiyuanhui* or *renmin weiyuanhui*). The crucial factors were swiftness of action, proper use of the class line, and strict adherence to the equalitarian principle (in quality and quantity) in land redistribution. A temporary disruption of the rural economy was a necessary evil. After redistribution, the peasants could be mobilized to increase production. The rural economy would quickly recover from any temporary decline.

In spite of the radical turn in the new policy, the party still exercised great caution so as not to antagonize the gentry. Some gentry were allowed to keep a piece of land. With the exception of local tyrants, traitors, returned armed gentry, and GMD secret agents, the instruction said, landlords and rich peasants, like everyone else, were entitled to some land. In fact, party directives still ordered cadres to cement their relations with some progressive gentry members. They were to cultivate the support of the "respected gentry" (*xian*) and to use their personal connections to recruit the progressive gentry for village leadership.

Having learned from past experience, the party was careful not to let the land reform program get out of control. It tried to prevent excessive actions of the overzealous "left." Although the policy clearly focused on a reliance on poor peasants as leaders and on the poor gaining political power in the villages, the basic emphasis was still on forging a class alliance with the middle peasants. The provincial party reiterated Mao's policy of reliance on these peasants in social revolution. Should the policy run into opposition from the middle peasants, the directive said, cadres should yield to these cultivators. The party also warned rural mobilizers not to make mistakes in classifying peasants. It instructed them to always conduct rural social surveys, rather than simply relying on personal preconceptions of local class structure (cadres frequently misclassified laboring rich peasants, or classified as a landlord anybody who hired a couple of farmhands). It alerted cadres that mistakes in rural classification invariably led to class conflict and disruption, which would adversely affect the outcome of the land reform program.[30]

In their mobilization, the Communists always employed simple, down-to-earth, easy-to-remember slogans. The most popular one, of course, was Sun Yatsen's "Land to the tillers." Other reform slogans included "Dig up the root of poverty; pursue the source of wealth," "Taking back the land is legal," "Right the wrongs; avenge and settle accounts," "Everybody has a piece of land to till; everyone has rice to eat," and "Peasants have the right to their land. Owner-cultivators should not be left alone. Landlords should be progressive and give up their land for redistribution."[31]

Three methods were adopted by the party to repossess land:

1. Class struggle (*douzheng*) involved direct seizure of landlords' land. This tactic was directed only against the most oppressive landlords.

2. Buying back the land (*daodi*) applied to land owned by middle and small landlords. The measure called for a buy-back of land peasants had sold to these landlords during the agrarian crisis of the Sino-Japanese War. Peasants were allowed to buy back their land at the selling price.

3. Land donation (*xiandi*) was aimed at "progressive" landlords supportive of the revolution. They were urged to voluntarily give up their land for redistribution. Cadres were ordered to clearly distinguish between the various rural classes—the big, middle, and small landlords—and also between "tyrants" and "non-tyrants." The reform policy was not directed at the rich peasants this time, obviously a measure to secure their neutrality, if not their support, in the fight against landlords. The party might have learned from its mistakes in the implementation of the "rich peasant policy" in the Eyuwan period. It also urged cadres to make allowances in policy implementation in different areas, for example, in Communist-controlled areas (*laoqu*, old areas) and newly liberated areas (*xinqu*, new areas).[32]

Although the party exercised great caution this time, the last-minute land reform was still hastily implemented and restricted in scope. A directive from the Central Plain Bureau stated that out of the 30 million people under Communist control, only 4 million (about 13.3 percent) had actually undergone land reform.[33] Even in established Communist areas, that is, the First, Second, and Third districts in the Yuwansu border base, land reform was far from thorough. In the newly occupied areas, where Communist authority was weak, village struggles were limited to seizures of money and grain from "local tyrants and the bullies" by Communist troops, an early predatory form of collective violence.[34]

In May 1948, party secretary Wu Zhipu reported at a military and financial meeting of the Yuwansu border base that the land reform program had many faults and caused much confusion. Wu said that the October decision was incorrect, particularly the policy of equal redistribution of land. In some areas, Wu said, land reform was carried out in great haste. Without carefully examining the rural classes, cadres mechanically applied the principle of "onetime equal distribution" (*yici pingfen*) or "absolutely equal redistribution" (*juedui pingfen*). The rule of thumb was that every individual was entitled to 2.4 *mu* of land. The new holdings were not registered. No one knew where his land was. A piece of land was supposed to be divided by three individuals but no one was able to figure out how to partition it. Without clear land rights, peasants refused to fertilize the land.[35]

The land reform policy encountered stiff resistance from locally entrenched landlords. To defend their own interests, the gentry allied with local bandits and built up village militia. They then used their legal position as heads of the local armed forces to strengthen the *baojia* system, link up with the GMD, resist land reform, and kill Communist cadres. Thus the Communists might have captured a village, but the underlying communal authority, the *baojia* system, remained intact. The *baojia* still had tremendous authority over the peasants. Communist reports indicated that even after an area had undergone land reform, changes were made in name only.

The difficulties stemmed from the chronic problem of a cadre shortage in the countryside, especially in the newly liberated areas. Because of the lack of cadres, when the Communists captured a village the party was forced to recruit cadres from the reputable progressive gentry, a method known as "a search for the able and the virtuous" (*fangxian*). Since Communist power was weak in the area, these new gentry cadres often struck a compromise with whatever local power holders happened to be in the area. Some even attacked the middle and poor peasants.[36] In certain regions, newly recruited cadres actively courted landlord support. In Dagao Ying in Shenqiu county, for instance, cadres were reported to be working closely with local gentry. Only one out of ten cadres was reportedly "clean."[37] Public notices were put up calling upon landlords, even those "guilty of the most heinous crimes," to return home and register with the new government. The cadres promised that as long as these bad gentry admitted past mistakes and vowed never to sabotage the land reform program, they would be guaranteed government protection.[38]

Landlords and *baojia* heads also used their legal and official positions to sabotage land reform. Many adopted the tactic of false compliance. They "voluntarily" redistributed grain among villagers and clansmen, undoubtedly giving more to their own clients. They then reported to the government that redistribution had been successfully carried out in an amiable atmosphere. They set up their own gentry-dominated peasant associations and used territorial feelings to drive a wedge between native poor peasants and outsiders.[39] In another case, the gentry coerced peasants to form a mutual nonaggression pact with them: "If the Guomindang comes, we will protect you, but in the meantime, while the Eighth Route Army remains in the area, you give us protection."

By insisting on a completely equal land redistribution, the party had broadened its scope of attack and created problems. In some villages, 40 percent of the landholders were forced to give up land.[40] Cadres sometimes took shortcuts. Instead of following instructions and taking a survey before drawing up class identification categories, they simply designated "owners of three *mu* of land as middle peasants, five *mu* as rich peasants, and ten *mu* as 'good for nothing.' " Seldom did they check the economic standing of households or the types of exploitative relationship present in the particular locality. As a directive pointed out, the basic problem was cadre "left impetuosity." Cadres were determined to complete the land reform in six months. Some wanted a "one-shot solution" to all existing problems, or to make a blanket attack on all enemies. In their hasty way of implementing change, these cadres found no time for social surveys and investigations.

Cadres once again overestimated the social revolutionary potential of the masses. Many mistook the growing demands of a few peasant activists for the rising consciousness of the peasant class. But villagers did not have faith in Communist rule. They were uncertain as to whether the Communists were there to stay; many therefore remained unresponsive to Communist appeals and kept their distance. Timid peasants were reported to have refused even the grain and money cadres gave them, not to mention the land.[41] Popular trust and legitimacy presented a problem. Traditionally, peasants had a strong respect for authority; to them, petty landlords and rich peasants, who still controlled the rural *baojia* system, remained the rural authority figures. Moreover, the Communists found that after a protracted period of warfare and destruction, peasants longed for peace and order. They sought a government that could bring political stability to the area. They had no interest in being leaders of a revolution. Asking them to head the government, to collect the grain and taxes, and to execute people without a trial was completely alien to their conservative thinking.[42]

Without peasant commitment and active participation, the Communists reported, land reform was conducted with "party paternalism." The reform was imposed on the peasants by force. Cadres had a simplistic notion that mass mobilization was merely a matter of material exchange for political support. If coercion did not achieve the desired results, they would resort to brute force. Thus, in some areas, peasants complained that Communist rule was "worse than that of the first Qin emperor" (Qinshihuangdi) and compared the Communists with the "King of Hell" (Yanwang). As in all social revolutions, things frequently got out of control, and the land reform program was accompanied by killings. Reportedly, on average three persons were executed in each village—about 1,500 in the three districts under Communist control—most without the approval of party superiors. Some landlords were said to have been buried alive. Among those executed were middle and even poor peasants, often accused by cadres of being "bandits and hooligans."[43] When accused of these crimes, some cadres answered that it was impossible not to harm the middle peasants in such a major revolutionary change.

From a tactical point of view, the hasty transfer of wealth to the rural poor was detrimental to the revolutionary process. A handful of peasant activists often became the primary beneficiaries of the reform. An early transfer of land, cash, and grain to a small group of activists took away the party's ability to build up sufficient resources to sustain the final campaign. The burden of financing the war fell heavily on the shoulders of the middle peasants. Moreover, without having firmly established their authority in the countryside and before exercising tight control over it, Communist cadres were not in an authoritative position to handle the large volume of disputes generated by the land reform program. The countryside was thus thrown into a state of confusion.[44]

Apparently following a policy change that was evolving in the party center at this time, high-ranking cadres such as Wu Zhipu, who had opposed the last-minute reform, condemned the radical land policy as purely "leftist opportunism."[45] He warned that such drastic agrarian actions would only push peasants toward the GMD and give the local gentry a chance to organize peasants in sectarian defense groups to oppose the Communist government. Wu argued that the radical policy would also cause severe damage to the United Front at the village level. In the long run, Wu insisted, not only would the party be unable to hold on to the newly won areas, in which Communist control was far from firmly established, but radical economic reform would surely lead to a collapse in the old areas already under Communist rule.[46] Moreover, land seizures and the landlord exodus from rural areas would harm agricultural production. Frequently, farmlands were not redistributed to cultivators immediately after seizure. Most of the arable acreage lay waste, which apparently accounted for the overall drop in production in the region.[47]

Because the land reform program had caused so many problems and so much disruption, in April 1948, the Central Plain Bureau issued an order for the immediate cessation of the practices of "onetime equal distribution" and "equal redistribution by making it up from both ends" (*liangtou pingfen*, that is, keeping middle peasant holdings intact and redistributing land from the landlords and rich peasants to the poor peasants).[48] At the military and finance meeting in May, Wu severely reprimanded radical cadres for their "leftist sense of haste."

A more moderate policy was now adopted by the party. First, in "bandit-suppression" areas, where heavy fighting was still going on and the CCP and GMD were contending for control, the main party objective was to consolidate political power. Class struggle was narrowly restricted to seizing and redistributing grain. Only when there was an unmistakable sign that the peasant masses wanted land redistribution were cadres allowed to promote land reform. Second, in areas where land reform had already been carried out, cadres were instructed to do their best to mediate land disputes, then to move on and focus on production. Third, in areas bordering on GMD areas, cadres were to aim at mobilizing peasants in the anti-puppet nationalistic movement and in defensive actions against GMD grain seizures. Their duty was to provide peasants with armed protection during the harvest. In both the new and old areas, the major emphasis was on agricultural production and rural reconstruction. Peasants were encouraged to gain access to cultivated land, not through class struggle, but by reclamation.

Wu urged cadres to swiftly mend fences with the middle peasants by publicly announcing the party's stated policy of never infringing on their rights. Party directives repeatedly underscored its stance of neutralizing the rich peasants. Losses experienced by the middle peasants in previous class struggles were to be made up immediately from the confiscated property in government hands. To highlight the party's middle peasant focus, cadres were urged to encourage middle peasants to join the peasant associations. Government policy stipulated that at least a third of the leadership in peasant associations had to come from the middle peasants. The Poor Peasant Corps, which had earlier formed the vanguard of the social revolution, were abolished, and poor peasants were incorporated into the peasant associations. The targets of attack were revised and clearly confined to big landlords and big bullies. The new policy toward middle and small landlords was to "neutralize these elites by playing on the differences between these petty landlords and the big landlords."[49]

In a dramatic turnabout, the party also adopted new measures to entice landlords who had fled the area to come back. As long as landlords agreed to give up their arms and to be law-abiding citizens, they were allowed to return to their villages without reprisal. The party guaranteed them protection if they promised to pay taxes and reduce interest payments and rent. They were also entitled to a piece of land and a share of the redistributed grain, like every other resident. Business interests were carefully guarded by law and children from elite backgrounds were guaranteed a good education in the Communist schools. The party also fell back on the old *baojia* system rather than rely on the new Communist government to clear the area of "counterrevolutionaries." The new emphasis in village transformation was on "democratic ways" rather than the confrontational politics adopted at the end of the Sino-Japanese War.[50] The key word was moderation, an approach in line with overall United Front policy.

By the winter of 1948, the Central Plain Bureau had completely abandoned the radical land program and had returned to the mild social reform of rent and interest reduction. The movement's focus shifted back to resistance to unfair taxation (*fan tanpai*). As the peasants were still weak, the party argued, the "democratic allotment" tax program (*minzhu tanpai*) was to be implemented with the assistance of the traditional "feudal village power holders." Even in areas where Communist control was well established, cadres were told to be flexible. A small number of "local tyrants and their agents" remained the prime targets of attack. The Central Plain Bureau, however, instructed cadres to leave the land the way it had already been redistributed; they were allowed to change leases only when there was an urgent request from local peasants. Issuing title deeds for the newly redistributed land was to be postponed.[51] Given the political instability and weakness of Communist control in the localities, the party was forced to modify its policy and to seek accommodation with local gentry and rich peasants. It had to give up its lofty ideals of absolute economic equality and radical class struggle in transforming the countryside.[52]

The final outcome of the radical land reform varied from area to area depending on the degree of Communist military and political control. Communist reports provide some hard data on the results of the reform. In the old area of the Sui-Qi-Tai border base, land reform had a rather considerable impact on the countryside. In the four brief months of land reform in 335 villages, 19,700 peasants received 48,569 *mu* of redistributed land. In Fugou and Tongxu counties, 13,000 peasants received 80,000 *mu* of land. In the Yellow River floodplain, the flood had wiped out practically everything. Farmlands were without boundaries. In this area, Communist authorities had no problems applying the principle of complete equality. The cadres took land from the landlords, most of whom had fled when the area was flooded, and redistributed it to the poor. Each individual received 5 *mu* of land, thus fully implementing Sun Yatsen's principle of "land to the tillers." In some areas, the class struggle was intense but limited to the most obvious targets—spies, corrupt officials, and village bosses. In other areas which had gone through land reform but had been retaken by GMD troops, the class struggle was very fierce. Peasants saw the fruits of their struggle taken away from them and heeded the Communist calls for a resettling of accounts with the landlords.[53]

As was to be expected, land reform was more successful in the old areas, where Communists had tight political control, and in the inundated areas, where the flood had helped clear away the feudal village power structure and thus enabled the Communists to start afresh and implement their own program. The success of the social revolution was highly dependent on the weakness of the rural elite. The party had greatly provoked the peasants in the fight for their economic interests, and some of them did actively respond to Communist appeals, because of the subsistence crisis caused by war and flooding, but the Communists' radical land program was greatly hampered by internal policy conflicts and sometimes by a lack of coordination. Even though on the eve of national liberation the Communists had redoubled their efforts to trade material benefits for the peasants' political support, this effort was hindered by the peasants' lack of confidence in the probability of Communist military success. In many areas, the Communists still faced stiff resistance from entrenched rural elites.

Problems in Taking Over the Cities

According to the Communist strategy, the takeover of the cities was to proceed in two distinct stages. It took roughly a month to restore social order and to reassure the urban public following the takeover. In this first stage, the Communists exercised great caution. The main objectives, the party stated, were to unite the urban classes and to avoid any disruption of commerce and industry by a radical labor movement. The central function of the party was to stabilize the area. This phase of stabilization was followed by a period of consolidation of power and institution building. In the second stage, the Communists conducted propaganda campaigns, tracked down bandit gangs and GMD secret agents, set up "people's governments," and revived production. The party envisaged that urban workers would assume leadership in the new government. The second stage was essentially a stage of transformation.

At the outset of the takeover, disarming the enemy and tracking down GMD agents did not present too much of a problem for the party. After their military defeat, many GMD officials and secret agents had fled the area. But GMD underground operations remained very active in large urban centers such as Zhengzhou. There, agents operated clandestinely as "underground armies" (*dixia jun*) and "guard units" (*shouwei jun*).[54] The Communists tried their best to avoid alarming the enemy with mass arrests. They used the police and public security bureau files to track down underground GMD agents individually. They kept a watchful eye on members of the GMD and small parties such as the Minshe Party (*Minshe dang*) and the Youth Party (*Qingnian dang*). When these tried to obtain government permission to legally become a Friendship Society (*lianyi hui*), their request was immediately denied. The party then outlawed and disbanded these political organizations.[55] Property belonging to high-ranking GMD officials was registered by and placed under the custody of the Communist government. Commercial enterprises and the property of "small bureaucrats, city employees, and landlords" were usually left alone.[56] All bandit and gentry armed forces in suburban areas sympathetic toward the GMD were either reorganized or disbanded.

In the meantime, the Communists made an all-out effort to propagate their revolutionary cause among local elites. Schools were reopened after the takeover. Communist papers were published and placed in libraries to influence the urban public. Soldiers were ordered to hold discussions with local elites, to espouse Communist policies, and to destroy the public concept of the legitimacy of the GMD government and the belief in the imminent return of Nationalist rule. Communist propaganda campaigns also aimed at providing urban citizens with information on the international situation and appealing nationalistically to the public to support the war.

Another way to change the public's ideas about the Communist government was through education. This had two purposes: to impart to urban elites the basic concepts of communism, and to get them to participate in the revolution. Due to the shortage of urban-oriented leadership, the party adopted various stopgap measures to mass-recruit local elites. Two- to six-month crash courses were set up to recruit college students, the military, and accountants. Party schools and worker training classes were created for the recruitment of leaders for local party branches, labor unions, and peasant associations. Newly trained party members were placed in urban centers to oversee commerce and industry. The Communists retained teachers in local schools, combined schools with low enrollments into a single unit, and appointed a committee or an acting principal as a transitional administrative agent.[57]

The party exercised moderation and proceeded with great caution so as not to offend urban elites and citizens. Except for wresting local armed forces from the people, the overall party policy was one of extreme leniency (*kuanda zhengce*): "Chief offenders are to be punished, but followers to be spared, and the meritorious to be rewarded." "Punishment for the chief offenders," the party elaborated, "does not mean capital punishment." Offenders were to be isolated and the punishment administered at an appropriate time. "Reactionaries" were to be tracked down and put under constant observation. Cadres were to try to persuade criminals to give themselves up.[58]

Such a moderate policy was practical and necessary since the Communists were operating in a new environment. Most cadres had little or no urban experience and the party had to make adjustments for that fact. Except for a few underground Communist activists who had an urban or mixed background, Communist cadres came from rural areas and were familiar with guerrilla operations in the countryside. Administering urban centers was highly complex and required a large influx of cadres, which the party was unable to provide. The Communists were in dire need of leaders with expertise in commerce, industry, public security, and government administration. The shortage of urban-oriented leaders forced the party to send only three cadres to take over the Longhai and Beiping-Hankou railroads and the telegraph and telegram bureau. Of these three cadres, only one had any knowledge of running these enterprises. The Communists had to rely on the existing staff to run the post office, the roadway bureau, the museum, and the city library.

Part of the problem stemmed from the ingrained rural mentality of the cadres. Cadres failed to develop the skills and attitudes needed for urban work following the Communists' protracted exclusion from the cities. Mao's concept of a rural revolution "encircling the cities from the countryside" had put an inordinate emphasis on rural operations. In time, rural-based cadres developed a disdain for urban work and refused to send fellow cadres to work in the urban centers. Sometimes local parties stubbornly resisted relocation of their headquarters to the county seat after the military takeover. Some rural leaders refused to dispatch troops to garrison cities. Despite the Communist policy that explicitly directed local parties to swiftly transfer large numbers of cadres into the cities, some urban centers were still run by only a few cadres. Shangqiu, site of the major Longhai rail station and a city with a population of 100,000 people, was run by only 33 cadres. The party repeatedly complained that cadres neglected urban areas and major transport lines. A report confirms that the Communists were drawing their economic and military resources mainly from the countryside, not from the cities.[59]

To change the cadres' outlook and improve their urban aptitude, the party immediately organized them into work sessions and gave them a crash course in urban skills. The party also issued directives underscoring the significance of urban work. Liu Zijiu, propaganda head of the Central Plain Bureau, told cadres that Communist urban policies had undergone fundamental changes because the growing Communist power at the national level had completely altered the military and political balance in the cities. Communist strength in urban areas forced the enemy to voluntarily give up their arms and gravitate toward the Communist side. "Formerly, cadres had to take to the hills after the collapse of an urban uprising. Today, the party has to rely on the cities as bases for launching strikes against the GMD. Previously, our policy was encircling the cities from the countryside; today the cities are leading the countryside in a revolution. Formerly, the Communist Party was a clandestine organization; today it is the ruling party in the cities." Liu urged cadres to quickly learn how to function in the cities: how to do business, and how to manage the factories, railroads, and schools in urban centers. But he warned cadres that urban operations differed radically from rural operations. The cities, he said, were complicated, cosmopolitan, literate, and dominated by transport facilities, while the countryside was straightforward, simple, illiterate, and remote.[60]

But the takeover of the cities generated even more complex problems and greater confusion than the Communists anticipated. Changes in currency resulted in a sudden stoppage of trade in some areas, causing severe shortages of many daily items. As a measure to relieve Kaifeng, a metropolis of 330,000 people, the Communists were forced to import two million *jin* of grain to stabilize food prices. Many of Kaifeng's 29,000 workers were unemployed.[61] Although a third of the 30,000 Kaifeng students had left with the GMD, those who remained were dependent on the government. The municipal government was running on a deficit. Urban expenditures were C$20 million a month, while urban income was a mere C$8 million. Right from the time of the takeover, urban centers relied heavily on the countryside to survive.[62]

On the whole, the Communists failed to secure the support of businessmen and citizens in the cities. Despite a policy of moderation and protection for the petty and national bourgeoisie, the Communists' class actions against landlords during the radical land reform program had terrified those in business circles. Despite the party's later order for cessation of land reform and for compensation for landlords, the psychological impact of fear and anxiety about Communist radicalism lingered and reverberated in urban centers. County towns had been ruined during the takeover fighting. In Taikang county, street vendors practically disappeared. Paradoxically, party leniency and its protection of commerce antagonized some urban citizens, like workers, who, apparently still influenced by GMD propaganda, harbored a particular animosity toward the Communists. In the cities, there was still a great deal of fear and hatred directed toward the Communists. When a cadre working in the Huaiyang bureau of commerce and industry was killed by a bandit, urban residents vented their anger against the Communists by mutilating the corpse. In the third district, citizens voluntarily buried GMD officials but refused to do the same for cadres killed in the war.[63]

In some areas, handicraft industries were revived and petty merchants were again active. But merchant leaders were always hesitant in their support for Communist rule. Many cities had traditionally been consumer and administrative centers, yet without the presence of government functionaries, these urban centers looked rather deserted. In smaller towns, where the economy was linked more directly to the countryside and therefore less affected by the fighting, shortages of grain and coal were less severe. The Communists were able to exert tighter control over these areas. In big cities, on the other hand, problems like the fluctuating prices of grain and other daily items made Communist rule less attractive. Popular support for the Communists quickly dwindled.[64]

The Communists were confronted with another urban problem: the support of the urban proletariat and of small traders. With prolonged GMD and Japanese control in the low-level urban centers, Communist urban networks had been successively dismantled by the enemy. But in the metropolises of Kaifeng, Zhengzhou, and Shangqiu, the Communists still maintained a certain degree of influence among the workers. There was a sizable population of urban workers in these cities—29,000 in Kaifeng, 20,000 in Zhengzhou, and 10,000 in Shangqiu. Most of these laborers were traditionally employed by the railroads, the postal service, telegraph and telegram offices, flour mills, cigarette factories, and iron foundries. Many of them had some education and technical skills. A large number of them, however, had been unemployed during the war. Some were displaced by workers who came to the area with the GMD from Chongqing; others were thrown out of work because the GMD had stripped the factories of machinery before they left. The rest lost their jobs when industry closed down at the time of the Communist takeover.

Right after the takeover, urban industry was indeed in shambles. Factories closed down for lack of funds or because of the collapse of markets. More importantly, workers' repeated demands for higher wages (in one case, three pay raises within six months) practically put businesses out of existence.[65] The cost of materials also went up. The resulting increase in retail prices drove customers away. Factory owners were frequently fined by labor unions under the control of "ruffian foremen." The growing tension in labor relations in urban areas often led to a complete collapse of industry and commerce, which in turn caused widespread urban unemployment. A survey of the textile labor union in Hexia in Huaxian county reported that 140 of its 246 members—57 percent—were unemployed.[66]

Another problem was caused by the Communist radical urban policy adopted at the end of the Sino-Japanese War. In line with the radical land reform policy in the rural areas, the party also instituted a radical reform of the market system, which was to be controlled by poor peasants in the urban centers. Private trading was abolished and replaced by trading through "commodity exchange bureaus" (*jiaoyi suo*), organizations dominated by poor peasants. Rural markets were either combined or abolished. This drastic Communist policy drove businessmen and capital out of urban areas. In some towns, many stores went out of business; those that remained open were operated by "middle and petty merchants."[67] Wealthy merchants usually sought refuge and GMD protection in the cities. Merchants, fearful of Communist confiscation, hid raw materials. Many major industries, such as the brewing industry in Suixi, collapsed.[68]

The canceling and combining of rural markets and the forced alteration of market schedules (for example, from a morning to an evening market) also greatly affected the lives of small traders. That vendors were driven out of the closing markets alienated many rural traders. Schedule changes disrupted marketing routines and inconvenienced traders. The combining of rural markets forced peddlers to travel longer distances. Itinerant merchants protested against such disruptions, saying there was no difference between the New Fourth Army and the GMD Eighteenth Army. Urban dwellers also complained that the New Fourth Army was "taking care of the countryside at the expense of the cities."

The "poor peasant line" adopted by the party in rural markets completely destroyed the traditional market system. Commodity exchanges eventually fell under the control of urban "hooligans." Middle and poor peasants refused to buy goods from the commodity exchange bureaus. The fact that peasants were required to obtain a "purchase license" before making purchases from the bureaus was too troublesome and seriously hampered market transactions. Added to that was the problem of bureaucratism. Some peasants applied to the government office nine times without getting a license. Yet when they were caught operating without one, traders were heavily fined, and in some cases their stores were confiscated by Communist authorities. Because of the disruption, trading activities in rural markets practically came to a halt. Communist cadres reported that this marketing policy was "suicidal" and demanded immediate changes.

In May 1948, faced with the reality of a depressed market, the party was forced to reverse its policy. In the third district, 101 rural markets previously abolished by the party were rehabilitated. The commodity exchange bureaus were abandoned. Small traders were encouraged to form cooperatives and jointly transport goods. Individuals were given the freedom to open and own stores, as long as they agreed not to spy and not to oppose the Communist land reform program, and to stop using GMD currency. With the new policy and a gradual revival of rural markets, commerce began to thrive. A quantity of salt that had cost C$800 now cost only C$400. The transport industry became active once again. Confiscated stores were returned to merchants. Members of a merchant's family were given the right to repossess property if the owner had fled the area because of the radical policy and refused to come back. Many unmanned stores were pooled into village cooperatives. The rightful owners, who did not want to return to run the businesses, became shareholders. Three months after the implementation of the new policy, the Communists reported that the number of business enterprises in the 58 markets in six counties had doubled.[69]

Although Communist policy had always emphasized that proletarians were the revolutionary vanguard, and cadres were constantly urged to mobilize them in the revolution, worker loyalty to the party was not automatic. Laborers undoubtedly had legitimate grievances against the GMD. Under Nationalist rule, workers were exploited by merchants and labor gangs. Many were forced to pay fees amounting to as much as 20 percent of their wages to labor bosses. Many middle and low-level employees had to bribe bosses to get a raise or a promotion. On the other hand, GMD-created "yellow" labor unions did perform some useful functions. The unions fought hard to gain benefits for workers. They frequently forced employers to build bathhouses, theaters, and barber shops for the workers, and schools for their children. Railway workers did not have to pay for travel by rail, nor for the coal they used. Urban labor unions had long been infiltrated by GMD secret agents, and intense GMD indoctrination had had a tremendous impact on labor. Workers often looked upon the Communists with mistrust and fear. Most of the time they stayed away from the cadres, not knowing whether Communist power would last.

Rural-based cadres had little or no knowledge of running a union. Unlike during the 1920s, when Communist labor leaders jumped at every opportunity and mobilized workers in class struggles, rural cadres now showed no enthusiasm for promoting labor movements. After the urban takeover they had created a couple of trade union preparatory offices in the major cities, restored bathhouses, and deducted the transport cost of coal for workers. The Communists also instituted some minor reforms. They abolished the "gifts" and fees laborers were forced to pay bosses, which had constituted the principal grievance in labor relations. But urban workers complained that the Communists were more on the side of the employers than on that of the laborers. In order to stabilize the cities and to induce merchants and industrialists to go back into production, the party put off all labor movements for the time being. The only form of labor movement they promoted was the struggle against GMD secret agents in the unions, but this was conducted out of political consideration rather than a concern for the economic welfare of urban workers.[70]

Communist reports indicate that workers and the urban poor were among the strongest critics of the Communists' urban policies. The urban poor lamented that the Communist Party had forgotten them once it moved into the cities. They resented the overconcern of the party for industrial production, which resulted in its directing most of its attention to the business and industrialist class, rather than to the urban poor. Communist propaganda, they pointed out, did not even mention the urban poor. The party had completely ignored the labor movement and cadres did not have the social and economic welfare of workers in mind. When workers lost their jobs and when wages were cut, the party did not lead them to fight for their interests. In some cases, the Communists even allowed GMD secret agents to remain in the unions.[71]

The party was particularly concerned about the railroads, which were vital for troop mobilization. Zhengzhou city in particular, where the Beiping-Hankou and Longhai railroads intersected, was an important strategic military center. The Nationalists had infiltrated the railway unions with their agents before the Sino-Japanese War. After the Communists took over Zhengzhou, the GMD agents mobilized the workers and seized the union. It took the Communists some time to find this out. They immediately replaced the GMD agents with their own cadres.

The railroads were not only strategically significant for troop mobilization in wartime, they also formed a direct link between liberated areas and GMD-occupied areas, and were therefore ideal lines for Communist infiltration. Railway workers and postmen were often in contact with workers and activists in urban centers in the Jiangnan region. The party therefore used the rail network to penetrate southern cities and pave the way for eventual liberation of these areas. Since the Communists were faced with high unemployment in the cities, they used unemployed workers as grass-roots infiltrators. Workers were paid and trained to set up contacts and to gather intelligence in central China. This not only partly solved the unemployment problem in the north, it also facilitated the takeover of cities in the south.[72]

Since the party did not have time to train enough cadres for urban work, it had to rely on existing urban elites to rebuild the cities. Communists mass-recruited technical experts and distinguished citizens and put them into urban leadership positions. Those with industrial backgrounds formed the very "backbone" of the urban renewal program.[73] Cadres were also forced to draw on existing elites to staff important positions in the municipal administration.[74] To maintain Communist control of these organizations, a dual management system was set up in all institutions and industrial enterprises. In strategic industries, such as the railroads and postal and telegraph services, Communist cadres normally headed the bureaus to ensure maximum party control over them; incumbents were retained as deputies. In areas where Communists lacked expertise, incumbents were allowed to stay on as heads, but were given military commissars as deputies. Communist deputies were given broad administrative power in personnel appointments and decision making.[75] In this way, the party hoped to prevent any disruption in production while their men were given time to pick up the necessary skills.

To protect the urban economy, the party had to make compromises. All forms of labor unrest were indefinitely suspended. High-ranking administrative elites kept their high salaries, a policy that infuriated many workers. Workers felt betrayed. Communist policies, they argued, were supposed to champion their economic rights, protect their interests, and help them in the struggle for higher wages. Instead, the party had systematically compromised with the capitalists for the sake of increased production and political stability. Communist appeasement of employers also angered middle and low-ranking employees, who felt that they were the real losers (the "unlucky ones," in their own words) in the revolution. Cadres quickly mended fences with the workers by explaining to them that such measures were only temporary, necessary evils in the transitional period. The party quickly assured urban workers that their wages would be adjusted in the future.[76]

Despite all these complications, Communist moderation had achieved favorable results in disarming and enlisting the support of urban elites. Bandits, Peace Preservation Squads, and landlords who controlled local militia voluntarily gave up their arms and joined the Communist camp. Policemen, teachers, and government functionaries began to apply and register for government services.[77] But in keeping the incumbents in office, the party, at least for the time being, had to close its eyes to the corrupt practices prevalent under GMD rule.[78] It was not until the 1950s that the Communists could move against the urban elites and effectively eradicate these problems. Appeasing urban elites also dampened worker class consciousness. Class conflict, which the revolution was designed to foster as a means to address workers' interests, had to be put on hold temporarily.

War Mobilization

Another urgent task for the Communist Party was war mobilization (*zhanqin*). Between November 16, 1948, and January 10, 1949, the CCP army fought a major battle against GMD forces in the Henan-Anhui-Jiangsu-Shandong area bordered by Haizhou (Jiangsu) in the east, Shangqiu (Henan) in the west, Lincheng (present-day Xuecheng in Shandong) in the north, and the Huai River in the south, a war zone centered at Xuzhou. The campaign, known as the Huaihai Campaign, was conducted under the leadership of such well-known officers as Deng Xiaoping, Liu Bocheng, Chen Yi, Su Yu, and Tan Zhenlin. The success of the campaign, in which, according to Communist statistics, the Nationalists suffered 550,000 casualties, led to the liberation of most of the areas in Henan and all of eastern China north of the Yangzi River. From then on, Communist troops posed a direct military threat to the two major GMD-controlled metropolises of Shanghai and Nanjing.[79]

The Communists had to make sure that they had adequate food supplies and labor conscripts to sustain such a major campaign. On November 9, 1948, the party ordered an all-out mobilization for war. It called upon cadres to actively organize transport corps and stretcher-bearers for the battlefront, to collect grain and fodder for the troops, and to mobilize the public to support the armies. A hierarchy of organizations was created to oversee the mobilization effort: the war service command headquarters in the county and war service committees in the villages. All able-bodied citizens between the ages of 16 and 55 were liable for military service. Young adults and the elderly were assigned to temporary and light labor. Able-bodied men between the ages of 18 and 45 were ordered to perform heavy military work. Women were mobilized to perform such tasks as making noodles, manufacturing military uniforms and shoes, and providing laundry services. Other groups were to be organized when necessary to provide guides, receptionists, cooks, and people to care for the wounded and sick.

The Communists tried to make the labor conscription system as fair as possible. Traditional labor conscription had been done by the allotment (*tanpai*) system based on landownership, and was a constant source of friction between the state and localities. The new Communist labor conscript system was based on village households. All citizens, except those already assigned to village defense, were to participate in the war effort. It was mandatory for each household to set aside 20 to 30 *jin* of grain for government use, for which the Communists promised to reimburse the lenders after the war. All households were required to provide oil, salt, bean curd, and bean sprouts for the armed forces.[80]

Despite intense preparation and mobilization, the party found itself unable to enlist popular support in urban centers and to effectively tap urban resources. Communist authority was in its infancy in the cities, and the party had very little command over the railroads, highways, telephones, and sewing and medical services. It even had difficulty wresting control of local means of transport, such as automobiles and horse-drawn carts, from urban residents. Ultimately, the Communists had to fall back on the countryside for logistic support. A major mobilization such as the Huaihai Campaign required almost a million laborers and innumerable draft animals for the transport of war materiel. The traditional corvée system of drafting labor and animals was highly ineffective. In areas where that system was adopted to conscript labor, desertion was widespread. For instance, the Communists had successfully organized 50,000 pairs of stretcher-bearers for the Huaihai Campaign, but on their way to the battlefront, half of these conscript laborers fled. In some districts, military desertion was as high as 60 percent. The party finally solved the problem by recruiting laborers directly from its old rural bases, for example, the Third District, where the party-peasant relationship was strong and where peasants, through prolonged participation in Communist programs, had developed a firm commitment to the revolutionary cause.[81]

In some cases, the party had to resort to the contract labor system to obtain workers needed for the war. Village governments paid workers three *jin* of grain a day for the work. Hired labor was widely used in rear areas and for transporting the injured.[82] But the system had unforeseen problems. Hauling heavy military materiel by ox-cart over a great distance was slow, and casualties among the draft animals were high.[83] Sometimes cadres thought that as long as peasants were paid for their services, tasks would be carried out properly. Yet because the peasants lacked supervision, draft animals often died in the snow. The party also attempted to use water transport. Urban transport companies refused to work for the Communists. Due to their lack of experience in urban work, the party neglected to register these companies. Fearful of suffering damage and losses in the war, transport companies evaded service. Transport in the rear area was a bit easier. Contract labor worked well there, and military materiel did reach the front. Cadres occasionally contracted an entire village for transport, a method that proved highly effective. Villagers performed well as a community and often cooperated with great enthusiasm.[84]

But the effectiveness of the contract labor system hinged on the party's ability to obtain enough resources, particularly grain, to pay for labor. Expansion of the Communist base in this period helped solve the problem. One tactic was to simply coerce the rich into paying for the war. Under the so-called grain borrowing program, Communist authorities systematically extracted food grains from landlords and rich peasants. Some grain was also obtained from the confiscated granaries of absentee landlords and from "native returnees" (*fanxiang tuan*). Penalties levied on GMD officials and the seizure of enemy strongholds also helped provide some of the badly needed grain resources.

Food supplies were vital to military combat. The Communist Party imposed a strict quota on every region. In Huaibei, local authorities and the army were ordered to gather at least 500,000 *jin* of grain three months before the summer harvest.[85] The Communist governments in the base areas were told to exercise their authority to gather grain. In guerrilla areas, troops were to collect it through the grain borrowing program. In border areas where the Communists had tenuous control, soldiers were to live off the area by getting food from "reactionary landlords." Gradually, the party built up its grain reserves.[86]

Citizens were asked to contribute grain according to ability: 40 percent of their grain stock if they were landlords (more than 40 percent if extremely wealthy), 20 percent if rich peasants, and 10 percent if middle peasants, with poor peasants exempted. As mentioned earlier, 40 percent of the grain confiscated in the class struggle went directly to the war chest. The grain, and all other military booty the army seized from the cities, was moved to nearby hilly areas for future use.[87] The party also used a tax collection campaign to extract resources for the war. Intense pressure was exerted on local authorities to collect taxes. Quotas were set for each collection period. All members of government agencies, not only officials but also army units and plainclothesmen, were told to use their power to drum up tax payments. The military was also financed by the funds obtained through selling war booty and landlord property.[88]

The Communists found that intense propaganda before a campaign served to raise village consciousness and win popular support. The most effective propaganda tactic was still to capitalize on village security and the need for physical protection. The Communists also made the peasants believe that the Huaihai Campaign was the last battle to bring down the GMD, and therefore would provide peasants with the thing they desired most—peace. Five days of political indoctrination in Changge and Weichuan counties enabled the Communists to retain 80 to 90 percent of their military recruits. On the other hand, deception did not work. Cadres in the Fifth District deceived peasants by saying that the government required them to perform only five days of war service. When the cultivators found that it took them longer just to reach the front, there were a great many desertions. Only 30 percent of peasant recruits eventually reached the battlefront.

The party confronted another problem in the peasants' customary attachment to community. Even though they were committed to the cause, few peasants were willing to travel and perform military service in far-off places. The Communists solved this problem by setting up a relay system. Peasants were organized into relay teams and asked to perform services only in or near their hometowns. In one county, the party rotated peasants and required each individual to serve thirteen days. These mobilization tactics achieved results. Peasants usually viewed this as the traditional collective defense that had always been required to protect their community. By identifying community security with the Communist revolutionary war, peasant political consciousness was heightened. Many participated actively in the war and later joined the Communist Party. Some even became Communist cadres.[89]

Conclusion

After the success of the Huaihai Campaign, the Central Plain Bureau immediately embarked on the task of forming a provincial government in Henan. On January 12, 1949, the Bureau issued a directive ordering all local parties to organize cadre training classes to build up their leadership. Quotas were set for each locality to train at least 200 low-level cadres and 150 district (*qu*) cadres by the autumn harvest. Finally, the party was able to transfer (probably forcibly) a large number of cadres from the border bases to Kaifeng, in preparation for the establishment of the new government in January.

In early March, a Central Plain Temporary People's Government was formed in Kaifeng, headed by Deng Zihui, political commissar of the New Fourth Army. The temporary government began work on the five overriding goals it set itself: increasing production in the cities, mobilizing the masses in the countryside, reviving the provincial economy, reorganizing local finance, building a local armed force of 100,000 men, and expanding party membership to 150,000. It simultaneously took up the immediate task of raising resources needed for the liberation of areas south of the Yangzi River by the People's Liberation Army. When Xinyang, the southernmost city on the Beiping-Hankou railroad, was finally liberated on April 1, the Communists decided to set up a permanent provincial authority. On May 10, 1949, the Henan provincial government was formed. Wu Zhipu, the Communist revolutionary who started out as a Red Spears mobilizer in the Sui-Qi-Tai area during the Northern Expedition, became its first governor. From then on, a new phase of the revolutionary process in Henan had begun, one focused on consolidation and reconstruction of the province rather than on struggle to seize state power, and on ruling the province from the urban center rather than on mobilizing the masses in the countryside to take over the cities.[90]

As we have observed in this chapter, taking over the cities was not simply a matter of positional warfare. Urban takeover involved gradually extending Communist influence in the cities, subverting urban enemy forces, and assembling sufficient resources to finance and sustain the war before finally mounting the campaign against the cities. All this required a lengthy period of preparation. Although the Communists had been driven out of the cities by the Japanese and the puppet troops and forced to operate in the countryside, the party had never given up on the urban centers as areas of operation. It realized that in the final stage of the revolution, seizure of state power meant capturing the cities. Mao had called for an "encircling of the cities from the countryside."

For the Communists, the primary focus of their urban work was army subversion. This entailed the employment of various tactics: extensive use of social ties to set up personal contacts with military officers; exploitation of factional power competition and internal friction in the enemy camp to divide, isolate, and finally destroy the enemy; and political negotiations to obtain the neutrality and defection of army officers. This was accomplished by intense diplomatic overtures at the top to provide effective cover for gradual infiltration and cooperation at the bottom. It was not until enemy forces were disintegrating through internal dissension and defections that encircling and taking over the cities was possible. In this military game, the Communists made the best possible use of the traditional military tactic of internal insurgency and external assault.

The Communists' urban work was greatly enhanced by Japan's defeat in the international war, which resulted in a substantial weakening of the defense capability of the puppet troops. Internal dissension and conflicts within the puppet army opened the way for intense political negotiations. Due to the previous conflict between Chiang Kaishek and Feng Yuxiang, Northwest Army officers were apprehensive of the Guomindang, and this blocked effective compromise between the Nationalists and these officers. Suspicion of the Nationalists offered the Communists an ideal opportunity for political intrigue and power games. The absorption of puppet armed forces considerably strengthened the revolutionary army.

The Communists were convinced that an all-out mobilization for war must link the military effort with improving the peasants' livelihood. Addressing rural poverty and the peasants' problem of access to land could generate popular support to further the war effort. Land reform could serve to strengthen the political alliance between the party and the peasants. Solving rural social and economic problems would encourage peasants to redouble their efforts to support the war. Moreover, through social revolution, the party could systematically extract from the landed upper classes the resources needed to finance and sustain the civil war against the Guomindang. The land revolution could also spearhead rural economic recovery and increases in production.

As the war against the Guomindang intensified, the Communists launched a last-minute radical land program to provoke peasants into social revolutionary actions. The objective was to achieve a synthesis between Communist military activities and the social revolution in the countryside. Once again, the party found that it had overestimated the social revolutionary potential of the peasantry. The response of these normally timid peasants was a rather passive one. The party had also underestimated the political and military strength of the entrenched rural elites, many of whom had been recruited into or had infiltrated the Communist government and mass organizations. From their official positions, the elites put up stiff resistance against Communist social reform.

Even though the party had drawn on the lessons of the Eyuwan period and had avoided attacking rich peasants, restricting its targets to a few big landlords and rural bosses, the radical social revolution it launched in this period was still hampered by a hasty policy implementation, a lack of coordination, an insistence on the Marxist ideal of absolute economic equality, and the taking of shortcuts, like onetime equal distribution, to achieve quick results. The radical land policy produced confusion and negatively affected agricultural production. Confronted with rural instability and a damaged economy, the party had to cancel the land reform and finally went back to the moderate wartime policy of rent and interest reduction and equitable taxation. But in certain favorable terrains, especially in the inundated floodplain and in base areas where Communist political control was strong, land reform produced visible results. It enabled the Communists to gather more grain resources, which helped further the mobilization.

After its protracted seclusion from the cities, the party found it difficult to adjust to the urban environment and to cope with urban problems after the takeover. Its work in the cities was inhibited by an acute shortage of cadres with urban backgrounds, and the problem was not solved by giving rural cadres quick training in urban work. Prolonged operations in the countryside had given rural cadres a "guerrilla mentality," and they failed to develop the skills and outlook required for leadership in the cities. Marxist ideology produced in them a disdain for the urban lifestyle. These cadres found it very hard to adjust to such a different operational environment. The shortage of urban-oriented cadres forced the party to rely heavily on existing urban elites to run the government and operate commercial and industrial enterprises.

The party policies of protecting the national and petty bourgeoisie and their enterprises, and the need to stabilize the urban economy and to increase industrial production, led the Communists to adopt urban-centered strategies favorable to capitalists and employers. Workers' needs and welfare were systematically compromised for the sake of political stability, economic recovery, and increases in production. The labor movement was temporarily suspended. Wage increases were postponed. The party failed to address the socioeconomic deprivation of petty employees and urban workers. All these adopted measures defeated the original revolutionary goal of social reform in the cities. The workers felt that they had been betrayed. A revolution is not a straightforward political, social, and economic change. It is a zigzag process that frequently results in compromises with ruling elites and produces unintended and sometimes undesirable outcomes.

Conclusion

In this study, we have traced step-by-step the Chinese Communist revolution in Henan province. Essentially, the revolution was a sociopolitical process of mobilizing the masses in the cities and the countryside to achieve certain revolutionary goals. Building the revolution took 30 years. It was an incremental process. During this time, the Chinese Communist Party, mainly through trial and error, evolved, improvised, improved, and gradually built up a store of revolutionary experience. Its mobilization tactics and modes of collective action changed over time. Some tactics were retained and modified; others were devised to meet the needs of a specific time and place. Initially, the Communists based their revolution in the cities, but they were driven out of the urban centers by repressive state forces. They then took refuge in the countryside, and it was in the rural areas that they eventually settled down and began mobilizing the peasants in a social revolution. The center of revolutionary activities shifted to the countryside. The revolutionary drama concluded with the capture of and return to the cities. The revolutionary process thus went full circle.

The Communist Party emerged as China was going through a process of political disintegration. Internal strife, first among the warlords and then between the warlords and the Nationalists, followed by the international war with Japan, brought about the political breakdown. Operating in an environment of internal turmoil, societal fragmentation, political rivalries and foreign intrusion, the Chinese Communists seized every political opportunity to further their revolution. They successfully penetrated the countryside, built an army, set up various territorial bases, and consolidated political power. They also organized local residents in defense organizations, changed the rural sociopolitical structure, integrated the communities, and mobilized the masses in a monumental effort to rebuild the rural economy. In the process, they gradually rebuilt the nation.

The course of the Communist revolution was certainly not smooth. Rural mobilizers had to overcome one obstacle after another, and they made numerous mistakes. The only thing certain about the revolution was the unpredictability of the outcome. Revolutionary action all too frequently brought about unanticipated and undesirable results. Revolutionary tactics and programs designed to attack certain problems often gave rise to entirely different sets of problems. The process of mobilizing peasants was full of surprises. As we follow the course of the revolution we find revolutionary idealism, revolutionary excesses, intra-party policy disputes, inadequate planning, hasty implementation of programs, cadre favoritism, corruption, inept and ineffective leadership, and, at times, despair and confusion. But we also witness a deep concern on the part of the Communists for the poor and the downtrodden, as well as flexibility and adaptability in policy implementation, patience and perseverance in times of hardship, participatory leadership, brilliant military tactics, skillful employment of coalition politics, effective organization and mobilization, revolutionary resiliency, and a strong will to overcome all odds. There are both positive and negative aspects to this revolutionary drama.

The Chinese Communists were trying to accomplish two major goals in the revolution: to seize political power and to promote socioeconomic reform in the countryside. The revolution was essentially a dual process: a political power game and a social revolution. In playing power politics, the Communists seized every favorable opportunity to advance their objectives. In May 1925, they made use of their alliance with the Guomindang and Feng Yuxiang to launch labor strikes in the cities. In 1930, they exploited the political differences between Chiang Kaishek and the Guominjun to penetrate the countryside and carve out a rural base in Eyuwan. They then used the Japanese disruption of Guomindang power to revitalize the movement, mass-recruit patriotic students, and rebuild their bases behind Japanese lines. After the Japanese overextended themselves in the Pacific war and were forced to withdraw troops from the region, the Communists immediately seized the chance to inflict heavy damage on the weak puppet forces. Undoubtedly, favorable political opportunities opened a way for the Communists to build power and to expedite the process of seizing control of the state.

The Communist revolution was also facilitated by international military intervention. Foreign intrusions or defeats in war often contribute to the outbreak of revolutionary crises. Japanese imperialism had a direct impact on the Communist revolution in China. The Japanese invasion gave rise to a political power crisis in the region. The origin of this regional power crisis can be traced back to the warlord period, when political rivalries among militarists shattered local society. The subsequent power struggle between Chiang Kaishek and the Guominjun further differentiated rural elites into rival factions. In the fierce contest for power, each group of local power holders was sharply pitted against another. The fragmentation of the elite and the political power crisis were intensified by foreign invasion and wartime anarchy.

Japanese expansionism significantly undercut the political authority of the Nationalist government. With the Nationalists retreating into inland China, state control was substantially relaxed, opening the way for radical transformation of the regional political structure. Weak regional power holders, who had been reluctant allies of the Guomindang, immediately seized this opportunity to move away from the Nationalist camp. Many began to assert power in the region and to form new political clusters. The threat of Japanese attacks compelled these weak power holders to seek physical protection and military assistance. Skillfully making use of these favorable political conditions, the Communists forged new relationships with local elites and regional militarists, drawing them into political alignments.

It was through skillful employment of political strategy that the Communists managed to entrench themselves in rural areas and build an army. Armies are indispensable in a revolutionary movement; they are needed to pin down enemy forces, to seize power, to create territorial bases, and to enforce government legislation and reform programs. The Communists' tactics for building the army also changed over time. In the beginning, like other rebels who possessed no military forces, the Communists created an army by absorbing and co-opting existing armed forces. In the Northern Expedition, the party adopted an en bloc incorporation approach. Direct political alliances were forged between the party and Red Spears chieftains, who were then employed in local power struggles. This approach to army building had advantages and shortcomings. An instant en bloc takeover of existing armed irregulars enabled the Communists to create a huge military force in a short time and at a relatively low cost. However, when the political situation changed, for example in the 1927 GMD-CCP split, the state could use the same forces to repress the party.

In the early 1930s, the party tried a very different approach. With the creation of a relatively secure border base in Eyuwan, the Communists used land redistribution to recruit peasants into the Red Army. The method was highly successful. Class benefits, such as access to land, were an effective force for motivating peasants to join the Communist army. But the newly created Red Army was almost decimated by Nationalist troops in the extermination campaigns. Part of the Red Army did break loose and eventually joined Mao Zedong in the Long March to Yan'an. The remaining forces, weak and disorganized, scattered over the area, and their members became guerrilla fighters.

When Sino-Japanese hostilities broke out, the Communists gathered these surviving guerrilla forces in an attempt to form a coherent army. But they had to rebuild the army practically from scratch. In this stage of their reemergence, the Communists adopted tactics similar to those they used in the Northern Expedition. The party utilized coalition politics to absorb and co-opt all available existing armed forces in the region. These armed forces included the friendly Northwest Army and an array of local forces such as bandit gangs, sectarian groups, clan bands, anti-Japanese guerrillas, and local militia. The party skillfully capitalized on the fear of war and the political instability in the area to recruit students and peasants into self-defense programs. Step by step, they built up their local militia. Instead of simply taking over these forces en bloc as they had done in the earlier period, the Communists disengaged these troops and reorganized them into the New Fourth Army. Remaining local armed forces were turned into local irregulars and used for community defense. Simultaneously, the party launched an army subversion program in the cities to secure defections from puppet armies. In short, the party formed tactical alliances.

All these were achieved through the effective use of United Front tactics. The war with Japan had created a fluid and more dynamic political environment. Military power in the region was highly fractured, which made political realignments feasible. In subverting enemy forces and in playing the coalition game, the party adopted both top-down and middle-out approaches. The Communists made political compromises with high-ranking warlord commanders and GMD commissioners so that cadres could gain access to their armies and secure official positions in county administrations. In the top-down approach, the party erected a "framework" of cordial relations, or *da jiazi*, to provide political cover for the smooth execution of revolutionary programs at the grass-roots level. The Communists were very much aware of the unreliability and vacillating political attitudes of these high-ranking officers, but even short-term political compromise with these regional power holders could ease tension and bring political rewards.

In the meantime, the party concentrated on extending its influence in subcounty armed forces and administration. Under the pretext of collective defense, it employed native cadres to infiltrate local defense networks by providing gentry with military assistance they badly needed for the creation of clan bands and local militia. They also helped neighborhood and village pacts build local security forces and then reorganized these forces into the Communist army. Using the subcounty forces under their control as political capital, Communist commanders successfully competed for county and subcounty administrative positions.

The party continually made use of corporate kinship, standard household units (neighborhoods, or *bao*), villages, and local communities as organizational units for collective action. These collective units usually exhibited the kind of "conservative solidarity" noted by Barrington Moore.[1] They were solid community institutions normally controlled by such conservative elements as local gentry, rich peasants, and *bao* heads, who commanded human and material resources. These units had traditionally served as tax administration units or communal collective defense units. In the revolution, they became solid units for action. They formed the very basis of Communist rural mobilization and were the community institutions the Communists utilized to seize state power.

Mobilization at the local level was greatly facilitated by the party's extensive use of indigenous leaders. As members of the rural elite, native Communist intellectuals not only possessed the social ties required for local contacts and for recruitment of "progressive" gentry into the movement; native students could also be used to win the confidence of the peasantry. The corporate kinship to which they belonged had under its control the manpower and material resources needed to sustain the revolution. Communist recruitment of these rural patriotic intellectuals, however, had been greatly facilitated by the Japanese military threat and brutal repression in the countryside. Students had been dislocated by the war. Given Nationalist inaction toward Japanese aggression, it is not surprising that these students actively responded to the Communists' nationalistic appeals. Many were favorably disposed toward the revolution not so much because they subscribed to Marxist revolutionary ideology but because the Communist movement was an acceptable alternative to Guomindang inaction. Once the war broke out, the party immediately set up crash military training programs to absorb these patriotic students. Afterward they were sent back to their hometowns as seeders, rural mobilizers, and party builders.

The Communists' party-building tactics usually involved a gradual diffusion of their influence "from a key point outward over a broad surface" (*you dian dao mian*).[2] This entailed choosing a key town or village as the incipient center, one where the party found favorable conditions in terms of availability of elite seeders and a weak state/elite repressive power. After setting up an organization there, the party then radiated from that centrality outward in a "ripple effect." Effective political networking depended on the continuous employment of personal and community ties as a means of leadership recruitment. When a specific area was permeated with party cells, it was then integrated into a regional hierarchy. The revolutionary movement, however, remained centrally directed by the party located in the original key center (the key village, *jiben cun*, or the central district, *zhongxin qu*).

The Communists' success at building party organizations and mobilizing the peasantry in the countryside depended very much on the inability of the state and its supportive rural elites to use repressive power against the movement. The prewar Communist failure stemmed not so much from an inability of the party to mobilize the peasant masses as from a highly effective state repressive power. The rapprochement between the left and right Guomindang in 1927 enabled the Nationalists to drive the Communists out of the cities. The conclusion of the civil strife between Chiang Kaishek and the warlords permitted the Nationalists to direct all their military resources at combating Communist influence in Eyuwan. Effective state repression eventually forced the Communists to retreat from their base areas and run for cover. The Communist movement would have been nothing more than a series of sporadic, irritating riots had it not been for the wartime collapse of state control and the weakening of the Nationalist political position as a result of the Japanese invasion.

Although substantially weakened, the Guomindang was far from impotent militarily. With the support of regional warlords, the Nationalists still possessed enough military power to inflict heavy damage on Communist bases. Japanese motorized assaults also brought high casualties and rural disruption to the bases, and confusion to the Communist Party. But by actively promoting collective defense and socioeconomic reforms in the rural areas, the party was able to entrench itself in the countryside and enlist peasant support in the revolution. Against all odds and in the face of overwhelmingly superior Nationalist and Japanese forces, the Communists made the best of their guerrilla and mobile warfare capabilities. The party conducted resilient retreats and organized rural residents to fight a war of attrition against the Japanese. It capitalized on the daily menace of war and mobilized local communities in resistance efforts. It fully utilized its staying power and employed a wait-it-out strategy while Communist armed forces attacked soft enemy targets to wear them out. After the Japanese were tied down in a wider international conflict, and later, when Japanese troops moved out of the region, the Communists sprang into action to defeat the remaining weak puppet forces. The party was able to reassert military and political dominance in the region.

While the Communists were building party organizations and competing with the Guomindang for power, they were also actively mobilizing peasants in a social restructuring of the countryside. They had to begin by undermining the power of rural elites. The party had stressed repeatedly in its directives that the breakdown of "old feudal ruling authorities" was a prerequisite to effective rural mobilization.[3] But the power of the entrenched elites was formidable, and was backed by political authorities, local armed forces, the judicial system, and an efficient intelligence service. In their attempts to blunt class attacks, the gentry frequently used threat, rumor, deceit, clan power, and all sorts of material benefits to entice peasants to join their side.

Local peasants were invariably subjected to the control of elite power. Peasants frequently felt completely impotent in confronting landlords. A Yuwansu peasant told a cadre, "If you want me to redistribute my landlord's land, you had better get me a coffin first." Another peasant said, "Like a skinny horse with long hair and round hoofs, a poor man's words are worth no more than a penny. One sentence from the landlord carries as much weight as a poor man's utterances over half a year." Other typical peasant reactions included: "You take care of the reactionaries [the gentry] first, and leave the land redistribution to us." "If I redistribute his land, he will want my head. Tell me, what is more important, my head or the land?" "Comrade, you can always leave the area [if something goes wrong], but I can't."[4] Peasants were always under the landlords' dominance. Only when the power of the rural gentry had been substantially eroded could rural peasants, whether tenants or freeholding middle peasants, obtain the autonomy needed for social revolutionary action.

Yet the power of the rural elites was not monolithic. With the intensification of political struggles in the region, elite power became increasingly fragmented as rural gentry were sharply differentiated in rival political/military factions. As the political breakdown deepened, a new power structure began to emerge in the countryside. New political configurations and social clusters came into existence. In this highly fragmented and volatile society, the Communists could always find "free bourgeoisie" or "enlightened gentry" who were willing to join forces with them, either for the purpose of gaining power or to fight common enemies. The military commanders of the Northwest Army, the left Guomindang, and reformist gentry entrepreneurs were the Communists' ideal allies. Although cadres were repeatedly warned of the "wavering" and "conservative" attitudes of these agrarian upper classes, the party nevertheless insisted that the "enlightened gentry" constituted a useful revolutionary force and ordered all cadres to make every effort to win them over as temporary allies. As we observed in the Houjiao Village struggle, the party skillfully exploited gentry rivalries as a means of securing alliances with out-groups. The party never ceased to manipulate the gentry to gain power.

If gentry power had already splintered in the prewar period, it went through further fragmentation in wartime. Warfare, Japanese military threat, and security problems further weakened gentry positions in the villages and seriously undermined their authority. The party continued to exploit gentry division and doubled its efforts to draw sympathetic gentry into the revolutionary movement. With the powerful gentry having fled the war, the lesser gentry lacked the means or resources and were less disposed to challenge the Communist power. Moreover, the party offered them the necessary organizational and military skills to build up collective defense forces for protecting their families and communities. Some rural elites saw the Communist movement as an opportunity for political advancement and actively sought Communist accommodation. Others joined the revolutionary movement simply out of patriotism. Although class struggle still remained the predominant form of rural power politics, Communist United Front tactics and policy changes, from radical land redistribution to moderate reforms such as rent reduction, debt rationalization, and graded taxation, helped win over the rural upper classes. Gentry cooperation, whether voluntary or coerced, was crucial to the smooth implementation of Communist social programs.

It is true that peasants were not motivated to join the revolution by a reorganization of national politics or lofty ideological ideals, as Skocpol and others have observed, and that rural cultivators were invariably motivated by immediate, concrete interests, such as easy access to land, low taxes, and light labor conscription.[5] But peasants' immediate, concrete interests vary with time and place. It remains debatable whether peasant-based revolution is ecologically determined or not. But if Communist revolutionaries were mobilizing the peasantry by addressing the cultivators' immediate needs, then the type of ecological environment, the form of socioeconomic grievances, the particular needs of the peasantry in a specific locality and time would ultimately define not only the mode of rural mobilization but the tactics with which the Communists prosecuted the revolution.

In this study, we do find peasants' immediate, concrete interests to be localistic and region-specific. Objective material conditions and local politics invariably dictated the form of mobilization strategy to be adopted. In the Rivereast, for instance, the basic peasant concerns were war-induced anarchy and a lack of security. Consequently, the Communists focused their energy mainly on mobilizing the masses in collective defense. In the Huaibei lakeside areas where class tension was high, Communist programs concentrated on addressing the questions of concealed lakeside landholding and the registration of these properties for tax purposes. The Communists also attacked such collective issues as water conservancy, land reclamation, and increasing agricultural productivity. In the predominantly smallholder Taihang area, Communist redistributive programs were not very successful because of the low tenancy rate and peculiar land tenure arrangements in the area. Communist mobilization excelled in areas such as agricultural production and economic recovery.

There is no doubt that rural poverty and war-induced subsistence crises were significant factors in rural revolutionary mobilization. One must admit that the political anarchy of wartime and man-made flooding devastated the rural economy and caused a great deal of misery in the countryside. Political disintegration also gave rise to rural social tensions that frequently energized peasants into rebellious actions. In the past, peasants had reacted indignantly to material deprivation and at times rose up in large-scale rebellions to alleviate their suffering. But relative deprivation alone is not sufficient to generate large-scale, organized peasant revolution. The peasant-based revolution in China, although undertaken with active peasant support, was by no means generated by the peasant masses. There was little peasant revolutionary impulse unless provoked. Admittedly, there was revolutionary potential in the peasantry, but potential only. The Chinese revolution must be perceived as a movement deliberately and systematically fomented, organized, and built by the Chinese Communist Party. It was the outcome of purposive actions taken by the party and the party, in fact, stage-managed the revolution. External elite intervention was therefore a significant factor in the Chinese revolution.

Unlike their Russian and French counterparts, Chinese peasants did not possess the kind of institutional arrangements, such as the French *terroir* or the Russian *obshchina*, that could be used as units of solidarity for collective class action. In Chinese villages, cross-class social units such as corporate lineages, sectarian groups, community self-defense organizations, tax-based neighborhoods, and territorial groupings were pervasive. These units bonded landlords and peasants vertically in a clientelist relationship. In these types of collective communal institutions, gentry power was always predominant. Peasant class action was viable only after rural elite power had collapsed.

Social revolutionary situations and peasant autonomy usually emerged with the creation of a secure territorial base and the establishment of a legitimate Communist power. Peasant class actions succeeded only with the full backing of Communist authorities and military power. The Chinese Communists did use solid communal institutions such as villages, sectarian groups, and neighborhood pacts in the revolution. But these community units were used mainly as instruments for the seizure of state power, seldom for collective class action. The mass organizations the Chinese peasants employed as collective units for class action had to be purposively created by the party.

Without deliberate Communist arousal and mobilization, peasant moral outrage alone could not produce a large-scale, organized social revolution in this region. Peasant violence and militant impulse could flare up, and at times attained explosive proportions. But such violent behavior was spontaneous, sporadic, and subsided after the immediate objectives were achieved. Rebellions were frequently suppressed by superior government forces. Others failed as a result of internal strife and lack of organizational cohesion. It is true that individual peasants did take action to fight for a subsistence livelihood, and peasants do have a sense of social and economic justice. But rural elites have traditionally exerted nonreciprocal claims on peasant production, and peasants usually accepted that. It is hard for us to perceive peasants as moral communitarians, capable of taking collective action to fight for a moral standard without outside assistance. It is difficult to envision North China peasants forming a separate collectivist peasant community, sharing and fighting for a set of moral norms. Our vision of Chinese peasants is essentially one of masses of highly differentiated rural cultivators working for very diverse interests. Peasants often belonged to communal institutions that included and were invariably dominated by rural elites.

In antistate political actions, it was usually the lesser gentry who organized and directed the peasants. Unlike that in southern China, the tenancy rate in northern China was relatively low. The majority of the collective violence in this region was directed against the state or undisciplined troops misusing their military power. Most of the violence in the region came in the form of antitax movements, rather than rent resistance movements. As members of the corporate neighborhood or village unit liable for tax payment, rural elites and peasants had a common economic interest. Antitax movements were invariably multiclass actions, usually mounted under the leadership of local elites. Elite leadership was indispensable in antistate and antimilitary collective actions. Even in Eyuwan, where one finds a relatively high tenancy rate, class actions, as we have seen, assumed the form of poor lineages pitted against rich lineages, not poor peasants as a class fighting rich peasants and landlords.

Moreover, village communities were traditionally governed by a "norm of obligatory collective action."[6] In times of natural disasters, bandit attacks, and military abuse of power, all agrarian classes, rich and poor, were obligated to act collectively to defend their communities. Peasant cooperation with rural elites in such collective endeavors frequently gave rise to rather congenial class relations. These collective actions served to defuse some peasant economic grievances and mitigate violent class action toward the upper classes. Effective class action, as mentioned before, was only feasible when gentry power was sufficiently eroded, and when this action was fomented, organized, and prosecuted by party authorities in a secure environment.

Peasant involvement in the revolution should not be interpreted as a simple formula of exchange of material benefits for peasant political support. All peasants make rational economic decisions and strive for private and family welfare. The Communists were well aware of that. Party directives repeatedly stressed that addressing peasant material interests was the sole means of sustaining peasant involvement in the revolutionary movement. If they failed to address the concrete economic interests of the peasantry, the party argued, rural movements would ultimately flounder. Even though the Communists made every effort to motivate the peasantry with concrete material benefits, again and again we see examples of peasant timidity, passivity, and indifference to Communist economic appeals. In the case of the Taihang region, peasant indifference stemmed from the fact that the redistributive programs benefited merely a minor segment of the peasant population. At other times, factors such as political uncertainty, inadequate planning, kinship and community obligations, and the disruptive effects of reform programs prohibited peasants from participating.

Aside from making use of elite contacts and military defectors to jump-start and revitalize the movement, the Chinese Communists mobilized all kinds of peasants in the revolution: the propertyless, the land-short, tenant families, freeholding middle peasants, and sometimes rich peasants. In the 1920s, the party used all types of peasant followers under the sectarian chieftains to build up its fighting force. In the 1930s and 1940s, Communist revolutionaries were as successful in mobilizing the land-hungry peasants in Eyuwan as they were the freeholding middle peasants in the Taihang. Even though the party's policies repeatedly emphasized the significance of the middle peasantry as its main target of appeal, it continuously fought for the propertyless and, at the same time, made compromises with the rich peasants. It seems that only when Communist power was extremely weak (as in the guerrilla war period, when the movement was almost crushed by the GMD) did the party make more use of the poorer segment (the déclassé and social bandits) of the peasant population.

From time to time, out of a sense of justice and as a means of rapid power building, the party utilized radical programs to energize the masses by capitalizing on the socioeconomic grievances of the underprivileged. Redistributive economic programs such as "eat-ins," grain seizures, fines on the rich, and land redistribution could provoke poor peasants into swift action. At such times, party policies focused primarily on individual and class benefits. Party programs aimed at satisfying the peasants' private interests (*ziji de liyi*), such as access to land and seizure of landlords' food stocks and money. They allowed the party to swiftly amass the necessary resources for the revolution. They also enabled the Communists to sustain mass involvement with little cost and organization. Such radical programs, however, were disruptive and class-divisive.

However, a successful revolution entails not only class-based appeals and economic redistribution but also revolutionary reconstruction and economic production. As the revolution deepened, the party had to rebuild society and integrate communities. It had to address not only class interests but collective communal interests (*gongtong yaoqiu*), or as the Communists put it, "the common demands of the majority of the masses."[7] At that stage, the party had to appeal to not only the poor segment of the peasant population but also the freeholding middle peasants, the rich peasants, and the "progressive" landed elites. The party had to make skillful use of the dual tactic of struggle and compromise, particularly in the period of reconciliation during the Second United Front.

In order to reintegrate the countryside and reconstruct the economy, the Communists had to mobilize all segments of rural communities to engage in agricultural production work. In the promotion of such communal projects as land reclamation, water conservancy, and spring planting, the party found it increasingly crucial to stress communitarian bonds and inter-village cohesion instead of the disruptive and divisive issues in rural society. They turned also to nationalism, security benefits, and collective benefits as appeals to the people. Nevertheless, during the reconstruction period, the Communists never ceased fighting for class benefits. Social leveling, however, took on the more moderate and less disruptive form of progressive taxation and rent reduction. It was only when the party was militarily very strong and its bases well established that it reverted to the class-confrontational policy of land repartition.

It is interesting to note that the Communists were less successful in community-divisive programs and had better success in community-cohesive and production programs. The Eyuwan land reform had to be modified and the "rich peasant policy" was eventually abandoned so as to bring order back to the base area. In the civil war period, land reform was immediately called off when it produced disruptive effects in the area. Radical redistributive programs invariably alienated rural elites and turned them into formidable enemies of the party. Class struggle could bring instant political and economic benefits to the poor, but also societal disruption and damage to productive forces. Rural economic recovery could only be achieved with a certain degree of societal stability and voluntary cooperation from local elites.

That is why, even on the very eve of Communist liberation, party directives still warned cadres about revolutionary impetuosity (*jixingbing*). Deng Zihui, the army's propaganda head, told cadre mobilizers, "Today, the immediate needs of the broad masses in Henan are not land reform, nor even rent and interest reduction, but bandit suppression, equitable taxes, and a settling of accounts with the bullies."[8] The targets of class attack were accordingly restricted to a minority of outstandingly evil rural bosses and their agents. Class benefits were minimized to make way for security benefits and collective benefits.

The party did obtain some tactical advantages by operating in marginal geographical areas in the early stage of power contention. It did find the rural poor and social bandits in the mountain redoubts ready audiences for an appeal for social revolution. But the revolution was essentially made possible by the support of the peasantry in settled communities. It was in these settled peasant communities that the party secured control of a tax base, organized local people in community defense, and mobilized rural residents collectively in production. To locate the areas of intense Communist activity, I suggest we look into the "urban fringe" areas, defined not as suburban areas but as the immediate urban hinterland. It was in the countryside contiguous to urban centers, such as Hankou-Xinyang (the Eyuwan base), Xinyang (the Yunan base), and Kaifeng-Shanqiu-Xuzhou (the Sui-Qi-Tai, and later, its extension into the Yuwansu base) that we find the centers of revolutionary activity.[9] Typically, each Communist base analyzed in this study was located not far from an urban center.

The urban fringe areas possessed a number of conditions conducive to the birth and development of revolutionary activities. Eric Wolf has stated that a revolution cannot evolve from a position of complete impotence.[10] Urban centers usually supplied the movement with the initial revolutionary forces: an ideology, student leadership, and Communist organizations. As we have seen, the birth of a Communist movement in a certain locality depended on infiltration of the area by urban-educated indigenous leaders. Student intellectuals were the indispensable "seeders" of a revolution. Since urban Communist leaders were drawn mostly from the adjacent countryside, the "urban fringe" areas thus became the fertile ground for Communist penetration. The proliferation of indigenous leaders in the urban fringe also allowed the party the flexibility of shifting its headquarters in accordance with the political atmosphere. Party branches located in the fringe areas possessed the advantage of maintaining constant contact with party headquarters in the cities, and the Communists could easily send student leaders down to revitalize the movement.

Moreover, urban fringes were normally areas of sharper social tension and class contradiction. The relatively more commercialized section located right next to the core of an urban center contrasts sharply with the less developed peripheral hinterland. In China, both society and the economy in the commercialized section were undergoing a major transformation. The social friction between commercial-reformist elites in the modernized section and traditional landed elites and rural bosses in the hinterland was intense. As the economic gaps between the peasants in the relatively underdeveloped section and the commercialized section widened, social tension intensified. As indicated in the analysis of the Eyuwan base area, the Communist Party was able to appeal to both the progressive elite in the commercialized fringe as well as impoverished peasants in the less commercialized hinterland.

According to Mao Zedong, the final stage of revolution involves an "encirclement of the cities from the countryside"; urban fringe areas are the ideal locations for such tactical military maneuvers. Urban centers are invariably transport nodes, loci of troop concentration and military maneuvers, strategically significant in a revolutionary war. Urban fringe areas are ideal springboards for the capture of these strategic centers. Thus, in studying peasant-based revolutions, one should refrain from focusing simply on the countryside. Peasant-based revolution moves back and forth between cities and countryside. The revolution is normally directed from the cities; urban centers provide ideology, leadership, and organization. The countryside provides human and economic resources. The hinterland is where rebels usually seek refuge in times of adversity. Revolutionary movement is always in a state of flux, moving toward the cities in times of strength and outward to the periphery in times of weakness. The cities and the countryside complement each other, and urban fringe areas form the ideal urban-rural link.

Did capitalist imperialism cause peasant-based revolution in China? There is no doubt that the Communists' ability to seize power in China was directly related to Japanese imperialism and the changing international situation. But capitalist imperialism had only a minor impact on the North China rural economy. There is no indication in Henan of any extensive commercialization setting in motion fundamental economic changes that disrupted the rural economy and dramatically increased the revolutionary potential of the peasantry. In the Hubei segment of the Eyuwan border base, where we do find a penetration of market forces and growing agrarian commercialization, peasants tended to be indifferent to Communist appeals to social revolution. Social ties between enterprising peasants and the merchant gentry were strengthened by their common economic interests. The economic interdependence of these two agrarian classes was strengthened with increasing commercialization. To our surprise, it was the reformist merchant gentry who were more disposed to the Communist revolution. However, capitalist imperialism did have another impact: imperialistic aggression wrecked the rural economy and caused untold economic hardship in the countryside. This disruption gave the Communists an opportunity to draw the peasants into defense alliances. In addition, chronic fighting dislocated rural cultivators, and many displaced peasants eventually ended up in the revolutionary camp.

In the course of the revolution, the Communists relentlessly educated the peasants in an attempt to heighten their class consciousness. Were the peasants able to arrive at a state of class consciousness? Class consciousness is not simply an expression of social tension. Some disaffected peasants might have perceived a clash of interests between themselves and the landlords. But others were tightly linked to the landed elites by common interests. Material welfare of villages often cut across class lines. Peasant political aims are vague, diverse, and localistic. Many peasant political actions were nothing but short outbursts. Class issues have to be inculcated in the peasantry by outside elites, such as the Communist revolutionaries.

Throughout the revolution, Communist cadres used organizational devices, political/economic programs, and propaganda to bring the peasantry to an awareness of their common interests. In the process, the party never ceased to assemble cultivators in mass organizations and mobilize them in political and economic programs. When rural elite power had been weakened and peasants found themselves facing a crisis, peasant consciousness began to rise. Protected by the Communist authorities, peasants gained independence from the landed elites. They also began to act as a class. The Communists always provided leadership and guidance to bring peasants to cooperative actions. In class struggle sessions and in land redistribution meetings, the Communists never failed to identify for the peasantry a community of material interests which, they insisted, differed from those of the landed elite. The cadres supported the peasants in their confrontation with landlords. In this way, peasants were able to face their class enemies as a solid collective unit. Through continuous politicization and collective participation, peasants became more "outward oriented."[11] The Communists' repeated articulation of their goals, party guidance, and peasant collective action finally enabled the timid, passive, and localistic peasants to move out of their traditional mode of thinking, overcome their limitations, and arrive at a state of class consciousness. In the course of the struggle, the peasantry was gradually transformed into a dynamic revolutionary force.

REFERENCE MATTER

Notes

Introduction

1. Skocpol 1979; Wolf 1966; Walton 1984.
2. George Pettee uses the term "great revolution" to describe the French and Russian revolutions. See Pettee 1974; Stone 1974.
3. For instance, the studies of the Vietnamese revolution by James Scott and Samuel Popkin. Scott 1976; Popkin 1979. Also see Wolf 1969; Paige 1975.
4. For the aggregate-psychological approach, see Joseph Zygmunt in Denisoff 1974; Gurr 1972; Davies 1972; Gurney and Tierney 1982; McAdam 1982. For the resource mobilization perspective, see Tilly 1978; McCarthy and Zald 1977; Ferree and Miller 1985; McAdam 1982. For moral economy, see Scott 1976; Little 1989. For social exchange theory, see Popkin 1979; Migdal 1974; Little 1989. For the social structural perspective, see Skocpol 1979; Paige 1975.
5. Tilly 1978.
6. McCarthy and Zald 1977: 1212–41.
7. The concept of "guided political action" comes from Teodor Shanin. According to him, there are three types of peasant political action: autonomous class action, guided political action, and amorphous political action. Shanin 1987: 359–61.
8. Yung-fa Chen 1986; Levine 1987; Hartford and Goldstein 1989. The term "countervailing factors" comes from Hartford and Goldstein 1989: 24.
9. Steven Levine concludes in his work on the Communist revolution in Manchuria by saying, "Organization as the key to victory emerges as a central conclusion of this study when one reflects upon the way in which the CCP attacked and overcame the initial superiority of locally entrenched rural elites in the Northeast. Levine 1987: 244. Yung-fa Chen also says, "I show the difficulties of isolating peasant motivation from the problem of organization. Moreover, organizational weapons did more than just 'structuring mass mobilization' as Johnson claims. The growing organization facilitated mass mobilization, giving peasants more reason to join the ranks of rebels, but also spearheaded the Party's penetration into rural societies." Yung-fa Chen 1986: 14.
10. C. Johnson 1962; Kataoka 1974.
11. C. Johnson 1962: vii.

12. For instance, in his work on the Communist revolution in eastern and central China, Yung-fa Chen undervalues socioeconomic forces. He concludes his work by saying, "I am unable to offer much on the issue of peasant support in terms of socioeconomic environment. . . . The materials merely require us to view tenancy as an important, but minor, problem in CCP-occupied central and eastern China. A revolution built solely on it would never take off." Yung-fa Chen 1986: 516.

13. See Doug McAdam's critique of the resource mobilization approach in McAdam 1982: 25–32. Also see McCarthy and Zald 1977; Ferree and Miller 1985.

14. Skocpol 1982: 157–58.

15. Wilson 1973; Wilkinson 1971; Lofland 1985.

16. Gurr 1972.

17. Davies 1972. For the relative deprivation theory, see also Gurney and Tierney 1982; McAdam 1982.

18. Marks 1984.

19. C. Johnson 1962: 14–19.

20. Kataoka 1974: 308–11.

21. Selden 1971: 35.

22. Scott 1976.

23. Popkin 1979.

24. Migdal 1974.

25. Thaxton 1981, 1982, 1983: 227.

26. Levine 1987: 9.

27. Thaxton 1983: 228.

28. Levine 1987: 229–35, 242–48.

29. Levine acknowledges, "The CCP came to the Northeast as an existing organization with a large number of trained cadres, a well articulated program of social change, and extensive experience in rural organizing. The problems it faced differed substantially from those of a fledgling revolutionary organization attempting to start up operations for the first time." Ibid., 232.

30. Skocpol 1979: 115.

31. Skocpol 1979; Wolf 1969; Skocpol 1982.

32. Stinchcombe 1961; Zagoria 1974.

33. Paige 1975.

34. Wolf 1969.

35. Hofheinz 1969: 59.

36. John Lewis and Robert McColl emphasize geographical continuity, while Mark Selden argues that there was a shift of revolutionary location from advanced to remote areas. See Lewis 1966; McColl 1967a; Selden 1971: 36–37.

37. Little 1989: 25–26.

38. Yung-fa Chen 1986: 18.

39. Schram 1963: 288.

40. McColl 1967a, 1967b. See Selden 1971: 36–37, n. 26, for the discussion of geographical continuity of peasant revolution.

41. Wolf 1969. For a discussion of overemphasis of the revolutionary potential of peasantry, see Walton 1984: 14–22.

42. For example, by Mark Selden and Ralph Thaxton. Yung-fa Chen is an exception.

43. Polachek 1983.

44. Wou 1984.

45. Thus, the Chinese Communists have not strictly followed the standard Marxist interpretation which identifies the masses as "those people in the

society who comprise the working classes—the factory proletariat and the peasantry—as well as marginal intellectuals, who perceive their purpose not primarily as the achievement of their particular class needs but as the elevation of an entire mass of 'oppressed' persons." This is similar to Mao's definition of the "basic masses." Horowitz 1970: 7.

46. Deng Zihui, "Lun qunzhong yundong" (On mass movement), Nov. 1, 1948. In *P:jiefangqu*: 229.

47. See Yung-fa Chen 1986.

48. For information on party archival materials and Henan local history materials, see Wou 1987.

Chapter 1

1. Meisner 1967: 253–54; Alavi 1987: 190–91.

2. Shorter and Tilly 1974; Edwards 1981; Tilly 1978; Welch 1972; Tilly et al. 1975.

3. *P:dashiji*: 4–9; Wou 1978: chap. 8.

4. At the end of 1921, foremen on the Longhai line declared a strike when they came into conflict with the Franco-Belgian owners. In August 1922, a strike broke out on the southern section of the Beijing-Hankou line over the question of the reinstallment of three foremen dismissed by the Belgian railway officers. Chesneaux 1986: 484.

5. The dollars (C$) given in this book are silver dollars (*yuan*). The exchange rate varied from period to period, averaging roughly 300 copper cash to one silver dollar. *P:5/30*: 188.

6. *LH:5/30*: 266–67.

7. Lin Delong 1980.

8. *Zhongguo qingnian* no. 101 (Nov. 7, 1925): 16–18; *LH:5/30*: 266–68; Xue Yi 1982: 43–47, 68.

9. Liu Yingxian 1983: 131–32; *LH:5/30*: 271; *P:5/30*: 184–85.

10. *LH:5/30*: 209.

11. We have no actual figure for the number of miners in the Zhongyuan mines in the 1920s. According to Chesneaux, the estimate was 11,200. By 1929, the figure had dropped to 2,000. Chesneaux 1968: 38; *LH:Jiaozuo*: 108.

12. In 1931, a survey of the standard of living of hired laborers was conducted by Xu Jingshan and Pan Jingwu. They surveyed 1,109 laborers (only 1 female). According to their findings, 128 were living at subsistence level. The survey was published in *Henan Zhongyuan meikuang gongsi huikan* (Journal of Henan Zhongyuan Mining Company) no. 2 (Apr. 1931). *LH:Jiaozuo*: 93–95.

13. *LH:Jiaozuo*: 9.

14. See Shan Gen, "Xiuwu meikuang zi gongtou zhi" (The contract labor system in the collieries in Xiuwu county). *Meizhou pinglun* (Weekly critique) no. 4 (Jan. 20, 1919). In *LH:Jiaozuo*: 69–70.

15. *LH:Jiaozuo*: 97.

16. *Henan Zhongyuan meikuang gongsi huikan* no. 2. In *LH:Jiaozuo*: 9, 80–88.

17. For example, in the contract mining system of the Zhongyuan Company,

six workers contracted with six mines in the first district and another thirteen miners contracted with ten mines in the second district.

18. See the report by the Henan Labor Committee of the Chinese Youth League on workers in the western mines of the Fuzhong Mining Company in *LH:Jiaozuo*: 157–64.

19. Wou 1978: chap. 8; Yang Peng 1989; Xia Zilun 1989; Pang Shouxin 1989; "Henan difang dangshi ruo gan wenti yanjiu zongshu" 1989.

20. The theory of the opportunity to act together comes from Charles Tilly. See Tilly 1978: chap. 4.

21. Mackeras 1982: 296.

22. How 1985–86; Guo and Chen 1987: 92–94.

23. Zhang Jiang 1982: 57.

24. Nie and Shi 1984: 15.

25. Qu Wu was a Peking University student and the son-in-law of Yu Youren, a Guomindang veteran. Qu was assigned by Li Dazhao to work with Hu Jingyi in Kaifeng. *P:dashiji*: 10–11.

26. According to Qu Wu, he met Li Dazhao on December 20, 1925. At that time, Li was not sure if he could make the trip to Kaifeng. Qu then went with his father-in-law, Yu Youren, to see Sun Yatsen in Tianjin. At the end of December, Li Dazhao left for Kaifeng in the company of Qu Wu. See Zhang Jiang 1982.

27. At first, the negotiations with Hu Jingyi were conducted by Li Dazhao and Qu Wu. Qu Wu later left for Shaanxi, and the talks were concluded by Liu Yunchen, Hu's staff officer, and Hu Jingquan, Hu Jingyi's brother and a Guominjun brigade commander. Zhang Jiang 1982: 16; He Yang 1982: 20; *P:dashiji*: 10–11; Han and Yao 1987: 169.

28. Hu's delegates were a General Liu (probably Liu Tianzhuang, a Communist), Yu Youren, and Li Dazhao. See How 1985–86: 12; Han and Yao 1987: 178.

29. How 1985–86: 12.

30. In January 1925, a resolution on party organization was passed in the Fourth Party Congress which directed members to set up party branches in urban and industrial centers in Manchuria, Henan, Sichuan (Chongqing), Jiangxi (Jiujiang), Anhui (Wuhu), and Fujian (Fuzhou). Zhang Jiang 1982: 57.

31. Zhang Jiang 1982: 57; He Yang 1982: 20.

32. How 1985–86: 12, 14.

33. Yue Weijun was appointed Henan governor on April 14, 1925.

34. He Yang 1982: 20.

35. *P:dashiji*: 12; He Yang 1982: 20.

36. For complexity within the Guominjun, see Wen Gongzhi 1962, 2: 175–89, and Liu and Wang 1983, 4: 23–45. For the role of the Guomindang in the Second Guominjun, see Yu Shude's report to the Second Congress of the Guomindang in January 1926. Yu Shude 1981: 407–15.

37. *Jing bao*, June 12, 1925; *Minguo ribao* (Shanghai), June 9 and 22, 1925, July 2, 5, and 20, 1925, Aug. 1, 1925; *Shishi xinbao*, June 30, 1925: 2; *Xinwen bao*, July 5, 1925: 3; *Chen bao*, July 9, 1925. In *LH:5/30*: 279–83. Also see *P:5/30*: 49–50, 60, 70, 72, 81, 96, 101, 106, 108, 111, 116.

38. *Shishi xinbao*, June 15, 1925: 2, June 19, 1925: 2; *Jing bao*, July 5, 1925: 5; *Minguo ribao* (Shanghai), June 17, 1925, July 9 and 19, 1925, Aug. 11, 1925;

Chen bao, June 25, 1925: 3, July 17, 1925: 4; *Xin Zhongzhou bao*, Nov. 12, 1925: 2. In *LH:5/30*: 284–93.

39. *Minguo ribao*, July 9, 1925, in *LH:5/30*: 287–88. See also *Chen bao*, July 13, 1925, in *P:5/30*: 243.

40. Zheng Xiang, or Zeng Sicheng, was commander of the First Cavalry Brigade of the Second Guominjun. *Henan tongsu jiaoyu bao* (Henan public education newspaper), Oct. 5, 1925: 7. In *LH:5/30*: 247–48.

41. In Deng Baosan's division, Peng Zexiang, a student who had returned from the Soviet Union, served as interpreter for the Soviet adviser. See Luo Renyi's reminiscence, written in May 1959, of his activity in 1925 in the Anyang Communist Party. Originally published in *P:Anyang*: 1. See also *P:5/30*: 300–308.

42. Xu Xiangqian, a military instructor in the training regiment of Gong Fukui's army in Anyang, was from the Whampao Military Academy. According to Xu, he spent most of his time working for the movement, giving students in the Eleventh High School military training during their summer vacation and recruiting them for the academy. He even formed a student battalion in Anyang. See Xu Xiangqian 1984: 35–39; *P:5/30*: 310.

43. *LH:5/30*: 54–60.

44. See Zhao Zhongtao's letter to the manager of the British-American Tobacco Company in Hankou dated Aug. 17, 1925. *P:5/30*: 411. There is a discrepancy in the amount Zhao paid. One source gives C$2,000, but according to Zhao's own account, it was C$5,000. Cf. Liu Yingxian 1983: 131.

45. In Shangcheng, students confiscated cigarettes from retailers and fined them C$200. Retailers in Changgongguan paid a C$20 fine, and those in Liulin paid C$100. There were also seizures of BAT products in Anyang, Xinyang, Guangzhou, Zhengzhou, Yuncheng, and Shangguan. For confiscation and fines against the BAT between June and September 1925, see *P:5/30*: 410.

46. *Chen bao*, July 7, 1925: 6. In *LH:5/30*: 58.

47. *Shishi xinbao*, Dec. 2, 1925. In *P:5/30*: 213–14.

48. Chesneaux 1968: 177–210. For the February 7, 1923 Beijing-Hankou railway strike, see Lin Delong 1980; Deng Zhongxia 1949: 85–108.

49. On the Beijing-Hankou line, the Anyang union had 450 members (rehabilitated before Feb. 7, 1925); the Beijing-Hankou union, 1,200 members (rehabilitated Feb. 7, 1925); the Yancheng union, 338 members (rehabilitated Mar. 1925); the Zhumadian union, 420 members (rehabilitated Mar. 1925); the Xinyang union, 800 members (rehabilitation date unknown); the Yellow River union, 170 members (rehabilitated June 15, 1925). There are no data on membership in the Kaifeng, Luoyang, and Xuzhou unions on the Longhai line, which were all rehabilitated in the summer of 1925. On the Daoqing line, the general union had 1,000 members and was rehabilitated in May 1925. *LH:5/30*: 235–47.

50. According to a party source, all these affiliated unions were set up in a matter of twenty days. See Ma Wenyan, "Huiyi Henan zong gonghui de jianli" (A recollection of the establishment of the Henan General Union), n.d. In *P:5/30*: 152–53.

51. In the beginning, it was suggested that the headquarters of the All-China Labor Union should be located in Zhengzhou, the point of interchange between the Beijing-Hankou and the Longhai. Finally Kaifeng, the political, economic, and cultural center of the province, was chosen. *P:5/30*: 153–56.

52. According to Zeng Guangxing, the Henan-Shaanxi Regional Committee was created in mid- or late October 1925 (after the Second Enlarged Plenum of the Fourth Party Congress, held in October 1925), not June 1925, a month after party leader Wang Ruofei came to the province. See Zeng Guangxing 1984: 109–10.

53. The provincial origins of the Henan leadership was as follows: Wang Hebo, head of the All-China Union, was from Fujian; Li Zhenying, secretary of the Beijing-Hankou General Union, Tianjin; Ma Wenyuan, secretary of both the CYL (Kaifeng) and the provincial labor union, Shaanxi; Zhang Kundi, leader of the provincial labor union, Hunan; and Liu Wensong, executive committee member of the Beijing-Hankou union, Hubei.

54. Huang Pingwan, secretary of the Zhengzhou party, Tang Shaoyu, secretary of the Kaifeng party and of the Zhengzhou Guomindang, and Li Lisan, leader of the Beijing-Hankou railroad, held membership in both the CCP and the GMD.

55. Li Zhenying, for instance, was an organizer of the Tianjin student association and an active participant in the May Fourth Movement. Man Qian, Sun Yousan, and Xiao Shen, "Li Zhenying." In Zhonggong Henan shengwei dangshi gongzuo weiyuanhui et al., 5: 179–211.

56. Li Wensong was vice president of the All-China Railwaymen's General Union in May 1922. Zhang Kundi was an inspector on the Beijing-Hankou line in 1922. See Chesneaux 1968: 259 and Lin Delong 1980: 44.

57. See Zhonggong dangshi renwu yanjiu hui 1983, 12: 39–64.

58. Yang Jieren had to report to Li Zhenying, the head of the Beijing-Hankou General Union stationed at Changxindian, who in turn reported to Li Dazhao.

59. *P:5/30*: 302.

60. The school network included the Eleventh High School and the Sanyu Girls' High School in Anyang. See Luo Renyi, "Huiyi yijiu erwu nian dang zai Anyang de geming douzheng" (A recollection of the party's revolutionary struggle in Anyang in 1925), May 1959, "Wusa yundong zai Anyang Sanyu nu zhong" (The May 30th Movement in Sanyu Girls' High in Anyang), n.d. In *P:5/30*: 300–308, 311–14.

61. *P:5/30*: 302.

62. See Luo Renyi's recollection of Communist activities in Anyang in 1925 in *P:5/30*: 300–304.

63. See the account by Geng Yuru, Zhan Zhongheng, and Li Zunyao of the 1925 Huaxin textile factory strike in Weihui in *P:5/30*: 328–30.

64. The provincial origins of the Jiaozuo Communist leadership were Liu Changyin, party secretary, from Hunan; Gong Yiqing, head of propaganda, Anhui or Sichuan; Wang Zeming, a later party secretary, Hubei or Hunan; Luo Siwei, also a later party secretary, Hubei; Zhu Jintang, party committee member, Hunan; Yang Tianran, CYL secretary, Hebei; and She Liya, head of the Daqing union, Yunnan. The provincial origins of Mr. He, who was in charge of propaganda, and He Zhizheng, technical secretary, are unknown. *P:5/30*: 153; *LH:Jiaozuo*: 304, 351.

65. The heads of the student union were Wu Huizhi (Sichuan), Qin Menghu (Jiaozuo), and Wu Guangrong (Hankou). At the lowest level, Jiang Tian (CCP member working on the Daoqing line), Li Mingqiu, (a miner later recruited into the Jiaozuo Society for the Support of the Shanghai Incident), Guan Yongfu

(educational director of the Jiaozuo miners' union), Cui Changyong (president of the Jiaozuo chefs' union), Liu Qinghai (CCP member and party liaison between Jiaozuo and Xiuwu), and He Daolin (in charge of miners' union pickets) were all natives of Henan. *LH:Jiaozuo*: 303–5; 350–52.

66. *LH:Jiaozuo*: 2.

67. See Lin Zhuangzhi's recollection in *LH:Jiaozuo*: 303.

68. See Zhang Fanglai's reminiscence on Jiaozuo underground activities in *LH:Jiaozuo*: 308.

69. See Mu Xiangshun's recollection in *LH:Jiaozuo*: 351.

70. See the recollections of Lin Zhuangzhi, Zhang Fanglai, and Mu Xiangshun in *LH:Jiaozuo*: 303, 308, 351, 409.

71. It was through Li Mingqui, a miner, that Luo Siwei got in touch with ten or so lower-level foremen. When Li's activity was discovered by the head foreman, he was fired. Luo, however, recruited him into the Society for the Support of the Shanghai Incident and charged him with the responsibility of giving out strike money to workers. Li was later sent by the party to Canton to study at the Whampao Military Academy. See Li's statement in *LH:Jiaozuo*: 371.

72. The chefs were reported to have donated C$100 to the strike fund, the largest amount collected among workers.

73. The three bankers who joined the party were Zhu Zhufeng, Lin Zhuangzhi, and Jiang Zuo. See Lin Zhuangzhi's recollection in *LH:Jiaozuo*: 303.

74. The leaders who came to Jiaozuo were Luo Zhanglong, Wang Zhongxiu, Zhang Yintao, and Ma Shangde (Yang Jingyu) of the CYL.

75. The First Congress of the CCP was held in Shanghai on July 23, 1921. See Zhang Fenglai's recollection on the underground struggle in Jiaozuo in *LH:Jiaozuo*: 309.

76. They were Luo Zhanglong, Zhang Yintao, Wang Zhongxiu, and Ma Shangde.

77. The miners' union had an elaborate structure. It had one chairperson, two deputies, one secretary, two persons in charge of communication, two propagandists, two treasurers, and four men responsible for organizing pickets. The chefs' union was relatively simple, consisting of one chairperson, four deputies, and one person in charge of pickets.

78. They were Wang Hebo (head of the All-China Railwaymen's General Labor Union), Li Zhenying (secretary of the Beijing-Hankou Railway General Union), Ma Wenyan (secretary of the Henan labor union), Yang Jieren (head of the Anyang party), and He Shuheng.

79. Some of the machines in the Peking Syndicate Collieries were dismantled by strikers and transferred to the Zhongyuan mines. See Wang Ziying's reminiscence in *P:5/30*: 292. (Original document in the provincial *Wenshi ziliao*.)

80. See Mu Xiangshun's "Kuangshan fengbao" (Storms in the mines) in *LH:Jiaozuo*: 356. According to Mu, the government had given C$23,000 to support the strike.

81. The first team, under Luo Siwei, was responsible for the area south of the Yellow River. Members went to Xiuwu, Zhengzhou, Luoyang, Xinyang, and Kaifeng. The money they raised was sent to Jiaozuo through the trade unions. The other team, led by Xu Siqian, covered the area north of the Yellow River, including major cities such as Anyang and Weihui.

82. Pickets were paid C$2 a day, and each received C$3 more from the provincial and county governments. See He Daolin's recollection in *LH:Jiaozuo*: 372–73.

83. *LH:Jiaozuo*: 302–41, 349–417; *P:5/30*: 232–93; *LH:5/30*: 171–204; *P:dashiji*: 14.

84. The activists included Luo Zhanglong, head of the Beijing-Hankou union; a Mr. Wu (Wu Huizhi?); a Mr. Qin; Jiang Tian, a Zhongyuan miner; Mr. Zhang, a Daoqing line worker; and Mr. Hu, a postman from the Peking Syndicate mines.

85. The original document, dated Aug. 16, 1925, is in the Henan Security Bureau. See *LH:5/30*: 197–201.

86. See Luo Renyi's recollection of CCP revolutionary activities in Anyang in 1925, written in May 1959 and first published in the *Anyang dangshi ziliao* (Anyang party history) no. 1. In *P:5/30*: 300–308.

87. See Wang Ziying's recollection written in September 1982 (original document in the *Wenshi ziliao* archives). See *P:5/30*: 293–94.

88. The two female workers were Li Shuixiang and Li Peizhi. The Beijing-Hankou workers were Han Yushan and Wang Changbao.

89. Wages for two-thirds of the workers were 20 cash a day for a twelve-hour workday. Management paid the new workers 30 cents a day.

90. Seventy-three foremen and mechanics received one month's paid vacation and a one-month bonus. Ex-provincial mechanics and foremen could receive travel expenses to return to their native provinces. For example, natives of Jiangsu were given C$30; the train ticket itself cost only C$20. These privileged workers were known as *da zhezi*, or "big accounts." See the autobiography of Chao Senxin, secretary of the Yufeng union, original document in the party history archives in Zhengzhou, part of it published in *P:5/30*: 225–26.

91. Li Dazhao, in the company of Yu Youren, came to Kaifeng to dissuade Yue Weijun from implementing his expansionist policy (see *P:dashiji*: 15). *Jing bao* (Aug. 14, 1925) reported that a Russian was directing the strike. Liu Yingxian identifies the Russian as Mikhail Borodin. Liu reports that Borodin even donated C$100 to the strike fund. See *LH:5/30*: 212–13 and Liu Yingxian 1983: 131–34.

92. The two who died in the incident were Han Yushan and Wang Changbao, the Beijing-Hankou workers sent to organize the Yufeng union. One account states that C$2,000 in union funds were lost.

93. A 40-cash increase for those earning 400 cash a day; 30 cash for 500; 20 for 600; and 10 for 700.

94. *Minguo ribao* (Shanghai), Sept. 6, 1925. In *LH:5/30*: 270.

95. Wang Liuxian et al. 1985, 1: 61–74.

96. These included the Youth Cooperative, Youth Textile Factory, Girls' School Auxiliary Association, Youth Publication, Youth Sericulture Association, Volunteer Corp, and Insect Extermination Squad.

97. "Xihua xian mofan cun nongmin relie hua Hu" (Active support for the Shanghai incident by the peasants in the model village in Xihua county). *Shishi xinbao*, June 16, 1925. In *P:5/30*: 384–86.

98. "Xihua ge jie dui Hu an zhi biaoshi" (The attitude of civic organizations in Xihua county toward the Shanghai Incident). Originally entitled "Kaifeng ge jie gonggei zhanfei shi wan yuan" (A sum of C$100,000 "war fund" provided by various civic organizations in Kaifeng). *Chen bao*, June 14, 1925. In *P:5/30*: 384.

99. "Xihua xian qingnian gongxue zhi qingnian xuesheng jun zuzhi dagang" (Organizational outline of the Young Student Army of the Youth Public School in Xihua county). *Chen bao*, July 25, 1925. In *LH:5/30*: 145–46.

100. I would like to thank Joseph Esherick for calling my attention to the significance of the CCP's concentration on skilled workers in its proletarian movement.

Chapter 2

1. Lo Baoxuan 1982; Li Guoqiang 1984, 1986; Pang Shouxin 1984; Wang Quanying 1983.

2. In Buddhist thought, a kalpa is an era lasting hundreds of thousands of years. The end of the kalpa is usually accompanied by a cosmic holocaust and the arrival of Buddha as a savior. Naquin 1976: 11–12.

3. Esherick 1987; Perry 1980; Naquin 1976; Heu-Tam Ho Tai 1983.

4. Baba Takeshi 1974, 1976; Dai Xuanzhi 1973; Perry 1980.

5. Han Sheng 1928; Liu and Wang 1983.

6. These troops comprised the Second and Third National Army and the Jianguo Yu jun (Nation-Building Henan Army).

7. These were officers from the Second and Third Guominjun who were former Wu subordinates.

8. *Chen bao*, Mar. 16, 1927. In Liu and Wang 1983.

9. They controlled the public fund bureau (gongkuan ju) and the military provisions bureau (zhiying ju) in the county. These were the bureaus that yielded most of the funds for sustaining the war.

10. *Minguo ribao* (Hankou), June 23, 1927. In Liu and Wang 1983: 46.

11. Zhu Xinfan, "Zhongguo nongcun jingji guanxi ji qi tese" (Economic relations and their characteristics in Chinese villages). In Liu and Wang 1983: 44.

12. Wang Shijun 1982: 154–65; *Chongxiu Xinyang xianzhi* 1934.

13. *Chongxiu Xinyang xianshi* 1934. See the *dashiji* (major historical events) and *bingzhi* (military affairs) sections.

14. *Minguo ribao* (Hankou), Feb. 17, 1927. In Liu and Wang 1983: 31.

15. For instance, rural elites had constructed the Yigeng and Guan stockades in Xiping county.

16. The county police force was known by various names, such as the household clearance bureau (*qingxiang ju*) in 1914, guard squads (*jingbei dui*) in 1915, patrol regiment (*xunji ying*) in 1918, and armed police (*quzhuang jingcha*) or peace-keeping squads (*bao'an dui*) in 1932. See *Chongxiu Xinyang xianzhi* 1934, *bingzhi* (military affairs) section.

17. *Chongxiu Xinyang xianzhi* 1934.

18. *Chongxiu Runan xianzhi* 1938, 15: 805. See the *bingbei* (military preparation) section.

19. *Zhengyang xianzhi* 1936. See May 1923 in the *dashiji* (major historical events) section.

20. *Zhengyang xianzhi* 1936; *Chongxiu Runan xianzhi* 1938, 15: 805; *Guangshan xianzhi yuegao* 1936 (see *bingzhi* [military affairs] section, 3a).

21. For the Eight Trigrams uprising, see Naquin 1976.

22. In another (unpublished) study, I have traced the influence of the Elder Brother Society on these sectarian groups in the greater Kaifeng area. The 1911 revolutionaries had transformed and integrated these sectarians into a secret society known as Ren-yi hui, the Benevolent and Righteous Society. The society was in fact composed of a great variety of religious groups, for instance the Eternal Mother or the Yellow Way, the Boxers in the Zhoujia kou area, and the Red Spears pervasive east of Kaifeng. More research needs to be done to find out what impact the Taiping and the Heaven and Earth Society had on sectarians in this area.

23. *Chen bao*, Oct. 8, 1925. In *LH:RS*: 26.

24. The sacrificial attendants of the sectarians were Wan Yunlong, Hu Deqi, Han Liner, Liu Futong, Xu Shouhui, Zhang Tingbi, Zhou Yuji, Huang Santai, Yang Xiangwu, and Zhang Wenxiang. Those of the Heaven and Earth Society and the Red Spears were Wang Zhong, Kong Wanxiu, and Sheng Wen.

25. Zhen Zhen, "Henan de Hongqiang hui" (Red Spears in Henan). Originally in *Juewu* (Awareness), a supplement to *Minguo ribao* (Shanghai), Dec. 8, 9, 10, and 14, 1928. In *LH:RS*: 61–65.

26. For the Boxers, see Esherick 1987 and Purcell 1963.

27. According to Joseph Esherick, if the teachers of the Red Spears sectarians came mostly from Caozhou prefecture in Shandong, it is very likely that they were linked to the Big Swords. But it seems that like the Boxers, they had multiple origins. See Esherick 1987.

28. For information on the Armor of the Golden Bell or the Iron Shirts, see Naquin 1976: 30–31; Esherick 1987: 96–123.

29. *Chen bao*, Sept. 22, 1925, Aug. 24, 1926; *Xin Zhongzhou bao*, Jan. 17, 1926; *Yi Jing* 25 (Mar. 1937): 77; *Minguo ribao* (Shanghai), Jan. 11, 1926. In *LH:RS*: 25, 27, 36, 65, 72.

30. *Chen bao*, Sept. 22, 1925; *Xin Zhongzhou bao*, Jan. 17, 1926. Ji Fan (Zhang Jifan, member of the Henan-Shaanxi committee in 1926), "Jieshao Henan Hongqiang hui" (Introducing the Red Spears in Henan). *Zhongguo qingnian* 6, no. 1 (June 10, 1926): 9–17. Wen Huiji, "Hongqiang hui" (Red Spears). *Yi Jing* 25 (Mar. 1937): 77. In *LH:RS* 25, 27–30, 65.

31. Xiang Yunlong 1927; *LH:RS*: 51.

32. See Chai Huazhou 1984.

33. *LH:RS*: 63–64. The terms first teaching-brother (*da shixiong*), second teaching-brother (*er shixiong*), etc., used in martial arts organizations, are very different from the leadership terms first brother (*da ge*), second brother (*er ge*), etc., used in secret societies. This may be an indication that the Red Spears were indeed martial arts organizations.

34. Dai Xuanzhi 1973: 104–5.

35. *Xin Zhongzhou bao*, Jan. 17, 1926; *Chen bao*, Sept. 22, 1925. In *LH:RS*: 25–27. Nine Dragon Mountain was reportedly in Guangdong. See Zhongguo diyi lishi dangan guan 1985: 191; Wei Jianyou 1985: 456.

36. *LH:RS*: 27.

37. When Wu Peifu was ruling Henan, one of his subordinates, Zhang Zhigong, lured a Red Spears leader into a lumberyard and had him killed. In 1925, a Red Spears leader named Mr. Huang staged an uprising. At the end, Huang was killed and his adherents scattered over the countryside in the Luoyang area.

38. Wen Gongzhi 1962, 2: 180–99; Chai Huazhou 1984: 70.
39. Wen Gongzhi 1962, 1: 175–89.
40. *Chen bao*, Sept. 22, 1925. In *LH:RS*: 25–26.
41. Chai Huazhou 1984: 72; Li Mingxi 1983: 66.
42. After that, Red Spears in this area numbered their militia on their red flags. Many joined Yue Weijun's bandit suppression campaign. The Haizu zhen militia, one of the Red Spears chapters, defeated three bands of brigands and was awarded C$1,000 and a couple of pigs by Governor Yue. These Red Spears were organized by district (*qu*). The chapters were becoming more visible and powerful. When three Red Spears were killed in a battle at Li Family Tower, a well-publicized memorial service, attended by Red Spear leaders from all nine districts in Luoyang, was held at the Temple of the God of Wealth.
43. The Eighteenth Route Army was named after the army of eighteen feudal princes who launched a joint attack on Henan in the Zhou dynasty.
44. Wang Lingyun n.d.: 164–65.
45. *Dagong bao* (Changsha), Feb. 15, 1926. In *LH:RS*: 74.
46. *Dagong bao* (Tianjin), Jan. 17, 1927; a survey of the Red Spears in Henan by the Northern Expeditionary Army was published in *Minguo ribao* (Hankou), May 9 and 10, 1927. In *LH:RS*: 39, 45–47.
47. Local residents were paying advance taxes for 1932 in 1927.
48. Chai Huazhou 1984: 73–79; Li Mingxi 1983: 66.
49. *Xin Zhongzhou bao*, Mar. 9, 1927. In *LH:RS*: 86.
50. In Queshan county, the traditional household unit was a *pai* ("door plate") consisting of ten households. Depending on the size of the village, a *pai* could be between six and fifteen households. As village population increased, more and more household units had more than 15 households, the maximum according to the regulation. The extra households (*pai yu*) were then grouped together, waiting to be organized into a new *pai*. In the winter of 1922, Queshan county had 49,051 households grouped into 5,095 *pai*. See *Queshan xianzhi* 1928.
51. Queshan county had 41 *bao*.
52. *LH:Beifa*: 340. The commanding generals of Queshan county were eastern route: Ouyang Bingyan, western route: Liu Shiyan, southern route: Li Shuzeng, and northern route: Xu Yaocai.
53. *Chongxiu Shangcai xianzhi* 1944.
54. The gentry commanders in these regiments took on traditional military titles. Wu Tingbi, for example, was known as *zongdai* (commander general), while other stockade commanders assumed the title of *tongdai* (regiment commander). *Chongxiu Shangcai xianzhi* 1944.
55. A survey of village names in Tongxu county indicates that 30 villages in the 15 subdistricts (*xiang*) bore the surname Liu. Some were monoclan villages; others were dominated by a single lineage. *Tongxu xianzhi* 1934, 2: 48b–55a.
56. The clan history indicates that it had three presented scholars (*jinshi*), five licentiates, two prefects, two military officials, one judge, one assemblyman, one university and several high school and normal school graduates. Besides Liu Xing, the clan added another presented scholar to its list in both the Ming and Qing dynasties. Liu Jiping was an assemblyman in Tongxu county.
57. Liu Guilin, the garrison commander, donated part of his salary to build a school for minorities in Hubei. Local assemblyman Liu Jiping taught for five

years in a charity school and also set up a model school, the National Primary School, for the county. In 1929, eight members of the Liu clan, including Liu Yuanping, a Red Spear and Communist leader, raised money to set up the Number Five County Primary School. The school was built right outside the West Gate of Four Towers. See biography of Liu Jiping in *Tongxu xianzhi* 1934, 2:60b, 6:54b–55a. Clan members were also known for their knight-errant spirit (*xia yi*) and charitable deeds. See biography of Liu Mengcun, *Tongxu xianzhi* 1934, 6: 53.

58. Liu Zongan was appointed patrol commander (*qing zong*) for his achievement in the battle in eastern Turkistan. Liu Guilin, a presented scholar, served in the Tongzhi period as imperial bodyguard and later received an appointment as battalion commander in Hubei. Liu Heping was a major in the Republican army. See the biography of Liu Guilin in *Tongxu xianzhi* 1934, 6: 43b–44b.

59. The *baowei tuan* (protective regiment) was a small contingent of 100 mounted and foot soldiers jointly supervised by ten regiment commanders and deputies from the five (central, north, south, east, west) districts. Their headquarters was located in the Temple of God of War (Guan di miao) inside the county seat. Funding for this militia came from a surchange paid by holders of fifteen *mu* or more of property. The command of both the central and eastern districts was held by the Lius, even though the post of deputy was held by other clans. When the militia was renamed the local patrol (*xunji dui*) in 1918, the clan lost its control. But during its three-year term as head of the militia, the Liu clan had built up its connections and consolidated its power in local defense. *Tongxu xianzhi* 1934, 10: 20b–21b.

60. See the inscription on the stone stele erected by the natives of Qixian, Tongxu, and Chenliu counties in 1931 in memory of Liu Boxun. *P:SQT*: 46–47.

61. The Liu regiment (*tuan*) consisted of 2,000 to 3,000 men, subdivided into large squads (*da dui*) and again broken down into smaller companies (*xiao dui*) of 30–50 men. See Han Xiaoting 1984: 84. The three networks controlled the following areas in the eastern and northeastern sections of the county: Shangwan, Xiawan, Sisuoliu, Changzhi, Yundian, Liuying, Yuezhai, and Wuzhai.

62. According to Perry, "The Red Spears were an association forged along settlement rather than kinship lines." Perry 1980: 156.

63. See Lo Wen (Liu Yuanfu), "Pianduan de huiyi," (Fragmentary recollection). *P:SQT* 1: 124–25.

64. A coalition was formed between Liu and three other clan-dominated regiments: the Cao regiment, centered at Transport Shop Village (Yundian cun) and headed by Cao Jinlin, the Liu regiment at White Tower (Bai ta), headed by Liu Xilu, and the Xu regiment at Ye Village (Ye zhuang), with Xu Number Five (Xu lao wu) as leader. Each of these regiments controlled one or two market towns. There were six towns and villages in Qixian under Liu Xilu's control, Wanggu, Shawo, Baita, Yangzhuang, E'gang, and Xiaoyao zhai; five towns and villages under Xu Number Five, Dayun suo, Gegang (town), Yezhuang, Pingcheng (town), and Baiqiu in northern Qixian.

65. *Chen bao*, May 18 and 19, 1926, in *LH:RS*: 129–31. *P:SQT* 1: 24–47.

66. They included Xu Xiangqian, Kong Zhaolin, Zhao Rongzhen, and Bai Longting. *P:dashiji*: 299.

67. Xu Xiangqian 1984: 35–39.

68. Zhang Jiang 1982: 58–60.
69. Zhang Jiang 1982: 59–60.
70. See *P:GZPM*: 20–61. For the first three classes, the Peasant Training Institute enrolled students only from Guangdong. After the third class, Institute leaders decided to extend enrollment outside Guangdong. Altogether, there were 478 graduates in the first five classes. Upon graduation, they were sent back to their home provinces to promote peasant movements. See Guo Shaoyi 1980: 49.
71. Pang Shouxin 1984: 2; *P:dashiji*: 18; He Yang 1982: 23.
72. For Xiao Rengu, see Niu Yuqian 1982.
73. As far as we can identify them, the group included Hu Lun (head of the GMD propaganda section), Dai Peiyuan (native of Hebei and former secretary of the Zhengtai railway union, transferred to Zhengzhou in July 1925 to lead the Zheng-Xing-Mi network as head of the western route propaganda team), Xiao Rengu, Wang Hebo (railroad union leader), Wang Zhongxiu (activist in the May 30th Movement in Luoyang and a mine organizer in Jiaozuo), Zhang Zhaofeng (CCP member introduced by the party in Baoding to work as regiment commander in Hu Jingyi's Guominjun), Tang Shikui (editor of a small paper in the propaganda section in Luoyang), and Huo Yunfu. The surveyors included Dai Peiyuan, Tang Shikui, and Hu Lun. The result of the survey was used by Li Dazhao in his article "Land and the Peasants," published in December 1925. Although the article dealt with peasants in China in general, a large part of it was based on the survey in eight villages in Xingyang, Mixian, and Qixian. It detailed the number and types of farm households, the amount of acreage, and the kinds of taxes in these three counties. Also see Liu Yingxian 1984: 106; Zhonggong zhongyang shujichu 1980: 652–62.
74. Thus one of the characteristics of peasant movements in this area was the mingling of laborers and peasants. Peasants frequently participated in labor strikes, while peasant uprisings were frequently directed by labor leaders from the city. In July 1925, Dai Peiyuan, a Hubei native and secretary of the Zhengtai railroad, was sent by the party to Zhengzhou to mobilize the peasants; Hu Lun, head of a Guomindang propaganda team, was one of the leaders in the peasant movement. See Liu Yingxian 1984: 107–8.
75. Liu Yingxian 1984: 106–7; Pang Shouxin 1984: 3. For the Red Spears in Xingyang, see *Chen bao*, Aug. 24, 1926. In *LH:RS*: 35–36.
76. *P:PM*: 69.
77. *P:PM*: 69.
78. "Zhang Jifan gei tuan zhongyang xin—shicha Xingyang xian Shuangliuguo zhen nongyun de qingkuang" (A letter from Zhang Jifan to the central committee of the Communist Youth League—On the investigation of the peasant movement in Shuangliuguo township in Xingyang county), Dec. 26, 1925. In *P:PM*: 69–72.
79. *P:PM*: 409.
80. Even at the age of 74, Ma still remembered some of the revolutionary songs he learned during the Northern Expedition period. Ma, together with other peasant youths in the Young Pioneers, participated in the song competition organized by the Communist Party in Shuangliuguo township.
81. For instance, one of the leaders of the peasant association had two family

members, his uncle and brother, in the Red Spears, and it was through them that the party set up its contacts.

82. Tang Shikui, "Dui da geming shiqi Xingyang nongmin yundong de huiyi" (A reminiscence of the peasant movement in Xingyang county during the Northern Expedition), and Zhang Mashuan, "Da geming shiqi Xingyang xian nongmin chang de jishou geming gequ" (A few revolutionary songs sung by the peasants in Xingyang during the Northern Expedition), n.d. *P:PM*: 408–17.

83. Han Xiaoting 1984: 87–88.

84. Prominent in the Qi county group were Zhang Haifeng, Wu Zhipu (later governor of Henan), and Han Shaoting. Other members of the group included Wang Kexin, Yang Tianren, Jiang Daozhong, Liu Gengchu, Yan Fengshu, Zhang Shengting, Zhao Xiaguang, Su Wenhuan, Jin Shoushan, Gao Guanglu, and Kong Yinchu.

85. The party moved to the Song Stockade in mid-1927, when the county launched a crackdown on the Communists. Liu Gengchu (Liu Kaitian, party secretary in Qi county), "Youguan Qixian diwei de yixie qingkuang" (some information about the Qixian Local Committee), 1985. *P:SQT* 1:89–91.

86. *P:SQT* 1: 110–12.

87. *P:SQT* 1: 73–75.

88. *P:SQT* 1: 73–75.

89. In another case, Yu came to know a Red Spear leader through his Qi county connections. Through that Red Spear leader he came into contact with other Red Spears. *P:SQT* 1: 73–88.

90. The branch was headed by Zhang, who was a native of Zhumadian and a Shanghai University graduate, and two other Henanese, Zhang Shaozeng and Wang Xinheng of Kaifeng and Xuchang counties.

91. The Queshan special party branch controlled Queshan itself (including the railroad town of Zhumadian) plus the neighboring subnetworks in Suiping and Runan counties. A county party was formed in March 1927 under Li Mingqi and four others. It oversaw seven districts (*qu*) and twenty subdistricts (*qu fenbu*). The second party branch (*qu dangbu*) was set up on May 3, 1927, in Zhumadian. It had four subdistricts, headed by Feng Shouting and Guo Fengxiang. Total membership (including four women) was 80 (worker-peasants 30 percent, merchants 20 percent). Pang and Wang 1981; Li Zeqing 1982: 32; Pan Yuqing 1985: 11–13.

92. They were Zhang Yaochang, Ma Shangde (Yang Tingyu), Liu Jianzhao, Zhao Zile, Li Panlin, Xu Zirong, Xu Zhonghe, and Zhang Zhicai.

93. See Li Zeqing 1982: 33.

94. Zhang Yaochang and Ma Shangde, both natives of northern Queshan county, were responsible for winning over two other Red Spear chiefs, Zhang Guanghan and Xu Yaocai. Zhang Yaochang and Xu Yaocai were relatives; later, through Xu Yaocai, Zhang Guanghan was recruited to the revolutionary camp.

95. See Lo Shaozheng's report in *LH:Beifa*: 286–87.

96. *LH:Beifa*: 332.

97. *LH:Beifa*: 352.

98. *LH:Beifa*: 317.

99. *LH:Beifa*: 316.

100. "Yi erzhan shiqi Xinyang diqu de Hongqiang hui" (The Xinyang Red

Spears in the first and second revolutionary war periods), n.d. In *P:Fengbei* 6: 276.

101. Red Spear chiefs such as Zeng Qingcheng, Liu Shun of Xinyang, Wang Yujiu of Shangcheng, Gu Lanhua and Hu Tingbi of Xixian, and Fang Fanjiu of Luoshan joined the Communist Party; Communist activists such as Zhou Shibin, Bao Zikuan of Xinyang, Du Shouzhi, Cheng Yi of Huangchuan, and Li Ziguang and Wang Guangrong of Xixian became Red Spear leaders.

102. The leaders of the coalitions were Li Lanzhi, Li Kejing, Ren Zixiang, Shou Laobao, and Zhao Tianlu of Xixian; Wang Jieying, Wang Ziyou, Zhang Shu, Liu Jingshan, Feng Chenglin, and Ding Zeqing of Xinyang; Wang Tanyuan of Shangcheng; Wen Kaizhou and Chen Xulun of Luoshan; and Bi Bashao, Su Shaowen, and Zhang Yangwu of Huangchuan.

103. "Yi erzhan shiqi Xinyang diqu de Hongqiang hui." *P:Fengbei*: 276–78.

104. *LH:Beifa*: 316.

105. Li Dazhao, "Tudi yu nongmin" (Land and the peasants). In Zhonggong zhongyang dangxiao dangshi jiaoyan shi 1979, 2:178–91. Zhonggong zhongyang shuji chu 1980: 652–62.

106. Chen Duxiu 1926.

107. Originally published in *Chen Yun wenxuan* in 1984. See *LH:RS*: 4–5.

108. Li Dazhao [1936] 1959: 546. See also *LH:RS*: 5–9.

109. At the beginning, the party only sent 28 Henanese to the Institute. In June 1926, two more students were transferred from the Whampao Military Academy. Later one dropped out because of illness, making a total of 29 Henanese.

110. Xue Yi 1983: 25–28.

111. See document 30, "Resolution on the Red Spears Movement," in Wilbur and How 1956.

112. *LH:RS*: 106.

113. For a report on the formation of the Henan Provincial Peasant Association, see *Zhong guo nong min* (Chinese peasants) 8: 4–55 in *LH:RS*: 108–14. By June 1926, four counties (Xinyang, Qixian, Xuchang, and Xingyang) had county peasant associations; seven counties (Changge, Mixian, Suixian, Yencheng, Anyang, Xiuwu, and Qixian) had district (*qu*) peasant associations. In such major cities as Kaifeng, Luoyang, and Zhengzhou, defunct parties had been rehabilitated. See *P:dashiji*: 24.

114. *P:dashiji*: 27.

115. *P:dashiji*: 27; Wang Tianjiang et al. 1990: 260; *P:PM*: 8.

116. Originally in *Minguo ribao* (Hankou), Mar. 19, 1927. See *LH:Beifa*: 227–33.

117. Below Xiao Rengu were five committee members overseeing the eastern, western, northern, southern, and central parts of Henan. *Minguo ribao* (Hankou), Mar. 22, 1927. In *LH:Beifa*: 234–35.

118. Lin Zhuangzhi 1985: 7.

119. Lin Zhuangzhi, 1985: 8; Pan Yuqing 1985: 19–20.

120. The targets of attack were four prominent gentry: a provincial assemblyman and heads of the local militia, bureau of public funds, and corvée bureau.

121. They notified the Red Spears in Suiping, Runan, Zhengyang, and Xinyang counties.

122. Pan Yuqing 1985: 23–32; Lin Zhuangzhi 1985: 8–9; Li Hongbin 1979: 7–10; Li Zeqing 1982: 34–38.

123. *P:dashiji*: 28.

124. *Minguo ribao* (Hankou), Mar. 4, 1927, May 17 and 22, 1927. In *LH:Beifa*: 243, 246–49, 294–95.

125. See the report on the Henan peasant movement by the War Zone Peasant Movement Committee, *Minguo ribao* (Hankou), May 22, 1927. In *LH:Beifa*: 295.

126. See report on the work between Xinyang and Suiping filed by the General Headquarters of the Political Department (May 21, 1927, at Zhumadian). *Minguo ribao* (Hankou), May 28–June 8, 1927, in *LH:Beifa*: 317.

127. Report on work at Zhumadian by the party affairs section of the headquarters of the political department. *Minguo ribao* (Hankou), May 23, 1927, in *LH:Beifa*: 313.

128. See the section on survey of local party affairs in the report on work between Xinyang and Suiping filed by the general headquarters of the political department (May 21, 1927, at Zhumadian). *Minguo ribao* (Hankou), May 28–June 8, 1927, in *LH:Beifa*: 317.

129. See the section on work in Runan in the work report on Henan filed by the political department of the Eleventh Army of the National Revolutionary Army. *Minguo ribao* (Hankou), June 11, 1927, in *LH:Beifa*: 351–52.

130. *Minguo ribao* (Hankou), May 13 and 22, 1927, June 11, 1927. In *LH:Beifa*: 255–56, 292–93, 295–96, 304.

131. The propaganda materials included peasant manifestos, manifestos of armed Henan peasants, resolutions on peasant problems, banners, and printed slogans.

132. For the role of "Representatives of the Nationalist Government for Consoling the Military and Civilians in Henan," see *Minguo ribao* (Hankou), Apr. 1 and 3, 1927, May 5, 1927. In *LH:Beifa*: 281–88.

133. *Minguo ribao* (Hankou), Apr. 3, 1927, May 23, 26, and 28, 1927, July 1, 1927. In *LH:Beifa*: 305–6, 310–11, 313–28.

134. See the section on propaganda in the report on work between Xinyang and Suiping by the political department of the general headquarters (May 21, 1927, in Zhumadian), *Minguo ribao* (Hankou), May 28–June 8, 1927. In *LH: Beifa*: 319–20.

135. *Minguo ribao* (Hankou), May 5 and 22, 1927, June 2, 11, and 17, 1927. In *LH:Beifa*: 289–90, 298–305.

136. *Minguo ribao* (Hankou), June 2, 1927, in *LH:Beifa*: 300. *P:dashiji*: 28–29.

137. Li Zeqing 1982: 40–42.

138. Li Hongbin 1979; Li Zeqing 1982; Lin Zhuangzhi 1985; Pang and Wang 1981; Pan Yuqing 1985.

139. Pan Yuqing 1985: 40–42.

140. *P:dashiji*: 29; Wang Tianjiang et al. 1990: 264.

141. *P:SQT* 1: 48–124.

142. Perry notes in her work on rebels and revolutionaries in North China, "In stressing the discontinuity between rebellion and revolution, this book again parts company with those who would look to the secret society as a bridge spanning 'traditional' and 'modern' styles of peasant protest. The contention

that the sectarian was a 'primitive revolutionary' whose actions were 'necessary for a transition to more "developed" or "advanced" revolutionary organizations' seems, in the case of Huai-pei, at variance with the historical record." Perry 1980: 255–56.

Chapter 3

1. Moore 1966; Skocpol 1979.

2. The Eyuwan revolutionary region was divided into two separate bases, or soviet areas. One was the Henan-Hubei section, composed of Guangshan and Luoshan counties in Henan and Macheng and Huangan counties in Hubei. This section was centered at Qiliping, a town in northern Huangan. The other was the Henan-Anhui section. It included Liu'an county in Anhui province, and Huoshan and Shangcheng counties in Henan. It was centered around Jinjia zhai in Anhui. This chapter focuses on the Henan-Hubei section only.

3. On peripheral location as a factor in peasant-based revolutions, see Wolf 1969: 292–93.

4. Shang Shiying et al. 1985: 25–27; *P:Xinxian*: 1.

5. *Shina kenkyu so sho* 1918; 1: 206–7, 210, 218–27.

6. *Henan sheng nongcun diaocha* 1934: 86–87.

7. For example, in Zhengyang county, Yuan Naikuan owned 20,000 *mu* of land. In Luoshan county, Liu Jietang, a former governor-general of Yunnan, was proprietor of 25,000 *mu* of high-quality land. A landlord in Gushi county is said to have been able to travel 120 *li* (43 miles) to town without even stepping on other people's property.

8. The area includes Xinyang, Luoshan, Guangshan, Huangchuan, Gushi, Shangcheng, and Xixian counties. See *Henan sheng nongcun diaocha* 1934: 86. Yet we have a conflicting source: Xue Chao stated in his study of tenancy in Henan that rental arrangements in south Henan (Yunan) were cash rent 5 percent, crop rent 75 percent, and sharecropping 20 percent. He was probably talking about southwestern Henan, particularly Zhengping county, where he did the survey. In Zhengping, sharecropping predominated. Xue Chao, "Henan zudian jidu niao kang" (A bird's-eye view of the tenancy system in Henan). In Feng Hefa 1933, 2: 582. On rental arrangements in Zhengping, see Feng Hefa 1935, 1: 192.

9. *Henan sheng nongcun diaocha* 1934: 68. According to John Buck, the distribution of rental arrangements in Xinyang was sharecropping 75 percent, cash rent 7 percent, and cash-crop rent 18 percent. See table 24 in Buck [1937] 1956: 61.

10. Feng Hefa 1933, 2: 690–92; *Henan sheng nongcun diaocha* 1934: 87; Amano Gennosuke 1935: 39.

11. *P:Xinxian*: 4–6.

12. According to Chen Honggen, 60 percent of the villagers were tenants and 40 percent landowners. Chen Honggen 1934: 52.

13. Fixed rent was commonly known as *sike* or *sizu*, literally "dead rent." Unfixed rent was referred to as *kanke* ("inspecting the harvest") or *huozu* ("unfixed rent").

14. Tenant labor service consisted of doing construction and repairs and

helping with weddings, funerals, and moving. Tenants sometimes served as sedan chair carricrs and cart pullers. Occasionally they were required to participate in clan fights. Gift rent (*zuke*) included fish, poultry, and fruit.

15. *Di er ci Zhongguo laodong nianjian* 1933–34: 156; Zeng Jianquan 1927.

16. Arrigo 1986. The issue of the impact of capitalism in the countryside remains controversial. Intrusion of capitalism did bring higher farm wages to the countryside, but as Joseph Esherick pointed out to me, "Note that while farm wages may rise in these conditions, farm laborers with no claims on land at all increase. There is, thus, a Marxist polarization between landed and landless." More research needs to be done to determine whether the impact of market forces in the Chinese countryside was beneficial or damaging.

17. For example, in the Qiting area, there were five households with 1,000 *mu* of land. The number of households owning several hundred or tens of *mu* of land was triple that of the north.

18. The majority of hired farmhands earned 200 strings of cash a year, and all of them earned at least 150–160 strings (each string was 1,000 cash).

19. "Macheng xianwei baogao" (A report from the Macheng county committee), May 1929. *P:EYW* jia 5: 238–40.

20. According to a report of the Huangan county committee, "About 10 percent of the southern part of the county is capitalized. There are plenty of merchants. The number of hired laborers (*gu nong*) is inordinately high. But both farm wages and living standards are high. In other areas, except for a lack of freedom, their living standard is sometimes higher than that of the poor peasants. But most of them are single." "Huangan xianwei baogao" (A report from the Huangan county committee), 1929. *P:EYW* jia 5, 204–15. Unfortunately, we have no information on whether these "hired farmhands" were the absentee landlords' tenants or actual hired labor. If they were hired labor, they would have been more dependent on the landlord and this might have explained their behavior.

21. "E dongbei tewei He Yulin gei zhongyang de baogao" (A report to Party Central from He Yulin of the northeastern Hubei special committee), May 7, 1929. *P:EYW* jia 5: 45.

22. "Macheng xianwei baogao." *P:EYW* jia 5: 238.

23. *P:EYW* jia 5: 236.

24. Although Communist forces had destroyed their rural power base, landlord-merchants in southern Huangan could still maintain their political power in urban centers. Many conducted trade in Beijing, Shanghai, and Wuhan.

25. "Eyu bian tewei gei zhongyang de baogao, bian zi di yi hao" (A report to Party Central from the Hubei-Henan border special committee, bian no. 1) Jan. 10, 1930. *P:EYW* jia 2: 89.

26. Normally, five subdistrict peasant committees (*xiang nongmin weiyuan hui*) were integrated into a district peasant committee (*qu nongmin weiyuan hui*).

27. The *chongyang* festival falls on the ninth day of the ninth lunar month and is a time the Chinese honor their deceased. When people go to the cemetery to pay respect to the dead, they also take the occasion to "sweep clean the graves."

28. "E dongbei ge xian di er ci lianxi hui nongmin yundong jueyi an" (Resolu-

tion on peasant mobilization passed at the Second Joint Conference of Northeastern Hubei Counties), June 9, 1929. *P:EYW* jia 5: 105–8.

29. Skocpol 1979: 112–17, 147–60.

30. Guo and Chen 1987: 146.

31. Guo and Chen 1987: 144–202; Sheridan 1966: 240–67; Gillin 1967: 110–17.

32. The designations for subdistricts varied from county to county. For example, in Huangan the subdistrict was known as *hui*, in Macheng as *kui*, and in Guangshan in Henan as *li*. Each of these subdistricts was under a head known as the "*hui* head," "*kui* head," or "*li* head." These were probably designations of tax units in the *lijia* tax system.

33. "Huangan xianwei baogao." *P:EYW* jia 5: 207.

34. For cooperation between the Guominjun and the Communists, see How 1985–86.

35. There are numerous examples of conflict among local elite groups. In Luoshan county, in a fight over local taxes, Ding Yingkun disarmed Liu Shanpu's military forces. In Guangshan county, Yi Benying seized the arms of the gentry-dominated county militia. In Macheng county, a powerful gentry member named Guo Shandong coerced middle and small landlords to contribute C$35,000 to his war chest. Xia Douyin, a Macheng militarist, tried to reorganize the county armed forces into his army, but ran into stiff opposition from the village gentry. Macheng militia also fought against each other. In Huangan county, a landlord prepared for combat by selling his grain in Hankou and procuring arms. Huangan landlords were involved in all kinds of litigation. In Huangpi county, gentry Red Spears and Green Spears fought each other. One group of gentry tried to force another to contribute to the military buildup, but the other group refused. See "Eyu bian tewei zonghe baogao" (A comprehensive report from the Hubei-Henan border special committee), Dec. 1930, and "Eyu bian tewei gei Hubei shengwei de baogao" (A report from the Hubei-Henan special committee to the Hubei provincial committee), Sept. 20, 1930. *P:EYW* jia 2: 124, 141–43.

36. In Huangan, the village-clearing squad in Seven Miles battled the village-clearing squad of Purple Cloud. Seven Miles squad members accused the Purple Cloud squad of raiding their area not to drive out the Communists but to seize the grain stock.

37. In Guangshan, the gentry considered the Communist Party in northeastern Hubei the "old party" (*lao dang*) and themselves the "new party," and they refused to launch an assault on the "old party."

38. "Eyu bian tewei gei zhongyang de baogao, bian zi di yi hao." *P:EYW* jia 2: 83–109.

39. For example, in Arrow River (Jianhe), the dominant gentry in the eastern, western, northern, and southern sections of the village were Peng Songchen, Wang Jian, Li Wanlan, and Shi Ziqian, respectively.

40. Many of these were powerful clans or official families in the locality, like the Shih family in Arrow River. Shih Ziqian, a local landlord, had paid 300 taels of silver for a licentiate degree. His brother obtained a "filial, modest, square and upright" decoration by paying 200 silver taels. In Zhou River (Zhou he), a landlord named Peng Songchen purchased the official position of assistant

department director for 200 *shi* of grain in the late Qing. He served under Yuan Shikai as assistant secretary in the Ministry of Finance and later headed the salt bureau in Lingbao county. Huang Jian of Kaifeng was an official whose eldest son, a landlord, was a son-in-law of the mayor of He county in Jilin province. The younger son, through marriage, was able to form an alliance with the politically powerful Wang family. Wang Ziguo, head of the Wang family, was a powerful landlord in Luoshan county and a county mayor in Anhui.

41. In an armed conflict in Guangshan, the powerful Hu, Fan, and Cheng clans jointly mobilized several thousand of their clan members to fight the Communists. Clan leaders promised a reward of C$300 to anyone who killed a Communist. Over 100 Communists were killed in the conflict, but the clan heads went back on their word.

42. For example, Huang Jian made use of his official position to force local peasants to pay for stockade construction. In Zhou River, Peng Songchen ordered each family to provide fifteen labor units to guard the stockade. Those who failed to comply were fined C$60. Each household also had to contribute C$60 for the acquisition of weapons for village defense.

43. Wu Weicun, head of a powerful lineage, ordered other lineages, when they divided their family property, to set aside one portion as lineage land, the proceeds of which would be used for sacrifices to ancestors. These lands from various lineages were to be managed by him, and he was to be given sole power to lease these lands to members of the lineages. He frequently pocketed the sacrificial money.

44. Communist reports indicate that local armed forces in Huangan were composed mainly of members of gentry families (*zidi,* or sons and brothers). Many of these clan bands had previously been under Communist attack, and as a result were strongly anti-Communist. There were few tenant peasants in these clan bands. See "Eyu bian tewei zonghe baogao." *P:EYW* jia 2: 144.

45. "Xiaowei xianwei baogao" (A report from the Xiaowei county committee), May 26, 1929. *P:EYW* jia 5: 224.

46. In Luoshan, Guangshan, and Shangcheng, the anti-Communist forces were mostly bandits. Some were secret societies, for instance the Red Gang (Hong bang) and Green Gang (Qing bang). There were very few peasants. "Eyu bian tewei zonghe baogao." *P:EYW* jia 2: 144.

47. "Macheng xianwei baogao." *P:EYW* jia 5: 244–45.

48. *P:EYW* jia 5: 74.

49. Most of these groups were under the local gentry known as *laoye* (master) or *hushou* (household head) and *zuzhang* (clan head). They were both territorial and kinship-based organizations. Each was integrated under a system of patronage. Communist reports referred to the members as "son-and-brother soldiers" (*zidi bing*). "Huangan gongzuo baogao" (Huangan work report), Dec. 14, 1927. *P:EYW* jia 5: 1–2. The Red Spears were not the only blood-oath fraternity in the area. Another variant was the Benevolent and Righteous Society. This sectarian organization originated in the 1911 Revolution and was particularly popular in the upper Huai River area. Some of its organizations included half the county residents. In Huangpo and Xiaowei counties, it dominated county politics. See "E dongbei ge xian di er ci lianxi hui: muqian zhengzhi xingshi yu E dongbei qudang de renwu jueyi an" (Second joint conference of north-

eastern Hubei counties: Current political conditions and resolution on the tasks for the northeastern Hubei regional committee), June 9, 1929. *P:EYW* jia 5: 74.

50. In the 1930s, the Nationalist garrison commander stationed in the area was Dai Minquan, who had under him four regiments.

51. "Eyu bian di qu yi ci quanqu daibiao dahui qunzhong yundong jueyi an" (Resolution on mass movement passed in the First Representative Conference of the Hubei-Henan border area), Dec. 2, 1929. *P:EYW* jia 2: 39–50.

52. "E dongbei ge xian di er ci lianxi hui bingshi yundong jueyi an." *P:EYW* jia 5: 99.

53. For example, there were two networks in Guangshan under Yi Benying and Liu Jianpu, three networks in Luoshan under Hou Xiangpu, Ding Yingkun, and Liu Shanpu, one network in Shangcheng under Gu Jingzhi, one network in Macheng under Zheng Qiyu, and one network in Huangpi under Chen Zuoqin.

54. Villagers had to pay a string of cash and urban citizens a dollar to purchase a badge. The proceeds were used for arms procurement.

55. See "Eyu bian tewei zonghe baogao." *P:EYW* jia 2: 143.

56. Ni Zhongwen 1982.

57. Tan and Jiang 1983.

58. Zhang Guotao (Chang Kuo-t'ao) mentions in his memoir that he saw villages incorporated into Communist guerrilla areas. For instance, there was a monoclan village composed of 26 families about eight *li* outside of Li Family Town that was sympathetic toward the revolution. See Chang Kuo-t'ao 1972, 1: 178.

59. See *P:Xinxian*: 29.

60. Hou Zhiying et al. 1982.

61. For example, Yu Menghen received his education in Jiangxi. He returned to his native Yu Inn in 1926 to set up a school at the clan ancestral temple to recruit student activists. *P:Xinxian*: 22.

62. In Zhengbian, all defense leaders belonged to the Wu clan. In Zhan Bay, the leader was Zhan Yixian; in Wu Bay, Wu Weirong; in Lu Hill, Lu Xiandian; in Xiao Bay, Xiao Lihua; in Shi Mound, Shi Shengyong; in Zhao Mound, Zhao Jiyong. See *P:Xinxian*: 23.

63. Leadership in the Cao Gate Peasant Association, the one created by Wu Huanxian, remained within the Wu family. Except for the chairman, Geng Jiyong, who was a garment factory worker and an outsider, committee members came from the Wu clan: Wu Weilong (organization), Wu Xianshen (propaganda), Wu Xianyun (land), and Wu Xian'en.

64. In Wang Bay village in Fodder Hill, Wang Zhiren, the Huangan party secretary, had already started a Communist movement by creating a chapter of Red Spears at the time of the Northern Expedition. Wang was killed in the Huang-Ma uprising. When the Communists moved to Wang Bay in 1928, they used Wang Zhiren's brother and other members of the Wang family to seize control of the area. Using this as a base, the party extended its influence into the neighboring villages of Hu Bay, Chen Bay, and Big Wu Family. In Cao Bay, Cao Xue used the firecracker store belonging to his wife's uncle as party headquarters, conducting clandestine revolutionary activities from there. He also recruited members of the Cao family as Communist Party members. See *P:Xin-*

xian: 61–62. For Fodder Hill Neighborhood, see Yang Jingqi 1982: 463; Yang Jingqi 1985; Chen and Lin 1981.

65. "Macheng xianwei baogao." *P:EYW* jia 5: 245–46.

66. "E dongbei ge xian di er ci lianxi hui." *P:EYW* jia 5: 74.

67. "E dongbei ge xian di er ci lianxi hui nongmin yundong jueyi an" (Resolution on peasant mobilization passed by the second joint conference of northeastern Hubei counties), June 9, 1929. *P:EYW* jia 5: 105–8.

68. "Huangan gongzuo baogao." *P:EYW* jia 5: 5.

69. "Eyu bian di yi ci quanqu daibiao dahui qunzhong yundong jueyi an." *P:EYW* jia 2: 47.

70. "Hu Yanbin gei zhongyang de baogao" (Hu Yanbin's report to the Central Committee), June 29, 1929. *P:EYW* jia 5: 115–17. The self-defense squads were directly under the command of the secretary of the Special Committee.

71. "E dongbei tebie qu weiyuanhui gei zhongyang de baogao" (A report from the northeastern Hubei special committee to Party Central), Sept. 8, 1929. *P:EYW* jia 5: 142.

72. For example, Wu Huanxian's Red Spears units were later reorganized into the Red Army.

73. The area under attack spanned 100 *li*. It was located in the eastern, western, and northern sections of the county seat of Macheng. The targets were the following clans: Chen, Zhu, Yan, Wang, Fang, Yu, another Chen, Shuai, Hu, and Bao. According to the Macheng gazetteer, 3,000 people were killed and 6,000 houses were demolished. The insurrection was finally crushed by thirteen county divisions. See *wubi* (military preparation) and *bingshi* (military events) sections in *Macheng xianzhi xubian* 1935, 5: 27b–28a.

74. *P:Xinxian*: 61–65.

75. *P:EYW* jia 2: 24–33.

76. *P:EYW* jia 5: 232.

77. Chang Kuo-t'ao 1972, 2: 186.

78. "Xiaowei xianwei baogao." *P:EYW* jia 5: 223–29. In repression in Huangchuan and Guangshan counties, 250 villagers were killed. After that, the Communists found other villagers were unwilling to rise up, and instead wanted the Red Army to do the fighting for them. When the Red Army came to the area, as many as 100 peasants volunteered to be guides. See "Eyu bian tewei zonghe baogao." *P:EYW* jia 2: 158.

79. "E dongbei tewei He Yulin gei zhongyang de baogao." *P:EYW* jia 5: 52.

80. For example, cadres in the Huangkang, Yunmeng, and Anlu areas avoided using the term.

81. "E dongbei ge xian di er ci lianxi hui." *P:EYW* jia 5: 74. Eight to nine months after the Communists took over Huangan county, only an area of 30 by 40 *li* had experienced land reform. In Macheng, the land reform program had not been implemented seven months after the takeover. See "He Yulin gei zhongyang de baogao" (He Yulin's report to Party Central), Sept. 7, 1929. *P:EYW* jia 5: 125. The Communist terminology for social banditry was "burning and killing," or *shao sha*.

82. "Hu Yanbin gei zhongyang de baogao." *P:EYW* jia 5: 115–17.

83. According to one report, after the capture of the county town of Huangan,

the Communists proposed, but never implemented, land reform. Only after they later returned and exercised control over the area was some form of land reform carried out. With some of the landlord gentry fleeing Communist rule, the land they left behind was redistributed to the peasantry. "Eyu bian geming weiyuanhui baogao" (Report of the revolutionary committee at the Hubei-Henan border area), 1929. *P:EYW* jia 2: 60–63.

84. "Eyu bian qu di yi ci quanqu daibiao dahui qunzhong jueyi an." *P:EYW* jia 2: 39–50.

85. "E dongbei ge xian di er ci lianxi hui nongmin yundong jueyi an." *P:EYW* jia 5: 105–8.

86. "Eyu bian tewei zonghe baogao." *P:EYW* jia 2: 175.

87. "Eyuwan tewei Zeng Zhongsheng gei zhongyang de baogao" (A report from Zeng Zhongsheng of the Eyuwan special committee to the Party Central), Feb. 10, 1930. *P:EYW* jia 2: 233.

88. This happened in the districts of Yongan and Bali in Huangan county.

89. This happened in the central and Song districts in Macheng.

90. For example, in Huangan county, when peasants failed to provide cadres with a good meal, the cadres forced them to pay a grain tax (*zhengfa*).

91. "Eyu bian tewei zonghe baogao." *P:EYW* jia 2: 175.

92. "Eyu bian tewei gei Hubei shengwei de baogao." *P:EYW* jia 2: 128–30.

93. "Eyu bian tewei zonghe baogao." *P:EYW* jia 2: 156–58.

94. Skocpol 1979: 253–54.

95. In 1930, the Red Army consisted of three divisions stationed in three subbases (Huang-Ma, Shangcheng, and Jin-jia-zhai) of the Eyuwan border region. The army originated from a variety of armed forces. The First Division of the Huang-Ma area, the area studied here, originated from the peasant self-defense army the Communists created at the time of the Northern Expedition. There were some defected soldiers within this division. The Second Division came from the local militia in Shangcheng and included a high percentage (40 percent) of bandits. The Communists report that it was "a feudal coalition" of neighborhood units, clan bands, and bandit gangs. The Third Division was a spin-off from the Second Division composed mostly of peasant guerrillas. There was also a small group of bandits within this division. "Eyu bian tewei zonghe baogao." *P:EYW* jia 2: 193.

96. In his memoir, Zhang Guotao also confirmed that the independent regiment in Huangan came from the peasant self-defense army (mostly local militias made up of settled peasants). Zhang writes in his memoir, "The staff officers and clerks in the regimental headquarters were low-class local intellectuals (some of them were apprentices to Taoist priests; some of them had been schooled in private tutorial classes or in primary schools)." Chang Kuo-t'ao 1972, 2: 182–85.

97. Polachek 1983.

Chapter 4

1. Huntington 1968.

2. See Shanin 1987: 384–86.

3. See "Peasantry in the Eyes of Others," Shanin 1987: 382–90.

4. Huntingon 1968: 302.
5. Peter Saunders et al. 1978: 55–86.
6. Marx 1987.
7. "Guangshan xian Suweiai zhengquan de chuangjian" (The founding of soviet political power in Guangshan county), Dec. 1985. *P:Fengbei* 13: 57–66.
8. The core section was composed of the following districts: White Sparrow, Splash River, Brick Bridge, Double Wheel, Summer Clear, and Dou Hill. The soviet government was located in Ding Li Bay and, in 1931, was moved to Xu Farm. In mid-1931, a peripheral zone was set up consisting of View City, Chen Awning (Chen Peng), and Yang Fan. See "Yijiu wuyi nian Eyuwan lao genju di Henan bufen diaocha cailiao jielu" (Excerpts of 1951 investigation materials on the Henan section of the old Eyuwan base). *P:Fengbei* 13: 67.
9. For instance, the headquarters of View City soviet (Wangcheng) was located in Wang South Hollow (Wang nan wa), in the mansion of landlord Wang Zuoting. The Xiandong soviet headquarters was set up in the house of wealthy landlord Xu Fuyuan. The Qianjin district soviet headquarters was located in an ancestral temple in Yang Inn, and the district soviet headquarters of the Kafang soviet was located inside the main hall of the Dongtang temple. See appendices in "Guangshan xian Suweiai zhengquan de chuangjian" and "Xinxian Suweiai zhengquan de jianli" (The establishment of Xinxian soviet authority), Sept. 1985. *P:Fengbei* 13: 57–79.
10. The Communist Party selected 30 dedicated cadres from the central and northern parts of the county and had them trained for the White Sand Pass revolt. In this way, the Communists were able to secure a base in that area. Nine cadres from the south and four from Huangan and Macheng counties were sent north to infiltrate the area. Their duty was to mobilize and help local peasants set up peasant associations and Red Guards. "Guangshan xian Suweiai zhengquan de chuangjian." *P:Fengbei* 13: 60.
11. For instance, the Qianjin district soviet, except for chairman Shi Chuansheng, was dominated by members of the Yang clan: Yang Jiashun, secretary, and Yang Deyu, economic committee member. In Kafang village, important soviet positions were dominated by the Hu, Lin, and Jiang clans. The officials were Hu Tingjie, a native of Hu River, chairman; Hu Daquan, treasurer; Jiang Zichen, secretary; Jiang Zilan, women's committee; Lin Peifa, member of standing committee; Lin Daosheng, local armed forces; and Lin Zhengyi and Ye Daozeng, propaganda. See "Qianjin xiang laoren Yang Guanglu, Yu Dinghuai deng huiyi" (A recollection of two old men of Qianjin village, Yang Guanglu and Yu Dinghuai), "Kafang xiang Tan Youbo de huiyi" (A recollection of Tan Youbo of Kafang village). Appendices 2 and 7 in "Xinxian Suweiai zhengquan de jianli." *P:Fengbei* 13: 77–79.
12. "Eyu bian geming weiyuanhui baogao" (Report of the revolutionary committee of the Hubei-Henan border area), 1929. *P:EYW* jia 2: 64.
13. For village authority, see Dobrowolski 1987 and Maccoby 1967.
14. "He Yulin gei zhongyang de baogao" (He Yulin's report to the Central Committee), Sept. 7, 1929. *P:EYW* jia 5: 124.
15. *P:EYW* jia 5: 124.
16. *P:EYW* jia 5: 127.
17. *P:EYW* jia 5: 128.

18. *P:EYW* jia 5: 125. According to the report, all the problems in Guangshan were referred to Cao Xuejie, the commander in the area. Other heroic leaders included Xu Pengren, secretary of the Special Committee in northeastern Hubei, and Dai Jiying, secretary of the Huangan county committee.

19. *P:EYW* jia 5: 126–27.

20. "Eyu bian tewei zonghe baogao" (A comprehensive report of the Hubei-Henan border area Special Committee), Dec. 1930, and "Eyuwan tewei Zeng Zhongsheng gei zhongyang de baogao" (A report from Zeng Zhongsheng of the Eyuwan special committee to Party Central), Feb. 10, 1931. In *P:EYW* jia 5: 174–99, jia 2: 203–37.

21. In 1929 in Huangan, the social composition of party members was peasants 85 percent, intellectuals 5 percent, and artisans 5 percent. The social composition of party members in Macheng was reported to be similar. In Fodder Hill Neighborhood, Guangshan county, party members were mostly peasants. See "E dongbei tewei He Yulin gei zhongyang de baogao" (A report to Party Central from He Yulin of the northeastern Hubei special committee), May 7, 1929. *P:EYW* jia 5: 57.

22. For example, in 1929, party members (700, including 10 women) in Macheng county were composed of 80 percent peasants, and 15 percent "petty bourgeoisie" and intellectuals. Only 20 percent of the members were active. Except for party branches, all leaders at the county and district levels were intellectuals. "Macheng xianwei baogao" (A report from the Macheng County Committee), May 1929. *P:EYW* jia 5: 246.

23. "E dongbei tewei He Yulin gei zhongyang de baogao." *P:EYW* jia 5: 58.

24. Hobsbawm 1959; Hobsbawm, "The Social Bandit as a Pre-Capitalist Phenomenon," in Shanin 1987: 338–39.

25. "He Yulin gei zhongyang de baogao." *P:EYW* jia 5: 124.

26. "E dongbei tewei He Yulin gei zhongyang de baogao." *P:EYW* jia 5: 58.

27. The screening eliminated 300 members in Huangan and 200 in Macheng. In September 1929, party membership was 800 in Huangan, 500 in Macheng, 300 in Huangpi, 300 in Xiaowei, 300 in Yingshan, 200 in Guangshan, 100 in Luoshan, and 60 to 70 in Luotian. Figures for Anlu and Shangcheng are unavailable. "E dongbei tebie qu weiyuanhui gei zhongyang de baogao" (A report from the northeast Hubei special committee to Party Central) Sept. 8, 1929. *P:EYW* jia 5: 132–78.

28. They were Zhou Chunquan, a worker who had some education and was a committee member in Huangan, and Wei Zusheng, a peasant who became party secretary in Xiaowei county.

29. "E dongbei tebie qu weiyuanhui gei zhongyang de baogao." *P:EYW* jia 5: 152.

30. "He Yulin ge zhongyang de baogao." *P:EYW* jia 5: 123.

31. For example, when the party in Xiaowei county requested assistance from the northeastern Hubei party, the Hubei Special Committee only sent C$150 a day to Xiaowei.

32. "He Yulin gei zhongyang de baogao." *P:EYW* jia 5: 128.

33. *P:EYW* jia 5: 130.

34. *P:EYW* jia 5: 122.

35. "Eyuwan tewei Zeng Zhongsheng gei zhongyang de baogao." *P:EYW* jia 2:

203–37. Zeng Zhongsheng was the party secretary of the Special Committee in Eyuwan.

36. "E dongbei tebie qu weiyuanhui gei zhongyang de baogao." *P:EYW* jia 5: 132–58.

37. "E dongbei tewei He Yulin gei zhongyang de baogao." *P:EYW* jia 5: 60.

38. *P:EYW* jia 5: 58.

39. "E dongbei ge xian di er ci lianxi hui nongmin yundong jueyi an" (Resolution on peasant mobilization passed at the second joint conference of northeastern Hubei counties), June 9, 1929. *P:EYW* jia 5: 105–8.

40. "E dongbei tewei He Yulin gei zhongyang de baogao." *P:EYW* jia 5: 58.

41. "He Yulin gei zhongyang de baogao." *P:EYW* jia 5: 124.

42. Newby 1978: 6.

43. "Xinxian tudi geming qingkuang jianshu" (A brief account of the land revolution in New County), n.d. *P:Fengbei* 13: 90–91.

44. Auyang Zhiliang 1982: 355.

45. In March 1929, the Guangshan Communist Party recruited several hundred "revolutionary elements" from such areas as White Sparrow (Bai que), Brick Bridge (Zhuan qiao), Splash River (Po he), Yan River (Yan he), Scholar-tree Inn (Huai dian), and Wenshu for special training in Fodder Hill. Afterward, these "seeders" were sent back to their hometowns to carry out land reforms.

46. From June to November 1929, land reform was conducted in only three neighborhoods—Fodder Hill, Goddess of Mercy (Guanyin bao), and Official Weir (Guanyan bao)—all located in the southern part of Guangshan.

47. *P:Xinxian* 1985: 84.

48. *P:Xinxian* 1985: 84.

49. In Splash River, classes were identified in the following way: Boat-towers, cart-pushers, peddlers, coolies, long-term laborers, and landless peasants were identified as wage laborers; tenants who owned a small piece of land were considered poor peasants; owner-cultivators who were not exploiting others were defined as middle peasants; middle peasants engaging in some exploitative activities were identified as rich middle peasants; rich peasants were those who tilled the land but derived part of their income from exploitation; landlords were non-productive agrarian residents.

50. "Eyu bian geming weiyuanhui baogao." *P:EYW* jia 2: 60–63.

51. These included Yan District (Yanqu), White Sparrow, Double Wheel (Shuanglun), Brick Bridge, Splash River, Scholar-tree Inn (Huaidian, that is View City/Wangcheng), and Yan River (present-day Xiaqing/Summer Clear). All are presently located in southern Guangshan, but in 1930 were located in central Guangshan.

52. In the village of Huang Valley Farm (Huanggu fan), for instance, agrarian classes were defined as follows: the dirt poor were the landless peasants; poor peasants were owners of 1.67 *dou* of land; middle peasants were holders of 2 *dou* of land. Middle peasants were subdivided into 3 categories, depending on their living standard. Rich peasants were holders of 5 *dou* of land who engaged in the following types of exploitation—leasing land, hiring wage laborers, and lending money. Those who had 5 *dou* of land but did not engage in exploitative activities and whose living standard was poor were defined as "bankrupt rich peasants." Landlords were those who held more than 5 *dou* of land, owned fish ponds,

bamboo groves, lumberyards, oil extraction mills, and large agricultural implements and engaged in the three types of exploitative activities stated above. Landlords who did not engage in exploitative activities were known as "bankrupt landlords." *P:Xinxian* 1985: 85.

53. The motto was, "Do not touch the middle, only even out both ends," meaning leave the holdings of middle peasants unchanged and take land from the rich and redistribute it to the poor.

54. "Guangshan xian de tudi geming yundong" (The revolutionary land movement in Guangshan county), n.d. *P:Fengbei* 13: 84–85.

55. Little 1989: 50.

56. "Guangshan xian de tudi geming yundong." *P:Fengbei* 13: 81–84.

57. "Xinxian tudi geming qingkuang jianshu." *P:Fengbei* 13: 92–93.

58. *P:Fengbei* 13: 92.

59. The Li Lisan line refers to the policy of armed insurrection of the urban proletariat in preparation for the new "rising tide" in the revolution. It was adopted after the GMD-CCP split in 1927 by Li Lisan, then secretary general of the CCP.

60. Wang Quanying 1982: 373.

61. "Xinxian tudi geming qingkuang jianshu." *P:Fengbei* 11: 93.

62. "Guangshan xian de tudi geming yundong." *P:Fengbei* 13: 86–87.

63. "Xinxian tudi geming qingkuang jianshu." *P:Fengbei* 13: 93.

64. Wang Quanying 1982: 275.

65. "Eyuwan tewei Zeng Zhongsheng gei zhongyang de baogao." *P:EYW* jia 2: 223.

66. Wang Quanying 1982: 376.

67. There was an initial debate within the party over the question of whether functionaries in the soviet government should be given a piece of land. Qu Qiubai decided later that cadres should receive a piece of the repartitioned land.

68. "Eyu bian geming weiyuanhui baogao." *P:EYW* jia 2: 60–63.

69. These state farms had a minimum of twenty *shi* of cropland. Sometimes state farms encroached on the farmland of middle peasants. Since soviet regulations strictly stipulated that government should not take away the property of the middle peasants, the soviet government had to find a way to persuade middle peasants to swap lands.

70. "Eyu bian tewei zonghe baogao." *P:EYW* jia 2: 193.

71. For instance, Li Mingrui, one of the Guangxi generals, staged a coup and retreated to Guangshui area. The 31st Division used the chance to retake some of the cities and expanded its force from 130 to 400. See Hou and Cai 1990: 80.

72. In the guerrilla war conducted by the 32nd Division in May 1929 around Shangcheng, the Red Army defeated the local militia and captured its arms. An enemy company under the leadership of Wu Yunshan defected to the Communist side, bringing with it 109 men and 99 firearms. Hou and Cai 1990: 105.

73. Hou and Cai 1990: 153; Wang Tianjiang et al. 1990: 288.

74. Hou and Cai 1990: 163.

75. In the taking of Yingshan county seat, for example, the Red Army killed and wounded 1,000 enemy soldiers and captured 1,000 weapons.

76. Wang Tianjiang et al. 1990: 304, 309. See Nov. 7, 1931, and June 1932.

77. Expenses for the Red Army were C$10,000 a month. The two special task

teams were able to raise C$3,000 a month. The remaining C$7,000 probably came from local Red Guards. See "E dongbei hongjun sanshi yi shi shiwei hui de baogao" (A report from the committee of the 31st Division of the Red Army in northeastern Hubei), June 1929. *P:EYW* jia 5: 118–20.

78. *P:EYW* jia 5: 118–20; also see "Eyu bian tewei zonghe baogao," *P:EYW* jia 2: 191.

79. *P:EYW* jia 2: 191.

80. *P:EYW* jia 2: 172.

81. *P:EYW* jia 2: 199.

82. Tilly 1978: 98–114.

83. "Eyu bian tewei guanyu chengli Eyu bian geming weiyuanhui jingguo baogao" (A report by the special committee of the Hubei-Henan border base on the setting up of the Hubei-Henan border revolutionary committee), early 1930. *P:EYW* jia 2: 60–68.

84. Only four extermination or encirclement campaigns actually took place in the Eyuwan area: the first was launched in December 1930, the second in February 1931. The third campaign planned never got off the ground. The fourth took place in July 1931, and the fifth in April 1934.

85. "Eyu bian tewei gei zhongyang de baogao, bian zi di yi hao" (A report to Party Central from the Hubei-Henan border special committee, bian no. 1), Jan. 10, 1930. *P:EYW* jia 2: 83–109.

86. The Communists were able to bring down dozens of enemy fortified strongholds in the area, seizing 400–500 rifles and capturing several hundred enemy soldiers. Through propaganda, they persuaded a few enemy troops to defect. But they were unable to capture much in the way of food supplies.

87. "Eyuwan tewei Zeng Zhongsheng gei zhongyang de baogao." *P:EYW* jia 2: 207–17.

88. Colburn 1989: xiv.

Chapter 5

1. Kataoka 1974: 1.

2. C. Johnson 1962: 2.

3. *P:dashiji*: 89, 98.

4. *P:kangzhan*: 50–55.

5. The Northwest Army consisted of remnants of Feng's Guominjun who had been defeated in the civil war by Chiang Kaishek in 1930.

6. According to Polanyi, we can "distinguish two forms of feudalism: the one, a progressive, healthy development in early society, connected with its territorial expansions; the other associated with the dissolution with empires. The first we call primitive feudalism; the second feudalism of decay." See Polanyi 1971: 141–47.

7. The stations the Japanese occupied were located on the Beiping-Hankou, Longhai, and Tianjin-Pukou railroads. The major cities under Japanese occupation were Kaifeng, Shangqiu, Xuzhou, Huaiyang, Zhoukou, and Bengbu.

8. For example, Japanese troops took over the county seats of Dangshan, Yongcheng, Xiayi, Zhecheng, Haoxian, and Woyang, all adjacent to the city of Shangqiu at the Henan-Anhui-Jiangsu border.

9. For information on Zhang Lanfeng, see *P:ZLF*.

10. The first offensive was conducted in support of the "Southern Anhui Incident" (Wannan shibian). Tant Enbo mobilized 200,000 soldiers from both the Nationalist forces and local auxiliary forces in a major assault on the Communist bases. The combat lasted three months. At the end, Communist forces were driven out of the area and the party moved eastward across the Tianjin-Pukou railroad. The second offensive was in 1943, when Li Xianzhou and 20,000 troops from his 92nd Army launched an attack against the Communists in southern Shandong and in the Hebei-Shandong-Henan (Ji-Lu-Yu) base. Li was defeated and fled to northern Anhui. In the third offensive, Zhang Gong and Geng Mingxuan mobilized their Rivereast Forward Army (Shuidong tingjin jun) to attack the Communists in the Sixth Region of the Ji-Lu-Yu base. Their army was decimated by the Communists, and Zhang and his officers were captured. The fourth offensive took place in October 1944, when Wang Yuwen attacked the New Fourth Army with his 28th Army and 20,000 local auxiliary forces. Wang was driven south of the Sha River by the Communists.

11. In Taikang county, the puppet troops stationed at Yu Township (Yu zhen) adjacent to the Japanese stronghold of Dragon Canal market town were an example. The Japanese recruited five bandit armed forces (*tufei wuzhuang*) to form an Anti-Communist Peace and National Salvation Army. See Duan Pei, "Sui-Qi-Tai duli tuan zenyang zhansheng liao diren" (How did the independent regiments in Suixian, Qixian, and Taikang win a victory against the enemies?). First published in *Fuxiao bao*, June 18, 1940. In *P:SQT* 2: 39–41.

12. Chen Zizhi, "Shuidong dulituan yijiu sisi nian gongzuo zongjie" (A comprehensive report on the Rivereast Independent Regiment in 1944), 1945? *P:SQT* 2: 230–31.

13. Zhu Guangren of Minquan county was a pro-CCP county defense commander. Zhang Shaoru of Gaocheng county was a "special CCP member." See Wang Feixiao, "Kang Ri zhanzheng shiqi Yuwansu qu di wei wan wuzhuang budui gaikuang" (A survey of the Japanese, puppet, and GMD troops in Yuwansu during the Sino-Japanese War), Aug. 24, 1983. *P:Shangqiu* 2: 139–54.

14. The Blueshirts (so named because they wore coarse blue cotton shirts) were members of a secret organization originally formed by Whampao cadets and encouraged by Chiang Kaishek. They adhered to a disciplinary code and were used by Chiang as his secret police. The CC Clique was the "organization clique" headed by brothers Chen Guofu and Chen Lifu. The Chens were responsible for building up the Central Political Institute and training civil servants in the Nationalist government.

15. For information on community forces, see Tan Youlin, "Yuwansu bianqu de qingkuang huibao" (Comprehensive report on conditions in the Henan-Anhui-Jiangsu border base), Aug. 1941. *P:YWS* 1: 18–44.

16. *P:SQT* 2: 191.

17. In addition to Tan Youlin's work, see Yin Mingdan, "Manhua Yudong lunxian de jinxi" (Brief report on the past and present of eastern Henan after the Japanese occupation), III *Minguo ribao* (Henan), Aug. 13, 1939. In *P:SQT* 2: 191.

18. When Communist troops passed through Haozhou, the Japanese were about to launch an attack on that county. The Haozhou county mayor pledged to raise some provisions for the Communist troops in return for their defense of

the county against the Japanese. After the Japanese army was driven out of the area by the Communists, the mayor intended to use the Red Spears to drive the Communists out. The Red Spears leader, however, informed the Communists of the mayor's intention so that the Communists could move out of the area. Peng Xuefeng, "Yuwansu bian sannian lai tongzhan fangzhen zhi jingyen jiaoxun" (Three years of experience and lessons in United Front tactics in the Henan-Anhui-Jiangsu border base), Dec. 3, 1940. *P:YWS* 1: 121.

19. Yin Mingdan, "Manhua Yudong lunxian de jinxi" III. In *P:SQT* 2: 191. The Communist policy toward the Red Spears was not one of elimination but one of appeasement. Most of the time, the Communists regarded them as purely local defense forces. Even though some Red Spears opposed them, the party tried its best to win them over. For instance, a group of Red Spears attacked the Communists' main force and was defeated. Traditionally, the winning army would massacre the villagers and the Red Spears and set fire to the village. But in order to win the Red Spears support, the Communists not only refrain from destroying the area, they sent a representative to attend the funeral of the Red Spears killed in the battle. Peng Xuefeng, "Wei jianshe tie de dangjun er douzheng" (Struggle to set up an iron party army), Oct. 21, 1940. *P:YWS* 1: 109.

20. Tan Youlin, "Yuwansu bianqu de qingkuang huibao." *P:Yuwansu* 1: 18–44. See also Yin Mingdan, "Manhua Yudong lunxian de jinxi." II *Minguo Ribao*, (Henan) Aug. 9, 1938. In *P:SQT* 2: 187.

21. Li Xueshun of Cao Mount in Fugou county was a graduate of the Japanese Military Officers Academy. He had been a regiment commander of the Northwest Army. Li Wenyuan (also known as Li Number One) of Qi county was a Red Spears chief and former bandit head. Zhang Shian of Sesame Hollow in Taikang county had served as secretary and later division adjutant of the Northwest Army. Zhang Jishi, also of Sesame Hollow in Taikang, was a battalion commander. Huang Xiangbin of Huang Village in Taikang had been an adjutant in the Northwest Army.

22. For example, Zhang Anshi of Sesame Hollow, the leader of the community forces of seven villages, had been a follower of Feng Yuxiang.

23. The leaders of the band included Huang Xiangbin, Huang Xiangjiu, and Huang Xiangxian, all obviously members of the Huang clan in Huang Village. Huang based his headquarters in nearby Cui Bridge Township and recruited his people from the surrounding villages.

24. For example, after the death of Zhang Jishi, his followers were led by Zhang Jichuan, and were reorganized into the "Peace Preservation Squad" of the twelfth zone of Henan.

25. Li Xueshun's force disintegrated and Li himself joined the puppet forces of Zhang Lanfeng and served as Zhang's division commander. Both Zhang and Li graduated from the Japanese Military Officers Academy. For Zhang Lanfeng, see Wang Xiangjiu 1980: 136–52.

26. For example, when Huang Xiangbin's forces grew from several hundred to about a thousand men, he took them across the county to Suixian. Local landlords resisted Huang's encroachment, brought in Japanese troops, and had him defeated. Huang Xiangbin was killed in the battle and two small segments of his troops fled back to Huang Village. For more information on the anti-Japanese guerrilla squads in this area, see Zhang Zhongheng 1983: 148–52.

27. "Peng Xuefeng bao Mao, Zhou, Ye dian: Muqian Yudong dake fazhan nidai de erqi jiaodao dui biye ji ke chudong" (A telegram from Peng Xuefeng to Mao Zedong, Zhou Enlai, and Ye Ting: We can mobilize and expand now, but should wait until after the graduation of the second session of the training unit), Sept. 17, 1938. *P:Zhugou*: 58–59.

28. Yin Mingdan, "Manhua Yudong lunxian de jinxi." II *Minguo ribao* (Henan), Aug. 9, 1939. See *P:SQT* 2: 187–88. An example of this type of joint defense battalion was the one operating in the Fourth District of Sui county, right next to the Japanese occupied region.

29. *Ji-Lu-Yu ribao*, May 30, 1945. In *P:SQT* 2: 98–99.

30. Zhu Lizhi was a native of Nantong, Jiangsu province. He received his education in economics and was very active in the underground Communist movement at Qinghua University. In April 1927, he became a member of the Chinese Communist Party. Arrested by the Guomindang in 1928, Zhu was not released from prison until April 1930. For the next five years, Zhu devoted his energy to organizing the anti-Japanese student movement in Shanghai and Beiping. In March 1935, he was transferred to Shaanbei and became the key central representative in carrying out the ultra-left rectification (or *sufan*) movement, in which he arrested Liu Zhidan and Gao Gang and executed 200 other Communist members. According to his biographer, he later regretted his action. During that time, he was also actively involved in the Shaanbei land reform movement.

In 1936, Zhu was ordered by Party Central to focus on army subversion work in Sian, with the 107th Division of Zhang Xueliang's Northeastern Army (Dongbei Jun) as the target. The army subversion work and the student national salvation movement promoted under his leadership in the "Work committee of the Chinese Communist Northeastern Army" might have had an impact on Zhang Xueliang's decision to place Chiang Kaishek under house arrest in the Sian Incident. Because of his experience in coalition work in the white zone, Zhu was invited to participate in a white zone work conference in Yenan in April 1937. There he devised a detailed plan for building up the guerrilla forces in Henan by incorporating bandits and using coalition politics to forge strong relations with the "enlightened gentry" and county governments in Henan. His plan called for utilizing legal means in this period to set up anti-Japanese forces in Henan.

In mid-July 1937, Zhu was ordered by the party to proceed to Red Army headquarters in Sanyuan county in Shaanxi to set up a training class for educating Henan party members in underground work in the white zone. At the end of August 1937, because of his close working relations with the Henanese, Zhu was dispatched to Kaifeng to assist the Communists in Henan in setting up a provincial committee. See Chen Mu and Zhang Wenjie, "Zhu Lizhi," in Zhonggong Henan shengwei dang shi gongzuo weiyuanhui and Henan Zhonggong dangshi renwu yanjiuhui 1987, 3: 19–47.

31. Zhu was given authority to oversee a broad area covering Henan, northwestern Anhui, and two border (Henan-Hubei and Jiangsu-Shandong) regions. At that time, he had 460 cadres under him. Henan was divided into south, north, central, east, and southeast sectors, each under a special party branch; there were also two municipal party branches in Kaifeng and Nanyang. See Chen and Zhang, "Zhu Lizhi" (n30).

32. Directly under the special branches were the centrally administered counties (*zhongxin xian*). Of the 22 counties in western Henan, 5 were designated as centrally administered. There were 3 centrally administered counties in eastern Henan. See Zhu Lizhi's "Yi nian lai de Henan gongzuo" (One year of work in Henan), 1938. In *P:shengwei*: 34–39. Zhu Lizhi was then the provincial party secretary.

33. See Liu Zijiu's "Henan gongzuo baogao" (Henan work report) in *P:shengwei*: 69. The report was given to the Central Committee on May 28, 1940, by Liu, head of the propaganda section in Henan and one of the provincial representatives from Henan attending the Seventh National People's Congress in Yenan at that time.

34. They were Zhu Lizhi, who set up a Henan cadre training class in Sanyuan in Shaanxi, and Liu Zijiu, the head of the work committee (*gong wei*), who also created a summer vacation membership training class in western Henan.

35. Zhu Lizhi, "Guanyu kang Ri zhanzheng shiqi de Henan shengwei" (The Henan provincial party at the time of the anti-Japanese War). In *P:shengwei*: 240. The section on the provincial party in Zhugou was written as reminiscence on June 11, 1958, and was published in the *Hongse Zhugou* (Red Zhugou).

36. Zhu Lizhi, "Yi nian lai de Henan gongzuo." *P:shengwei*: 35.

37. These figures were given by Zhu Lizhi in his work report to the Central Committee. *P:shengwei*: 22.

38. For details on the Henan Wartime Educational Work Promotion Squad, see *P:Kangzhan*: 27–34.

39. Zhu Lizhi, "Yi nian lai de Henan gongzuo." *P:shengwei*: 30.

40. Ren Ziheng, "Xin nan kang Ri fengbao—Yi Tan jia he ziwei dadui" (The anti-Japanese windstorm in southern Xinyang—A recollection of the self-defense regiment in Tan Family River). *P:Yu-E*: 268–85. Ren Ziheng was head of the political section of the "Southern Xinyang People's Anti-Japanese Self-Defense Regiment" at the time of the Sino-Japanese War.

41. Wei Gongzhi, "Guanyu Yunan wuzhuang gongzuo buchong baogao" (Supplementary report on the work of organizing armed forces in southern Henan), June 7, 1940. *P:Zhugou*: 106–18.

42. Ulmer 1971: 301. In the study, Ulmer distinguishes coalitions from cliques. A clique is perceived as a "persistently cohering group (or sub-group) organized around and reflecting long-range interests. It follows that a clique is identified by a value-consensus and end-orientation which coalition lacks."

43. During the third session of negotiation, the GMD special commissioner and the GMD-appointed county mayor of Queshan, fearful of an increase in Communist power in the area, attempted to arrest Zhou Junming, but their attempt failed.

44. Li Lin 1991, no. 3: 32–36.

45. Wang Tianjiang et al. 1990: 337–42.

46. See Peng Xuefeng's telegram to Teng Daiyuan, "Henan sheng wo dang lingdao xia de wuzhuang liliang qingkuang he fazhan gei sheng gongzuo yijian" (Personal view on military power under the party leadership and its development in Henan), June 9, 1938. *P:Zhugou*: 28. Peng Xuefeng was chief commander in Henan.

47. The militarists targeted included Wei Fenglou, Hu Xiaochu, Hou Xiangshan, and Qu Shenting.

48. Wang Qimei was a Hunanese who was educated in Beijing. After joining the Communist Party, Wang was placed in charge of army, worker, and student movements. At the outbreak of the Sino-Japanese War, he was dispatched by the Northern Bureau to serve as party secretary in centrally administered Xihua county. His official position was headmaster of the Communist-run Puli (a homophone of the Russian pronunciation of "proletariat") School. Assisting him in the Anti-Japanese National Salvation Training Class was Liu Zuofu, a Kangda graduate. Yang Juren 1985: 22.

49. *P:YWS* 1: 78–79, 84–89.

50. Shen Dongping was secretary of the east Henan Special Committee. He had been county party secretary of Xuchang. In early 1934, Shen came to Xihua, working undercover in the Communist-run Puli School. There he recruited four local elites into the party. In October 1936, with party approval, he set up an eastern Henan Special Committee in Xihua. The movement later expanded to include the neighboring counties of Huaiyang and Fugou. *P:kangzhan*: 45. At the outbreak of the war, there were two Special Committees in eastern Henan, one overseeing Xihua, Huaiyang, and Fugou, with Shen Dongping as secretary, and another in charge of Suixian, Qixian, and Taikang counties, with Wu Zhipu as secretary. Yang Juren 1985: 25, footnote.

51. *P:YWS* 1: 89.

52. Shen Dongping moved some of them to Suixian county and reorganized them into the East Henan Guerrilla Army.

53. Wang Qimei's army was a semipublic force based at the border of Qixian and Taikang counties. Wang came to the area with a couple of cadres. The party sent him 60 semiliterate party members. Other areas also supplied him with soldiers. Under his leadership, a student unit was formed, headed by an old cadre from the Eighth Route Army. Three-quarters of his troops were peasants. They possessed 160 rifles, 12 handguns, and 2 light machine guns. Half of these were modern weapons, the rest old-fashioned firearms. Xue Puruo, the district head of Huaiyang county, gave Wang a monthly subsidy of C$100. See *P:YWS* 1: 93–95.

54. After the Japanese attack and with the county inundated by floodwater, Xihua was abandoned and had no mayor. *P:YWS* 1: 89.

55. Wang Tianjiang et al. 1990: 261.

56. See *P:Zhugou*: 1–15.

57. Zhao Benren (Zhao Jinxian), "Guanyu Xinyang, Queshan, wuzhuang gongzuo baogao" (A report on military work in Xinyang and Queshan counties), Mar. 16, 1940. *P:Zhugou*: 89–90.

58. All of south and southwestern Henan was divided into two United Front zones: the western front (Tanghe, Nanyang, Zhenping, and Neixiang counties) was supervised by Liu Guanyi, and the eastern front (Queshan, Xinyang, Minggang, Zhumadian, Suiping, and Runan counties) was under Wang Enjiu. See Liu Guanyi, deputy chief of the United Front Committee in Zhugou, "Huiyi yi Zhugou wei zhongxin de tongzhan gongzuo" (Reminiscence on the United Front operation center at Zhugou), n.d. *P:Zhugou*: 293–97.

59. Li Mingzhong, a Northwest commander, also fled to southwestern Henan after the Japanese occupied eastern Henan. He might have acted as a go-between

in the negotiation, given the cordial relations the Communists had developed with Feng Yuxiang in the May 30th period.

60. Li Zijian, "Huiyi tong Dongbei jun Zhou Fucheng shi fasheng tongzhan guanxi de shishi" (A recollection of the historical facts of the alliance with Zhou Fucheng, commander of the Manchurian army), 1985. *P:Zhugou*: 175–80. Li Zijian was head of the propaganda department of the provincial party committee at the Hubei-Henan border at the time of the Sino-Japanese War.

61. Wei Gongzhi, "Guanyu Yunan wuzhuang gongzuo buchong baogao." *P:Zhugou*: 103–5. Wei Gongzhi was organization chief of the Henan provincial party at the time of the Sino-Japanese War.

62. Zhang Wangwu and Zhou Qingming, "Hongse jidi—Zhugou" (Red base—Zhugou), n.d. *P:Zhugou*: 185–86.

63. Communist guerrillas engaged in predatory activities too. By this time, the Communists had narrowed their attack targets. The new party policy changed from "Attack the local tyrants and divide their lands" (*da tuhao, fen tiandi*) to "Attack evildoers" (*da huaihuo*), meaning only outstandingly evil landlords and their bullies.

64. Wen Minsheng, "Huiyi zai Yunan de geming huodong" (A recollection of revolutionary activities in southern Henan), Nov. 5, 1983. *P:Zhugou*: 251–54. Wen was head of the political department of the Southern Henan Independent Regiment, and after 1949, governor of Henan.

65. For example, the Sixth Company of the independent regiment in the Eyuwan border area was headed by Liu Shiyao, a former bandit chief who brought with him 40 guns when he joined the Communist force in 1938, after the party recruited him under the United Front tactic. Zhang Qingping, "Eyuwan bianqu budui gongzuo baogao" (A report on the work of the troop in the Hubei-Henan-Anhui border area), Jan. 1938. *P:Zhugou*: 17.

66. Liu Kuangqi, "Huiyi Peng Xuefeng shoubian An, Duan tuan he zhengqu Xia tuan de qingkuang" (A recollection of how Peng Xuefeng reorganized the An Kexing-Duan Qixiang regiments and how he won over the Xia regiment), Nov. 1962. *P:Zhugou*: 298–301. Zhang Zhen, "Cong Linfen dao Zhugou" (From Linfen to Zhugou). *P:Zhugou*: 243–50. The article was written by Zhang in February 1980 in Beijing. Zhang was chief of staff in the Communists' Zhugou headquarters in 1938, and deputy chief of staff of the People's Liberation Army after 1949.

67. "Xinbian disi jun disi zhidui diba tuandui qishi" (Notice from the Eighth Regiment of the Fourth Detachment of the newly organized New Fourth Army). *Xinhua ribao*, Apr. 29, 1939. In *P:Zhugou*: 23.

68. For example, in Deng Village Town, Li Yaotang, the GMD-designated neighborhood pact chief, was asked by the Communists to win over a gang of 1,000 bandits by preaching to them about the Chinese tradition of social banditry. See Zhang Wangwu and Zhou Qingming, "Hongse jidi—Zhugou." *P:Zhugou*: 188–89.

69. There was a conflict of interest between Xu Jingxian, the head of the neighborhood pact (*lianbao zhuren*), and Luo Shili and Mao Xiyou, leaders of two bandit bands. The party formed an alliance with Luo and Mao in a move to eliminate Xu. Zhou Qingming, "Huiyi Zhugou wuzhuang baodong" (A recollection of armed insurrection in Zhugou), n.d. *P:Zhugou*: 205.

70. For example, in the Communist command center in the mountainous

area southwest of Zhugou, small groups of bandits often moved out of their lairs to disrupt the area. The Communists mobilized the armed forces in Zhugou and the peasant self-defense forces in two adjacent villages in a bandit suppression. See Zhang Wangwu and Zhou Qingming, "Hongse jidi—Zhugou." *P:Zhugou*: 194. For a detailed account, see Zhou Qingming, "Huiyi Zhugou wuzhuang baodong." *P:Zhugou*: 202–10.

71. Wen Minsheng, "Huiyi zai Yunan de geming huodong." *P:Zhugou*: 251.

72. Peng Xuefeng, "Muqian zai Henan yinggai zuoxie shenmo" (What we should do in Henan now), June 6, 1938. First published on June 14, 1938, in *Xinhua ribao*. See *LH:YWS*: 7.

73. Peng Xuefeng, "Pingyuan youji zhan de shiji jingyan" (The actual experience of fighting guerrilla war on the plain), May 30, 1939. First published on June 25, 1939, in *Balu jun junzheng zazhi* (The military administration magazine of the Eighth Route Army) 1, no. 6. See *LH:YWS*: 128–38. Conflicts between the Red Spears and Communist forces persisted into the Sino-Japanese War period. Some sectarian groups were incorporated into the puppet troops. After the fall of Luyi and Haoxian counties, Communist-controlled community forces were attacked by the Red Spears, resulting in the loss of a large number of rifles.

74. "Zhonggong Henan shengwei qiyue zhi bayue de gongzuo jihua" (The July-August work plan of the Henan provincial committee), 1938. *P:YWS* 1: 46.

75. Wu Zhipu, "Minzhu geming shiqi Henan dang de jianshe he kaizhan douzheng de yixie qingkuang" (A brief account of the party's construction and struggle in Henan in the democratic revolutionary period), Apr. 11, 1956. *P:SQT* 1: 68.

76. See "Zhonggong Yudong diwei baogao" (Eastern Henan local Communist Party report), 1940. *P:YWS* 1:78. When Communist cadres used the traditional rituals of "sworn brotherhood," they were praised by the party for being tactically skillful. Another Chinese term for "sworn brotherhood" was *jiebai ba xiongdi*. The rituals had not changed from the time of the Northern Expedition; they included incense burning, kowtowing to the patriarch, and drinking out of a shared cup filled with wine mixed with rooster blood. But in the war period, the fraternity oath was slightly different, often laced with nationalistic sentiment. For instance, "Share joys and sorrows. Unite and be moral. Fight the Japanese to the end. Always remain faithful. May heaven strike me down if I am disloyal." See Ren Ziheng, "Xin nan kang Ri fengbao." *P:Yu-E*: 272.

77. *P:Yu-E*: 272–73.

78. Wu Zhipu, "Kangzhan chuqi de Yudong douzheng" (Struggle in eastern Henan at the beginning of the Sino-Japanese War). In *LH:Zhanzheng*. This is probably part of Wu's 1956 biography.

79. Lu Weiping, "Jiuwang yundong zai Weichuan" (The national salvation movement in Weichuan county). *Feng Yu* (Windstorm) no. 27, May 8, 1938 (see *tongxun*, new dispatches). In *P:SQT* 2: 27–31.

80. "Zhonggong Yudong diwei wuzhuang gongzuo baogao" (A report of the military work of the local committee in eastern Henan), May 25, 1940. *P:YWS* 1: 91. The village pacts reportedly had many firearms in their possession. On community forces, see Tan Youlin, "Yuwansu bianqu de qingkuang huibao." *P:YWS* 1: 18–44.

81. Wen Qing, "Women shi zenyang ba nonghui zuzhi qilai de—Suixian tongxun" (How did we organize the peasant association? A dispatch from Suixian). First published on Apr. 9, 1938, in *Fengyu* (Windstorm) no. 24. See *P:SQT* 2: 22–25.

82. There was a group of defeated GMD soldiers in the town of Wagang, not far from Wu's native village. They were the men of Cao Fulin, commander of the GMD regular army (*zhongyang jun*). After they were defeated by the Japanese, the soldiers were trapped in the flood area. Wu sent a man to invite them to join the Communist forces. Later, when Wu's forces moved to Yangliu for a reorganization, the two platoons of defeated soldiers planned a mutiny. However, with the help of other Communist-controlled militia, Wu had them disarmed. The Communists gained 2 machine guns, 30 rifles, 40 hand grenades, and 4,000 rounds of ammunition. Yang Juren 1985: 33–34.

83. A group of twenty Japanese soldiers came to He Stockade to seize grain and livestock from the peasants. Wu's guerrilla fighters ambushed them in the village. Three Japanese soldiers were killed, and the Communists obtained some arms, ammunition, and a horse-drawn cart. They recovered from the Japanese 2,000 *jin* of wheat, 2 pigs, and 10 chickens. The Communists were using local defense not only to build their armed strength, but to promote an image as village defenders. Wu also led his guerrillas in an attack on Japanese puppet Zhang Xinzhen in Changgang township. Zhang was a member of the Guomindang CC Clique, assigned to guard the strongly fortified stockade town. The Communists besieged the town, cut off the water supply, and let it fall. They took 50 prisoners of war, 100 guns, and 5 horses. Yang Juren 1985: 39–40.

84. Zhu Lizhi, the party secretary, reported that Wu's three detachments were very loosely organized. Peng Xuefeng, a commander in the New Fourth Army, said that Wu's troops were composed partly of disbanded soldiers. Of the 4,000 men under his command, only 1,000 were reliable. See Zhu Lizhi's Aug. 9, 1938 report and Peng Xuefeng's Aug. 9, 1938 report. In *P:YWS* 1: 48, 59.

85. See Peng Xuefeng's Aug. 9, 1938 report. In *P:YWS* 1: 59.

86. Wu Zhipu, "Kanzhan chuqi de Yudong douzheng." In *LH:Zhanzheng*. *P:YWS* 1: 48, 59. *P:SQT* 1: 68; 2: 22–25.

87. In Big Cao village, the family defense force was commanded by brothers Li Dalun and Li Dazhou; in Big Zhao village, the force was headed by Zhao Jinxian's family; and in the market town of Xinan, the Communists set up family forces in the households of Wang Guozhi (a district party secretary), Li Qigyun, and Li Jingrang. Military drills were conducted at Big Cao village.

88. Niu Desheng, "Daru Queshan jingchaju" (Infiltrate the Queshan police bureau), n.d. *P:Zhugou*: 282–92. Niu Desheng had been working under Zhao Jinxian in the Queshan police bureau. According to Niu, Zhao, formerly a deputy regiment commander under Feng Yuxiang, was instructed by the party to go back to his village to set up a community force in accordance with the party policy of conducting mass movement at the grass-roots level.

89. *P:Zhugou*: 284.

90. Wang Jingrui and Pan Youge, "Queshan xian renmin kang Ri youji dadui de dansheng he chengzhang" (The beginning and development of the Queshan county anti-Japanese guerrilla squad), Oct. 15, 1981. In *P:Zhugou*: 262–67.

Wang was the county party secretary in Zhugou and Pan was an anti-Japanese propagandist in the same area.

91. Yang Juren 1985: 354, footnote 1.

92. "Geng Wu Liu panbian shijian" (The revolt of Geng Yunzhai, Wu Xinrong, and Liu Ziren), n.d. *P:kangzhan*: 178–81.

93. Li Diping, "Guanyu Liu, Geng, Wu wuzhuang panbian de huiyi" (A recollection of the revolt of Liu Zhiren, Geng Yuzhai, and Wu Xinrong), Sept. 1983. *P:YWS kang Ri*: 102–18. "Geng Wu Liu panbian shijian." *P:kangzhan*: 178–81.

Chapter 6

1. For the impact of war on society, see Allmand 1973; J. Johnson 1964; Bramson and Goethals 1964; Wright 1964.

2. C. Johnson 1962.

3. See C. Johnson 1962: 1–30.

4. *LH:huoYu*: 160–62.

5. For example, 300 were killed in the northeastern corner of Huaxian on March 29, 1938; 200 young men were shot in Zhongshan Park in the city of Jiaozuo on April 5, 1938; and 4,500 died in the takeover of Xunxian on March 29, 1938. Chen Chuanhai 1983: 60–62.

6. Chen Chuanhai 1983: 60–62.

7. The Japanese arrested 53 persons in Huaiyang county, 22 of whom were buried alive in the yard of the Girls' Normal School. The rest became crippled after having been tortured by troops. *Xinhua ribao*, Mar. 28, 1939. In *LH:huoYu*: 100.

8. Twenty *li* east of Qi county, 1,000 women were herded into a temple and raped. *Henan Minguo ribao*, June 10, 1938. In *LH:huoYu*: 96.

9. Old county gazetteers have recently been compiled and republished in the People's Republic of China.

10. Wang Futang, "Ri kou zai Shangqiu xian Lao Nanguan da tusha ji shi" (An eyewitness account of the massacre by Japanese bandits at Old South Gate in Shangqiu county), Aug. 4, 1985. *P:Shangqiu* 2: 128–30.

11. When the Japanese occupied Huting Village, one *bao* head was shot, another buried alive. Two other *bao* heads managed to escape, but their savings and belongings were confiscated by the Japanese. A neighborhood pact office messenger was arrested. A guard was cut into three pieces by a Japanese soldier with a fodder chopper. "Xin si jun liu zhidui zhengzhi bu gao gejie minzhong shu" (A public notice from the political department of the Sixth Detachment of the New Fourth Army), May 16, 1940. *LH:YWS*: 62.

12. *Henan Minguo ribao*, June 17, 1938. In *LH:huoYu*: 93.

13. *Henan Minguo ribao*, Jan. 31, 1941. In *LH:huoYu*: 108.

14. *Henan Minguo ribao*, Aug. 15, 1938, Jan. 31, 1941. In *LH:huoYu:* 95, 108.

15. According to company reports, Mitsui exported seven million *shi* of rice from China in 1939, and nine million *shi* in 1940. Zhao Boyan 1985.

16. In 1941, one allotment for Fengtai, a flooded area, was C$3,200, four mules (each worth C$1,000), and three donkeys (worth C$800 each). The grain tax was levied by land (3.5 *jin* or 1.75 kilograms per *mu*). Each household was

required to give the Japanese four *sheng* (four liters) of husked rice. Altogether, the allotment for the neighborhood was worth C$20,000. See "Xin si jun di si shi zhengzhi bu gao Wobei minzhong shu" (A public notice from the political department of the Fourth Division of the New Fourth Army), Apr. 13, 1941. First published on the same date in *Fuxiao bao*. See *LH:YWS* 1985: 92.

17. Adults received less than a *jin* (ten *liang*) of grain a day. Children under 6 and adults over 56 were given only a few *liang*. Each individual could purchase from the cooperative four *liang* of kerosene a month and five matches a day.

18. *Xinhua ribao* (Chungking), June 17, 1943. In *P:SQT* 2: 49. There were other exchanges: two peanut cakes for one *mu* of land, or four catties of yam leaves for a catty of wheat. See Li Zhongyi, "Zai zhandou zhong chengzhang de Yu dong" (East Henan, growing up during the war). *Ji-Lu-Yu ribao*, Feb. 25, 1945. In *P:SQT*: 94.

19. The Japanese acquired their cotton from Zhengzhou (Henan), Jinan (Shandong), and Tianjin (Hebei) markets. The price they paid was C$38 a *dan*; the market price then (in the autumn of 1938) was C$65. In 1942, the price they paid for wheat was C$27.85, the market price C$45. Zhao Boyan 1985.

20. For example, Huidefeng Fabrics in Sui county folded once the Japanese started to charge them several hundred dollars a month in taxes.

21. *Xinhua ribao* (Chungking), July 25, 1938. In *P:SQT* 2: 46.

22. *P:SQT* 2: 41–43.

23. *Xinhua ribao*, Mar. 7, 1945. In *LH:huoYu*: 246.

24. There were provincial garrison surcharges, county garrison surcharges, local surtaxes, and "temporary business" taxes. *Jiefang ribao*, June 19, 1943. In *LH:huoYu*: 244.

25. *Xinhua ribao* (Chungking), Apr. 8, 1941. In *P:SQT* 2: 48.

26. *LH:huoYu*: 243.

27. In Wu'an county, each neighborhood was mandated to deliver 300 catties of iron and 200 catties of steel. *Xinhua ribao* (Chungking), June 17, 1943. In *P:SQT* 2: 49.

28. In February 1939, wealthy leaders in Kaifeng were beaten and executed by the Japanese for refusing payment. The entire business community in Bo'ai county was locked up until they paid their taxes. Li and Jiang 1987: 61.

29. *LH:huoYu*: 211.

30. *Xinhua ribao*, Jan. 28, 1938. In *P:SQT* 2: 44–45.

31. Wang Tianjiang et al. 1990: 360.

32. On July 4, 1938, the Nationalist government called upon every person in the nation to donate a day's wages for the relief of flood victims. On July 18, it informed four counties in the inundated area that the government intended to resettle 100,000 flood victims in Huanglong shan in Shaanxi province. It also relocated 5,000 victims to Deng county in southwestern Henan. The Nationalists claimed they had spent C$255,583 on rebuilding the dike and C$200,000 on relief. Obviously, this government action was not enough to cope with a man-made disaster of that magnitude. Wang Tianjiang et al. 1990: 349–56.

33. According to the statistics given by the Nationalist publication *Henan Tongji yuekan* (Henan statistics monthly), the population of the twenty counties in the Huangfan district flood area in 1936 was 6,619,658, but by 1946, it had gone down to 5,368,643. Within that period, five counties reported a com-

bined increase of 244,121 persons, while fifteen counties registered a combined drop of 1,495,136, a total decrease of 1,251,015. See Zhao Boyan 1985: 303.

34. The 1939 flood caused a famine in 85 counties. It destroyed 1,310,000 homes and claimed 12,272 lives. Of the total of 6.8 million victims, more than 4.5 million sought government relief. In 1942, Nationalist statistics reported that only 10–20 percent of regular crop production was attained because of flooding; shortages of food caused 1.5 million persons to die of starvation and 3 million victims to flee to other provinces. The 1943 famine accounted for 3 million deaths, 2 million refugees, and 15 million people starving. See Zhao Boyan 1985: 304.

35. *Fugou xianzhi* 1986.

36. *Shenqiu xianzhi* 1987: 119.

37. *LH:huoYu*: 60–80.

38. Deng Zihui, "Zai Huaibei gaogan hui shang de fayan, jielu" (A talk at the high-ranking cadre conference in Huaibei, excerpt), June 1943. *P:YWS* 1: 334.

39. Peng Xuefeng, "Pingyuan youji zhan de shiji jingyan" (The actual experience of fighting guerrilla war on the plain), May 30, 1939. First published on June 25, 1939, in *Balu jun junzheng zazhi* (The military administration magazine of the Eighth Route Army) 1, no. 6. See *LH:YWS*: 128–38.

40. Peng Xuefeng explained the maneuvers in detail. Short, swift thrusts: sudden unexpected assaults on the enemy at dawn or dusk, or during stormy nights. Back thrust: an abrupt swing around to catch the enemy off guard, requiring constant breaking up of the force into smaller bands and reassembling for concerted attacks. Concerted assaults: avoiding the strong and attacking the soft targets, launching an assault when the enemy is tired, weakening the enemy by destroying their houses, fortified strongholds, and command posts. Deception: making a feint to the east and attacking from the west, using flags, sound, and firecrackers to create a smoke screen; employing "sparrow warfare," that is, conducting rapid movements of small guerrilla bands to give the impression of a large formation. Mislead the enemy by going around in circles; ambush the enemy, first luring him into the base or the mountain and onto unfamiliar terrain; bypass close enemy forces and attack distant ones, giving one's own forces time to recuperate, regroup, and retrain. Peng Xuefeng, "Youji zhanshu de jige jiban zuozhan yuanze" (A few basic fighting principles in guerrilla tactics), July 7, 1938. *P:Zhugou*: 33–53. This comes from the outlines of a lecture given by Peng Xuefeng on that date.

41. See *P:Zhugou*: 33–53 and Atkinson 1981: 120–43.

42. The "Southern Anhui Incident" refers to the military conflict between the New Fourth Army and the Nationalist forces in Jingxian (Anhui) in early January 1941. In that incident the Nationalist troops decimated an entire contingent of the Communist army, and Commander Ye Ting was taken prisoner.

43. Zhang Zhen, "Yuwansu kang Ri genjudi zong shu" (A summary of the Yuwansu anti-Japanese base), Apr. 14, 1983. *P:YWS* 1: 6–8.

44. The first zone was Kaifeng and its vicinity, the second Shangqiu and nearby counties, and the third was on the Anhui-Jiangsu border.

45. Peng Xuefeng and Deng Zihui, "San ge yue fan wan douzheng zhong di si shi gaikuang" (The situation of the Fourth Division of the New Fourth Army in the anti-GMD struggle), Dec. 31, 1941. *P:YWS* 1: 167–68. Originally this was

part of a lengthy report entitled "Si shi gongzuo zongjie baogao" (A comprehensive report on the work of the Fourth Division) submitted by Peng and Deng.

46. *P:YWS* 2: 171

47. Peng and Deng, "San ge yue fan wan douzheng zhong di si shi gaikuang." *P:YWS* 1: 159–79.

48. Chen Yi, "Xin si jun di si shi fanwan zhandou zongjie" (A summary of the anti-GMD struggle of the Fourth Division of the New Fourth Army), 1942. *P:YWS* 1: 186.

49. According to Peng Xuefeng, the Communists troops not only were able to fight a guerrilla war but began to adapt themselves to mobile warfare in the three months of fighting the GMD. He insisted that the quality of the troops greatly improved and the commanders began to pick up the skill of planning and organizing a campaign. One problem, he said, that worked against them was the commanders' indecisiveness as to whether to fight the enemy or retreat from an area. Peng Xuefeng, "San ge yue lai junshi douzheng jiantao" (An examination of the military struggle in the last three months), May 20, 1941. *P:YWS* 1: 123–27.

50. Peng and Deng, "San ge yue fan wan douzheng zhong di si shi gaikuang." *P:YWS* 1: 178.

51. Zhang Zhen, "Yuwansu kang Ri genjudi zong shu." *P:YWS* 1: 9.

52. Deng Zihui, "Guanyu si shi san nian lai zai Yuwansu bianqu douzheng zongjie, jielu" (A comprehensive report on the struggle of the Fourth Division of the New Fourth Army in the Yuwansu border area in the past three years), July 1941. *P:YWS* 1: 129–30. This was originally a report given by Deng when representing the Central Plain Bureau in a cadre meeting.

53. For the Hundred Regiments Offensive, see C. Johnson 1962: 56–59; Beijing shifan xueyuan lishi xi Zhongguo jinxiandai shi jiaoyanshi 1985, 2: 590–91. There is a discrepancy in the number of soldiers and regiments employed by the Communists in this campaign. According to Johnson, it was 400,000 troops and 115 regiments, but the Communist source gives 300,000 troops and 105 regiments.

54. *P:YWS* 2: 171.

55. Peng Xuefeng, "Zai Huaibei Suwan bianqu di er jie canyi hui shang de junshi gongzuo baogao, jielu" (A report on the military in the second consultative conference in the Huaibei Suwan border region), Oct. 14, 1942. *P:YWS* 1: 214–39.

56. It was reported that the Japanese vehicles could travel only eight *li* per hour because of Communist destruction of roads.

57. Peng Xuefeng, "Sanshi san tian fan saodang zhanyi shulue" (A brief account of 33 days of the anti-mop-up campaign), Feb. 13, 1943. *P:YWS* 1: 257–71.

58. Wen Minsheng, "Huiyi zai Yunan de geming huodong" (A recollection of revolutionary activities in southern Henan), Nov. 5, 1983. *P:Zhugou*: 252.

59. *P:YWS* 2: 272.

60. *P:YWS* 2: 274, 275.

61. Peng Xuefeng, "Sanshi san tian fan saodang zhanyi shulue." *P:YWS* 1: 273–75.

62. *P:YWS* 2: 275.

63. "Zhonggong Huaibei qu dangwei guanyu zhunbei xin saodang zhong jianshao renli wuli sunshi de zhishi" (A directive from the Huaibei regional

party committee on preparation for a new mop-up campaign as a move to reduce the loss of manpower and materials), Dec. 30, 1942. *P:YWS* 1: 242–45.

64. See the appendix in Peng Xuefeng, "Sanshi san tian fan saodang zhanyi shulue." *P:YWS* 1: 281.

65. *P:YWS* 1: 257–81.

66. *P:YWS* 1: 277.

67. *P:SQT* 2: 5.

68. *P:SQT* 2: 5–6.

69. Chen Zizhi, "Shuidong duli tuan yijiu xisan nian gongzuo baogao" (River-east Independent Regiment work report), 1943. *P:SQT* 2: 197–221.

70. Of these 166 strongholds, Japanese forces controlled only 18, and the puppet forces 148.

71. *P:SQT* 2: 197–202.

72. Wang Yanzhang 1984: 74–78.

73. This was typical in such places as New Village (Xin zhuang) and Hu Village, both devastated by the militarists, or Ma village (a bandit lair near county borders that was used as a base for the New Fourth Army). New Village was raided by the "special commissioner" seven times before Communist troops arrived.

74. When Communist forces passed Nie Village, *baojia* heads came out to welcome them, offered them meat, and begged them to drive out the troops of the "special commissioner," who had reportedly sent a 50-man force to the village to obtain meat and wine from villagers. The *jia* head in the village had been arrested by the GMD army. In the vicinity of Minzhao Village, local peopled offered Communist troops 100 cash and food to entice them to help build a joint defense force for the purpose of defending villagers against bandits and local militarists.

75. The gentry were most willing to form house-watching squads, but they were apprehensive of giving them a Communist-sounding name. Most of them had families and properties in the village and were afraid that such a name would attract the attention of GMD troops and make them targets of attacks.

76. If villagers asked "Are there two of you?" the password from the Communists was "Three." If villagers asked "Is that my elder brother?" the password was "Younger brother." (These are actual passwords the Communists used to enter villages.)

77. The family would provide the fighters with food, usually yams, wheat bran, carrots, sometimes cotton seed buns. Occasionally, when troops stayed at the heart of the base, which was relatively free from enemy disruption and where peasants were able to produce more food, the soldiers could have a meal with meat. Sun Weihe, "Sun Weihe riji" (Sun Weihe's diary), Nov. 14, 1942 to Dec. 31, 1942. In *P:SQT* 2: 303–22.

78. Some villages, such as Ma village, refused to join the Communist collective defense program. These villages were probably headed by pro-GMD elite.

79. For example, in Cypress Stockade (Bai zhai), a cadre beat up a peasant for refusing to provide him with a cart for transport. Although Cypress Stockade was already under Communist influence—the party had employed the United Front tactic to form an alliance with local power holders—this rash action aroused a great deal of local resentment. The party lost the support of the village

and as a result troop movement was greatly delayed. The Communists also had the potential to mobilize the residents of Qibu Village, an area devastated by bandit and military attacks, but their high-handed extraction of two items, oil and salt, turned the people against them. Although the party had issued an order forbidding such extraction, it found it virtually impossible to prevent cadres from taking such basic necessities from the people.

80. For example, in Daxing Village, a village close to the roadway and devastated by war, as indicated by Sun.

81. The types of fighting engaged in by the Rivereast Independent Regiment in 1943 included offensive assaults (57), skirmishes (15), surprise attacks (21), defensive battles (24), enemy attacks (13), ambushes (5), pursuit attacks (7), and interceptions (4), a total of 167. See Chen Zizhi, "Shuidong duli tuan yijiu sisan nian gongzuo baogao." *P:SQT* 1:209.

82. *P:YWS* 1: 200.

83. For example, in the confrontation in Zhangchang Village, the enemy destroyed a third of the village's crop.

84. *P:SQT* 2: 202.

85. *P:SQT* 2: 216.

86. Xie Shengkun, "Guanyu si shi de gongji gongzuo" (The work of military provisioning for the Fourth Division of the New Fourth Army), June 30, 1942. *P:YWS* 1: 199–201.

87. *P:SQT* 2: 225.

88. Chen Zizhi, "Shuidong duli tuan yijiu sisan nian gongzuo baogao." *P:SQT* 2: 218–19.

89. This comes from a survey of 128 cadres above the rank of company and regiment commander. The survey indicated the percentage of cadres guilty of these offenses: beating and scolding people (10.8 percent); requesting leave (18 percent); insisting on retraining (6.3 percent); saying things in an irresponsible manner (28.8 percent); exhibiting strong familism (16.2 percent); being suspected of corruption (6.3 percent); being politically unreliable (9 percent); defecting to the enemy (4.5 percent); getting married without informing the party (12.6 percent); and executing people without permission from the party (27 percent). *P:SQT* 2: 218–19.

90. The following is a survey conducted by the army of cadres above the rank of company and battalion commander. The total number surveyed was 90. Of the military leadership, 24 percent were literate, 59 percent could read a newspaper, and 14 percent were illiterate. Twenty percent of the cadres were recruited before the war, 79 percent after the war; 84 percent were party members and 16 percent nonmembers. Thirty-four percent were young men, 63 percent middle-aged, and 2 percent older; 54 percent were Henanese, 37 percent were natives of North China, and 9 percent were recruited from southeastern China. Thirty-seven percent had no training at all and 59 percent had some training. *P:SQT* 2: 216.

91. For example, a cadre by the name of Hu asked the party for C$15 for intelligence gathering. Others requested that the party solve their families' food problem before they would work. In some cases, the quality and the amount of work cadres would render were dependent on the amount of reward they obtained. *P:SQT* 2: 219.

92. *P:SQT* 2: 196–221.

93. Wang Yanzhang, "Dang zai Sui Qi Tai diqu de geming douzheng zongshu" (A general description of the Communist revolutionary struggle in the Sui-Qi-Tai area), n.d. *P:SQT* 2: 8–9.

94. *P:SQT* 2: 225.

95. *P:SQT* 2: 228.

96. *P:SQT* 2: 8.

97. Chen Zizhi reported that 80 percent of the battles fought in 1944 were offensive warfare. Chen Zizhi, "Shuidong duli tuan yijiu sisi nian gongzuo zongjie" (A summary of the work of the Rivereast Independent Regiment in 1944), n.d. *P:SQT* 2: 234.

98. See the detailed report on the Hediling campaign submitted by the command headquarters of the twelfth military zone in "Yijiu sisi nian Shuidong diqu zhandou xiangbao yu zhanli zongjie" (Detailed report of campaigns and summaries of examples of battles in the Rivereast area in 1944), n.d. *P:SQT* 2: 254–58.

99. Six of these raids were conducted by GMD forces and seven by the puppets. See "Shuidong duli tuan yijiu sisi nian dashiji" (Major events of the Rivereast Independent Regiment in 1944), n.d. *P:SQT* 2: 239–44.

100. Chen Zizhi, "Shuidong duli tuan yijiu sisi nian gongzuo zongjie." *P:SQT* 2: 226–27.

101. *P:SQT* 2: 224.

102. *P:SQT* 2: 231.

103. C. Johnson 1962: 158.

104. Wu Zhipu, "Luxi diqu de qunzhong gongzuo" (Mass work in the railroad-west area), 1945. *P:YWS* 1: 461.

105. Weber 1976: 243.

106. Duan Pei, "Zhandou zhuo de Sui-Qi-Tai" (The battling Suixian, Qixian, and Taikang counties), first published in *Fuxiao bao*, Jan. 18, 1940. *LH:YWS*: 351.

107. "Jinggao Yuwansu bianqu fulao xiongdi jiemei shu" (A letter respectfully reporting to our elders, brothers, and sisters in the Yuwansu border area), first published in *Fuxiao bao*, Aug. 23, 1944. *LH:YWS*: 124.

108. For Communist propaganda methods, see *LH:YWS*: 34–127.

109. There are similar corporate community institutions serving as an organizational basis for local mobilization and insurrection in Japan. These are the villages (*mura*), the official unit of taxation. But in the Japanese case, the relationship within these institutions is less paternalistic and less of a patron-client relationship. See Vlastos 1986.

110. Little 1989: 179.

Chapter 7

1. Yung-fa Chen 1986; Levine 1987.

2. Wright 1964: 238–56; Leiden and Schmitt 1968: 55–75, 170–75.

3. See Liu Ruilong's report of the second meeting of the assembly of the Huaibei border region, "Huaibei Suwan bianqu san nian lai de zhengfu gongzuo, jielu" (Three years of government work in the Jiangsu-Anhui border area in the Huaibei region, excerpt), Oct. 1942. *P:Anhui* 2: 102.

4. See Lei Ming's report, "Suwan bianqu caijing gongzuo zongjie" (A comprehensive report on financial and economic work in the Jiangsu-Anhui border area), Nov. 16, 1941. *P:Anhui* 2: 45, 51. The Communists had to set up an inspection station network, reinforced with armed guards, to eliminate the problem of salt smuggling.

5. Liu Chongguan, "Huaibei Suwan bianqu yijiu sisan nian de shengchan jianshe zongjie" (A summary of production and reconstruction in the Suwan border base in Huaibei in 1943), Nov. 5, 1944. *P:Anhui* 2: 242. One *qing* is equal to 100 *mu*.

6. See Hu Keming's report, "Siyang xian de shengzhan jiuhuang yu cungeng yundong" (The famine relief and spring planting movement in Siyang county), Apr. 18, 1942. *P:Anhui* 2: 85.

7. See Zhao Min's report, "Huaibei Suwan bianqu xingzheng gongshu zhishu qu ershi wu tian de liangshi gongzuo zongjie" (A comprehensive report submitted by the administrative office of the Suwan border base in the Huaibei region of 25 days of tax grain work in the directly administered area), Nov. 1, 1941. *P:Anhui* 2: 28.

8. In one area in Siyang county, total wasteland was 33,995 *mu*. Of this, 68.9 percent was virgin land and 31.1 percent was cultivable wasteland; 36.9 percent was public and 63.1 percent was private land. Hu Keming, "Siyang xian de shengzhan jiuhuang yu cungeng yundong." *P:Anhui* 2: 88.

9. *P:Anhui* 2: 87–88.

10. Zhao Min, "Huaibei Suwan bianqu xingzheng gongshu zhishu qu ershi wu tian de liangshi gongzuo zongjie." *P:Anhui* 2: 28.

11. "Huaibei Suwan bianqu xingzheng gongshu guanyu fanghan jiuhuang de jinji xunling" (Emergency order on drought prevention and famine relief issued by the administrative office of the Jiangsu-Anhui border area of the Huaibei region), June 11, 1945. *P:Anhui* 2: 291.

12. According to statistics gathered by the Nationalist land committee, in Huoqiu county, there were thirteen households owning between 25,000 and 80,000 *mu* of land. In Wuhe county, there were six landlords with more than 3,000 *mu*; in Sixian county, four households with holdings between 2,000 and 25,000 *mu*; in Lingbi county, three households with 6,000 to 15,000 *mu*; in Mengcheng county, four households with 10,000 *mu*; in Woyang county, four households with holdings between 5,000 and 10,000 *mu*; in Haoxian county, seven households with holdings between 1,000 and 4,000 *mu*; in Taihe county, one household with 10,000 *mu*; and in Fuyang county, sixteen households with holdings between 3,000 *mu* and 10,000 *mu*. See Zhu Chaonan et al. 1985: 6.

13. Zhao Min, "Huaibei Suwan bianqu xingzheng gongshu zhishu qu ershi wu tian de liangshi gongzuo zongjie." *P:Anhui* 2: 30.

14. The type of tenancy arrangement in which the rentier provide the seeds, agricultural implements, and fertilizer was known as *daizhong di* (land cultivated on behalf of the landlord). See "Huaibei Suwan bianqu tudi zudian tiaoli" (Regulations on tenancy in the Jiangsu-Anhui border area of the Huaibei region), promulgated on May 27, 1943. In *P:Anhui* 2: 121–25.

15. "Huaibei qu dangwei guanyu cungeng shengchan yundong de buchong

zhishi" (Supplementary directive on the spring planting production movement issued by the party committee of the Huaibei region), Mar. 25, 1944. *P:Anhui* 2: 190.

16. "Huaibei Suwan bianqu xiuzheng gaishan renmin shenghuo ge zhong banfa" (Various methods of improving the people's livelihood in the Jiangsu-Anhui border area in the Huaibei region), Dec. 25, 1941. *P:Anhui* 2: 75. This document was first published by the Huaibei administrative office in *Zhengfu gongzuo* (Government work) no. 5.

17. *P:Anhui* 2: 72–73.

18. *P:Anhui* 2: 208.

19. "Huaibei bianqu de er jie caizheng huiyi jueyi" (Resolution of the second financial meeting of the Huaibei border region), Nov. 4, 1943. *P:Anhui* 2: 154.

20. "Huaibei Suwan bianqu xingzheng gongshu guanyu tudi fucha wenti de xunling" (An order on the question of the land resurvey issued by the administrative office of the Jiangsu-Anhui border area of the Huaibei region), May 28, 1944. *P:Anhui* 2: 208.

21. See Liu Chongguang's report, "Huaibei Suwan bianqu yijiu sisan nian de shengchan jianshe zongjie." *P:Anhui* 2: 235.

22. See Liu Ruilong's report, "Huaibei Suwan bianqu san nian lai de zhengfu gongzuo, jielu." *P:Anhui* 2: 105.

23. Zhao Min, "Huaibei Suwan bianqu xingzheng gongshu zhishu qu ershi wu tian de liangshi gongzuo zongjie." *P:Anhui* 2: 34. See also An Ming's report, "Shixing zhengliang zhengce de jiantao" (An evaluation of the implementation of the tax policy), Nov. 1, 1941. *P:Anhui* 2: 38.

24. Hu Keming, "Siyang xian de shengzhan jiuhuang yu cungeng yundong." *P:Anhui* 2: 85.

25. Liu Ruilong, "Huaibei Suwan bianqu san nian lai de zhengfu gongzuo, jielu." *P:Anhui* 2: 109.

26. Yang Juren 1985: 205–10; Zhu Chaonan et al. 1985: 27.

27. *LH:YWS* 1985: 1–6; Zhang Zhen, "Yuwansu kang Ri genjudi zongshu" (A comprehensive narrative of the Henan-Anhui-Jiangsu anti-Japanese base), Apr. 14, 1983. *P:YWS* 1: 1–17.

28. Liao Yuan, "Suwan bianqu di caijing gongzuo" (Financial and economic work in the Jiangsu-Anhui border region), Nov. 16, 1941. *P:Anhui* 2: 56.

29. Liu Ruilong, "Huaibei Suwan bianqu san nian lai de zhengfu gongzuo, jielu." *P:Anhui* 2: 95–97. Also see Lei Ming, "Suwan bianqu caijing gongzuo zongjie" (*P:Anhui* 2: 42–54), and Zhu Chaonan et al. 1985: 33–37.

30. The "crack troops and simplified administration" program was a reform carried out by the CCP during the Sino-Japanese War. The program downsized the Communist Party, administration, and army, especially administrative and non-combat army personnel. Such streamlining was necessary because of dwindling resources. The administrative office went through three stages of streamlining the government. The second stage cut 72 percent of the functionaries, saving 16,500 *jin* of grain, 33,000 *jin* of fodder, and C$4,262 in military pay. Zhu Chaonan et al. 1985: 49.

31. Liu Chongguang, "Huaibei Suwan bianqu yijiu sisan nian de shengchan jianshe zongjie." *P:Anhui* 2: 231–32.

32. Liao Yuan, "Suwan bianqu de caijing gongzuo." *P:Anhui* 2: 55–64.

33. See Liu Yuzhu's report, "Huaibei Suwan bianqu qiuji gongliang dongyuan de renwu ji qi zhengce, jielu" (The duties and policy of cadre mobilizers for autumn tax collection in the Jiangsu-Anhui border area in the Huaibei region), Oct. 1, 1941. *P:Anhui* 2: 6. See also Lei Ming, "Suwan bianqu caijing gongzuo zongjie." *P:Anhui* 2: 46.

34. Liao Yuan, "Suwan bianqu de caijing gongzuo." *P:Anhui* 2: 55. Liu Ruilong, "Qieshi zhengdun liangzheng baozheng junxu minshi" (Effectively reorganize the grain tax to guarantee military provisions and public food supply), Nov. 4, 1943. *P:Anhui* 2: 138.

35. From 1939–41, the Communists were collecting land taxes in cash. The tax rates were very low: eight, ten, and twelve cents per *mu*. In 1941, the party switched to payment in kind. The land tax was about 2 percent of yield. In the Huaibao area, total tax revenue was 20,000 *shi*.

36. For the families of the New Fourth Army and the independent battalions, the reductions were 20 percent for upper households and 50 percent for middle and lower households. For families of the local militia and government functionaries, it was 10 percent for upper households, 20 percent for middle households, and 50 percent for lower households.

37. There were three types of payment: in a single crop, for example large sorghum; in two crops, for example half large and half small sorghum; and in three crops, for example a third each in large and small sorghum and beans. The type of payment varied depending on the type of crop produced in the locality.

38. Liu Yuzhu, "Huaibei Suwan bianqu qiuji gongliang dongyuan de renwu ji qi zhengce, jielu." *P:Anhui* 2: 5–16.

39. Meng Dongbo, "Zhengliang gongzuo zhong de liang ge wenti" (Two problems in grain tax collection work), Oct. 16, 1941. *P:Anhui* 2: 23.

40. "Huaibei Suwan bianqu xingzheng gongshu guanyu tudi fucha wenti de xunling." *P:Anhui* 2: 207–14.

41. An Ming, "Shixing zhengliang zengce de jiantao" (A critique on the implementation of the tax grain policy), Nov. 1, 1941. *P:Anhui* 2: 40.

42. These are traditional devices for measuring land, probably bow-shaped (perhaps the reason they were referred to in Chinese as *gong*, literally "bow"), that gave a unit of length equal to five *chi*.

43. "Huaibei Suwan bianqu xingzheng gongshu guanyu tudi fucha wenti de xunling." *P:Anhui* 2: 212.

44. For example, in Head Gate Village (Toumen cun), the 38 *mu* of land Yuan Chaodou owned was scattered over fourteen locations.

45. The party discovered that some cadres at the natural village and subdistrict levels did not take the deeds to the government for evaluation of land quality. It was through the peasants that the government was able to uncover holdings owned by usurers. "Changsheng xiang tudi fucha jingyan jie shao" (An introduction to the experience of land resurvey in Changsheng subdistrict), July 10, 1944. *P:Anhui* 2: 215–17. The material was written by Chen Aihua and first published on the same date in *Fuxiao bao*.

46. In some areas, landlords and rich peasants were classified as middle or lower households, while poor and middle peasants were rendered as upper

households. Other areas set 6 percent for upper households, 4 percent for middle, and 2 percent for lower, thus undertaxing the entire region.

47. Meng Dongbo, "Zhengliang gongzuo zhong de liang ge wenti." *P:Anhui* 2: 23.

48. *P:Anhui* 2: 34.

49. An Ming, "Shixing zhengliang zhengce de jiantao." *P:Anhui* 2: 40.

50. Meng Dongbo, "Zhengliang gongzuo zhong de liang ge wenti." *P:Anhui* 2: 19–24.

51. In the fifth *bao* of Newly Created (Xinjian) village, a *bao* head classified his as a middle household, even though he had a foreman and two hired farmhands working for him and had never participated in production. He should have been classified as a rich peasant belonging to an upper-class household. In a *bao* in Four Rivers (Sihe) village, a group of cadres jointly requested a reclassification of themselves from middle-class to lower-class households. See An Ming, "Shixing zhengliang zhengce de jiantao." *P:Anhui* 2: 41.

52. Some cadres held the view that the basic principle behind the survey was to single out culprits for punishment. In Four Rivers village, cadres penalized three households even before they had conducted their surveys. Some thought that they should set an example at the beginning to cow people into submission, a tactic that ended up in indiscriminate use of penalties.

53. In Huaisi county, Communist cadres made the mistake of forcing a gentry member to carry half the local tax burden. This alienated the gentry, who insisted that the Communist government was working only for the poor. They spread rumors that cadres would cut in half all long gowns (an outfit for the well-to-do and a status symbol in the countryside) or take away 80 percent of the land owned by the rich. Such rumors had an immense impact on rich peasants, whose support the Communists tried to cultivate.

54. Liu Yuzhu, "Huaibei Suwan bianqu qiuji gongliang dongyuan de renwu ji qi zhengce, jielu." *P:Anhui* 2: 9–10.

55. In the ward directly under the jurisdiction of the administrative office, one-third of the leadership positions in the neighborhood and subdistricts were occupied by landlords and rich peasants. Should there be an impasse in the neighborhood assembly, the case would be referred to a group of adjudicators composed of powerful households, poor households, and government functionaries or cadres, each with a third of the representation. The Communists also used the three-thirds system in the water conservancy committee. Of the fifteen members of the Production Salvation Committee, four were party members, four "progressive" gentry, and seven "neutralists." Of the 89 committee members at the neighborhood level in Huaibao county, only 31, about a third, were party members. Also see the chart of social composition and educational background of cadres at the *bao* and *xiang* levels in Zhao Min, "Huaibei Suwan bianqu xingzheng gongshu zhishu qu ershi wu tian de liangshi gongzuo zongjie." *P:Anhui* 2: 31. See also Hu Keming, "Siyang xian de shengzhan jiuhuang yu cungeng yundong." *P:Anhui* 2: 86.

56. Many of the rich households had a bad harvest because their land was inundated by floodwater. Some did not harvest as much grain that year as a middle household, but still were forced by cadres to pay taxes at the rate of

upper households. The cases were publicly debated in the neighborhood meeting and later corrected.

57. Zhao Min, "Huaibei Suwan bianqu xingzheng gongshu zhishu qu ershi wu tian de liangshi gongzuo zongjie." *P:Anhui* 2: 28–37.

58. Hu Keming, "Siyang xian de shengchan jiuhuang yu cungeng yundong." *P:Anhui* 2: 87–88.

59. Liao Yuan, "Suwan bianqu de caijing gongzuo." *P:Anhui* 2: 64–65.

60. Public and private wastelands (*gonghuang*) were defined as virgin wasteland and arable land abandoned for more than two years.

61. "Huaibei Suwan bianqu kenzhi zanxing tiaoli" (Temporary regulations for reclamation in the Suwan border area in Huaibei), Mar. 13, 1942; "Fu: Hubei Suwan bianqu xingzheng gongshu xiuzheng kenzhi zanxing tiaoli, jiexuan" (Appendix: Revised temporary regulations for reclamation issued by the administrative office of the Suwan border area in Huaibei), Apr. 18, 1942; and "Huaibei Suwan bianqu xingzheng gongshu kenzhi shishi banfa" (Method of implementation of land reclamation issued by the administrative office of the Jiangsu-Anhui border area in Huaibei), Apr. 18, 1942. *P:Anhui* 2: 76–77, 93–94. These regulations were first published by the administrative office in *Zhengfu gongzuo* (Government work) nos. 5 and 7.

62. "Huaibei xingzheng gongshu guanyu kaizhan shengchan jianshe de jueding" (A decision by the Huaibei administrative office on launching a movement for production and reconstruction), Nov. 1943. *P:Anhui* 2: 165.

63. Liu Chongguang, "Huaibei Suwan bianqu yijiu sisan nian de shengchan jianshe zongjie." *P:Anhui* 2: 138–39.

64. In the Houju area, 200 of the 400 households were families of new migrants. In Hongze Lake, there was a 101 percent increase in population.

65. See Liu Ruilong's address in the joint meeting of the party, the army, and the people, "Jin yi bu gonggu tuanjie jianshe Huaibei genju di" (One step further to consolidate, unify, and develop the Huaibei base), Dec. 29, 1944. *P:Anhui* 2: 270.

66. See Liao Yuan, "Suwan bianqu de caijing gongzuo." *P:Anhui* 2: 65.

67. "Huaibei xingzheng gongshu guanyu kaizhan shengchan jianshe de jueding." *P:Anhui* 2: 163.

68. Of the fifteen members of the Huaibao committee, four were party members, four "progressive gentry," and seven "middle elements." Of the 89 committee members in the nine districts (*qu*), only 31 were party members. See Liu Chongguang's report, "Huaibei Suwan bianqu yijiu sisan nian de shengchan jianshe zongjie." *P:Anhui* 2: 236.

69. *P:Anhui* 2: 237.

70. A project to combat flooding of the Huai River required a total of 5,500 men (2,000 natives and 3,500 outsiders), 78,756 cubic meters of earth, and 40 work days. But the project saved 540 *qing* (approximately 3,510 hectares) of land, which produced 25,000 *shi* of food grain. *P:Anhui* 2: 238.

71. Liu Ruilong, "Huaibei Suwan bianqu san nian lai de zhengfu gongzuo, jielu." *P:Anhui* 2: 101.

72. Liu Chongguang, "Huaibei Suwan bianqu yijiu sisan nian de shengchan jieshe zongjie." *P:Anhui* 2: 233.

73. "Deng Zihui tongzhi zai Huaibei gaogan hui shang de fayan, jielu" (The

speech given by Comrade Deng Zihui in the Huaibei high-ranking cadre meeting, excerpt), June 1943. *P:Anhui* 2: 127.

74. Liu Chongguang, "Huaibei Suwan bianqu yijiu sisan nian de shengchan jianshe zongjie." *P:Anhui* 2: 233–34.

75. In spite of dredging, the Xin River of Xufengjia and the two rivers in Sinan county overflowed after a heavy rain because of inadequate preliminary planning. Local people were angry at the government. In the Huaisi county project, inadequate planning led to constant changes of plan and much confusion. *P:Anhui* 2: 234.

76. "Huaibei xingzheng gongshu guanyu kaizhan shengchan jianshe de jeuding." *P:Anhui* 2: 162.

77. *P:Anhui* 2: 162–63.

78. Hu Keming, "Siyang xian de shengchan jiuhuang yu cungeng yundong." *P:Anhui* 2: 88.

79. Liu Ruilong, "Huaibei Suwan bianqu san nian lai de zhengfu gongzuo, jielu." *P:Anhui* 2: 101.

80. *P:Anhui* 2: 235.

81. According to regulations, the regular wage for water conservancy work was 8 *jin* of grain per square foot of construction. In some areas, local cadres paid the workers as much as 36 *jin*.

82. Liu Chongguang, "Huaibei Suwan bianqu yijiu sisan nian de shengchan jianshe zongjie." *P:Anhui* 2: 235–36.

83. *P:Anhui* 2: 232–38.

84. Zhu Chaonan et al. 1985: 92–95. See chart.

85. Zhu Chaonan et al. 1985: 85–100.

86. "Huaibei Suwan bianqu xingzheng gongshu zhishi xin—guanyu jiajin cungeng yundong nuli shengzhan" (A letter of directives from the administrative office of the Huaibei Jiangsu-Anhui border area—Concerning the movement to step up spring planting and actively expand production), Mar. 13, 1942. *P:Anhui* 2: 78–82. The letter was written by Liu Ruilong, the head of the base, and was originally published in *Zhengfu gongzuo* (Government operation). It also included the "three don'ts and four do's: don't borrow money if you are not in need, don't force others to borrow money, and don't be idle; do put everything down in a contract, do pay back a loan on time, do have security, and do pay interest." The government also made good use of propaganda teams and theatrical troupes for propaganda purposes in the countryside.

87. Altogether, they reclaimed 33,995 *mu* of land. With combined government and private effort, 74,397 trees were planted in three neighborhoods and one township. There were 385 combatants' families in the county that needed assistance. The production team completed one plowing for them in the second lunar month and gathered 2,341 *jin* of steamed buns, 135 *jin* of fish, 121 *jin* of meat, 17 *jin* of noodles, 230 *jin* of tofu, and 108 *jin* of bean sprouts. The government also made sure that enough seedlings would be raised for these families in the third lunar month for spring planting.

88. Hu Keming, "Siyang xian de shengzhan jiuhuang yu cungeng yundong." *P:Anhui* 2: 85–94.

89. Skocpol 1979: 262.

90. Wright 1964: 245.

91. Watson 1973: 117–31.
92. Shanin, "Peasantry in Political Action." In Shanin 1987: 357–63.
93. For the concept of the public arena, see Freitag 1989: 169–98.
94. Weber 1976: 242.

Chapter 8

1. Popkin 1979; Migdal 1974; Race 1974; Levine 1987.
2. For social exchange theory, see Popkin 1979; Little 1989; Easton 1973; Waldman 1973a, 1973b.
3. Race 1974.
4. Migdal 1974: 254.
5. CCP membership in Henan took a nosedive, dropping from around 2,000 during the Northern Expedition to 96 on the eve of the Sino-Japanese War. The provincial party was destroyed twice during the Nationalist period. Whatever Communist activities there were, were conducted clandestinely. For party membership figures and CCP activities in Henan during the Nationalist period, see *P:dashiji*: 1–88.
6. For a brief history of Communist influence in the Taihang area, see "Taihang kang-Ri genjudi" (Taihang anti-Japanese base), n.d. *P:Taihang* 1: 1–10.
7. The figure 1,621 represents total acreage in the village and probably included both private and unowned land, or land owned by public institutions such as the village government, temples, and clans. The actual amount of land owned by various classes totaled 1,516.5 *mu* (see Table 8.1). No figure is cited, however, for the amount of land owned by merchants or wage laborers (although the latter probably did not own any land), nor is this omission explained. Figures provided by the Communist revolutionaries are sometimes inaccurate or approximate.
8. In other parts of Henan, owners of 100–499 *mu* of land were designated small landlords, owners of 500–1,000 *mu* were middle landlords, and owners of over 1,000 *mu* were big landlords. In Houjiao, the largest landowner had a holding of only 26 *mu*. In other areas, landownership was much more concentrated and class conflict much more intense. For instance, in Huixian, 50 percent of the land was owned by landlords and rich peasants. In Houjiao, the figure was only 10.6 percent. See *Henan sheng nongcun diaocha* 1934: 4, 7.
9. For the Heavenly Gate Society, see Liang Xinming 1984; Du Dazhong 1984; Hou Wuzhao 1984; Mu Zhongyue 1984; Cui Zuze 1984. Also see Zi Zhen 1927; *Chongxiu Linxian zhi* 1932, vol. 14, chronological events; Li Jianquan 1932. *Xu Anyang xianzhi* 1933, vol. 1, chronological events; He Min 1985.
10. "Linxian qunzhong yundong zongjie baogao" (A comprehensive report on the mass movement in Lin county), Dec. 26, 1944. *P:JJLY-CJ* 3: 515–16.
11. *P:JJLY-CJ* 3: 516.
12. *P:JJLY-CJ* 3: 516.
13. *P:JJLY-CJ* 3: 517.
14. *P:JJLY-CJ* 3: 518.
15. See C. Johnson: 1962.
16. For example, when cadres trained members of the peasant association, the

content of the training still focused on anti-Japanese activities (*fan weichi*). Rent and interest reductions were secondary. *P:JJLY-CJ* 3: 495–520.

17. For a summary of the mass movement in Houjiao, see appendix 2, "Houjiao cun douzheng zongjie baogao" (Comprehensive report on the struggle in Houjiao Village) in "Linxian qunzhong yundong zongjie baogao." *P:JJLY-CJ* 3: 514–20.

18. See Race 1974: 179.

19. "Diwu zhuanshu dui guomin jingji diaocha yanjiu de cailiao" (Survey material on the national economy by the Fifth Prefectural Commissioner's Office), May 15, 1945. *P:JJLY-CJ* 3: 136.

20. Surpluses in the first Communist-designated region were 20–27 percent, 17 percent in the second region, and 15 percent in the third region. There seems to have been little or no surplus in the remote mountainous region.

21. *P:JJLY-CJ* 3: 136–55.

22. There are two figures for the per capita availability of land for the province. Zhao Jinsan 1934 gives a figure of 2 *mu* for 1934, while the statistics published by the Communist government in Henan sheng tongji xuehui et al. 1986 give a provincial average of 4.4 *mu*.

23. Population in 1943 was 381,646 and arable land was 608,801 *mu*, giving a per capita availability of land (in *mu*) of 1.6. In May 1945, a land survey by the Communists indicated the per capita availability of land in the following counties: She county, 1.76; Ciwu, 2.27; Linbei, 2.08; and Anyang, 3.04, an average of 2.29 for the entire area.

24. Zhao Jinsan 1934. See chart on p. 13561.

25. *P:JJLY-CJ* 3: 316–18.

26. Thaxton 1981, 1983.

27. *P:JJLY-CJ* 3: 501.

28. The social composition of the rentiers was as follows: in Beimujing village, of 11 rentier households, 4 were landlords; in Yangjia zhai village, of 5 rentier households, 2 were rich peasants, 2 middle peasants, 1 a poor peasant; in Yanhuashui village, of 7 rentier households, 5 were landlords, 1 a middle peasant, and 1 a household with too few able-bodied laborers for cultivation work. See "Linxian qunzhong yundong zongjie baogao." *P:JJLY-CJ* 3: 499.

29. The social composition of the renters was as follows: in Nanweidi village, 23 of 38 renters were middle peasants, 15 poor peasants; in Yangjiazhuang village, 14 of 21 renters were middle peasants and 6 poor peasants; in Yanhuashui village, 2 of 26 renters were middle peasants and 6 poor peasants; in Beimujing village, a third of the 31 renters were poor peasants. *P:JJLY-CJ* 3: 499.

30. The social composition of rentiers and renters of radish land in Yangjiazhai village in 1944 was as follows: of 9 rentier households, 4 were rich peasants, 1 a middle peasant, and 1 a poor peasant; of 49 renter households, 1 was a rich peasant, 21 were middle peasants, and 27 were poor peasants. *P:JJLY-CJ* 3: 499.

31. For Mao's "mass line," see Schram 1963: 70–71, 315–18.

32. Thaxton 1981.

33. The struggle of Wei Shaohua, a landlord, is an example. Wei insisted that his land was purchased and not withheld (*kuoya*) from a peasant. The question

was then thoroughly discussed in the tenants' meeting. The cadres followed up the discussion by pointing out to the peasants the evil and exploitative nature of the old feudal society. They then effectively mobilized the peasants in a struggle against the Wei family.

34. *P:JJLY-CJ* 3: 504.

35. *P:JJLY-CJ* 3: 502.

36. *P:JJLY-CJ* 3: 419.

37. *P:JJLY-CJ* 3: 421.

38. *P:JJLY-CJ* 3: 510–11. See appendix 1.

39. In the 33 mass movements the Communists conducted in the area, the targets of attack were 12 *baojia* heads, 2 sectarians, 6 *she* and *bao* heads, 1 village intellectual, 3 foremen, 11 GMD members, and 12 others, making a total of 47 targets. When broken down by class, the targets were 2 landlords, 3 landlord creditors, 2 managerial landlords, 4 managerial landlord creditors, 2 managerial landlord merchants, 12 rich peasants, 9 rich peasant creditors, 3 rich peasant merchants, 6 rich middle peasants, 1 rich middle peasant merchant, and 3 middle peasants. *P:JJLY-CJ* 3: 498.

40. The cases include 93 cases of land problems, 53 loan payments, 34 corruption cases, 17 anti-bully cases, and 129 miscellaneous cases.

41. "Linbei xian yijiu sisi nian dong jianzu yundong zongjie—Yao Guang zai zhuan xian kuangda ganbu hui shang de baogao" (A comprehensive report on the rent reduction movement in winter 1944 in northern Lin county—A report given by Yao Guang in the enlarged county cadre meeting), May 28, 1945. *P:JJLY-CJ* 3: 424.

42. In the Sixth District in Lin county, 411 tenant households in 20 villages were affected by the rent reduction movement. Before the movement, the class status of these tenant households were 3 rich peasant households (data on number of individuals not available), 126 middle peasants, 225 poor peasants, and 57 extremely poor peasants. After the rent reduction, there was a change of class status. The new status was 34 rich peasants, 157 middle peasants, 183 poor peasants, and 37 extremely poor peasants. Many of the poor and extremely poor peasants had moved up the social ladder.

There was also a slight reduction in the amount of land rented. Before the movement, 2,052 *mu* of village land were owned by owner-operators and 1,554 *mu* were rented. After the movement, owner-cultivators owned 2,171 *mu* and 1,316 *mu* were rented. The total amount of rent paid by tenants was halved; before the movement, total rent was 914.7 *shi* of grain, but after the movement it was 438 *shi*. *P:JJLY-CJ* 3: 423.

43. For the theory of moral economy, see Scott 1976.

44. See Scott and Kerkvliet 1977.

45. Surveys by the Communists of nine natural villages in the First District indicate a drop in population of 23–28 percent; in the nine villages in the Second District, the population decrease varied from 22–35 percent. See "Linbei jiuzai weiyuanhui gongzuo zongjie ji jinhou fangzhen yu zuofa" (A comprehensive report and future policies and practices for the disaster relief committee of northern Lin county), June 2, 1943. The document was originally published on Nov. 5, 1944, in the first volume of *Taihang dangshi jicun* (A collection of Communist party materials in the Taihang). *P:JJLY-CJ* 3: 334–35.

46. Negotiating through peasant associations, the government was able to get nine villages in the Old Fort (Gucheng) area to loan C$11,492, 3.1 *shi* of rice, and 5 *shi* of wheat to Pan Mountain (Pan shan) and other villages. For the famine relief work of the Communist Party in northern Henan, see *P:JJLY-CJ* 3: 334–40.

47. *P:JJLY-CJ* 3: 347.

48. For the grain borrowing movement, see *P:JJLY-CJ* 3: 345–53.

49. "Diwu fenqu shengchan gongzuo baogao" (A report on production work in the Fifth District), May 1944. *P:JJLY-CJ* 3: 79.

50. In Upper Stockade village (shangzhai cun) in the Sixth District of Ciwu county, a total of 52.3 *mu* of land was cultivated with vegetables. Of that total, 17.5 *mu* belonged to rich peasants, 31 *mu* to middle peasants, and 3.8 *mu* to poor peasants.

51. *P:JJLY-CJ* 3: 79–81.

52. For example, in Sang'er zhuang in the First District, only 77 percent of the spinning and weaving households were famine victims. A breakdown of the participating households in Baotai Village by class shows the following: all 52 poor peasant households participating were famine victims, as were 7 of the 52 middle peasant households, but none of the 30 rich middle peasant or the 3 rich peasant households participating were famine victims. *P:JJLY-CJ* 3: 341.

53. *P:JJLY-CJ* 3: 341.

54. *P:JJLY-CJ* 3: 87–93.

55. In the Sixth District, for example, there was a 56 percent decrease in the number of draft animals from 1941 to 1944, and in the Seventh District, a drop of 36 percent.

56. *P:JJLY-CJ* 3: 170.

57. Some of the problems leading to the failures of the mutual aid teams listed in their reports were an undemocratic way of conducting business; peasants' refusing or being afraid to speak their minds; one party perceiving an exchange to be unfair; and lack of planning, with decisions being made on the spot.

58. On the mutual aid teams, see "Diwu zhuanqu ban nian lai shengchan gongzuo gaikuang" (A brief account on production in the second half of the year in the Fifth Special District), July 15, 1945. *P:JJLY-CJ* 3: 170–77.

59. The local party held labor hero meetings (*yingxiong dahui*) to elect "labor heroes," who were awarded pennants for their achievements. According to Communist reports, "labor heroes" were the most effective propagandists for the government. "One sentence from them was ten times more effective than ten sentences from the government," one report says. See *P:JJLY-CJ* 3: 84–87.

60. The counties were Shende, Licheng, Pingshun, Liaoxian, Qinzhou, Yangcheng, and Huixian.

61. The silk price was reported to be C$9–C$12 per *jin*. With an increase in the price of grain in this period (1911–26), the handicraft industry in the area went through a decline.

62. In 1944, the government sold 600 shares to 918 households in the spring and 1,392 shares to 1,234 households in the winter. The social composition of the autumn shareholders was 128 rich peasant households (10.4 percent); 517 middle peasant households (41.9 percent); and 589 poor peasant households (47.7 percent).

63. "Linbei shan can fuhuo liao" (Resurrection of the mountain sericulture

industry in northern Lin county), Sept. 1, 1944. First published by the government of northern Lin county in *Bianqu zhengbao* (Border political news) no. 41. See *P:JJLY-CJ* 3: 381–400.

64. See Easton 1973.

65. See Turner 1988. He divides the social interaction theory into motivational processes, interactional processes, and structuring processes.

Chapter 9

1. Kau 1974: 267.

2. Wang Tianjiang et al. 1990: 422–26.

3. *P:dashiji*: 145–56.

4. *P:YWS* 1: 491.

5. Deng Zihui, "Guanyu chengshi gongzuo de ji ge jiban wenti, jielu." (A couple of basic problems in urban work, excerpt), 1945. *P:YWS* 1: 490–501. This is part of the comprehensive report Deng Zihui presented in 1945 at the first city work conference in the Huaibei Suwan border base.

6. *P:ZLF*. See also Wang Feixiao, "Liyong maodun cuihua Zhang Lanfeng Yang Shusan huoping—dixia gongzuo shiling ziyi" (Using contradiction to intensify armed conflicts between Zhang Lanfeng and Yang Shusan—No. 1 of the tidbits of underground work), Dec. 1982. *P:Shangqiu* 2: 76–77.

7. *P:Shangqiu* 2: 78–79. Yang Mingxun and Xie Gongyi, "Wo dang zai weijun Zhang Lanfeng bu junyun gongzuo gaishu" (A brief account of the party's military work in Zhang Lanfeng's puppet army), Mar. 1985. *P:Shangqiu* 2: 67.

8. Li Subo was a native of Dongming county in Shandong province. He received his high school education in Kaifeng, Henan. In 1937, he returned to and conducted revolutionary activities in his home province. In 1944 and 1945, he was party committee member in the Hebei-Shandong-Henan region. Acting as the representative of the Eighth Route Army, Li was appointed by the party to negotiate with Zhang Lanfeng. See "Li Subo," n.d. *P:Shangqiu* 3: 103–4.

9. Miao Zesheng was a native of Sui county in Henan. He was a Red Spears mobilizer in his hometown during the Northern Expedition. After 1931, he continued his revolutionary activities underground and was later made secretary of the Sui county Communist Party. During the war, Miao commanded an independent regiment in Rivereast. See "Miao Zesheng," n.d. *P:Shangqiu* 3: 111.

10. Yang Mingxun and Xie Gongyi, "Wo dang zai weijun Zhang Lanfeng bu junyun gongzuo gaishu." *P:Shangqiu* 2: 64–74. Li Subo, Jiang Dasheng, Miao Zesheng, Liu Xuekong, Dai De, and Li Zimu, "Yu Zhang Lanfeng de san ci tanpan" (The three negotiations with Zhang Lanfeng), May 1983. *P:Shangqiu* 2: 59–63.

11. Tilly 1974.

12. Wang Feixiao was a native of Zhecheng county in Henan, the home of Zhang Lanfeng. After graduating from Huaiyang High School, Wang joined the Northwest Army as a soldier. After the capture of Zhecheng county by the Japanese in June 1938, Wang gathered Zhecheng natives and organized a guerrilla force to fight the Japanese. Unfortunately, the unit was defeated and swallowed up by the bandits. Wang left his native land to study at Kangda in Yan'an.

In October 1938, he joined the Communist Party. After graduation, Wang was assigned to work in his hometown, at first under Chen Ziliang. In March 1941, he was instructed by the Rivereast Communist Party to assist Du Xinmin in his "military mobilization" (*junyun*) and to infiltrate Zhang Lanfeng's army. See Xie Gongyi and Lo Liangshen, "Wang Feixiao," n.d. *P:Shangqiu* 3: 86–87.

13. Yang Mingxun, "Du Xinmin zhuanlue" (A brief biography of Du Xinmin), n.d. *P:Shangqiu* 3: 38–42. The biography was first published in the philosophy/social science section of *Henan daxue xuebao* (Henan university journal) no. 3, 1985.

14. Lu Wei (Chen Zhensheng), "Da ru wei shiba shi kaizhan qiyi de zhunbei gongzuo" (The work of infiltrating the puppet Eighteenth Division and preparing it for an uprising). *P:Shangqiu* 2: 28–32.

15. Wang Ziguang, "Zhengcheng qiyi" (The uprising in Zhengcheng). *P: Shangqiu* 2: 94–107.

16. Yang Mingxun and Xie Gongyi, "Wo dang zai weijun Zhang Lanfeng by junyun gongzuo gaishu." *P:Shangqiu* 2: 74.

17. Wang Feixiao, "Liyong maodun cuihua Zhang Lanfeng Yang Shusen huoping." *P:Shangqiu* 2: 76–85.

18. Wang Feixiao, "Cuihua maodun xiaomie Wang Jinxuan—dixia gongzuo shiling zi san" (To intensify the contradiction and to eliminate Wang Jinxuan—No. 3 of the tidbits of underground work). *P:Shangqiu* 2: 86–89.

19. This was decided in the meeting of the standing committee of the branch bureau on December 7, 1945. See Liu Ruilong's report on the meeting in "Xunsu fangshou fadong xin jiefang qu qunzhong, jielu" (Swiftly and freely mobilize the masses in the newly liberated areas, excerpt), Dec. 7, 1945. *P:Anhui* 3: 18–20. The report first appeared in *Huazhong tongxun* no. 1, 1946. Liu Ruilong was head of the finance and economic office of the party committee in the Yuwansu region.

20. "Suwan bianqu moshou hanjian tudi fangling banfa" (Methods of redistributing holdings confiscated from the "traitors" in the Jiangsu-Anhui border area), Apr. 1946. *P:Anhui* 3: 82–83.

21. *P:dashiji*: 149–50.

22. *P:dashiji*: 152–53.

23. "Land to the tillers" was first suggested by Sun Yatsen as a revolutionary slogan. The policy was defined by Liu Ruilong in a statement issued on June 10, 1946. Liu insisted that it differed from the concept of "land equalization" (*pingfen tudi*). It was not a policy designed to level holdings of the rich and middle peasants, nor was it a policy of forceful seizure of landlords' holdings. It only seized land from "traitor landlords" and transferred this land to the peasants. It was a moderate policy, using mainly rent and interest reductions to protect the interests of the tenants while guaranteeing a livelihood for the landlords. Therefore, according to Liu, it was different from the Guomindang land policy of "equalization of land rights" (*pingjun di quan*).

Nor was it a nationalization of land. The policy aimed at consolidating the interests and arousing the consciousness of wage laborers and poor peasants. It solidified the middle peasants, but absolutely would not encroach on their interests. It would not affect the owner-cultivated part of rich peasant holdings, only the exploitative part. As for the landlords, it clearly distinguished the wealthy from the middle and small landlords, and the tyrants from the progressives. The policy singled out traitors, wealthy gentry, local tyrants, and big landlords as targets of attack. Although the excess land of managerial, middle, and small landlords was to be redistributed, the policy underscored moderation and mediation between classes in land conflicts. It encouraged progressive landlords to voluntarily donate land to the pool of land to be redistributed. Despite the call for confiscation of temple, clan, and community lands, it did allow kinship groups and religious institutions to retain a portion of their land for sacrificial and religious purposes. For a detailed definition of "land to the tillers," see Liu Ruilong, "Lun gengche you qi tian, jielu" (Land to the tillers, excerpt), June 10, 1946. *P:Anhui* 3: 95–119. First published in *Zhonghua tongxun* no. 4, June 1946.

24. "Zhonggong Huazhong fenju guanche dang zhongyang wusi guanyu tudi zhengce xin jueding de zhishi" (Directive from the central China branch bureau of the Chinese Communist Party on thoroughly carrying out the May Fourth land reform decided on by the Central Committee), May 28, 1946. *P:Anhui* 3: 89–95. First published in *Huazhong tongxun* (Central China newsletter) no. 4, 1946.

25. "Yuwansu qu dangwei guanyu zhixing Jin-Ji-Lu-Yu zhongyang ju guanyu tudi gaige de zhishi de zhishi" (Directive from the party committee of the Yuwansu region on the "Land Reform Directive" issued by the central bureau of the Jin-Ji-Lu-Yu region), Aug. 1, 1947. *P:YWS45–49*: 53–54. The Yuwansu area was at that time under the jurisdiction of the Jin-Ji-Lu-Yu region. In May 1948, it was transferred to the Zhongyuan ju (central bureau).

26. In areas that had already gone through land reform, such as Qi county, landlords were allowed to own 4–5 *mu* of land, while peasants had only 3 *mu*. In Taikang county, landlords' holdings were 4.5–5 *mu* and peasants' 2.8–3.1 *mu*. The directive points out that with their concealed land and money, landlords must have been leading a very comfortable life.

27. "Yuwansu qu dangwei guanyu tudi gaige de zhishi, jielu" (Directive on land reform from the party committee of the Yuwansu region, excerpt), Sept. 1947. *P:Anhui* 3: 207–10. This document was included in *Xuefeng tongxun* (News dispatches from Pang Xuefeng) no. 4, 1947.

28. *P:dashiji*: 159–60.

29. "Zhongyuan yezhan jun houfang silingbu guanyu Huaixi tugai zhong douzheng celue de baogao" (A report by the rear command headquarters of the Zhongyuan field army on struggle tactics in the land reform in western Huai River), Feb. 13, 1948. *P:jiefangqu*: 35–37. Li Xuefeng, "Guanyu xinqu douzheng delue ji zuzhi xingshi wenti de baogao" (A report on struggle tactics and problems of forms of organization in newly liberated areas), Feb. 13, 1948. *P:jiefangqu*: 38–41.

30. The directive points out a number of "leftist" tendencies: a preconceived idea of who the landlords and rich peasants were; classifying as a landlord anyone who came from a landlord background dating back three generations, even if the individual was presently a cultivator; classifying a laboring household as non-laboring household because the labor was considered secondary, or because the household hired a couple of farmhands; and classifying a rich peasant as a landlord if he owned a calf or a sheep. For local directives, see

"Yuwansu qu dangwei guanyu guanche tudi gaige de zhishi" (Directives on thoroughly carrying out the land reform, issued by the party committee of the Yuwansu region). *P:YWS45–49*: 74–82. Also see *P:Anhui* 3: 237–46.

31. *P:YWS45–49*: 108.

32. "Yuwansu qu dangwei guanyu tudi gaige de zhishi" (Directive of land reform issued by the party committee of the Yuwansu region), May 10, 1948. *P:YWS45–49*: 108–13.

33. The population in the Zhongyuan area was 45 million. About 20 million lived in the Communist-occupied areas and 10 million in the guerrilla zones. "Zhongyuan qu guanyu zhixing zhonggong zhongyuan tugai he zhengdang gongzuo zhishi de zhishi" (A directive from the Zhongyuan bureau on the party central directive on carrying out land and party reforms), June 6, 1948. *P:jiefangqu*: 76.

34. "Liu Ruilong, Wu Zhipu tongzhi guanyu tugai wenti gei Zheng Hua tongzhi de xin" (A letter from Comrades Liu Ruilong and Wu Zhi-pu to Comrade Zheng Hua on the problems of land reform). *P:YWS45–49*: 85–88. Liu Ruilong was then head of finance and economy in the Yuwansu region; Zheng Hua was secretary of the first district of Yuwansu.

35. The example was taken from the village of Changli ying in Lianci, Shenqiu county, an area said to have been very effective in its land redistribution. See "Du Runsheng tongzhi jian cha Shenqiu yici pingfen faxian de ji ge wenti zhi Wu Zhipu tongzhi dian" (Telegram from Comrade Du Runsheng to Comrade Wu Zhipu on problems discovered in the inspection of "onetime equal distribution" in Shenqiu county), Apr. 27, 1948. *P:YWS45–49*: 2–3. Du Runsheng was then secretary of the fourth local committee of Yuwansu. Wu Zhipu was party secretary for Yuwansu. This telegram was appended to Wu Zhipu's telegram to the Central Plain Bureau.

36. *P:YWS45–49*: 3.

37. In some villages, Communist officials were said to have lived off the local people, or in Communist terms, *chi daguo fan*.

38. The notice was posted in the Fifth District. See "Li Xuefeng tongzhi dui Yuwansu wu fenqu baogao de piping yijian" (Comrade Li Xuefeng's critical view of the notice posted in the Fifth District in the Yuwansu region), May 11, 1948. *P:YWS45–49*: 9. Li Xuefeng was head of the organization section of the Central Plain Bureau.

39. Li Xuefeng, "Guanyu Huaixi qu liang ge yue gongzuo jingyan de baogao" (A report on work experience in the last two months in the western part of the Huai River), Feb. 27, 1948. *P:jiefangqu*: 42–45.

40. In the Fifth District, 20–40 percent of households were attack targets. In the Third District, 20–30 percent of households gave up some land, and 50–60 percent were recipients. In some villages, cadres strictly applied the policy of absolute equality, taking a tiny bit from one household and giving it to another. Frequently, the attack extended to the middle peasants, who were coerced to dispense grain to the poor. Many even went on their knees and cried. See "Cao Diqiu zai Jianghuai qu diyi ci tudi huiyi shang de baogao" (Cao Diqiu's report in the first meeting of land reform in the Jianghuai area), June 26, 1948. *P:Anhui* 3: 284–90.

41. "Wu Zhipu tongzhi zai Yuwansu bianqu jianjun-caijing huiyi shang de

zongjie baogao" (Wu Zhipu's comprehensive report in the military and finance meeting of the Yuwansu border region), May 16, 1948. *P:YWS45–49*: 117–19.

42. "Zhongyuan qu guanyu zhixing zhonggong zhongyang tugai he zhengdang gongzuo zhishi de zhishi." *P:jiefangqu*: 77, 80.

43. In one village, one middle peasant and six poor peasants, identified as "bandits and hooligans," were executed.

44. "Zhongyuan qu guanyu zhixing zhonggong zhongyang tugai he zhengdang gongzuo zhishi de zhishi." *P:jiefangqu*: 79.

45. In December 1947, the Central Executive Committee of the CCP had already held a meeting to discuss the problems of the land reform. On February 1, 1948, the central bureau of the Jin-Ji-Lu-Yu border base issued a directive "on land reform, party reorganization, and democratic movement" severely criticizing "leftist" tendencies in the movement. Wu Zhipu might have been following the direction from the center in his opposition to excesses in the land redistribution movement. See *P:dashiji*: 164, 168; Wang Tianjiang et al. 1990: 475.

46. "Wu Zhipu tongzhi zai Yuwansu bianqu jianjun-caijing huiyi shang de zongjie baogao." *P:YWS45–49*: 119–21.

47. "Yuwansu qu dangwei guanyu muqian gongzuo de zhishi" (Directive from the party committee of the Yuwansu region concerning present party work), 1948. *P:YWS45–49*: 163–66.

48. "Zhongyuan ju zhi Wu Zhipu tongzhi dian" (A Telegram to Comrade Wu Zhipu from the Central Plain Bureau), Apr. 27, 1948. *P:YWS45–49*: 1–2. Also see the appendix in "Du Runsheng tongzhi jian cha Shenqiu yici pingfen faxian de ji ge wenti zhi Wu Zhipu tongzhi dian." *P:YWS45–49*: 3.

49. "Zhongyang qu guanyu zhixing zhonggong zhongyang tugai he zhengdang gongzuo zhishi de zhishi." *P:jiefangqu*: 87.

50. "Zhongyuan ju dui Yuwansu tugai huiyi de fushi" (Directive from the Central Plain Bureau in answer to the decision made by the land reform meeting held in the Yuwansu area), May 29, 1948. *P:YWS45–49*: 10.

51. "Zhongyuan ju guanyu dong cun wuxiang gongzuo ruhe jiehe wenti gei Yuwansu fenju de fushi" (A response directive from the Central Plain Bureau to the Yuwansu branch bureau on the question of how to integrate the five items in the policy in winter-spring work, 1948–1949), Nov. 8, 1948. *P:YWS45–49*: 13–16.

52. "Wu Zhipu tongzhi zai Yuwansu bianqu jianjun-caijing huiyi shang de zongjie baogao." *P:YWS45–49*: 122–28.

53. See *Renmin ribao*, June 19, 1947. In *P:SQT* 2: 82–83.

54. Zhang Jichun, "Zai Zhengzhou shi ganbu hui shang de jiang hua" (A talk in the Zhengzhou cadre meeting), Oct. 31, 1948. *P:jiefangqu*: 199. Zhang Jichun was a deputy committee member and head of the political department in the Zhongyuan military region.

55. "Guanyu Kaifeng jige wenti de chuli yijian" (Suggestions for dealing with a couple of problems in Kaifeng), Nov. 12, 1948. *P:YWS45–49*: 17–18. This was a telegram sent by Liu Bocheng, Chen Yi, and Deng Xiaoping to the Central Plain Bureau.

56. "Zhongyuan ju guanyu zhanling Zheng-Bian de jidian zhishi" (Directive

from the Central Plain Bureau on taking over Zhengzhou and Kaifeng), Oct. 26, 1948. *P:YWS45–49*: 11–12. Also see *P:jiefangqu*: 189–90.

57. "Jieguan Zhengzhou Kaifeng de jingyan yu Zhongyuan xinqu de nongcun gongzuo" (The experience of taking over Zhengzhou and Kaifeng cities and rural work in the newly liberated areas in Henan), Jan. 12, 1949. *P:YWS45–49*: 43–44.

58. "Zhongyuan ju guanyu zhuli difang renyuan de zhengce wenti fu Kaifeng Shiwei" (An answer from the Central Plain Bureau to the Kaifeng municipal committee on the question of dealing with enemy personnel), Dec. 1, 1948. *P:YWS45–49*: 32–33.

59. "Jieguan Zhengzhou Kaifeng de jingyan yu Zhongyuan xinqu de nongcun gongzuo." *P:YWS45–49*: 46–47.

60. Liu Zijiu, "Cong renshi chengshi dao xuehui chengshi gongzuo" (From knowing the cities to learning to work in the cities), Nov. 30, 1948. *P:jiefangqu*: 309–12.

61. This includes 6,000 workers from the railroad, postal, and communication services. There were about 23,000 workers in other enterprises.

62. "Kaifeng shoufu hou de gongzuo qingkuang" (Working conditions after the takeover of Kaifeng), Nov. 27, 1948. *P:YWS45–49*: 29–30.

63. In Huaiyang, the southern part of the city was still occupied by the enemy. The Communists based themselves near the city's north gate. The city itself was still a guerrilla zone. In Zhoukou, a secondary urban center on the Huai River, there was still intense fighting going on.

64. "Song Renqiong tongzhi guanyu chengshi gongzuo zhanqin qiuzheng ji zhengli caizheng jidu gei Mao zhuxi zhongyang ju de disan hao zonghe baogao" (Comprehensive report no. 3 from Comrade Song Renqiong to Chairman Mao and the Central Plain Bureau on the work in the cities, war services, autumn taxes, and reorganization of the financial system), Dec. 24, 1948. *P:YWS45–49*: 219–21.

65. Workers in a sock factory forced employers to give them three raises between October 1945 and April 1946. The cost of production became very high, C$140 a dozen, while the retail price was only a few dollars more. The factory was forced to close.

66. "Huazhong fenju guanyu gongzi he gonghui gongzuo de zhishi" (Directive from the Central China branch bureau on workers' wages and labor unions), Apr. 8, 1946. *P:Anhui*: 3: 61–64. The directive was first published in *Huazhong tongxun* (Central China newsletter) no. 3.

67. In Yimen township, 142 of the original 406 enterprises, mostly small shops owned by vendors, stayed open. One hundred and eighteen remained closed but stayed in the area.

68. Of the 28 brewing industries in Suixi city, only one remained. Most of the merchants fled the area.

69. The survey indicated that up to August 20, 1948, the number of rural workshops jumped from 2,193 to 4,950 in the 58 markets in six counties in western Anhui province. For Communist policies on rural markets, see "Yuwansu san fenqu huifu gongshang ye de gaikuang" (The condition for revival of commerce and industry in the Third District in the Yuwansu area), Sept. 1948. *P:Anhui*: 3: 343–50.

70. Deng Zihui, "Jieguan Zhengzhou, Kaifeng de jingyan yu Zhongyuan xinqu de nongcun gongzuo" (The experience of taking over Zhengzhou and Kaifeng cities and rural work in the newly liberated areas in Henan), Jan. 12, 1949. *P:jiefangqu*: 345–55.

71. "Jieguan Zhengzhou Kaifeng de jingyan yu Zhongyuan xinqu de nongcun gongzuo." *P:YWS45–49*: 44–46.

72. "Zheng-Bian zhuli dixia gongzuo ganbu de jidian jingyan" (The experience of dealing with underground cadres in the Zhengzhou-Kaifeng area), Dec. 14, 1948. *P:YWS45–49*: 35–37. This is a report sent by the Central Plain Bureau to Party Central.

73. "Zhongyuan ju dui Kaifeng jige wenti de dafu" (Answer from the Central Plain Bureau on a few questions on Kaifeng), Nov. 23, 1948. *P:YWS45–49*: 27–28.

74. For example, Xu Ganqing, former headmaster of Kaifeng High School, was given the position of head of the educational bureau; Pei Luren, director of the school of medicine at Henan University, was appointed head of the health bureau; Zhou Huanan was made head of the justice department, and Wang Lingxiao deputy of the security bureau. These people were "sympathetic" to the Communist cause.

75. In the Zhengzhou railway bureau, an administrative committee was set up to provide transitional leadership and give the party time to investigate the administration before making official appointments.

76. "Jieguan Zhengzhou Kaifeng de jingyan yu Zhongyuan xinqu de nongcun gongzuo: Deng Zihui tongzhi yi yue fen gei Mao zhuxi de zonghe baogao" (The experience of taking over Zhengzhou and Kaifeng cities and rural work in the newly liberated areas in Henan: A comprehensive report from Comrade Deng Zihui to Chairman Mao Zedong on the first month of the year), Jan. 12, 1949. *P:YWS45–49*: 41–43. Deng Zihui was the third secretary of the Central Plain Bureau.

77. "Kaifeng shoufu hou de gongzuo qingkuang." *P:YWS45–49*: 29–30. According to this report sent by the Central Plain Bureau to Party Central on November 27, 1948, 3,000 bandit gangs and Peace Preservation Corps gave up their arms. The report says that recruiting many existing administrative personnel might be a mistake, since it gave the citizens the impression that the old administration was still in operation.

78. For example, at Zhuji, a market town on the Longhai railroad in Shangqiu county, the head of police under the GMD was reappointed deputy head of the security bureau in the new administration. This resulted in widespread corruption and the protection of GMD secret agents in the area.

79. Beijing shifan xueyuan lishi xi Zhongguo jinxiandai shi jiaoyanshi 1985: 651–52.

80. "Yuwansu qu dangwei guanyu jiaqiang zhanqin gongzuo de zhishi" (Directive from the party committee on strengthening the work of war service in the Yuwansu area), Nov. 9, 1947. *P:YWS45–49*: 55–58.

81. "Yuwansu zhongyang fenju guanyu Huaihai zhanyi zhiqian gongzuo de chubu zongjie baogao" (A preliminary comprehensive report by the central branch bureau of the Yuwansu area on battlefront support in the Huaihai campaign), Feb. 25, 1949. *P:YWS45–49*: 237. Another report gave the figure for

desertion at the front as 70 percent. According to Song Renqiong, 5,000 pairs of stretcher-bearers were recruited in the Fourth, Fifth, and Seventh districts, but only 1,500 pairs arrived at the front. See "Song Renqiong tongzhi guanyu chengshi gongzuo zhanqin qiuzheng ji zhengli caizheng jidu gei Mao zhuxi zhongyang ju de disan hao zonghe baogao." *P:YWS45–49*: 222.

82. *P:YWS45–49*: 221–23.

83. In the Fourth District, peasants lost 500 head of draft animals hauling supplies to the Wo River.

84. "Yuwansu zhongyang fenju guanyu Huaihai zhanyi zhiqian gongzuo de chubu zongjie baogao." *P:YWS45–49*: 240–43.

85. "Huaibei dang-zheng-jun weiyuanhui guanyu kefu jinhou caizheng jingji kunnan de jueding" (Resolution by the party-administration-military committee in Huaibei on overcoming present and future financial difficulties), Mar. 10, 1947. *P:Anhui*: 3: 154–55.

86. Troops gathered 150,000 *jin* of grain in Sinan county, another 150,000 *jin* from Huaisi, 100,000 *jin* in Sisu and Siling, and 50,000 *jin* from Siyang. See "Huaibei dang-zheng-jun weiyuanhui guanyu kefu caizheng kunnan de buchong zhishi" (Supplementary directive from the party-administration-military committee of Huaibei on overcoming financial difficulties), Mar. 23, 1947. *P:Anhui*: 3: 156–57.

87. "Wanxi gongwei guanyu dangqian caijing gongzuo de zhishi" (Directive from the working committee in western Anhui on present financial work), Oct. 6, 1947. *P:Anhui*: 3: 210–13.

88. In the three months before the summer harvest of 1947, the army and local authorities were required to raise C$300 million to support the war, C$100 million from taxes and C$200 from the sale of military spoils. "Huaibei dang-zheng-jun weiyuanhui guanyu kefu jinhou caizheng jingji kunnan de jueding." *P:Anhui*: 3: 155.

89. In Jieshou, peasants who participated in four months of fighting jointly formed a "Committee for the Support of the War Front and Protection of Families." The party recruited 130 party members and 40 cadres. "Yuwansu zhongyang fenju guanyu Huaihai zhanyi zhiqian gongzuo de chubu zongjie baogao." *P:YWS45–49*: 237–40.

90. *P:dashiji*: 173–84; Wang Tianjiang et al. 1990: 492–508.

Conclusion

1. Barrington Moore clearly distinguishes two types of local community solidarity: "conservative solidarity," in which the community is dominated by local elites, and "radical solidarity," in which peasants control the resources. Moore 1966: 475–76.

2. Deng Zihui, "Lun qunzhong yundong" (On mass movement), Nov. 1, 1948. *P:jiefangqu*: 260.

3. *P:jiefangqu*: 232–34.

4. *P:jiefangqu*: 233, 236.

5. Skocpol 1982: 163.

6. The term comes from Stephen Vlastos. See Vlastos 1986: 17.

7. Deng Zihui, "Lun qunzhong yundong." *P:jiefangqu*: 236.

8. *P:jiefangqu*: 236.

9. Although the Henan-Hubei section of the Eyuwan base was about 100 kilometers from Hankou, the influence of a large metropolis such as Wuhan covered a very wide area. As demonstrated in this study, a sizable number of the elite leaders in Macheng and Huangan in the Eyuwan base received their educational training in the Wuhan area. Commercialization that was closely linked to business activities in Hankou also greatly transformed the southern segment of the Eyuwan base area. Guangshan was intellectually and economically linked to the Beijing-Hankou rail town of Xinyang.

10. Wolf 1969: 290.

11. The term "outward oriented" is borrowed from Joel Migdal. See Migdal 1974.

Bibliography

Abbreviations

CHINESE COMMUNIST PARTY DOCUMENTS

P:Anhui. Anhui sheng caizheng ting (Anhui Finance Department) and Anhui sheng dangan guan (Anhui Province Party Archives), eds. 1983. *Anhui geming genjudi caijing shiliao xuan* (Selected materials on the financial history of the Anhui revolutionary base). 3 vols. Hefei: Anhui renmin chubanshe.

P:Anyang. *Anyang dangshi ziliao* (Anyang party history materials). 1983. Anyang: Henan renmin chubanshe.

P:dashiji. Zhonggong Henan shengwei dangshi ziliao zhengji bianzuan weiyuanhui (Compilation Committee for Historical Materials of the Henan CCP), ed. 1986. *Zhonggong Henan dangshi dashiji* (Chronological events of the Henan CCP). Zhengzhou: Henan renmin chubanshe.

P:EYW. Zhongyang dangan guan (Central Party Archives), Hubei sheng dangan guan (Hubei Province Party Archives), Henan sheng dangan guan (Henan Province Party Archives), and Anhui sheng dangan guan (Anhui Province Party Archives), eds. 1985. *Eyuwan suqu geming lishi wenjian huiji, 1929–1934* (A collection of documents on the revolutionary history of the Hubei-Henan-Anhui soviet area). 5 vols. N.p.

P:Fengbei. Zhonggong Xinyang diwei dangshi ziliao zhengbian weiyuanhui (Compilation Committee for Historical Materials of the Xinyang CCP), ed. 198?–87. *Fengbei* (Monument). 15 vols. Xinyang: Zhonggong Xinyang diwei dangshi ziliao zhengbian weiyuanhui.

P:5/30. Li Guangyi and Li Guoqiang, eds. 1985. *Wu sa yundong zai Henan* (The May 30th Movement in Henan). Zhonggong Henan dangshi ziliao congshu (Henan CCP historical materials series). Zhengzhou: Henan renmin chubanshe.

P:GZPM. Zhongguo Guangdong shengwei dangshi yanjiu weiyuanhui bangongshi (Office of the Committee of Party Studies of the Guangdong Communist Party) and Mao Zedong tongzhi zhuban nongmin yundong jiangxi suo jiu zhi jinianguan (Mao Zedong Peasant Training Institute Museum), eds. 1983. *Guangzhou nongmin yundong jiangxi suo wenxian ziliao* (Documentary materials on the Guangzhou Peasant Training Institute). Guangdong dangshi ziliao zongkan (Guangdong party historical materials series). N.p.

P:jiefangqu. Zhonggong Henan shengwei dangshi gongzuo weiyuanhui (Party History Working Committee of the Provincial Committee of the Henan CCP), ed. 1987. *Zhongyuan jiefang qu* (The liberated areas in Henan). Zhonggong Henan dangshi ziliao congshu (Henan CCP historical materials series). Zhengzhou: Henan renmin chubanshe.

P:JJLY-CJ. Henan sheng caizheng ting (Henan Finance Department) and Henan sheng dangan guan (Henan Province Party Archives), eds. 1985. *Jin-Ji-Lu-Yu kang Ri genjudi caijing shiliao xuanbian, Henan bufen* (Selected historical materials on the finance and economy of the Shanxi-Hebei-Shandong-Henan anti-Japanese base, Henan section). Zhengzhou: Henan dangan chubanshe.

P:JLY. Zhonggong Henan shengwei dangshi ziliao zhengji bianzuan weiyuanhui (Compilation Committee for Historical Materials of the Henan CCP), ed. 1985. *Ji-Lu-Yu kang Ri genjudi* (Hebei-Shandong-Henan anti-Japanese base). Zhengzhou: Henan renmin chubanshe.

P:JLY-ZL. *Zhonggong Ji-Lu-Yu bianqu dangshi ziliao xuanbian* bianji zu (Compilation Committee for the *Selected materials on the party history of the Hebei-Shandong-Henan border base*), ed. 1985. *Zhonggong Ji-Lu-Yu bianqu dangshi ziliao xuanbian* (Selected materials on the party history of the Hebei-Shandong-Henan border base). 2 vols. Jinan: Shandong daxue chubanshe.

P:kangzhan. *Henan kangzhan shi lue* bianxie zu (Compilation Committee for the *Brief history of the Sino-Japanese War in Henan*). 1985. *Henan kangzhan she lue* (A brief history of the Sino-Japanese War in Henan). Zhengzhou: Henan renmin chubanshe.

P:minzhu. Zhonggong Henan shengwei dangshi ziliao zhengji bianzuan weiyuanhui (Compilation Committee for Historical Materials of the Henan CCP), ed. 1986. *Zhonghua minzhu de zhuangju*: *Henan sheng jinan kang Ri zhanzheng shengli sishi zhou nian wenji* (The heroic deeds of the Chinese race: A collection of essays in memory of the 40th anniversary of victory in the Sino-Japanese War in Henan). Zhengzhou: Henan renmin chubanshe.

P:PM. Zhonggong Henan shengwei dangshi gongzuo weiyuanhui (Party History Working Committee of the Provincial Committee of the Henan CCP), ed. 1987. *Yizhan shiqi Henan nongmin yundong* (The Henan peasant movement during the First Revolutionary War). Zhengzhou: Henan renmin chubanshe.

P:PXF. Zhonggong Henan shengwei dangshi ziliao zhengbian weiyuanhui (Compilation Committee for Historical Materials of the Henan CCP), ed. 1986. *Gong chui zuguo: Jinian Peng Xuefeng tongzhi xisheng sishi zhounian zhuanji* (Meritorious deeds set an example for the nation: Special collection in memory of the 40th anniversary of the heroic death of Comrade Peng Xuefeng). Zhengzhou: Henan renmin chubanshe.

P:Shangqiu. Wu Bingli, Jin Yiguan, Yang Mingxun, and Xie Gongyi, eds. 1985–87. *Dang de guanghui zhao qianqiu* (The glory of the party radiates through the ages). Vols. 2–4. Shangqiu: Zhonggong Shangqiu xianwei dangshi bangongshi.

P:shengwei. *Kangzhan shiqi de Henan shengwei* bianxie zu (Compilation team for the *Provincial Committee of the Henan CCP during the Sino-Japanese War*), ed. 1986. *Kangzhan shiqi de Henan shengwei* (Provincial Committee of the Henan CCP during the Sino-Japanese War). Zhengzhou: Henan renmin chubanshe.

P:SQT. Sui-Qi-Tai dangshi bianxie zu (Compilation team for the Suixian-Qixian-Taikang Party History), ed. 1985. *Sui-Qi-Tai diqu shiliao xuan* (Selected historical materials on the history of Suixian, Qixian, and Taikang counties). Zhonggong Henan dangshi ziliao congshu (Henan CCP historical materials series). 2 vols. Zhengzhou: Henan renmin chubanshe.

P:Taihang. Zhonggong Henan shengwei dangshi ziliao zhengji bianzuan weiyuanhui (Compilation Committee for Historical Materials of the Henan CCP), ed. 1986. *Taihang kang Ri genjudi* (The Taihang anti-Japanese base). 2 vols. Zhengzhou: Henan renmin chubanshe.

P:WQY. Wang Quanying, ed. 1984. *Zhonggong Henan dangshi ziliao* (Henan party history materials). Vol. 3, Eyuwan suqu ziliao xuanbian zhi yi (Selected materials on the Hubei-Henan-Anhui soviet area). Zhengzhou: Henan renmin chubanshe.

P:Xinxian. Xinxian wen guan hui (Xinxian Documents Management Society) and Henan daxue (Henan University), eds. 1985. *Xinxian geming shi: Eyuwan genjudi shoufu* (A history of revolution in Xinxian: The capital of the Hubei-Henan-Anhui border base). Zhengzhou: Henan renmin chubanshe.

P:Yu-E. *Yu-E bian kang Ri genjudi* bianxie zu (Compilation team for the *Henan-Hubei anti-Japanese base*), ed. 1986. *Yu-E bian kang Ri genjudi* (Henan-Hubei anti-Japanese base). Zhengzhou: Henan renmin chubanshe.

P:YWS. Yuwansu bian dangshi bianxie zu (Compilation team for the party history of the Henan-Anhui-Jiangsu border base), ed. 1985. *Yuwansu kang Ri genjudi* (Henan-Anhui-Jiangsu anti-Japanese base). Vol. 1. Zhengzhou: Henan renmin chubanshe.

P:YWS45–49. Henan sheng dangan guan (Henan Province Party Archives), Henan sheng shehui kexue yuan lishi yanjiu zuo (Historical Research Institute, Henan Academy of Social Sciences), comps. 1984. *Yuwansu bianqu geming lishi dangan ziliao xuan bian (1945–1949)* (A selection of archival materials on the revolutionary history of the Henan-Anhui-Jiangsu border base). Zhengzhou: Henan Academy of Social Sciences.

P:YWS kang Ri. Yuwansu san fenqu dangshi ziliao zhengji bangongshi (Compilation Office of Party Historical Materials of the Third District of the Henan-Anhui-Jiangsu border base), ed. 1988. *Yuwansu bian kang Ri fenghuo: geming douzheng shi ziliao xuanbian* (War flames over the Henan-Anhui-Jiangsu border: Selected historical materials of revolutionary struggle). N.p.: Yuwansu san fenqu dangshi ziliao zhengji bangongshi.

P:Zhugou. Zhonggong Zhumadian diwei dangshi ziliao zhengbian weiyuanhui (Compilation Committee for Historical Materials of the Zhumadian CCP), ed. 1985. *Kangzhan shiqi de Zhugou* (Zhugou during the Sino-Japanese War). Zhengzhou: Henan renmin chubanshe.

P:ZLF. Wu Bingli, Jin Yiguan, Yang Mingxun, and Xie Gongyi, eds. 1984. *Zhang Lanfeng qi ren* (Zhang Lanfeng: The man). Shangqiu: Zhonggong Shangqiu xianwei dangshi bangongshi.

HENAN LOCAL HISTORY MATERIALS

LH:Beifa. Zeng Guangxing and Wang Quanying, eds. 1985. *Beifa zhanzheng zai Henan* (The Northern Expedition in Henan). Henan shizhi ziliao congbian zhi qi (Henan local history materials series, no. 7). Zhengzhou: Henan renmin chubanshe.

LH:5/30. Pang Shouxin, ed. 1986. *Wu sa yundong zai Henan* (The May 30th Movement in Henan). Henan shizhi ziliao congbian zhi wu (Henan local history materials series, no. 5). Zhengzhou: Henan renmin chubanshe.

LH:Henan-ZL. Henan sheng difang shizhi bianzuan weiyuanhui (Compilation Committee of Henan Local History), comp. 1983–85. *Henan shizhi ziliao* (Henan local history materials), 9 vols. zhengzhou: Henan sheng difang shizhi bianzuan weiyuanhui. From vols. 1–5, known as *Henan difang zhi zhengwen ziliao xuan* (Collected materials for the Henan local gazetteer).

LH:huoYu. Chen Chuanhai, Xu Youli, Liu Haitao, Su Zhigang, and Zhang Binyuan, eds. 1986. *Ri jun huo Yu ziliao xuanbian* (Selected materials on the calamity that Japanese troops brought to Henan). Henan shizhi congbian zhi si (Henan local history materials series, no. 4). Zhengzhou: Henan renmin chubanshe.

LH:Jiaozuo. Henan sheng zong gonghui gongyun shi yanjiu shi (Research Institute for Labor Movements, Henan General Labor Union), ed. 1984. *Jiaozuo meikuang gongren yundong shi ziliao xuan bian* (Selected materials on the miners' movement in Jiaozuo). Zhengzhou: Henan renmin chubanshe.

LH:1911. Wang Tianjiang, ed. 1986. *Henan Xinhai geming shishi changbian* (Long version of events of the 1911 Revolution in Henan). Henan sheng shizhi ziliao congbian zhi san (Henan local history materials series, no. 3). 2 vols. Zhengzhou: Henan renmin chubanshe.

LH:RS. Chen Chuanhai, Wang Weiping, Liu Guangming, Wu Xiongliang, Guo Liping, and Li Guoqiang. 1984. *Henan Hongqiang hui ziliao xuan bian* (Selected materials on the Red Spears in Henan). In *LH:Henan-ZL*, vol. 6.

LH:YWS. Feng Wengang, ed. 1985. *Yuwansu bian wenxian ziliao xuanbian* (Selected documentary materials on the Henan-Anhui-Jiangsu border base). Henan shizhi ziliao congbian zhi liu (Henan local history materials series, no. 6). Zhengzhou: Henan renmin chubanshe.

LH:zhanzheng. Henan sheng difang zhi bianzuan weiyuanhui (Compilation Committee of Henan Local History) and Henan sheng difang shizhi xiehui (Association of Henan Local History), eds. 1985. *Kang Ri zhanzheng shiqi de Henan* (Henan during the anti-Japanese war). Zhengzhou: Henan sheng difang zhi bianzuan weiyuanhui and Henan sheng difang shizhi xie hui.

References

Alavi, Hamza. 1987. "Peasantry and Capitalism: A Marxist Discourse." In Shanin, pp. 185–96.

Allmand, C. T., ed. 1973. *Society at War*. New York: Barnes & Noble.

Amano Genosuke. 1935. "Shinno kosaku seido no kenkyu, ni" (A study of tenancy systems in China). *Toa* (East Asia) 4: 19–32; 5: 37–56; 6: 41–77; 8: 42–87.

Atkinson, Alexander. 1981. *Social Order and the General Theory of Strategy*. London: Routledge.

Arrigo, Linda G. 1986. "Landownership Concentration in China: The Buck Survey Revisited." *Modern China* 12: 259–360.

Auyang Zhiliang. 1982. "Eyu bian geming genjudi shiqi tudi zhengce chuxi" (A preliminary analysis of land policy in the Hubei-Henan border revolutionary base). *Eyuwan suqu lishi yanjiuhui di san jie lunwen xuanji* (Proceedings of the third research conference on the history of the Eyuwan soviet area), pp. 352–64. Zhengzhou.

Averill, Stephen C. 1987. "Party, Society and Local Elite in the Jiangxi Communist Movement." *Journal of Asian Studies* 46: 179–303.

———. 1990. "Local Elites and Communist Revolution in the Jiangxi Hill Country." In *Chinese Local Elites and Patterns of Dominance*, Mary B. Rankin and Joseph W. Esherick, eds., pp. 282–304. Berkeley: University of California Press.

Baba Takeshi. 1974. "Kosokai undo josetsu" (Introduction to the Red Spears). *Chugoku minshu hanren no sekai* (The world of Chinese popular uprisings). Tokyo.

———. 1976. "Kosokai" (Red Spears). *Shakai keizaishi gaku* (The study of social economic history), vol. 42, no. 1: 59–83.

Baker, Hugh D. R. 1979. *Chinese Family and Kinship*. New York: Columbia University Press.

Ball, Howard, and Thomas P. Lauth, Jr., eds. 1971. *Changing Perspectives in Contemporary Political Analysis*. London: Prentice-Hall.

Barnett, A. Doak, ed. 1969. *Chinese Communist Politics in Action*. Seattle: University of Washington Press.

Beijing shifan xueyuan lishi xi Zhongguo jinxiandai shi jiaoyanshi (Teaching and Research Section on Contemporary and Modern China, Department of History, Beijing Normal Institute). 1985. *Jianming Zhongguo jinxiandai shi cidan* (A concise dictionary of contemporary and modern Chinese history). 2 vols. Beijing: Zhongguo qingnian chubanshe.

Billingsley, Phil. 1981. "Bandits, Bosses, and Bare Sticks: Beneath the Surface of Local Control in Early Republican China." *Modern China* 7, no. 3: 235–88.

———. 1988. *Bandits in Republican China*. Stanford, Calif.: Stanford University Press.

Bramson, Leon, and George W. Goethals. 1964. *War*. New York: Basic.

Brocheux, Pierre. 1983. "Moral or Political Economy? The Peasants Are Always Rational." *Journal of Asian Studies* 42, no. 4: 791–804.

Buck, John Lossing. [1937] 1956. *Land Utilization in China*. Reprint. New York: Council on Economic and Cultural Affairs.

Chai Huazhou. 1984. "Luoyang diqu Hongqiang hui de xingqi yu xiaomie" (The rise and fall of the Red Spears in the Luoyang area). *Henan wenshi ziliao* (Henan historical materials) 10: 66–79.

Chang Jianqiao, Zhu Youwen, and Shang Xingfeng. 1985. *Henan sheng deli* (Henan geography). Zhengzhou: Henan Jiaoyu chubanshe.

Chang Jui-te. 1987. *Ping-Han telu yu Huaibei de jingji fazhan* (The Beijing-Hankou railroad and economic development in North China, 1905–1937). Zhongyang yanjiu yuan jindai shi yanjiu suo zhuan kan 55 (Institute of Modern History, Academia Sinica, monograph series no. 55). Taipei: Zhongyang yanjiu yuan.

Chang Kuo-t'ao. 1972. *The Rise of the Chinese Communist Party: The Autobiography of Chang Kuo-t'ao*. Lawrence: University Press of Kansas.

Chen Chuanhai. 1983. "Kang-Ri zhanzheng shiqi de Henan lunxian qu he Guomindang tongzhi qu qingkuang jianjie" (A brief account of the situation in the Japanese-occupied areas and Guomindang-controlled areas in Henan during the anti-Japanese war period). In *LH:Henan-ZL* 4: 60–80.
Chen Duxiu. 1926. "Hongqiang hui yu Zhongguo de nongmin baodong" (The Red Spears and Chinese peasant uprisings). *Xiangdao zhoubao* (Guided weekly) 158: 1543–44.
Chen Honggen. 1934. "Wo guo zudian wenti zhi niao kang" (A bird's-eye view of the tenancy question in our country). *Shiye tongji* (Industrial statistics) 2, no. 5: 40–62.
Chen Shinong and Lin Huanfen. 1981. "Juyou difang tedian de gong nong wuzhuang geju zhengce: Chaishan bao genjudi de kaipi chu tan" (The policy of worker-peasant hegemony with a regional cast: A first look at the development of the Fodder Hill base). *Henan shida xuebao* (Henan Normal University Journal) 1: 15–22.
Chen Weiru. 1980. "Huanghe Huayuan Kou jueti jingguo" (The breaking of the Yellow River dike at Huayuan Kou). *Henan wenshi ziliao* (Henan historical materials) 4: 168–69.
Chen, Yung-fa. 1986. *Making Revolution: The Communist Movement in Eastern and Central China, 1937–1945*. Berkeley: University of California Press.
Cheng, Ronald Ye-lin, ed. 1973. *The Sociology of Revolution: Readings on Political Upheaval and Popular Unrest*. Chicago: Regnery.
Chesneaux, Jean. 1968. *The Chinese Labor Movement, 1919–1927*. Trans. H. M. Wright. Stanford, Calif.: Stanford University Press.
———, ed. 1972. *Popular Movements and Secret Societies in China, 1840–1850*. Stanford, Calif.: Stanford University Press.
———. 1973. *Peasant Revolts in China, 1840–1949*. New York: Norton.
Chi'i Hsi-sheng. 1976. *Warlord Politics in China, 1916–1928*. Stanford, Calif.: Stanford University Press.
———. 1982. *Nationalist China at War: Military Defeats and Political Collapse, 1937–1945*. Ann Arbor: University of Michigan Press.
Chongxiu Linxian zhi (A revised edition of the Linxian county gazetteer). 1932.
Chongxiu Runan xianzhi (A revised edition of the Runan county gazetteer). 1938.
Chongxiu Shangcai xianzhi (A revised edition of the Shangcai county gazetteer). 1944.
Chongxiu Xinyang xianzhi (A revised edition of the Xinyang county gazetteer). 1934.
Cohen, Paul. 1984. *Discovering History in China*. New York: Columbia University Press.
Colburn, Forrest D., ed. 1989. *Everyday Forms of Peasant Resistance*. Armonk, N.Y.: Sharpe.
Colby, Scott D. 1969. "The Oyuwan Soviet: An Early Chinese Communist Rural Base." Unpublished master's thesis, Columbia University.
Cui Zuze. 1984. "Tianmen hui zai Huixian" (The Heavenly Gate Society in Hui county). *Henan wenshi ziliao* (Henan historical materials) 11: 80–86.
Dai Xuanzhi. 1973. *Hongqiang hui* (The Red Spears). Taibei: Shihuo chubanshe.
Davies, James C. 1972. "Revolution and the J-Curve." In Welch and Taintor.

Davis, Fei-Ling. 1971. *Primitive Revolutionaries of China: A Study of Secret Societies in the Late Nineteenth Century*. Honolulu: University of Hawaii Press.

Deng Zhongxia. 1949. *Zhongguo zhigong yundong jianshi* (A brief history of the Chinese labor movement). Beijing.

Denisoff, R. Serge, ed. 1974. *The Sociology of Dissent*. New York: Harcourt Brace.

Di er ci Zhongguo laodong nianjian (Second Chinese labor yearbook). 1933–34. Shanghai: Shiye bu.

Dobrowolski, Kazimierz. 1987. "Peasant Traditional Culture." In Shanin, pp. 261–77.

Du Dazhong. 1984. "Wo tong Tianmen hui shouling Han Yuming deng de jiechu" (My contacts with Han Yuming, leader of the Heavenly Gate Society, and others in the Society). *Henan wenshi ziliao* (Henan historical materials) 11: 32–54.

Eastman, Lloyd. 1984. *Seeds of Destruction: Nationalist China in War and Revolution*. Stanford, Calif.: Stanford University Press.

Easton, David. 1973. "Some Limits of Exchange Theory in Politics." In Effrat, pp. 129–48.

Edwards, P. K. 1981. *Strikes in the United States, 1881–1974*. New York: St. Martin's.

Effrat, Andrew, ed. 1973. *Perspectives in Political Sociology*. Indianapolis, Ind.: Bobbs-Merrill.

Elvin, Mark, and G. William Skinner, eds. 1974. *The Chinese City Between Two Worlds*. Stanford: Stanford University Press.

Esherick, Joseph W. 1983. "Symposium on Peasant Rebellions: Some Introductory Comments." *Modern China* 9, no. 3: 275–84.

———. 1987. *The Origins of the Boxer Uprising*. Berkeley: University of California Press.

Feeny, David. 1983. "The Moral or the Rational Peasant? Competing Hypotheses of Collective Action." *Journal of Asian Studies* 42, no. 4: 769–90.

Feng Hefa, ed. 1933. *Zhongguo nongcun jingji ziliao* (Materials on the Chinese rural economy). Zhongguo jingji shiliao zongshu (Historical materials on Chinese economy series) 1, no. 2. 2 vols. Taibei: Huashi chubanshe.

Ferree, Myra M., and Frederick D. Miller. 1985. "Mobilization and Meaning: Toward an Integration of Social Psychological and Resource Perspective on Social Movements." *Sociological Inquiry* 55: 38–61.

Feuerwerker, Albert. 1975. *Rebellion in Nineteenth-Century China*. Ann Arbor: Center for Chinese Studies, University of Michigan.

Freedman, Maurice. 1958. *Lineage Organization in Southeastern China*. LSE Monographs on Social Anthropology, no. 18. London: Athlone.

———. 1966. *Chinese Lineage and Society: Fukien and Kwangtung*. LSE Monographs on Social Anthropology, no. 33. London: Athlone.

Freitag, Sandria B. 1989. "Popular Culture in the Rewriting of History: An Essay in Comparative History and Historiography." *Peasant Studies* 16, no. 3: 169–98.

Fugou xianzhi (Fugou county gazetteer). 1986.

Gamson, William A. 1975. *The Strategy of Social Protest*. Homewood, Ill.: Dorsey.

Gillin, Donald. 1964. "Peasant Nationalism in the History of Chinese Communism." *Journal of Asian Studies* 23, no. 2: 269–89.

———. 1967. *Warlord: Yen Hsi-shan in Shansi Province, 1911–1949*. Princeton, N.J.: Princeton University Press.

Guangshan xianzhi yuegao (A draft of the Guangshan county gazetteer). 1936.

Guggenheim, Scott E., and Robert P. Weller, 1982. "Introduction: Moral Economy, Capitalism, and State Power in Rural Protest." In Weller and Guggenheim, pp. 3–12.

Guo Shaoyi. 1980. "Huiyi Guangzhou di liu jie nongmin yundong jiangxi suo" (Recollections of the 6th Class of the Peasant Training Institute in Guangzhou). *Dangshi yanjiu* (Studies of party history) 5: 49–53.

Guo Xuyin and Chen Xingtang. 1987. *Aiguo jiangjun Feng Yuxiang* (Feng Yuxiang, the patriotic general). Zhengzhou: Henan renmin chubanshe.

Gurney, Joan Neff, and Kathleen J. Tierney. 1982. "Relative Deprivation and Social Movement: A Critical Look at Twenty Years of Theory and Research." *Sociological Quarterly* 23: 33–47.

Gurr, Ted R. 1972. "Psychological Factors in Civil Violence." In Welch and Taintor.

Han Sheng. 1928. "Zhongguo nongmin fudan de fushui" (The taxes borne by the Chinese peasants). *Dongfang zazhi* (Chinese miscellany) 25, no. 19: 9–10.

Han Xiaoting. 1984. "Yu dong Tongxu, Qixian, Suixian Hongqiang hui huodong gaikuang" (A survey of Red Spear activities in Tongxu, Qixian, and Suixian in eastern Henan). *Henan wenshi ziliao* (Henan historical materials) 10: 82–89.

Han Yide and Yao Weidou. 1987. *Li Dazhou shengping jinian* (A chronological biography of Li Dazhou). Harbin: Heilongjiang renmin chubanshe.

Harrell, Stevan, and Elizabeth J. Perry. 1982. "Syncretic Sects in Chinese Society: An Introduction." *Modern China* 8, no. 3: 283–304.

Harrison, James P. 1969. *The Communists and Chinese Peasant Rebellions: A Study in the Rewriting of Chinese History*. New York: Atheneum.

———. 1972. *The Long March to Power: A History of the Chinese Communist Party, 1921–72*. New York: Praeger.

Hartford, Kathleen J. 1980. "Step by Step: Reform, Resistance, and Revolution in Chin-Ch'a-Chi Border Region, 1927–1945." Ph.D. diss., Stanford University.

Hartford, Kathleen, and Steven M. Goldstein, eds. 1989. *Single Sparks: China's Rural Revolution*. Armonk, N.Y.: Sharpe.

He Min. 1985. "Liyong Tianmen hui yu Ri kou zuo douzheng: Kang Ri zhanzheng shiqi Yu bei dixia gongzuo diandi" (Using the Heavenly Gate Society in a struggle against the Japanese invaders: Some information on the underground activities in Northern Henan in the anti-Japanese resistance war). *Henan wenshi ziliao* (Henan historical materials) 9: 50–56.

He Yang. 1982. "Wang Ruofei yu Yu-Shan qu dangwei" (Wang Ruofei and the Henan-Shaanxi Regional Committee). *Guizhou wenshi congkan* (Guizhou literature and history series) 2: 19–27.

"Henan difang dangshi ruo gan wenti yanjiu zongshu" (A summary of a number of questions on the study of Henan party history). 1989. *Henan dangshi yanjiu* (Study of Henan party history) 1: 33–45.

Henan sheng difang zhi bianzuan weiyuanhui (Compilation Committee for

Henan Local History), ed. *Henan renwu* (Henan historical figures). 3 vols. Zhengzhou: Henan sheng difang zhi bianzuan weiyuanhui.

Henan sheng nongcun diaocha (An investigation of Henan villages). 1934. Nanjing.

Henan sheng tongji xuehui (Henan Provincial Statistics Society), Henan sheng tongji ju "tongji zhi" bianzuan bangongshi (Compilation Office for the "Statistics Gazette," Henan Provincial Statistics Bureau), and "Henan tongji" bianji bu (Editorial Board of the "Henan Statistics"), eds. 1986. *Minguo shiqi Henan sheng tongji ziliao* (Henan statistical materials: The Republican period). N.p.

Henan sheng wenzheng ting (Administrative Department, Henan Provincial Government), ed. 1979–87. *Lieshi yongsheng* (Long live the martyrs). 12 vols. Zhengzhou: Henan renmin chubanshe.

Hobsbawm, Eric J. 1959. *Primitive Rebels*. New York: Norton.

———. 1973. *Revolutionaries*. London: Quartet.

Hofheinz, Roy Jr. 1969. "The Ecology of Chinese Communist Success: Rural Influence Patterns, 1923–45." In Barnett.

———. 1977. *The Broken Wave: The Chinese Communist Peasant Movement, 1922–1928*. Cambridge, Mass.: Harvard University Press.

Horowitz, Irving Louis, ed. 1970. *Masses in Latin America*. New York: Oxford University Press.

Hou Wuzhao. 1984. "Tianmen hui shimo lue" (A brief history of the beginning and end of the Heavenly Gate Society). *Henan wenshi ziliao* 11: 55–73.

Hou Zhiying and Cai Kangzhi, eds. 1990. *Dabeishan fengyun lu: Yu dongnan tudi geming zhanzheng shi gao* (The storm in the Dabie Mountains: A draft history of the revolutionary land war in southeastern Henan). Zhengzhou: Henan renmin chubanshe.

Hou Zhiying, Chen Shinong, and Yin Zhongjun. 1982. "Wu Huanxian zai Eyuwan diqu de geming huodong" (Wu Huanxian's revolutionary activities in the Hubei-Henan-Anhui area). *Eyuwan suqu lishi yanjiu hui di san jie nian hui lunwen xuanji* (Proceedings of the third research conference on the history of the Hubei-Henan-Anhui soviet area), pp. 275–301. Zhengzhou.

How, Julie Lien-ying. 1985–86. "Soviet Advisers With the Kuominchun, 1925–1926." In *Chinese Studies in History*, Li Yu-ning, ed., vol. 19, nos. 1–2. Armonk, N.Y.: Sharpe.

Hsiao, Kung-chuan. 1960. *Rural China: Imperial Control in the Nineteenth Century*. Seattle: University of Washington Press.

Hsiao, Tso-liang. 1969. *The Land Revolution in China, 1930–1934: A Study of Documents*. Seattle: University of Washington Press.

Hsieh, Winston. 1974. "Peasant Insurrection and the Marketing Hierarchy in the Canton Delta, 1911." In Elvin and Skinner.

Huaiyang xianzhi (Huaiyang county gazetteer). 1934.

Huang, Philip C. C. 1985. *The Peasant Economy and Social Changes in North China*. Stanford, Calif.: Stanford University Press.

———. 1990. *The Peasant Family and Rural Development in the Yangzi Delta, 1350–1988*. Stanford, Calif.: Stanford University Press.

Huntington, Samuel P. 1968. *Political Order in Changing Societies*. New Haven, Conn.: Yale University Press.

Johnson, Chalmers A. 1962. *Peasant Nationalism and Communist Power: The Emergence of Revolutionary China, 1937–1945*. Stanford, Calif.: Stanford University Press.

———. 1966. *Revolutionary Change*. Boston: Little, Brown.

Johnson, John J. 1964. *The Military and Society in Latin America*. Stanford, Calif.: Stanford University Press.

Jordan, Donald A. 1976. *The Northern Expedition: China's National Revolution of 1926–1928*. Honolulu: University of Hawaii Press.

Kataoka, Tetsuya. 1974. *Resistance and Revolution in China: The Communists and the Second United Front*. Berkeley: University of California Press.

Kau, Ying-mao. 1974. "Urban and Rural Strategies in the Chinese Communist Revolution." In Lewis, pp. 253–70.

Keyes, Charles F. 1983. "Peasant Strategies in Asian Societies: Moral and Rational Economic Approaches—A Symposium. Introduction." *Journal of Asian Studies* 42, no. 4: 753–68.

Kuhn, Philip A. 1970. *Rebellion and Its Enemies in Late Imperial China: Militarization and Social Structure, 1796–1864*. Cambridge, Mass.: Harvard University Press.

Leiden, Carl, and Karl M. Schmitt, eds. 1968. *The Politics of Violence: Revolution in the Modern World*. Englewood Cliffs, N.J.: Prentice-Hall.

Levine, Steven I. 1987. *Anvil of Victory: The Communist Revolution in Manchuria, 1945–1948*. New York: Columbia University Press.

Lewis, John W. 1966. "The Study of Chinese Political Culture." *World Politics* 18, no. 3: 507–12.

———, ed. 1974. *Peasant Rebellion and Communist Revolution in Asia*. Stanford, Calif.: Stanford University Press.

Li Dazhao. [1926] 1959. "Lu Yu Shan deng sheng de Hongqiang hui" (The Red Spears in Shandong, Henan, and Shaanxi). [Originally published on Aug. 8, 1926 in *Zhengzhi shenghuo* (Political life) no. 80/81.] *Li Dazhao xuan ji* (Selected works of Li Dazhao), p. 546. Renmin chubanshe.

Li Guoqiang. 1984. "Lue lun yi zhan shiqi Hongqiang hui zai Henan nongmin yundong zhong de lishi zuoyong" (A brief discussion on the historical effect of the Red Spears in the peasant movement in Henan during the First Revolutionary War period). *Shixue xizuo* (Historical exercises), pp. 23–29.

———. 1986. "Hongqiang hui yu Henan nongmin yundong" (The Red Spears and the peasant movement in Henan). *Zhongzhou jin gu* (Henan, past and present) no. 6: 32–35.

Li Guozhong and Jiang Shulin. 1987. "Lue shu Ri jun dui Henan de jingji luedo" (A brief account of the Japanese economic pillage in Henan). *Henan dangshi yanjiu* (Henan party history study) 5: 58–61.

Li Hongbin. 1979. "Zui zao de nongmin baodong" (The earliest peasant uprising in Henan). *Henan wenshi ziliao* (Henan historical materials) 2: 7–10.

Li Jianquan. 1932. "Tianmen hui shi mo" (The beginning and end of the Heavenly Gate Society). *Chongxiu Linxian zhi* (A revised edition of the Lin county gazetteer), vol. 14 (Chronological events).

Li Lin. 1991. "Kangzhan chuqi Zhonggong Henan zhuzhi da fazhan de tedian he jingyan jiaoxun" (The characteristics, experience, and lessons of the rapid development of Henan party organizations in the early period of the Sino-

Japanese War). *Henan dangshi yanjiu* (The study of Henan party history) no. 3: 32–36.

Li Mingxi. 1983. "Luoyang Hongqiang hui zhi qi luo" (The ups and downs of the Red Spears in Luoyang). In *LH:Henan-ZL* 1: 65–66.

Li Shanyu and Yang Shusheng. 1985. "Li Dazhao yu Guominjun" (Li Dazhao and the Guominjun). *Qilu xuekan* (Shandong journal) 2: 72–78.

Li Zeqing. 1982. "Da geming shiqi de Queshan nongmin yundong" (Peasant uprisings in Queshan at the time of the Great Revolution). Recorded by Wang Quanying. *Henan wenshi ziliao* (Henan historical materials) 7: 31–44.

Liang Xinming. 1984. "Da geming shiqi beifang mongmin qiyi—Tianmen hui" (Peasant uprisings in North China during the Great Revolution period). *Henan wenshi ziliao* (Henan historical materials) 11: 12–31.

Lin Delong. 1980. "Shi lun Jing-Han tielu gongren da bagong" (On the Beijing-Hankou railwaymen's strike). *Zhengzhou daxue xuebao* (Zhengzhou University journal) 1: 24–47.

Lin Zhuangzhi. 1985. "Juesheng yu qian li zhi wai—ji Zhou Enlai zhidao xia de Queshan nongmin baodong" (Determine the victory thousands of *li* away—peasant uprisings in Queshan directed by Zhou Enlai). *Zhongyuan fenghuo* (Battles in Henan), Zhou Weisong, ed., pp. 1–10. Zhengzhou: Henan renmin chubanshe.

Linxian zhi (Linxian county gazetteer). 1932.

Little, Daniel. 1989. *Understanding Peasant China: Case Studies in the Philosophy of Social Science*. New Haven, Conn.: Yale University Press.

Liu Yingxian. 1983. "Yijiu erwu nian Zhengzhou Yufeng shachang gongren da bagong" (The 1925 strike of Yufeng textile workers in Zhengzhou). *Zhongzhou xuekan* (Henan journal) no. 6: 131.

———. 1984. "Da geming shiqi de Zheng Xing Mi nongmin yundong" (The peasant movement in Zhengzhou, Xingyang, and Mixian at the time of the Great Revolution). *Zhongzhou xuekan* (Henan journal) no. 5: 84–85, 106–8.

Liu Yongzhi and Wang Quanying. 1983. "Minguo nianjian Henan bingzai zhanhuo xuanbian" (Selected materials on Henan warfare in the Republican period). In *LH:Henan-ZL* 4: 23–45.

Lo Baoxuan. 1982. "Diyi ci guonei geming zhanzheng shiqi de Hongqiang hui" (The Red Spears during the First National Revolutionary War). *Shehui kexue zhanxian* (Social science battlefront) 4: 132–36.

Lofland, John. 1985. *Protest: Studies of Collective Behavior and Social Movements*. New Brunswick, N.J.: Transaction.

Lu Jingzhi. 1990. "Henan sheng zhan shi sunshi diaocha baogao" (Investigation report on the losses in Henan province during the Sino-Japanese War). *Minguo dangan* (Republican archives) 21: 7–12.

Maccoby, Michael. 1967. "Love and Authority: A Study of Mexican Villagers." In Potter, Diaz, and Foster, pp. 336–45.

Macheng xianzhi xubian (Continued edition of the Macheng county gazetteer). 1935.

Mackeras, Colin. 1982. *Modern China: A Chronology from 1842 to the Present*. San Francisco: W. H. Freeman.

Mao Zedong. 1990. *Report from Xunwu*. Trans. Roger R. Thompson. Stanford: Calif.: Stanford University Press.

Marks, Robert. 1984. *Rural Revolution in South China: Peasants and the Making of History in Haifeng County, 1570–1930*. Madison: University of Wisconsin Press.

Marx, Karl. 1987. "Peasantry as a Class." In Shanin, pp. 331–37.

McAdam, Doug. 1982. *Political Process and the Development of Black Insurgency, 1930–1970*. Chicago: University of Chicago Press.

McCarthy, John D., and Mayer N. Zald. 1977. "Resource Mobilization and Social Movement: A Partial Theory." *American Journal of Sociology* 82, no. 6: 1212–41.

McColl, Robert. 1967a. "A Political Geography of Revolution: China, Vietnam, and Thailand." *Journal of Conflict Resolution* 11, no. 2: 153–67.

———. 1967b. "The Oyuwan Soviet Area, 1927–1932." *Journal of Asian Studies* 27, no. 1: 41–60.

McDonald, Angus W., Jr. 1978. *The Urban Origins of Rural Revolution: Elites and the Masses in Hunan Province, China, 1911–1927*. Berkeley: University of California Press.

Meisner, Maurice. 1967. *Li Ta-chao and the Origins of Chinese Marxism*. Cambridge, Mass.: Harvard University Press.

Migdal, Joel S. 1974. *Peasants, Politics, and Revolution: Pressures Toward Political and Social Change in the Third World*. Princeton, N.J.: Princeton University Press.

Moore, Barrington, Jr. 1966. *Social Origins of Dictatorship and Democracy: Lord and Peasant in the Making of the Modern World*. Boston: Beacon.

Mu Zhongyue. 1984. "Yijiu sansan nian Linxian Tianmen hui xiaomie jingguo" (The collapse of the Heavenly Gate Society in Linxian in 1933). *Henan wenshi ziliao* (Henan historical materials) 11: 74–79.

Naquin, Susan. 1976. *Millenarian Rebellion in China: The Eight Trigrams Uprising of 1813*. New Haven, Conn.: Yale University Press.

———. 1982. "Connections Between Rebellions: Sect Family Networks in Qing China." *Modern China* 8, no. 3: 337–60.

———. 1985. "The Transmission of White Lotus Sectarianism in Late Imperial China." In *Popular Culture in Later Imperial China*, David Johnson, Andrew J. Nathan, and Evelyn S. Rawski, eds. Berkeley: University of California Press.

Newby, Howard, ed. 1978. *International Perspective in Rural Sociology*. Chichester, Eng.: Wiley.

Ni Zhongwen. 1982. "Zheng Weisan tongzhi tan Eyuwan suqu lishi de diaocha he bianxie" (Interview of Comrade Zheng Weisan on the investigation and writing of the history of the Hubei-Henan-Anhui soviet area). *Eyuwan suqu lishi yanjiuhui, di san nian hui lunwen xuanji* (Proceedings of the third research conference on the history of the Hubei-Henan-Anhui soviet area), pp. 1–26. Zhengzhou.

Nie Yuansu and Shi Xiaosheng. 1984. "Li Dazhao yu Henan gong nong geming yundong" (Li Dazhao and the worker-peasant revolutionary movement in Henan). *Lishi jiaoxue* (The teaching of history) 7: 13–18.

Niu Yuqian. 1982. "Zhuoyue de zhanshi—ji Henan zao qi nongmin yundong lingdao ren zi yi—Xiao Rengu" (Outstanding warrior—one of the leaders in the early peasant movement in Henan—Xiao Rengu). *Lieshi yong sheng* (The immortal martyrs) 3: 13–16. Zhengzou: Henan renmin chubanshe.

Paige, Jeffery M. 1975. *Agrarian Revolution: Social Movement and Export Agriculture in the Underdeveloped World*. New York: Free Press.

Pan Yuqing. 1985. "Zhenjing zhong wai de Queshan nongmin baodong" (The Queshan peasant uprising that shook the country and the world). *Zhongyuan fenghuo* (Henan battles), Zhou Weisong, ed., pp. 11–42. Zhengzhou: Henan renmin chubanshe.

Pang Shouxin. 1984. "Di yi ci guonei geming zhanzheng shiqi de Henan nongmin yundong" (Henan peasant movement during the First National Revolutionary War). In *LH:Henan-ZL* 5: 1–16.

———. 1989. "Shilun Wusa yundong zai Henan de lishi diwei" (Preliminary analysis of the historical significance of the May 30th Movement in Henan). *Henan dangshi yanjiu* (Study of Henan party history) 1: 23, 27–32.

Pang Shouxin and Wang Quanying. 1981. "Henan zuizao de xian nong gong zhengfu" (The earliest peasant-worker county government in Henan). *Zhongzhou xuekan* (Henan journal) 2: 25–29.

Pepper, Suzanne. 1978. *Civil War in China: The Political Struggle, 1945–1949*. Berkeley: University of California Press.

Perry, Elizabeth J. 1980. *Rebels and Revolutionaries in North China, 1845–1945*. Stanford, Calif.: Stanford University Press.

———. 1983. "Social Banditry Revisited: The Case of Bai Lang, a Chinese Brigand." *Modern China* 9, no. 3: 355–82.

Pettee, George. 1974. "Revolution—Typology and Process." In Denisoff, pp. 372–84.

Polachek, James M. 1983. "The Moral Economy of the Kiangsi Soviet (1928–1934)." *Journal of Asian Studies* 42, no. 4: 805–30.

Polanyi, Karl. 1971. "Primitive Feudalism and the Feudalism of Decay." In *Economic Development and Social Change: The Modernization of Village Communities*, George Dalton, ed., pp. 141–47. New York: Natural History Press.

Popkin, Samuel. 1979. *The Rational Peasant: The Political Economy of Rural Society in Vietnam*. Berkeley: University of California Press.

Potter, Jack M., May N. Diaz, and George M. Foster, eds. 1967. *Peasant Society: A Reader*. Boston: Little, Brown.

Purcell, Victor. 1963. *The Boxer Uprising: A Background Study*. Cambridge, Eng.: Cambridge University Press.

Queshan xianzhi (Queshan county gazetteer). 1928.

Race, Jeffrey. 1974. "Toward an Exchange Theory of Revolution." In Lewis, pp. 169–206.

Saunders, Peter, Howard Newby, Colin Bell, and David Rose. 1978. "Rural Community and Rural Community Power." In Newby, pp. 55–86.

Schram, Stuard R. 1963. *The Political Thought of Mao Tse-tung*. New York: Praeger.

Scott, James C. 1976. *The Moral Economy of the Peasant: Rebellion and Subsistence in Southeast Asia*. New Haven, Conn.: Yale University Press.

Scott, James C., and Benedict J. Kerkvliet. 1977. "How Traditional Rural Patrons

Lose Legitimacy: A Theory with Special Reference to Southeast Asia." In *Friends, Fellows and Factions: A Reader in Political Clientelism*. Steffen W. Schmidt et al., eds. Berkeley: University of California Press.

Selden, Mark. 1971. *The Yenan Way in Revolutionary China*. Cambridge, Mass.: Harvard University Press.

Shang Shiying, Liu Zuwang, Chang Jianqiao, Zhu Youwen, and Shang Xingfeng, eds. 1985. *Henan sheng dili* (A geography of Henan). Zhengzhou: Henan jiaoyu chubanshe.

Shanin, Teodor, ed. 1987. *Peasants and Peasant Societies*. Oxford, Eng.: Blackwell.

Shek, Richard. 1982. "Millenarianism Without Rebellion." *Modern China* 8, no. 3: 305–36.

Shenqiu xianzhi (Shenqiu county gazetteer). 1987.

Sheridan, James E. 1966. *Chinese Warlord: The Career of Feng Yu-hsiang*. Stanford, Calif.: Stanford University Press.

Shina kenkyu so sho (China studies series). 1918. Tokyo: Toa Jisshinsha.

Shorter, Edward, and Charles Tilly. 1974. *Strikes in France, 1830–1968*. Cambridge, Eng.: Cambridge University Press.

Skocpol, Theda. 1979. *States & Social Revolutions: A Comparative Analysis of France, Russia, & China*. Cambridge, Eng.: Cambridge University Press.

———. 1982. "What Makes Peasants Revolutionary?" In Weller and Guggenheim, pp. 157–79.

Slawinski, Roman. 1972. "The Red Spears in the Late 1920s." In Chesneaux 1972.

Stinchcombe, Arthur L. 1961. "Agricultural Enterprise and Rural Class Relations." *American Journal of Sociology* 67: 165–76.

Stone, Lawrence. 1974. "Theories of Revolution." In Denisoff, pp. 385–98.

Tai Hsuan-chih. 1985. *The Red Spears, 1916–1949*. Trans. Ronald Suleski. Michigan Monographs in Chinese Studies, no. 54. Ann Arbor: University of Michigan.

Tai, Hue-Tam Ho. 1983. *Millenarianism and Peasant Politics in Vietnam*. Cambridge, Mass.: Harvard University Press.

Taikang xianzhi (Taikang county gazetteer). 1942.

Tan Kesheng and Jiang Kangmei. 1983. "Lun geming zhishi fenzi zai chuangjian Eyuwan suqu de lishi zuoyong" (On the historical role of the revolutionary intellectuals in the founding of the Hubei-Henan-Anhui soviet area). *Huazhong shiyuan xuebao* (Central China Normal University Journal) 6: 56–63.

Thaxton, Ralph. 1981. "The Peasants of Yaocun: Memories of Exploitation, Injustice and Liberation in a Chinese Village." *Journal of Peasant Studies* 9: 3–46.

———. 1982. "Mao Zedong, Red Miserables, and the Moral Economy of Peasant Rebellion in Modern China." In Weller and Guggenheim, pp. 132–56.

———. 1983. *China Turned Rightside Up: Revolutionary Legitimacy in the Peasant World*. New Haven, Conn.: Yale University Press.

Tiedemann, R. G. 1982. "The Persistence of Banditry: Incidents in Border Districts of the North China Plain." *Modern China* 8, no. 4: 395–434.

Tilly, Charles. 1974. "Town and Country in Revolution." In Lewis, pp. 271–302.

———. 1978. *From Mobilization to Revolution*. Reading, Mass.: Addison-Wesley.

Tilly, Charles, Louise Tilly, and Richard Tilly. 1975. *The Rebellious Century, 1830–1930*. London: J. M. Dent.

Tongxu xianzhi (Tongxu county gazetteer). 1934.

Turner, Jonathan H. 1988. *A Theory of Social Interaction*. Stanford, Calif.: Stanford University Press.

Ulmer, S. Sydney. 1971. "Toward a Theory of Sub-group Formation in the United States Supreme Court." In Ball and Lauth, pp. 299–314.

Van Slyke, Lyman P., ed. 1952. *The Chinese Communist Movement: A Report of the United States War Department, July, 1945*. Stanford, Calif.: Stanford University Press.

———. 1967. *Enemies and Friends: The United Front in Chinese Communist History*. Stanford, Calif.: Stanford University Press.

Vlastos, Stephen. 1986. *Peasant Protests and Uprisings in Tokugawa Japan*. Berkeley: University of California Press.

Waldman, Sidney R. 1973a. "Exchange Theory and Political Analysis." In Effrat, pp. 101–28.

———. 1973b. "Response to Easton." In Effrat, pp. 149–56.

Walton, John. 1984. *Reluctant Rebels: Comparative Studies of Revolution and Underdevelopment*. New York: Columbia University Press.

Wang Jinyu. 1985. "Shuidong kang Ri genjudi de chuangjian he fa zhan" (The building and development of the anti-Japanese base in the Rivereast). *Zhengzhou daxue xuebao* (Henan University journal) 2: 97–101.

Wang Lingyun. N.d. "Yu xi jiu shehui junfei hengxing de gaikuang" (The rampage of military bandits in traditional society in western Henan). *Wen shi ziliao xuan ji* (Selections from the historical materials) 38: 158–75.

Wang Liuxian, Song Guanyi, Wu Cangzhou, Wang Yuru, Fan Longzhang and Fan Tiren. 1985. "Fan Zhongxiu he Jianguo Yu jun" (Fan Zhongxiu and the Henan Reconstruction Army). *Henan wenshi ziliao* (Henan historical materials) 1: 61–74.

Wang Quanying. 1982. "Eyuwan suqu tudi zhengce de yanbian" (A transformation of the land policy in the Hubei-Henan-Anhui soviet area). *Eyuwan suqu lishi yanjiuhui di san jie lunwen xuanji*. (Proceedings of the third research conference on the history of thc Hubei-Henan-Anhui soviet area), pp. 365–84. Zhengzhou.

———. 1983. "Da geming shiqi de Henan Hongqiang hui" (The Henan Red Spears during the First Revolutionary War period). *Zhongzhou xuekan* (Henan journal) 2: 133–37.

Wang Shijun. 1982. *Beiyang junfa tongzhi shiqi de bingbian* (The army mutinies in the warlord period). Zhongguo di er lishi dangan guan (Second Historical Archives), ed. Zhonghua minguo shi dangan ziliao zongkan (Archival materials on Republican China series). Shanghai: Jiangsu renmin chubanshe.

Wang Tianjiang, Pang Shouxin, Wang Quanying, and Feng Wengang. 1990. *Henan jindai dashiji, 1840–1949* (Major events in modern Henan, 1840–1949). Zhengzhou: Henan renmin chubanshe.

Wang Xiangjiu. 1980. "Wo zuo zhidao de Zhang Lanfeng" (The Zhang Lanfeng I know). *Henan wenshi ziliao* (Henan historical materials) 3: 136–52.

Wang Yanzhang. 1984. "Sui-Qi-Tai diqu dangshi yanjiu zhong de jige wenti" (A few problems in the study of the party history of the Suixian-Qixian-

Taikang base area). *Henan dangshi yanjiu* (Research on Henan party history) 4: 74–78.

Watson, Goodwin. 1973. "Resistance to Change." *In Processes and Phenomena of Social Change*, Gerald Zaltman, ed. New York: Wiley.

Weber, Eugene. 1976. *Peasants into Frenchmen: The Modernization of Rural France, 1870–1914*. Stanford, Calif.: Stanford University Press.

Wei Jianyou. 1985. *Zhongguo huidang shilun zhu huiyao* (Abstract of historical writings on secret societies in China). Tianjin: Nankai daxue chubanshe.

Welch, Claude E., Jr., and Marvis B. Taintor, eds. 1972. *Revolution and Political Change*. North Scituate, Mass.: Duxbury Press.

Weller, Robert P., and Scott E. Guggenheim, eds. 1982. *Power and Protest in the Countryside: Studies of Rural Unrest in Asia, Europe, and Latin America*. Durham, N.C.: Duke University Press.

Wen Gongzhi. 1962. *Zuijin sanshi nian Zhongguo junshi shi* (Chinese military history of the last thirty years). 2 vols. Taibei: Wen sheng shudian.

Wilbur, C. Martin. 1983. *The Nationalist Revolution in China, 1923–1928*. London, Eng.: Cambridge University Press.

———. 1988. "The Beginnings of the Farmers' Movement in Kwangtung, 1924–1926." *Zhongyang yanjiuyuan jindai shi yanjiusuo jikan* (Journal of the Institute of Modern History, Academia Sinica), 17, no. 1: 311–96.

Wilbur, C. Martin, and J. L. Y. How. 1956. *Documents on Communism, Nationalism, and Soviet Advisers in China, 1918–1927*. New York: Columbia University Press.

———. 1989. *Missionaries of Revolution: Soviet Advisers and Nationalist China, 1920–1927*. Cambridge, Mass.: Harvard University Press.

Wilkinson, Paul. 1971. *Social Movement*. New York: Praeger.

Wilson, John. 1973. *Introduction to Social Movement*. New York: Basic.

Wolf, Eric R. 1966. *Peasants*. Englewood Cliffs, N.J.: Prentice-Hall.

———. 1969. *Peasant Wars of the Twentieth Century*. New York: Harper & Row.

Wou, Odoric Y. K. 1978. *Militarism in Modern China: The Career of Wu P'ei-fu, 1916–1939*. Folkstone, Eng.: Dawson/Australian National University Press.

———. 1984. "Development, Underdevelopment and Degeneration: The Introduction of Rail Transport into Honan." *Asian Profile* 12, no. 3: 215–30.

———. 1985. "The Boxer Uprising and Its Aftermath: The Impact on Honan." *Proceedings on the Sixth International Symposium on Asian Studies, 1984*. Vol. 1, *China*. Hong Kong: Asian Research Service.

———. 1987. "Bibliographic Sources for Henan Local History in the People's Republic of China." *Gest Library Journal* 2: 31–38.

Wright, Quincy. 1964. *A Study of War*. Chicago: University of Chicago Press.

Xia Zilun. 1989. "Jing-Han tielu zong gonghui chengli dahui wei he zai Zhengzhou zhaokai" (Why the meeting of the Beijing-Hankou Railway General Union was called in Zhengzhou). *Henan dangshi yanjiu* (Study of Henan party history) 1: 7, 24–26.

Xiang Yunlong. 1927. "Hongqiang hui de qiyuan ji qi shanhou" (The origin and aftermath of the Red Spears). *Dongfang zazhi* (Chinese miscellany), 24, no. 21: 35–41.

Xihua xianzhi (Xihua county gazetteer). 1928.

Xu Anyang xianzhi (A revised edition of the Anyang county gazetteer). 1933.

Xu Fuling. 1979. "Jiang Jieshi zai Huanghe shang fanxia de taotian zuixing" (The heinous crimes committed by Chiang Kaishek in the Yellow River area). *Henan wenshi ziliao* (Henan historical materials) 1: 1–9.

Xu Xiangqian. 1984. *Lishi de huigu* (A look back at history). Beijing: Jiefang jun chubanshe.

Xu Youchun. 1984. "Kan Ri zhanzheng chu qi Huanghe juekou zhenxiang qian xi" (A preliminary analysis of the breaking of the dike of the Yellow River in the beginning of the Sino-Japanese War). *Jianghai xuebao* (Jianghai journal) 2: 102–4.

Xue Yi. 1982. "Daoqing tielu zaoqi gongren yundong" (The early Daoqing railroad labor movement). *Shixue yuekan* (Historical studies monthly) 2: 43–47, 68.

———. 1983. "Guangzhou de liu jie nongmin yundong jiangxi xuo zhong de Henan xueyuan" (The Henan students in the 6th class of the Peasant Training Institute in Canton). In *LH:Henan-ZL* 2: 25–28.

Yang Jingqi. 1982. "Chaishan bao kao" (Research on Fodder Hill Neighborhood). *Eyuwan suqu lishi yanjiuhui de san jie lunwen xuanji* (Proceedings of the third research conference on the history of the Hubei-Henan-Anhui soviet area), p. 463. Zhengzhou.

———. 1985. "Henan Xixian Chaishan bao kao" (Research on Fodder Hill Neighborhood in Xi county). *Shixue yuekan* (Historical study monthly) 5: 30.

Yang Juren. 1985. *Feng yu Zhongyuan* (Windstorm in the central plain). Zhengzhou: Henan renmin chubanshe.

Yang Peng. 1989. "Shixi Jing-Han tielu da bagong de yuanyin" (A preliminary analysis of the cause of the Beijing-Hankou railway strike). *Henan dangshi yanjiu* (Study of Henan party history) 1: 20–23.

Yin Wentang. 1979. "Zhen Song jun shi mo" (The beginning and end of the Zhen Song army). *Henan wenshi ziliao* (Henan historical materials) 2: 84–112.

Yu Shude. 1981. "Yu Shude tongzhi de beifang zhengzhi zhuangkuang baogao" (Comrade Yu Shude's report on political conditions in North China). *Dangshi yanjiu ziliao* (Party historical research materials) 2: 407–15.

Zagoria, Donald S. 1974. "Asian Tenancy Systems and Communist Mobilization of the Peasantry." In Lewis, pp. 29–60.

Zeng Guangxing. 1984. "Zhonggong Yu-Shan quwei jianli shijian bianzheng" (A debate over the timing of the establishment of the Henan-Shaanxi regional committee of the CCP). *Zhongzhou xuebao* (Henan journal) 5: 109–10.

Zeng Jianquan. 1927. "Guangshan" (Guangshan county). *Dongfang zazhi* (Chinese miscellany) 24, no. 16: 136–38.

Zhang Jiang. 1982. "Li Dazhao zai Kaifeng" (Li Dazhao in Kaifeng). *Shixue yuekan* (Historical study monthly) 5: 47, 57–60.

Zhang Zhongheng. 1983. "Yudong Fu-Tai-Tong-Qi xi xian bianqu de kangchu youji dui" (Guerrilla squads for resisting the Japanese and removing the puppets in the border region of Fugou, Taikang, Tongxu, and Qixian counties). *Henan wenshi ziliao* (Henan historical materials) 8: 148–52.

Zhao Boyan. 1984. *Minguo shiqi Henan sheng tianfu gaikuang* (Land taxes in Henan in the Republican period). In *LH:Henan-ZL* 5: 73–75.

———. 1985. "Kangzhan shiqi Henan nongcun jingji gaikuang" (An account of the agricultural economy in Henan during the Sino-Japanese War). In *LH:zhanzheng*: 300–305.

Zhao Jinsan, ed. 1934. *Henan tudi zhengli wenti* (Problems of reorganizing the land in Henan). Zhongguo dizheng yanjiu shuo cong kan (Chinese land administration research institute series), Xiao Zheng, ed. Taibei: Wencheng chubanshe.

Zhengyang xianzhi (Zhengyang county gazetteer). 1936.

Zhonggong dangshi renwu yanjiuhui (Research Society on Historical Figures in the CCP), ed. 1983. *Zhonggong dangshi renwu chuan* (Biographies of historical figures in the CCP). Xian: 12 vols. Shaanxi renmin chubanshe.

Zhonggong Henan shengwei dangshi gongzuo weiyuanhui (Party History Working Committee of the Henan CCP) and Henan Zhonggong dangshi renwu yanjiuhui (Research Society on Historical Figures in the Henan CCP), eds. 1987. *Henan dangshi renwu zhuan* (Biographies of historical figures in Henan party history). 10 vols. Zhengzhou: Henan renmin chubanshe.

Zhonggong zhongyang dangxiao dangshi jiaoyan shi (Section for Research and Teaching of Party History, Central Party School of the CCP), ed. 1979. *Zhonggong dangshi cankao ziliao* (Reference materials on the history of the CCP). Beijing: Renmin chubanshe.

Zhonggong zhongyang shuji chu (Secretariat of the CCP Central Committee), ed. 1980. *Liu da yi quan—dang de lishi cailiao* (Before the sixth national people's congress—historical materials of the party). Beijing: Renmin chubanshe.

Zhongguo di yi lishi dangan guan (First Historical Archives) and Beijing shifan daxue lishi xi (History Department, Beijing Normal University), eds. 1985. *Xinhai geming qian shi nianjian minbian dangan shiliao* (Archival materials on the uprisings in the ten years before the 1911 Revolution). 2 vols. Beijing: Zhonghua shuju.

Zhongguo qingnian (Chinese youth).

Zhu Chaonan, Yang Huiyuan, and Lu Wenpei. 1985. *Huaibei kang Ri genjudi caijing shigao* (A draft history of the finance and economy of the Huaibei anti-Japanese base). Hefei: Anhui renmin chubanshe.

Zi Zhen. 1927. "Fan-Feng zhanzheng zhong ai Yubei Tianmen hui" (The Heavenly Gate Society during the Anti-Fengtian War). *Xiangdao* (The guide weekly) no. 197: 2163–64.

Index

In this index an "f" after a number indicates a separate reference on the next page, and an "ff" indicates separate references on the next two pages. A continuous discussion over two or more pages is indicated by a span of page numbers, e.g., "57–59." *Passim* is used for a cluster of references in close but not consecutive sequence.

Library of Congress Cataloging-in-Publication Data

Wou, Odoric, Y. K.
Mobilizing the masses : building revolution in Henan /
Odoric Y. K. Wou.
p. cm.
Includes bibliographical references and index.
ISBN 0-8047-2142-4
1. Honan Province (China)—History. 2. Communism—China—Honan
Province—History. I. Title.
DS793.H5W6 1994
951'.18042—dc20 93-20624 CIP

∞ This book is printed on acid-free paper. It has been
typseset in 10/12½ Trump by Keystone Typesetting, Inc.